THEORIES OF
TYRANNY
FROM PLATO
TO ARENDT

ROGER BOESCHE

THEORIES OF
TYRANNY
FROM PLATO
TO ARENDT

The Pennsylvania State University Press
University Park, Pennsylvania

Library of Congress Cataloging-in-Publication Data

Boesche, Roger.
    Theories of tyranny from Plato to Arendt / Roger Boesche.
        p.   cm.
    Includes bibliographical references and index.
    ISBN 0-271-01457-1 (cloth)
    ISBN 0-271-01458-X (paper)
    1. Despotism.   2. Dictatorship.   I. Title.
    JC381.B65   1996
    321.9—dc20   94-42591
                                                        CIP

It is the policy of The Pennsylvania State University Press to use acid-free paper
for the first printing of all clothbound books. Publications on uncoated stock satisfy the minimum requirements of American National Standard for Information
Sciences—Permanence of Paper for Printed Library Materials, ANSI Z39.48–1992.

With love to my daughter, Kelsey
May she never know tyranny

CONTENTS

PREFACE

This book grew naturally from my writings on Tocqueville, especially my attempts to understand his fear of a qualitatively new despotism. After reading Tocqueville, I was intrigued by Tacitus's analysis of Roman *dominatio*, or absolute rule, and the similarity between Tocqueville's fear and Tacitus's analysis was striking. Could it be that Tocqueville's supposedly "new" despotism was not dramatically different from previous tyrannies? Could there be continuity between ancient and modern tyrannies? What other thinkers might have analyzed the tyrannies of their own time? Could this be a little noticed discourse in the history of European political thought? Might the problem of tyranny be one of those perennial problems that political theorists come back to again and again? And thus an idea and a book began to grow.

The work on this project began with a National Endowment for the Humanities Fellowship in 1986–87. The book was helped along by an enhanced sabbatical from Occidental College in 1989–90, by a 1991 Faculty Fellowship from the John Randolph Haynes and Dora Haynes Foundation, and by a Totten Anderson Fellowship in 1994. I am grateful for all of this support.

Friends and colleagues have been very helpful. Sheldon Wolin, Jack Gunnell, Sandy Thatcher, Peter Breiner, Nina Gelbart, and Bernard Yack have each read all or parts of the manuscript, and their comments and suggestions have been instrumental in making this a better book. Sheldon Wolin, in particular, read the entire book at an earlier stage and made especially detailed and insightful suggestions. Keith Monley did a superb job of copyediting the book.

Thanks especially to Jean Viggiano and Luisa Reyes for helping me get all the versions of the manuscript safely in and out of computers. What would I have done without their help? Many very capable students—Amy

Ash, Eugene Sheppard, Dan Curran, Janet Blum, Chris Gamble, Jennifer Moulton, and Michael Rooney—helped me so patiently and thoroughly with library sources. And thanks to my students in my course How Tyrannies Work; they gave me many insights, helping me to clarify my ideas.

Because I have been battling severe rheumatoid arthritis for more than thirty years now, it seems like I need a whole team of superb physicians—many of whom are surgeons—to keep me in the field of play. I promised myself that if I finished this book, I would thank these doctors, so I wish to express sincere thanks to Reginald Friesen, Peng Thim Fan, Stephen Read, John Garner, George Mulfinger, Andrea Cracchiolo, Richard Merrill, Elaine Evans Constantz, and Victor Kovner.

Most of all I would like to thank my best friend and wonderful wife, Mandy, for a marvelous twenty-five years.

INTRODUCTION

Many write about freedom; few analyze tyranny. And yet at any given moment in history, surely tyrannies have greatly outnumbered states we would call just or free. Moreover, tyrannies and tyrants tug at our imaginations because so many tyrants stride across the streams of history and leave marks. From Alexander to Julius Caesar, from Louis XIV to Napoleon, from Hitler to Stalin, from Mao to Marcos, and from Pinochet to Saddam Hussein, tyrants fill our history books and our headlines as they both repel us and intrigue us. They seem unconstrained and unconcerned about our persistent questions of morality; they seem powerful in a world in which most of us feel powerless; they seem to act, while we seem to drift; they do not seem bent over by the winds of history, but rather they stand firm, stand out from history, and sometimes change history. However terrifying and odious, they also excite. We watch them like we watch a fire.

This book introduces the story of tyrannies in the European tradition. It tells how they work and, by implication, how they can be defeated. And it does so by considering tyranny as a perennial problem in our history and by demonstrating how a number of great political philosophers have tried to analyze and explain this phenomenon of tyranny that never seems to disappear.

In undertaking analyses of tyranny or formulating theories of tyranny, political thinkers ask at least some of the following questions: How does one define a tyranny? Or what constitutes a tyranny? Is tyranny the opposite of freedom, or perhaps the opposite of virtue or justice? Is a tyranny always the rule of one person, or can one have, to take two examples, a class tyranny or a tyranny without an identifiable tyrant? Do men and women always oppose tyranny, or do they sometimes welcome it? What historical changes help bring about tyranny? What are the political and economic preconditions for a viable tyranny? Is property a defense against tyranny or a buttress to it? How have modern factories and the administration of modern bureaucracies altered the forms of tyranny? Why are some tyrannies successful and long-lasting, whereas others burn themselves out rapidly? Why are some tyrannies static and tranquil, whereas others are brutally expansionistic? How can a tyrant rely on military and paramilitary forces without risk of being supplanted by them? How important is fear and violence? Or is a tyranny sometimes more successful bribing the population with comforts and pleasures? Which classes should a tyrant rely upon? How can he or she rely on one class without offending others? How does a tyrant make use of political parties and factions? Is religion an obstacle to tyranny, or does it assist tyranny? How does a tyranny make use of the legal system? education? the media? language? ethnic tension? What role does the family play in sustaining tyranny? What can we learn about tyranny by examining the status of women? And finally, what are the most successful strategies for preventing or opposing tyranny?

Sadly, the story of tyranny is a long one with no end in sight, but at least in the European tradition, we know its beginning. The seventh-century Greek poet Archilochus has left European historians the earliest known passage in which the word *tyrannos* (tyrant) appears. The narrator in the poem says, "I do not care about the wealth of Gyges, there is no envy in me, I am not jealous of the works of the gods, nor do I desire to be a great tyrant." Gyges was a king of Lydia (c. 685–657 B.C.E.), although he had not gained the throne by inheritance but rather by force of arms. The word *tyrannos* probably came to the Greeks and thus to Europe from Lydia, and the word is probably not Indo-European in origin. Initially the word may have meant something like "usurper," someone who did not attain power by traditional or constitutional means, which would of course describe Gyges accurately. This can be true only if one can strip the word *usurper* of any pejorative connotations, because scholars agree that the word *tyrant* originally carried a neutral meaning, without the suggestion of sinister wickedness associated with it later. As the historian M. I. Finley put it, "Originally a neutral word, 'tyrant' signified that a man seized and held power without legitimate constitutional authority (unlike a king); it implied no judgment about his quality as a person or ruler."[1]

1. Quoted in A. Andrewes, *The Greek Tyrants* (London: Hutchinson & Co., 1956), 21; M. I. Finley, *The Ancient Greeks: An Introduction to Their Life and Thought* (New York: Viking, 1964), 25; John V. A. Fine, *The Ancient Greeks: A Critical History* (Cambridge, Mass.: Harvard University Press, 1983), 105; Raphael Sealey, *A History of the Greek City States ca. 700–338 B.C.* (Berkeley and Los Angeles: University of California Press, 1976), 38; Chester G.

Finley's claim is slightly inaccurate for two reasons. First, although his distinction between king and tyrant is generally true, the contrast is too sharp. From the seventh century through the fifth century, many writers used the words *king* and *tyrant*—*basileus* and *tyrannos*—interchangeably, as if they were synonyms. This is certainly true of the poets Aeschylus (c. 525–456), Pindar (518–438), and Sophocles (c. 496–406), although of course poets have a greater fondness for synonyms, but it is also true of the historian Herodotus (c. 490–430). Second, Finley is right in saying that the word *tyrant* originally held a neutral meaning. Indeed, many of the early Greek tyrants, such as Pisistratus (c. 600–527) of Athens, were quite popular and in many ways progressive, so much so that one recent writer has called Pisistratus "a truly great man." Nevertheless, the word was capable, even as early as the sixth century, of carrying the connotation of evil and odium that it carries today. Three sixth-century writers—Alcaeus, Solon, and Theognis—all occasionally used the word *tyrant* to condemn absolute power, and from the end of the sixth century, we have a line from a drinking song that praised those who committed tyrannicide as liberators. "Your fame will last forever, . . . because you killed the tyrant and made Athens equal in law." Thus, even though the word *tyrant* generally carried a neutral meaning, as a synonym for the word *king,* from the seventh through the fifth centuries, from its earliest usage the word gradually accumulated, almost as a parallel development, connotations of wickedness.[2]

Only in the fourth century did the words *tyrannis* (tyranny) and *tyrannos* come to have, in an emphatic way, the modern connotations of a harsh and lawless government in which the ruler does not govern for the general good. Only now was it unequivocally an insult and a condemnation to describe someone as a tyrant. Xenophon, Plato, Aristotle, and probably Socrates all held the view that a kingship was a good form of monarchy, whereas a tyranny was a bad form. Plato, of course, put forth this view most dramatically, by offering a theoretical analysis of the ty-

---

Starr, *The Economic and Social Growth of Early Greece, 800–500 B.C.* (New York: Oxford University Press, 1977), 178; Mary White, "Greek Tyranny," *The Phoenix* (Toronto) 9, no. 1 (1955): 1–18, esp. 1–2. Robert Drews gives the most detailed account of Gyges and the political turmoil surrounding his rule. See "The First Tyrants in Greece," *Historia* (Germany) 21, no. 2 (1972): 129–44, esp. 136–40. All dates in the introduction that refer to Greece are, of course, B.C.E.

2. Fine, *The Ancient Greeks*, 219; Sealey, *A History of the Greek City States*, 38–39; Andrewes, *Greek Tyrants*, 7, 20–28; Fine, *The Ancient Greeks*, 105; Lionel Jehuda Sanders, *Dionysius I of Syracuse and Greek Tyranny* (London: Croom Helm, 1987), 132. White saw the earliest tyrants as so progressive and popular, by and large, that she declared later generations looked back to these tyrannies as "a golden age." White, "Greek Tyranny," 18.

rant as an "ogre of wickedness," a theory that tried to encompass both
the tyrants of the seventh and sixth centuries and contemporary tyrants
like Dionysius I of Syracuse (c. 430–367). There is some truth to Plato's
argument that tyrants of the second and third generations tended to become more cruel and to commit greater evil. The sons of Pisistratus, after
a period of peace and prosperity, became brutal and were overthrown,
and this pattern was a familiar one. "Uncontrolled military power was
inherently an evil; if not in the first generation then in the second or third
the tyrants usually became what the word now means."[3]

When we learn that the word *dēmokratia* probably did not exist before
the fifth century, and when we see all the ambiguities and changes that
accompanied the word *tyrant* as it journeyed from the seventh to the
fourth century, it becomes clear that the ancient Greek universe of political concepts was not always a stable one, that new words emerged to
meet new needs while old words adopted new meanings. Of course, the
meanings of political concepts change during times of crisis and transition, and this was certainly true of the word *tyrant.* So many tyrants
sprang up in ancient Greece during the seventh and sixth centuries that
this period has been called the "age of tyrants," a somewhat inaccurate
label because ancient Greek tyrannies hardly confined themselves to
these centuries. In retrospect it appears that tyranny in ancient Greece
was a transitional form of government, that tyrannies generally served to
weaken or eliminate aristocratic government, manage rapid economic
change, and improve the lot of a broader base of citizens. Thus, tyrants
frequently hastened a Greek city-state from a traditional aristocracy to
the fifth- or fourth-century polis more familiar to us, a polis with a government usually called either an oligarchy or a democracy. Because tyranny was a transitional form of government that emerged in times of
crisis, ancient Greek tyrannies appeared once more in great numbers
with the breakdown of the polis in the period from the fourth to the second centuries. These later tyrannies tended to rely on a more narrow
class base and to use a brutal military rule, and thus writers could use
the words *tyrant* and *tyranny,* with their modern connotations of evil and
cruelty, to describe them accurately.[4]

Aristotle often depicted early tyrants, as Andrewes notes, as champions

3. Andrewes, *Greek Tyrants*, 18; Finley, *The Ancient Greeks*, 25, 28–29; Andrewes, *Greek
Tyrants*, 19–21, 28–30, 101; Fine, *The Ancient Greeks*, 133. Sanders has succeeded in reha-
bilitating the reputation of Dionysius I somewhat. See *Dionysius I of Syracuse and Greek
Tyranny*, 174–77.

4. Andrewes, *Greek Tyrants*, 35, 147–50; Fine, *The Ancient Greeks*, 105, 133; Finley, *The
Ancient Greeks*, 29; Starr, *Economic and Social Growth of Early Greece*, 180–81.

"of the many and the poor against the few and the rich," and even though this claim is much too strong, historians do agree that early tyrants, in serving this transitional function, did come into opposition with traditional aristocracies. In Solon's time, the word *tyrant* seemed to have this connotation. Solon several times lamented that he was asked to become a tyrant by some of his supporters, and it is clear that these supporters wanted him to do something like Cypselus and Periander had done in Corinth, that is, either weaken or destroy the aristocracy and then redistribute its lands. It is sad to note that despite Solon's wisdom and fairness, Athens needed the force of Pisistratus to push forth both economic and political change.[5]

> Indeed, being a tyrant, [Pisistratus] could accomplish what Solon could not, and it was in his reign that the peasantry finally obtained a reasonably secure and independent position on the land, with financial assistance when required, that the civil strife was abated, and that the political monopoly of the aristocratic familes was broken once and for all. . . . Solon may have thought that he "stood covering both parties with a strong shield," but it was Pisistratus and Hippias [his son] who in fact had the necessary strength. Solon was followed by a renewal of the old civil war; Hippias, after a very short struggle lasting less than two years, by a wholly new, democratic state.[6]

Two more points are important. First, no tyrant intended to bring about ancient democracy. Tyrants were generally aristocrats themselves who sought power, fame, and wealth, but to succeed they had to rely on newly emerging classes and thus decisively had to weaken traditional aristocracies. Second, not all tyrants fit this pattern. Even the early tyrants of Syracuse, for example, often ruled brutally in defense of the old order.[7]

Nearly all scholars would agree with the claim that "in the great majority of cases the basic cause for the rise of tyrannies was opposition to the social, economic, political, and religious monopoly of power exercised by the aristocrats." But what brought about such opposition in so many Greek city-states at approximately the same time? One explanation with widespread, although hardly unanimous, support is the so-called hoplite theory, which focuses on economic and especially military changes in the seventh and sixth centuries. Warfare before the age of tyrants was the

5. Aristotle is paraphrased in Andrewes, *Greek Tyrants*, 18; see also 22, 90, 103, 43–53.
6. Finley, *The Ancient Greeks*, 28–29.
7. Ibid., 29; Starr, *Economic and Social Growth of Early Greece*, 180; Andrewes, *Greek Tyrants*, 134–42.

province of a "military aristocracy." Fighting was the responsibility of aristocratic warriors, experts in the art of war and in a more individual method of combat in which the bulk of the population had little role. As time passed, this method of fighting proved inadequate, and military aristocracies lost decisively to more disciplined and broader-based armies of hoplites, because the hoplite method of fighting relied upon "a greater number of trained fighters accustomed to acting as a team and not showing off their individual prowess." Hoplites were those nonaristocratic citizens wealthy enough to supply their own weapons and armor, which means they were generally wealthier peasant farmers, traders, and artisans. Although it strikes me as presumptuously modern to describe hoplites as "the new business class," it seems somewhat accurate to call them "a sort of middle class" composed both of wealthier farmers and of citizens "wealthy in movables rather than in land."[8]

It seems logical that with substantial economic power and much greater military responsibility, the hoplites would demand increased political power. Even though some historians caution us that the evidence for the hoplite theory is partial, while others are leery of projecting modern theories of class struggle back into the ancient world, it is probable that tyrants frequently allied themselves with hoplites in wrenching power from traditional aristocracies. With economic and military change, the base of the citizenry was widened, allowing tyrants and hoplites to form an alliance of self-interest, a development that would explain the oft-repeated claim by Herodotus, Plato, and Aristotle, that tyrants were champions of the *dēmos*. The term *dēmos* was certainly ambiguous; sometimes it referred to the entire population, sometimes to those who were citizens only, sometimes to the poorer part of the population and not the rich. Aristotle, however, noted that rule by the hoplites was once called *dēmokratia*, and it seems reasonable to see the word *dēmos* as referring to hoplites, to this wider base of the citizenry, and not to the poorest parts of the population. It is in this sense quite likely that tyrants were frequently champions of the *dēmos*, because in their quests for power and fame, they leaned upon the hoplite class, thus unintentionally bringing hoplites more extensive political power as they weakened the power of the aristocracy.[9]

8. Fine, *The Ancient Greeks*, 106; Andrewes, *Greek Tyrants*, 34; Fine, *The Ancient Greeks*, 131–32; Sealey, *A History of Greek City States*, 39; White, "Greek Tyranny," 5–7. The much-maligned pioneering study by P. N. Ure, which unsuccessfully linked the rise of tyrants to coinage, finance, and business, also made the same point that a change in warfare helped bring new classes more political power. See Ure, *The Origin of Tyranny* (New York: Russell & Russell, 1962 [1922]), 300.

9. Andrewes, *Greek Tyrants*, 34–38; Sealey, *A History of Greek City States*, 39, 57–58; Starr, *Economic and Social Growth of Early Greece*, 179; Fine, *The Ancient Greeks*, 108. Drew

While there are drawbacks in making generalizations, especially because historians have more information about tyrannies in Athens and Corinth than those in other city-states, it is still worthwhile trying to characterize these early tyrannies. First, early Greek tyrannies frequently ended factional strife, brought order to the city-state, and unified a polis that before was often a loose collection of villages. To do this, tyrannies necessarily strengthened the role of government. "Tyranny increased the power of the state; that was indeed its most lasting effect."[10] Second, ancient tyrannies apparently were, in many ways, both effect and cause of increasing prosperity, the development of trade and manufacturing, and a growing urbanization. Whereas it is completely false to conclude that the early tyrants "were one and all first-class businessmen," early tyrannies did frequently, and perhaps inadvertently, bring order to the economic system and thereby help those classes devoted to commerce, manufacturing, and finance. And with state loans to small farmers, and perhaps occasionally with some redistribution of land, the early tyrannies frequently promoted a new prosperity among agricultural classes.[11]

Third, with a new independence for those in agriculture and trade, and with the emerging end to debt bondage, tyrannies often brought Greece to the edge of democracy, although it is one of history's sad ironies that newly won freedom for some brought servitude for others. Outside the city-state, early tyrants often established colonies for purposes of trade, but this original commercial intent led later to empire, to the military and political dominance of some city-states by others. And inside the city-state, commercial and agricultural growth coupled with an end to bondage for debt brought a demand for cheap labor and thus the introduction of slavery into ancient Greece. "The final paradox, therefore, of archaic Greek history is this march hand in hand of freedom and slavery."[12] Fourth, the early tyrants frequently embarked on massive building programs. On the one hand, they used public money to develop what we might call the infrastructure of the economy. They often built roads, improved harbors, constructed aqueducts to bolster the water supply, and established drainage systems. On the other hand, they built lasting monuments that both fostered and symbolized the greatness and the unity of

---

avoids economic and sociological theories of the origin of tyranny and attributes the rise of tyranny to "the desire for power and prestige," but admits that tyrants shrewdly took advantage of hoplite armies. Drew, "The First Tyrants in Greece," 131.

10. Sealey, *A History of Greek City States*, 57; Starr, *Economic and Social Growth of Early Greece*, 101, 177–81; Fine, *The Ancient Greeks*, 219–20; Andrewes, *Greek Tyrants*, 7, 26.

11. Ure, *The Origin of Tyranny*, 301; Andrewes, *Greek Tyrants*, 111–12; Fine, *The Ancient Greeks*, 100, 132; Starr, *Economic and Social Growth of Early Greece*, 23, 102; Sealey, *A History of Greek City States*, 139; White, "Greek Tyranny," 10.

12. Finley, *The Ancient Greeks*, 30; Sealey, *A History of Greek City States*, 50–52, 139.

the polis. As Finley pointed out, the early tyrants did not build palaces for themselves, but rather public monuments, like temples for the community. All such building programs had the net effect of something like a "full employment policy," although it is likely that those who labored to build the roads and temples did so under severe and often cruel conditions.[13] Fifth, tyrants frequently encouraged, and relied upon, the systematic development of religious institutions, not only for the good of the community but also to help pacify the population. Sixth, tyrants often patronized the arts, not only architecture, sculpture, and painting but also poetry and drama.[14]

Seventh, the fourth-century definition of a tyrant—a lawless ruler who governed an unwilling population and whose rule was not in the general interest—was only a partially accurate description of the early Greek tyrants. Sometimes tyrants were not entirely lawless—for example, they did not always abolish traditional councils, which were at least vaguely representative—and sometimes, as in the case of Pisistratus, who established a system of judges who traveled the countryside, tyrants helped rationalize the legal system. Sometimes the population was far from unwilling to obey and was indeed eager to follow a strong and popular leader. And sometimes tyrants unintentionally promoted something like the general good. Despite all these qualifications, early Greek tyrants generally did seize power illegally, ruled lawlessly, and reigned "in defiance of any constitution that had existed previously." When the Greeks of the fifth and the fourth centuries claimed themselves to be free, they thought of freedom as "an ordered existence within a community which was governed by an established [legal] code respected by all." Free government, in other words, was lawful government that protected citizens against both rapacious nobilities and cruel tyrants.[15]

Eighth, tyrants frequently ruled by fear instead of law. Although some tyrants, such as Pisistratus, were popular, this was not the general pattern. Tyrants came to power with violence, and most ruled with military and paramilitary forces that, when necessary and sometimes when not,

13. Andrewes, *Greek Tyrants*, 51; Fine, *The Ancient Greeks*, 132–33, 113; Finley, *The Ancient Greeks*, 31; Starr, *Economic and Social Growth of Early Greece*, 102.

14. Fine, *The Ancient Greeks*, 219; Finley, *The Ancient Greeks*, 28–36; Sealey, *A History of Greek City States*, 52.

15. Andrewes, *Greek Tyrants*, 7; Finley, *The Ancient Greeks*, 41; W. R. Newell, "Tyranny and the Science of Ruling in Xenophon's 'Education of Cyrus,'" *Journal of Politics* 45, no. 4 (1983): 889–905, esp. 890; Andrewes, *Greek Tyrants*, 16, 28, 109; Sealey, *A History of Greek City States*, 40, 48, 139; Sanders, *Dionysius I of Syracuse and Greek Tyranny*, 92; Starr, *Economic and Social Growth of Early Greece*, 32; Max Pohlenz, *Freedom in Greek Life and Thought*, trans. Carl Lofmark (Dordrecht: D. Reidel, 1966), 3–9, 24, 34.

did not hesitate to murder and exile rivals, instill fear in the population, and sack neighboring cities.[16] Ninth, not given to restraint, most tyrants undertook ostentatious displays of power and wealth and boasted of their delight in sensual pleasures. In this, some proudly saw themselves as imitating Persian despotism.[17] Finally—a chilling and sobering thought for the late twentieth century—some early Greek tyrants made overt racial appeals and exacerbated existing racial or ethnic divisions, generally between Dorian and pre-Dorian portions of the population, in order to solidify their rule.[18]

The record of seventh- and sixth-century Greek tyrants was a mixed one, which explains why originally the word *tyrant* could have both neutral and negative connotations. In seeking power and fame for themselves, they ended the domination of traditional aristocracies, they broadened the base of the citizenry, they brought increased unity to Greek city-states, they fostered considerable economic development and an expanding prosperity, and thus in general they laid the social, economic, and political groundwork for the classical polis of the fifth and fourth centuries. Nonetheless, they ruled with violence and fear, they defied legal and constitutional restraints, and thus their momuments to the future, both literally and figuratively, resulted from the oppression and exploitation of slaves, women, and others with little or no property. By the fourth century, when writers such as Plato and Aristotle were analyzing tyranny, most ambiguity had disappeared, precisely because the record of these later tyrants was not such a mixed one. Thus the word *tyranny,* shorn of its neutral meaning, could enter the Greek and European lexicon of political and politicized words with all the connotations of evil and cruelty that it retains some twenty-four centuries later.

Of course, a connotation—and for that matter, an idea or a concept or a word—is one thing, while an analysis is another. Even though it is accurate to say that since the time of Plato the word *tyranny* has signified a wicked form of government that does not act in the general interest, such a vague statement tells us little, and it certainly does not mean that the examples of tyranny and the analyses of tyrannical government have not changed and developed, have not altered and shifted, over the centu-

16. Newell, "Tyranny and the Science of Ruling," 891, 904; Fine, *The Ancient Greeks*, 131; Andrewes, *Greek Tyrants*, 51; Sanders, *Dionysius I of Syracuse and Greek Tyranny*, 175; White, "Greek Tyranny," 8. Acquiring a bodyguard or a private military force seems to be a key characteristic of a Greek tyrant. Drew, "The First Tyrants in Greece," 135.

17. Sealey, *A History of Greek City States*, 39, 45, 58; Andrewes, *Greek Tyrants*, 25; Sanders, *Dionysius I of Syracuse and Greek Tyranny*, 9.

18. Andrewes, *Greek Tyrants*, 54–65; Fine, *The Ancient Greeks*, 122; Sealey, *A History of Greek City States*, 39.

ries. And so has the vocabulary of tyranny. *Despotēs* was already a term competing with the word *tyrannos* for the Greeks; Tacitus labeled the rule of Tiberius a *dominatio*; Machiavelli analyzed "princely tyrannies"; Montesquieu introduced the word *despotisme* into European discourse; Tocqueville rejected both *despotisme* and *tyrannie* as inadequate to describe what he feared, and thus fell back on words like *oppression* and *servitude;* Marx explored the "despotism of capital"; Freud analyzed what he thought was a natural "tyranny of the superego" imposed by the family; and Weber feared "bureaucratic domination" (*Herrschaft*).

To say that confusion reigned in the vocabulary of tyranny is a wild understatement. By the time of the *Declaration of Independence*, Jefferson could use the words or phrases *tyranny, absolute tyranny, absolute despotism,* and *absolute rule* as if they were synonymous. By the mid-nineteenth century, influenced by the rule of Napoleon and entire changes in the European understanding of time and history, the words *tyranny, despotism,* and *dictatorship* had become virtual synonyms, as *dictatorship* shed itself of the previous connotation of absolute authority circumscribed by a legally established framework of time.[19] In the late twentieth century, the political vocabulary we use to describe governments we regard as oppressive has continued to drift far from its historical moorings, severing itself from time-honored concepts and analyses put forth by numerous past thinkers who sought to describe and analyze what they regarded as oppressive and tyrannical governments. This muddle in our political vocabulary appears readily in the chaotic ways we label governments that we condemn. While writers and politicians frequently refer to governments as "totalitarian," "fascist," "dictatorial," "autocratic," or "authoritarian," it would almost seem quaintly anachronistic or awkwardly forced to call Pinochet's Chile a tyranny or Deng Xiaoping's China a despotism. It is possible, of course, that a more systematic political analysis has simply necessitated a more complicated political lexicon, that our voluminous vocabulary signifies precision rather than confusion, but a close reading of ancient and early modern writers quickly makes us doubt that we have illuminated much of what formerly was only dimly perceived.

Studies that attempt to make distinctions between fascism and totalitarianism, and between dictatorships and authoritarian regimes, are both many and useful.[20] This book makes no attempt to enter this debate, and

19. Reinhart Koselleck, *Futures Past* (Cambridge, Mass.: MIT Press, 1985 [1979]). See "'Neuzeit': Remarks on the Semantics of the Modern Concepts of Movement," 231–66, esp. 261–62.

20. For some examples, see Renzo de Felice, *Interpretations of Fascism* (Cambridge,

thus offers little help in clarifying the muddied waters of our political vocabulary. Rather, two arguments underlie this study. First, as Karl Bracher suggested, while it is of great importance both to make conceptual distinctions and to use a consistent vocabulary, ultimately the analyses of individual regimes are more important than general theories and the refining of definitions. "The weaknesses and limits of general theories are obvious: neither the theory of fascism nor the theory of totalitarianism, both of which lend themselves to political abuse, fully live up to their claim of furnishing a common denominator for *the* phenomenon of dictatorship in the twentieth century." Second, this study sees as much similarity as dissimilarity, as much continuity as discontinuity, between the tyrannies of the ancient and early modern world and those of the twentieth century. Leonard Schapiro, one of few recent scholars to analyze twentieth-century forms of tyranny with an awareness that ancient authors such as Aristotle and Machiavelli could teach us much about our judgments, has argued persuasively that tyranny has been a persistent problem and that twentieth-century variants of tyranny are not so qualitatively different as to be unrecognizable, like some startling biological genus tossed up anew into the natural world. "For totalitarianism is in truth," wrote Schapiro, "tyranny or despotism—but it is the tyranny or despotism of the age of mass democracy."[21] Obviously the Third Reich tyrannized over its population otherwise than did the Roman Empire, and clearly Franco had more sophisticated methods of rule than did Louis XV, yet the similarities are also striking. Or, to keep the biological metaphor: yes, there are new species or new political developments and mutations, but with significant genetic similarities to the old. The word *tyranny*— which always lurks in the background of modern analyses, because even-

---

Mass.: Harvard University Press, 1977); Ernst Nolte, *Three Faces of Fascism* (New York: Holt, Reinhart, & Winston, 1966); A. James Gregor, *Interpretations of Fascism* (Morristown, N.J.: General Learning Press, 1974); Eugen Weber, *Varieties of Fascism* (New York: D. Van Nostrand, 1964); Walter Laquer, ed., *Fascism: A Reader's Guide* (Berkeley and Los Angeles: University of California Press, 1976); Stanley G. Payne, *Fascism: Comparison and Definition* (Madison: University of Wisconsin Press, 1980); Carl J. Friedrich and Zbigniew K. Brzezinski, *Totalitarian Dictatorship and Autocracy*, 2d rev. ed. (New York: Praeger, 1965); Karl Dietrich Bracher, *The German Dictatorship* (New York: Holt, Rinehart & Winston, 1970); Amos Perlmutter, *Modern Authoritarianism: A Comparative Institutional Analysis* (New Haven: Yale University Press, 1981); Leonard Schapiro, "The Concept of Totalitarianism," *Survey* 70/71 (winter-spring 1969): 93–115; Wolfgang Sauer, "National Socialism: Totalitarianism or Fascism?" *American Historical Review* 73, no. 2 (1967): 404–24.

21. Bracher, *The German Dictatorship*, 491; Schapiro, "The Concept of Totalitarianism," 115 and passim. For another argument in favor of continuity in the phenomenon of tyranny, see Alan Bullock, *Hitler: A Study in Tyranny*, rev. ed. (New York: Harper & Row, 1962), esp. chap. 7.

tually authors call totalitarianism or fascism or authoritarianism a "tyrannical" form of government—should not be discarded, because it has stood for some twenty-four centuries as a condemnation of oppressive government, and our modern vocabulary, as Schapiro maintained, only explores variants of tyrannical government.

While this study is not an attempt to straighten out a twisted political lexicon, it is also not a study in the history of ideas, that is, some history of the "idea" of tyranny. Scholars in the United States associate the history of ideas with the work of Arthur Lovejoy, who argued for the study of "unit-ideas," which are something like irreducible components of the intellectual universe, similar to elements on a periodic table. Lovejoy maintained that "the number of essentially distinct philosophical ideas . . . is— as the number of really distinct jokes is said to be—decidedly limited." Although he acknowledged that "essentially novel conceptions" do emerge from time to time in intellectual history, "absolute novelty" is quite rare, and what is original and distinctive is usually a new pattern or combination of ideas, like a new chemical compound composed of different elements. Lovejoy encouraged scholars to trace these ideas over time—and certainly his most famous accomplishment is the history of the idea of "the great chain of being"—by reading not only so-called masterpieces but also "minor writers"; and by inferring from what he says about sources, one can with confidence conclude that he would not be averse to having scholars read pamphlets, letters, diaries, and other documents that have lately been the province of social historians.[22]

This book is not a history of the idea of tyranny for three reasons. First, even Lovejoy would eschew such a task, because complex phenomena including virtually all isms—presumably despotism, and hence tyranny— are not "unit-ideas," but rather compounds of ideas; and thus, according to Lovejoy, one would have to break the compound down into its elemental parts in order to begin a successful study. Thus Lovejoy himself would regard a history of the idea of tyranny as impossible unless it transformed itself into a mammoth history of many unit-ideas.[23] Second, Quentin Skinner has, in my opinion, argued persuasively that there are no "timeless ideas" and "timeless concepts" that appear and disappear, remain hidden or reappear, as the stream of history flows on. Declaring himself a "sworn

---

22. Arthur O. Lovejoy, *The Great Chain of Being: A Study of the History of an Idea* (Cambridge, Mass.: Harvard University Press, 1936), 3–6, 19–20. See also Melvin Richter, *"Begriffsgeschichte* and the History of Ideas," *Journal of the History of Ideas* 48, no. 2 (1987): 258–63; and for a recent defense of Lovejoy, see Francis Oakley, "Against the Stream: In Praise of Lovejoy," in *Omnipotence, Covenant, and Order: An Excursion in the History of Ideas from Abelard to Leibniz* (Ithaca: Cornell University Press, 1984), 15–40.

23. Lovejoy, *The Great Chain of Being*, 5–7.

foe" of such projects as a history of the nature of a just state, a history that examines the work of at Plato, Hobbes, Rousseau, and the like, Skinner rightly maintained that there are no timeless concepts such as "nature," "justice," or "state," but rather "only a variety of statements made with the words by a variety of different agents with a variety of intentions" in a variety of very different political and economic contexts. Searching assiduously for timeless ideas and concepts, we all too often end up projecting our "prejudices" onto the past, and thus history "becomes a pack of tricks we play on the dead." Or, as Sheldon Wolin put it, we "impoverish the past by making it appear like the present." Certainly this book makes no claim that there is a timeless idea of tyranny, but rather only multivarious forms of tyranny analyzed in different ways by different thinkers. And this book also seeks to look at significant analyses or theories in some depth, rather than assume the existence of a timeless concept of tyranny and recount in snippets what dozens of European thinkers have said about such a concept, as has been done in a recent history of the idea of progress.[24]

Finally, this book is not a contribution to the history of ideas, because the notion of timeless ideas assumes some nearly absolute identity and continuity, whereas I can only argue for similarity and partial continuity. If there are no timeless and unchanging ideas or doctrines, if there is no continuity from age to age of such ideas as progress or the separation of powers, if history only offers examples of the same word or phrase being used in different ways in different contexts, then any endeavor to trace the history of some idea across time is a "spurious" enterprise based on a "fundamental philosophical mistake." We are left with studying different authors located in specific historical contexts at specific moments in history using a vocabulary concerned with their own specific problems, not ours and not those of some earlier time. "For it is the very fact that the classic texts are concerned with their own quite alien problems," Skinner contended, "and not the presumption that they are somehow concerned with our own problems as well, which seems to me to give not the lie but the key to the indispensable value of studying the history of ideas."[25] His-

---

24. Quentin Skinner, "Meaning and Understanding in the History of Ideas," *History and Theory* 8, no. 1 (1969): 3–53, see esp. 5, 13–14, 38, 53; idem, "A Reply to My Critics," in *Meaning and Context: Quentin Skinner and His Critics*, ed. James Tully (Princeton: Princeton University Press, 1988), 231–88, esp. 283; Sheldon S. Wolin, "Political Theory as a Vocation," *American Political Science Review* 63, no. 4 (1969): 1062–82, esp. 1077; Robert Nisbet, *History of the Idea of Progress* (New York: Basic Books, 1980).

25. Skinner, "Meaning and Understanding in the History of Ideas," 7, 10–12, 35–37, 52; Reinhart Koselleck, "*Begriffsgeschichte* and Social History," *Economy and Society* 11 (1982): 409–27, esp. 413–15.

tory therefore offers not timeless and unchanging ideas, but rather a great measure of discontinuity and dissimilarity. We do not glide along the trail of timeless doctrines, but we lurch anew into each distinctive era. Two widely cited studies of despotism and tyranny fail, in my opinion, because they too fervently claim identity and continuity over time. Karl Wittfogel saw a nearly absolute continuity between ancient "oriental despotism" and the "unchangeable" Communism of twentieth-century China and the Soviet Union (whose "unchangeability" has now been exposed as absurd), whereas Eli Sagan's anthropological approach is too ready to see modern forms of oppression already writ large in preindustrial societies, so much so that "the forms of tyranny . . . have remained remarkably unvaried over thousands of years."[26]

If this book is not a contribution to the history of ideas, neither is it an exercise in conceptual history. Conceptual history, or *Begriffsgeschichte*, is generally associated with the gigantic German project called *Geschichtliche Grundbegriffe*, a project that will eventually have six volumes detailing the ways key concepts have changed their meanings over time. Although the entries look at the origins of concepts and, if appropriate, their meanings in the ancient, medieval, and Renaissance worlds, the focus is on the tumultuous change in German and, by extension, European political vocabularies from roughly the early eighteenth to the mid-nineteenth centuries.[27] Despite the fact that there are very good examples of conceptual history in the English language, they are certainly not as extensive and ambitious as those in German.[28] The results of conceptual history are often startling in their importance. Whereas we take the word

26. Karl A. Wittfogel, *Oriental Despotism: A Comparative Study of Total Power* (New York: Vintage Books, 1981 [1957]), xxvii; Eli Sagan, *At the Dawn of Tyranny: The Origins of Individualism, Political Oppression, and the State* (New York: Knopf, 1985), 278.

27. Otto Bruner, Werner Conze, and Reinhart Koselleck, eds., *Geschichtliche Grundbegriffe: Historisches Lexikon zur politisch-sozialen Sprache in Deutschland* (5 vols. in print; Stuttgart: Klett-Cotta, 1972–). A similar study is Joachim Ritter and Karlfried Grunder, eds., *Historisches Wörterbuch der Philosophie* (6 vols. in print; Basel: Schwabe & Co., 1971–). For an introduction to *Begriffsgeschichte*, see Koselleck, "*Begriffsgeschichte* and Social History"; Keith Tribe, "The *Geschichtliche Grundbegriffe* Project: From History of Ideas to Conceptual History," *Comparative Studies in Society and History* 31, no. 1 (1989): 180–84; Melvin Richter, "Conceptual History (*Begriffsgeschichte*) and Political Theory," *Political Theory* 14, no. 4 (1986): 604–37; Jeremy Rayner, "On *Begriffsgeschichte*," *Political Theory* 16, no. 3 (1988): 496–501; Melvin Richter, "Understanding *Begriffsgeschichte*: A Rejoinder," *Political Theory* 17, no. 2 (1989): 296–301; Jeremy Rayner, "On *Begriffsgeschichte* Again," *Political Theory* 18, no. 2 (1990): 305–7.

28. See Terence Ball, *Transforming Political Discourse: Political Theory and Critical Conceptual History* (Oxford: Basil Blackwell, 1988), and Terence Ball, James Farr, and Russell L. Hanson, eds., *Political Innovation and Conceptual Change* (New York: Cambridge University Press, 1989).

patriot to mean one with an unquestioning devotion to one's nation, the word originally signified those with courage enough to oppose a nation's policies; and whereas we look upon the word *revolution* as signifying a complete upheaval tossing a nation in entirely new directions, the word originally had a conservative connotation in that a full revolution, or "revolving," of 360 degrees would restore a nation to a former order.[29]

Reinhart Koselleck, the remaining editor of *Geschichtliche Grundbegriffe,* has suggested that there are three different groupings of concepts. First, "traditional concepts such as those of Aristotelian constitutional thought"—presumably including the concept of tyranny—whose meanings have changed comparatively little over the centuries. Second, concepts like "patriot" and "revolution," whose meanings have changed so drastically, especially in the period from roughly 1700 to 1850, that "despite the existence of the same word as a shell the meanings are barely comparable." And finally, a whole group of neologisms, or new words—*despotism, individualism, socialism, bureaucracy*—that have emerged as reactions to new political and economic circumstances. Those writing conceptual history have concentrated on the last two groupings.[30]

However fascinating, conceptual history is not an end in itself, but rather it assists scholarship in three ways. First, and most obvious, it is indispensable for understanding texts. If one seeks to understand the seventeenth-century political thinker James Harrington on revolution, or Weber's use of the concept of "legitimacy," clearly an understanding of the shifting meanings of such concepts is imperative.[31] Second, conceptual history is an alternative to the history of ideas. The proponents of conceptual history argue, of course, that there are no timeless and unchanging concepts, but rather concepts change with history, and indeed they both reflect social and political change and also help to cause, or at least to circumscribe, such change. Terence Ball has suggested that conceptual history is simultaneously "critical, creative, and conservative": critical because political actors must call into question established political vocabularies; creative because men and women must remake such vocabularies; and conservative because conceptual change always occurs with reference to established language and thus "tends to be piecemeal

29. Mary G. Dietz, "Patriotism," in *Political Innovation and Conceptual Change*, ed. Ball et al., 177–93; Reinhart Koselleck, "Historical Criteria of the Modern Concept of Revolution," in *Futures Past*, 39–54; Ball, *Transforming Political Discourse*, 16; idem, introduction to *Political Innovation and Conceptual Change*, ed. Ball et al., 4.

30. Koselleck, "*Begriffsgeschichte* and Social History," 417.

31. Ibid., 412, 423, 425–26; Richter, "Conceptual History and Political Theory," 632.

and gradual, sometimes proceeding at an almost glacial pace." Thus, in contrast to the history of ideas, conceptual history shows a linguistic universe constantly changing, although the weight of the past presses for considerable continuity. As Koselleck put it, concepts are rooted in the past, but "they reach for the future."[32] And finally, conceptual history goes hand in hand with social history. Proponents of conceptual history maintain that conceptual change is always linked to social and political change, and—particularly in times of crisis—classes, groups, and individuals clash over the meanings of concepts. "The struggle over the 'correct' concepts becomes socially and politically explosive." In reminding us that language is forever politicized, conceptual historians must show "the emergence and transformation of concepts as outcomes of actors using them for political purposes." By investigating linguistic battles waged in great books and minor works—as well as in pamphlets, speeches, letters, and diaries—conceptual history lives symbiotically with social history. Moreover, conceptual historians argue, when we witness the battles over words like *revolution, progress, state, politics, republic,* and the like, we discover "the contours of a new conceptual topography which, when taken together, constitute 'modernity.'"[33]

Aside from some writers who cast into question virtually all concepts,[34] there are three main criticisms of conceptual history, none of which seems insurmountable. First, in a notable passage, Skinner argued that while Milton certainly had the concept of "originality" in his writings, he did not have the word. How, then, does one do conceptual history? Koselleck's answer, that conceptual historians must look at words and "parallel expressions," seems to be an inadequate response that sets an impossible task.[35] Second, how does the conceptual historian decide upon

---

32. Ball, introduction to *Political Innovation and Conceptual Change*, ed. Ball et al., 3; Koselleck, "*Begriffsgeschichte* and Social History," 413, 415, 420; James Farr, "Understanding Conceptual History Politically," in *Political Innovation and Conceptual Change*, ed. Ball et al., 24–49, esp. 31–32; Richter, "Conceptual History and Political Theory," 618. On the issue of concepts both reflecting and causing change, see also Quentin Skinner, "Language and Political Change," in *Political Innovation and Conceptual Change*, ed. Ball et al., 6–23, see esp. 20–22.

33. Koselleck, "*Begriffsgeschichte* and Social History," 413–14; Farr, "Understanding Conceptual History Politically," 31–32, 38; Tribe, "The *Geschichtliche Grundbegriffe* Project," 181–83; Ball, *Transforming Political Discourse*, 16; Richter, "Conceptual History and Political Theory," 610, 618–19; Richter, "*Begriffsgeschichte* and the History of Ideas," 253.

34. Alasdair MacIntyre, "The Essential Contestability of Some Social Concepts," *Ethics* 84, no. 1 (1973): 1–9.

35. Skinner, "Language and Political Change," 7–8; Koselleck, "*Begriffsgeschichte* and Social History," 418–21. Interestingly, Lovejoy recognized this problem, although Skinner accused him otherwise. See Paul Oskar Kristeller, "History of Philosophy and History of Ideas,"

the most "meaningful" or most "important" sources for his or her studies? Does every scrap of paper count equally in this sort of history, or only "major" works of literature, philosophy, law, and so forth?[36] And finally, is the concept the best unit of analysis for intellectual history? Skinner has maintained for more than twenty years that it is a mistake "to write histories of ideas tracing the morphology of a given concept over time." Indeed, in a recent essay, he has declared, "I remain unrepentant in my belief that there can be no histories of concepts as such; there can only be histories of their uses in argument." According to Skinner, we should focus not on major texts and not on concepts but instead "on the more general social and intellectual matrix out of which both arose." In doing so, the intellectual historian will situate a concept into its "intellectual context," explore the surrounding "vocabulary" by understanding the "general vocabulary of the age," and thus write a "history of ideologies." Only then will we understand a writer, a text, or a concept.[37] To an outside observer, the difference between Skinner's approach and that of conceptual historians does not seem so dramatic, because surely a good conceptual history necessarily explores the surrounding vocabulary and the contexts—intellectual, social, and political—out of which concepts arise.

This book is not a study in conceptual history. Indeed, it is doubtful that a conceptual history of tyranny could be written, because even in ancient and early modern times, the words are dauntingly voluminous— *tyrannis, dominatio, despotisme, absolutisme, dictator, oppression, servitude,* and so forth. Beyond this fundamental problem, this study does not seek to understand incremental changes in concepts over some manageable period of time, and it does not focus on the meanings or definitions of words and concepts; rather, it focuses on a limited number of profound and complex analyses or theories of tyranny. To accomplish this latter

Journal of the History of Philosophy 2, no. 1 (1964): 1–14, esp. 12; and Skinner, "Meaning and Understanding in the History of Ideas," 35–37.

36. Richter, "Conceptual History and Political Theory," 627–28.

37. Skinner, "Meaning and Understanding in the History of Ideas," 48; idem, "A Reply to My Critics," 283; idem, *The Foundations of Modern Political Thought*, vol. 1, *The Renaissance* (London: Cambridge University Press, 1978), ix–xiv; idem, "Language and Political Change," 8. Similarly, J.G.A. Pocock has argued that intellectual historians should focus not on concepts but on the "conceptual vocabulary," the "language," or the "discourse" within which concepts function. See Pocock, *The Machiavellian Moment: Florentine Political Thought and the Atlantic Republican Tradition* (Princeton: Princeton University Press, 1975), vii–ix, 84–86; also idem, "Political Ideas as Historical Events: Political Philosophers as Historical Actors," in *Political Theory and Political Education*, ed. Melvin Richter (Princeton: Princeton University Press, 1980), 139–58; John G. Gunnell, *Political Theory: Tradition and Interpretation* (Cambridge, Mass.: Winthrop, 1979), 96–103; and Richter, "Conceptual History and Political Theory," 620.

task, it seems reasonable, though perhaps not essential, to concentrate on what the tradition of European political thought has called major writers, instead of on minor works, pamphlets, and so on.

It is fair for the reader to ask, if this book is neither the history of an idea nor conceptual history, what is it? It is the story of a perennial problem in our history and how various political philosophers have sought to analyze and explain this ever-recurring threat of tyranny. In an essay written near the end of his life, Franz Neumann, who gave us the first great theoretical analysis of the structure of Nazi Germany, wrote, "Strange though it may seem, we do not possess any systematic study of dictatorship. . . . There is no analysis that seeks to generalize not only from the political experience of the twentieth century, but from the political systems of the more distant past."[38] Three decades later, this statement remains largely true. Despite an enormous and varied literature that has examined Hitler's Germany and Stalin's Soviet Union, despite many attempts to make distinctions among so-called totalitarian regimes and so-called authoritarian regimes, no study has sought to put modern theories of tyranny into historical perspective. What Neumann sought, an analysis of modern forms of tyranny in light of ancient and modern theories of tyranny, has remained elusive. As a consequence, this book makes a cautious and preliminary effort to fill this void by examining over time the perennial problem of tyranny.

Wolin has argued that in the European tradition of political thought one can find a "fairly stable vocabulary" that addresses a "core of problems" examined in a variety of ways by successive political thinkers from ancient Greece to the twentieth century. In suggesting that the European political tradition "discloses the continual reappearance of certain problem-topics," Wolin was of course not maintaining that these problems were identical from one century to the next, and he certainly noted loud disagreement about possible solutions to these problems. "What is important is the continuity of preoccupations, not the unanimity of response."[39] This book starts from the premise that the phenomenon of tyranny is one of these recurring problems, and although it is rarely the central preoccupation of any thinker, it is almost always a secondary or tertiary concern. Of course, the problem of tyranny is not identical over time; Pisistratus did not rule as did Hitler. But there are enduring similarities over time, so much so that if we can liken tyranny to an ever-

38. Franz Neumann, "Notes on the Theory of Dictatorship," in *The Democratic and the Authoritarian State* (Glencoe, Ill.: Free Press, 1957), 233–56, esp. 233.

39. Sheldon S. Wolin, *Politics and Vision: Continuity and Innovation in Western Political Thought* (Boston: Little, Brown, 1960), 27, 23, 3.

recurring and very frightful melody, then it is reasonable to conclude that history records frequent variations and considerable innovation on a familiar theme. And of course the concept of tyranny has shifted significantly over time, as has even the vocabulary of tyranny, but some concepts, as Wolin has suggested, "retain some contact with common meanings and experience," and tyranny is just such a concept, with a common core of meaning that has been "refashioned" to fit the new needs of each age.[40]

One could undertake to understand theories of tyranny in a great variety of ways. One could look at more thinkers in less depth, one could narrow the time framework to focus more carefully on what one regards as both major and minor works, and one could certainly look at brilliant theorists outside the European tradition of political thought. But I am most familiar with the European tradition, and I have chosen to look at what I regard as a small collection of great writers, not because it is necessarily the best way to explore theories of tyranny, but because it is at least one way to begin. Can I offer an unassailable defense of my selection of these dozen thinkers and not others, for example, my inclusion of Montesquieu and exclusion of Locke? Of course not. But in a preliminary journey one must begin somewhere; one cannot visit all unexplored territory.

As John Gunnell has suggested, "it is perfectly possible to approach [the history of political theory] as a series of perspectives on perennial and fundamental issues of political life which challenge and teach the reader to think about these issues." And, as a further justification for this approach, I do think there are great political thinkers with something called genius, and it is worth examining them in some detail. These men and women have what Wolin called "vision"—they see clearly and often from a new perspective, and they offer to their contemporaries, usually in times of crisis, some combination of warning, prophecy, and imagination, all as they refashion concepts and reformulate theories in order to criticize their times and, usually, to offer a promise of something new.[41]

Because, in Wolin's words, the "political experience of one age is never precisely the same as that of another," political theorists are first and foremost focused on problems of their own time. While they may think of themselves as writing for the future, as did Thucydides, or while they may quite consciously borrow from the past, as did Machiavelli, their gaze does not stray for long from present concerns. Thus, inevitably fastened

40. Ibid., 14; also, 6, 25.
41. Gunnell, *Political Theory: Tradition and Interpretation*, 134; Wolin, *Politics and Vision*, 1–27; idem, "Political Theory as a Vocation."

to a moment in time, political thinkers always reflect their times, which is why situating such thinkers in their intellectual, social, and political contexts can help us understand them. Nevertheless, great political thinkers stand out from their times, partly because they are great thinkers and partly because they often seek to say something enduring and thus make a "contribution to the continuing dialogue of Western political philosophy." Rooted in the present but taking stock of the past, great political thinkers frequently call to mind Old Testament prophets warning us about the future—and thus all great writing operates on three levels simultaneously.[42]

This means, according to Wolin, that there is both something conservative and something highly original in the best political thinking. The tradition of political theory—its problems, its questions, its vocabulary—is, to the theorist, both a help and a restraint. As Wolin has maintained, "in the act of philosophizing, the theorist enters into a debate the terms of which have been largely set beforehand," thus "compelling those who would participate in the Western political dialogue to abide by certain rules and usages." Machiavelli wanted a new order of things, Hobbes sought to begin anew, and Marx urged his followers to discard the past by listening to the "poetry of the future," but in the end, their dreams and endeavors were dragged down by the weight of historical developments. But they were also forced to talk about a new future in the language of the past, in some cases hindered by the baggage of the past, thereby ensuring more continuity than discontinuity. Nevertheless, side by side with this conservative tradition one finds innovative originality, which is why we read great political thinkers, not because of antiquarian interests, but because they help us see the world with fresh eyes. In the history of European thought, "genius has not always taken the form of unprecedented originality," but rather, genius usually revolves around the two qualities of vision, seeing critically and prophetically from a new perspective, and of imagination, asking old questions in new and provocative ways. Thus, according to Wolin, political thinkers "unfasten established ways of thinking and [thrust] on their contemporaries and posterity the necessity of rethinking political experience."[43]

My approach challenges claims that Skinner made in his famous 1969 article, "Meaning and Understanding in the History of Ideas." Skinner

---

42. Wolin, *Politics and Vision*, 25–27. Although it is woefully old-fashioned, there is something to Kristeller's claim that, in all great thinkers, one finds something "dated" and something timeless—not timeless answers, to be sure, but perhaps questions. See Kristeller, "History of Philosophy and History of Ideas," 11.

43. Wolin, *Politics and Vision*, 23–24, 27.

maintained that there are no "perennial problems," that there are instead only problems specific to a given moment in time. Doubtless it is true that there are no *identical* problems that reappear from age to age, but it strikes me that there is enough continuity in the phenomenon of tyranny to call it a perennial problem. No matter how dramatically different tyrannies seem to be, there are what Wittgenstein would call family resemblances among them. Skinner also argued that there are no "lessons" to be learned from the past, precisely because the problems of past thinkers were very different from ours and specific to their times. As a consequence, "the classic texts cannot be concerned with our questions and answers, but only with their own." It is naïve and fruitless, Skinner suggested, to rely on thinkers from the past to help solve problems in the present. Rather, "we must learn to do our thinking for ourselves." Taken literally, as Joseph V. Femia, one of Skinner's critics, has said, this argument "would reduce the history of thought to little more than a sterile celebration of intellectual pedigree." Obviously, classic texts are not concerned with our problems, but whenever thinkers confront the problems of their own times, they invariably lean on the past by reformulating old analyses and by refashioning an old vocabulary. There is no reason we cannot try to do something similar. In doing so, we do not learn complete lessons, but instead partial lessons, as Gunnell has suggested, we do not find timeless truths, but we do find insight and education—and these more modest goals are important. "What seems to have been forgotten," Wolin has argued, "is that one reads past theories, not because they are familiar and confirmative, but because they are strange and therefore provocative."[44]

So what exactly am I trying to accomplish in writing this book? What I maintain is that there is a little-noticed discourse in the history of European political thought that addresses the perennial problem of tyranny. While the problem of tyranny is not the chief concern of any individual thinker, at least until we come to Neumann and Arendt, it is usually an important concern. In analyzing tyranny and in offering theories of tyranny, these political thinkers are certainly reacting to problems of the

---

44. Skinner, "Meaning and Understanding in the History of Ideas," 50–53 (Skinner later modified his positions somewhat; see Skinner, "A Reply to My Critics," 283–88); Joseph V. Femia, "An Historicist Critique of 'Revisionist' Methods for Studying the History of Ideas," in *Meaning and Context*, ed. Tully, 156–75, esp. 158; Wolin, "Political Theory as a Vocation," 1077; Gunnell, *Political Theory: Tradition and Interpretation*, 134–35. Kenneth Minogue put it this way: "Just as one finds aesthetic value in the Parthenon, the Sistine Chapel, and *The Magic Flute* . . . so one may also find philosophical value in works of earlier writers." See Minogue, "Method in Intellectual History: Quentin Skinner's *Foundation*," in *Meaning and Context*, ed. Tully, 176–93, esp. 178.

moment. Tacitus wondered what made Rome travel from the republic of
Cato to the absolute rule (*dominatio*) of Tiberius; Montesquieu latched on
to the new word *despotisme* in order to criticize the power of the encroaching French monarchy; Marx responded to the brutalizing poverty of
nineteenth-century capitalism; and Weber marveled at and feared the
stultifying force of emerging bureaucratic domination. Each of these
thinkers was shouting warnings in times of dangers; almost all were like
prophets in moments of crisis.[45] What makes this a discourse is the fact
that, although situated in specific moments in time and reacting to specific historical developments, each thinker borrowed from the past, entered into an established dialogue, in order to analyze the present. While
I am mindful of Skinner's admonition that it is virtually impossible to
prove that one thinker influenced another,[46] I still think the evidence is
persuasive. Both Aristotle and Tacitus openly acknowledged borrowing
from Plato; Montesquieu frequently quoted Tacitus and Machiavelli;
Tocqueville delighted in contemporary comparisons of his work with that
of Tacitus and Montesquieu; Marx clearly acknowledged the importance
of Aristotle, Machiavelli, and Montesquieu; and Freud regarded Plato as
the greatest of psychologists, the one who best saw the politics, and potential tyranny, of the mind. Although late-twentieth-century scholars
have inadequately explored this tradition in political theory—this discourse in which political thinkers refashioned both the vocabulary of tyranny and thus the theories of tyranny—the thinkers examined in this
book certainly explored this tradition of political thought well.

Parts of five chapters of this book have been published, but in general
the individual chapters are not especially original. In this sense, this book
is not for the specialist. One who has spent years studying Greek thought
will find little, if anything, original in the chapters on Plato and Aristotle;
a scholar who has studied Marx closely will find little, if anything, new in
that chapter. But in another sense, this book is written for a world of
specialists insofar as I have attempted—however successfully—to climb
out of a comfortable corner of specialization and synthesize far-ranging
theories of tyranny, hoping to provide some increment of insight to students and scholars who might also feel confined by the narrow world of
modern academics. Thus, to the extent that this book has any originality,
it is more in the aggregate than the individual parts; it is in taking a
slightly different perspective from this little noticed corner in the history
of European political thought.

---

45. Wolin, *Politics and Vision*, 8, 13; Gunnell, *Political Theory: Tradition and Interpretation*, 135, 142–43.

46. Skinner, "Meaning and Understanding in the History of Ideas," 26.

One final thought. This book is emphatically not a handbook for tyrants, because tyrants already know what is central to this book. Rather, like all the thinkers in this tradition, like all those who have formulated theories of tyranny, my wish is to write for those who do not know—in Gramsci's words—so that they may guard against tyranny and resist it.

1

PLATO

The Political Psychology of Tyranny

Plato offered us the first great theoretical analysis of tyranny, a fact that often remains both overlooked and unexamined. Even though the nature and structure of tyranny persisted as chief concerns throughout his life, even though as a young student he was happy to see the fall of the Thirty Tyrants and as an elderly philosopher sought twice to reform Dionysius II, who was tyrant of Syracuse, modern commentators pay comparatively little attention to his descriptions and analyses of both tyrants and tyrannies. Our selectivity would surprise classical writers. Both Aristotle and Tacitus, to use but two examples, regarded Plato's analysis of tyranny as a solid foundation upon which to build their own theoretical and descriptive constructs. There are probably many reasons why too many twentieth-century critics have ignored Plato's discussions of tyranny: perhaps his theory of justice is of such gigantic stature that it seizes not just center stage but nearly the entire stage whenever we discuss Plato; or perhaps his political ideas seem so unrealistic that we cannot picture him as offering us a realistic portrait or analysis of tyranny; or perhaps because he himself was so hostile to our own democratic ideals, and in fact impresses us as rather authoritarian, we cannot imagine him as either opponent or critic of tyranny.

Nevertheless, Plato's theory of tyranny is, as both Freud and Arendt, for example, understood quite well, neither thoroughly unrealistic nor merely of antiquarian interest, and this first great analysis of both the psychology and the political culture of tyranny deserves greater scrutiny. Tyrants fascinated Plato for the same reasons they fascinate us—think of the endless refocusing of our attention on Hitler, Stalin, Pinochet, Mao Zedong, and more recently Saddam Hussein—because they shatter ordinary political life, because they are individuals who unhesitatingly break through traditional moral boundaries in an attempt to initiate a new order of things by extraordinary political action, and because they are powerful and sometimes brilliant individuals who willingly choose evil, usually out of self-interest scantily justified by ideological trappings, when they might have undertaken great good. Evil giants to be sure, but at least they are giants. Having recognized that the early tyrants were innovators who transformed Greek city-states, having seen for himself that the heirs to these tyrants had fallen into cruelty and degradation, and having come to the conclusion that the tyrant was frequently the potential philosopher-ruler gone astray, Plato not surprisingly groped for an analysis of the phenomena of tyrants and tyrannies.

Tyranny as Both Disharmony and Disease

Plato, of course, regarded tyranny as the opposite of justice, and he thought of justice as a harmonious arrangement of conflicting parts of the city and of the soul.[1] This answer, that justice is what produces and ensures harmony, has struck Plato's audiences, then and now, as both unusual and unexpected. When Glaucon and Adeimantus pleaded with Socrates at the beginning of book 2 of the *Republic* to show them why justice is worthwhile, they probably expected a list of just actions or at least some clear criteria by which to make such a list. Plato, however, rejected this approach. Instead, Plato sought to build a moral theory, or a theory of justice, by discovering and describing the just city and the just person, arguing, in fact, that the just act in any given situation is simply what the just person would do. This is neither as circular nor as fruitless

1. Plato, *Republic*, trans. Allan Bloom (New York: Basic Books, 1968), 430e, 435b–c, 443a–444a. All translations of Plato's dialogues, except for the translations of the *Republic* and the *Laws*, can be found in *The Collected Dialogues of Plato*, ed. Edith Hamilton and Huntington Cairns (Princeton: Princeton University Press, 1961).

as it seems, because Plato suggested, rather convincingly, that no list of just actions, and no formula by which we might judge an action to be just, can possibly help us in all times, places, and circumstances. Indeed, Plato looked upon most of the acts that we ordinarily call just as simply signs that justice is active, much as happiness and stamina are not equivalent to health but merely symptomatic of good mental and physical health. Conversely, most of the actions that we would ordinarily call injustice are, according to Plato, symptoms of a deeper illness.[2]

Harmony, for Plato, is a condition, a cause, and a result of justice. In the just city, each of three classes—philosopher-rulers, warriors or auxiliaries, and the producing classes—will perform its proper function, thus producing a harmonious order guided by the knowledge of the philosophers. The philosopher-rulers bring wisdom to the city, the auxiliaries bring courage, and the producing classes bring only the more commonplace moderation, but when each class performs the role appropriate to it by nature, justice is the result. "[A] city seemed to be just when each of the three classes of natures present in it minded its own business." Similarly, harmony, in this case psychic harmony, is the chief characteristic of the just individual. In the just individual, again, each of the three parts of the soul—the reasoning part, the spirited part, and the desiring part—performs its proper function under the careful guidance of reason.[3] The just individual "arranges himself, becomes his own friend, and harmonizes the three parts, exactly like three notes in a harmonic scale. . . . Then, and only then, he acts. . . . In all these actions he believes and names a just and fine action one that preserves and helps to produce this condition, and wisdom the knowledge that supervises this action."[4] The just ac-

2. The following book provided key ideas in this paragraph: Julia Annas, *An Introduction to Plato's Republic* (Oxford: Oxford University Press, 1981), see esp. 122, 157–64. See also Gregory Vlastos, "Justice and Happiness in the *Republic*," in *Ethics, Politics, and Philosophy of Art and Religion*, vol. 2 of *Plato: A Collection of Critical Essays*, ed. Gregory Vlastos (Garden City, N.Y.: Doubleday, 1971), 66–95.

3. *Republic*, 435b, 433a–b.

4. *Republic*, 443d–e. See also Terence Irwin, *Plato's Moral Theory: The Early and Middle Dialogues* (Oxford: Oxford University Press, 1977), chap. 2, 177–248. For a good discussion of the spirited part of the soul and its relation to philosophy, see Mary Nichols, "The *Republic*'s Two Alternatives: Philosopher-Kings and Socrates," *Political Theory* 12, no. 2 (1984): 252–74. For recent debate whether Plato regarded women as equal, see Annas, *An Introduction to Plato's Republic*, 181–85; Susan Moller Okin, "Philosopher Queens and Private Wives: Plato on Women and the Family," in *Feminist Interpretations and Political Theory*, ed. Mary Lyndon Shanley and Carole Pateman (University Park: Pennsylvania State University Press, 1991), 11–31; and an intriguing article on Plato's discourse by Wendy Brown, "'Supposing Truth Were a Woman . . .': Plato's Subversion of Masculine Dialogue," *Political Theory* 16, no. 4 (1988): 594–616.

tion both emanates from and preserves this inner harmony of the individual.

If harmony is the central metaphor in Plato's discussion of justice, then the metaphor of health is almost as important because justice is analogous to health. At least as early as the dialogue *Gorgias,* Plato likened justice to health,[5] and in the *Republic,* he looked upon justice as producing the greatest psychic health for the individual. Like Freud, who thought that mental health involved a proper balance of ego, superego, and id, Plato maintained that justice was a form of mental health and a proper balance of the soul.[6] Plato was suggesting, in fact, that human beings have an "essential need" for justice,[7] that to have justice is to be "completely fulfilled," to attain "the right condition of the human soul," to find "the spiritual harmony resulting from perfect self-control," and to live a "genuine" life.[8] With this argument, Plato hoped to demonstrate that an individual would find justice worthwhile and would seek justice for the same reason he or she would seek health, and having demonstrated this, he sought to show that his ideal city, the just city that is in fact a prerequisite for the existence of just individuals, is the city that best meets the needs, both physical and psychical, of its citizens. All of this, of course, like any attempt to recount Plato's lively dialogues, remains rather lifeless and formulaic, but it remains a necessary prelude to a discussion of Plato's analysis of tyranny.

Tyranny, by contrast, is obviously both disharmony and disease, by which Plato meant that both the tyrant and the city ruled by the tyrant suffer from disharmony, both in the parts of the soul and in the parts, or classes, of the city. Although Plato suggested that all constitutions, other than his ideal republic, are somewhat ill, it is tyranny that embodies the

5. Plato, *Gorgias,* trans. W. D. Woodhead, 477a-478b. See also Irwin, *Plato's Moral Theory,* 129.

6. Anthony Kenny, "Mental Health in Plato's *Republic,*" in *The Anatomy of the Soul* (Oxford: Basil Blackwell, 1973), 1–27. See also John M. Cooper, "The Psychology of Justice in Plato," *American Philosophical Quarterly* 14, no. 2 (1977): 151–57; and G.M.A. Grube, *Plato's Thought* (Boston: Beacon Press, 1958 [1935]), chap. 4, 120–49.

7. Ernest Barker, *The Political Thought of Plato and Aristotle* (New York: Dover, 1959), 102. See *Republic,* 369c, where Plato suggests that the ideal city is founded on human needs, of which justice turns out to be our most essential need. See also Jerome Neu, "Plato's Analogy of State and Individual: *The Republic* and the Organic Theory of the State," *Philosophy* 46, no. 177 (1971): 238–54.

8. Annas, *An Introduction to Plato's Republic,* 132; Barker, *The Political Thought of Plato and Aristotle,* 101; Paul Shorey, "Plato's Ethics," in *Plato,* ed. Vlastos, 2:15; and Plato, *Letter VII,* trans. L. A. Post, 327d. (If *Letter VII* is not authentic, my overall argument would remain the same, but it would be more difficult to construct.) See also Plato, *Apology,* trans. Hugh Tredennick, 30a-b.

"extreme illness of a city." Similarly, just as disease constitutes the chief evil of the body, so injustice, of which tyranny is the extreme manifestation, constitutes "an evil condition of the soul." While Plato took great care to describe the tyrant, he thought that there was no qualitative difference between the tyrant and the subjects—hardly citizens—ruled by the tyrant, because the dispositions of men and women both create and reflect the political order in which they live. "Or do you suppose that the regimes arise 'from an oak or rocks' and not from the dispositions of the men in the cities?" Indeed, no healthy individual can grow from the soil of tyranny. After describing the immorality and license of Syracuse, Plato noted that "[i]n such an environment no man under heaven, brought up in self-indulgence, could ever grow to be wise. So marvelous a temperament as that is not in nature."[9] Both tyrant and subjects mirror each other, reinforcing their common subjection and their common illness.

In book 8 of the *Republic,* when Plato offered a theory both of revolution and of history, he presented it less as a political, economic, or class analysis and more as a medical diagnosis. Gradually the patient, in this case his ideal city, grows older and declines, for nothing can resist natural decay.[10] Illness, however, hastens this decline, and this disease passes through various stages until it reaches the fever pitch of tyranny, the complete collapse of the healthy city. The stages of decline that Plato described are, of course, familiar; the ideal city moves first to timocracy, animated by a love of honor, then to oligarchy, animated by a love of wealth, then to democracy, animated by a love of license that has the appearance of freedom, until finally it founders in tyranny, which is simply a state of limitless desiring.

At a political level, this decline entails an increasing discord, or disharmony, of the various parts and classes of the city. On the one hand, Plato certainly meant that neither individuals nor classes attend to their proper, specialized functions. Democratic individuals, for example, do whatever pleases them at the moment, according to Plato, which can only result in a life of wandering and dabbling as these individuals attempt to learn a bit of philosophy, soldier for a while, sometimes try their hand at being a producer, but mostly gratify whimsical and transient desires. Classes, too, mingle and meddle in the proper functions of their counterparts. "Meddling among the classes, of which there are three, and exchange with one another is the greatest harm for the city and would most correctly be called extreme evil-doing."[11]

9. *Republic*, 544c, 477b–c, 544d–e; *Letter VII*, 326c.
10. *Republic*, 546a.
11. *Republic*, 434b–c; also 551e–552a, 561c–d.

On the other hand, Plato feared open civil conflict, something far more serious than this meddling. Whereas, in the best city, people shun political and economic power, in the various diseased cities we see a struggle among individuals and classes for power and all its apparent advantages. "For it is likely that if a city of good men came to be, there would be a fight over not ruling, just as there is now over ruling."[12] Harmony and unity collapse, as we can see in Plato's description of oligarchy: "Such a city's not being one but of necessity two, the city of the poor and the city of the rich, dwelling together in the same place, ever plotting against each other." Such discord Plato described as illness, and he warned against the oligarchic or democratic city that has a tendency to "fall sick and do battle with itself, and . . . become divided by faction."[13]

The collapse from republic to tyranny results both from the rulers' lack of wisdom and from the susceptibility of the many whose desires lead them to embrace the appearance of happiness in lieu of the reality. Change comes largely because ruling elites are unable to rule with wisdom, thus becoming morally unfit for rule. "Change in every regime comes from that part of it which holds the ruling offices."[14] Although Plato blamed the ruling classes harshly, he suggested that they had eager accomplices from among the people, because the "madness of the many" cheerfully chases after appearances. The many race toward democracy, which appears to offer the most freedom, despite the fact that it really offers only the "license" to pursue one's desires in all directions. "Just like a many-colored cloak decorated in all hues, this regime, decorated with all dispositions, would also look fairest, and many perhaps, . . . like boys and women looking at many-colored things, would judge this to be the fairest regime."[15]

The real force behind this political transformation is desire, because political decline is "pushed on by desire," just as democracy edges over into tyranny because of an "insatiable desire" to do what one pleases.[16] Indeed, revolution, according to Plato, is unavoidable once a city is ruled, not by reason, but by desire. "Neither can a city be free from unrest under any laws, be those laws what they may, while its citizens think fit to spend everything on excesses . . . banquets and drinking bouts and

12. *Republic*, 347d; also 520e–521a. For Plato's views on the roles of intellectuals and philosophers in political rule, see Blair Campbell, "Intellect and the Political Order in Plato's *Republic*," *History of Political Thought* 1, no. 3 (1980): 361–89.

13. *Republic*, 551d, 556e.

14. *Republic*, 545d; see also *Laws*, trans. Thomas Pangle (New York: Basic Books, 1980), 683e.

15. *Republic*, 496c, 557b–c.

16. *Republic*, 548b, 562c.

painstaking attention to the gratification of lust. It is inevitable that in such cities there should be an unending succession of governments— tyranny, oligarchy, democracy—one after another, while the very name of just and equal government is anathema to those in control."[17] All of this political change, however, is simultaneously cause and symptom of psychological change within both tyrant and subjects, because political discord signifies the more profound illness of individual psychic disharmony.

All of this political discord is symptomatic of disorder within the souls of not only the tyrant but also the subjects of tyranny. If the just person has achieved a harmony among the three parts of his or her soul, with reason certainly predominant, the unjust person experiences psychic "dissonance" and a soul that refuses to obey the dictates of reason. Whereas the just individual "becomes his own friend," the unjust individual possesses a soul at war with itself, a soul whose various parts are enemies to one another, endlessly engaging in "civil strife." The unjust man "is a faction and not of one mind with himself," as well as "an enemy both to himself and to just men." Just as Plato used psychological terminology to analyze political change, he used a political vocabulary to describe what happens in the soul that has lost all harmony. In the democratic individual, for example, "faction and counterfaction arise in him and he does battle with himself."[18]

With this argument, Plato maintained that the tyrant and the city ruled by the tyrant suffered from extremes of disharmony, from a sort of feverish and almost delirious illness in which the guidance of reason and the admiration for honor had been pushed aside in pursuit of boundless desire. "Musn't [injustice], in its turn, be a certain faction among those three [parts of the soul]—a meddling, interference, and rebellion of a part of the soul against the whole?"[19] In other words, tyranny, for Plato, is a political order in which both tyrant and subjects are caught up in an endless, if unsatisfying, cycle of desire and gratification, a political culture of hedonism. As a result, Plato's greatest contribution to the interrelated theories of tyranny we find in the European tradition is his insight that political and economic power both cause and reflect a culture and a psychology of tyranny. Tyranny, for Plato, is more than simply a frightening abuse of power; tyranny must lean upon a political culture that teaches us how to behave, to think, and even to feel.

---

17. *Letter VII*, 326c–d.
18. *Laws*, 691a, 689b; *Republic*, 443d; Kenny, "Mental Health in Plato's *Republic*," 8; *Republic* 352a, 560a.
19. *Republic*, 444b.

Desires Out of Control

Plato's tyrant is, by definition, a person governed by desire. In the dialogue *Gorgias,* for example, Polus says that were he a tyrant, he would be "at liberty to do what I please in the state—to kill, to exile, and to follow my own pleasure in every act,"[20] a definition that meshes well with Plato's discussion in the *Republic.* Callicles, however, in his description of those who are "naturally" stronger and better, portrayed most clearly Plato's image of the tyrant, a description later partially adopted by Nietzsche while distinguishing between master and slave moralities.

> The naturally noble and just is what I now describe to you with all frankness—namely that anyone who is to live aright should suffer his appetites to grow to the greatest extent and not check them, and through courage and intelligence should be competent to minister to them at their greatest and to satisfy every appetite with what it craves. But this, I imagine, is impossible for the many; hence they blame such men through a sense of shame to conceal their own impotence. . . . Luxury and intemperance and license, when they have sufficient backing, are virtue and happiness, and all the rest is tinsel, the unnatural catchwords of mankind, mere nonsense and of no account.[21]

Possessing a soul thoroughly out of balance, the tyrant is the person who is indifferent to both reason and honor and whose soul lusts after gratification until it is enslaved to desire, the soul's "most depraved and maddest" part.[22]

Plato just about defined madness as a state in which desire dominates us completely; he quoted Sophocles to the effect that sexual desire is a "frenzied and savage master"; he agreed with Cephalus, who condemned desires as "many mad masters"; he spoke of being "addicted" to desires; he labeled the desiring part of the soul a "mob-like beast"; and he talked of "this tyrannic man maddened by desires and loves."[23] Plato did not, of

20. *Gorgias*, 469c.

21. *Gorgias*, 491e–492c. Callicles' description of the tyrant, which is similar to the portrait put forth by Glaucon and Adeimantus at the beginning of book 2 of the *Republic*, is really the one Plato uses, not the more defensible description by Thrasymachus. See T. Y. Henderson, "In Defense of Thrasymachus," *American Philosophical Quarterly* 7, no. 3 (1970): 218–28. For elaboration on Callicles' view of justice, see R. E. Allen, "The Speech of Glaucon in Plato's *Republic*," *Journal of the History of Philosophy* 25, no. 1 (1987): 3–11.

22. *Republic*, 577d.

23. *Republic*, 329c, 329d; *Letter VII*, 331c; *Republic*, 590b, 578a.

course, seek an individual who had no desires, because even his just person desires courage, wisdom, and the health resulting from a harmonious soul. Instead, Plato distinguished between good and bad desires, or rational and unnecessary desires,[24] and he seemed to associate the latter with physical gratification that goes beyond the simple needs for physical and psychical health. Metaphorically, unnecessary desires are those bold enough to saunter forth in our dreams, because in our dreams the desiring part of the soul "dares to do everything as though it were released from, and rid of, all shame and prudence. And it doesn't shrink from attempting intercourse, as it supposes, with a mother or with anyone else at all . . . or attempting any foul murder at all." Like Freud, Plato suggested that our dreams reveal the lascivious and homicidal wishes that we both possess and repress, or, as Plato put it, "surely some terrible, savage, and lawless form of desires is in every man, even in some of us who seem to be ever so measured."[25] The tyrant is the one who pursues in the light of day those desires the rest of us only dream about at night.

Plato had only disgust and contempt for the tyrannic city, and indeed for the democratic city, which invariably consecrates itself to the obsessive chase for unnecessary desires. "After the fashion of cattle, always looking down and with their heads bent to earth and table, they feed, fattening themselves, and copulating; and, for the sake of getting more of these things, they kick and butt with horns and hoofs of iron, killing each other because they are insatiable."[26] Subjects of tyranny passionately chase what is pitifully insubstantial. Surprisingly, although Plato had only contempt for the subjects of the tyrannic city, he had a certain disconsolate admiration for the tyrant because the tyrant is generally the great person—indeed a potential philosopher-ruler—gone bad, the potentially best person who has been cultivated in a perverted and unnatural manner. "Won't we say for souls too . . . that, similarly, those with the best natures become exceptionally bad when they get bad instruction? Or do you suppose an ordinary nature is the source of great injustices and unmixed villainy? Don't you suppose, rather, that it's a lusty one corrupted by its rearing, while a weak nature will never be the cause of great things either good or bad?"[27] This accords well with Socrates' claim in the *Crito* that ordinary people have the capacity neither for great harm nor great

24. *Republic*, 561b–c, 571b; Irwin, *Plato's Moral Theory*, 191–95, 213–17. Plato suggested that people must be trained or educated to desire what is good. Irwin, *Plato's Moral Theory*, 201–2.

25. *Republic*, 571c–d, 572b.

26. *Republic*, 486a–b. For a view of Plato's pessimism about what human beings can attain, see E. R. Dodds, "Plato and the Irrational Soul," in *Plato*, ed. Vlastos, 2:206–29.

27. *Republic*, 491e; also 495b.

good, an idea that Plato repeated much later in the *Statesman*.[28] As a consequence, the potential tyrant is also a potential philosopher-ruler because only those souls capable of unmitigated injustice are strong enough to recognize justice and desire it, or, as Socrates put it in an early dialogue, "And is it not the soul which has the greater power and wisdom also better, and better able to do both good and evil in every action?"[29] This explains, in part, Plato's claim in the *Laws* that it is the tyrant who can most easily bring about the best city, because the tyrant, having proved strong enough to master and shape himself or herself, is strong enough to shape an orderly city.[30] Ironically, the link between the philosopher-ruler and the tyrant is desire. Desire obsesses both, but while the tyrant pursues unsatisfying and unnecessary physical desires, the philosopher, drawn by powerful Eros or love or what Plato called "heaven-sent madness," is impelled irresistibly to desire what is immortal, knowledge of the good.[31]

Although the tyrant and the subjects of that tyrant chase their desires, they only get what they think they want and never what they really want. What holds for tyrants holds for the tyrant's subjects. "Doesn't the city that is slave and under a tyranny least do what it wants? . . . And therefore, the soul that is under a tyranny will least do what it wants."[32] For Plato, this was an obvious deduction. Whereas the philosopher-ruler pursues rational desires and most specifically the desire for justice or psychic health, a condition that satisfies the single most essential human need, the tyrant remains ignorant of his or her need for the health brought by justice, that is, remains ignorant of what he or she really needs and wants, and instead chases "unnecessary" and ultimately unsatisfying pleasures.[33] Put simply, the tyrant wastes his or her enormous talent and energy chasing only the shadow of satisfaction, what is apparently satisfying and not what is really satisfying.

Plato argued in at least three ways that the tyrant was the unhappiest individual. First, the tyrant seeks only what is transitory and not what is enduring, an argument that leads eventually to Plato's theory of the

28. Plato, *Crito*, trans. Hugh Tredennick, 44d; Plato, *Statesman*, trans. J. B. Skemp, 303a.

29. Plato, *Lesser Hippias*, trans. Benjamin Jowett, 375e.

30. *Laws*, 709a–711e.

31. Plato, *Phaedrus*, trans. R. Hackforth, 244a-245e; Plato, *Symposium*, trans. Michael Joyce, 206b-212a. On the notion of irony and its relation to the ways in which Plato used the word *eros*, see Paul Friedlander, *Plato: An Introduction*, 2d ed., trans. Hans Meyerhoff (Princeton: Princeton University Press, 1969), chap. 7, 137–53.

32. *Republic*, 577d–e.; also, *Gorgias*, 466d.

33. *Republic*, 559c. See also Jerome Schiller, "Just Men and Just Acts in Plato's *Republic*," *Journal of the History of Philosophy* 6, no. 1 (1968): 1–14, esp. 6–11.

Forms. Second, the tyrant is literally unbalanced, torn this way and that by the demanding and conflicting desires of his or her soul, never at peace and always tormented, unable to control a soul that "teems with ten thousand such oppositions arising at the same time." The tyrant, pestered by the "stings" of multiple desires, is the person in whom "many terrible and very needy desires sprout up . . . every day and night." And third, the tyrant can find no lasting satisfaction because, by definition, to be desiring is to feel an "emptiness," a "hunger," and a yearning, conditions that Plato described as "painful."[34] Even the most powerful tyrant, one who is able to gratify every desire almost instantaneously, must waste his or her life in a cycle of desire and gratification followed by more desire and more gratification, a cycle that ensures the tyrant spends at least half of a lifetime in a state that is empty and painful.

Driven on by desires that seem to have no limit, the tyrant is the individual who is least free, and in fact Plato referred to such people as "dominated by desire and enslaved to pleasure." The "license" of democracy, which appears to the democratic citizen as freedom, is no more than the slavery of the reasoning part of the soul to the desiring part, and the tyrant is the one who "not having control of himself attempts to rule others." With both reason and honor dominated completely by insatiable desire, "the real tyrant is, even if he doesn't seem so to someone, in truth a real slave."[35]

To the twentieth century, accustomed to equating democracy and freedom, it is difficult to agree that Plato's tyranny is the opposite of freedom, because it is so difficult to think of Plato's ideal city as a political order embracing freedom. Not only does his *Republic* strike us as authoritarian, but Plato offered passages in other works that seem chillingly tyrannical: for example, "it follows that there should be a schedule regulating how all the free men spend all their time, beginning almost at dawn and extending to the next dawn and rising of the sun."[36] Perhaps we should simply conclude that, for Plato, the opposite of tyranny is not freedom but justice or virtue. This depends, however, on how one uses the word *freedom*. Consider three possible definitions.[37] First, we might equate freedom

34. *Republic*, 603d, 573d–e, 585b–c, 585a–b; *Gorgias*, 496c–d. One can find most of the arguments why a tyrant is an unhappy person in Xenophon's short treatise *Hiero or Tyrannicus*, although Xenophon's portrait of the tyrant is more moralistic and less insightful than Plato's. See Leo Strauss, *On Tyranny* (Ithaca: Cornell University Press, 1963), a book that includes the work by Xenophon as well as commentaries by Strauss and Alexandre Kojève. No translator is listed for the work by Xenophon.

35. *Phaedrus*, 238e; *Republic*, 563e–564a, 579c–d, 442a–b, 579d.

36. *Laws*, 807d–e.

37. In the following discussion, I am borrowing from, and building upon, J.M.E. Moravcsik,

with democratic freedom, the ability of all citizens to participate in political decisions that affect their lives. Second, we might look upon freedom as the ability to do what we want. And third, we might regard freedom as something approximating Kantian autonomy, as the reasoned choice of how we should order our lives; or, as Plato put it, "the good are those able to rule themselves."[38] Although Plato had no use for the first definition, he certainly thought his philosopher-rulers attained freedom as defined in the second and third instances, and indeed, he thought these last two definitions intersected neatly, since the philosopher ruler who ordered his or her life with reason was the one who had the ability to do what he or she really wanted.

Tyranny as Cookery

We know by now that statesmanship brings unity to a city, that the statesman "weaves all into its unified fabric with perfect skill," but the best ruler, according to Plato, concerns himself or herself with the souls of the city's citizens. "[W]hen you embark upon a public career, pray will you concern yourself with anything else than how we citizens can be made as good as possible?" Plato, in fact, defined politics as "the art whose business it is to care for souls,"[39] a definition extremely foreign to our liberal tradition and one that sounds to us like dangerous manipulation, although Plato would reply that all societies shape the souls of their citizens and that to pretend otherwise ignores what social scientists now more tamely call the socialization process. Not only will the best rulers do what is beneficial for the entire community, but these rulers will involve themselves in shaping the characters of their citizens. "What matters is that . . . the ruler does what is really beneficial. . . . all is well if he passes this test. . . . The ship's captain fixes his attention on the real welfare at any given time of his ship and crew. . . . By rulers with this sound attitude of mind no wrong can possibly be done so long as they keep firmly to the one great principle, that they must always administer impartial justice to their subjects under the guidance of intelligence and the art of government. Then they will not only preserve the lives of their subjects, but reform their characters too, so far as human nature permits

---

"Plato and Pericles on Freedom and Politics," *Canadian Journal of Philosophy*, supplementary vol. 9 (1983): 1–18.

38. *Laws*, 644b; also 626e.

39. *Statesman*, 305e; *Gorgias*, 515b–c; *Laws*, 650b; *Gorgias*, 464b; *Protagoras*, trans. W.K.C. Guthrie, 319a.

of this."[40] Because the best rulers avoid simply giving their citizens what they desire, but instead teach them what they ought to desire, such rulers are indeed like doctors who, "when a man is well, . . . allow him to satisfy his appetites, eating as much as he wishes when hungry or drinking when thirsty, but when he is sick, practically never allow him to take his fill of what he craves."[41] Jacqueline de Romily suggests, with some reason, that the *Republic* is a medical treatise.[42]

Not only does politics invariably concern itself with shaping souls, it is, in the eyes of Plato, an elitist occupation, and he frequently likens political leaders to captains of ships as well as to doctors, that is, people with expert knowledge. Leaders, captains, and doctors guide people toward justice and psychic health, teaching the few how to live lives of reason and the many how to control themselves with moderation. "Aren't these the most important elements of moderation for the multitude: being obedient to the rulers, and being themselves rulers of the pleasures of drink, sex, and eating?"[43] Sometimes Plato's elitism frightens us, as if he is offering a license to a brutal elite that will claim to rule us in the name of our own health. "It makes no difference whether their subjects be willing or unwilling. . . . We do not assess the medical qualification of a doctor by the degree of willingness on our part to submit to his knife or cautery or other painful treatment. . . . So long as they control our health on a scientific basis. . . . They may purge the city for its better health by putting some of the citizens to death or banishing others."[44] Still, Plato's point remains, because, if the goal of a society is moral health, then statesmen must be like doctors.

By contrast, tyrants resemble cooks who maintain power over us by pleasing our corrupted tastes. Even though Plato certainly recognized and condemned tyrannies for cruelty and the use of "violent control," and even though he noted that tyrants routinely destroy their enemies, embark upon wars so that their subjects will think they need a leader, and

40. *Statesman*, 296d–297b.

41. *Gorgias*, 505a; see also 515a–e. Plato was certainly ambivalent about doctors, because the very presence of doctors in the city implies imperfect health in the citizens. Kenny, "Mental Health in Plato's *Republic*," 6.

42. Jacqueline de Romily, *Thucydides and Athenian Imperialism*, trans. Ph. Thody, (Oxford: Basil Blackwell, 1963), 365; cited in Moravcsik, "Plato and Pericles on Freedom and Politics," 14–15.

43. *Republic*, 389d–e. At times, Plato's demand that political leadership teach us how to control ourselves and our desires seems inordinately stuffy, when, for example, he wanted someone to control laughter and not "[let] himself go" (*Republic*, 388e); and at other times, Plato's insistence on control is unsettling, when, for example, he suggested that "it's necessary to fetter [the child] with many sorts of bridles" (*Laws*, 808e).

44. *Statesman*, 293a–d.

impoverish their people so that, having to work simply to stay alive, their people will have little time to oppose the tyranny,[45] nevertheless Plato stressed that tyrannies are lasting to the extent that they are not harsh but pleasing. His analogy of the cook is clever and insightful. "Rhetoric [is] to justice what cookery is to medicine," Socrates argues in the *Gorgias,* and later in the same dialogue announces, "My trial will be like that of a doctor prosecuted by a cook before a jury of children." Just as patients and children do not know what is best for them and reach for the short-term pleasure promised by the cook instead of the long-term health offered by the doctor, so the subjects of a tyranny—at least the tyranny Plato envisioned—eagerly embrace their servitude and willingly chase after the pleasures of licentiousness. Pleasure is a "bait" deftly dangled by the tyrant, and thus "cookery has impersonated medicine and pretends to know the best foods for the body."[46]

In reality, according to Plato, tyrants do not in fact rule, because both subjects and tyrants are mutually caught up in a cycle of servitude, "slaves being doctored by slaves." Tyrants retain what power they have only so long as they engage in "flattery" of the multitude, promising to please the crowd and ultimately resembling the crowd, a weakness, in Plato's opinion, both of democracy and tyranny. The tyrant is only the democratic individual who has lost his or her last ounce of restraint, and to win power in such a feverish city, the tyrant must not only resemble the multitude but must also promise them that they can enjoy the inexhaustible license that all are joyfully applauding as freedom. No one "in the world will deliver you to an art which will win you great power in the city, unless either for better or for worse you resemble its government."[47] In the following passage, Plato was probably likening the democratic multitude of Athens to a great beast that politicians must please and flatter, but ultimately the tyrant must learn to cook for this beast.

> It is just like the case of a man who learns by heart the angers and desires of a great, strong beast he is rearing, how it should be approached and how taken hold of, when—and as a result of what—it becomes most difficult or most gentle, and, particularly, under what conditions it is accustomed to utter its several sounds, and, in turn, what sort of sounds uttered by another make it tame and angry. When he has learned all this from associating and spending time with the beast, he calls it wisdom. . . .

45. *Statesman,* 276e; *Republic,* 566e–567a.
46. *Gorgias,* 465c, 521e; 464d.
47. *Laws,* 857c; *Gorgias,* 463a–465a, 513a–b.

Knowing nothing in truth about which of these convictions and desires is noble, or base, or good, or evil, or just, or unjust, he applies all these names following the great animal's opinions—calling what delights it good and what vexes it bad. . . . So, does this man seem any different from the man who believes it is wisdom to have figured out the anger and pleasures—whether in painting, music, or, particularly, in politics—of the multifarious many who assemble?[48]

To the extent that the tyrant makes political decisions that are pleasing, though unhealthy, for the multitude, the tyrant is indeed like the cook; but to the extent that the tyrant must learn to tame, flatter, and satisfy this beast, the tyrant must be a skillful rider on a dangerous animal, and it is worth asking what skills the tyrant must have.

The Economics of Tyranny

The successful tyrant most of all must encourage his or her subjects to love money and property above virtue, honor, and even moderation, an achievement that is not terribly difficult for a tyrant, since, by definition, the subjects of tyranny have been pushed by desire to love pleasure and money above all else. The tyrant must only pander to present vices. In his conviction that tyranny and love of money are interconnected, Plato demonstrated his distaste for wealth and commerce and his belief that property is good only to the extent that it is a means to a good life, never as an end in itself. In the Laws, he wrote: "Because of the wickedness due to nature and lack of education, money has the power to engender tens of thousands of erotic desires for its insatiable and limitless acquisition. . . . The noblest and best thing of all for every city is that the truth be told about wealth, namely, that it is for the sake of the body, and the body is for the sake of the soul."[49] Although Plato greatly opposed a life devoted to the acquisition of wealth, he saw no advantage to poverty, and he ultimately advocated a life of moderation, a mean between poverty and luxury. Two enemies of all lawgivers are "wealth and poverty, . . . since

---

48. Republic, 493a–d. Plato thought that deciding public policy by popularity was equivalent to judging poetry by a show of hands; in each case the result was mediocrity and ignorance (Laws, 659a–c).

49. Laws, 870a–b.

the one produces luxury, idleness, and innovation, while the other produces illiberality and wrongdoing as well as innovation."[50]

If love of money is the tyrant's greatest weapon, the best means of exacerbating desire, then this love of money is also the greatest enemy to virtue, and in fact, when Plato described the transformation of society from republic to tyranny, it was money that eventually destroyed timocracy, oligarchy, and democracy. The eclipse of timocracy occurs when citizens love the honor that comes from battle less and wealth more. "There is . . . no other transformation so quick and so sure [as that] from a young man who loves honor to one who loves money." Oligarchy collapses in a similar fashion; at first, oligarchs attain great wealth only by means of some inner discipline over immediate desires, but in the long run, having taught the city a desire for wealth, they are powerless to condemn the many whose desires are even stronger and less disciplined than theirs. Ultimately the desire for wealth, which facilitates most other desires, batters down all restraints, even the last remnants of moderation one finds in democracy. "Isn't it by now plain that it's not possible to honor wealth in a city and at the same time adequately to maintain moderation among the citizens, but one or the other is necessarily neglected?"[51]

In this analysis, which really amounts to a theory of history, Plato demonstrated his hostility to wealth, a hostility due to the continual conflict between wealth and virtue. "[I]sn't virtue in tension with wealth, as though each were lying in the scale of a balance, always inclining in opposite directions?" Love of wealth is capable of transforming good, solid citizens into men and women whom Plato despises. Love of wealth "turns those human beings who are orderly by nature into merchants, commercial ship traders, and complete servants, and makes those who are courageous into pirates, housebreakers, temple robbers, warriors, and tyrannical types."[52] While Plato's link of merchants to pirates tugs at the curiosity of a twentieth-century audience, even more important for our purposes is his link between wealth and tyranny because both tyrannical cities and tyrannical individuals are feverishly in love with wealth. Plato took it for granted that both subjects and rulers in tyrannical states such as Persia had abandoned virtue in favor of wealth, but when we ask what exactly does love of wealth accomplish for the tyrant, we see that it dissolves all unity in the city and isolates and depoliticizes individuals.

Plato regarded disunity as the greatest of all possible evils for a city.

---

50. *Republic*, 422a; also *Laws*, 679b–c.
51. *Republic*, 553d, 555c–d; also 549a–b, 555b.
52. *Republic*, 550e; *Laws*, 831e–832a, also 695e–696a.

"Have we any greater evil for a city than what splits it and makes it many instead of one?"[53] If unity and harmony are signs of a healthy city, then multiplicity and disorder are signs of an unhealthy city, and Plato thought the surest route to disunity and discord was an obsessive love of wealth. He made this argument, for example, when he defended the common and austere living arrangements of his philosopher guardians. "Whenever they'll possess private land, houses, and currency, they'll be house-holders and farmers instead of guardians, and they'll become masters and enemies instead of allies of the other citizens; hating and being hated, plotting and being plotted against, they'll lead their whole lives far more afraid of the enemies within than those without. Then they themselves as well as the rest of the city are already rushing toward a destruction that lies very near."[54] In fact, Plato was only willing to call his ideal city a true city because all other imperfect cities fragment easily into conflicting factions quarreling over property. "For each of them is very many cities but not a city. . . . There are two, in any case, warring with each other, one of the poor, the other of the rich. And within each of these there are very many." For example, he described oligarchy as two cities, "the city of the poor and the city of the rich, . . . ever plotting against each other," and democracy comes about when the poor, after no longer recognizing any legitimate basis for the privileges accorded the rich, takes power for itself.[55]

Beyond fostering this class conflict, tyrannies fling individuals into their private worlds of personal economic affairs and isolate them from each other. Each individual, thinking only of how he or she might augment a personal fortune, gives little concern to the functioning of the city as a whole. "The treasure house full of gold . . . which each man has, destroys the regime," or, as he put it later in the *Laws,* "the common binds cities together, while the private tears them apart." So much did Plato fear that the private pursuit of gain would tear citizens apart that he called it a "darkness" that will "completely fill . . . the whole city with everything bad." As a consequence, Plato argued that his philosopher guardians should own property in common, or otherwise all will live sep-arated one from another in their private worlds, a natural result in a tyranny: "[o]ne man dragging off to his own house whatever he can get his hands on apart from the others, another being separate in his own house with separate women and children, introducing private pleasures and griefs." Such disunity, isolation, and privatization is exactly what oc-

53. *Republic*, 462a–b.
54. *Republic*, 417a–b.
55. *Republic*, 422e–423a, 551d, 556d.

curs in corrupted forms of government. "And such men . . . will have walls around their houses, exactly like private nests, where they can make lavish expenditures on women." While each subject tends to his "private nest," the tyrant is afraid to leave the house to travel, and thus "stuck in his house for the most part, he lives like a woman."[56] (Of course, Plato here, perhaps inadvertently, acknowledges that the typical woman in ancient Greece was tyrannically confined to the household.)

If one is seriously interested in political reform, wrote Plato, one should pick fifty men from a population of ten thousand, "summon [them] from their homes with entreaties and offers of the greatest possible honors," and ask them to become lawgivers.[57] Again we see the notion that one must extract oneself from one's private affairs to pay attention to the public good. Other political thinkers will argue that love of wealth isolates citizens, but these thinkers—such as Tacitus, Machiavelli, and Tocqueville—will object to this isolation for political reasons, that is, because such isolation renders political cooperation nearly impossible and consequently makes citizens powerless while simultaneously strengthening tyranny. Plato, however, objected for moral reasons. People isolated from one another cannot achieve the unity and harmony that he regards as symptomatic of justice.

Torn apart by class conflict, feverish from all the material self-seeking, and replete with individuals who are envious of one another as they busy themselves with their private affairs, a tyranny is a dismal place, hardly a unified city and more like a swarm of disconnected individuals. It is—and this constitutes Plato's greatest moral condemnation—a place where real friendship cannot exist. "Therefore, they live their whole life without ever being friends of anyone, always one man's master or another's slave. The tyrannic nature never has a taste of freedom or true friendship."[58] In arguing against Callicles in the *Gorgias,* Socrates uses the key argument that a man who is self-seeking and constantly desiring cannot consider the welfare of another and therefore is incapable of friendship,[59] but in the *Republic,* Plato has given us a dreary picture of tyranny as a world in which all, bent on private pleasures and wealth, are self-seeking strangers who cannot experience friendship. Dionysius II, tyrant of Syracuse, "was in want of tried and true friends, and there is no surer sign of a man's moral

---

56. *Republic*, 550d; *Laws*, 875a–c; *Republic*, 464c–d, 548a–b, 579b–c. In a city where people have an "erotic love of wealth," citizens care only about their private affairs and are unable to undertake any "noble and good activity." *Laws*, 831c–e.

57. *Letter VII*, 337b–d.

58. *Republic*, 576a.

59. *Gorgias*, 507e–508a.

character than this, whether he is or is not destitute of such friends."
Similarly, the Persians "destroyed the friendship and community within
the city," because they ruled with "an excess of slavery and despotism."[60]
Certainly Plato acknowledged that the strength that accompanies friendship is a political threat to the tyrant,[61] just as he recognized that a tyrant
must eliminate all honest and courageous citizens (thus condemning himself to be surrounded by mediocrity),[62] but again this was not his major
concern. Obsessive love of wealth, isolation of citizens from one another,
and the absence of friendship are all signs that tyranny is the least just
and most feverishly unhealthy of all possible cities.

Tyranny as the Unmasking of All Authority

Plato argued that the very presence of lawyers and doctors in a city is
symptomatic of political illness. "When licentiousness and illness multi-
ply in a city, aren't many courts and hospitals opened, and aren't the arts
of the law court and medicine full of pride." The illness that worried Plato
was not only lack of political harmony but also an absence of the individual internalized discipline that leads people to obey the reasonable authority of the city. Because the driving force within a tyranny is a desirous self-interest, neither subjects nor tyrant have any such internalized
discipline, and thus they regard all authority as simply a bothersome hindrance in their chase for desires. Tyranny, then, is a state in which all
forms of authority are regarded as illegitimate. In speaking of subjects
under an oligarchy, a state with a remnant of moderation, Plato said "they
will harvest pleasure stealthily, running away from the law like boys from
a father." In the transition from democracy to tyranny, however, one finds
no shame whatsoever in questioning and disobeying all forms of authority. For example, while sons have no respect for fathers, fathers fear their
sons and wish to be like them, just as teachers fawn over their pupils,
while pupils "make light" of their teachers. In such a world, all authority
seems to be slavery. "Do you notice how tender they make the citizen's
soul, so that if someone proposes anything that smacks in any way of

60. *Letter VII*, 332c; *Laws*, 697c–698a. When we read Plato's phrase "an excess . . . of
despotism"—a loose translation at best, because the Greeks did not have the word *despotism*—it reminds us that the words *despot* and *despotic* did not have the same connotation
for Plato as they do for us, because we regard any despotic act as excessive, whereas he did
not think of a despot as always inappropriate and entirely evil.
61. *Symposium*, 182c.
62. *Republic*, 567a–d.

slavery, they are irritated and can't stand it? And they end up, as you well know, by paying no attention to the laws, written or unwritten, in order that they may avoid having any master at all."[63]

Even though these subjects may grudgingly submit to the power of the tyrant in order to bring order from chaos, it is impossible to imagine that they will regard their submission to the tyrant's authority as more than a temporary bow to self-interest, certainly not an authority that is morally legitimate; and thus, every tyranny, according to Plato, remains without real authority and potentially chaotic. A free, orderly, and harmonious political order can exist only if subjects feel a certain "awe" in the presence of authority, regarding it, of course, as legitimate. This awe or respect for authority—for the authority of laws, leaders, parents, friends, and so forth—can help bind a city together and enable it, as a unity, to accomplish great deeds. Free people are "voluntarily enslaved, in a certain sense, to the laws," much as justice involves the acceptance of the authority of philosopher-guardians as fully legitimate, which is itself rather like submitting oneself to the expert authority of a doctor.[64]

Since the city is unstable, refusing to acknowledge the authority of reason or law or any kind of leadership, then the citizens of this city are also constantly changing until, in Plato's words, there is nothing natural or "genuine"[65] about them and they become mere actors playing any role that best suits their transitory self-interest. We know from the previous discussion that Plato sought a unified city in which each person did the job suited to his or her nature. Plato was suggesting that each person has one natural function to fulfill, one task or job allotted to him or her by nature, and that to find this function and fulfill it is conducive both to psychic health and to lasting happiness. Such a political conviction might read: one person, one role. To try and go beyond the function allotted to us by nature is to violate the natural order of things, with the result that we lose the psychic health and stability that comes from knowing our places.[66] Individuals become divided, with different desires pulling each in different ways, ultimately creating a city of what Plato called "double men." To avoid this, "each of the other citizens too must be brought to that which naturally suits him—one man, one job—so that each man, practicing his own, which is one, will not become many but one." The

---

63. *Republic*, 405a (see also *Laws*, 630e–631a); *Republic*, 548b, 562c–563d.

64. *Laws*, 647b, 699b–d, 700a; Moravcsik, "Plato and Pericles on Freedom and Politics," 15.

65. *Letter VII*, 327d.

66. *Republic*, 374b; also 370a–b. Plato suggested that the "play" of children can give us insight into the nature of each child (*Laws*, 643b–d).

jack-of-all-trades, the person who tries to engage "in farming, money-making and war-making at the same time,"[67] is in some sense unnatural, never sincere, and unhappy. Democracy, the mother of tyranny, produces such meddling to an extreme, but tyranny, as the offspring of democracy, cannot avoid this fate of personal instability and insincerity.

If the just city is the one in which each individual is, in some sense, sincere or acting out the role allotted to him or her by nature, then in a tyranny, Plato suggested, no one is natural or genuine, and all become hypocritical role-players, playing to the crowd in order to further material self-interest. This is one reason Plato sanctioned the censorship of poets, playwrights, and actors. For citizens in a just city to watch people act out roles, or to imitate people they are not, might lead to widespread imitation and eventually to citizens' choosing roles not allotted to them by nature. "Or haven't you observed that imitations, if they are practiced continually from youth onwards, become established as habits and nature." Once this happens, all becomes sham; people do not honestly and sincerely show themselves as they really are, but they only try to deceive others and appear something they are not. Even in democracies, people try to deceive each other by distorting language, "calling insolence good education; anarchy, freedom; wastefulness, magnificence; and shamelessness, courage." Tyrants, Plato added, would try to give the appearance of justice and would "pretend to be gracious and gentle to all." In the *Statesman,* Plato complained of "this strange cry of players acting their part," because they are like Sophists who are deceivers, and "such impersonators are hard to distinguish from the real statesmen and kings."[68] Plato's ideal city is in some sense a dramatic production, but it is a drama that is thoroughly sincere because the roles have been outlined by nature. In the *Laws,* some actors approach the city, and to these Plato says, "Best of strangers . . . we ourselves are poets who have to the best of our ability created a tragedy that is the most beautiful and the best; at any rate, our whole political regime is constructed as the imitation of the most beautiful and best way of life, which we at least assert to be really the truest tragedy. Now you are poets, and we too are poets of the same things; we are your rivals as artists and performers of the most beautiful drama, which true law alone can by nature bring to perfection."[69] In a tyranny, all are actors in a tragedy that is far from the health, harmony, and sincerity that nature recommends.

All of this points, finally, to the fact that in a tyranny nothing is stable

67. *Republic,* 397d–e; also 423d, 551e–552a.
68. *Republic,* 395c–d, 560e–561a, 566e; *Statesman,* 291b–d.
69. *Laws,* 817b–c.

and unchanging—not the regime itself, which is subject to revolution; not the tyrant's goals, which change as quickly as his or her desires; not the jobs or roles of the subjects, which change because they never satisfy; and not even the psychic balance of individuals who, although dominated by desire, once in a while boastfully bluster brief moments of courage or wisdom. Tyranny may look stable, but incipient chaos hovers over every part of a tyranny at every moment. For Plato, who longed for the unchanging world of the Forms, constant change was tyranny's worst possible feature. "Change, we shall find, is much the most dangerous thing in everything except what is bad—in all the seasons, in the winds, in bodily habits, and in the characters of souls."[70] Although there is always a chance that a given tyranny will change for the better and reform, this chance remains remote, and Plato gloomily depicted tyranny as everything unnatural and everything unhealthy, a chaos of restless desire.

Conclusion

Plato's theory of tyranny is more like a logical deduction and less like a theoretical hypothesis that he sought to test with empirical observation, and despite his brilliant insights, this theoretical analysis of tyranny has the weaknesses of a purely deductive approach. For example, however grateful we are to Plato for offering us one of the first great theories of history, and however intellectually pleasing and tidy is his theory of political decline from republic to tyranny, we never can grasp exactly how each political transformation takes place. Does oligarchy always follow timocracy, and democracy always precede tyranny? If not, then how does he explain other patterns of historical change?

Or again, although Plato has produced an intriguing moral and psychological analysis of tyranny, we wish for a more detailed political analysis. What is the tyrant's source of power? Does this tyrant rule alone, or does this tyrant need advisers? What does a tyrant try to do with the system of education and the means of communication? How does a tyrant control the army? How does religion either undermine or support tyranny? Will class conflict not make this tyranny extremely short-lived? If tyranny always borders upon chaos, will this city not be perpetually threatened by invasion from external enemies? How will the tyrant provide material gratifications to his or her subjects if the economy is threatened by an

---

70. *Laws*, 797b–e; also *Republic*, 424c. Plato even showed some admiration for the fact that Egyptian art and music had not changed in hundreds of years (*Laws*, 656e–657b).

absence of personal discipline? Finally, to liken tyranny to madness is powerfully persuasive, but of only limited use to us. Certainly some tyrants have been apparently insane—Caligula comes quickly to mind—but most tyrants are hard-nosed political realists capable of controlling armies, waging wars, inventing propaganda, co-opting religious authorities, stimulating economies, and suppressing dissent. As Julia Annas put it, Plato's tyrant, enslaved to desire, "would not last a week."[71]

The weaknesses of Plato's analysis are so obvious that they too often obscure the strengths. It is worth remembering, for example, that when Tacitus sought to explain the despotism of Tiberius, he relied upon Plato's theoretical approach; that when the philosophes of the eighteenth century wanted to challenge the tyranny of the French monarchy, they returned both to Plato and to Tacitus; and, finally, that when Arendt sought to explain the horrors of Nazi death camps, she used images of madness and of sadistic desires out of control and of acting out in the light of day what others dream about nightmarishly at night, all images that remind us of Plato and Freud, one of Plato's finest students. In this, Plato constructed a foundation from which subsequent theories of tyranny were willing to build.

Although I am certain that one could lengthen such a list, it is easy to see several of Plato's ideas that other theorists later borrowed and expanded upon. First, notwithstanding the fact that Plato's psychology of tyranny seems overblown or exaggerated, there remains a valuable kernel of truth to it. Tyrants and their subjects frequently do seem caught up in a relentless chase for desires and power—a drive for self-interest to the exclusion of any concern for the common good—if not to the point of madness, at least frequently to the point of obsession. There is something to be said for the idea that disordered and troubled individuals and classes are both cause and consequence of tyranny. The myth of ordered and tranquil tyranny surely has been exploded by the chaos we have witnessed in so-called totalitarian governments. Second, there is merit in the idea that successful tyranny resembles cookery. Not only are tyrannies often more enduring to the extent that they gratify and please their subjects, but also citizens often long for the promised pleasures of tyranny; that is, we too frequently wish for what is bad for us, just as we eagerly seek tasty but unhealthy cooking. Third, Plato recognized that commerce and wealth play a key role in satisfying and pacifying the subjects of tyranny, that tyrants must ally themselves with one or more classes against the rest. Fourth, under tyrannies each house is a separate house; subjects remain isolated from one another, alone and friendless.

71. Annas, *An Introduction to Plato's Republic*, 304, 294–95.

Fifth, tyrannies do seem to originate sometimes from a questioning of all authority, although the most lasting tyrannies certainly find ways to institute new forms of accepted authority. Sixth, as Tacitus elaborated after Plato, the subjects under tyranny often discover that in order to survive, they must play roles and hide their real feelings and convictions. Seventh, as we know from experience in our own century, it is terrifyingly easy for ordinary people to participate in the crimes of tyranny, while it is disturbingly difficult to be a good person living in an evil regime. And finally, Plato took the first bold steps in outlining a theory of tyranny, a tyranny that is more than simply rule by one individual and more than straightforward class domination. Rather, Plato regarded tyranny as a whole whose parts are interrelated—here is a thinker who believed that a change in the music of a society will have a rippling effect that will cause change throughout that society—a system in which the politics of tyranny is interwoven with class struggle, economic development, religion, literature, art, and the ways we live and think. This is a monumental achievement in the history of ideas.

2

ARISTOTLE
Tyranny as Unnatural

Aristotle, who wrote on everything from politics to poetics and from physics to the parts of animals, wrote comparatively little on tyrannies. In all of the volumes of Aristotle's writings that have come down to us, one can find the word *tyranny* on no more than a few dozen pages, and he gave us a sustained discussion of tyranny, by which I mean only a section of perhaps four or five successive pages, just once in the *Politics* and once in *The Constitution of Athens*. Nevertheless, almost in passing, Aristotle formulated the ancient world's most enduring political analysis of tyranny, bequeathing this analysis first to key Roman thinkers such as Tacitus, then to medieval and Renaissance political theorists, and ultimately to the eighteenth century, where philosophes such as Montesquieu substantially altered it to suit their own pressing political needs. Such is the influence of history's most brilliant thinkers, whose almost parenthetical thoughts serve as fundamental conceptual tools for subsequent generations. A single five-page chapter in the *Politics*,[1] based most certainly on

---

1. Aristotle, *Politics*, trans. B. Jowett, bk. 5, chap. 11. All translations of Aristotle's works, except for the translation of *The Athenian Constitution*, can be found in *The Complete Works*

years of empirical observation of tyrannies, served as the best single study of the structure and practice of tyranny (and perhaps even as the best advice to a tyrant wishing to create a lasting regime), at least until Machiavelli.

Aristotle classified governments by who ruled and for what purpose. Either the one, the few, or the many rule, according to Aristotle, and if the rulers govern in the general interest, then rule by one is monarchy, rule by the few is aristocracy, and rule by the many is called constitutional government. If, however, the rulers govern only in their own private interest, then they pervert the proper purposes of government, and rule by one becomes tyranny ("For tyranny is a kind of monarchy which has in view the interest of the monarch only"),[2] rule by the few becomes oligarchy, and rule by the many becomes, in Aristotle's lexicon, democracy. Although Aristotle later modified these classifications and certainly elaborated upon them in much greater detail, he kept these principles of classification more or less intact, and indeed, as so often with Aristotle, these classifications corresponded roughly to the common wisdom of his time.[3] Actually, when he later refined his classifications by outlining subdivisions under each form of government, he described three different kinds of tyranny—the monarchy that rules despotically over barbarians, who deserve no better; the elective tyranny or dictatorship of ancient Greece; and finally a pure form of tyranny, the perverse "counterpart of the perfect monarchy," which is the kind of tyranny that receives all of his subsequent attention. This pure tyranny retained the basic definition of selfish rule by a single individual. "This tyranny is just that arbitrary power of an individual which is responsible to no one, and governs all alike, whether equals or better, with a view to its own advantage, not to that of its subjects, and therefore against their will. No freeman willingly endures such a government." Since Aristotle defined a free person as one "who exists for himself and not for another"—or, as he put it elsewhere, "it is the mark of a free man not to live at another's beck and call"—tyranny is clearly the government that most denies freedom.[4]

---

of Aristotle, ed. Jonathan Barnes, the revised Oxford translation, 2 vols. (Princeton, New Jersey: Princeton University Press, 1984).

A large part of this chapter has previously been published as "Aristotle's 'Science' of Tyranny," *History of Political Thought* 14, no. 1 (1993): 1–25.

2. *Politics*, 1279b6–7.

3. *Politics*, 1279a22–1279b10; Richard Mulgan, *Aristotle's Political Theory* (Oxford: Clarendon Press, 1977), 60.

4. *Politics*, 1279b6–7, 1285a18–1285b3, 1295a17–19, 1295a19–23; Aristotle, *Metaphysics*, trans. W. D. Ross, 982b26–27; Aristotle, *Rhetoric*, trans. Rhys Roberts, 1367a31–32; *Politics*, 1285a18–1285b3.

Despite the fact that all of these definitions and classifications, which remind us of Aristotle's brilliant biological taxonomy, influenced political thinking about tyranny for more than twenty centuries, they strike us as rather stale and skeletal—stale because these dry classifications tell us little about the terrifying political dynamics of tyrannies, and skeletal because these classifications capture little of Aristotle's rich analysis of the moral and political consequences of tyranny. To understand what Aristotle saw as the political dynamics of tyranny, I must examine how his scientific mind described the political and economic prerequisites for a stable tyranny. But first, to understand the consequences of tyranny, I must place Aristotle's analysis of tyranny within the broader context of his philosophy as a whole because, in fact, one cannot really extricate his discussion of tyranny from his political, moral, psychological, and metaphysical arguments, because, with Aristotle, all of these are always interrelated.

Tyranny as Unnatural

Because Aristotle's ethical and political discussions are inseparable from his metaphysics,[5] it is essential to review in a summary fashion what we know about this part of his philosophy. To look at the world through the spectacles of Aristotle's metaphysics is to see a world in which everything is constantly changing and developing; nothing is static, because every part of the natural world is acting to attain some goal or purpose or end. "Therefore action for an end is present in things which come to be and are by nature." Since nature does nothing in vain[6] and every part of nature is acting to attain some purpose, Aristotle quite literally presents a picture of the world in which trees are trying to grow higher, animals to become stronger, and the heavenly bodies to continue performing their perfect heavenly functions. "By gradual advance in this direction we come to see clearly that in plants too that is produced which is conducive to the end—leaves, e.g. grow to provide shade for the fruit. If then it is both by nature and for an end that the swallow makes its nest and the spider its web, and plants grow leaves for the sake of the fruit and send

5. T. H. Irwin, "The Metaphysical and Psychological Basis of Aristotle's Ethics," in *Essays on Aristotle's Ethics*, ed. Amelie Oksenberg Rorty (Berkeley and Los Angeles: University of California Press, 1980), 35–53.

6. Aristotle, *Physics*, trans. R. Hardie and R. K. Gaye, 199a7–8; also *Politics*, 1342b18–19, and Sir Ernest Barker, *The Political Thought of Plato and Aristotle* (New York: Dover, 1959 [1906]), 208, 220, 353.

their roots down (not up) for the sake of nourishment, it is plain that this kind of cause is operative in things which come to be and are by nature."[7] Aristotle called the ends that nature attempts to attain "final causes," although they are not really causes, at least in the sense that we use the word *cause*, but rather, a final cause explains why something occurs, or some purpose or purposes that underlie nature.[8]

Aristotle distinguished between that which is actually and that which is potentially. For example, an acorn is in actuality a seed, but it is potentially a mighty oak tree, and as the acorn passes from seed to sapling to tree, that is, as it attains its proper end, it is said to actualize its potentiality.[9] When something attains its end, when it actualizes its potentiality, it becomes what in one sense it really is, because it attains its most essential or defining characteristics, its essence. "For a thing is more properly said to be what it is when it exists in actuality than when it exists potentially." If we know the essence of something, then we know the end outlined for it by nature, and to know the end or purpose of something is to know what is good. "For what each thing is when fully developed, we call its nature, whether we are speaking of a man, a horse, or a family. Besides, the final cause and end of a thing is the best."[10] Because human beings are also part of nature and thus have an end, or purpose, because there is a human essence that we should strive to attain, if we know this essence or the end and purpose appropriate to human beings, we will answer a great number of ethical and political questions about how we should act and what sort of political institutions are conducive to actualizing our human potential. Not surprisingly, tyranny obstructs all efforts at attaining this potential.

Aristotle began his inquiry into the end, or purpose, of human existence by asking if there is one end human beings desire above all others, because, if we can discover this end determined for us by nature, we can know what is best for human beings. As he put it in a passage thoroughly

7. *Physics*, 199a23–30.

8. *Metaphysics*, 994b9–10; *Physics*, 194b32–195a3. Aristotle did acknowledge that sometimes the ends or purposes attained are not determined by nature, but by the intentions of human beings.

9. See, for example, *Metaphysics*, 1017a35–1017b9.

10. *Physics*, 193b7–9; *Politics*, 1252b32–1253a1; also, *Metaphysics*, 982b5–8, 1015a10–11, 1032b1–2. For a modern defense of Aristotle's argument for a human essence, see Martha C. Nussbaum, "Human Functioning and Social Justice: In Defense of Aristotelian Essentialism," *Political Theory* 20, no. 2 (1992): 202–46. For an examination of how Aristotle reasoned that women lacked this human essence, see Arlene Saxonhouse, "Aristotle: Defective Males, Hierarchy, and the Limits of Politics," in *Feminist Interpretations and Political Theory*, ed. Mary Lyndon Shanley and Carole Pateman (University Park: Pennsylvania State University Press, 1991), 32–52.

familiar to all who have read Aristotle: "If, then, there is some end of the things we do, which we desire for its own sake (everything else being desired for the sake of this), . . . clearly this must be the good and the chief good. Will not the knowledge of it, then, have a great influence on life? Shall we not, like archers who have a mark to aim at, be more likely to hit upon what we should?"[11] Of course, human beings pursue many ends, from pleasure to wealth to knowledge, but is there one end we pursue for its sake alone and not for the sake of anything else? Happiness, Aristotle suggested, is the end we pursue for its sake alone. "Now such a thing happiness, above all else, is held to be; for this we choose always for itself and never for the sake of something else, but honour, pleasure, reason, and every excellence we choose indeed for themselves, . . . but we choose them also for the sake of happiness."[12] Aristotle here used the Greek word *eudaimonia,* and our word *happiness* does not capture his meaning, which is ultimately untranslatable. Others have suggested that we translate *eudaimonia* as "well-being" or "human flourishing," and these renderings are useful to the extent that they convey the notions of good fortune and prosperity,[13] but all of these translations, including "happiness," which I will keep, fail to capture the idea that *eudaimonia* is not a transitory mood but a lasting state, that it is not a feeling but an activity.[14] It also indicates a moral accomplishment, or, as Aristotle put it, "the happy man lives well and fares well."[15]

Outlining the shortcomings of the various definitions of *eudaimonia* is minimally helpful in understanding how we attain this happiness. Borrowing from Plato, Aristotle suggested that people have commonly identified happiness with either a life of sensual and material pleasure, a political life, or contemplation,[16] and to settle this question, Aristotle set out to discover if nature has outlined a specific function for human beings to perform, for if there is such a function, then surely it will coincide with the happy life. "Presumably, however, to say that happiness is the chief

11. Aristotle, *Nicomachean Ethics*, trans. W. D. Ross and revised by J. O. Urmson, 1094a18–25.

12. *Nicomachean Ethics*, 1097a35–1097b5.

13. Sir David Ross, *Aristotle*, rev. ed. (London: Methuen & Co., 1949), 190; A.W.H. Adkins, "The Connection Between Aristotle's *Ethics* and *Politics*," *Political Theory* 12, no. 1 (1984): 29–49, esp. 31; see also Abraham Edel, *Aristotle and His Philosophy* (Chapel Hill: University of North Carolina Press, 1982), 259, and W. F. R. Hardie, *Aristotle's Ethical Theory* (Oxford: Clarendon Press, 1968), 20.

14. Hannah Arendt, *The Human Condition* (Garden City, N.Y.: Doubleday, 1959 [1958]), 172.

15. *Nicomachean Ethics*, 1098b20–21.

16. *Nicomachean Ethics*, 1095b14–20.

good seems a platitude, and a clearer account of what it is is still desired. This might perhaps be given, if we could first ascertain the function of man. For just as for a flute-player, a sculptor, or any artist, and, in general, for all things that have a function or activity, the good and the 'well' is thought to reside in the function, so it would seem to be for man, if he has a function. Have the carpenter, then, and the tanner certain functions or activities, and has man none? Is he naturally functionless?"[17] Aristotle concluded that human beings do have a function, which is to live according to reason, and that the life that most corresponds to this function is a life of contemplation, a life that should offer "the complete happiness of man." Although this seems to be Plato's conclusion, Aristotle quickly added that "such a life would be too high for man" and that the life of contemplation is nearly divine; and despite urging us to try "so far as we can, [to] make ourselves immortal, and strain every nerve to live in accordance with the best thing in us,"[18] Aristotle never seems convinced that the life of contemplation is really either the best possible life or the one most likely to bring happiness.

Aristotle himself was too political, and he remained so convinced that human beings by nature are political, that he rarely stated that a life devoted solely to contemplation is the happiest, but instead indicated in a myriad of ways that a life that pursues both contemplation and political action is best. When Aristotle stated that happiness is an activity, praised the Olympic Games as an example of such activity, and declared that "those who act rightly win the noble and good things in life," it is hard to imagine that contemplation is what he had in mind. When he stated that "political science spends most of its pains on making citizens to be of a certain character, viz. good and capable of noble acts," we do not immediately think that he wants to create contemplative citizens. Although he did declare that contemplation is the "highest" excellence, he also suggested in a nearby passage that it is excellent "to do noble and good deeds." And finally, when he offered examples of people who had led good lives, he mentioned the eminently political Solon and Pericles, two people who certainly led lives that involved both contemplation of what is good and political action. Solon, said Aristotle, maintained that a happy person was one who had moderate wealth, did "the noblest acts, and lived temperately," whereas Pericles deliberated well "about what sorts of thing conduce to the good life in general" and translated such thoughts into political action.[19] Although Aristotle was undoubtedly a Platonist and

---

17. *Nicomachean Ethics*, 1097b22–30.
18. *Nicomachean Ethics*, 1177b24–25, 1177b27–35; also 1098a3–18.
19. *Nicomachean Ethics*, 1098b30–1099a5, 1099b30–33, 1177a11–18, 1176b6–8, 1179a9–

acknowledged that a life of contemplation was superior, he also bowed, time after time, to the common wisdom of his day, and indeed he probably did not escape the notion that the best life is not only one of wisdom but also one of political and military leadership. In this, his description of the good life is not that far from Homer's description of Hector as a speaker of great words and a doer of great deeds.

Once we understand that Aristotle thought the good life could develop only in the polis (or the Greek city-state), we can see not only that the best political system is necessary for the best life but also that tyranny, or the worst political system, is an unnatural political order that undermines the proper development of human potential. When Aristotle said that "the state is a creation of nature, and that man is by nature a political animal," he meant both that nature intended human beings to live in a polis and that human beings can develop their potentials or come to perfection only in a Greek polis (which makes this undeniably an ethnocentric argument).[20] Just as an acorn can actualize its potential to become a mighty oak only in the proper soil and the proper climate, so human beings can attain their end, or perfection, only in the soil of the Greek polis, an argument that penultimately rests on biological assumptions about human beings and ultimately on a philosophy that sees purposes built into the world by nature. Within the proper setting of a good polis, human beings can attain greatness, but living without a polis or in a corrupt political environment such as a Persian despotism, human beings cannot develop completely. "For man, when perfected, is the best of animals, but, when separated from law and justice, he is the worst of all." Elsewhere in the same chapter, Aristotle suggested that an individual without a state "is either a bad man or above humanity" or, later, "either a beast or a god." Since human beings need the nurturing and education of a good polis in order to attain their proper ends and indeed the good life, then it will be nearly impossible for a person to become good in an evil

---

12, 1140a24–1140b11. See Amelie Oksenberg Rorty, "The Place of Contemplation in Aristotle's Nicomachean Ethics," in *Essays on Aristotle's Ethics*, ed. Rorty, 377–94; also W.F.R. Hardie, "The Final Good in Aristotle's *Ethics*," in *Aristotle: A Collection of Critical Essays*, ed. J.M.E. Moravcsik (Notre Dame, Ind.: University of Notre Dame Press, 1968 [1967]), 297–322; Marcia L. Homiak, "The Pleasure of Virtue in Aristotle's Moral Theory," *Pacific Philosophical Quarterly* 66, nos. 1 and 2 (1985): 93–110, esp. 99–100; also Charles M. Young, "Aristotle on Temperance," *Philosophical Review* 97, no. 4 (1988): 521–42. For good discussions of this topic, see Thomas Nagel, "Aristotle on *Eudaimonia*," and J. L. Ackrill, "Aristotle on *Eudaimonia*," in *Essays on Aristotle's Ethics*, ed. Rorty, 7–14 and 15–33. For a balanced view on how much Aristotle valued political participation, see Richard Mulgan, "Aristotle and the Value of Political Participation," *Political Theory* 18, no. 2 (1990): 195–215.

20. *Politics*, 1253a1–3; Mulgan, *Aristotle's Political Theory*, 3, 23.

political order, just as an oak cannot grow in desert sand. "For only a great soul can live in the midst of trouble and wrong without itself committing any base act."[21]

To understand the end and purpose of the polis, or city-state, Aristotle, again thinking biologically, examined the origin and natural development of human association, because "he who thus considers things in their first growth and origin, whether a state or anything else, will obtain the clearest view of them." The first stage, both biologically and historically, in the development of human association was the union of male and female, or the family, because "the family is the association established by nature for the supply of men's everyday wants." Next came the village, a union of several families, which Aristotle described as an "association [that] aims at something more than the supply of daily needs." The village, however, was still an association that Aristotle regarded as prepolitical both because it still aimed only at meeting the everyday physical needs of its inhabitants and because the villagers had little common purpose and thus lived "dispersedly, as was the manner in ancient times,"[22] or, as Aristotle put it literally, they lived alone as did the Cyclopes of Homer. In a strict Aristotelian sense, a political union of people must involve a common purpose and must aim at something higher than mere perpetuation of existence, two reasons Aristotle regarded a tyranny as unnatural. Transcending both family and village, the city-state, or polis (poorly translated here as the "state"), is the end, or "completion," of the process of development in human association,[23] just as the oak is the completion of the acorn's growth. "When several villages are united in a single complete community, large enough to be nearly or quite self-sufficing, the state comes into existence, originating in the bare needs of life, and continuing in existence for the sake of a good life. And therefore, if the earlier forms of society are natural, so is the state, for it is the end of them, and the nature of a thing is its end. For what each thing is when fully developed, we call its nature, whether we are speaking of a man, a horse, or a family. Besides, the final cause and end of a thing is the best, and to be self-sufficing is the end and the best."[24] No single passage in Aristotle more

21. *Politics* 1253a31–32, 1253a3–4, 1253a29–30; Aristotle, *Economics*, trans. E. S. Forster and G. C. Armstrong, bk. 3, chap. 1. There is some doubt whether Aristotle wrote this treatise on economics, but I do not think this affects my overall argument.

22. *Politics*, 1252a24–26,1252b11–12, 1252b15–17, 1252b23.

23. William J. Booth, "Politics and the Household: A Commentary on Aristotle's *Politics* Book One," *History of Political Thought* 2, no. 2 (1981): 203–26, esp. 210.

24. *Politics*, 1252b27–1253a1. To translate the Greek word *polis* as "state" is probably misleading, since it brings to mind much larger, modern nation-states. Aristotle could have used the word *ethnos*, a word that we would translate as nation, but he regarded such an

clearly demonstrates how his metaphysical thinking, his conviction that all in nature acts toward some end or purpose, penetrates into his political thought. The polis is "a creation of nature," the political environment in which human beings can attain their purpose, or, as Aristotle put it in subsequent passages, "a state is a body of citizens sufficing for the purposes of life," and "a state exists for the sake of a good life, and not for the sake of life only."[25] While the village is too small and cannot provide the leisure necessary for the good life, and while an empire such as Persia is too large and cannot provide the opportunities for citizenship necessary for the good life, the polis is the perfect environment for satisfying all human needs. (Of course, size is not the only reason the polis is best for the good life.)

Aristotle called politics both "the master art" and the "science" whose "end must be the good for man," and he indicated that a people that succeeds in its political life attains the highest good possible and even lasting greatness, for "though it is worth while to attain the end merely for one man, it is finer and more godlike to attain it for a nation or for city-states."[26] In contrast to Anglo-American assumptions that the role of the political order is, for the most part, merely the protection of persons and property, Aristotle argued that "statecraft" aims at the creation of "character," that statecraft addresses itself to "the best good, and the best in the sense of the best for us."[27] Any political order, according to Aristotle, that concerns itself solely with the negative functions of protecting persons and property is not truly a polis, which, by definition, must concern itself with engendering human excellence (aretē). "Whence it may be further inferred that excellence must be the care of a state which is truly so called, and not merely enjoys the name: for without this end the community becomes a mere alliance." Because Aristotle thought nature assigned a positive role to the polis in developing human potential, he wanted the polis to teach us to love what is good and indeed to "make the citizens good by forming habits in them."[28] Some readers wince at the positive role that Aristotle assigned to the political community, as, for

---

entity as too large to be an environment for human development. See G.E.R. Lloyd, *Aristotle: The Growth and Structure of His Thought* (Cambridge: Cambridge University Press, 1968), 249–50.

25. *Politics*, 1253a2, 1275b20–21, 1280a31–32.

26. *Nicomachean Ethics*, 1094a27, 1094b7–8, 1094b8–10.

27. Aristotle, *Magna Moralia*, trans. St. G. Stock, 1181b25–27, 1183a7–8. Even if *Magna Moralia* is not by Aristotle, I do not think this hurts my overall argument.

28. *Politics*, 1280b5–8; *Nicomachean Ethics*, 1103b2–4, 1104b11–13. See also M. F. Burnyeat, "Aristotle on Learning to Be Good," in *Essays on Aristotle's Ethics*, ed. Rorty, 69–92, esp. 79.

example, when he said "neither must we suppose that anyone of the citizens belongs to himself, for they all belong to the state,"[29] but I take this to indicate the obligation each citizen should feel to a polis that has been necessary to the development of his or her intelligence, morality, and excellence. Despite the positive role Aristotle bestowed upon the polis, it is hard to see this community as imposing and threatening; Sir Ernest Barker described it well when he said Aristotle's polis "is an association of friends mutually provoking one another to virtue."[30]

While Aristotle certainly condemned tyranny because it denies personal freedom and is violently cruel, he opposed it most because it violates the natural order of things, because it is an unnatural political order inhibiting the development of human morality and excellence. To hope that human beings can flourish and achieve greatness under a tyranny is very much like hoping that an oak tree can grow tall without sunlight, and thus Aristotle despised tyranny not just because it is brutal but most of all because it murders in human beings precisely what Aristotle regarded as most beautiful, the natural tendency to grow toward greatness. "For there is by nature both a justice and an advantage appropriate to the rule of a master, another to kingly rule, another to constitutional rule; but there is none naturally appropriate to tyranny, or to any other perverted form of government; for these come into being contrary to nature." If the goal of a true polis is the good life, then the goal of a tyranny is at best mere life, something even the household can provide (and tyranny of course even threatens to end this), and if statesmen in a true polis "aspire to do . . . great deeds," then tyrants strive first and foremost to secure their selfish "protection." Aristotle, who regarded tyranny as the "worst" form of government, was even willing to declare "great is the honour bestowed . . . on him who kills a tyrant."[31]

In Aristotle's suggestion that tyranny is unnatural, we doubtless find the shadow of Plato. When Aristotle said that human beings have an end, or purpose, outlined by nature, when he argued that the best polis most completely meets our biological needs, he had in mind, as did Plato, the notion that human beings tend by nature to develop toward a state of "perfect health," which entails both citizenship and a life of reason. Aristotle, as K. Von Fritz and E. Kapp noted, used "nature" in the same way as

---

29. *Politics*, 1337a27–28. Aristotle also said that the polis should use education to see that citizens are "moulded to suit the form of government under which [they live]" (*Politics*, 1337a11–13). Although this may sound authoritarian, surely it is descriptive of almost any society's practices.

30. Barker, *The Political Thought of Plato and Aristotle*, 271.

31. *Politics*, 1287b37–41; *Rhetoric*, 1391a24, 1366a6; *Politics*, 1289b2, 1267a15–16.

Plato used the ideas of the just and the good.[32] For Plato, a life according to reason is healthy and just; for Aristotle, it is healthy and natural. Tyranny, according to Aristotle, is unnatural, precisely because it arises either from disease or from stunted growth. Of Solon, Aristotle wrote, "[T]hat he had the opportunity to become tyrant is evident from the diseased state of affairs."[33] The most evil and ignorant people, those who predictably live under tyrannies, are those whose natural capacities have had no opportunity for development. Political communities make mistakes because the *politikē,* or science of the polis that statesmen use to bring about human excellence, is invariably imprecise, a mixture of what we would call art and science, and ultimately resembles most of all the science of medicine, that hybrid discipline that attempts to make people better and bring health, not only physical health but also mental well-being.[34] As Stephen G. Salkever noted, exaggerating considerably, "social science as Aristotle understood it is a sort of psychiatry," but, as Aristotle himself put it, "the master of the house and the ruler of the state have to consider about health."[35] Of course, Plato and Aristotle did not have identical concepts of health; Aristotle advocated a kind of political participation and citizenship that Plato would not have countenanced.

Nevertheless, the unnatural and unhealthy state of tyranny that Aristotle described invariably reflects a Platonic heritage. For example, a wicked man, according to Aristotle, is one whose "soul is rent by faction, and one element in it by reason of its wickedness grieves when it abstains from certain acts, while the other part is pleased, and one draws [him] this way and the other that, as if they were pulling [him] in pieces." For Aristotle as well as Plato, both tyrants and tyrannies know nothing of a life guided by reason, as nature intended, but instead are driven by desire. Tyrants "begin at dawn and pass whole days in sensuality" and are content to encourage "license" among their subjects and to allow "everybody to live as he likes," which makes tyranny a very popular form of government, "for most persons would rather live in a disorderly than in a

32. K. Von Fritz and E. Kapp, "The Development of Aristotle's Political Philosophy and the Concept of Nature," in *Ethics and Politics*, vol. 2 of *Articles on Aristotle*, ed. Jonathan Barnes, Malcolm Schofield, and Richard Sorabji (New York: St. Martin's, 1978), 113–34; see 116–18.

33. Aristotle, *The Athenian Constitution*, trans. J. Rhodes (New York: Penguin, 1984), chap. 6. Although Rhodes himself argues that Aristotle most likely did not write this book, I think most modern scholarship is persuasive in attributing this work to Aristotle.

34. Stephen G. Salkever, "Aristotle's Social Science," *Political Theory* 9, no. 4 (1981): 479–508; see 479, 495–97, 501–3. See also *Nicomachean Ethics*, bk. 2.

35. Salkever, "Aristotle's Social Science," 503; *Politics*, 1258a31–32. Aristotle himself noted that ethical knowledge is imprecise, just like medical knowledge. See *Nicomachean Ethics*, 1104a3–5.

sober manner."[36] Aristotle thought most people were "slaves of their pleasures," and he described the many as obsessed with chasing apparent,
but of course invariably unsatisfying, pleasures. For the many to seek
wealth and sensual pleasure is all too common, but when the rulers of a
polis are driven by desire, such excess leads easily to tyranny, for once
released, these desires know no limits. "For desire is a wild beast, and
passion perverts the minds of rulers, even when they are the best of
men." Because both tyrant and subjects are driven by desire, tyranny,
which "is not limited by anything," is capable of any evil. "The fact is, that
the greatest crimes are caused by excess and not by necessity. Men do
not become tyrants in order that they may not suffer cold."[37] Although
Aristotle certainly had in mind here violent crimes against ordinary citizens, in effect he thought of tyranny as committing an even greater crime,
because he regarded tyranny as a violation of nature, or, to be more
precise, as an obstacle to the natural development of human capacities. If
a good polis is a natural setting that promotes citizenship and a life of
reason, then tyranny is an unnatural environment that stunts human development and promotes everything that is vicious and evil in human
beings. It is with a similar analysis that Montesquieu condemned French
absolutism, that Marx excoriated what he called the despotism of capital,
and that Weber warned against a new bureaucratic tyranny.

Tyranny as a Household: The Elimination of Politics and the Primacy of Economics

Aristotle criticized Plato for trying, in his *Republic,* to transform a polis
into a family, or household (*oikia*). Although both polis and household
are essential to human development,[38] their functions, according to Aristotle, are very different, and the kind of rule one finds in a polis, where
citizens meet as equals, differs significantly from the hierarchical relations of the household. Consider first how rule in the polis differs from
rule in the household. Despite more than once praising monarchy and
aristocracy, in general, when Aristotle discussed political rule, or the kind
of rule one finds in a good polis, he described a government by equals
and praised citizenship. Such rule he labeled "constitutional rule," that

36. *Nicomachean Ethics*, 1166b19–22; *Politics*, 1314b30–31, 1319b25–32. See also Homiak,
"The Pleasure of Virtue in Aristotle's Moral Theory."
37. *Politics*, 1287a30–32; *Rhetoric*, 1366a1–3; *Politics*, 1267a13–14.
38. Hardie, "The Final Good in Aristotle's *Ethics*," 303; M. I. Finley, "Aristotle and Economic Analysis," in *Articles on Aristotle*, ed. Barnes et al., 2:140–58, esp. 144.

kind of government "which is exercised over freemen and equals by birth." Because Aristotle accepted so many of the assumptions of his contemporaries, he always assumed that the number of adult male citizens would be small compared to the total population of the polis, and to this extent he was not defending what he called "extreme democracy" but was suggesting that those lucky enough to be citizens did meet in the public assemblies as equals. "But in most constitutional states the citizens rule and are ruled by turns, for the idea of a constitutional state implies that the natures of the citizens are equal." Equality did not imply for Aristotle that citizens were all alike, having the same interests and opinions, because a polis by nature is "composed of unlikes."[39] If Plato sought one big harmonious family united in its common opinion of and pursuit of justice, Aristotle pictured citizens differing and deliberating in the assembly about the common good.

Despite his conservatism, despite defending monarchy at times,[40] Aristotle often displayed genuine faith in the political participation and intelligence of ordinary citizens. In talking of the deliberations of popular assemblies, he said, "[N]ow any member of the assembly, taken separately, is certainly inferior to the wise man. But the state is made up of many individuals. And as a feast to which all the guests contribute is better than a banquet furnished by a single man, so a multitude is a better judge of many things than any individual." In a good polis, suggested Aristotle, the many are less subject to passion than an individual—"it is hardly to be supposed that a great number of persons would all get into a passion and go wrong at the same moment"—and quite able to judge music, poetry, and political decisions, following the common maxim that even if ordinary people do not have sufficient knowledge to cook a feast or craft a shoe, they know how the former tastes and the latter fits.[41] For that reason, Aristotle was willing to define a citizen as "one who shares in governing and being governed." More precisely, a citizen "shares in the administration of justice, and in offices," and "has the power to take part in the deliberative or judicial administration" of the polis. The good citizen should "know how to govern like a freeman, and how to obey like a freeman."[42] In this argument, the man who left the

39. *Politics*, 1277b8–9, 1277b3–4, 1259b4–6, 1277a5.

40. See H. Kelsen, "Aristotle and Hellenic-Macedonian Policy," in, *Articles on Aristotle*, ed. Barnes et al., 2:170–94; Ellen Meiksins Wood and Neal Wood, *Class Ideology and Ancient Political Theory: Socrates, Plato, and Aristotle in Social Context* (New York: Oxford University Press, 1978), 209–57.

41. *Politics*, 1286a28–31, 1286a34–35; bk. 3, chap. 11.

42. *Politics*, 1283b42–1284a1, 1275a21, 1275b19–20, 1277b15–16; also 1332b26–27, 1333a1–2.

private world of the household entered the public world of politics and political deliberation as an equal among his fellow citizens, and while Aristotle was hardly a full-fledged democrat, he did offer a lasting defense of citizen participation in the governance of the polis. Citizenship, for Aristotle, is essential to the development of human excellence.

Whereas the government of a good polis involves a high degree of equality and participation, the household, by contrast, is a hierarchical social system involving not only the immediate family but also servants and slaves, and as a result, household government must be monarchical. "The rule of a household is a monarchy, for every house is under one head; whereas constitutional rule is a government of freemen and equals." Even within the household, Aristotle described two different kinds of rule—royal rule over those who by nature are free, such as one's wife and children, and despotic rule over those who by nature are servants or slaves.[43] The word *despotēs* also connotes rule in one's own interests, so the master of the household who abuses his responsibilities and rules the entire household selfishly is said to rule despotically.[44] Strictly speaking, a despot (*despotēs*) is a master who rules over people who are slaves by nature, and such despotic rule is in a sense appropriate not only for most servants and slaves within a household but for all, such as barbarians, who are unable by nature to be free. "For barbarians, being more servile in character than Hellenes, and Asiatics than Europeans, do not rebel against a despotic government."[45]

In effect, tyrants turn the political world upside down. Even though free men should share in the government of the polis, tyrants treat free men as slaves and rule despotically; even though citizens should govern as equals, tyrants rule hierarchically; even though government should be in the common good, tyrants rule selfishly; and even though the political rule of the polis should be the proper soil in which human excellence can flourish, tyrants transform the polis itself into a household, which can sustain mere life but not the good life. Aristotle noted that monarchy greatly resembled household management. "For as household management is the kingly rule of a house, so kingly rule is the household management of a city." By extension, he certainly regarded tyranny, the perverted form of monarchy, as the cruel misrule of a household. Just as the master of a household uses his servant as a tool, or an

---

43. *Politics*, 1255b19–20, 1254b1–1255a3. See also Arendt, *The Human Condition*, 23–34.

44. Mulgan, *Aristotle's Political Theory*, 36, 44. See also John F. Wilson, "Power, Rule, and Politics: The Aristotelian View," *Polity* 13, no. 1 (1980): 80–96.

45. *Politics*, 1285a19–21. I have used Jowett's original translation of *barbaros* as "barbarian," instead of the revised translation of "foreigner."

"instrument,"[46] by using the labor of the servant to provide himself with leisure, so tyrants use their subjects as tools in their selfish pursuits.

This means that tyrannies reverse the proper functions of the household and the polis. In the development of human excellence, the function of the household was to free the citizen from the labor process, so that the citizen would have leisure, or free time, almost literally time in which to be free, to strive for both political and intellectual excellence. "Property is a part of the household, and the art of acquiring property is a part of the art of managing the household; for no man can live well, or indeed live at all, unless he is provided with necessaries."[47] Athens had about 40,000 to 45,000 adult male citizens out of a total population of about 250,000, perhaps slightly more,[48] which means that the labor of the great majority—slaves, servants, and women—was providing the necessary leisure for comparatively few adult male citizens. Aristotle saw no alternative; if the development of human excellence requires freedom from the labor process, then for any to be free, others must labor. The only other option Aristotle recognized was for all to labor and none to be free, although he did fantasize that if fields could plow themselves and shuttles could weave on their own, then masters would not need slaves,[49] a passage that Marx quoted many centuries later when he dreamed of a world in which machines freed us all from necessary, or forced, labor.[50] Knowing nothing of modern dreams of automation, and faced with an economy of scarcity, Aristotle regarded *oikonomikē,* or household management, as an inferior, but nonetheless essential, economic task furthering the possibility of freedom for citizens. "Hence those who are in a position which places them above toil have stewards who attend to their households

46. *Politics,* 1285b31–33, 1253b30–34.

47. *Politics,* 1253b23–26.

48. M. I. Finley, *The Ancient Greeks: An Introduction to Their Life and Thought,* (New York: Viking, 1964), 38, 55.

49. *Politics,* 1253b33–1254a1.

50. See Karl Marx, *Capital: A Critique of Political Economy,* trans. Samuel Moore and Edward Aveling (New York: Modern Library, 1906), pt. 4, chap. 14, sec. 3, b (445–46): "'If,' dreamed Aristotle, the greatest thinker of antiquity, 'if every tool, when summoned, or even of its own accord, could do the work that befits it, just as the creations of Daedalus moved of themselves, or the tripods of Hephaestos went of their own accord to their sacred work, if the weavers' shuttles were to weave of themselves, then there would be no need either of apprentices for the master workers, or of slaves for the lords.'. . . Oh! those heathens! . . . They perhaps excused the slavery of one on the ground that it was a means to the full development of another. But to preach slavery of the masses, in order that a few crude and half-educated parvenus, might become 'eminent spinners,' 'extensive sausage-makers,' and 'influential shoe-black dealers,' to do this, they lacked the bump of Christianity."

while they occupy themselves with philosophy or with politics."[51] It is worth noting that neither in constitutional government nor in tyranny should women, in Aristotle's view, have any measure of citizenship.

The household was designed by nature to provide the economic means to a political and moral end, and it was itself a primitive form of government that could suffice for mere life but not for the good life. In this, Aristotle clearly regarded the economic (*oikia*) as subservient to the political (*polis*). By Aristotle's definition, the tyrant eliminates what is political—citizenship, participation, popular assemblies, and deliberation—and transforms political rule into household management or *oikonomikē* (from which we get our word *economics*). Aristotle maintained that with tyranny we see the eclipse of politics and the primacy of economics, an argument later borrowed and elaborated by Machiavelli, Tocqueville, and Arendt.

The Consequences of Avarice and Tyranny

For Aristotle, wealth was a means to the good life and not an end to be pursued for its own sake alone. Although no person can live well without a moderate amount of property, any person who pursues superfluous amounts of property is morally deficient and ignorant of the proper ends of life because, just as we must sometimes engage in war but only as a means to peace, we must only undertake "business for the sake of leisure."[52] Unfortunately, too often people misperceive the purposes of life and regard the accumulation of wealth as an end and not a means. "Hence some persons are led to believe that getting wealth is the object of household management, and the whole idea of their lives is that they ought either to increase their money without limit, or at any rate not to lose it. The origin of this disposition in men is that they are intent upon living only, and not upon living well; and, as their desires are unlimited, they also desire that the means of gratifying them should be without limit."[53] Although Aristotle criticized Plato's communalism and touted the economic efficiency of each taking the responsibility for his or her private

51. *Politics*, 1255b35–38. For a good summary of Aristotle's view of slavery, see Wayne Ambler, "Aristotle on Nature and Politics: The Case of Slavery," *Political Theory* 15, no. 3 (1987): 390–410.

52. *Politics*, 1333a35–36; Barker, *The Political Thought of Plato and Aristotle*, 382–84.

53. *Politics*, 1257b38–1258a2. See also Aristotle, *Fragments*, trans. Jonathan Barnes and Gavin Lawrence, F 52 R³, B 53: "It is slave-like to desire to live rather than to live well, to follow the opinions of the many instead of expecting the many to follow one's own, to seek money but to show no concern at all for what is noble."

property, saying, for example, "how immeasureably greater is the pleasure, when a man feels a thing to be his own," nevertheless he wished "that property should be private, but the use of it common." By common use, Aristotle meant a great deal of sharing among citizens—of such things as produce, land, tools, and animals—following the familiar Greek proverb that said "friends will have all things common." Common use would limit private avarice, teaching citizens that happiness lies in intellectual and political pursuits that require only moderate amounts of wealth. "And the avarice of mankind is insatiable; . . . men always want more and more without end. . . . The beginning of reform is not so much to equalize property as to train the nobler sorts of natures not to desire more."[54]

In a brilliant analysis, M. I. Finley suggested that Aristotle did not have a systematic and modern economic analysis, mainly because he regarded economics as a necessary but subservient function to be carried out by foreigners, household stewards, and slaves.[55] In fact, Aristotle despised commerce, regarding it as a life unfit for a free citizen and considering, for example, "retail trade" as an "unnatural" occupation in which people use one another for profit.[56] Plutarch recorded a passage in which Aristotle complained not just of people who become obsessed with the pursuit of wealth, but also of people who waste their lives bowing to the demands of their business. "For of the majority of people, as Aristotle says, some do not use it [sc., wealth] through meanness, and others misuse it through extravagance—the latter spend their lives as slaves to every passing pleasure, the former to their business."[57] So much did Aristotle dislike commerce that if a people came together only to further prosperity, Aristotle refused to call such an association a polis, since a polis must have a higher goal than wealth. "But a state exists for the sake of a good life, and not for the sake of life only. . . . Nor does a state exist for the sake of alliance and security from injustice, nor yet for the sake of exchange and mutual intercourse. . . . Let us suppose that one man is a carpenter, another a farmer, another a shoemaker, and so on, and that their number is ten thousand: nevertheless, if they have nothing in common but exchange, alliance, and the like, that would not constitute a state."[58] Since Aristotle pictured the polis as friends who are seeking the

---

54. *Politics*, 1263a40–1263b1, 1263a38, 1263a21–1263b6, 1263a30–31, 1267b1–7.
55. Finley, "Aristotle and Economic Analysis."
56. Aristotle, *Eudemian Ethics*, trans. J. Solomon, 1215a26–32; *Politics*, 1258a38–1258b2. See also Mulgan, *Aristotle's Political Theory*, 49.
57. *Fragments*, F 56 R³.
58. *Politics*, 1280a31–36, 1280b20–24.

good life together, and since this pursuit of excellence is what they share and have in common, then a political order whose primary purposes are the protection of property and the assurance of order so that people can pursue their private economic interests (and here one easily thinks of modern thinkers such as Locke and Smith) is not a polis, at least in the eyes of Aristotle, but merely an economic alliance or a commercial treaty. The tyrant is someone who, treating the polis as if it were a household, ignores the proper role of the polis and regards it instead as an economic alliance designed to produce wealth mainly for himself or herself. "As of oligarchy so of tyranny, the end is wealth (for by wealth only can the tyrant maintain his guard and his luxury)." Like Plato, Aristotle pictured a tyrant as driven by desires for power, pleasure, and wealth. The tyrant's "aim is pleasure, the aim of a king, honour . . . the tyrant accumulates riches, the king seeks what brings honour."[59]

Although such desire for riches tends to make tyrannies unstable and short-lived, tyrants, while they last, control their subjects to some extent by encouraging in them a similar love of wealth. Aristotle mentioned two broad ways in which this happens, and in both cases, the tyrants use economic incentives to depoliticize their subjects. First, tyrants promise to gratify the desires of the many by bringing prosperity. In recounting the history of Athens, Aristotle wrote that "since Cleophon there has been an unending succession of popular leaders whose chief desire has been to be outrageous and to gratify the masses, looking only to considerations of the moment." Cicero, who of course lived in a time during which Rome was spending money to pacify the lower classes, reported that Aristotle had complained about this method by which ruling classes controlled the population. "How much more serious and true is Aristotle's criticism of us for not being astonished at these vast sums of money spent on captivating the populace."[60] In this first way, tyrants provide moderate gratification to forestall popular discontent. Second, tyrants play upon this love of wealth to confine people to their private affairs, thus leaving no time, opportunity, or desire for them to attend to public matters. In his description of Pisistratus, Aristotle noted that he encouraged agriculture, in part because the people "should have reasonable means of subsistence, and should concentrate on their private affairs and have neither the desire nor the leisure to take an interest in public affairs." Pisistratus consolidated his power and won over the many "by his help for their private concerns." In another context, Aristotle suggested that tyrannies sometimes "impoverish" their subjects so that "the people, having to keep

---

59. *Politics*, 1311a9–11, 1311a3–6.
60. *The Athenian Constitution*, chap. 28; *Fragments*, F 89 R³.

hard at work, are prevented from conspiring."[61] Ironically, both poverty, which compels people to work so hard that they have no time for political affairs, and affluence, which distracts people from political concerns, work to the advantage of the tyrant. In each case, a life of economic activity helps to subvert possible political opposition to the tyranny, and this dichotomy of the economic life versus the political life, with tyrants encouraging the former and forbidding the latter, will reappear again and again—for example, with Machiavelli, Montesquieu, Tocqueville, and Arendt—in subsequent theories of tyranny.

Whether a tyranny pacifies the population with material gratification or distracts people by encouraging them to busy themselves with private affairs, it misuses, or even eliminates, genuine leisure time. For Aristotle, this was disastrous, because leisure time is a prerequisite for intellectual development, political activity, and human excellence in general; citizens who have been freed from the labor process occupy themselves with philosophy and politics. The best state, according to Aristotle, will not allow ordinary laborers and artisans to be citizens, because the word *citizen* can apply "only to those who are freed from necessary services."[62] Although this seems harsh to our modern ears, Aristotle was arguing that leisure is essential to the development of intelligence and excellence, and a person who must labor from sunrise to sundown cannot have such leisure, remains dominated by necessity, and ultimately resembles a tool for labor or a beast of burden rather than a human being.[63] Human beings can attain their proper ends of a life of reason and citizenship only on the other side of necessity. In the best polis, "the citizens must not lead the life of artisans or tradesmen, for such a life is ignoble and inimical to excellence. Neither must they be farmers, since leisure is necessary both for the development of excellence and the performance of political duties."[64]

Even though leisure may be necessary for the good life, it is hardly sufficient, since people with leisure must use it well, a task perhaps even more difficult, according to Aristotle, than attaining leisure in the first place. "The first principle of all action is leisure . . . and therefore the question must be asked, what ought we to do when at leisure? Clearly we ought not to be amusing ourselves, for then amusement would be the end

---

61. *The Athenian Constitution*, chap. 16; *Politics*, 1313b19–21.
62. *Politics*, 1278a10–11; also 1255b36–37.
63. Arendt, *The Human Condition*, 74.
64. *Politics*, 1328b37–1329a2. See Adkins, "The Connection Between Aristotle's *Ethics* and *Politics*," 43–44.

of life."[65] Under a tyranny, this is precisely what happens; while tyrants use leisure time to amuse themselves with coarse pleasures, most of their subjects busy themselves with commerce, and as this commerce becomes an end in itself, they deny themselves the opportunity for genuinely fruitful leisure. In a passage referred to above, Aristotle described Pisistratus as encouraging his subjects in their private affairs so that they would have neither desire nor "leisure" to participate in political affairs.[66]

Something much more serious is at issue here in Aristotle's analysis of the way tyranny misuses leisure. First of all, the elimination of leisure time threatens intellectual development. Aristotle noted on several occasions that leisure was necessary for science and philosophy, that only after certain classes in society had conquered necessity did they turn to artistic and intellectual pursuits. "Hence when all such inventions were already established, the sciences which do not aim at giving pleasure or at the necessities of life were discovered, and first in the places where men first began to have leisure."[67] Second and more important, leisure is necessary to deliberation about what constitutes the good life. As a consequence, when tyrannies misuse or eliminate leisure, they simultaneously eliminate what Aristotle called practical questions, or questions about how a society might attain a good life. With this elimination of all practical questions, all assume, from tyrant to the poorest subject, that the good life consists in the pleasures and amusements that preoccupy the ruling classes, that there is no alternative to the status quo (all of which brings into question Aristotle's claim that the rule of a tyrant is always endured involuntarily). Nevertheless, closing off a discourse of practical questions—as Weber and Habermas have noted in the twentieth century—is one of the most powerful buttresses of any tyranny.

Aristotle maintained that "statecraft" by definition must inquire into and "speak about" the good life, or what is best for human beings, and he defined a citizen as one who participated in these deliberations about how to achieve the best life. "In the best state [a citizen] is one who is able and chooses to be governed and to govern with a view to the life of excellence." At the beginning of the *Politics,* when he suggested that human beings are political animals who attain their perfection within a Greek polis, Aristotle attempted to prove this by citing the human capac-

65. *Politics,* 1337b30–36. I have returned to the original Jowett translation, substituting "amusement" for "play." See also *Politics,* 1334a36–39: "If it is disgraceful in men not to be able to use the goods of life, it is peculiarly disgraceful not to be able to use them in time of leisure—to show excellent qualities in action and war, and when they have peace and leisure to be no better than slaves."
66. *The Athenian Constitution,* chap. 16.
67. *Metaphysics,* 981b21–23; also 982b23–28.

ity for speech. Since nature does nothing in vain, and since human beings are the only animals endowed with speech, then nature intended for human beings to live in political societies and to use "the power of speech . . . to set forth the expedient and inexpedient, and therefore likewise the just and the unjust." In other words, human beings can attain their proper end of excellence only if they can deliberate, as citizens of a polis, about the good life and how to achieve it. Not only did he applaud the fact that "assemblies meet, sit in judgment, deliberate, and decide,"[68] but he thought such action was indispensable to the development of human potential, and he wanted such assemblies to deliberate about the most serious moral and practical questions. What we both attain and apply in such political deliberation is what Aristotle called *practical wisdom.* "Now it is thought to be a mark of a man of practical wisdom to be able to deliberate well . . . about what sorts of thing conduce to the good life in general." *Phronēsis,* customarily translated as "practical wisdom," is an elusive term that suggests knowledge of the proper ends to human life, as well as the best ethical and political means by which to attain these ends. When Aristotle sought an example of a person who had attained practical wisdom, he used Pericles, who knew "what is good for men in general" but also knew how to translate this knowledge into political practice.[69] To be precise, Aristotle said in this passage that Pericles "and men like him" have practical wisdom, and this is consistent with the way he used this notion of practical wisdom throughout his works, because clearly not just one statesman but citizens in general, at least in a good polis, can possess practical wisdom.

If citizens in a good polis both develop and apply practical wisdom through their deliberations, then a tyranny, again by definition, can have no practical wisdom, although a tyrant might well have technical wisdom (*technē*) regarding how best to preserve the tyranny. (Weber made the distinction between substantive reason [about ends] and instrumental reason [about the technical means to achieve chosen ends] central to his philosophy.) Obviously a tyrant and most likely his subjects are ignorant of the good life, but Aristotle was saying something more important. The subjects of a tyranny have lost the ability to ask practical questions, to deliberate about the good life and how they might attain it. Cicero recorded a fragment of Aristotle that supports this conclusion. "Eloquence

68. *Magna Moralia,* 1183a3–8, 1183a34–35; *Politics,* 1284a1–3, 1253a7–18, 1286a26–27.

69. *Nicomachean Ethics,* 1140a25–28, 1140b7–11; see also Hardie, *Aristotle's Ethical Theory,* 234–35; Mulgan, *Aristotle's Political Theory,* 9–10; and, for a good discussion of *phronēsis,* Peter Simpson, "Contemporary Virtue Ethics and Aristotle," *Review of Metaphysics* 45, no. 179 (March 1992): 503–24, esp. 510–18.

is the companion of peace, the ally of leisure, and, so to say, the offspring of a well-ordered state. And for this reason, Aristotle says, it was when the tyrants in Sicily had been removed" that Sicilians could develop the art of eloquence;[70] that is, in the absence of tyranny citizens could finally turn to the practical questions they had previously been unable to ask. The subjects of a tyranny are unable to ask these questions not only because such questions would threaten the privileged position of the tyrant and any ruling class but also because the entire polis has accepted, according to Aristotle, the idea that the good life consists in attaining power, wealth, and pleasure. A tyrant who has eliminated all deliberations about the good life, who has managed to rule over a populace unable to question whether there is a better life or an alternative to the status quo, has found one of the most powerful weapons any tyrant can wield in the interest of stability and longevity. This idea of limiting discussion leads eventually to Tocqueville's tyranny of the majority, Marx's ideology of class, and Arendt's ideologies of political movements.

Tyranny and the Disappearance of Community

When Aristotle outlined the development of the polis, he said that the polis is an association of households, but he had already described the household as an association, so, in a sense, a polis is an association of associations.[71] The Greek word that we sometimes translate as "association" is *koinōnia,* but our word *association* cannot capture the richness of the original word. While our use of the word *association* suggests some degree of passivity in belonging to a group (for example, the National Association of Manufacturers), the word *koinōnia* suggests active participation, and while *association* to us may well connote hierarchy, *koinōnia* implies a greater degree of equality. Indeed, *koinōnia* suggests to us words such as *community* and *sharing,* and probably the best translation is *partnership* because this conveys the quality of active participation by equals in some common enterprise.[72] When we say that a polis is a community and a partnership, we immediately sense people actively embarking upon some common undertaking together, and that is probably the picture Aristotle wanted us to have of a polis. The polis, said Aristotle, "is a community of families and aggregations of families in well-being, for the

70. *Fragments,* F 137 R³.
71. *Politics,* 1252b10–1253a2.
72. Mulgan, *Aristotle's Political Theory,* 13. Elsewhere Jowett translates Aristotle as saying a state is a "partnership of citizens" (*Politics,* 1276b1–2).

sake of a perfect and self-sufficing life." Aristotle maintained that a community, or partnership, must have two other characteristics—justice and friendship—and indeed the more perfect the community, the more perfect will be the justice and friendship in that community. "For in every community there is thought to be some form of justice, and friendship too. . . . And the extent of their association is the extent of their friendship, as it is the extent to which justice exists between them. And the proverb 'what friends have is common property' expresses the truth; for friendship depends on community."[73]

Aristotle might just as well have turned this around, however, and said that community depends on friendship, because he more than once declared that the best polis is a community, or partnership, among friends and that "friendship seems . . . to hold states together."[74] When Aristotle said, "[W]ithout friends no one would choose to live, though he had all other goods," he was indicating not only that friendship is a key component of a good life but also that friendship is of supreme importance to any community, including the polis, because "there is nothing so characteristic of friends as living together." On the one hand, Aristotle meant by this that nature intends human beings to live together in a polis and that we can neither become happy nor attain excellence alone. "For no one would choose to possess all good things on condition of being alone, since man is a political creature and one whose nature is to live with others." Human beings naturally live in communities based on friendship, communities that overcome loneliness and help to develop human excellence.[75] On the other hand, Aristotle simply meant that friendship is one of the most enduring sources of human joy. "Further, men believe a friend to be among the greatest of goods, and friendlessness and solitude to be most terrible." If we have friends, we naturally want to enjoy their company, and thus Aristotle suggested that friends "contemplate in common and feast in common," as well as drink together, play dice together, and study philosophy together, "for since they wish to live with their friends, they do and share in those things as far as they can."[76] He might just as

73. *Politics*, 1280b33–35; *Nicomachean Ethics*, 1159b27–32.

74. *Nicomachean Ethics*, 1155a21–22; also *Eudemian Ethics*, 1242b21–37, and Edel, *Aristotle and His Philosophy*, 311. The Greek word *philia*, which we translate as "friendship," has a broader range of meanings than our word, including, for example, "relations among family members." For our purposes, "civic friendship," or friendship among equals, is most important. See John M. Cooper, "Aristotle on Friendship," in *Essays on Aristotle's Ethics*, ed. Rorty, 301–40, esp. 301–3.

75. *Nicomachean Ethics*, 1155a5–6, 1157b19–20, 1169b17–19; Cooper, "Aristotle on Friendship," 321–30.

76. *Eudemian Ethics*, 1234b32–1235a1, 1245b4–5; *Nicomachean Ethics*, 1172a1–8.

well have added that friends go to the assembly together and even go to battle together, because these too are consistent with the picture he gave of a good polis as a partnership, or community, distinguished most of all by friends acting in common.

In a tyranny, however, the relations between individuals are despotic; that is, they resemble the relation of a master to household servants, and by definition, this is not a relation involving friendship. "But in the deviation-forms [of government], as justice hardly exists, so too does friendship. It exists least in the worst form; in tyranny there is little or no friendship. For where there is nothing common to ruler and ruled, there is not friendship either, since there is not justice; e.g. between craftsman and tool, soul and body, master and slave. . . . For there is nothing common to the two parties; the slave is a living tool and the tool a lifeless slave."[77] It would be a mistake to conclude that Aristotle was simply depicting tyranny as an unfriendly place to live, for his picture is far gloomier than that. Because a tyranny is a political order that has lost all sense of community, all sense that people must work together toward the common goal of a good life, the relations in tyranny are marked by selfishness, exploitation, enmity, suspicion, and ultimately loneliness, which both Tocqueville and Arendt saw as key components of tyranny. If by definition we wish a friend well and share our prosperity with him or her, then in a tyranny we look upon another only as someone to be used for selfish advantage. Finally, in such a world we see only conflict between rich and poor, the former ruling despotically and the latter knowing only how to obey like slaves. "Thus arises a city, not of freemen, but of masters and slaves, the one despising, the other envying; and nothing can be more fatal to friendship and good fellowship in states than this."[78]

Aristotle used a complex class analysis, although it is difficult at times to tell exactly what he meant by the word *class*. Sometimes he referred to key occupational groups as classes—groups such as farmers, merchants, warriors, and magistrates—and at other times he talked of the rich and the poor as forming distinct classes.[79] After offering a pessimistic analysis that indicated frequent class conflict between rich and poor, Aristotle sought to solve this problem by encouraging the creation of a large middle class, literally "those in the middle," which would smooth possible conflict between rich and poor. His constitutional government, or polity, for example, which he called the best possible government for most states, was a fusion of democracy and oligarchy, with a large middle class

77. *Nicomachean Ethics*, 1161a30–1161b4.
78. *Politics*, 1295b21–26.
79. *Politics*, bk. 4, chaps. 4 and 11.

helping to bring stability to the polis.[80] Without a middle class, one class will generally dominate the other and rule "despotically." Although Aristotle is often regarded as a conservative who defended the position of the ruling classes, he actually argued that "the encroachments of the rich are more destructive to the constitution than those of the people," and warned that securing "gentle treatment for the poor is not an easy thing, since a ruling class is not always humane."[81] Under the oligarchic constitutions of ancient Athens, "the poor were enslaved to the rich," and class conflict originated in the "love of money and arrogance" embraced by the ruling class.[82]

Aristotle maintained that tyrannies benefit from modest class conflict, and as long as such conflict does not break into recurring violence, tyrannies will foster divisions between rich and poor. "Another art of the tyrant is to sow quarrels among the citizens; friends should be embroiled with friends, the people with the notables, and the rich with one another." Encouraging class conflict is a dangerous game for tyrants, however, because such conflict eventually leads to revolution. "Love of gain in the ruling classes was always tending to diminish their number, and so to strengthen the masses, who in the end set upon their masters and established democracies." In general, tyrannies must find ways to please both classes, to pretend to be the benefactor of each class and to appear to be ruling to the advantage of each class, and because this too is a dangerous game, it demonstrates that establishing and maintaining a lasting tyranny is not easy. When Aristotle advised tyrants to "win the notables by companionship, and the multitude by flattery," he was very consciously giving advice that corresponded to the practices of Pisistratus, whom Aristotle described as winning over "the notables by his friendly dealings with them, and the people by his help for their private concerns."[83]

In arguing that tyrannies benefit from quarrels between classes, and in noting that one finds little friendship and a great deal of animosity in a tyranny, Aristotle was suggesting that tyrannies are lasting to the extent

80. *Politics*, 1293b33–34, 1295b35–1296a9. See Mulgan, *Aristotle's Political Theory*, 76, 106; Andrew Lintott, *Violence, Civil Strife, and Revolution in the Classical City, 750–330 BC* (Baltimore: Johns Hopkins University Press, 1982), chap. 7, 239–51; Andrew Wheeler, "Aristotle's Analysis of the Nature of Political Struggle," in *Articles on Aristotle*, ed. Barnes et al., 2:159–69; and Wood and Wood, *Class Ideology and Ancient Political Theory*, 214–15.

81. *Politics*, 1295b20, 1297a11–12, 1297b9–10. Contrast these statements with the argument that Aristotle is only a conservative defending the privileged. See Wood and Wood, *Class Ideology and Ancient Political Theory*, and Kelsen, "Aristotle and Hellenic-Macedonian Policy."

82. *The Athenian Constitution*, chaps. 2 and 5.

83. *Politics*, 1313b17–19, 1286b16–18, 1315b3–4; *The Athenian Constitution*, chap. 16.

that they create and maintain divisions between their subjects. Divide and conquer remains a time-honored maxim for all tyrannies, and Aristotle knew this well. Aristotle noted at the beginning of the *Politics* that in prepolitical villages families live "dispersedly," in contrast to the polis, where people establish a vibrant community; and in a sense, tyrannies try to return to this prepolitical state of dispersal, confining people to their private affairs and to the household and depriving them of all opportunity for public and political action. After Aristotle no theorist of tyranny could overlook this isolation in the private world as the single most essential characteristic of tyranny. Without question, this is Aristotle's most important contribution to theories of tyranny.

After Pisistratus seized power by deceiving people into surrendering their arms, wrote Aristotle, he told the people that "they should not be startled or disheartened but should go and attend to their private affairs, and that he would take care of all public affairs." Aristotle also observed that Pisistratus isolated people from one another by encouraging them in agriculture, which took them out of the city, where they might organize themselves politically, and scattered them across the countryside, a common practice of tyrannies. "Both [tyrannies and oligarchies] agree too in injuring the people and driving them out of the city and dispersing them."[84] It was Aristotle who established that this practice of isolating citizens from one another is a central feature of any tyranny. Indeed, when Aristotle used his political science, which I examine more closely in the next section, to determine how tyrannies might make themselves more stable and more lasting, he suggested most of all a number of ways tyrannies might perpetuate divisions among the people. For example, tyrants should use spies and informers, which divide people because individuals cannot speak honestly with one another; they should divide families by encouraging women and slaves to inform against the head of the household; they should "sow quarrels among the citizens," separating citizens and breaking apart friendships; they "must not allow common meals, clubs, education," or any "meetings," because these activities might bring people together; they should "take every means to prevent people from knowing one another (for acquaintance begets mutual confidence)"; and finally, tyrants should create "mistrust among [their subjects]; for a tyrant is not overthrown until men begin to have confidence in one another."[85] Two consequences of all this are immediately striking.

---

84. *The Athenian Constitution*, chap. 15; *Politics*, 1311a12–14. Pisistratus encouraged his subjects in agriculture, "so that they should spend their time not in the city but scattered about the countryside." *The Athenian Constitution*, chap. 16.

85. *Politics*, 1313b10–17, 1313b33–38, 1313b17–19, 1313a41–1313b3, 1313b4–6, 1314a17–18.

First, if subjects are isolated from one another and mistrustful of one another, if suspicion and animosity have destroyed all friendship, then these subjects will be powerless to act politically in opposition to the tyranny. "The tyrant desires that his subjects shall be incapable of action, for no one attempts what is impossible, and they will not attempt to overthrow a tyranny if they are powerless."[86] Second, such divisions among citizens signify the complete destruction of the partnership, or community, that should constitute a polis, and once again, tyranny not only dominates and exploits, but it also destroys the political environment that is essential for the natural unfolding of human excellence.

Aristotle's Science of Tyranny

Aristotle was the ancient world's most outstanding natural scientist, a tireless observer of the natural world and one who devoted much of a lifetime to gathering facts from these empirical observations.[87] As I indicated above, Aristotle saw great continuity between his studies of the physical and biological worlds and his studies of the political world because he saw the polis, designed to develop the capacities of these human beings, as natural, even biologically demanded. Aristotle's science strikes our century as unusual because he thought he could use his science to discover not only facts but also moral imperatives; once we know that the natural end, or purpose, of human development is a life of reason and citizenship, and once we know that human beings develop these potentials within a polis, then our scientific investigation has yielded moral and political knowledge and tells us how we ought to act to promote human excellence. It is, as I said above, a science, much like medicine, that knows health is good and how to bring it about. Despite the fact that his science is not exactly like the political science of the twentieth century, Aristotle's scientific respect for empiricism sets him apart from Plato. In recounting Plato's analysis that the republic will pass from timocracy to oligarchy to democracy and ultimately end in tyranny, Aristotle refuted him with empirical evidence! Borrowing from his empirical studies of various states, Aristotle suggested that democracy is more likely to pass into oligarchy than into tyranny. When he sought the origin of tyrannies, he offered not a theoretical (or even psychological) analysis but historical examples. Tyrants have generally been chosen by the peo-

---

86. *Politics*, 1314a22–25.
87. Jonathan Barnes, *Aristotle* (New York: Oxford University Press, 1982), 14–17.

ple purportedly to protect the people from the outrages of the notables; "history shows that almost all tyrants have been demagogues who gained the favour of the people by their accusation of the notables."[88]

Aristotle's political science sought to know four things: the ideal government in the abstract, the best *possible* government (a not so subtle criticism of Plato), the best government relative to a nation's given circumstances, and, finally, how statesmen might form a government and preserve it.[89] This latter goal, how best to make a government both stable and lasting, led him to analyze how one might preserve a tyranny. Although this analysis is somewhat startling to us, since he seemed to be offering advice to benefit tyrants, Aristotle's prodigious curiosity simply led him to ask a technical question in regard to what makes a tyranny lasting, much as a physician might wonder under what conditions disease will spread most rapidly. He even likened his study to a medical investigation. "For as healthy bodies and ships well provided with sailors may undergo many mishaps and survive them, whereas sickly constitutions and rotten ill-manned ships are ruined by the very least mistake, so do the worst forms of government require the greatest care." Aristotle offered a good deal of general advice about preserving and improving the stability of any constitution, such as securing the habit of obedience to all laws and educating young people into the "spirit of the constitution,"[90] but he also made specific observations about how tyrants might best preserve tyrannies.

In distilling Aristotle's specific advice for stabilizing tyrannies, I find four broad recommendations, the first two of which have already appeared in preceding sections of this chapter. First, Aristotle recommended, in a variety of specific ways, that tyrants depoliticize their populations. Not only will citizens then busy themselves with their private economic concerns, but they will also forgo asking practical questions about alternatives to the status quo. Second, Aristotle gave a host of detailed suggestions about how a tyrant might divide citizens to prevent them from organizing politically against the tyranny. In this, the effective tyrant will try to destroy community and friendship, isolating people from one another in an attempt to render them powerless. Third, tyrants must know how to use violence, and fourth, they must be adept at deception.

---

88. *Politics*, 1310b15–16; also bk. 5, chap. 12. And see Raymond Weil, "Aristotle's View of History," in *Articles on Aristotle*, ed. Barnes et al., 2:202–17, esp. 209; and Kurt Von Fritz, "Aristotle's Contribution to the Practice and Theory of Historiography," *University of California Publications in Philosophy* 28, no. 3 (1958): 113–38, esp. 137.

89. *Politics*, bk. 4, chap. 1.

90. *Politics*, 1320b34–37, 1307b25–34, 1310a12–22.

On three different occasions Aristotle either related or referred to a story about Periander, a tyrant of Corinth, who, when asked advice, "said nothing, but only cut off the tallest ears of corn till he had brought the field to a level," a symbolic gesture indicating that tyrants must use violence against all the outstanding individuals who threaten their power. Although Aristotle preferred to see a tyrant use ostracism to eliminate potentially powerful opponents, he readily admitted that an effective tyrant must be capable of violence. "The tyrant should lop off those who are too high; he must put to death men of spirit."[91] Add to this violence the use of spies and informers, and it is easy to see that Aristotle thought that tyrants needed both fear and violence to maintain their rule. The problem is especially acute for those who inherit tyrannical power, for "most of those who have acquired, have retained their power, but those who have inherited, have lost it, almost at once; for, living in luxurious ease, they have become contemptible." Whereas Pisistratus was a model of moderation, his sons became more violent as their tyranny became more unstable. All tyrannies, however, engage in violence, frequently when there is no pressing need. After the Thirty Tyrants of Athens had consolidated their rule by pretending to be moderate, they "put to death those who were outstanding for their wealth, birth or reputation, cunningly removing those whom they had cause to fear and whose property they wanted to plunder. Within a short space of time they had killed no fewer than fifteen hundred." This is an extraordinary number of people for a city-state numbering perhaps 250,000, and it belies Aristotle's suggestion that the forceful and violent means of tyrants are merely "Persian and barbaric arts."[92]

If tyrants must wield violence against their subjects, they must make sure that they have a monopoly on the means of violence, which first of all means that they must "deprive [their subjects] of their arms." Pisistratus began one of his reigns of tyranny by tricking the people into giving up their arms; after he pretended that they all must go to the Acropolis to hear him speak, the citizens went and appropriately left their weapons outside, whereupon followers of Pisistratus simply collected them.[93] While it is fine to have a monopoly of arms, a tyrant must also have men willing to use them, and thus one of the first steps of any tyrant lies in establishing a bodyguard or paramilitary force. Pisistratus con-

---

91. *Politics*, 1284a29–31; also 1311a20–22, 1313a39–41. On ostracism, see *Politics*, bk. 3, chap. 13. Here Aristotle acknowledged that both democracies and oligarchies must also know how and when to use violence.

92. *Politics*, 1312b21–25j; *The Athenian Constitution*, chaps. 19 and 35; *Politics*, 1313b10.

93. *Politics*, 1311a11–12; *The Athenian Constitution*, chap. 15.

vinced the Athenians that because he was in danger, he needed a body-guard, and then he promptly "took the men called club-bearers, and with their aid rose against the people and seized the Acropolis." In distinguish-ing between a king and a tyrant, Aristotle noted that "kings rule according to law over voluntary subjects, but tyrants over involuntary; and the ones are guarded by their fellow-citizens, the others are guarded against them"; and he mentioned later that "the guards of a king are citizens, but of a tyrant mercenaries."[94] As general advice to all regimes, Aristotle sug-gested that rulers "invent terrors" and "bring distant dangers near," so that "citizens may be on their guard, and, like sentinels in a night-watch, never relax their attention." In advice directed more specifically at ty-rants, he observed that "the tyrant is also fond of making war in order that his subjects may have something to do and be always in want of a leader."[95] Despite the fact that he did not explain exactly how a tyrant organizes an army, or even a personal bodyguard, all of Aristotle's advice has a sadly familiar ring to it well into the twentieth century, although we, unlike Aristotle, have gained insight from Machiavelli's warnings about the dangers of relying on mercenaries and foreigners to oppress citizens.

Aristotle regarded violence as inevitably necessary for a tyrant but also as a sign of instability, and he certainly regarded deception as a more effective means to make a tyranny lasting. Aristotle seemed genuinely fond of relating stories involving deception. Not only did Pisistratus trick the citizens of Athens into giving up their weapons, but in order to con-vince them that he needed a bodyguard, he wounded himself! Another tyrant, faced with a demand from Persia for tribute, assembled his sub-jects and asked them for money; having planted in the crowd certain subjects who promised to pay generously, he tricked the wealthiest into paying even more.[96] On more general and important matters, Aristotle's persistent advice to tyrants was that they maintain the appearance of constitutionality even as they rule arbitrarily, that they maintain the ap-pearance of generosity even as they tax voraciously, and so on, the sort of advice we almost automatically associate with Machiavelli. The Thirty Tyrants, to take another case, at first "pretended that their aim was the traditional constitution," and even when they moved to violence against the population, they first introduced and passed new laws, all to sustain the appearance of legality. Just as tyrants must make bows toward legal-ity, they must appear religious even as they use religion to their own

94. *The Athenian Constitution*, chap. 14; *Politics*, 1285a26–28, 1311a6–7. Aristotle also noted that tyrants like to keep company with foreigners. *Politics*, 1314a9–11.
95. *Politics*, 1308a28–31, 131b28–30.
96. *The Athenian Constitution*, chaps. 14–15; *Economics*, 1348a4–11; *Politics*, 1292b17–21.

ends. Pisistratus once pretended that Athena was reinstating him, found a "tall and impressive" Thracian woman, rode into the city with the woman at his side, and "the people in the city worshipped and received him with awe."[97] If this story sounds to us far-fetched and difficult to believe, it illustrates Aristotle's suggestion that tyrants must make use of religion. A tyrant "should appear to be particularly earnest in the service of the gods; for if men think that a ruler is religious and has a reverence for the gods, . . . they are less disposed to conspire against him, because they believe him to have the very gods fighting on his side."[98]

Aristotle's ultimate advice to the tyrant was to maintain power by appearing to rule like a king. "But though power must be retained as the foundation, in all else the tyrant should act or appear to act in the character of a king."[99] Although it is difficult to know whether Aristotle was merely giving the time-honored and usually fruitless advice to a tyrant, that his or her regime will be lasting if he or she becomes more just and moderate, or was really counseling, as it seems, that appearing to rule like a king is simply the final and most effective deception, in either case he was suggesting that both some moderation and the appearance of even more moderation were in the best interests of the tyrant. Such advice falls into clear categories. First, tyrants should "appear, not harsh, but dignified," and should wish that their subjects look upon them not with fear but with reverence. Aristotle acknowledged that this might entail deception, for he observed that "at least [the tyrant] should maintain the character of a great soldier, and produce the impression that he is one."[100] Second, tyrants should be moderate in their desires, "or at any rate should not parade [their] vices to the world," and should not offend the modesty of modest women or the honor of honorable men. Third, as stated above, tyrants should appear religious, even if they are not. Fourth, a tyrant "should pretend concern for the public revenues," use tax money only for public purposes, not waste money on extravagance or presents for favorites, keep a good account of revenues and expenditures, and "adorn and improve his city, as though he were not a tyrant, but the guardian of the state." In general, the tyrant should "seem to be a steward of the public" and should "make himself the guardian and treasurer of

---

97. *The Athenian Constitution*, chaps. 35–37, 14; Dionysius I of Syracuse fooled the people by claiming Demeter appeared before him, requesting that all women bring to the temple their jewelry, which of course Dionysius promptly collected himself. *Economics*, 1349a14–24.

98. *Politics*, 1314b38–1315a4.

99. *Politics*, 1314a38–40.

100. *Politics*, 1314b19–24, 1314b24–36, 1315a14–20.

[tax monies], as if they belonged, not to him, but to the public."[101] Fifth, tyrants should distribute honors themselves but make lesser officials incur hatred for inflicting punishments; make certain to "honor men of merit," making these people believe that no free government would give them as much distinction; raise up to distinction not one person, who might offer the tyrant opposition, but "two or more," so that they watch one another; and avoid not only elevating to positions of power individuals of "bold spirit" but also depriving a person of power suddenly rather than gradually.[102] Finally, tyrants should appear to rule to the advantage of both rich and poor, make each class think its security depends upon the tyrant, and ally themselves with the strongest of the two classes, which will obviate the necessity of disarming the citizens.[103] Aristotle ended this section with a general summary of his advice to tyrants who have an enlightened sense of their own self-interest.

> He ought to show himself to his subjects in the light, not of a tyrant, but of a steward and a king. He should not appropriate what is theirs, but should be their guardian; he should be moderate, not extravagant in his way of life; he should win the notables by companionship, and the multitude by flattery. For then his rule will of necessity be nobler and happier, because he will rule over better men whose spirits are not crushed, and who do not hate and fear him. His power too will be more lasting. His disposition will be virtuous, or at least half virtuous; and he will not be wicked, but half wicked only.[104]

Because it is difficult to believe that any tyrant who followed this advice would remain a tyrant, it is possible that Aristotle himself sought to entice or to deceive a tyrant into becoming a king. His hope that tyrants would prudently become kings might explain why Aristotle gave such fine advice for the promulgation of evil. It is also possible that he had Pisistratus in mind, whom Aristotle regarded as "humane" and "mild" and who, once in power, "administered the city's affairs moderately, and more like a citizen than like a tyrant."[105] In many details, Aristotle's description of Pisistratus resembles his advice to the tyrant who would appear to rule as a king.

101. *Politics*, 1314b1, 1314b14–15, 1314b1–5, 1314b5–6, 1314b37–38, 1314b6–7, 1314b16–19.

102. *Politics*, 1315a5–7, 1315a4–5, 1315a8–10, 1315a10–14.

103. *Politics*, 1315a31–40.

104. *Politics*, 1315a40–1315b10.

105. *The Athenian Constitution*, chap. 16.

Aristotle did not pretend that his political science could be as empirically accurate and verifiable as mathematics, astronomy, or physics. We can see that his science of tyranny either resembles the prudence or common sense gathered by a brilliant person with long experience in the political world or, perhaps, as I noted earlier, resembles that blend of art and science that we call medicine. If it resembles the latter, we are not at all sure, of course, that we want the physician to prolong the life of the tyrannical patient. At any rate, with his political science, Aristotle moved some distance away from Platonic moralizing and toward an objective analysis of this phenomenon of tyranny.

Conclusion

With Aristotle we find ourselves in a political and economic world that we largely recognize. He gave us a clear definition of tyranny and cited specific goals that a tyrant pursues as well as the means needed to achieve them. Whereas both Plato and Aristotle gave us sophisticated theoretical arguments about what tyranny does to its subjects, Aristotle was much more effective in explaining *how* tyrannies do this and, by implication, how we might resist the disease of tyranny. It is his bent toward empirical investigation that most separates Aristotle from Plato, and by using his own metaphysical and moral reasoning—which at root are admittedly Platonic—along with his empiricism, Aristotle firmed up the groundwork for all subsequent theories of tyranny.

But problems and questions remain. To begin with, we encounter the problem of defining tyranny. Although it seemed rather simple for Aristotle to say that a tyrant is one who rules in his or her own interest, it turned out to be very complicated; to discover what Aristotle regarded as the proper "interests" of human beings, we had to swim up and down the stream of Aristotle's entire philosophy. Ultimately, Aristotle defined a tyranny as the political order that makes human beings the least healthy or, to put it another way, the political order that least satisfies human beings' highest psychic and biological needs. Are we satisfied that Aristotle's investigations have established these needs? Can modern physical and social sciences perhaps do a better job?[106] If we could rank human needs as Maslow has tried to do, then we could categorize the severity of tyrannies

---

106. To see the difficulty in establishing objectively some set of human needs, see the excellent overview discussion by Patricia Springborg, *The Problem of Human Needs and the Critique of Civilisation* (London: George Allen & Unwin, 1981).

by the kinds of needs they deny, but we leave Aristotle feeling we are a long way from such an intriguing goal.

While we feel very much at home when Aristotle talks of the political and economic foundations of tyranny, his definition of tyranny sounds strange to our modern ears, because we want to speak of tyrannies as denying natural rights, violating agreements or contracts, and suspending democratic freedoms. We tend implicitly to define a tyranny as a country that denies basic "democratic rights and freedoms." But Aristotle would have tremendous difficulty in talking about democratic rights and freedoms. He would not see freedom as the companion to democracy, and he certainly would not see democracy as the opposite of tyranny. For Aristotle, the opposite of tyranny is not a political order that protects rights and allows voting, but rather a political order that creates virtue and excellence in individuals. It is immediately apparent how far from us is Greek political discourse and how much we learn that is new and provocatively puzzling by seeing tyranny through Aristotle's eyes.

Another problem emerges. Why did Aristotle define and confine tyranny to rule by one person? As an admirer of Pisistratus, he may have assumed such a definition almost unthinkingly, again accepting common Greek political discourse as his starting point. But would a ruthless oligarchy not rule tyrannically? Would such an oligarchy not use all the means of depoliticizing a population that a tyranny does—the violence of spies and paramilitary forces, deception, isolating individuals by banning groups, and so forth? Aristotle here betrayed his own very sophisticated class analysis, falling back on the notion that for power to be tyrannical it must be in the hands of one person. A variety of thinkers in the modern world have since sought to escape the confines of this definition and have looked at a variety of tyrannies—class-based tyrannies, military juntas, faceless bureaucracies, and so on.

Aristotle's analysis helps us identify yet another problem that all tyrannies face. Although his advice to a tyrant seems terrifyingly effective as we read it, it becomes apparent that it is not easy to establish and maintain a lasting tyranny, and it is no wonder that Aristotle said "no forms of government are so short-lived as oligarchy and tyranny."[107] Seemingly countless problems surface. If tyrants attempt to pacify their populations with prosperity, will prosperity not lead to the leisure necessary for political activity? If tyrants disarm their subjects, how will they control both their private paramilitary forces and the general army? How reliable are mercenaries? Aristotle admitted that insults to honorable men are dangerous because such people might be led by passion or anger to attempt

107. *Politics*, 1315b12.

an assassination, with no concern for their own survival,[108] but how can any tyrant avoid insulting honorable men? How does a tyrant with arbitrary power keep up appearances of, say, legality? How does a tyrant make use of religious authorities without yielding to them significant power? And finally, how can a tyrant please the rich, the middle classes, and the poor all at once? If the tyrant pleases the poor, will the rich not threaten the tyranny? If the tyrant pleases the rich and middle classes, will their newly found economic power not endanger the tyrant's political power? And how long can a tyrant stave off rebellion by the oppressed poor? While it seems, to the outside observer, as if the tyrant's life is an easy one, Aristotle began to make a good case that the tyrant's life is a juggling act in which at least one of the balls in the air must finally fall.

All of these questions should obscure neither the brilliance of Aristotle's analysis nor the often striking familiarity this ancient analysis brings to any modern reader. Without trying to summarize an entire chapter, I wish to point out several major characteristics of tyranny that certainly apply to our own century. First, a tyranny encourages its citizens to avoid politics. Aristotle, of all ancient thinkers, most dramatically drew the distinction between the public, political realm and the private, economic sphere; between the polis and the household. One cannot be a citizen and one cannot organize opposition if one is confined to and isolated in the private sphere, and thus tyrants try to transform citizens into subjects by eliminating public and political life. Aristotle actually mentioned several ways of confining subjects to the private and economic life of the household. A tyrant might do this by force—for example, by banning all public gatherings—but perhaps more effectively, a tyrant might divert subjects from political affairs either by enticing them with prosperity into their private worlds or by forcing them to labor long hours on their private economic affairs in order to overcome poverty (a practice we have seen in this century in Communist countries). Without question, this is Aristotle's greatest contribution to theories of tyranny, and Tacitus, Machiavelli, Montesquieu, Tocqueville, and Arendt all learned from Aristotle, at least indirectly, that tyrants must depoliticize citizens by confining them and isolating them in the private household. (In other words, tyranny reduces male citizens to the status of women and servants, for whom despotic rule, in Aristotle's opinion was appropriate.)

Second, tyrannies fill leisure time with amusements, so people will not focus on political matters. Third, tyrannies eliminate practical questions, that is, speculative deliberation about what constitutes the good life, until people cannot even raise questions about alternatives to the status quo.

108. *Politics*, 1315a25–31.

Fourth, tyrannies monopolize the means of violence and are willing to use this violence to serve their purposes. Finally, tyrannies maintain appearances, for example, of legality or of being religious, even when they betray both. One reads Aristotle's analysis sadly, for it is easy to conclude that since the tyrannies he analyzed so carefully still haunt us in one form or another today, a tyranny is a monstrous species of rule that will perhaps never become extinct. To any modern reader with only passing acquaintance of Hitler's Germany, one passage must stand out as horrifyingly prophetic and appropriate to our own age. An evil man might be safer and wiser, suggested Aristotle, if he committed "crimes so great and terrible that no man living could be suspected of them: here too no precautions are taken. For all men guard against ordinary offences, just as they guard against ordinary diseases; but no one takes precautions against an offence that nobody has ever yet committed."[109]

---

109. *Rhetoric*, 1372a25–29.

3

TACITUS

Tyranny as a
Politics of Pretense

Although Plato and Aristotle each outlined a theory of tyranny, the writer in the ancient world who offered the best political analysis of tyranny was perhaps the historian Tacitus. Political theorists of past centuries knew this well. In the Renaissance, both Machiavelli and Guicciardini leaned upon the political wisdom of Tacitus.[1] In the French Enlightenment, Montesquieu borrowed from Tacitus again and again, while d'Alembert, Rousseau, and Diderot, each seeing in Tacitus an exemplary analysis of tyranny, took the time to translate him.[2] In the American tradition, Tacitus was a favorite political writer of both Jefferson and Adams.[3]

The writings of Tacitus tell many stories, but underlying each of these

---

1. Burke, "Tacitism," in T. A. Dorey, ed., *Tacitus* (New York: Basic Books, 1969), 149–50. A version of this chapter has previously been published as "The Politics of Pretense: Tacitus and the Political Theory of Despotism," *History of Political Thought* 8, no. 2 (1987): 189–210.

2. Orest Ranum, "D'Alembert, Tacitus, and the Political Sociology of Despotism," *Studies on Voltaire and the Eighteenth Century* (Transactions of the Fifth International Congress of the Enlightenment II) 191 (1980): 547–58, esp. 553.

3. Donald Dudley, *The World of Tacitus* (Boston: Little, Brown, 1968), 237.

seems to be one central question, namely, why did Rome travel from *principatus* to *dominatio,* from the principate of Augustus to the absolute rule, the tyranny, or the despotism—and "despotism" is probably the best translation of *dominatio*[4]—of emperors from Tiberius to Domitian.[5] Although historians have agreed that Tacitus exaggerated the despotism of Tiberius,[6] this conclusion does not hinder us from examining the ways in which Tacitus analyzed the structure and characteristics of despotism, or what one writer called the "anatomy of tyranny."[7] Under Augustus, the word *principatus* was a descriptive term suggesting government by one person, a word without pejorative connotations. Exhausted by civil wars, the Roman people genuinely welcomed the order and stability brought to them by Augustus (27 B.C.E.–14 C.E.). To the Romans, the principate of Augustus was still a *res publica,* a government concerned with the common good, and it was not a form of government from which *libertas* was entirely absent. From the time of the early republic, the word *libertas* had overlapping meanings. On the one hand, *libertas,* or liberty, necessarily entailed *civitas,* or citizenship, and all the duties and privileges that accompanied citizenship, including participation in popular assemblies. On the other hand, *libertas* referred to the rights of person and property protected by Roman law. By the time of the principate of Augustus, the liberty associated with republican government and citizen participation had

---

4. As will be clear in Chapter 5, the word *despotism* was not invented until the seventeenth century, and it most forcefully entered into our political vocabulary with Montesquieu's famous discussion in the eighteenth century. Tacitus did not have at his disposal any Latin word derived from the Greek word *despotēs,* a word that signified one who ruled over servants in the household or over barbarian subjects, who were supposedly not fit for freedom. Nor did he frequently make use of the Latin word *tyrannus.* Instead, Tacitus called the absolute role of Tiberius a *dominatio* and Tiberius himself a *dominus.* It would probably be best to translate *dominatio* as "absolute rule" and *dominus* as "absolute ruler," but that would be awkward, so, to differentiate from the discussions by Plato and Aristotle of tyrannies and tyrants, I have somewhat reluctantly chosen to use the words *despotism* and *despot.* Most modern translators agree with this rendering, for good reason, because, just as *despotēs* suggested rule over a household, so do the words *dominus* and *dominatio.* See R. Koebner, "Despot and Despotism: Vicissitudes of a Political Term," *Journal of the Warburg and Courtauld Institutes* 14 (1951): 275–302. For an introduction to the concept of despotism, see Melvin Richter, "Despotism," in *Dictionary of the History of Ideas,* 5 vols. (New York: Scribner's, 1974), 2:1–18.

5. Herbert W. Benario, *An Introduction to Tacitus* (Athens: University of Georgia Press, 1975), 141.

6. Michael Grant, *The Ancient Historians* (New York: Charles Scribner's Sons, 1970), 288; Colin Wells, *The Roman Empire* (Stanford: Stanford University Press, 1984), 36.

7. B. Walker, *The Annals of Tacitus: A Study in the Writing of History* (Manchester: Manchester University Press, 1952), 233.

disappeared, but at least to some shaky extent that part of liberty referring to the rights of person and property persisted.[8]

If *principatus* implied government by one person, *dominatio* implied absolute and unrestrained rule by one person, a rule that reduced all others to servitude. For the Romans, *dominatio* was in every conceivable way antithetical to liberty.[9] In fact, under a *dominatio* (or despotism) the *dominus* (or despot) treated the nation like a *res privata*, and despots worried not about the common good but only about their private goods, treating what once was a commonwealth as if it were the despot's private wealth. Both liberty as citizen participation in the assemblies of a republic and liberty as embodying rights of person and property were entirely absent under a *dominatio*, and if liberty under despotism meant anything for someone like Tacitus, it was but a remnant of real liberty, nothing more than the courage to keep one's dignity alive in the face of despotism.[10] It was in delineating the characteristics of this despotism, beginning with that of Tiberius (14–37 C.E.), that Tacitus became the political theorist who offered to his readers an unparalleled understanding of the tyranny of the Roman Empire. "When there was democracy, it was necessary to understand the character of the masses and how to control them. When the senate was in power, those who best knew its mind—the mind of the oligarchs—were considered the wisest experts on contemporary events. Similarly, now that Rome has virtually been transformed into an autocracy, the investigation and record of these details concerning the autocrat may prove useful. Indeed, it is from such studies—from the experience of others—that most men learn to distinguish right and wrong, advantage and disadvantage."[11]

Despotism as Administration and the Eclipse of Politics

Near the opening of *Agricola*, his first work, Tacitus described the political development fundamental to almost every page of his writing. "Rome of old explored the utmost limits of freedom; we have plumbed the

8. Ch. Wirszubski, *Libertas as a Political Idea at Rome During the Late Republic and Early Principate* (London: Cambridge University Press, 1969), 3, 121–29.

9. Herbert W. Benario, "Tacitus and the Principate," *Classical Journal* 60, no. 3 (1964): 102.

10. Wirszubski, *Libertas as a Political Idea*, 121, 159–67.

11. Tacitus, *The Annals of Imperial Rome*, trans. Michael Grant, rev. ed. (New York: Penguin, 1977), bk. 4, sec. 33 (henceforth cited by book and section as 4.33).

depths of slavery."[12] The first and most obvious characteristic of this new servitude was the concentration of power into the hands of one man, and Tacitus declared in the first pages of the *Annals* that this concentration of power, perhaps unavoidable, began with Augustus: "Then he gradually pushed ahead and absorbed the functions of the senate, the officials, and even the law. Opposition did not exist. War or judicial murder had disposed of all men of spirit." Whereas Augustus and his successors were wise enough to maintain the appearance of republicanism, the illusion of freedom, Tacitus was eager to have his readers penetrate past the charade. He wrote, for example, that Tiberius allowed the senate only the "pretenses of freedom" and "a shadow of its ancient power."[13] Tacitus was maintaining that hypocrisy and deception are invaluable even to the most entrenched despot, that the most powerful ruler is more appealing if he or she pretends to be no more than a servant of the people, with all the trappings of legitimacy. "Otho, too, played his part well. He would hold out his hands, bow to the mob and throw them kisses, in everything aping the slave in order to become the master."[14] The senate still deliberated, the law courts functioned, and magistrates decreed, but all this was only the illusion of popular government because, behind the veil, power rested in the hands of the emperor.[15] As Tacitus put it, "The impressiveness of the Republican facade only meant that the slave-state . . . would be all the more loathesome."[16]

Tacitus was suggesting that the Roman state was no longer political, but instead administrative. If the word *politics* refers to popular decision making or at a minimum public deliberation by someone—if even just the senate—about the common good, then the Roman state under the empire had eliminated politics. Consider the debate in "A Dialogue on Oratory" on the question of why oratorical eloquence had declined since the time of the republic. Maternus claimed that great political speaking emerges when one finds great political battles; in past times of civil disorder one found great orators, but, said Maternus, under the empire one thankfully could exchange political eloquence for order, peace, and prosperity. In this debate, Messala declared political eloquence had declined because of a loss of ancient morality and because of poor education or training by parents. Although in each case the fabric in the debate between Maternus

12. Tacitus, *The Agricola*, in *The Agricola and the Germania*, trans. H. Mattingly and S. A. Handford (New York: Penguin, 1970), 2.

13. *Annals*, 1.2, 77; 3.60.

14. Tacitus, *The Histories*, trans. Kenneth Wellesley (New York: Penguin, 1975), bk. 1, sec. 36 (henceforth cited by book and section as 1.36).

15. Wells, *The Roman Empire*, 131–32.

16. *Annals*, 1.81.

and Messala was different, a common thread was present in each argument: great eloquence has disappeared (1) because no one other than the emperor can act politically and make political decisions, and (2) because serious political questions about the common good are no longer debated, but administratively decided. Maternus contended that there was no longer any political debate, because "the best men are soon of one mind," that is, the emperor's, and Messala suggested that there were no longer any orators, because subjects (hardly citizens) could no longer openly debate "good and evil . . . right and wrong."[17] While public discourse disappeared, private decree remained; while politics vanished, administration thrived.

All this coincides exactly with what we find in Tacitus's other writings. Tacitus noted that Tiberius suppressed the popular assemblies, and he related that senators "were too busy calculating their private prospects to worry about the public interest."[18] In a more significant passage, Tacitus used irony and innuendo—so well documented by other scholars[19]—to enable the reader to see that the Roman senate could only discuss trivial matters, not substantive political questions. Under the despotism of Nero (54–68), the senate passed a measure that authorized the city of Syracuse to increase attendance at gladiatorial contests. Thrasea opposed the measure, and Tacitus quoted unidentified critics who mocked Thrasea's opposition to such an insignificant decree. "If, they said, Thrasea believes Rome needs a free senate, why does he pursue such trivial matters? Why does he not argue one way or the other about questions of war and peace, taxation, legislation, and other matters of national importance? . . . If significant matters are passed over and ignored, surely trivialities ought to be left alone?"[20] What is the effect of such a passage on the reader? The reader becomes well aware of Tacitus's admiration for the courage of Thrasea, for Thrasea's republican and Stoic opposition to Nero, which ended in death. No reader caught up in the prose of Tacitus could possibly agree with the critics of Thrasea. The effect of the passage is to emphasize to the reader that the senate under the despotism of Nero could only deal with trivial administrative affairs, not with political questions. Even the repetitive, questioning style of Tacitus in this passage forces the reader to ask himself or herself why the senate could not deal with genu-

17. Tacitus, "A Dialogue on Oratory," in *Complete Works of Tacitus*, trans. Alfred John Church and William Jackson Brodribb (New York: Modern Library, 1942), 41, 31; also 30, 1, 15.

18. *Histories*, 1.19; *Annals*, 1.15.

19. Donald Sullivan, "Innuendo and the 'Weighted Alternative' in Tacitus," *Classical Journal* 71, no. 4 (1976): 312–26.

20. *Annals*, 13.49.

ine political questions of war and peace and taxation. Why indeed are "significant matters" ignored? And the reader must conclude that if a courageous man like Thrasea could not engage in genuine political debate, then political deliberation and political decisions were impossible under the despotism of Nero, who had transformed political questions into imperial and administrative decrees. Tacitus, living in the Roman Empire, caught one of the earliest glimpses of administrative tyranny, an idea that would be far more central to the theories of tyranny offered by Tocqueville and Weber, both of whom despaired at seeing political life supplanted by a new and far-reaching bureaucratic tyranny.

The Overt Means of Control

If we ask ourselves how one man concentrated the power of Rome in his hands alone, we begin with the most obvious of tyranny's characteristics, that is, the control of force, which first and foremost meant the army. Augustus could concentrate power only because of the unquestioned loyalty of the army, and it is no accident that Tiberius, who extended this power, was supreme commander of the military well before he formally ruled.[21] Even before Augustus died, Tacitus noted, Tiberius had a private army whose soldiers escorted him to and from the senate,[22] suggesting that private paramilitary forces loyal to a leader must exist alongside the army. Certainly the foundation of any despotism must be a near monopoly of the means of violence. And certainly the Roman Empire was violent. When the modern reader first encounters Tacitus's litany of death by murder, execution, suicide, and war, this violent time of empire appears grim indeed. And yet compared to a century in which genocide has been attempted more than once, the Roman Empire as described by Tacitus appears to have been a time when violence, however cruel, was frequently political and somewhat selective; and thus force alone cannot explain the tenacity of Roman despotism.

From the beginning of the *Annals,* Tacitus argued that a despotism is more effective to the extent that it appeals to self-interest, to the extent that it can coax rather than threaten. Augustus "seduced the army with bonuses, and his cheap food policy was successful bait for civilians. In-

21. Kurt Von Fritz, "Tacitus, Agricola, Domitian, and the Problem of the Principate," *Classical Philology* 52, no. 2 (1957): 86–87.

22. *Annals,* 1.7. On how emperors used urban violence to solidify their power, see Elizabeth Keitel, "Principate and Civil War in *Annals* of Tacitus," *American Journal of Philology* 105, no. 3 (1984): 306–25.

deed, he attracted everybody's goodwill by the enjoyable gift of peace. . . . Upper-class survivors found that slavish obedience was the way to succeed, both politically and financially." A successful despotism, Tacitus suggested, always involves more enticement than force, an idea expressed in one of his most famous passages about Britain. "And so the population was gradually led into the demoralizing temptations of arcades, baths, and sumptuous banquets. The unsuspecting Britons spoke of such novelties as 'civilization,' when in fact they were only a feature of their enslavement." If an emperor could control the armies by personal loyalty, military discipline, and bribes, he could also apply such a formula to leading citizens who might pose a threat. Tacitus indicated, for example, that Nero thought "he could bind everyone of importance to himself by generous presents."[23] And although historical evidence suggests that Roman historians underestimated the extent to which the Roman populace could loosely unite to express discontent,[24] Tacitus was at least partly correct in his implicit agreement with Juvenal that emperors controlled the Roman populace with bread and circuses, with bribes and entertaining diversions. To subvert that part of *libertas* that entailed republican participation, Roman despotism forcefully abolished popular assemblies and then contented a passive population with cheap food and depoliticizing amusements.

To undermine that part of *libertas* that referred to the rights of person and property, emperors had to subvert Roman law, and Tacitus dwelled on this at great length. Augustus himself began the trend to bribe judges, but later, under Tiberius, the legal system became one additional instrument for imperial despotism. "The legal system had provided no remedy against [abuses], since it was wholly incapacitated by violence, favouritism, and—most of all—bribery." For the corruption of Roman law, Tacitus blamed Tiberius, who began to sit in the law courts, thwarted just decisions, and "infringed on the independence of judges." Most pernicious of all, Tiberius accelerated the practice of using the *lex maiestas,* or treason law, to punish not merely traitorous acts but the spoken opinions of even the mildest critics. In the opinion of Tacitus, the treason law was a "disastrous institution—which Tiberius so cunningly insinuated, first under control, then bursting into an all-engulfing blaze."[25]

Force, bribery, and control of the legal system all are essential to an

23. *Annals*, 1.2; *Agricola*, 21; *Annals*, 13.28.
24. Z. Yavetz, *Plebs and Princeps* (Oxford: Oxford University Press, 1969), 5–23. See also, Michael Roberts, "The Revolt of Boudicca (Tacitus, *Annals*, 14.29–39) and the Assertion of *Libertas* in Neronian Rome," *American Journal of Philology* 109, no. 1 (1988): 118–32.
25. *Annals*, 1.2, 75, 73.

efficient despotism, but Tacitus regarded these as insufficient in explaining the profoundly far-reaching qualities of Roman despotism. We see this in a famous story he tells about Tiberius: "But this was a tainted, meanly obsequious age. The greatest figures had to protect their positions by subserviency; and, in addition to them, all ex-consuls, most ex-praetors, even many junior senators competed with each other's offensively sycophantic proposals. There is a tradition that whenever Tiberius left the senate-house he exclaimed in Greek, 'Men fit to be slaves!' Even he, freedom's enemy, became impatient of such abject servility."[26] Tacitus was asking, not why despots want to rule, but why Roman subjects were so eager to be ruled; not why emperors eliminated popular assemblies, but why Roman citizens no longer wanted political participation. "In spite of repeated popular pressure, Tiberius refused the title 'Father of his Country.'"[27] Tacitus was asking how individuals become eager for a leader to care for them like a father, comfortable with childlike obedience and accustomed to servitude, questions Freud and Fromm would address more systematically in the twentieth century.

Isolation and Privatization

Every political theorist who has written about tyranny, from Aristotle to Machiavelli and from Montesquieu to Arendt, has noticed one key characteristic of tyranny, a characteristic that might well be called the essential prerequisite for tyranny: tyrants must find some way to keep subjects isolated, unable to coordinate political opposition. This dictum of despotism is, of course, just a corollary to the commonsense military proposition that if one can divide, then one can more easily conquer. Tacitus recorded that Britons were unwilling to unite their forces against the Romans, and "thus, fighting in separate groups, all are conquered."[28] Surprisingly, isolation in the twentieth century might well be easier than in the first century because the architecture of our modern apartments and suburban homes necessarily isolates, whereas the shabby living conditions of ancient Rome forced many citizens to spend much time in public places such as city squares, baths, and amphitheaters.[29] Still, Tacitus de-

26. *Annals*, 3.65.
27. *Annals*, 1.72.
28. *Agricola*, 12.
29. Wells, *The Roman Empire*, 220. Montesquieu noted that in the early Roman Republic "[t]he houses . . . were very small, for the men were always at work or in the public square,

scribed both physical isolation and a psychological isolation born of fear and mutual suspicion.

According to Tacitus, the despotism of the empire extinguished all public and political life and forced people to concentrate on their private lives. Roman authority destroyed popular assemblies, the senate "wallowed in the most abject appeals," illegal gatherings were dispersed, and open debate disappeared as the treason laws "corroded public life."[30] In his "Dialogue on Oratory" Tacitus suggested, through the character Maternus, that there was no longer any great oratory because there were no public issues to debate and no public space in which to debate them. Even though Tacitus himself probably agreed that the price of peace was the loss of his public freedom,[31] he knew that under free government the orator found "incessant popular assemblies," whereas, under despotic government, affairs became entirely private and even the business of the law courts was "transacted almost in solitude."[32] Writing on the tribes of Germany, Tacitus wanted his Roman audience to contrast Germany's infant virtue to Rome's elderly decline. "On matters of minor importance only the chiefs debate; on major affairs, the whole community. . . . These same assemblies elect, among other officials, the magistrates who administer justice in the districts and villages."[33] In the end, Nero seized control of public space by means of force. "Nero became increasingly frightened. His guard had been redoubled. Indeed, the whole of Rome was virtually put in custody. . . . Roman public squares and homes, and even neighboring towns and country districts, were invaded by infantry and cavalry."[34]

Like Machiavelli, Tocqueville, and Weber later, Tacitus suggested that one could learn much about a regime by observing who literally occupies public space—if police and paramilitary forces occupy public places, one is probably observing a tyranny; if bureaucrats and administration, probably some kind of bureaucratic domination; and if citizens, and discussions among citizens, force open public space, one has probably found the freedom of a republic. With Roman violence controlling the public sphere, political organization and political opposition became virtually impossible, and although the Roman Empire witnessed many Stoic mar-

---

and hardly ever remained at home." *Considerations on the Causes of the Greatness of the Romans and Their Decline*, trans. David Lowenthal (Ithaca: Cornell University Press, 1968), 23–24.

30. *Annals*, 1.12; 2.27; also 14.17; 1.15.

31. Ronald Syme, *Tacitus*, 2 vols. (Oxford: Oxford University Press, 1958), 547.

32. "Dialogue on Oratory," 39–40.

33. Tacitus, *Germania*, 11–12. See also Lidia Storoni Mazzolani, *Empire Without End* (New York: Harcourt Brace Jovanovich, 1976), 164–68.

34. *Annals*, 15.57–58.

tyrs, it saw few leaders genuinely devoted to political opposition. When Tacitus related the story of a failed conspiracy to assassinate Nero, he indicated a mixture of admiration and distaste for Stoic suicide. After the plot against Nero was discovered, the supporters of Piso, who was a key conspirator, urged him to go both to the army and to the Forum and try to rally the people against Nero. "If your fellow conspirators rally round you . . . outsiders will follow. Once a move is made the publicity will be immense—a vitally important point in revolutions. . . . How much finer to die for the good of your country, calling for men to defend its freedom! The army may fail you, the people abandon you. But you yourself—if you must die early—die in a way of which your ancestors and posterity could approve!"[35] Piso ignored this advice, "shut himself in his house," and committed suicide, and Tacitus recorded all of this bitterly, as if this private but courageous death was all that a despotic age unaccustomed to public and political action could hope for. To Tacitus such Stoic suicide was a waste of courage, useful to no one but Nero, as we can see in the irony with which he wrote, "Seneca's death followed. It delighted the emperor."[36]

The eclipse of all public space meant that all Romans had become isolated, flung into their private worlds. In one instance, Tacitus recorded, "Rome resembled a captured city on the next day. The great houses were shuttered, the streets almost empty, the populace in mourning." Just as the people withdrew from the public sphere, so did the emperor, and thus public decision making became a private affair. Tacitus emphasized this by suggesting that Tiberius withdrew from Rome to seek "secretive pleasures" and by calling him the "secretive Tiberius." Roman power concentrated itself in the hands of a despot who led an "isolated, joyless life of gloomy watchfulness and sinister machinations."[37] In effect, because of isolation and the disappearance of popular assemblies, the public sphere was gone, and the Roman Republic, or *res publica,* had become the private concern of one man, in a sense, a *res privata.*[38]

In the ancient Greek lexicon, a *despotēs* was, strictly speaking, a master who ruled over the members of the household (*oikia*) and controlled the private affairs of that household. In Latin, the word *dominus* had a similar connotation, and in some instances the words *paterfamilias* and *dominus* were equivalent.[39] When Tacitus referred to a Roman emperor as a *domi-*

---

35. *Annals*, 15.59.

36. *Annals*, 15.60; see also Denis Henry and B. Walker, "Tacitus and Seneca," *Greece and Rome* 10, no. 1 (1963): 108, and Mazzolani, *Empire Without End*, 194–200.

37. *Histories*, 1.82; *Annals*, 4.57, 52; 3.37.

38. Wirszubski, *Libertas as a Political Idea*, 121.

39. R. Koebner, "Despot and Despotism," 276–78; also Hannah Arendt, *The Human Condition* (Garden City, N.Y.: Doubleday, 1959), 27, 307.

nus or to the rule of these emperors as *dominatio,* or despotism, he was claiming that the emperors ruled Rome as one would rule servants in a private household, that the emperors treated Rome as if it were their private property. When speaking of Nero, Tacitus argued this directly. "Nero himself now tried to make it appear that Rome was his favourite abode. He gave feasts in public places as if the whole city were his own home (*domus*)."[40]

In ancient Athens one left the household (*oikia,* from which we get our word *economics*) to be a citizen in a city-state (*polis*), and thus one left behind private economic matters to deliberate on public political affairs. Similarly, in the Roman Republic, one left the household (*domus*) to become a citizen (*civis*). Under the despotism of the Roman Empire, the public realm disappeared and with it any meaningful definition of citizenship; all became the private affair of the despot. Tacitus reminded his readers of this when he noted that, in Germany, when a young man comes of age, he "ceases to rank merely as a member of a household and becomes a citizen." By contrast, in despotic Rome each became merely a member of the emperor's household. Tacitus noted ironically and bitterly that Tiberius "issued an edict forbidding the disturbance of his privacy."[41]

Mutual Suspicion and the Control of the Private

When we ask ourselves how the Roman Empire managed to isolate people from one another, we think first of fear and force. Everywhere Tacitus, like Aristotle, mentioned spies and informers, the hated *delatores.* Romans "have indeed set up a record of subservience . . . robbed as we are by informers even of the right to exchange ideas in conversation." The fear of informers created mistrust and that, of course, drove citizens apart. In speaking of a unit of the army, he said, "Mutual suspicions began to undermine the solidarity between one brigade and another, between young and old. A sense of obedience gradually came back."[42] When each is isolated and no one acts in common, a despot can control people easily and ensure obedience. To isolate people effectively, however, one needs enough fear to divide families and dissolve friendships, and it is this psychological isolation that Tacitus found to be so devastatingly effective, a practice examined in great detail by Neumann and Arendt writ-

40. *Annals,* 15.37.
41. *Germania,* 13; *Annals,* 4.67.
42. *Agricola,* 2; *Annals,* 1.28.

ing about Nazi Germany. "It was, indeed, a horrible feature of the period that leading senators became informers even on trivial matters—some openly, many secretly. Friends and relatives were as suspect as strangers, old stories as damaging as new. In the Forum, at a dinner-party, a remark on any subject might mean prosecution. Everyone competed for priority in marking down the victim. Sometimes this was self-defence, but mostly it was a sort of contagion, like an epidemic."[43]

Tacitus regarded friendship as both a political and a military virtue, and he still admired the Roman ideal of soldiers resembling friends acting in common.[44] To break apart friendship, which Aristotle had of course regarded as a key political virtue, was to Tacitus perhaps the most odious accomplishment of Roman emperors, and it signaled how thoroughgoing and complete was this despotism. For example, he complained that his was a miserable age for a historian because, unlike previous historians, who could write about great battles and great deeds, he had to record "cruel orders, unremitting accusations, treacherous friendships, innocent men ruined." So despicable was his time that not only the influential and wealthy were in constant danger but even "those who had not an enemy in the world were ruined by their friends." And Tacitus knew why this had happened, for even selective terror freezes compassion for others and makes us want to withdraw to some illusory private safety. "Terror had paralysed human sympathy. The rising surge of brutality drove compassion away." The result of all this was isolation, suspicion, and mistrust. In speaking of a Roman settlement, Tacitus commented that in the past such settlements were communities "based on consent and comradeship" but that now colonists came from far and wide and were "unknown to each other."[45] Tacitus was also offering an appropriate description for Rome; by means of suspicion and isolation, what once was a city united at least in part by friendship and cooperation had become a city of strangers.

In reality, in this world where all was private, nothing was really private. People confined to a private sphere find that this privacy is easily invaded by despotic authority.[46] Germanicus complained that informers had entered his house and were watching him as he died, and spies reported "even private mutterings" of Germanicus's son Drusus. Spies had "insinuated themselves into all the great houses"; "the whole atmosphere was heavy with suspicion. Even the privacy of the home was hardly se-

43. *Annals*, 6.7.
44. *Annals*, 15.12.
45. *Annals*, 4.32–33; *Histories*, 1.2; *Annals*, 6.19, 14.27.
46. See Hannah Arendt, *The Origins of Totalitarianism*, 2d ed. (New York: World Publishing Co., 1958), 338–39.

cure."[47] Tacitus did not hide his disgust toward, and horror of, a world in which even Roman senators would clamor to become informers by hiding behind walls, a world in which mutual suspicion and frenzied fear made any private safety impossible. "At Rome there was unprecedented agitation and terror. People behaved secretively even to their intimates, avoiding encounters and conversation, shunning the ears both of friends and strangers. Even voiceless, inanimate objects—ceilings and walls—were scanned suspiciously."[48] But as I mentioned earlier, Tacitus did not believe that fear and force were sufficient to explain the strength of imperial despotism. For Tacitus, the pursuit of pleasure was both symptom and cause of this most thoroughgoing despotism.

The Fall of the Roman Ethic and the Pleasures of Empire

Tacitus did not think that laws and institutions by themselves had maintained the Roman Republic, nor did he believe that one could revitalize the empire with legislation. Whereas, in the time of the republic, Rome had attained greatness because of an internalized ethic of austerity and devotion to the community, during the empire, Rome reached the depths of servitude for want of any morality other than unrestrained hedonism and self-interest. In each case, Tacitus thought morality was more important than law. "Laws were most numerous when the commonwealth was most corrupt,"[49] a sentiment repeated later by Montesquieu and Tocqueville, two of Tacitus's greatest admirers. Tacitus wrote as Montesquieu did in the eighteenth century, longing for ancient virtue but resigning himself to tyrannical, centralized authority. The best his corrupt age

47. *Annals*, 2.70, 6.24; *Histories*, 1.85.

48. *Annals*, 4.69. Aleksandr Solzhenitsyn talks of how easy it was for a small number of secret police to arrest large numbers of isolated and powerless individuals who clung to the supposed security of their private homes. "And how we burned in the camps later, thinking: What would things have been like if every Security operative, when he went out at night to make an arrest, had been uncertain whether he would return alive. . . . Or, if, during periods of mass arrests, as for example in Leningrad, when they arrested a quarter of the entire city, people had not simply sat there in their lairs, paling with terror at every bang of the downstairs door and at every step on the staircase, but had understood that they had nothing left to lose and had boldly set up in the downstairs hall an ambush of half a dozen people with axes, hammers, pokers, or whatever else was at hand?" *The Gulag Archipelago*, trans. Thomas Whitney, (New York: Harper & Row, 1973), 3–23, esp. 13.

49. *Annals*, 3.27. For this very important passage, I have chosen to use the translation of Church and Brodribb (1942).

could hope for was an honest principate, and thus he welcomed Nerva (96–98) and Trajan (98–117), who could provide order and even a degree of freedom of speech. Tacitus could hope for no more because, though legal reform was possible, he could imagine no way to bring moral rejuvenation. "The country had been transformed, and there was nothing left of the fine old Roman character."[50] Nothing is more apparent to one who reads any section of Tacitus than his condemnation of the immorality and sometimes barbarity of his age. To select an extremely incomplete list, one sees Tacitus mention debauchery, slavish obedience, orgies, subserviency, homosexual indecencies, cruelty, and even gluttonous eating.[51] Tacitus was suggesting that the social order and the moral order of Rome had collapsed simultaneously. He would have scoffed at modern writers who approve of so-called victimless crimes, because he thought that private examples of immorality eventually lead to public moral decay. "The same destitution and indiscipline ruined man after man, driving them herd-like down the slope that leads to mutiny, dissension and, in the last resort, civil war."[52]

Tacitus was arguing that private immorality undermines any sense of public duty toward others, but we might ask how such private immorality originated. He offers a clue in at least one passage. "Moreover their vigour was sapped by pleasures, in a way totally at variance with old-fashioned ideas of discipline and tradition, which found a better basis for Roman steadiness *in character than in money*."[53] For Tacitus, luxury and wealth helped to undermine the Roman Republic. "It was easy to maintain equality when Rome was weak. World-wide conquest and the destruction of all rival communities or potentates opened the way to the secure enjoyment of wealth and an overriding appetite for it. This was how the smouldering rivalry between senate and people was first fanned into a blaze. . . . Rome and the Roman Forum had a foretaste of what civil war means. Then Gaius Marius . . . and Lucius Sulla . . . destroyed the republican constitution by force of arms. In its place they put despotism (*dominatio*)."[54] Throughout his writings Tacitus complained of excessive wealth, comfort, ease of living, and luxury. He sneered at "long-pampered Romans," disapproved of "sordid profits," and complained of usury that occurred because "patriotism comes second to private profits." When two

50. *Annals*, 1.4; also Wirszubski, *Libertas as a Political Idea*, 164; and Grant, *The Ancient Historians*, 295–97.
51. *Annals*, 2.33, 1.2, 4.67, 3.65, 5.3, 3.52; *Histories*, 3.33, 83.
52. *Histories*, 1.46; Walker, *The Annals of Tacitus*, 27–28.
53. *Histories*, 2.69 (emphasis added).
54. *Histories*, 2.38.

senators complained of luxuries such as gold, silver, silk, and lavish furniture, Tacitus noted his agreement by calling these luxuries signs of debauchery and extravagance. In a passage somewhat astonishing to twentieth-century political and economic assumptions, Tacitus claimed that peace undermined the Britons and comfort destroyed the Gauls. "But the Britons show more spirit: they have not yet been enervated by protracted peace. History tells us that the Gauls too had their hour of military glory; but since that time a life of ease has made them unwarlike: their valour perished with their freedom." Indeed, a German leader said that the Romans found it more effective to dominate others with "pleasures" than with "arms."[55]

Tacitus was noting a cruel irony that seems to accompany the human condition. Whereas Plato had argued that the good things of this world—knowledge, virtue, justice, courage, beauty, and so forth—accompany one another and can coexist in harmony, Tacitus agreed more with Thucydides, and he certainly would have agreed with Machiavelli and Weber, who knew that good can come from evil, and evil from good. For example, Tacitus praised both the Roman military ethic that brought imperial expansion and the frugal work ethic that brought self-discipline,[56] and yet both of these, merely by success, destroyed themselves and brought ruin. Rome conquered the Italian peninsula and much of the world with an austere work ethic and a military discipline that demanded self-sacrifice; with success came peace, comfort, and luxury, all of which undermined the original ethic and led to civil war and despotism. "Frugality used to prevail because people had self-control—and because we were citizens of one city. Even our domination of Italy did not bring the same temptations. But victories abroad taught us to spend other people's money."[57] Tacitus saw a world in which evil frequently came from good: peace and prosperity might well undermine virtue; military success could bring ruinous luxury; great oratory might come only with civil turmoil that brought great deeds; political freedom might necessitate disorder; order could bring mediocrity and boredom; and in Tacitus's case, knowledge of all this might bring despair.

---

55. *Annals*, 1.54, 4.62, 6.16, 2.33; *Agricola*, 11; *Histories*, 4.64.
56. *Annals*, 3.55.
57. *Annals*, 3.54. This quotation is from a speech by Tiberius; Tacitus seems to have approved the substance of the passage, but he apparently was criticizing Tiberius for being unwilling to address the problem. For a classic discussion of the relation between luxury and Roman political decline, see Montesquieu's *Considerations on the Causes of the Greatness of the Romans and their Decline* (1734). On the view that Tacitus saw the good things of the world often in conflict, see Syme, *Tacitus*, 107, 218.

The Tyranny of Desire

In the writings of Tacitus, there is nearly as much literature as history and political thought, and thus, a literary comparison is worthwhile. In *King Lear* Shakespeare depicted a world of disorder, and when the world cracks, chaos occurs simultaneously in the natural world (the storm), the political world (civil war), and the psychological world (Lear's madness). In Tacitus, unrelenting desire simultaneously spins both despot and subjects out of control. For example, he described Tiberius this way. "For his criminal lusts (*libido*) shamed him. Their uncontrollable activity was worthy of an oriental tyrant. Free-born children were his victims. He was fascinated by beauty, youthful innocence, and aristocratic birth. New names for new types of perversions were invented. Slaves were charged to locate and procure his requirements." And Nero, who "was already corrupted by every lust, natural and unnatural," still managed to refute "any surmises that no further degradation was possible for him."[58] These descriptions of despots enslaved to desires parallel closely the depiction of the tyrant offered by Plato, to whom Tacitus referred, and like Plato, Tacitus concluded that such a despot could not be happy, both because uncontrolled lust isolates one by ending all possibility of friendship and because such a tyrant feels an endless cycle of brief satisfaction followed by gnawing desire. Tiberius's "crimes and wickedness had rebounded to torment himself. How truly the wisest of men [i.e., Plato] used to assert that the souls of despots, if revealed, would show wounds and mutilations—weals left on the spirit, like marks on a body, by cruelty, lust, and malevolence. Neither [Tiberius's] autocracy nor isolation could save him from confessing the internal torments which were his retribution."[59]

Just as emperors became slaves to all their desires, so did Rome itself, most dramatically in the power struggles of the year 69 C.E., which Tacitus described as a time of "lust and violence," when "rape alternated with murder and murder with rape."[60] Somewhat less dramatically, in the time of Nero desire was unrelenting and led the city into every sort of immorality. "Taverns were built, and every stimulus to vice was displayed for sale. Moreover, there were distributions of money. Respectable people were compelled to spend it. The disreputable did so gladly. Promiscuity and degradation throve. Roman morals had long become impure, but never was there so favourable an environment for debauchery as among this filthy crowd. Even in good surroundings people find it hard to behave

58. *Annals*, 6.1, 15.37.
59. *Annals*, 6.6.
60. *Histories*, 3.33.

well. Here every form of immorality competed for attention, and no chastity, modesty, or vestige of decency could survive."[61] By contrast, German morality and especially sexual morality remained intact. "Good morality is more effective in Germany than good laws are elsewhere."[62] Later Machiavelli repeated Tacitus's strategy by contrasting virtuous Swiss republics to corrupt Italian city-states.

This tyranny of desire destroyed the social order in different ways. First, it confused license and freedom. In an interesting twist on Plato, Tacitus noted that "[i]n these promiscuous crowds, debauchees are emboldened to practise by night the lusts they have imagined by day." Tacitus agreed with this claim and added, "This license was just what most people approved—though they put it more respectably." Second, lust and self-interest, pursued in the private sphere, only contributed to that political isolation that despots find so useful. Third, people accomplished nothing great, because they only sought to satiate desires. "Contempt for fame means contempt for goodness." Fourth, forgetful of the past and oblivious of the future, people fastened themselves to present desires. Tacitus lamented that few knew anything of the old republic, and he repeatedly claimed that people acted "with total unconcern for the future." Obsessed with present gratification, a people can neither transmit a heritage from the past nor look with purpose toward the future, an argument Tocqueville repeated centuries later. Finally, hedonism undermined all common belief and led to nihilism. Tacitus spoke of civil war and an army in which "there was a diversity of wild desires, differing conceptions of what was lawful, and nothing barred," all reminiscent of Plato's fear that if nothing is believed, all is permitted.[63]

But what did Tacitus think caused such lust and immorality? How could he explain the corruption of Rome? What would cause desires to emerge uncontrolled? For Tacitus, the answer was simple: the disappearance of restraints. Tacitus regarded all desires, and especially the desire for power, as something like water behind a dam waiting to fall; remove the restraining wall and one lets loose a flood. One can see this best in his description of power and in his characterization of Tiberius. "From time immemorial," wrote Tacitus, "man has had an instinctive love of power. With the growth of our empire, this instinct has become a dominant and uncontrollable force."[64] The literary portrait that Tacitus gave of

---

61. *Annals*, 14.15.
62. *Germania*, 19.
63. *Annals*, 14.20–21, 4.38, 1.3; *Histories*, 3.31, 55–56, 33.
64. *Histories*, 3.38.

Tiberius, however doubtful historically,[65] offers an insight into the way in which Tacitus thought of the desire for power. While restrained by the laws of Augustus or by competition with Germanicus or even by the influence of his mother, the real personality of Tiberius could not appear, just as fear of Carthage had earlier restrained the moral decay of Rome. When the restraints collapsed, the real and despotic Tiberius emerged.[66] "While he was a private citizen or holding commands under Augustus, his life was blameless; and so was his reputation. While Germanicus and Drusus still lived, he concealed his real self, cunningly affecting virtuous qualities. However, until his mother died there was good in Tiberius as well as evil. Again, so long as he favoured (or feared) Sejanus, the cruelty of Tiberius was detested, but his perversions unrevealed. Then fear vanished, and with it shame. Thereafter, he expressed only his own personality—by unrestrained crime and infamy."[67] Long before Lord Acton's famous dictum, Tacitus claimed that Tiberius was "transformed and deranged by absolute power."[68]

The Corruption of Language

If we ask ourselves what Tacitus thought was the political result of absolute power, it is worth noting that he first mentioned the corruption of language.[69] At the very beginning of the Annals, Tacitus observed that ancient Rome and even the Rome of Augustus had great writers, "but then the rising tide of flattery (adulatio) exercised a deterrent effect. The reigns of Tiberius, [Caligula], Claudius, and Nero were described during their lifetimes in fictitious terms, for fear of the consequences." Not by coincidence did he also open his Histories with the same theme, telling us that written history under the emperors was unreliable largely because of a "passion for flattery." Happily he noted that under the principates of Nerva and Trajan, "we can think as we please, and speak as we think."[70] Tacitus's message was clear; by promoting flattery and servility, despotism corrupted language and brought dishonesty and hypocrisy to social

---

65. Dudley, The World of Tacitus, 83.
66. Ronald Martin, Tacitus (Berkeley and Los Angeles: University of California Press, 1981), 105–6; Grant, The Ancient Historians, 286.
67. Annals, 6.51.
68. Annals, 6.48.
69. Ranum, "D'Alembert, Tacitus, and the Political Sociology of Despotism."
70. Annals, 1.1; Histories, 1.1.

relations.[71] "Meanwhile at Rome, consuls, senate, knights, precipitately became servile. The more distinguished men were, the greater their urgency and insincerity. They must show neither satisfaction at the death of one emperor, nor gloom at the accession of another: so their features were carefully arranged in a blend of tears and smiles, mourning and flattery."[72]

The first and most obvious result of the distortion of language was the loss of honesty in public discourse. On a simple level, language was used to hide wrongdoing. "It was typical of Tiberius to use antique terms to veil new sorts of villainy." On another level, few were willing to be honest, for fear of being held accountable for firm opinions. As Tacitus said of one officer in the military, "His language was carefully chosen so that in the light of events he could either disclaim responsibility or take credit for success." On still another level, emperors protected power by concealing policy; that is, emperors found power in purposefully obscuring their language. Frequently lying and often cryptic, Tiberius kept senators fearfully confused when "his words became more and more equivocal and obscure." As a result, both honesty and any real understanding of governmental policy became extremely rare. The Stoic Helvidius won "great glory" simply by speaking honestly in public. And yet this was so rare that most often people were fooled by words, until they were unable to understand the world around them. Said one speaker, "[Y]ou attach great importance to mere words, and judge of good and evil according to the utterances of agitators rather than in the light of their real nature."[73]

The corruption of language meant that no one could speak of what the Greeks had called practical questions, questions about the purposes of society. In the republic, Brutus had "laid open the convictions of his heart frankly and ingenuously," but under despotism, one could not have great oratory, because one could not have honest debate; "the clever speakers of this day we call pleaders, advocates, counsellors, anything rather than orators."[74] In his "Dialogue on Oratory," both sides of the debate seemed to agree that Rome could boast of orators when men spoke of "vast issues" that judged of "right and wrong" in "popular assemblies [that] were continually before [their] eyes." By contrast, under Roman despotism, one saw only ignorant rhetoricians who spoke on "subjects remote from all reality." Distorted discourse that evades all practical and political subjects is a hallmark of despotism. No nation has practical debate or a clear

71. Ranum, "D'Alembert, Tacitus, and the Political Sociology of Despotism," 549.
72. *Annals*, 1.7.
73. *Annals*, 4.19; *Histories*, 3.52; *Annals*, 1.11; *Histories*, 4.4, 73.
74. "Dialogue on Oratory," 25, 1.

and unambiguous political language when all evince "willing obedience to authority."[75]

Long before Orwell wrote his brilliant essay "Politics and the English Language" and coined the word *Newspeak,* Tacitus noted that despotism used corrupted language to hide its reality. His most famous sentence tells us just that. "To robbery, butchery, and rapine, they give the lying name of 'government'; they create a desolation and call it peace." In the civil war of the year 69, Otho accused Galba of distorting language to hide his tyranny: "By a misuse of language, he describes cruelty as severity, greed as economy, and the execution and insults you have suffered as a lesson in discipline."[76] Tacitus knew well that in a world of despotic power those who wage war can call it an effort for peace, while those who enslave can do so under the banner of freedom. As one speaker said: "It is always the same motive that impels the Germans to invade the Gallic provinces—their lust, greed and roving spirit. What they have really wanted is to abandon their marshes and deserts, and gain control of this rich soil and of yourselves. But 'liberty' and other fine phrases serve as pretexts. Indeed, no one has ever aimed at enslaving others and making himself their master without using this very same language."[77] Words can become a "weapon," a "blood-stained" weapon serving despotic power.[78] Without question this analysis of distorted language is Tacitus's single most important contribution to theories of tyranny, an observation later repeated by Tocqueville, Marx, Neumann, and Arendt.

The Politics of Pretense: Insincerity, Hypocrisy, and Role-Playing

After recounting the death of Nero's mother, Tacitus described the emperor in this way: "Nero's insincerity took a different form. He adopted a gloomy demeanour, as though sorry to be safe and mourning for his parent's death."[79] Nero was pretending to be sorry for his mother's death, and this was but one example of a theme that pervades all of Tacitus's writings, that is, the idea that under despotism everyone becomes an actor and all of society wraps itself in insincerity, role-playing, and pretense.[80]

75. "Dialogue on Oratory," 37, 31, 34, 32, 35, 41.
76. *Agricola*, 30; *Histories*, 1.37
77. *Histories*, 4.73.
78. "Dialogue on Oratory," 12.
79. *Annals*, 14.10.
80. Walker, *The Annals of Tacitus*, 78.

In another instance, both senators and the people "cursed Galba, compli-mented the soldiers on their choice, and covered Otho's hand with kisses. These demonstrations were multiplied in proportion to their insincerity." Role-playing was a predictable defensive reaction, an attempt to survive in despotic times. When Nero offered what Tacitus considered disgraceful performances as a musician, spies watched and reported every expres-sion of the individuals in the audience. "There were many spies uncon-cealedly (and more still secretly) noting who was there—and noting whether their expressions were pleased or dissatisfied." Under such cir-cumstance, it is not surprising that people applauded the emperor and played the role required, with both emperor and citizens reduced to the status of mediocre actors and pretenders. By contrast, the virtuous Ger-mans spoke sincerely, "blurting out their inmost thoughts in the freedom of festive surroundings, so that every man's soul is laid completely bare."[81] In one instance, Galba said, "You will have to face up to flattery, honied words and the poison most fatal to sincerity—individual self-interest . . . the world will prefer to address us as emperors, not as ourselves." One addressed the role rather than the person, relationships lacked sincerity, and people focused more on appearance than on reality. In fact, all was pretense, and to Tacitus, most emperors were despots pretending to be leaders, tyrants offering the appearance of freedom. Tiberius engaged in "dissimulation" and "concealed his real self"; Otho managed "to learn the part of emperor" and "played his part well"; and Domitian "posed as a connoisseur of literature and poetry" in order "to hide his real character." Worst of all, the emperor Nero aspired quite literally to become an actor. For Tacitus, it was a sign of unmitigated "degradation" for an emperor to perform for the crowd and seek applause. "The climax"—perhaps of Rome's decay—"was the emperor's stage debut."[82]

For Tacitus, despotism substitutes appearance for reality, the playing of roles for sincere opinion, acting for genuine accomplishments. Tacitus wrote that the young men who joined Nero on stage "were grand and respected *as if they had done great things.*" Tacitus noted that critics, who in all likelihood expressed Tacitus's opinion, said, "Now they are compelling the Roman upper class to degrade themselves as orators or singers on the stage. It only remains to strip and fight in boxing-gloves instead of joining the army." Having delivered oneself to playacting, one can accomplish nothing great, and Rome substituted the circus for politi-cal assemblies and the boxing ring for the field of battle. Tacitus used humor and irony to make this point. "The crowd shouted that [Nero]

81. *Histories*, 1.45; *Annals*, 16.5; *Germania*, 22.
82. *Histories*, 1.15; *Annals*, 6.50–51; *Histories*, 1.33, 36; 4.86; *Annals*, 14.14–15.

should 'display all his accomplishments' (those were their actual words)."
As one character said in his "Dialogue on Oratory," once Rome had "a
liking for actors and a passion for gladiators," then "how little room [was]
left for worthy attainments!"[83]

In the end, under the despotism of emperors, the Roman political world
was a stage, and once proud Roman citizens were mere spectators. In one
of the most grotesque passages of his writings, Tacitus described the indifference of the Roman populace to civil war, as if this were just one
more spectacle to applaud. "Close by the fighting stood the people of
Rome like the audience at a show, cheering and clapping this side or that
in turns as if this were a mock battle in the arena. . . . The whole city
presented a frightful caricature of its normal self: fighting and casualties
at one point, baths and restaurants at another. . . . As if this were one
more entertainment in the festival season, they gloated over horrors and
profited by them, careless which side won and glorying in the calamities
of the state."[84] Rome had become a city of actors and spectators alike,
and however bloody and murderous, on this Roman stage all was pretense and hypocrisy. "So, with many solemn phrases, the senate was summoned as though the charges against Silius had a legal foundation—as
though Varro were a real consul, or Rome a Republic!" Despotism was the
cause of this hypocrisy, because despotism forced men and women to
play roles to please their masters. "Men had constantly to attune their
attitudes and expressions to the latest rumour: it would not do to appear
too upset by bad tidings and insufficiently gratified by good." Rome had
sacrificed "fame, glory, and genius" in rushing to imitate actors.[85] This
was, however, a drama without a playwright, a stage with actors only and
no director, a desperate improvisation with murderous results. This notion that under tyranny one must pretend and play roles to survive is
another of Tacitus's major contributions to theories of tyranny, one perhaps borrowed from Plato but certainly elaborated upon, and probably

---

83. *Annals*, 14.15 (emphasis added), 20; 16.4; "Dialogue on Oratory," 29. Rousseau, who
translated Tacitus, complained that the theater undermined republican virtue. "In giving our
tears to these fictions, we have satisfied all the rights of humanity without having to give
anything more of ourselves. . . . In the final accounting, when a man has gone to admire fine
actions in stories and to cry for imaginary miseries, what more can be asked of him? Has he
not acquitted himself of all that he owes to virtue by the homage which he has just rendered
it? What more could one want of him? That he practice (virtue) himself? He has no role to
play; he is no actor." *Politics and the Arts: Letter to M. d'Alembert on the Theater*, trans. Allan
Bloom (Ithaca: Cornell University Press, 1960), 25.

84. *Histories*, 3.83.

85. *Annals*, 4.19; *Histories*, 1.85; "Dialogue on Oratory," 26.

not analyzed in a thorough fashion again until the analyses of modern Communist governments.[86]

Conclusion

When we ask ourselves how thorough was Tacitus's theory of tyranny, we note some shortcomings. First, he paid too little attention to the relation of the military to domestic and foreign policies of imperial despotism. Second, his political sociology was too simplistic, for Tacitus really recognized only emperor, senate, and mob. As a result, he is not convincing when he suggests that all power was concentrated in the hands of one man, ignoring some power left to law courts, magistrates at all levels of state bureaucracies, those with enormous private economic power, elites close to the emperor, factions within ruling circles, and even classes with enough assertive power to be bothersome. Third, Tacitus's account of what caused republican freedom to become imperial despotism is intriguing, but not complex enough. Tacitus saw two main causes for despotism: an innate lust for power had broken through republican restraints, and wealth and luxury obtained from imperial successes abroad had undermined the old republican ethic of self-discipline. As one critic pointed out, Tacitus ignored "the impersonal forces in history," such as demographic changes in the city of Rome, changes in the class composition in governing bodies, changes in the economy over the last two centuries of the republic, and the transformation of the army from a civilian army to a professional one.[87]

In addition, with the wisdom of many hundreds of years of hindsight, we can point to characteristics of tyranny that Tacitus could not have known. First, he had a faith that truth cannot be destroyed, that the reality of despotism will always be passed to posterity by historians, and he wanted to "deride the stupidity of people who believe that today's authority can destroy tomorrow's memories."[88] In fact, modern nation-states can come perilously close to destroying even factual truth,[89] as, for example,

---

86. Note the strong similarity to the role-playing one undertakes to survive recent tyrannies, for example, the cycles of ideological change in China under Mao. Michel Oksenberg, "Getting Ahead and Along in Communist China: The Ladder of Success on the Eve of the Cultural Revolution," in *Party Leadership and Revolutionary Power in China*, ed. John W. Lewis (London: Cambridge University Press, 1970).

87. Von Fritz, "Tacitus, Agricola, Domitian, and the Problem of the Principate," 95.

88. *Annals*, 4.35.

89. Hannah Arendt, "Truth and Politics," in *Between Past and Future* (New York: Viking, 1968).

when Stalin wrote a history of the Bolshevik Revolution and omitted Trotsky. Second, Tacitus could not have known about modern propaganda techniques, that fear and spies are essential for controlling people, but that there are also other, even more effective means of doing so. Finally, Tacitus reported civil wars, military massacres, and the butchery of slaves, and yet these are usually passing references. In Tacitus, death is still personal and agonizing for Tacitus and his reader; the one who dies usually has a title and status because the most important death is the patrician death. For Tacitus, as for Hobbes and Montesquieu later, those who were anonymous were usually safe; he spoke of the ordinary soldier who "thought himself relatively safe, because unknown."[90] Tacitus described a world in which tyrants killed many, but he could not have known of a century with systematic slaughter and more than one attempt at genocide, directed toward those who are wholly innocent.

All theorists have shortcomings, and those of Tacitus should not diminish his contributions to subsequent theories of tyranny. Indeed, Tacitus also made quite a few entirely new contributions to European theories of tyranny. First, more than Aristotle, Tacitus observed that those who establish tyrannies try to preserve the appearance of freedom. While to the superficial observer in Rome the senate debated, the law courts functioned, and magistrates made decisions, in fact all this was the illusory remnant of a real republic and of genuine rule by law. Second, Tacitus, who of course emerged from the Roman tradition that put so much emphasis on protecting individual rights and liberty by laws and courts, emphasized how much a tyranny must subvert and control the judicial process and the legal system. Tiberius, who sat in on court decisions, did this dramatically. Third, although Tacitus knew the importance of law, he recognized that republics thrive on the basis of moral character and that the Roman *dominatio* flourished after the laws had been subverted, but also, and more important, after an ethic of duty to the public and an internalized morality of the individual Roman citizen had been replaced by lust and desire. Machiavelli, Montesquieu, and Tocqueville all elaborate on this analysis. Fourth, with the spread of lust and desire, a corrupt people focuses on present satisfaction, forgetting the principles of their ancestors and any hopes for a better future. Like Tocqueville, who argued this later, no people, said Tacitus, who forget the past and fail to envision a better future can be either free or great; they can only fasten themselves to the satiation of present enjoyments. Fifth, Tacitus emphasized that force is needed only peripherally in establishing tyranny, that as the

90. *Histories*, 3.31; Roland Barthes, "Tacitus and the Funerary Baroque," trans. Richard Howard, in *A Barthes Reader*, ed. Susan Sontag, (New York: Hill & Wang, 1983).

Britons were seduced into "enslavement" by "arcades, baths, and sumptuous banquets," so can a populace be enticed into servitude by the promise of diversions, pleasure, comfort, and security. Sixth, Tacitus was the first to ask Freud's later question—even if his answer is not fully satisfying—why at some moments in history some people wish to be ruled by a strong leader, wish to regress to the comfort of a childlike obedience.

Seventh, and one of his most important contributions, Tacitus is the thinker who most clearly articulated that under a frightening tyranny we all must become puppets and role-players, dishonest and insincere—a nation of play actors and hypocrites—in order to survive. Rome became a stage set, the emperor the key playwright. And finally, his most important contribution, Tacitus was the first to emphasize that tyrants must distort language to hide the reality from observers and to legitimize tyrannical authority. Tacitus suggested that genuine oratory, which asks the most important questions about freedom, morality, and the good life, thrives in republics and disappears in tyrannies. When oratory disappears, flattery flourishes. And in the late twentieth century, a century that has perfected the techniques of propaganda, Tacitus's warning that tyrants will seek to rule by pretense, that rulers will buttress tyrannies with sweet words of freedom, sounds not ancient by sadly modern.

4

MACHIAVELLI
Defeating Princely Tyrannies

Plato, Aristotle, and Tacitus analyzed tyrannies almost in passing; with Machiavelli, the analysis of tyranny emphatically took center stage. On the one hand, Machiavelli, like Tacitus, saw himself living in a "corrupt century" characterized by "extreme misery, infamy, and degradation," a century in which one could find no religious faith, no respect for law, and, most of all, no military discipline, but instead only "every species of the lowest brutality."[1] Because he repeatedly blamed the cruel incompetence of the Italian princes for the misery of Italy,[2] he was eager to analyze

---

1. Niccolò Machiavelli, *Discourses on the First Ten Books of Titus Livius*, trans. Christian E. Detmold, in *The Prince and the Discourses* (New York: Modern Library, 1950), bk. 2, chap. 19, 344 (henceforth cited by book, chapter, and page as 2.19.344); and bk. 2, introduction, 273. See also the prologue to Machiavelli's play *Mandragola*, in *Machiavelli: The Chief Works and Others*, 3 vols., ed. and trans. Allan Gilbert, (Durham, N.C.: Duke University Press, 1965), 778, which I have used for Machiavelli's works, except for the translations of *The Prince*, the *Discourses*, and the *Letters*. Page numbers to works other than *The Prince*, the *Discourses*, and the *Letters* refer to Gilbert's three volumes.

2. Machiavelli, *The Art of War*, bk. 7, 724; Machiavelli, *The Letters of Machiavelli*, ed. and trans. Allan Gilbert (New York: Capricorn Books, 1961), 218.

these princely tyrannies and hoped to offer a remedy for Italy's political illness. On the other hand, Machiavelli was by nature a political person, far more so even than any of the three previous thinkers examined here, and he was a passionate political observer, political participant, and per- haps even a political conspirator. Politics thus constituted an ineradica- ble part of his personality. "Fortune has determined that since I don't know how to talk about the silk business or the wool business, or about profits and losses, I have to talk about the government."[3] Because he wanted to diagnose the corrupt decline of his century, and because he was so political, it seems at first glance as if it should be easy to under- stand his analysis of tyranny, but in fact Machiavelli presents three spe- cial difficulties.

First, Machiavelli was more provocative than systematic, as evidenced by the fact that virtually every possible interpretation—from democrat to totalitarian and from devout Christian to wicked atheist—has been ap- plied to his writings. It is indicative of this less than systematic approach to analyzing politics that his key political words come to us with frustrat- ing ambiguity.[4] *Virtù, fortuna, necessità, libertà, ambizione,* and *gloria* are all extremely important words in Machiavelli's political vocabulary, but he used each of these words in such multivarious ways that each word causes confusion and requires interpretation, a pattern that certainly holds for *tirannide,* or tyranny. Second, Machiavelli contradicted himself frequently and in significant ways. Some examples here are illustrative. In *The Prince* Machiavelli advised new princes to endeavor to be both feared and loved, though if both of these are impossible, "it is much safer to be feared than loved"; but in his *History of Florence,* when Machiavelli re- counted the many errors of the duke of Athens who established a short- lived tyranny in Florence in 1342, he concluded that the duke mistakenly "wished to be feared rather than loved."[5] In *The Prince* Machiavelli di- rected a new prince to rely on the strength of the people and not to

---

3. *Letters,* 104. See also Martin Fleisher, "A Passion for Politics: The Vital Core of the World of Machiavelli," in *Machiavelli and the Nature of Political Thought,* ed. Martin Fleisher (New York: Atheneum, 1972), 114–47.

4. On the wide array of interpretations, see John H. Geerken, "Machiavelli Studies Since 1969," *Journal of the History of Ideas* 37, no. 2 (1976): 351–68. In his fine study of the word *lo stato,* J. H. Hexter noted the complaints about ambiguity in Machiavelli's use of key words, clarified the word *lo stato* extensively, but still acknowledged the remaining ambiguity. J. H. Hexter, "*Il Principe* and *lo Stato,*" *Studies in the Renaissance* 4, no. 1 (1957): 113–38.

5. Machiavelli, *The Prince,* trans. Luigi Ricci and E. R. Vincent, in *The Prince and the Discourses* (New York: Modern Library, 1950), chap. 17, 61; Machiavelli, *The History of Flo- rence,* bk. 2, chap. 37, 1133 (henceforth cited by book, chapter, and page as 2.37.1133).

establish a new order by turning to the nobles, but in the *Discourses* he gave the opposite advice and suggested that "whoever desires to establish a kingdom or principality" must set up and rely upon a number of "gentlemen" or nobles and give "them castles and possessions, as well as money and subjects."[6] More confusing still, when he wrote in 1520 his advice about remodeling the government of Florence, he again contradicted the advice given in *The Prince,* once more maintaining that to establish a princedom in Florence one would need to increase inequality and establish "noble lords" who would protect the prince with "their arms and their followers."[7] Finally, consider his advice about where military power should reside in a princedom. Once again, in *The Prince* Machiavelli urged Lorenzo de' Medici, in a famous passage, to arm his subjects, "for by arming them, these arms become your own, [and] those you suspected become faithful"; but elsewhere he suggested that a prince should disarm his subjects and rely on the armies of a few faithful nobles, the exact method used by Lorenzo's grandfather, Lorenzo the Magnificent.[8] It does not seem feasible to attribute such contradictory advice to the inconsistencies of an ordinary thinker, because Machiavelli was certainly one of the most brilliant political writers in history, and he would not simply change his mind casually on such issues as what classes a prince should rely upon or whom a prince should arm. Nor is it likely these contradictions are simply oversights or mistakes, because, if we can spot these inconsistencies with diligent reading, he would see them in a lightning's flash. An exasperated reader can only ask, What do these contradictions mean?

This leads to a third difficulty in reading Machiavelli: because of political persecution, and because he was a republican in a violent world of princes, he wrote deceptively, hid his beliefs, and contradicted himself on purpose. "For a long time," he wrote in a letter in 1521, "I have not said what I believed, nor do I ever believe what I say, and if indeed I do happen to tell the truth, I hide it among so many lies that it is hard to find."[9] When writing his *History of Florence,* he acknowledged that since he could not indict the Medici tyranny as he wished, he had to soften his language, criticize cryptically, and place his criticisms in the speeches of those who opposed the Medici. "If anyone nevertheless wants to under-

---

6. *The Prince*, chap. 9, 36–37; *Discourses*, 1.55.256.
7. Machiavelli, *A Discourse on Remodelling the Government of Florence*, 107.
8. *The Prince*, chap. 20, 77; *Discourses*, 1.55.256; *Letters*, 98.
9. *Letters*, 200.

stand Cosimo [de' Medici], let him observe well what I shall have his opponents say."[10]

Mary Dietz has suggested in a superb article that Machiavelli was deliberately practicing deception when he wrote *The Prince,* that he wished Lorenzo de' Medici to follow his advice, because Machiavelli thought this advice would lead to popular government. As Dietz noted, Machiavelli praised Junius Brutus in the *Discourses* for using deception in "destroying the kings [and] liberating his country," while in that same chapter he suggested that an adviser who could not oppose a prince openly could deceptively win the favor of a prince "by praising, speaking, seeing, and doing things contrary to your way of thinking, and merely to please the prince," all in order to destroy the prince's regime from within, thus doing one's part in restoring liberty to one's country.[11] Dietz's argument strikes me as persuasive, in part because it explains the contradictions mentioned above. If Lorenzo had taken Machiavelli's advice seriously, if he had made himself feared, if he had betrayed his noble friends who brought him to power, and if he had armed the people, then as time passed he would have unwittingly established a popular government. "But men with their lack of prudence," wrote Machiavelli midway through *The Prince,* "initiate novelties and, finding the first taste good, do not notice the poison within."[12]

If Machiavelli was deliberately using deception in *The Prince,* then it becomes devilishly difficult to discover his analysis of tyranny. All of his advice in *The Prince* could not be wrong, because then the book would be unbelievable. But which advice do we ignore and which advice is actually reliable advice for a prince who wants absolute power? As a general rule, if the advice given in *The Prince* is contradicted by the analyses Machiavelli offered elsewhere in the *Discourses, History of Florence,* or other works, then we should be suspicious of those contradictory passages in *The Prince.* Although this makes an examination Machiavelli's analysis of tyranny difficult, it does not make the examination impossible.

---

10. Cited by Allan Gilbert in his introduction to *History of Florence,* 1028.

11. *Discourses,* 3.11.403–4. See Mary Dietz, "Trapping the Prince: Machiavelli and the Politics of Deception," *American Political Science Review* 80, no. 3 (1986): 777–99. As much as I admire Dietz's excellent article, I must acknowledge that I first heard this argument informally about twenty years ago from my friend Professor Peter Breiner, now of SUNY at Albany. This argument also helps reconcile *The Prince* and Machiavelli's vigorous defense of republics in the *Discourses,* a problem outlined well by Hans Baron, "Machiavelli: The Republican Citizen and the Author of *The Prince,*" *English Historical Review* 76, no. 299 (1961): 217–53.

12. *The Prince,* chap. 13, 52.

Machiavelli's Break with
Classical Political Thought

Machiavelli claimed that through much experience and careful study he knew an extraordinary amount about political and military matters. "I have endeavored to embody in [the *Discourses*] all that long experience and assiduous research have taught me of the affairs of the world." Elsewhere he declared that he "knew well the nature of things" and that when he wrote *The Prince,* he had spent fifteen years studying "the art of the state." Machiavelli claimed that this knowledge was rare indeed, because "few there are who know this world." To Guicciardini he wrote, "I would say more, if I were talking to a man who did not know secrets and did not understand the world."[13] He seems to have meant that knowledge of the political world is itself a rare secret available only to a few. Machiavelli used a new approach to study political matters, in part to challenge political philosophers such as Plato and Aristotle. When he wrote in *The Prince* that "it appears to me more proper to go to the real truth of the matter than to its imagination; and many have imagined republics and principalities which have never been seen or known to exist in reality,"[14] he certainly saw himself breaking with the political speculation found in Plato's *Republic.* How admirable it was, noted Machiavelli, that Plato and Aristotle created free governments through strength of imagination, but how much more glorious, for Solon and Lycurgus, to create such governments in reality. "Aristotle, Plato, and many others . . . have wished to show the world that if they have not founded a free government, as did Solon and Lycurgus, they have failed not through their ignorance but through their impotence for putting it into practice."[15]

When Machiavelli announced at the beginning of the *Discourses* that "I have resolved to open a new route, which has not yet been followed by any one,"[16] this route was new in comparison with the political speculation of his contemporaries and also classical writers such as Plato, Aris-

13. *Discourses*, "Greeting," 101; *Letters*, 186, 144, 150, and 232.
14. *The Prince*, chap. 15, 56. When Florentine leaders wanted to know the plans of Caesar Borgia, Machiavelli wrote, "Your Excellencies must excuse me, and bear in mind that one cannot guess such things. . . . Anyone who does not want to write mere fantasies and fairy-tales, has to collate the facts, and this takes time." Cited by Roberto Ridolfi, *The Life of Niccolò Machiavelli*, trans. Cecil Grayson (Chicago: University of Chicago Press, 1963), 60–61. Since Machiavelli saw his approach to the study of political affairs as a challenge to Greek speculation, it is worth noting that he probably did not know Greek. See Ridolfi, *The Life of Niccolò Machiavelli*, 3.
15. *Remodelling the Government of Florence*, 114.
16. *Discourses*, bk. 1, introduction, 103.

totle, and Cicero. In taking a new route, Machiavelli sought to understand "the affairs of the world" by careful empirical observation of his own time and by studying the observations of intelligent writers from the past, most notably Livy and Xenophon. Twice Machiavelli advised political and military leaders to venture out into the countryside, note the topography, watch hills rise from plains, and follow the valleys, all while constructing hypothetical military dilemmas—what would we do if the enemy stormed over that hill? if we were compelled to march across that river? if we fought trapped in that valley? "And it is a fact that a man who has familiarized himself thoroughly with one country afterwards readily comprehends the nature of all other countries; for all countries resemble each other in their general conformation."[17] With historical and political observations, Machiavelli set out to do something very similar. Just as natural topographies do not vary dramatically, neither do political topographies. Since the future is always pregnant with the past, to know the past well is to anticipate the future accurately. "Wise men say, and not without reason, that whoever wishes to foresee the future must consult the past; for human events ever resemble those of preceding times."[18]

Moreover, by his very approach to understanding politics, he was suggesting that speculation, contemplation, and revelation can tell us little about the affairs of this world, but instead, to apply empirical observation to a specific problem—something he called prudence—is the most fruitful approach we can take to the world of politics. Machiavelli clearly was speaking a political language different from that of Plato, Christian political thinkers, and, to a lesser extent, Aristotle, when he seasoned his writings with phrases such as "experience has proved" and "history proves in a thousand cases what I maintain."[19] As a consequence of this approach, Machiavelli's writings adopt the flavor of hypothetical reasoning, and he apparently savored every kind of political and military dilemma, dilemmas that take the form of "If X is my goal, will Y help me attain it?" Hence, we find famous passages whose bluntness is initially shocking: for example, if one wants to establish a republic, one must destroy the landed nobility, whereas, if one wants to establish a tyranny, one must be willing to be "cruel and destructive of all civilized life."[20] Machiavelli did

17. *Discourses*, 3.39.524–25; *The Prince*, chap. 14, 54–55.
18. *Discourses*, 3.43.530, 1.39.216.
19. *Discourses*, 2.4.293, 2.10.311. Felix Gilbert noted how the bulk of Machiavelli's historical examples changed, from ancient ones in the *Discourses* to contemporary ones in *The Prince*. Gilbert, "The Composition and Structure of Machiavelli's *Discorsi*," *Journal of the History of Ideas* 14, no. 1 (1953): 136–56, esp. 154.
20. *Discourses*, 1.26.184, 1.55.256. As an example of his calculating, empirical method, Machiavelli talks about testing one's friends before engaging in a conspiracy. *Discourses*, 3.6.416.

not seek, as did Plato and Aristotle, a philosophical understanding of tyranny, but rather he wielded a political sociology that sought to know how tyrannies originated, how they worked, and how they could be overthrown.

Many have looked at Machiavelli's approach and seen only wickedness; as Strauss put it, "Machiavelli was a teacher of evil."[21] More commonly, commentators see Machiavelli's approach as offering a rudimentary science of society, with Machiavelli as a dispassionate clinical researcher whose laboratory is the world of politics. "Machiavelli studied political actions in the same way as a chemist studies chemical reactions. Assuredly a chemist who prepares in his laboratory a strong poison is not responsible for its effects."[22] Although there is much to be said for the latter view, this interpretation still presents problems. First, it is simply not true that Machiavelli studied political events "in the same way" as the chemist studies chemical reactions; even the most excited chemist does not feel as passionately about his or her conclusions as Machiavelli did about the results of his political studies. Second, because the chemist is studying physical and not moral phenomena in the laboratory, this scientist's moral standards stand somewhere outside his or her laboratory and remain grounded on some reasoning or some faith that bears no relation to the chemical research at hand. Such was not the case with Machiavelli. Because he carefully avoided applying Plato's Forms, Aristotle's teleology, Cicero's natural laws, and Christian revelation to the political world, Machiavelli saw little use in moral standards that stand timeless and above us—ready to be slapped down on political events—as guides to good action and as judges measuring results. Whatever moral standards Machiavelli used—and there certainly were such standards—were contingent upon experience and emerged from his personal interaction with the political and social world. Indeed, he would undoubtably have been amused at the modern wish to make him respectable by clothing him in the clean garb of a clinically detached social scientist.

Although Machiavelli did bury moral assumptions in his writings, as I indicate below, it is important to see that he was strongly critical of what we might call the Platonic conviction that there is a good in itself, an absolute moral standard applicable to all situations. Machiavelli had no use for any notion of an absolute good. First, he noted time and again in

21. Leo Strauss, *Thoughts on Machiavelli* (Glencoe, Ill.: Free Press, 1958), 9.

22. Ernst Cassirer, *The Myth of the State* (New Haven: Yale University Press, 1946), 154. See also H. Butterfield, *The Statecraft of Machiavelli* (New York: Macmillan, 1956), 15–25, 59–86. For the notion that Machiavelli was a political actor, not a scientific observer, see Neal Wood, "Machiavelli's Humanism of Action," in *The Political Calculus: Essays on Machiavelli's Philosophy*, ed. Anthony Parel (Toronto: University of Toronto Press, 1972), 33–57.

his commentaries about the political world that what we ordinarily call evil always seems inseparable from what we ordinarily call good, that evil clings to good, or, as one of his characters in *Mandragola* put it, "there's no honey without flies." Like John Adams, who remarked that he had never seen a rose without thorns, Machiavelli was arguing that nothing in this world can possibly be an absolute good, because every good seems to carry along a baggage of evil. "And thus it is seen in all human affairs, upon careful examination, that you cannot avoid one inconvenience without incurring another." Elsewhere he suggested that "all human institutions . . . contain some inherent evil." For example, republics may require poverty, and knowledge may come only with suffering. When Machiavelli quoted a passage by Sallust that "all evil examples have their origin in good beginnings," he was arguing that good and evil are all jumbled up in this world and that what we call good can never be neatly gleaned from what we call evil.[23] "So that this is one of those cases where the evil lies so near the good and is so commingled with it, that it is easy to encounter the one in thinking to take the other."[24] To think we can have what we ordinarily call good without what we ordinarily call evil is the silly result of the wishful imaginations of dreamy philosophers such as Plato and Aristotle.

Second, Machiavelli observed again and again that good consequences did not derive from what we ordinarily call good actions; too often evil followed from good. In part, this conviction emerged from Machiavelli's cyclical view of history, because even the finest nations move from initial growth to the development of excellence to eventual decay, and the final decay is linked directly to characteristics accompanying excellence.

> So always from good [countries] go down to bad, and from bad rise up to good. Because ability brings forth quiet; quiet, laziness; laziness, disorder; disorder, ruin; and likewise from ruin comes order; from order, ability; from the last, glory and good fortune. Therefore the discerning have noted that letters come after arms, and that in countries and cities generals are born earlier than philosophers. Because, after good and well-disciplined armies have brought forth victory, and their victories quiet, the virtue of

23. Machiavelli, *Mandragola*, act 3, scene 4, p. 796; *Discourses*, 1.6.127, 3.11.448, 1.46.232; also *The Prince*, chap. 21, 84.
24. *Discourses*, 3.37.520. Compare this claim to Nietzsche: "It might even be possible that *what* constitutes the value of those good and honored things resides precisely in their being artfully related, knotted and crocheted to these wicked, apparently antithetical things, perhaps even in their being essentially identical with them." Friedrich Nietzsche, *Beyond Good and Evil*, trans. R. J. Hollingdale (New York: Penguin, 1973), sec. 2, 16.

military courage cannot be corrupted with a more honorable laziness than that of letters. . . . Cato realized this; . . . he made a law that no philosopher should be received by Rome.[25]

Unlike Plato, who suggested in his cyclical theory of history that an initial small evil—lack of knowledge and of psychic harmony—multiplied and intensified until it produced the greatest evil, which is tyranny, Machiavelli argued that evil in fact comes from good qualities. This conviction that what we ordinarily call good too often produces what we ordinarily call evil (and vice versa) pervades Machiavelli's writings; to take another example, peace saps the vigor of nations and thus ensures that such nations will produce few great individuals.[26]

The consequences of this conviction for political action are unsettling. If what we ordinarily call good frequently brings about what we ordinarily call evil, and if what we call evil is sometimes necessary to produce what we call good, then we must toss aside philosophical and religious discussions about good and evil—as Nietzsche said, go beyond good and evil—and look at the particular situation. If "good" action X produces "evil" result Y, then in what sense can I call X good? If I must use "evil" means A to achieve "good" end B, then in what sense can I call A evil but B good? All of this is evident in the most famous advice he gave in *The Prince:* "For how we live is so far removed from how we ought to live, that he who abandons what is done for what ought to be done, will rather learn to bring about his own ruin than his preservation. A man who wishes to make a profession of goodness in everything must necessarily come to grief among so many who are not good. Therefore it is necessary for a prince, who wishes to maintain himself, to learn how not to be good, and to use this knowledge and not to use it, according to the necessity of the case."[27]

Machiavelli quite probably had in mind his friend Pietro Soderini, who was head of the Florentine Republic from 1502 to 1512. Twice in the *Discourses* Machiavelli maintained that because Soderini was a good man—patient, gentle, humane, pious, and respectful of the law—he brought ruin to himself and to the Florentine people. Even though Soderini knew that for the good of Florence he should destroy his enemies by attacking the Florentine nobility in general and the Medici in particular, his "goodness" prevented him, and as a result, he ruined the republic and paved the way for a return of the Medici tyranny. "Pietro Soderini . . . was in all

25. *History of Florence*, 5.1.1232.
26. *History of Florence*, 5.1.1233; *Art of War*, bk. 2, 622.
27. *The Prince*, chap. 15, 56.

his actions governed by humanity and patience. He and his country prospered so long as the times favored this mode of proceeding; but when afterwards circumstances arose that demanded a course of conduct the opposite to that of patience and humanity, he was unfit for the occasion, and his own and his country's ruin were the consequence."[28] Soderini's "goodness" brought evil; to bring a good result, he would have needed to be ruthless toward his enemies and "evil" in the eyes of the world, or, as Machiavelli advised in *The Prince,* he should have learned how and when not to be good. "It will be found that some things which seem virtues would, if followed, lead to one's ruin, and some others which appear vices result in one's greater security and well-being."[29]

The world is more complicated than it appears to be, and Machiavelli repeatedly maintained that people who do not understand the "affairs of this world" are easily fooled by appearances. In his chapter on liberality, he declared that initial appearances are deceiving; frugality, for example, by lessening the need for taxes, appears niggardly but really *is* liberality. In his chapter on cruelty, he noted that sometimes violence, by minimizing the chances of civil war, appears to be cruelty but really *is* humanity.[30] In his *History of Florence* he gave a chilling example. If the armies of Italy were more ruthless, if, when an army won a battle, it destroyed the losing army completely, as in ancient Roman times, instead of releasing prisoners and allowing the losing city to regroup and fight again the following year, then Italy would experience fewer wars and less suffering.[31]

All of this disturbs us deeply. While we admit that sometimes the use of cruelty lessens violence, we are reluctant to trust the political leader who wishes to try, and while we acknowledge that sometimes a destructive war brings peace, we are not *certain* that it will do so in any given situation. Machiavelli would probably respond that indeed this is the nature of the world—never to be certain—and that he did not cause the problem, but instead only described a perennial problem that invariably accompanies the human condition. Indeed, we wish to believe that always being decent and good will produce decent and good results, whereas always

28. *Discourses,* 3.9.442; also 3.3.405–6. In a similar discussion, Wood quite rightly likened Machiavelli's position to Sartre's claim that, to accomplish anything in this world, we need to dirty our hands. Wood, "Machiavelli's Humanism of Action," 53.

29. *The Prince,* chap. 15, 57. See Friedrich Meinecke, *Machiavellism: The Doctrine of Raison d'Etat and Its Place in Modern History,* trans. Douglas Scott (New Haven: Yale University Press, 1957). For further discussion on when violence must be used, see Paul Norton, "Machiavelli and the Modes of Terrorism," *Modern Age* 29 (fall 1985): 304–13.

30. *The Prince,* chap. 16, 57–60; chap. 17, 60–63.

31. *History of Florence,* 5.1.1284–85; also *The Prince,* chap. 12, 49.

being cruel and evil will bring cruel and evil consequences. But, as Weber put it, "it is *not* true that good can follow only from good and evil only from evil, but that often the opposite is true. Anyone who fails to see this is, indeed, a political infant."[32] Machiavelli shocks us precisely because he refused to let us remain political infants. A prince, he noted, must do what is considered good if at all possible, but a prince must also be able to do what is considered evil if compelled to do so, because there are some moments in the world of politics when, in order to accomplish something great and good, one must act against all the canons of decency. A prince "cannot observe all those things which are considered good in men, being often obliged, in order to maintain the state, to act against faith, against charity, against humanity, and against religion."[33] Machiavelli himself believed that the only way to regenerate a corrupt Italy, the only way to liberate Italy from the miserable anarchy of princely tyrannies, was to use popular violence that in the long run would reduce human suffering but in the short run would be seen as evil in the eyes of the world. "[The Florentine people] would like a preacher who would show them the road to Paradise, and I should like to find one who would teach them the way to go to the house of the Devil; they would like, besides, that he should be a man prudent, blameless, and true; and I should like to find one crazier than Ponzo, more crafty than Fra Girolamo [Savonarola], more of a hypocrite than Frate Alberto, . . . because I believe the true way of going to Paradise would be to learn the road to Hell in order to avoid it."[34] However disturbing the argument, Machiavelli was suggesting that the comparative "goodness" of Italian leadership had brought his country the hell of constant warfare, oppressive tyrants, and national disunity, whereas what Italy most needed was some "evil" force

32. Max Weber, "Politics as a Vocation," in *From Max Weber: Essays in Sociology*, ed. and trans. H. H. Gerth and C. Wright Mills (New York: Oxford University Press, 1946), 123. Contrast this with Plato: "Then the good is not the cause of everything; rather it is the cause of the things that are in a good way, while it is not responsible for the bad things." *Republic*, trans. Allan Bloom (New York: Basic Books, 1968), 379b.

33. *The Prince*, chap. 18, 65; also chap. 19, 71.

34. *Letters*, 198. Compare to Nietzsche: "These terrible energies—that which is called Evil—are the cyclopic architects and road-makers of humanity." *Human, All Too Human*, trans. Helen Zimmern (London: T. N. Foulis, 1909), sec. 246, 228. Compare also to Nietzsche's character Zarathustra, who claimed, "Man must grow better and more evil." *Thus Spoke Zarathustra*, trans. R. J. Hollingdale (New York: Penguin, 1969), pt. 4, "Of the Higher Man," 299. Finally, compare to Stendhal's character Julien, who said, "In a word, Mademoiselle, . . . must a man who wants to drive ignorance and crime off this earth pass through it like a whirlwind and do evil indiscriminately?" *Scarlet and Black*, trans. Margaret R. B. Shaw (Baltimore: Penguin, 1953), 309–10.

that would destroy Italy's princely tyrants and bring the comparative paradise of republican virtue, military glory, and national unification. Machiavelli, obviously, did not abandon all moral standards. Instead, he merely claimed that in an extraordinarily complicated world there is no clear moral code that one can apply to all situations, and that one must judge actions according to circumstances and by results, however difficult it might be to predict these results.[35] Writing to Soderini just after the fall of the Florentine Republic and the return to power of the Medici, Machiavelli said that he understood "the compass by which you navigate," a compass of prudence and decency, but that he felt "obliged in affairs to judge the result when they are finished, and not the means while they are going on." Similarly, in the *Discourses* he maintained that great deeds such as the founding of a republic require one to use "extraordinary means," but "it is well that, when the act accuses him, the result should excuse him."[36] Machiavelli meant no more than this when he said in *The Prince,* "in the actions of men, and especially of princes, . . . the end justifies the means."[37] To talk of judging moral actions by results

35. Machiavelli made moral assumptions or addressed the issue of morality in at least three additional ways. First, societies establish laws and moral systems out of a necessity to survive, which leads Machiavelli to have both a genealogy and sociology of morality. Common needs lead to similar moral rules across cultures—laws prohibiting murder, rape, incest, theft, and so forth—and so it is not surprising that Machiavelli refers to *jus gentium,* or laws of nations, laws, such as those mentioned above, that are common to all nations (*Discourses,* 2.28.379). Second, Machiavelli assumed that an individual would regard his or her nation as a higher good. Because he assumed that international relations would always involve war and conquest, he regarded it as hopelessly utopian—at least in almost all cases—to apply a moral standard that extended beyond national boundaries. He loved Rome and accepted that "the aim of Rome was empire and glory" (*Discourses,* 2.9.307). Twice he suggested that one cannot let considerations of morality endanger one's nation and one's fellow citizens. For example, "Where the safety of the country depends upon the resolution to be taken, no considerations of justice or injustice, humanity or cruelty, nor of glory or of shame, should be allowed to prevail" (*Discourses,* 3.41.528; also *The Prince,* chap. 18, 65–66). Finally, Machiavelli was intrigued by and admired all actions that are exemplary, actions that exemplify what human beings are capable of accomplishing. This is easily understandable when he admired acts of sacrifice and spoke of the "greatness" of Rome as an example for all time (*History of Florence,* 4.12.1199; *Discourses,* 1.6.127). But he also spoke of Caesar Borgia as an "example" of political virtuosity and political innovation (*The Prince,* chap. 7, 30) and clearly saw Borgia as an exemplary figure who mastered the political and military world with a skill that no other prince had been able to match (Ridolfi, *The Life of Niccolò Machiavelli,* 57–64). It is even more disconcerting to see Machiavelli speak of the "grandeur" of a crime or of the fact that the "greatness" of Rome was "made manifest by the extent of her executions," that is, by the astonishing measures Rome took to maintain military discipline (*Discourses,* 1.27.186, 3.44.539).

36. *Letters,* 97; *Discourses,* 1.9.139.

37. *The Prince,* chap. 18, 66. Allan Gilbert translates this passage thus: "As to the actions

seems reasonable, but Machiavelli is disturbing because of the openness with which he acknowledged that action in the political world so frequently involves using questionable means or getting one's hands dirty, as if he took delight in reminding us that one cannot, without sin, act effectively in the political world. "I believe, have believed, and will believe always," he wrote in a different context, "that it is true, as Boccaccio said, that it is better to act and repent than not to act and repent."[38]

As a matter of fact, Machiavelli criticized tyrants for misunderstanding the results of their actions, for miscalculating their interests. Although people with extraordinary ability could establish a republic or a just kingdom and "earn eternal glory," instead they "incline toward tyranny, without perceiving how much glory, how much honor, security, satisfaction, and tranquillity of mind, they forfeit; and what infamy, disgrace, blame, danger, and disquietude they incur." Whereas Romulus will forever be praised, Caesar will forever be condemned, and whereas Nerva and Trajan enjoyed reigns of comparative peace and well-being, Tiberius and Nero experienced only the ruin of their countries and deep personal torment. To choose tyranny instead of either founding a republic or ruling with justice is to be ignorant of the probable results of one's choice, which is as close as Machiavelli ever came to borrowing an argument from Plato; to found a republic is "to live securely and insure [oneself] glory after death," but to establish a tyranny is to live a life of "constant anxiety, and after death consign [oneself] to eternal infamy."[39] In a well-known passage in *The Prince,* Machiavelli said that "it cannot be called virtue to kill one's fellow-citizens, betray one's friends, be without faith, without pity, and without religion," and at first glance this appears to be a passage embracing a straightforward moral condemnation of evil, but he ended the passage with an appeal to self-interest. "By these methods one may indeed gain power, but not glory."[40]

The result that Machiavelli most sought was not an absolute and timeless good in itself but a changing common good or public good, variously expressed as *bene commune, publica utilità, commune utilità,* or *salute della patria* throughout the *Discourses* (although these phrases are almost

of all men and especially those of princes, . . . everybody looks at their result" (67). For an excellent discussion of judging political actions by results, see Sheldon Wolin's chapter "Machiavelli: Politics and the Economy of Violence," in his *Politics and Vision: Continuity and Innovation in Western Political Thought* (Boston: Little, Brown, 1960), 195–238, esp. 207–9, 220–28.

38. *Letters*, 158.
39. *Discourses*, 1.10.141–45.
40. *The Prince*, chap. 8, 32.

entirely lacking in *The Prince*).[41] What makes cities and nations great are rulers and citizens "whose object is to promote the public good, and not [their] private interests." Why did Rome attain such greatness? "The cause of this is manifest, for it is not individual prosperity, but the general good, that makes cities great; and certainly the general good is regarded nowhere but in republics."[42] And why has Italy fallen into such corruption? Because the Italian princes do not seek "true glory," which comes from acting for the "public benefit" instead of for private "avarice," and because the Italian princes betray the "common good" in favor of partisan interests, that is, the interests of a particular faction of the city.[43] Although certainly Plato and Aristotle sought the general good, they thought they could discover it by philosophical reasoning—such a contrast to Machiavelli, who assaulted this classical confidence in philosophy and sought instead to find a general good empirically, through experience in the world of politics. It was experience that taught him to love republics and to detest the princely tyrannies of his time.

Princes as Tyrants

Machiavelli thoroughly enjoyed the excitement of political participation as second chancellor of the republic, a job that also made him secretary of the republic,[44] but after the republic collapsed and the Medici tyranny continued to thrive, he became completely disenchanted with "this corrupt century," which refused to make use of his immense political talents. All of his major works reflect this anger and disenchantment, and in all of these writings he fled to the glory of the ancient world to escape the sordidness of his own time, an escape captured so well in one of his most famous letters.

> With these [people] I sink into vulgarity for the whole day, playing at *cricca* and at trich-trach, and then these games bring on a thousand disputes and countless insults with offensive words, and usually we are fighting over a penny, and nevertheless we are

---

41. These terms and others are listed by Russell Price in his "*Ambizione* in Machiavelli's Thought," *History of Political Thought* 3, no. 3 (1982): 383–445; see 430. See also Anthony Parel, "Introduction: Machiavelli's Method and His Interpreters," in *The Political Calculus*, ed. Parel, 3–32, esp. 5–7.

42. *Discourses*, 1.9.138, 2.2.282.

43. *History of Florence*, 2.1.1081, 3.5.1146; *Remodelling the Government of Florence*, 103. For a recent discussion of Machiavelli's concept of justice, see A. J. Parel, "Machiavelli's Notions of Justice: Text and Analysis," *Political Theory* 18, no. 4 (1990): 528–44.

44. Ridolfi, *The Life of Niccolò Machiavelli*, 15–21.

heard shouting as far as San Casciano. So, involved in these trifles, I keep my brain from growing mouldy, and satisfy the malice of this fate of mine, being glad to have her drive me along this road, to see if she will be ashamed of it.

On the coming of evening, I return to my house and enter my study; and at the door I take off the day's clothing, covered with mud and dust, and put on garments regal and courtly; and reclothed appropriately, I enter the ancient courts of ancient men, where, received by them with affection, I feed on that food which only is mine and which I was born for, where I am not ashamed to speak with them and to ask them the reason for their actions; and they in their kindness answer me; and for four hours of time I do not feel boredom, I forget every trouble, I do not dread poverty, I am not frightened by death, entirely I give myself over to them.[45]

If he could not regenerate his corrupt political world, for which he did not give up hope entirely, he wanted to escape his time, because he despaired of living in an era "when not the least trace of ancient virtue remains," an era when "there is only one country [probably Germany, perhaps Switzerland] in which we can say that free communities exist," an era boasting of "nothing that compensates for all the extreme misery, infamy, and degradation of a period where there is neither observance of religion, law, or military discipline." His beloved Italy—"poor, ambitious, cowardly"—had fallen to the bottom of the historical cycle. In the *Discourses* he tried to persuade princes that it was in their self-interest to rule justly (or even to establish republics) and depicted graphically the ruin of Italy under the evil emperors, possibly borrowing much of his description from Tacitus. "If now [a prince] will but glance at the times under the other Emperors, he will behold the atrocities of war, discords and sedition, cruelty in peace as in war, many princes massacred, many civil and foreign wars, Italy afflicted and overwhelmed by fresh misfortunes, and her cities ravaged and ruined. . . . He will see innumerable cruelties in Rome, and nobility, riches, and honor, and above all virtue, accounted capital crimes." To Machiavelli, and probably to much of his audience, this remained an accurate description of his own time, and for Italy's misery he blamed the princes. When writing his *History of Florence,* he noted, "I relieve myself by blaming the princes, who have all done everything to bring us here."[46]

45. *Letters*, 142.
46. *Discourses*, bk. 1, introduction, 104; 2.2.282; bk. 2, introduction, 273; *Letters*, 134; *Discourses*, 1.10.144; *Letters*, 218. For Machiavelli's analysis of Florence, the Medici, and espe-

When we come to Machiavelli's analysis of these troublesome princedoms, we immediately run into the problem of Machiavelli's unsystematic
approach to definitions and classifications.[47] In the first chapter of *The
Prince* he claimed that all governments are either republics or monarchies, although he quickly moved from monarchies to princedoms, thus
equating the two.[48] Later in *The Prince* he suggested three types of political orders: "absolute government [tyranny], liberty [republic], or license
[mob rule]."[49] Throughout his writings he assumed that governments are
either republics or princedoms and that the former are free and the latter
are generally tyrannical. "No firm government can be devised if it is not
either a true princedom or a true republic, because all the constitutions
between these two are defective." Florence had been plagued by political
troubles because it had a "defective" government, a hybrid that was neither republic nor princedom, and indeed quite often fell into license. Florence "has never been either a republic or a princedom having the qualities each requires, because we cannot call that republic well-established
in which things are done according to the will of one man [e.g., Cosimo or
Lorenzo de' Medici] yet are decided with the approval of the many."[50]

Machiavelli described three different kinds of princedoms, which I label
benevolent princedoms, whose rule, for a time at least, is for the common
good; *static princedoms,* characterized by a prince who rules self-inter-
estedly but who is satisfied with the pleasures of a tranquil state; and
mobilizing princedoms, which seek to mobilize the energy of the people
for the purposes of war and territorial expansion.

Machiavelli did describe what I have called a *benevolent princedom.*
Although nowhere does he write a chapter or even a long paragraph describing a prince who would rule in the common interest, he did sprinkle
throughout his writings arguments and exhortations urging princes to
rule in a restrained and benevolent manner. In other words, he seemed to
admit the possibility of a "well-governed kingdom" that was not tyranni-

---

cially Cosimo de' Medici, see John M. Najemy, "Machiavelli and the Medici: The Lessons of
Florentine History," *Renaissance Quarterly* 34, no. 4 (1982): 551–76.

47. Early in the *Discourses,* Machiavelli plagiarized Polybius by classifying every government as either a monarchy, an aristocracy, or a democracy, or the perverted form of each of
these—tyranny, oligarchy, licentiousness (*Discourses,* 1.2.111–12). Since he never made use
of Polybius's system of classification later, we can safely dismiss the mention of this system
in the *Discourses* as simply a commentary on an ancient author.

48. *The Prince,* chaps. 1 and 2, pp. 4–5.

49. *The Prince,* chap. 9, 36.

50. *Remodelling the Government of Florence,* 106 and 101. For a description of this hybrid
form of government, see Felix Gilbert, *Machiavelli and Guicciardini: Politics and History in
Sixteenth-Century Florence* (New York: W. W. Norton, 1984), 7–19.

cal, that is, the possibility of a "just and proper government" of a king or prince.[51] Such benevolent princes should curb their own passions by following the law, observe the "laws and ancient customs" of the people they rule, make certain to "conduct themselves prudently," display the utmost respect for "the property of the subjects," forgo extravagance and especially use of public money for private aggrandizement, avoid "pride, cruelty, or luxuriousness," control the people with examples of "humanity and benevolence," and strive to gain the "affections" of both soldiers and citizens.[52] In the late fifteenth and early sixteenth centuries, humanists of the Renaissance wrote literally dozens of polite treatises—advice books intended for princes[53]—urging princes to be benevolent both because benevolence was in the princes' self-interest and because it was the proper thing to do. Perhaps Machiavelli could not resist offering some of this advice, but he did so rarely, because he was convinced that benevolent princedoms could not last, that all princes invariably become tyrants.

Machiavelli defined tyranny as did Aristotle, namely, rule by one person in his or her own self-interest and in opposition to the general interest.[54] Despite the facade of republicanism, he certainly regarded Florence under Lorenzo the Magnificent as a tyranny. "Nonetheless Lorenzo, hot with youth and with power, wished to attend to everything and to have all Florence admit everything came from him."[55] There is ample evidence that Machiavelli equated princes with tyrants. When he spoke of "the Roman Emperors and other tyrants and princes," he treated them as nearly equivalent; when he said that Germany was the only free country in his time, he clearly regarded all Italian princedoms as forms of tyranny; and when he wrote a long chapter on conspiracies for the purpose of assassination, he used the words *prince* and *tyrant* interchangeably.[56] Finally, he flatly maintained that "the general good is regarded nowhere but in republics," whereas a prince is a ruler "whose private interests are gener-

---

51. *Art of War*, bk. 1, 577; *Discourses*, 2.24.365–66.

52. *Discourses*, 3.5.409, 3.19.471, 3.20.473, 3.20.472, 3.22.481; also 1.58.263–65, 3.5.408.

53. See Quentin Skinner, *The Renaissance*, vol. 1 of *The Foundations of Modern Political Thought* (New York: Cambridge University Press, 1978), 116–18. In effect, Machiavelli's *Prince* offered substantially new material in old familiar packaging. See Felix Gilbert, "The Humanist Concept of the Prince and *The Prince* of Machiavelli," *The Journal of Modern History* 11, no. 4 (1939): 449–83.

54. For examples of this use of the word *tyranny*, see Machiavelli's *History of Florence*, 3.17.1168 and 3.25.1180.

55. *History of Florence*, 8.3.1385.

56. *Discourses*, 1.58.262, 2.2.281–82, 1.55.253, 3.6.410–36, esp. 425–30. Strauss commented that Machiavelli "frequently [used] 'prince' and 'tyrant' as synonyms." *Thoughts on Machiavelli*, 272.

ally in opposition to those of the city, . . . [a] state of things [that] soon leads to a tyranny."[57]

Even if a prince is not always a tyrant, even if in theory a benevolent princedom is possible, for Machiavelli such benevolence can never last, and all princes more or less rapidly become tyrants. He suggested three reasons for this. First, the private interests of the prince come into conflict with the general interests of the community, and the prince necessarily becomes tyrannical in order to preserve power. Second, Machiavelli shared the assumption of Plato and Tacitus, and argued that power corrupts. Over time a ruler without restraints becomes tyrannical because "a prince who knows no other control but his own will is like a madman." Third, in a century of warfare, even a good prince must become authoritarian in order to survive. Whether it is a competition among individuals, classes, or states, there seems to be "a necessity either to oppress or to be oppressed,"[58] and even a good prince will feel this necessity. Indeed, Machiavelli depicted an almost Hobbesian state of nature in which even those trying to live tranquilly are forced into the cycle of violence. "Nature has created men so that they desire everything, but are unable to attain it; . . . as some men desire to have more, whilst others fear to lose what they have, enmities and war are the consequences." Under such conditions, a prince must become a tyrant in order to survive. "So to find a violent government joined with a good prince is impossible, because of necessity either they become alike or one by the other is quickly destroyed."[59]

Machiavelli described two very different kinds of tyranny, what I have called a *static princedom,* or a *static tyranny,* and what I have called a *mobilizing princedom,* or a *mobilizing tyranny.* These parallel closely Machiavelli's view of republics insofar as Machiavelli thought that one could have either a republic that was content to remain quietly within its borders, such as Sparta or Venice, or a republic that mobilized the people for imperial expansion, such as Rome.[60] In his analyses of princely tyrannies, Machiavelli seemed to sort them into *static tyrannies,* which were comparatively tranquil, defensive rather than expansive, and characterized by the dominance of local nobilities, and *mobilizing tyrannies,* ruled by

57. *Discourses,* 2.2.282–83.

58. *Discourses,* 1.58.265, 1.46.232 (here Machiavelli was quoting Livy), 2.2.282–83;

59. *Discourses,* 1.37.208; *History of Florence,* 2.34.1125.

60. *Discourses,* 1.6.127–30. In claiming that Venice was a republic, Machiavelli contradicted his claim that, in his time, only Germany was free. To understand Florentine attitudes toward Venice at this time, see Skinner, *The Foundations of Modern Political Thought,* 1:139–44.

princes eager to mobilize a citizen army for purposes of military expansion.

The Means of Violence

No writer has ever spoken more openly and frankly than Machiavelli about the political necessities of violence, and once again he judged the political use of violence by its result. "For he is to be reprehended who commits violence for the purpose of destroying, and not he who employs it for beneficent purposes."[61] One can oppose others either by violent means or by legal means, that is, either by means appropriate to beasts or by means appropriate to human beings, but in the political world few leaders can escape the necessity of using both violence and law. "It is therefore necessary for a prince to know well how to use both the beast and the man."[62] Machiavelli knew, however, that violence had limited effectiveness. Although Hannibal had much success, not despite but because of his "inhuman cruelty," Scipio was successful using "kindness" as well as "mercy, loyalty and piety"; although one must sometimes use force to defend the government against a violent opposition, such force has drawbacks because "the more cruelty [a man] employs the feebler will his authority become," just as the duke of Athens lost power quickly despite "frequent executions"; although it is useful for a ruler to be feared, Machiavelli thought it was better to be loved, despite advice to the contrary in *The Prince*.[63] Machiavelli regarded violence as a political medicine safe to use only in controlled doses, and hence he gave the famous advice that a ruler must "commit all his cruelties at once," whereas "benefits should be granted little by little."[64]

War offers another instance in which rulers necessarily use the means of violence, and certainly Machiavelli paid elaborate attention to circumstances that require war, although it is not true that Machiavelli was always spoiling for a good fight. "Arms and force . . . should be reserved as

61. *Discourses*, 1.9.139. Machiavelli was certainly attacking the vast majority of humanists who advocated traditional Christian virtue and the scrupulous avoidance of force and violence. See Skinner, *The Foundations of Modern Political Thought*, 1:128–38.

62. *The Prince*, chap. 18, 64.

63. *The Prince*, chap. 17, 62–63; *Letters*, 96–100; *Discourses*, 1.16.162; *History of Florence*, 2.36.1128. Machiavelli advised in *The Prince* that one should be feared rather than loved, if one could not attain both (*The Prince*, chap. 17, 61), but elsewhere he noted that the Duke of Athens, in trying to establish a tyranny, made the key mistake of wishing "to be feared rather than loved" (*History of Florence*, 2.37.1133.)

64. *The Prince*, chap. 8, 34–35.

the last resort when other means fail." Nor is it true that Machiavelli always romanticized war; in his poem "On Ambition," he described the results of war: "Wherever you turn your eyes, you see the earth wet with tears and blood, and the air full of screams, of sobs, and sighs." While he recognized the horrors of war, he also regarded war as inescapable, at least in his century, and he agreed with Savonarola, who said, "Peace, peace, and there will be no peace."[65] Still, Machiavelli sanctioned not merely defensive wars but also wars for national unification and wars for the purpose of attaining glory by "aggrandizing a republic and founding a great empire."[66] For Machiavelli, as for Thucydides and Weber, it was a fact of international relations that nations will conflict with each other for reasons of economic interest and political power. "It always has been, and it is reasonable that it should be, the object of those who go to war to enrich themselves and to impoverish the enemy, nor is victory sought for any other reason or gains wished for anything else than to make oneself powerful and weaken one's opponent." If a war furthered the common good of a nation, by defending the nation or by bringing glory and reputation to the nation or by enriching the public treasury, he seemed to approve, but he despised wars fought to foster the self-interest of particular individuals or classes, precisely the kind of wars fought by the Italian princes of his time. "These wars were undertaken to enrich [the wealthiest] citizens, and not from necessity."[67]

Machiavelli also recognized that violence, perhaps even extraordinary violence, would be needed to transform the political structure of any society. To reform or regenerate a corrupt state one cannot use ordinary means of legislation and education, but instead "it becomes necessary to resort to extraordinary measures, such as violence and arms." And to transform a state entirely, to take it, for example, from tyranny to republic, is a terrifying prospect no matter how noble the end result. "Every student of ancient history well knows that any change of government, be it from a republic to a tyranny, or from a tyranny to a republic, must necessarily be followed by some terrible punishment of the enemies of the existing state of things."[68] Machiavelli neither glorified such political transformations nor shrunk from describing graphically the terrible necessities that push such transformations, and he admitted that such vio-

65. *Discourses*, 2.21.354; Machiavelli, "Tercets on Ambition," 738; *Letters*, 134, 223.

66. *Discourses*, 2.19.345. For a good discussion of Machiavelli's approval of empire and imperial expansion, see Mark Hulliung, *Citizen Machiavelli* (Princeton: Princeton University Press, 1983), chap. 1, 3–30.

67. *History of Florence*, 6.1.1284, 4.14.1202.

68. *Discourses*, 1.18.170–71, 3.3.405.

lence may devour those who begin such revolutions. "Nobody should start a revolution in a city in the belief that later he can stop it at will or regulate it as he likes"—a comment reminiscent of Weber's suggestion that a revolution is "not a cab, which one can have stopped for one's pleasure."[69] For example, to introduce a republic in a nation that is accustomed to rule by a prince, one must be willing to destroy the landed nobility in order to establish the requisite equality, but "the greatness of the enterprise frightens men so that they fail even in the very beginning."[70]

Machiavelli's empirical mind also recognized the immense violence necessary to establish most tyrannies, a necessity either ignored or obscured by Plato and Aristotle. While it is comparatively easy to establish a tyranny in a nation ruled by a monarch or by another prince, the aspiring tyrant must still make certain he or she kills the former king or destroys the former prince and his entire family. More frightening still is the task of the tyrant who wishes to establish a tyranny over a free people, for "whoever becomes the ruler of a free city and does not destroy it, can expect to be destroyed by it."[71] The list of violent measures such a would-be tyrant must undertake is chilling: such a tyrant must "organize the government entirely anew"; appoint new officials with new titles; make certain that "there should be neither rank, nor grade, nor honor, nor wealth, that should not be recognized as coming from him"; "destroy the old cities and build new ones"; transfer the population to new provinces just "as shepherds move their flocks from place to place"; attempt to obliterate the old religion and replace it with a new one; and, if possible, even establish a new language, the best means of effacing all memory of past freedoms.[72] After acknowledging that these measures are "neither Christian nor human" and certainly "cruel and destructive of all civilized life," Machiavelli suggested that "the life of a private citizen" would be preferable to ruling "at the expense of the ruin of so many human beings." Such rule is also risky, as Machiavelli indicated by quoting Juvenal's dictum that "tyrants never die a natural death."[73]

If Machiavelli maintained that all governments, and especially tyrannies, need to use violence, then how did he envision tyrants organizing the means of violence? To start with, as Aristotle and Tacitus maintained, every tyrant must have not only a bodyguard but also a loyal paramilitary force for extralegal violence against selected enemies. The duke of Athens

---

69. *History of Florence*, 3.10.1154.; Weber, "Politics as a Vocation," 119, 125.
70. *Discourses*, 1.55.256; see also 1.16.163, 3.4.406–7; *The Prince*, chap. 3, 7.
71. *The Prince*, chap. 5, 18–19.
72. *Discourses*, 1.26.183–84, 2.5.296–97.
73. *Discourses*, 1.26.184, 3.6.412.

employed "armed retainers on foot and on horseback," and Lorenzo the Magnificent was "accompanied by many armed men."[74] However, all of a nation's accomplishments are of no account if the nation cannot defend itself, and thus Machiavelli regarded the art of war as of primary importance and concerned himself most of all with how a prince, or a tyrant, might organize an army for war, again a topic virtually ignored by Plato and Aristotle. "A prince should therefore have no other aim or thought, nor take up any other thing for his study, but war and its organization and discipline."[75] The twin foundations of any state are "good laws and good armies," which means that the absence of military discipline is a sure sign of decline, something Italian princes should have known well, since their poor military performance had "reduced Italy to slavery and degradation."[76] Best of all is a prince willing to command his armies in person; princes incapable of command Machiavelli called "feeble." The Roman Empire collapsed at the moment the emperors preferred "the shade of the palace to the sun of the camp," and Italy's princes similarly were distinguishing themselves, not by military virtue, but by witty sayings, luxurious attire, and "wanton pleasures."[77]

Armies need not only prudent commanders but also disciplined and spirited soldiers, for wars are won with good soldiers and not with money, with iron and not with gold. Machiavelli tirelessly repeated that a nation should not use mercenaries, because they do not remain loyal, they become a threat to the government if they are victorious, and they do not fight with the spirit of free citizens. Nor should a nation pay for certain citizens to compose a professional army, an army that becomes a threat to the nation, but instead should rely only on citizen soldiers.[78]

But should static tyrannies and mobilizing tyrannies organize armies in identical ways? The answer is no, though Machiavelli's writings on this point are contradictory. His advice to any tyrant who seeks tranquility and not military expansion is to disarm the people, and he noted that Augustus and Tiberius disarmed the people (although they kept armies on the frontiers to continue their expansions), as did the duke of Athens and Lorenzo the Magnificent.[79] Since static tyrannies can rely neither on a popular army nor on mercenaries, they must rely on the armies of a nobility willing to receive from the tyrant honors and material reward and in

74. *History of Florence*, 2.36.1128, 8.9.1393; see also *Discourses*, 1.40.223–24.
75. *The Prince*, chap. 14, 53; *Art of War*, dedication, 566.
76. *The Prince*, chap. 12, 44, 49; *History of Florence*, 5.1.1232.
77. *Discourses*, 1.30.192, 1.19.173, 2.30.386; *Art of War*, bk. 7, 724.
78. *Discourses*, 2.10.309–10, 1.43.227; *The Prince*, chaps. 12–13, pp. 44–53; *Art of War*, bk. 1, 575.
79. *Art of War*, bk. 1, 578; *History of Florence*, 2.35.1127; *Letters*, 98.

return offering this tyrant security. "In order to have a princedom in Florence, where equality is great, the establishment of inequality would be necessary; noble lords of walled towns and boroughs would have to be set up, who in support of the prince would with their arms and their followers stifle the city and the whole province."[80] Machiavelli, of course, gave just the opposite advice in *The Prince*. "A new prince has never [!] been known to disarm his subjects, on the contrary, when he has found them disarmed he has always armed them, for by arming them these arms become your own, those you suspected become faithful [!]"[81] Here Machiavelli suggested that the prince form a popular army, because he envisioned a tyranny, or princedom, that would harness this popular energy for military expansion and national unification. As he wrote in a letter, "the best armies are those of armed peoples; and they cannot be resisted except by armies similar to themselves."[82]

Because Machiavelli so flagrantly contradicted himself, and even lied openly when he said no princes had ever disarmed their subjects, we wonder immediately what he thought might happen if a tyrant formed a popular army. Certainly Machiavelli hoped that such an army could unify Italy, and he repeatedly said that an excellent army was the key to such unification.[83] He probably also thought that a popular army would diminish the power of the nobility; in the *History of Florence*, after recounting an incident when the people armed themselves and took to the public square, Machiavelli noted that "the nobles, seeing all the people armed, did not dare to take arms, and each man remained in his mansion."[84] When Machiavelli suggested that a citizen army keeps a city "free" and "uncorrupted," when he used Sparta and Rome to exemplify nations that flourished with citizen armies,[85] we begin to suspect that princes who establish a mobilizing tyranny set the stage for popular government. Indeed, Machiavelli thought that political power closely followed or paralleled military power, that those with military might eventually rule. "It is not reasonable to suppose that one who is armed will obey willingly one who is unarmed; or that any unarmed man will remain safe among armed servants."[86] When we recognize Machiavelli's assumption that political power follows military power, when we see him announce that "all armed

80. *Remodelling the Government of Florence*, 107; also *Discourses*, 1.55.255–57.
81. *The Prince*, chap. 20, 77. Virtually the entire *Art of War* was written to persuade a prince to mobilize a citizen army.
82. *Letters*, 136.
83. For example, *Letters*, 128–29.
84. *History of Florence*, 2.39.1135.
85. *Art of War*, bk. 1, 585.
86. *The Prince*, chap. 14, 54.

prophets have conquered and unarmed ones have failed,"[87] we begin to suspect that a mobilizing tyrant who establishes a popular army might inadvertently bring about popular government. We then suspect that this is precisely what Machiavelli wanted. The war that Machiavelli most wanted was a popular war against princely tyranny, something we can see in a speech given by an opponent of Cosimo de' Medici, precisely the speeches that Machiavelli said expressed his opinions.

> No man should condemn in all conditions weapons that citizens turn against their native place. . . . Just as in simple bodies diseases often appear which cannot be healed without fire and steel, so in cities many times there are such disorders that a merciful and good citizen, when steel is the necessary remedy, would sin much more in leaving them untreated than in treating them. In the body of a republic what illness can be more serious than servitude? What medicine is more necessary than that which relieves it from this disease? Only those wars are just that are necessary; and arms are holy when there is no hope apart from them.[88]

If just one city in Italy could raise a disciplined citizen army, then that city could attain the greatness of the ancients, and one should not despair of this, because Italy "seems born to raise up dead things, as she has in poetry, in painting, and in sculpture," and as she might well do both in politics and the art of war. In other words, an ancient republic might well rise again, "because all the things that have been can, I believe, be again."[89]

Deception and Religion

Machiavelli assumed that deception was an inescapable part of the political world, and claiming to borrow from Xenophon, he spoke of the "necessity of deception" and said that "a prince who wishes to achieve great things must learn to deceive." Indeed, a prince, or a tyrant, must not only be strong like the lion but also clever like the fox, and a key element to this cleverness is the ability to be a "great feigner and dissembler"; if willing to deceive, one "will always find those who allow themselves to be

87. *The Prince*, chap. 6, 22.
88. *History of Florence*, 5.7.1242.
89. *Art of War*, bk. 7, 725–26; *Letters*, 180.

deceived."[90] In ruling a city, as Tacitus said, appearances become virtually everything, and thus, although it is not essential to be merciful, humane, and religious—indeed, at times one must act contrary to these virtues—it is important to *seem* merciful, humane, and religious. Machiavelli talked about deception in seemingly countless passages: he admired Pisistratus, who wounded himself so that Athens would provide him with the bodyguard needed to subdue the city-states; he noted that in battle one must learn deception to bewilder the enemy; and he even admired one tyrant who, having directed his minister to use cruelty to bring order, killed the minister brutally once order had been restored, all in order to convince the populace that he was just and that the cruelties committed had been the fault of the man who was killed.[91]

At first glance it appears to us that Machiavelli was suggesting the use of deception to anyone seeking to transform a republic into a tyranny, much as Tacitus had noted the deceptions used by Augustus and Tiberius in transforming Rome from republic to principate to despotism. "He who desires or attempts to reform the government of a state . . . must at least retain the semblance of the old forms; so that it may seem to the people that there has been no change in the institutions, even though in fact they are entirely different from the old ones. For the great majority of mankind are satisfied with appearances, as though they were realities, and are often even more influenced by the things that seem than by those that are."[92] Machiavelli quickly added, however, that such deception works for those who bring change slowly, but not for those wishing to change everything, to found a tyranny quickly, and to destroy free government entirely. For this, one needs a stomach for violence. Still, if the deception Machiavelli described is not useful in establishing a tyranny rapidly, if keeping the appearances of the old order will not be of much help when one needs to uproot the institutions and habits of free government, these deceptive appearances are useful to the tyrant who wants to consolidate rule and to move gradually but deliberately toward tyranny. Appius Claudius, for example, simply tried to stride too rapidly toward tyranny and should have relinquished less quickly the appearance of justice and benevolence. "For he who for a time has seemed good, and for purposes of his own wants to become bad, should do it gradually, and should seem to be brought to it by the force of circumstances." Thus, for any tyrant consolidating absolute power, deception is essential. "Everybody sees what

90. *Discourses*, 2.13.319; *The Prince*, chap. 18, 64–65.
91. *Discourses*, 3.6.432; *Art of War*, bk. 4, 653; *The Prince*, chap. 7, 27; chap. 18, 65.
92. *Discourses*, 1.25.182.

you appear, few feel what you are, and those few will not dare to oppose themselves to the many."[93]

Of all conceivable deceptions, however, Machiavelli—even more than Aristotle—regarded religion as the greatest and most important, a deception indispensable for any society. As a consequence, he concerned himself not with whether a religion was correct but with how it might be useful. One would almost literally have to return to ancient Roman writers, certainly pre-Christian writers, to find someone who would say, as Machiavelli did, "I love my native city more than my own soul," a sentence that indicates how much he subordinated religion to political priorities.[94]

Those who want to establish a republic or a tyranny that mobilizes the people must use the fictions of religion to discipline people so that they will devote themselves to the common good. Despite his intense admiration for Romulus, who was bold enough to found Rome through force of arms, Machiavelli gave even more credit to Numa for Rome's enduring success, because Numa founded the religion so crucial as a buttress to the Roman political and military ethic. Numa "established [the religion] upon such foundations that for many centuries there was nowhere more fear of the gods than in that republic." With belief in religion, or, as Machiavelli put it, "fear of the gods," citizens are more willing to consecrate themselves to the general good of society, more willing to adopt an internalized discipline imperative to a republic. To take one example Machiavelli used several times, citizens fear breaking oaths made in public, because these oaths are supposedly sanctioned by the gods. "Where religion exists," wrote Machiavelli, "it is easy to introduce armies and discipline. . . . In truth, there never was any remarkable lawgiver amongst any people who did not resort to divine authority." In his own time, only Germany had both "probity and religion," which enabled German communities to establish republics and to discipline themselves to observe their laws. Even though "so great a man" as Savonarola was wise enough to use religion to frighten and discipline the Florentine population and also to attack the Florentine nobility,[95] he ultimately failed because he forgot to mix religious motivation with military might, in Machiavelli's view the best possible recipe for political regeneration. It is easy to see that Machiavelli thought both republics and mobilizing tyrannies would do better

---

93. *Discourses*, 1.41.225; *The Prince*, chap. 18, 66.

94. *Letters*, 249. See J. Samuel Preus, "Machiavelli's Functional Analysis of Religion: Context and Object," *Journal of the History of Ideas* 40, no. 2 (1979): 171–90.

95. *Discourses*, 1.11.146–47; *Art of War*, bk. 4, 661; *Discourses*, 1.11.147, 1.55.253, 1.11.149; *Letters*, 86–87.

with a pagan religion that supported political expansion or, at the very least, with a drastically different and militant Christian ethic.

Static tyrannies found great consolation and support in the Christianity of Machiavelli's time for several reasons. First, Christianity in Machiavelli's time was otherworldly and taught the primacy of the next world—or, as Augustine had put it centuries earlier, this world is but the waiting room for the next—a belief perfect for making a tyrant's subjects indifferent to political matters. "For, as our religion teaches us the truth and the true way of life, it causes us to attach less value to the honors and possessions of this world; whilst the Pagans, esteeming those things as the highest good, were more energetic and ferocious in their actions."[96] Since most people have their eyes on the paradise of the next world, they willingly endure tyrannical oppression in this world. Second, by praising humility and contemplation, all while condemning pride and worldly action, the Christianity of the sixteenth century rendered subjects passive.

> Besides this, the Pagan religion deified only men who had achieved great glory, such as commanders of armies and chiefs of republics, whilst ours glorifies more the humble and contemplative men than the men of action. Our religion, moreover, places the supreme happiness in humility, lowliness, and a contempt for worldly objects, whilst the other, on the contrary, places the supreme good in grandeur of soul, strength of body, and all such other qualities as render men formidable; and if our religion claims of us fortitude of soul, it is more to enable us to suffer than to achieve great deeds.[97]

Third, Christianity facilitates obedience. In a passage full of irony, Machiavelli praised Saint Francis and Saint Dominic for revitalizing the Christian religion by returning Christianity to its first principles of self-control and "voluntary poverty" in opposition to the "licentiousness" of the papacy. As a result, "they obtained so much influence with the people, that they were able to make them understand that it was wicked even to speak ill of wicked rulers, and that it was proper to render them obedience and to leave the punishment of their errors to God. And thus these wicked rulers do as much evil as they please."[98] Although Machiavelli did dutifully and prudently suggest that a correct interpretation of Christianity would lead to patriotism and republican freedom,[99] his overall conclusion was

96. *Discourses*, 2.2.285; see also bk. 1, introduction, 104.
97. *Discourses*, 2.2.285.
98. *Discourses*, 3.1.401.
99. *Discourses*, 2.2.286.

certainly that Christianity was the most useful deception possible for any tyrant seeking only a static tyranny.

The Benefits of Corruption

When Machiavelli stated that any founder of a state must "start with assuming that all men are bad and ever ready to display their vicious nature," at first glance he appeared to be suggesting that human beings are simply evil, but in fact he had a more complicated view. Motivated by "love and fear," "animated by the same desires and the same passions," and pushed by desires that are ever "insatiable,"[100] human beings in all centuries and in all societies have always been the same, a statement that actually tells us perilously little about what they have the potential to be. The key is this: although Machiavelli acknowledged that "men are readier to evil than to good,"[101] he also recognized that depending on the education and training that people receive, they can attain the glories of ancient Rome or the degradations of the worst tyranny. Left alone and untrained, people tend toward petty evils, but educated and disciplined properly, people can attain wonders, which means that Machiavelli did not see people as always and everywhere wicked, but rather as always and everywhere having the potential for good and evil, greatness and pettiness.

Republics and tyrannies that want to mobilize their people must learn to educate, train, and discipline them. To begin with, this involves the recognition that people are "easily corrupted," and thus legislators must make laws with the hope of "restraining the passions of men, and depriving them of all hope of being able to do wrong with impunity." Thus, Machiavelli spoke of laws designed to "bridle" the population, that is, laws that would restrain the many who tend toward license and the nobles who tend toward tyranny.[102] Citizens should be taught—and like Plato, Machiavelli focused on the very young—to obey all laws without exception and to fear the laws, that is, to fear punishment for wrongdoing and to expect rewards for exceptional service.[103] Laws themselves are of only limited help unless they are fortified by customs and habits, as Tacitus had said and as Montesquieu and Tocqueville confirmed later, when they discussed *les moeurs.* One of Machiavelli's orators in his *History of*

---

100. *Discourses*, 1.3.117, 3.21.474, 1.39.216; bk. 2, introduction, 274.
101. *History of Florence*, 7.30.1375.
102. *Discourses*, 1.42.226; *History of Florence*, 2.32.1119, 4.1.1187.
103. *Discourses*, 1.45.229, 3.46.535; *Art of War*, bk. 1, 595 and 608; *Discourses*, 1.24.181.

Florence complained that "good laws, because they are ruined by bad customs, do not remedy this condition."[104] As a consequence, laws must be supported by the education and customs of the nation. "It is true that men are more or less virtuous in one country or another, according to the nature of the education by which their manners and habits of life have been formed." If the excellence of the country is evident in the manners and habits of its citizens, then republics and even tyrannies wishing to instill a military discipline might do well to emulate the ancient Roman censors. "For the Censors being the supreme arbiters of the manners and customs of the Romans, they became the most potent instrument in retarding the progress of corruption of Rome."[105]

The end result of good laws, good education, good habits, and good manners—all of which are necessary to military excellence—is an internalized morality or an internalized discipline that teaches one to consider the common good before his or her individual good, something Tacitus recognized had disappeared from the Roman character with the advent of empire. "When can [Italian soldiers of today]," asked Machiavelli, "be brought back to such discipline and such obedience and respect that a tree full of apples can stand in the middle of the camp and be left untouched, as we read many times happened in ancient armies?" Only the Germans of Machiavelli's time had such an internalized discipline and self-control, and although Machiavelli did not test the Germans with a tree glistening with apples, he did note that they lived up to their oaths and promises by paying taxes secretly and fully, without public scrutiny as a watchdog over private interest.[106] When Machiavelli wrote that Italy was less courageous than formerly because of "bad discipline," when he complained of cities neglecting both laws and training, when he spoke of soldiers being "disciplined by training," and when he suggested that "ancient examples show that in every country training can produce good soldiers," he was demonstrating that this internalized discipline is clearly a military virtue.[107]

If this ethic is a military virtue, it is also a political virtue, because it teaches each individual to consider the common good first. The Roman people, bridled by laws and disciplined from birth, were "lovers of the glory and common good of their country." And a popular army fights for its own glory and the glory of the public, not for the private ambition of

104. *History of Florence*, 3.5.1146.
105. *Discourses*, 3.43.530, 1.49.238–39.
106. *Art of War*, bk. 7, 723; *Discourses*, 1.55.253–54.
107. *Discourses*, 2.17.336; *Art of War*, bk. 2, 608; *Discourses*, 3.36.516; *Art of War*, bk. 1, 581.

some prince or some particular class.[108] Similarly, to promote concern for the common good, Machiavelli praised voluntary poverty, because citizens not preoccupied with gaining material wealth will pour themselves into increasing the grandeur of their nation. After citing the example of Cincinnatus, who left his small farm to serve Rome, Machiavelli indicated that he completely accepted the assumption that poor nations, not rich ones, attain greatness. "I might demonstrate here at length that poverty produces better fruits than riches,—that the first has conferred honor upon cities, countries, and religions, whilst the latter have only served to ruin them,—were it not that this subject has been so often illustrated by other writers."[109]

Any tyrant who wants to mobilize a popular army in order to undertake military expansion—and that was Machiavelli's advice both in *The Prince* and in *The Art of War*—must find a way to instill this internalized military discipline through education, customs, laws, and training. If this tyrant discovers that the nation is corrupt and lacking in this discipline, then the nation must be returned to its first principles or the original virtue that almost always accompanies nations in their infancy. All monarchies "must have within themselves some goodness, by means of which they obtain their first growth and reputation, and [since] in the process of time this goodness becomes corrupted," one must find a physician to restore the nation to health[110] (a very different use of the concepts of physician and health than in Plato and Aristotle). Sometimes such rejuvenation can be the work of one extraordinary individual, sometimes an external demand forces this return to first principles, and sometimes a nation is so corrupt that even a Cato cannot cure the illness. If a healthy discipline is essential to republics and mobilizing tyrannies, then the illness of corruption is wonderfully useful for static tyrannies.

Although tyrants must use violence to control their subjects, they often can dominate these subjects far more easily with the seductive pleasures of corruption, or, as Machiavelli advised in *The Prince*, "men must be either caressed or else annihilated."[111] Cities such as Florence, which

---

108. *Discourses*, 1.58.263, 1.43.226. On Machiavelli's attitude toward glory, see Russell Price, "The Theme of *Gloria* in Machiavelli," *Renaissance Quarterly* 30, no. 4 (1977): 588–631.

109. *Discourses*, 3.25.488.

110. *Discourses*, 3.3.397–98, 1.17.166. On Machiavelli's analysis of corruption, see S. M. Shumer, "Machiavelli: Republican Politics and Its Corruption," *Political Theory* 7, no. 1 (1979): 5–34. And on Machiavelli's notion of political health, see Gian Piero Barricelli, "Rereading *The Prince*: Philosophical Themes in Machiavelli," *Italian Quarterly* 13, no. 52 (1970): 43–62, esp. 48.

111. *The Prince*, chap. 3, 9.

boast of the "semblance of republican government," oscillate not between servitude and liberty, as many suppose, but between "slavery and license," that is, between the slavery that the nobles wish to impose upon the city and the license by which the people seek to gratify themselves.[112] This very license, however, makes tyranny both tempting and lasting. A thoroughly corrupt people, by which Machiavelli meant a people almost literally addicted to the pleasures of license, can never be free, no matter what measures one might take. Milan and Naples, for example, were doomed to servitude forever.[113]

And certainly Machiavelli thought that the licentiousness of Italian cities was a key component to the durability of princely tyrannies. One of Machiavelli's orators in his *History of Florence* described an Italy that had become depraved: "Truly in the cities of Italy all is collected that can be depraved and that can deprave any man: the young are lazy, the old licentious, and both sexes and every age abound in vile habits." Nations that become "enervated by pleasures and luxury" willingly trade their military discipline for "sensual pleasures" and are easy prey to any tyrant who will furnish gratifications. In losing their military strength, such nations become "effeminate," weak, and prone to domination.[114] Weakness, however, was not Machiavelli's primary concern; rather, he despaired that licentiousness and corruption channeled the passions and desires of citizens, particularly of the young men to whom he so often appealed, not into attaining glory or serving the common good, but instead into private gratification and into adapting oneself to tyrannical rule. We can see Machiavelli's scorn in his description of Florence in the time of Lorenzo the Magnificent. "The young men, more unrestrained than had been customary, spent without measure on dress, on banquets, on similar luxuries; and being without occupation, they wasted on gambling and whores their time and their property. Their ambition was to appear magnificent in their clothing, and to use speech that was pithy and clever."[115] If the finest ambition of Florentine young men was to "appear" magnificently

---

112. *History of Florence*, 4.1.1187.

113. *Discourses*, 1.17.165–66. The corruption that is so important to the stability of tyranny can only set its roots gradually in a free country. "To usurp supreme and absolute authority, then, in a free state, and subject it to tyranny, the people must have already become corrupt by gradual steps from generation to generation" (*Discourses*, 3.8.440).

114. *History of Florence*, 3.5.1145–46; *Discourses*, 2.19.348. See, for example, *Discourses*, 1.19.172, 2.2.285. For an intriguing discussion of the political implications of Machiavelli's assumptions about women, see Hannah Pitkin, *Fortune Is a Woman: Gender and Politics in the Thought of Niccolò Machiavelli* (Berkeley and Los Angeles: University of California Press, 1984), esp. chaps. 2 and 5, pp. 25–51, 109–37.

115. *History of Florence*, 7.28.1342.

dressed and not to accomplish magnificent deeds, then a corruption quite useful to Lorenzo's tyranny was complete.

In such a tyranny, both subjects and tyrant chase their desires with few restraints. Just as subjects lose all restraint at the sight of the pleasures that enslave them, so a prince "who knows no other control but his own will is like a madman," and here Machiavelli's analysis reminds us of Plato and Tacitus. Time and again in his *History of Florence*, Machiavelli noted tyrants who had lost all self-control or tyrants who were "lustful and cruel." The duke of Athens most offended the Florentine people by "the violence that he and his followers rashly used upon women." While it is not surprising that both tyrant and subjects come to resemble one another, it is not useful to tyrants to lose all of their control, because tyrants will need both prudence and discipline to maintain power. "When princes think more of luxury than of arms, they lose their state."[116]

What Machiavelli regarded as the cause of this corruption corresponds well with this class structure. "For such corruption and incapacity to maintain free institutions result from a great inequality that exists in such a state."[117] After discussing Germany's ability to remain disciplined and uncorrupted, Machiavelli gave two reasons: first, Germany remained uncorrupted by foreign (e.g., French and Italian) customs, and second, Germany maintained an extraordinary degree of equality.

> The other cause is, that those republics which have thus preserved their political existence uncorrupted do not permit any of their citizens to be or to live in the manner of gentlemen, but rather maintain amongst them a perfect equality, and are the most decided enemies of the lords and gentlemen that exist in the country; so that, if by chance any of them fall into their hands, they kill them, as being the chief promoters of all corruption and troubles.
>
> And to explain more clearly what is meant by the term gentlemen, I say that those are called gentlemen who live idly upon the proceeds of their extensive possessions, without devoting themselves to agriculture or any other useful pursuit to gain a living. Such men are pernicious to any country or republic; but more

---

116. *Discourses*, 1.58.265; *History of Florence*, 7.33.1379, 2.36.1127; *The Prince*, chap. 14, 53.

117. *Discourses*, 1.17.167. For a discussion of Machiavelli's belief that corruption is caused by inequality, and for an analysis that suggests that corruption is the opposite of military virtue, see J. G. Pocock, *The Machiavellian Moment: Florentine Political Thought and the Atlantic Republican Tradition* (Princeton: Princeton University Press, 1975), 204–11.

pernicious even than these are such as have, besides their possessions, castles they command, and subjects who obey them.[118]

It is easy to see why such gentlemen—whom Machiavelli ordinarily called nobles—are pernicious to a republic or to any tyrant seeking to mobilize a citizen army. Such gentlemen pursue their private self-interest to the detriment of the common interest, they use their extreme economic power to gain political power (just as Cosimo de' Medici used his "excessive wealth" to bribe his way to power),[119] and they set an example for the city that suggests riches, luxury, and pleasure should be pursued instead of austerity and sacrifice for the common good. For these very reasons, however, these gentlemen and the corrupting influence they bring are most useful for a static tyranny. Not only will such gentlemen use force to support such a tyrant, as long as the tyrant enables them to accumulate wealth and honor, but by their very examples of luxury and dissipation, they also plant the seeds of corruption. A static tyranny can find nothing more useful to its continued domination than moral corruption because a people seeking only the selfish pleasures of licentious behavior will forever be politically submissive to those who provide a panorama of gratifications.

Eliminating the Prerequisites for Popular and Public Political Action

Machiavelli offered a brilliant analysis of the prerequisites for popular political action, and in so doing, he also demonstrated how tyrants might stifle such political action. The scope and detail of Machiavelli's theories of popular political action are nowhere found in Plato, Aristotle, and Tacitus, and here Machiavelli made a major contribution both to theories of tyranny—in that tyrants must stop such political action—and to democratic theory. Early in the *Discourses* Machiavelli identified the turmoil of the Roman Republic, turmoil pitting patrician against plebeian, as the very source of Roman greatness: "I maintain that those who blame the quarrels of the Senate and the people of Rome condemn that which was the very origin of liberty, and that they were probably more impressed by the cries and noise which these disturbances occasioned *in the public*

---

118. *Discourses*, 1.55.254–55.
119. Cited by Allan Gilbert in his introduction to *History of Florence*, 1028.

places, than by the good effect which they produced."[120] Machiavelli suggested that in all republics there are two great parties, the party of the nobles and the party of the people, and the public clashes between these two parties preserve and enhance republican freedom. Indeed, "all the laws that are favorable to liberty result from the opposition of these parties to each other. . . . For good examples are the result of good education, and good education is due to good laws; and good laws in their turn spring from those very agitations which have been so inconsiderately condemned by many."[121] In this case public political action—and, as examples of such actions, Machiavelli mentioned debates in the assemblies, demonstrations, strikes and threatened strikes, threats to refuse to serve in the army, and even threats by the people to found a new city—made Rome great by bringing both energy and constitutional reform to the republic. What causes such action? Machiavelli answered that such action resulted because grand public issues brought people from their private homes and quite literally into public space—streets, parks, meeting halls, the seats of city governments, and so on—to debate reasonably and to clash turbulently.

Machiavelli did note that not all dissensions have this effect. Some dissensions are so violent that people retire back into their homes for the sake of security. Some dissensions, such as those pushed by the Gracchi in order to redistribute land, border on class warfare and are ruinous.[122] And finally some dissensions end by having one class win completely and dominate the other. If the people win, they tend toward anarchic license, whereas, if the nobles win, they establish a ruthless class tyranny over the people, and in either case, popular political action ceases. As long as dissensions and disturbances between the two classes do not end in complete victory for one of the classes, and as long as these clashes are concerned, not with a radical redistribution of property, but with the distribution of honors, with legal reform, with political reform, and even with selecting military strategy, then such clashes further popular political action and offer a healthy indication that the republic has vitality.

120. *Discourses,* 1.4.119 (emphasis added). Machiavelli never once used the word *politics* (*politica*), and there is not a single instance of a word from this root in *The Prince, The Art of War,* or *History of Florence.* He did occasionally use the adjective *political,* as in the phrase *political life* (*vivere politico*), in the *Discourses,* and he once used the adverb in the phrase *to live politically* (*vivere politicamente*). See J. H. Whitfield, "The Politics of Machiavelli," *Modern Language Review* 50, no. 4 (1955): 433–43, esp. 437–38.

121. *Discourses,* 1.4.119–20. Machiavelli's contemporaries were shocked by his praise of political turmoil. See Skinner, *The Foundations of Modern Political Thought,* 1:180–83, and Pocock, *The Machiavellian Moment,* 194–99.

122. *History of Florence,* 3.10.1154; *Discourses,* 1.37.210–12.

Machiavelli thought that the class that was able to dominate public discourse and the public sphere was the class with the most power. At times, Machiavelli meant this quite literally: whoever occupies the public arena or public space of a city is most powerful. After the people of Rome, for example, had seized the public space from the senate by means of their disturbances, they could extract concessions from the patrician class. When the people of Florence overthrew the tyranny of the duke of Athens, they "united and attacked the Public Square," while the duke's supporters "retired" to their private homes.[123] In the first draft of his *History of Florence,* Machiavelli expressed his hatred for the tyranny of Cosimo de' Medici more openly, and he depicted one of Cosimo's opponents as saying, "It is the duty therefore of a good citizen to find a remedy for this, to call the people to the Public Square, and to take over the government, in order to restore to the republic her liberty."[124] By contrast, the successful tyrant must dominate the public arena by eliminating it entirely, thus abolishing all public action and confining people to their private worlds. "The Duke [of Athens], when he had gained dominion, in order to deprive of influence those who were accustomed to act as liberty's defenders, forbade the Signors to hold their meetings in the Palace, and assigned them a private house."[125]

Public political action is extremely difficult to sustain, because the political world has dozens of centrifugal forces flinging people out of public space and into their private affairs. Great political issues do constitute one of the few countervailing centripetal forces because they demand—or a better word might be *necessitate*—that people engage in political action. "Men work either from necessity or from choice, and . . . virtue has more sway where labor is the result of necessity rather than of choice."[126] Political action occurs when citizens are pushed by necessity, by a *need* for a new order, not when people merely wish or dream or moralize about a new order. Machiavelli offered an excellent example of how difficult it is to sustain political action. After a defeat by the Gauls, many Romans went to live in Veii, but the senate soon commanded that they return by a certain time. At first, while united, they all ridiculed the senate's demand, but then each, one by one, "hastened to obey."

> And truly nothing can better illustrate the character of a multitude than this example; for they are often audacious and loud in

123. *History of Florence*, 2.37.1131; see also 2.39.1135.
124. Cited by Allan Gilbert in his introduction to *History of Florence*, 1028.
125. *History of Florence*, 2.36.1126.
126. *Discourses*, 1.1.107.

their denunciations of the decisions of their rulers, but when punishment stares them in the face, then, distrustful of each other, they rush to obey . . . and even if they are armed they will be easily subdued, if you can only shelter yourself against their first fury; for when their spirits are cooled down a little, and they see that they have all to return to their homes, they begin to mistrust themselves, and to think of their individual safety either by flight or submission. . . . United in one body they are brave and insolent, but when afterwards each begins to think of his own danger, they become cowardly and feeble.[127]

When people are united and together in public places, they will act politically, but when they return to their homes and begin to mistrust their fellow citizens and fear for their safety, they become passive and obedient. Those interested in popular action—which means only republics, because even mobilizing tyrannies cannot afford this sort of popular government—must recognize several prerequisites for political action. First, the people must have leadership. Second, the people must be united and organized, just as the plebeians were united and well organized in Rome. Similarly, an army will fight most effectively if the soldiers "know each other" and "have lived together for some time,"[128] phrases illustrating Aristotle's notion that political and military action must have the flavor of friends united and acting in common. Third, citizens must hold on to some public space—perhaps a park or a city square—that they occupy day and night, so that at any moment someone feeling anxious or afraid can join with at least some of his or her fellows. And finally, the people must feel a necessity to act in response to compelling political issues.

Over and over Machiavelli emphasized that great deeds by nations were usually a response to necessity (*necessità*) and rarely a reasoned decision. "Necessity compels [nations] to many acts to which reason will not influence them."[129] Just as the Venetians were "forced by necessity" to settle in the swamps for defensive purposes, the Romans became warlike out of a necessity to defend themselves against other peoples on the Italian peninsula. Necessity is not synonymous with inevitability, because the Venetians and the Romans had to respond intelligently to the demands at hand or perish, but still necessity compels action and frequently prompts great deeds. "We have already pointed out the advan-

127. *Discourses*, 1.57.259–60.
128. *Discourses*, 3.33.506.
129. *Discourses*, 1.6.129. On the concept of necessity, see F. Gilbert, *Machiavelli and Guicciardini*, 41.

tage of necessity in human actions, and to what glorious achievements it has given rise." In warfare, necessity is most apparent; "necessities may be many, but strongest is that which forces you to conquer or to die." Surrounded and threatened with death, even mediocre soldiers will be compelled by necessity to fight with "desperate fury," and thus "ancient commanders who well knew the powerful influence of necessity" sought to subject their own soldiers to necessity, while making certain that they did not turn a weak enemy into a powerful opponent by confronting this enemy with the same necessity. "Thus they often opened the way for the enemy to retreat, which they might easily have barred; and closed it to their own soldiers for whom they could with ease have kept it open."[130]

Tyrants can learn two lessons from this discussion of the prerequisites for political action. First, subjects will rebel only if pushed by necessity, so tyrants must never put subjects in such a situation. Second, successful tyrants must find ways to depoliticize people, remove them from the public arena, confine them to their private concerns, and content the people with private pleasures instead of public and political actions. In other words, a tyrant must take advantage of the welcome centrifugal forces that make sustaining political action so difficult.

Tyrants can accomplish these goals either by caressing or by annihilating their subjects, but caressing is probably far more effective; here Machiavelli offered observations similar to those of Aristotle and Tacitus, but elaborated them in much greater detail. The most successful tyrants are those who depoliticize their subjects in three different pleasurable ways: by allowing their subjects to amuse themselves, to busy themselves with acquiring goods, or to sequester themselves in the enjoyment of private pleasures. As to the first method, controlling the people through amusement, Machiavelli gave an example from the Medici rule of the fifteenth century. "While these disputes were boiling in the city, some of those grieved by the discords between the citizens decided to attempt to quiet them with some new pleasure." As a result, "the entire city was kept busy for many months" with festivals and celebrations, a strategy of pacifying and depoliticizing the people that Lorenzo the Magnificent used later in the century.[131] Machiavelli similarly advised in *The Prince* "to keep the people occupied with festivals and shows." The second method simply involves the recognition that people busy acquiring property have little time for political disturbances. Therefore, a tyrant "must encourage

---

130. *History of Florence*, 1.29.1068–69; *Discourses*, 3.12.450–51; *Art of War*, bk. 4, 662; *Discourses*, 3.12.451–53, also 1.45.231. For more on allowing an almost beaten enemy to retreat, see *Art of War*, bk. 6, 700–701.
131. *History of Florence*, 7.12.1352, 8.36.1433.

his citizens to follow their callings quietly, whether in commerce, or agriculture, or any other trade that men follow."[132] Finally, in a contribution not found in Plato, Aristotle, or Tacitus, Machiavelli acknowledged that romantic love, his legendary or infamous enjoyment of it notwithstanding, was a pleasant way to lose interest in political change. Once again in love, he wrote, "I have abandoned, then, the thoughts of affairs that are great and serious; I do not any more delight in reading ancient things or in discussing modern ones; they all turned into soft conversations, for which I thank Venus."[133] In employing these methods of "caressing" their subjects, tyrants make certain that their subjects feel no compelling necessity to undertake political action, and they confine their subjects to the private enjoyments of their private worlds. Thus, the public arena and public space remain strictly under tyrannical control.

Some tyrants will find it more effective to "annihilate" than to "caress," especially if they do not have wealth enough to buy a luxurious depoliticization. The key here is to disperse the subjects so that they cannot gather for common political action, much as dispersing a crowd leaves each person alone, fearful, and powerless. In his analyses, Machiavelli went well beyond Aristotle and Tacitus in examining what this really entails. Machiavelli noted that primitive peoples lived "dispersed" and thus formed cities for common defense; he praised Theseus, who "gathered the dispersed inhabitants" and formed Athens; and he noted that the Romans controlled some of their conquered territory by dispersing the former inhabitants.[134] Like Aristotle, Machiavelli regarded a dispersed people as almost literally a prepolitical people incapable of action. To keep the people isolated from one another and unable to organize may require fear and force. A tyrant must "destroy cities" and "transfer the inhabitants from one place to another"; similarly, "it will always be for his interest to keep the state disunited, so that each place and country shall recognize him only as master."[135] To control a conquered people determined to rebel, one must "scatter, disorganize, and destroy the people so completely that they can in no way injure you," because if you simply impoverish them, they still have weapons; if you take their weapons, they will fight you with sheer fury; and "if you kill the chiefs and continue to oppress the others, new chiefs will spring up like the heads of the Hydra." Within a city, one can somewhat effectively separate people and keep them from organizing simply by fear—for example, using spies, informers, and se-

132. *The Prince*, chap. 21, 85.
133. *Letters*, 165.
134. *Discourses*, 1.1.105–6, 2.23.359.
135. *Discourses*, 1.26.184, 2.2.283.

cret police—because people suspected of political opposition will be shunned by friends and relatives alike.[136]

Whether one who seeks a static tyranny keeps people out of the public arena by contenting them with the private pursuit of wealth and pleasure or by forcibly separating them so they cannot organize, either approach will eliminate the conditions of political action. The first plan has drawbacks because few tyrants will be generous enough to allow their people the enjoyments of festivals, commerce, and private pleasures. But the second plan may backfire because violence and terror may provoke the very necessity that drives subjects to desperate and rebellious action. These difficulties are minor and manageable, however, compared to those faced by a tyrant who seeks to mobilize the people for military action but simultaneously keep them quiet politically.

Parties, Factions, and Classes

As I have noted, Machiavelli saw in every republic two great parties opposed to one another, the party of the nobles and the party of the people. Machiavelli's discussion of the role of parties and classes in tyrannies was a major and unprecedented contribution to theories of tyranny. Although the party and class quarrels in Rome produced greatness, not all such conflict does. Consider first what happens if either of these great parties wins completely. Whereas the nobles desire to oppress, the people desire simply to avoid oppression. "For in every city these two opposite parties are to be found, arising from the desire of the populace to avoid the oppression of the great, and the desire of the great to command and oppress the people." Or, as he put it elsewhere, "since the people wish to live according to the laws and the powerful to control the laws, it is not possible for them to agree."[137] While the people want simply to live in freedom, and perhaps revenge themselves against their oppressors,[138] by contrast the ambition of the nobles is to dominate the state completely and oppress all other classes. To illustrate this, Machiavelli noted that the nobles of ancient Rome restrained themselves from oppressing the people as long as they needed the people to counterbalance the Tarquins, but once the Tarquins had been eliminated, the nobles revealed their natural "insolence" and resumed attacking the people.

---

136. *Discourses*, 2.24.363–64; also *The Prince*, chap. 5, 19; *History of Florence*, 7.17.1359.
137. *The Prince*, chap. 9, 35–36; *History of Florence*, 2.12.1093–94.
138. *Discourses*, 1.16.162–63.

The nobles seemed to have laid aside all their haughtiness and assumed popular manners, which made them supportable even to the lowest of the citizens. The nobility played this role so long as the Tarquins lived, without their motive being divined; for they feared the Tarquins, and also lest the ill-treated people might side with them. Their party therefore assumed all possible gentleness in their manners towards the people. But as soon as the death of the Tarquins had relieved them of their apprehensions, they began to vent upon the people all the venom they had so long retained within their breasts, and lost no opportunity to outrage them in every possible way.[139]

However much he hated the nobles, Machiavelli was not advocating a thoroughly democratic government, but rather a sharing or balancing of power between these two great antagonistic classes. The elimination of classes was for Machiavelli unthinkable, and the complete domination of either class was ruinous. Legislators must guard against both "the insolence of the nobles and the license of the populace" because, if a triumphant people would not be as oppressive as a victorious nobility, it would lead a city to another kind of oppression, a licentious servitude.[140] Ironically both classes clash under the banner of freedom, but freedom results only from the counterbalancing of the two.

Those cities, especially such as are not well organized, that are administered under the semblance of republican government [e.g., Florence], often vary their rulers and their constitutions not between liberty and slavery, as many believe, but between slavery and license. The promoters of license, who are the people, and the promoters of slavery, who are the nobles, praise the mere name of liberty, for neither of these classes is willing to be subject either to the laws or to men. . . . Such customs and laws [which restrain both classes] have been wanting to all those who have often varied their governments and are at present varying them from the tyrannical form to the licentious. . . . The tyrannical form does not satisfy good men; the licentious dissatisfies the wise. The first can do evil with ease; the second can do good with difficulty. In one, too much power is given to arrogant men; in the other, too much to stupid men.[141]

139. *Discourses*, 1.3.117–18, also 1.2.115–16, 1.37.211.
140. *Discourses*, 1.2.115.
141. *History of Florence*, 4.1.1187.

Like Marx, one of his finest pupils, Machiavelli offered a brilliant class analysis, but unlike Marx, Machiavelli regarded the elimination of classes as neither possible nor desirable, and instead saw only the inevitable clash of classes and at best a sharing of power.

Another development equally disastrous for a republic is conflict between factions. Plato and Aristotle spoke of factions, but never in so much depth. Whereas Machiavelli generally used the word *party* to indicate the organizations of the two great classes, nobles and people, within the republic, he used the word *faction* to indicate groups of partisans whose main focus was furthering the ambitions of a single individual, such as Julius Caesar or Cosimo de' Medici. Conflict between parties that represent a broad class vision of what is just in society is generally healthy for a republic, but a conflict between factions and their partisans is ruinous because it focuses all political concern not on what is best for the city as a whole but on the competition for narrow self-interest of individuals. "It is true that some divisions harm republics and some benefit them. Those do harm that are accompanied with factions and partisans; those bring benefit that are kept up without factions and without partisans."[142] Ancient Rome had grand parties clashing over general political principles and conflicting visions of the common good, whereas Renaissance Florence fell into self-seeking factions. "In Florence first there were factions among nobles, then factional struggles between the nobles and the middle class, finally between the middle class and the masses."[143]

How can a legislator know whether quarrels are beneficial or not? Machiavelli suggested that there are two ways to gain distinction in a republic, by acting for the common good (e.g., "winning a battle" or "advising the state wisely") and by acting only for personal self-interest (e.g., "doing favors to various citizens" or "pleasing the masses with games"). Citizens who gain great reputation by means of working for the common good will not form factions and seek partisans, whereas citizens who please the populace in order to further their personal ambitions will eventually form factions harmful to the general good. Whereas the early Roman Republic produced great citizens who worked for the common good and engaged in political disputes about what policies best served the republic, Florence produced ambitious individuals, leaders of fac-

---

142. *History of Florence*, 7.1.1336. Sometimes Machiavelli used the words *party* and *faction* interchangeably. For a somewhat different interpretation of Machiavelli's analysis of parties, see Harvey Mansfield Jr., "Party and Sect in Machiavelli's *Florentine Histories*," in *Machiavelli and the Nature of Political Thought*, ed. Fleisher, 209–66.

143. *History of Florence*, preface, 1031–32.

tions, scrambling for their own selfish interests.[144] In Florence, factions made "laws and statutes not for the public benefit but for their own; hence wars, truces, alliances [were] decided not for the common glory but for the pleasure of a few." Ambitious individuals in republics seek "partisans, and from partisans arise factions in cities, and factions cause [the cities'] ruin," but this can only happen if an individual is "exceedingly rich" and thus able to buy the support of partisan followers, which is exactly the description Machiavelli applied to Cosimo de' Medici. Cosimo used his "excessive wealth" to bribe "all the heads of the common people" and to ensure that Florentine "soldiers [were] all his partisans."[145]

Although Machiavelli twice said that to establish a republic one needs both "equality" and the destruction of the nobility,[146] he did not mean by this some sort of classless society, because, as we have seen, there will always be the two great classes in any society. He meant that these classes must share power, that members of each class must have access both to public office and to honors, and that powerful, aristocratic individuals cannot have political, economic, or military resources that allow them to stand outside the laws. By contrast, tyranny arises when one class dominates entirely and looks to one individual, the tyrant, to defend its interests. "The necessity of creating the tyranny of the Decemvirs in Rome arose from the same causes that generally produce tyrannies in cities; that is to say, the too great desire of the people to be free, and the equally too great desire of the nobles to dominate. And if the two parties do not agree to secure liberty by law, and either the one or the other throws all its influence in favor of one man, then a tyranny is the natural result."[147] Machiavelli continued by noting that any tyrant raised to power by the people will move first to destroy the nobility and then to crush the people. Nevertheless, eventually—and this is the central point—all tyrannies, according to Machiavelli, must rest on a class foundation, either on the people or on the nobility.

According to the principles of military organization discussed above, a mobilizing tyranny must rely on popular favor, and this is the advice that Machiavelli consistently gave openly in *The Prince* and by implication in the *Art of War*. Early in *The Prince,* Machiavelli said a prince can govern in one of two ways, either personally with the help of chosen ministers or by means of nobles who "have states and subjects of their own," and

144. *History of Florence*, 7.1.1337.
145. *History of Florence*, 3.5.1146; *Discourses*, 1.7.132, 1.34.202; cited by Allan Gilbert in his introduction to *History of Florence*, 1028. See also 7.2.1335, 7.10.1350.
146. *Discourses*, 1.55.256; *Remodelling the Government of Florence*, 106–7.
147. *Discourses*, 1.40.222; see also *The Prince*, chap. 9, 36.

Machiavelli quickly advised against relying on the nobility.[148] Again and again Machiavelli advised his prince to gain the favor of the people, to use the power of the people, and of course to arm the people. This is advice that he offered in other places; in *The Discourses,* he noted that "those tyrants who have the masses for friends and the nobles for enemies are more secure in the possession of their power, because their despotism is sustained by a greater force than that of those who have the people as their enemies and the nobles for their friends."[149] Whenever he gave this advice, however, he was advising a tyrant who, he hoped, would tap into the energy of the people for purposes of military expansion and national unification.

By contrast, Machiavelli advised anyone who wished to establish a static tyranny to establish "great inequality" and to dominate the people by means of a tamed nobility. "Whoever desires to establish a kingdom or principality where liberty and equality prevail, will equally fail, unless he withdraws from that general equality a number of the boldest and most ambitious spirits, and makes gentlemen of them, not merely in name but in fact, by giving to them castles and possessions, as well as money and subjects; so that surrounded by these he may be able to maintain his power, and that by his support they may satisfy their ambition."[150] Over and over, this is the kind of tyranny that Machiavelli described. Cosimo de' Medici relied on a handful of "great nobles," used his enormous wealth to bribe this nobility, and, despite maintaining the illusion that Florence was a republic, had in fact become the "buyer" of a republic eager to sell itself.[151] Even Caesar Borgia sought to control Rome by bribing key nobles within Rome and giving them offices and military commands. When Machiavelli wrote about how one might reorganize the government of Florence, he said that in order to establish a princedom, one would have to set up "noble lords of walled towns . . . , who in support of the prince would with their arms and their followers stifle the city and the whole province. A prince alone, lacking a nobility, cannot support the

148. *The Prince*, chap. 4, 15. For a discussion of Machiavelli's regime in which a prince rules with his appointed officials or ministers, see Harvey C. Mansfield, "Machiavelli's New Regime," *Italian Quarterly* 13, no. 52 (1970): 63–95.

149. *Discourses*, 1.40.223.

150. *Discourses*, 1.55.256–57.

151. *History of Florence*, 5.4.1237–38, 7.5.1342, 4.27.1220–21. Machiavelli was correct when he claimed that the Florentine nobility intermixed with the business classes (*The Natures of Florentine Men*, 1437), and the Medici did rule along with only a few members of the patrician class. See Gene Brucker, *Renaissance Florence* (New York: John Wiley & Sons, 1969), 85–89, 97, 102–5, 124, 257.

weight of a princedom."[152] In other words, tyrants who wish to enjoy life quietly need to surround themselves with nobles.

A number of lessons for tyrants emerge from this discussion. First, only in republics does one find the clash of grand parties that is so important to popular political action and free government. Second, tyranny is class rule, the domination of one class by another, with the tyrant as the focus of power but not necessarily the locus of power. Third, a static tyranny must rely on a few powerful nobles, who in turn contribute their own factions and their own partisans, to dominate the government and control the people. And finally, a mobilizing tyranny must rely on the people against the nobility.

Will a Mobilizing Tyranny Lead to Political Regeneration?

Although in Machiavelli's writings the analysis of tyranny did take center stage, Machiavelli wrote his analyses with a passion, with a wish that other actors, at that moment languishing in supporting roles, could hasten to center stage. In virtually all of Machiavelli's analyses, he was asking whether it was possible to bring about a political regeneration in Italy, by which he meant genuine republican government and genuine republican *virtù*. Could Italy find its way to a new beginning? No one deserved more praise than one who founded a new religion, a new republic, or a new kingdom, but nothing was more perilous. "It must be considered that there is nothing more difficult to carry out, nor more doubtful of success, nor more dangerous to handle, than to initiate a new order of things." However difficult, such a new order of things is possible; indeed, "not believing that anything can happen that has not happened" is only a very natural human defect.[153]

Who might bring about this political regeneration? (This is a question that Machiavelli had in common with Plato, but with a very different definition of "regeneration.") Not an Italian prince, since Machiavelli saw no prospect for a Moses, a Theseus, or a Romulus among the likes of the Medici. Machiavelli's hope for political regeneration lay with the people and and followed from the proposition that political power will follow military power; if a prince armed the people, he might relinquish power

152. *Remodelling the Government of Florence*, 107; on Caesar Borgia, see *The Prince*, chap. 7, 26.

153. *The Prince*, chap. 6, 21; *Letters*, 130; *Discourses*, 1.10.141.

to the people. Support for this argument comes from one of the finest commentators on Machiavelli, Federico Chabod, who looked upon Machiavelli's recommendation for a citizen army as a mistake: "However, [Machiavelli] fails to perceive that such a revolution in the military art must have its counterpart in a political and social regeneration. . . . The mere enunciation of the new military theory must inevitably entail the abandonment of the concept of the Prince."[154] Perhaps Machiavelli did not just make a mistake, but instead thought that, just possibly, a tyrant who mobilized a citizen army would sow the seeds of political regeneration.

At first glance, this thesis seems impossible, because Machiavelli said that founding new republics "must be the work of one man only." When he added, however, that such political transformation "never or rarely" happens otherwise, we begin to wonder whether there are rare moments when a people rejuvenates itself. Certainly much of the *Discourses* is a hymn to the virtues of the people. "Governments of the people are better than those of princes," said Machiavelli, because "the cities where the people are masters make the greatest progress in the least possible time," and because "the people are vastly superior [to princes] in all that is good and glorious." Although the people sometimes misjudge general matters, they are almost unfailingly correct on particular matters and the particular needs of the moment.[155] Indeed, Machiavelli endowed the people with great prudence and prescience. The "people are more prudent and stable, and have better judgment than a prince; and it is not without good reason that it is said, 'The voice of the people is the voice of God'; for we see popular opinion prognosticate events in such a wonderful manner that it would almost seem as if the people had some occult virtue, which enables them to foresee the good and the evil."[156]

Machiavelli loved republican institutions because they brought popular freedom but also because they served the common good and brought greatness, glory, and power. For four hundred years, the people of the Roman Republic were "lovers of the glory and common good of their country." Although the Roman Republic was unique, it is not unique to find that republics most easily attain greatness and best serve the com-

---

154. Federico Chabod, *Machiavelli and the Renaissance*, trans. David Moore (New York: Harper & Row, 1965), 16. Another reader of Machiavelli's *The Prince* also concluded that the advice would not really work; in one of his letters, Tocqueville wrote, "As I see it, the student of Machiavelli would be constantly encumbered in his own ruses; while trying to fortify himself on one side, he always opens himself somewhere else." Alexis de Tocqueville, *Selected Letters on Politics and Society*, ed. Roger Boesche, trans. James Toupin and Roger Boesche (Berkeley and Los Angeles: University of California Press, 1985), 110.

155. *Discourses*, 1.9.138, 1.58.264, 1.47.233–37.

156. *Discourses*, 1.58.263.

mon good. "Only those cities and countries that are free can achieve greatness," wrote Machiavelli, but it is "the general good that makes cities great; and certainly the general good is regarded nowhere but in republics."[157] Perhaps, under special circumstances, a people might well bring about its own political regeneration.

Certainly Machiavelli's sympathies in Florentine politics were with the people. We know from that famous letter in which he described how he spent his days, before he entered his study to escape to ancient times, that he spent his time with the working people—"a butcher, a miller, two furnace tenders"—of Florence. Similarly, Machiavelli confided to a friend that he saw the affairs of the world with the "[mirror] of the many."[158] There is even evidence that he wrote his works for the people. In his "Greeting" prefacing the *Discourses,* he said, "I . . . do not address myself to such as are princes, but to those who by their infinite good qualities are worthy to be such; not to those who could load me with honors, rank, and wealth, but rather to those who have the desire to do so, but have not the power. For to judge rightly, men should esteem . . . those who would know how to govern states, rather than those who have the right to govern, but lack the knowledge."[159] Surely the *Discourses* is a book that suggested that the people are those "worthy to be" princes, that the people are the ones who know "how to govern states," and if so, then the *Discourses* is a book addressed to the people. So, I argue, is *The Prince.* In just about the middle of *The Prince,* Machiavelli wrote, "But my intention being to write something of use *to those who understand,* it appears to me more proper to go to the real truth of the matter than to its imagination."[160] Who, we ask, are "those who understand"? Again we get a clue from the dedication. There Machiavelli said, "for in the same way that landscape painters station themselves in the valleys in order to draw mountains or high ground, and ascend an eminence in order to get a good view of the plains, so it is necessary to be a prince to know thoroughly the nature of the people, and one of the populace to know the nature of princes."[161] Thus, as it turns out, the people are "those who

---

157. *Discourses,* 1.58.263; 2.2.287, 282. For a discussion of what Machiavelli meant by the word *freedom* (*libertà*), see Marcia L. Colish, "The Idea of Liberty in Machiavelli," *Journal of the History of Ideas* 32, no. 3 (1971): 323–50.

158. *Letters,* 142, 97.

159. *Discourses,* "Greeting," 102.

160. *The Prince,* chap. 15, 56 (emphasis added).

161. *The Prince,* dedication, 4. Strauss noted that Machiavelli "teaches subjects what they should expect from their prince, or the truth about the nature of princes" (*Thoughts on Machiavelli,* 77). Although my view seems to be at odds with Gramsci's famous claim that Machiavelli wrote "to give a political education to 'those who do not know,'" I think these

understand," and *The Prince* was written for them. The people, however, understand princes just as one who lives in the valley understands the mountain, that is, because he or she is constantly affected by it—the shadow it casts, the weather it brings, and so on. Similarly, the people understand princes because they know the tyrannical results—the arrests, the cruelty, the taxes, and so forth. Machiavelli wrote *The Prince,* at least in part, so that those who know the effects of princes may know the day-to-day behavior of princes, so they may "go to the real truth of the matter [rather] than to its imagination." Because tyrants since time immemorial have known how to deceive, how to use religion, and when to be cruel, do they really need Machiavelli's book? All of this, however, adds additional meaning to Machiavelli's advice to learn "how steep the mountains are" and to ask oneself constantly such questions as, "If the enemy were on that hill and we found ourselves here with our army, which of us would have the advantage?"[162]

Even if this is true, how might the people bring about political regeneration? a question that leads to Machiavelli's famous uses of the words *fortuna* and *virtù.* What did Machiavelli mean when he used this word *fortuna*? Sometimes he used the word almost the way we would use the words *luck* or *chance,* as when he complained that people in his time yielded too readily to fortune and "let things be ruled by chance." At other times, in describing fortune as the "arbiter of all human things" or in depicting fortune's "furious onrush" that "shifts and reshifts the world's affairs," Machiavelli seemed to liken fortune to fate. In fact, Machiavelli saw fortune neither as blind chance to which we must resign ourselves nor as a fatalistic force to which we must submit, and he even complained of lazy leaders who do not even aspire to "rule" fortune.[163]

If we cannot control fortune entirely, neither are we always passive spectators buffeted by the winds of fortune's changes. "Nevertheless, that our freedom may not be altogether extinguished, I think it may be true that fortune is the ruler of half of our actions. . . . I would compare her to an impetuous river that, when turbulent, inundates the plains, casts down trees and buildings, . . . when it is quiet, men can make provision against

---

views are quite similar. I am suggesting that Machiavelli was writing for those who knew the oppressive effects of tyranny but did not know how to attain and hold political power; despite the difference in language, this is essentially Gramsci's argument. See Antonio Gramsci, "The Modern Prince," in *The Modern Prince and Other Writings,* trans. Louis Marks (New York: International Publishers, 1957), 135–88, esp. 142.

162. *The Prince,* chap. 14, 54–55. Again, I must acknowledge my debt to Professor Peter Breiner for the insights of the previous paragraph.

163. *The Prince,* chap. 25, 91; *The Life of Castruccio Castracani,* 533; "Tercets on Fortune," 748; *Art of War,* 624.

it by dykes and banks, so that when it rises it will either go into a canal or its rush will not be so wild and dangerous. So it is with fortune, which shows her power where no measures have been taken to resist her."[164] Fortune corresponds to what Machiavelli elusively called "the needs of the times" or the "time and circumstances" that surround us at any given moment.[165] Whereas at some times and in some circumstances a cautious person or a cautious nation will succeed remarkably, at other times and in other circumstances caution will fail because bold and daring action is required. Fortune is on your side if your temperament—cautious or daring, cruel like Hannibal or humane like Scipio—corresponds to the needs of the time. "That man is fortunate who harmonizes his proceedings with his time, but on the contrary he is not fortunate who in his actions is out of harmony with his time and with the type of its affairs." If people were wise enough and prudent enough to change their way of proceeding, if the cautious person could toss caution to the wind at just the right moment, then he or she could master fortune. "If one could change one's nature with time and circumstances, fortune would never change." Because few are wise enough and virtually no one is able to change his or her temperament at will, fortune too often "commands men, and holds them under her yoke." Savonarola was very successful as long as he could "keep on working with the times and making his lies plausible,"[166] but when the times changed and called for him to use different tactics, he could not change with the times and, as a consequence, failed. Both Hannibal and Scipio were fortunate because, had the former tried to conquer Italy with humanity and had the latter tried to conquer Spain with cruelty, both would have found their temperaments at variance with the needs of the times and would quite likely have failed.[167]

To the prudent and virtuous individual, fortune will eventually present an "occasion" or an "opportunity," a moment when that individual's temperament and way of proceeding accords with the time, a moment when wise action will succeed. "It certainly is the course of Fortune, when she wishes to effect some great result, to select for her instrument a man of such spirit and ability that he will recognize the opportunity which is afforded him."[168] Although Machiavelli described such a man as an "instru-

---

164. *The Prince*, chap. 25, 91.
165. *The Prince*, chap. 25, 92–93. See Thomas Flanagan, "The Concept of *Fortuna* in Machiavelli," in *The Political Calculus*, ed. Parel, 127–56.
166. *Letters*, 99, 98; *The Prince*, chap. 25, 93; *Letters*, 99, 88.
167. *Letters*, 100.
168. *Discourses*, bk. 2, introduction, 274; 2.29.382.

ment," nevertheless such a man must have spirit, ability, and insight in order to take advantage of the opportunity. Certainly Machiavelli saw himself as one waiting for an opportunity, a victim of fortune, a man of great ability who might have accomplished great deeds in another age. "And since Fortune wants to do everything, she wishes us to let her do it, to be quiet, and not to give her trouble, and to wait for a time when she will allow something to be done by men; and then will be the time for you to work harder, to stir things up more, and for me to leave my farm and say: 'Here I am.'"[169] At any rate, young men who are wise, prudent, and virtuous have the best chance of mastering fortune. In a famous passage, Machiavelli described fortune as a woman who was a friend to young men, a woman more likely to favor the bold over the cautious, the passionate over the coldly calculating. "Fortune is a woman, and it is necessary, if you wish to master her, to conquer her by force."[170]

People prepare against fortune and seek to master fortune with those twin qualities of the ancient Romans, "virtue and prudence."[171] Prudence (*prudenza*) is the wisdom of experience, the foresight needed by any leader, and the ability "to know the nature of the difficulties." Machiavelli said flatly, "Fortune's malice can be overcome with prudence."[172] Virtue (*virtù*) is the quality that Machiavelli most often juxtaposed to fortune, and when Machiavelli and his fellow Florentines used the word *virtue* it had a variety of connotations. It often had the connotation of serving the common good, but it did not correspond to the Christian meaning of virtue as goodness and even piety; it suggested energy, courage, daring, and strength of will, but it also suggested action from intelligence and insight; it suggested excellence, but also the resolve to put this excellence into effect; most of all the word *virtue* suggested mastery and control, both of oneself and of the situation, very much like our word *virtuosity*, but several significant steps away from Plato's and Aristotle's use of excellence or virtue, that is, *aretē*. Felix Gilbert put it well: "[B]asically *virtù* was an italianization of the Latin word *virtus* and denoted the fundamental quality of man which enables him to achieve great works and deeds."[173] Just as an individual can possess virtue, so can a nation, an

169. *Letters*, 140.

170. *The Prince*, chap. 25, 94; *Letters*, 98.

171. *The Prince*, chap. 3, 11.

172. *The Prince*, chap. 21, 84–85; *History of Florence*, 3.5.1148. On prudence, see Fleisher, "A Passion for Politics," 139.

173. F. Gilbert, *Machiavelli and Guicciardini*, 179. For more on Machiavelli's use of the word *virtù*, see John Plamenatz, "In Search of Machiavellian *Virtù*," in *The Political Calculus*, ed. Parel, 157–78; Pocock, *The Machiavellian Moment*, chap. 6, 156–82.

army, or a body of citizens, but most of all Machiavelli looked to what he called "innovators,"[174] who had the virtue required to seize an opportunity given by fortune and to change the world successfully.

Could it be that, for Machiavelli, the real innovators were not the princes but the people? Consider first that Machiavelli saw nations as always changing in a cyclical fashion, "either ascending or declining,"[175] and since Italy had declined about as far as it could, then quite possibly the cycle would turn and Italy would rise. "When [nations] have gone down and through their defects have reached the lowest depths, they necessarily rise, since they cannot go lower." And what pushes nations to change? The answer is *necessità*. "States naturally either rise or decline, and necessity compels them to many acts to which reason will not influence them."[176] In one passage Machiavelli said that "necessity teaches us," and in another passage he quoted Livy to the effect that necessity is "the last and most powerful weapon."[177] Machiavelli well knew that he could not persuade either corrupt princes or corrupt peoples to bring about a political regeneration. But suppose a situation arose in which necessity taught what Machiavelli could not teach, a situation in which a people felt first necessity and then opportunity for bold public and political action. Such action rarely occurs as a result of moral conviction and principled choice, but instead from necessity.

Machiavelli tried to establish just such a situation when he advocated, both in *The Prince* and in *The Art of War,* a prince or tyrant who would mobilize a citizen army for national unification. Surely Machiavelli knew that a clash between a tyrant who wanted political power and a people who had military power would ensue; and surely, after having advised his prince to be feared rather than loved and to use cruelty when necessary and not to keep faith with the people, since they will not keep faith with you, Machiavelli thought it possible that the people would feel a compelling necessity to rebel, that necessity would teach them of the possibility of popular government. For evidence to support this hypothesis, note that Machiavelli wrote *The Prince* in the second half of 1513, and at that moment in his letters he was describing the Swiss as being pushed by necessity to fight and achieve great deeds.

174. *The Prince*, chap. 6, 22. For a discussion of "innovators" in Renaissance Italian politics, see Pocock, *The Machiavellian Moment*, chap. 6, 156–82.

175. *Discourses*, bk. 2, introduction, 272. See Robert Orr, "The Time Motif in Machiavelli," in *Machiavelli and the Nature of Political Thought*, ed. Fleisher, 185–208.

176. *History of Florence*, 5.1.1232; *Discourses*, 1.6.129.

177. *History of Florence*, 3.13.1159; *Discourses*, 3.12.454. See Harvey C. Mansfield Jr., "Necessity in the Beginnings of Cities," in *The Political Calculus*, ed. Parel, 101–25.

You will see that at first it is enough for men to defend themselves and not to be mastered by others; from this they go on to injure others and to try to master others. For the Swiss it was at first enough to defend themselves from the dukes of Austria. . . . [Their success] has put in their minds an ambitious spirit and a desire to try carrying on war for themselves . . . they often talked among themselves about the efficiency of their military organization, and that it was like that of the Romans, and why could they not one day do as the Romans did? . . . as I said to you about something else, things go along gradually, and often men are led by necessity to do what it was not their intention to do, and the habit of bodies of people is to go slowly.[178]

Machiavelli noted in the *Discourses* that people fight first from necessity but afterward from ambition,[179] and just possibly, he thought, the clash between a tyrant who wished to rule absolutely and the citizen army the tyrant had mobilized would create a necessity for popular rebellion. Afterward, such a disciplined citizen army would fight for its own ambition and for the ambitions of a divided Italy. In other words, a mobilizing tyranny contains a contradiction that might destroy it. All of this sheds new light on the last chapter of *The Prince,* in which Machiavelli exhorted Italy to liberate itself from the "barbarians." In his *History of Florence* Machiavelli made it clear that he regarded the "barbarians" as the princes, or tyrants, who had divided and ruined Italy, and in the *Discourses* he described the only remedy for a tyrannical prince. "A licentious and mutinous people may easily be brought back to good conduct by the influence and persuasion of a good man, but an evil-minded prince is not amenable to such influences, and therefore there is no other remedy against him but cold steel."[180]

Conclusion

Machiavelli certainly made observations about tyranny similar to those made by Plato, Aristotle, and Tacitus. These include the facts that tyrants

---

178. *Letters*, 129, 136. The last sentence is from a second letter, also written in August 1513 and also to Francesco Vettori. On determining when Machiavelli wrote *The Prince*, see Chabod, *Machiavelli and the Renaissance*, 33–36.

179. *Discourses*, 1.37.208.

180. *Discourses*, 1.58.265. On Machiavelli's reference to Italian princes as barbarians, see *History of Florence*, 5.1.1233.

must make use of violence, and thus must have bodyguards, spies, police, and personally controlled paramilitary forces; must isolate subjects in their private homes, thus rendering them powerless to organize; should transform the state into a tyranny slowly, so that the tyrant can keep the appearances of legality, normalcy, and stability of the old order; must use deception in order at least to appear to be frugal, merciful, humane, and religious; should make certain that they use the authority of religion to buttress their own power and perceived legitimacy; must pacify the population by encouraging a corruption of morals and allowing subjects to chase private pleasures—wealth, comfort, sensual pleasure, and so forth—that are no threat to the regimes of tyrants.

As one of history's most brilliant political theorists, however, Machiavelli certainly made a number of original contributions to theories of tyranny, contributions either entirely new or new in emphasis and elaboration. First, Machiavelli's whole approach to studying political phenomena, including tyrannies, constitutes a major break with Plato, Aristotle, and to a lesser extent Tacitus. Machiavelli avoided almost entirely philosophical questions about what a tyranny is and why it is evil. Rather, he asked how tyrannies come about, how they work, how they change, how they can be overthrown, and so forth. Not Platonic speculation about tyranny, but instead a genealogy of tyranny. Machiavelli's genealogy is wrapped up in his concept of *necessità* because societies originate in response to necessity. The Venetians settled swamps out of a necessity for defense, Rome became warlike out of necessity, the Roman plebeians clamored for a republic out of necessity to avoid oppression, and a ruling class establishes a tyranny out of necessity for survival and privilege. While he avoided determinism with this concept, he did present a sophisticated political sociology. In talking about the origin of morality, Machiavelli gave us a genealogy of morals long before Marx and Nietzsche. After societies formed themselves, Machiavelli noted, and they originated in the "necessity for uniting themselves for defense," they chose leaders and established laws and rules of right and wrong in order to preserve society and punish those who injured others. Upon completing this discussion, Machiavelli announced, "such was the origin of justice."[181] How different from Plato!

Second, Machiavelli's discussions of terror and violence far surpass those of Aristotle and Tacitus both in scope and detail. Machiavelli discussed when terrorizing a population is useful and when it is counterproductive, when violence should be selective and when it must be all-

---

181. *Discourses*, 1.2.112.

encompassing, who must undertake the violence and how the tyrant should avoid appearing responsible, how violence against the nobility is necessary to establish a republic but violence against the people is necessary for a prince, and so on. It is an anatomy of the uses of violence so complete that it resembles Aristotle's biological classifications more than his passing thoughts on the role of violence in politics. Third, Machiavelli discussed more thoroughly than any previous thinker the link between tyrannical rule and military power. To take a few examples, he warned princes and republics not to rely on mercenaries, because they may not fight energetically and they may be unreliable; he noted that republics must arm the people and fight with a people's army; he maintained that princes must rely on the private armies of nobles, but that this is risky because every noble aspires to be the prince; he openly discussed how a tyrant must get the credit for victories but the generals blame for defeats; he warned that a prince plays a dangerous game if he relies on others to oversee the military, because political power often follows military power; and in his *Art of War* he discussed military strategy at length. No thinker before Machiavelli saw so clearly the difficulties of a tyrant's relying on military leaders without being supplanted by them.

Fourth, Machiavelli made an important distinction between what I have called static tyrannies and mobilizing tyrannies, a distinction not found in Plato, Aristotle, or Tacitus (whose Roman Empire was expanding less than it was maintaining its borders). Plato and Aristotle focused mainly on static, stay-at-home tyrannies, the kind they found in Greek city-states. Machiavelli knew these well because most of the Italian city-states of the Renaissance fit this description. To pacify their subjects static tyrannies use spies, informers, and fear, rely on a powerful nobility, depoliticize the population either from fear or by encouraging the private pursuit of wealth and pleasure, isolate citizens in their private spheres, and so on. Tyrants who want to rule mobilizing tyrannies, however, have the tricky task of harnessing popular energy for imperial and military expansion without losing control of the tyranny. Machiavelli had doubts that in fact a tyrant could ride this tyrannical steed without falling off, that just perhaps a tyrant who mobilized a people's army would inadvertently create a popular government such as a republic. But the notion of a mobilizing tyranny surely is necessary to begin to explain Alexander, Julius Caesar, Cromwell, Napoleon, Mussolini, Hitler, Stalin, Mao Zedong, Ho Chi Minh, and so on.

Fifth, Machiavelli's political vocabulary became more complex than that of classical thinkers because his analyses were more complex. One can see this particularly in his discussion of classes, political parties, and factions. Machiavelli argued that all societies are divided into at least two grand classes—one composed of the nobles and a second composed of the people. (When he spoke occasionally of a middle class, we suspect he knew this schema was somewhat simplified.) Whereas republics need to give considerable power to the people, a "prince alone, lacking a nobility, cannot support the weight of a princedom." Long before Marx, Machiavelli was arguing that political quarrels are class-based quarrels, a political sociology that takes him well past Greek discussions of rich and poor, or of the one, the few, and the many. Machiavelli also gave us our first sustained discussion of political parties, which, in his opinion, embrace the grand ideals as well as the self-serving ideas of one of these two classes, the class of the nobles or that of the people. He even argued that a counterbalancing and competition of these parties was healthy for republican government. By contrast, factions, which he defined as groups whose followers are dedicated to the private and selfish interests of some individual noble, tear apart republics, but may in fact buttress tyrannies. His differentiation between political parties and factions is similar to Tocqueville's distinction between great parties and little parties. Only Marx, Weber, and Neumann have given us a more sophisticated political sociology.

Sixth, Machiavelli is perhaps the greatest theorist of popular political action, which means he knew best how to thwart a tyranny that tries to eliminate such action. Machavelli suggested that one could measure the degree to which a state was republican by determining how much the people occupy public space—streets, parks, city halls, meeting halls of all kinds, and so forth. Princes and the nobility endeavor constantly to eliminate public space by pushing the people out of it by force, by turning politics into state rule in which administrators and not the people make political decisions, and by enticing people into private worlds with the gleam of wealth and pleasure. Isolated and powerless in their private worlds, the people become fearful, tame, and submissive in the face of class and state power. By contrast, popular government eliminates the "art of the state" and state administration and replaces this with popular decision making, and it forces open public space for public debates, even with the nobility, about the general good. While Machiavelli certainly absorbed Aristotle's distinction between the public polis and the private household, he analyzed the consequences of this distinction in much greater detail. Seventh and finally, Machiavelli returned to Plato's despairing question of how one brings political regeneration to a corrupt and tyrannical political order. Plato could only suggest banishing all above the age of ten and then educating the rest, leaving the question of who will educate the educators. Machiavelli saw the only possible political regeneration emerging from popular political action, action taken when a people, out of *necessità,* must attain *virtù* to establish an ethic, laws, and popular institutions to defend itself. In brief, if Machiavelli is perhaps the greatest theorist of tyranny, he is also the greatest theorist of how popular government can defeat tyranny.

5

MONTESQUIEU'S TWO THEORIES OF DESPOTISM

Fearing Monarchs and Merchants

Although he did not invent the word *despotism,* Montesquieu more than any other author established it in that lexicon of political and politicized words—words such as *individualism, socialism, capitalism, bureaucracy,* and *culture*—invented in the last three centuries in response either to specific political necessities or to more general political goals. In this case, the opponents of Louis XIV's arbitrary uses of power apparently invented the French word *despotisme* in the 1690s. The root of this word is, of course, Greek, and in ancient Greek usage, a despot (*despotēs*) was technically a master who ruled in a household over those who were slaves or servile by nature, including women. For Aristotle, however, the noun *despot* and the adjective *despotic* (*despotikos*) had political connotations because such despotic rule was in a sense appropriate not only for most servants and slaves within a household but for all, such as barbarians, who were unable to be free. "For barbarians," wrote Aristotle, "being more servile in character than Hellenes, and Asiatics than Europeans, do not rebel against a despotic government."[1] On occasion, Aris-

---

1. Aristotle, *The Politics*, 1285a19–21; also 1285b2–4 (B. Jowett translation).
 A large part of this chapter has previously been published as "Fearing Monarchs and Merchants: Montesquieu's Two Theories of Despotism," *Western Political Quarterly* 43, no. 4 (1990): 741–61.

totle even used the words *despotic* and *tyrannical* interchangeably, but when discussing the misuse of political power, Aristotle most often used the words *tyrant* (*tyrannos*) and *tyranny* (*tyrannis*) and focused his attention on analyzing the political phenomenon of tyranny. Because Latin writers in this case guarded their own political nomenclature, there were no Latin words derived from the Greek *despotēs,* that is, until thirteenth-century translations of Aristotle.

Not until the seventeenth century did the word *despotic* surface in an important way again—ironically at the hand of a sworn enemy of Aristotle—when Hobbes, thoroughly familar with Greek and ever mindful of defining terms carefully, quite consciously introduced the adjectives *despotic* and *despotical* into the political vocabulary of his tumultuous century. To Hobbes, despotic government was specifically that originating in conquest, which made it no less legitimate than any other government. If Hobbes, however, sought to erase the Greek connotation of despotic government as evil, his French counterparts, intent on attacking absolute monarchy, had no such wish. The French word *despotique* first emerged when the pamphleteers for the Fronde attacked Cardinal Mazarin, who was ruling in Louis XIV's name, but by the end of the seventeenth century writers, and again especially pamphleteers, were using such phrases as *monarchie despotique, pouvoir despotique, puissance despotique,* and *gouvernement despotique* in their protests against the extension of royal power. In 1704 Pierre Bayle apparently became the first writer of distinction to use the word *despotisme.* And now an old and altered Greek word served a new and political French purpose. Those who complained of the despotic power of Louis XIV—writers such as Fénelon and the Duc de Saint-Simon—were by and large defending the interests of the privileged; they protested against monarchical encroachments on the *parlements,* they supported the traditional privileges of the feudal nobility, and they complained of the moral corruption brought by mercantilism and the new commercial interests. These writers also knew both Aristotle and the Greek language well, and they were quite content, even eager, to suggest that *despotisme* was a political system appropriate to barbarians and Asians, especially to Turks, Persians, and Chinese. And thus, by warning that the French monarchy was becoming a despotism, they were suggesting that France was marching toward the alleged absolutism and unthinking uniformity of Asiatic servitude. Like Aristotle, Montesquieu used a caricature of non-European governments to analyze his own time.

By the time the concept of despotism came to Montesquieu in the first half of the eighteenth century, it had all of these connotations of aristocratic alarm over what was regarded as a French monarchy coming to resemble an Asian empire. Montesquieu did little to alter this concept of despotism; he only filled in gaps and smoothed over what was roughly defined. But in the process, he gave to his century an understanding of this word *despotisme* that had enormous intellectual and political consequences. The word *despotisme* "became a fundamental element in the political doctrine which contemporaries considered to be one of the greatest achievements of the modern age: [Montesquieu's] *De l'És-prit des lois*. This book caused the word [*despotisme*] to acquire a significance even more momentous than that intended for it by the critics of Louis XIV. It is no exaggeration to say that the concept of *despotisme* played a part in the intellectual and political unrest which drove the French monarchy down to the Revolution."[2] But is Montesquieu's theory of despotism as straightforward and clear as his commentators suggest?

Montesquieu's theory of despotism confronts the reader with contradictory claims. On the one hand, Montesquieu described a harsh despotism characterized by fear, violence, isolation, and a general poverty supporting at best a subsistence living. On the other hand, he depicted a despotism distinguished by avarice, pleasure, urbanization, and at least enough production and commerce to distribute luxuries to some significant portion of the population. Montesquieu, in fact, offered two theories of despotism. The first reflected his fear of an ever more powerful monarch, swallowing up intermediate institutions, subverting the judiciary, concentrating all power in the monarchy and its Intendants, and transforming nobles into commoners, all of whom would become equal in misery and servitude. This model of despotism, the standard interpretation of Montesquieu's theory, he presented clearly and analytically. The second model is scattered throughout his writings, never analyzed openly, and replete with ambiguities, but it reflected Montesquieu's fear that *les moeurs* of France, and of Europe in general, were becoming corrupted by the self-interest, luxury, and license that seemed to be the inseparable companions of the new commercial classes. In short, Montesquieu was an aristocrat with two theories of despotism based on his twin fears of monarchs and merchants.

---

2. R. Koebner, "Despot and Despotism: Vicissitudes of a Political Term," *Journal of the Warburg and Courtauld Institutes* 14 (1951): 275–302, 301–2. In these first three paragraphs I have relied extensively on Koebner's excellent article, and also on Melvin Richter, "Despotism," *Dictionary of the History of Ideas*, 5 vols. (New York: Scribner's, 1974), 2:1–18. Melvin Richter's *The Political Theory of Montesquieu* (Cambridge: Cambridge University Press, 1977), 44–47 and 71–79, provides an excellent discussion of the historical backdrop to the concept of despotism. Nannerl O. Keohane's *Philosophy and the State in France: The Renaissance to the Enlightenment* (Princeton: Princeton University Press, 1980) gives a superb account of the intellectual legacy from which Montesquieu borrowed.

The First Theory of Despotism:
Uniformity and Mediocrity

Montesquieu sorted the political world into republics, monarchies, and despotisms, and he sought to classify each type according to its *nature,* which indicates who rules and how, and according to its *principle,* which reveals what motivates the people who live under each type of government. Like a monarchy, a despotism is also controlled by one person, but the *nature* of a despotism is rule "in which a single person directs everything by his own will and caprice." The *principle* of this government, that is, its motivating force, or what Montesquieu called "the spring of this government," is merely fear.[3]

The goal of despotic government, according to Montesquieu, is nothing more inspiring than order and tranquillity. "As fear is the principle of despotic government, its end is tranquillity; but this tranquillity cannot be called a peace: no, it is only the silence of those towns which the enemy is ready to invade."[4] Whereas to an outsider the order and tranquillity of despotism might seem to signify harmony and happiness, in fact such order is merely repressed conflict waiting for an opportunity to

---

3. Montesquieu, *The Spirit of the Laws,* 2 vols. in 1, trans. Thomas Nugent (New York: Hafner, 1949), bk. 2, chap. 1; and bk. 3, chap. 9 (henceforth cited by book and chapter, followed by the volume and page number from the Nugent translation, as, for example, 3.9, 1:26). For Montesquieu's major works—*The Persian Letters, Considerations on the Causes of the Greatness of the Romans and Their Decline,* and *The Spirit of the Laws*—I have relied on available translations. For other works I have used Montesquieu, *Oeuvres complètes,* ed. Daniel Oster (Paris: Éditions du Seuil, 1964). This edition of Montesquieu's "complete" works does not have, however, Montesquieu's correspondence. For his letters, I have used *Oeuvres complètes de Montesquieu,* ed. André Masson, vol. 3 (Paris: Éditions Nagel, 1955). In the text, I have referred to these two collections as *Oeuvres* (Seuil) and *Oeuvres* (Nagel) respectively. Montesquieu outlined his classifications of governments in *The Spirit of the Laws,* bks. 2–4. For discussions of Montesquieu's method of classification, see Alan Baum, *Montesquieu and Social Theory* (Oxford: Pergamon Press, 1979), 83–119; Nannerl O. Keohane, "Virtuous Republics and Glorious Monarchies: Two Models in Montesquieu's Political Thought," *Political Studies* 20 no. 4 (1972): 383–96; Melvin Richter, "Comparative Political Analysis in Montesquieu and Tocqueville," *Comparative Politics* 1, no. 2 (1969): 129–60; and David Lowenthal, "Book I of Montesquieu's *The Spirit of the Laws," American Political Science Review* 53, no. 2 (1959): 485–98. For discussions of Montesquieu's general method and approach to political studies, see Emile Durkheim, *Montesquieu and Rousseau: Forerunners of Sociology,* trans. Ralph Manheim (Ann Arbor: University of Michigan Press, 1960), 1–18, 36–42; Raymond Aron, *Montesquieu, Comte, Marx, Tocqueville,* vol. 1 of *Main Currents of Sociological Thought,* trans. Richard Howard and Helen Weaver (Garden City, N.Y.: Doubleday, 1968), 13–72; and Louis Althusser, *Montesquieu, Rousseau, Marx: Politics and History,* trans. Ben Brewster (London: Verso, 1982), 17–30, 43–60.

4. *The Spirit of the Laws,* 5.14, 1:59.

burst forth. "But, in the concord of Asiatic despotism . . . there is always real dissension. . . . And, if we see any union there, it is not citizens who are united, but dead bodies buried one next to the other."[5] Although other governments use laws to promote justice or to encourage trade and commerce, what laws there are under a despotism aim only at preventing civil disorder and thus simply facilitate the "police" functions of the state. Indeed, Asiatic despotisms rely less on legislation and more on customs ingrained in individuals from birth. "We ought not to be surprised that the legislators of China . . . should confound the laws, manners, and customs. . . . The principal object which the legislators of China had in view was to make their subjects live in peace and tranquillity. . . . They therefore gave rules of the most extensive civility." The result of any successful despotism is a tranquil servitude; each subject knows only "passive obedience," each "blindly submits to the absolute will of the sovereign," and "man's portion here, like that of beasts, is instinct, compliance, and punishment."[6] Despite this bleak description of despotism, Montesquieu noted that no government and no despot was ever literally absolute; that is, despots can never have total control over their subjects and dominate every aspect of society. "It is an error to believe that any human authority exists in the world which is despotic in all respects. There never has been one, and never will be, for the most immense power is always confined in some way. . . . A king of Persia can easily compel a son to kill his father, or a father to kill his son; but as for making his subjects drink wine, he cannot do it. There exists in each nation a general spirit on which power itself is based, and when it shocks this spirit it strikes against itself and necessarily comes to a standstill."[7]

Although despotic government is never absolute, or in modern terminology "totalitarian," it is destructive enough to reduce its population to uniformity and mediocrity. Whereas moderate government is always an intricate configuration involving division of power and local limits on the central government, despotism is "uniform throughout," with centralized despotic power crushing down upon powerless subjects, while the subjects themselves are "all upon a level," all the same, "all slaves."[8] In *The Persian Letters* Montesquieu used a Persian seraglio—a "small empire" in which a prince dominated his wives by means of cruel eunuchs—as a

5. Montesquieu, *Considerations on the Causes of the Greatness of the Romans and Their Decline*, trans. David Lowenthal (Ithaca: Cornell University Press, 1968), 94.

6. *The Spirit of the Laws*, 5.15, 1:63; 19.16, 1:300; 3.10, 1:27.

7. *Considerations*, 210. See Leonard Krieger, *An Essay on the Theory of Enlightened Despotism* (Chicago: University of Chicago Press, 1975), 38.

8. *The Spirit of the Laws*, 5.14, 1:62; 3.8, 1:25.

metaphor to illustrate the dynamics and effects of despotism. The job of the eunuch, the agent of despotism, was to introduce silent uniformity to the seraglio. "The head eunuch, the strictest man I have ever seen in my life, ruled there with an iron hand. There was no breath of cabal or quarrel; a deep silence reigned everywhere. All the women were in bed at the same hour from one year's end to the next, and all arose at the same hour."[9] This means, of course, that where one finds equality one might find either a republic or a despotism, a lesson not lost on Tocqueville, because in the face of despotic power all live equally in servitude. "In republican governments, men are equal; equal they are also in despotic governments: in the former, because they are everything; in the latter, because they are nothing." The worst despotisms are those in which the despot claims ownership of all land in the realm, because here agricultural improvement is neglected, there is no incentive for private trade or industry, and families build houses that provide only for the most basic necessities. "Everything is drawn from, but nothing restored to, the earth; the ground lies untilled, and the whole country becomes a desert."[10] With the harshest despotisms, one finds uniformity in misery and poverty.

With poverty and servitude, the human race can attain none of that greatness of which it is capable, but instead declines into a stupefying mediocrity. "Men are like plants: they never grow well unless they are well cultivated. Among people living in poverty, the human race loses and even degenerates." Under a despotism, according to Montesquieu, no one has hope of attaining honors and rewards, because fear eliminates all hopes and aspirations, reducing all endeavors to the wish to survive. "Fear must therefore depress their spirits, and extinguish even the least sense of ambition."[11] Both despot and subject fall into unthinking ignorance. "Excessive obedience supposes ignorance in the person that obeys: the same it supposes in him that commands, for he has no occasion to deliberate, to doubt, to reason." Ultimately, human beings accustomed to servitude can accomplish certainly no great good and quite

---

9. Montesquieu, *The Persian Letters*, ed. and trans. J. Robert Loy (Cleveland: World Publishing Co., 1961), letters 64 and 9. For a discussion of the seraglio as a metaphor for despotism, see Aram Vartanian, "Eroticism and Politics in the *Lettres Persanes*," *Romanic Review* 60, no. 1 (1969): 23–33; E. J. Hundert and Paul Nelles, "Liberty and Theatrical Space in Montesquieu's Political Theory: The Poetics of Public life in *The Persian Letters*," *Political Theory* 17, no. 2 (1989): 223–46; and Richter, *The Political Theory of Montesquieu*, 45–50.

10. *The Spirit of the Laws*, 6.2, 1:74; 5.14, 1:59; also Montesquieu, *Mes pensées*, in *Oeuvres* (Seuil), 231, p. 877. This edition of Montesquieu's *Pensées* uses the numbers by Montesquieu's original editor, H. Barckhausen.

11. *Persian Letters*, 122; *The Spirit of the Laws*, 3.9, 1:26.

probably no great evil, but instead commit the crimes and languish in the vices appropriate to "feeble souls."[12]

Although despots must rely upon force and "violent passions" to establish a despotism,[13] once the despotism becomes lasting, despots leave the violence to those who rule in their names, while they fall into lethargy or "apathy" interrupted only by ceaseless rounds of sensual pleasures. The typical despot is "lazy, voluptuous, and ignorant"; for example, once Persian despots had chosen someone to administer the state, they abandoned "themselves in their seraglio to the most brutal passions, pursuing, in the midst of a prostituted court, every capricious extravagance." "Great God!" wrote one eunuch to another in *The Persian Letters*, "How much must be done to keep just one man happy!"[14] In Montesquieu's judgment, the despot is caught in some elaborate web of servitude like everyone else, even if the despot's servitude is considerably more delightful, because every tyrant is a slave to those who provide the pleasures and is constantly anxious lest the source of these pleasures should disappear.[15] Anxious sensuality at the top, coupled with tranquillity, uniformity, and misery at the bottom—this powerful but almost unbelievable portrait of despotism Montesquieu painted in order to draw a strong contrast between limited monarchical rule and what happens when rule by one person breaks through all constitutional and customary restraints.

The Administration of Despotism: Abolishing Intermediate Powers

All executive, legislative, and judicial powers are of course concentrated in the person of the despot because this is a prerequisite for arbitrary power. "In Turkey, where these three powers are united in the Sultan's person, the subjects groan under the most dreadful oppression." Because there is no give and take between people or institutions that share power, because there is no compromise between, say, provincial government and national government, politics under a despotism is always reduced to the intrigues of the court, to the whispering of secrets, and to the gossipy infighting of the seraglio. Politics "is reduced to reconciling the political and civil administration to the domestic government, the officers of state

---

12. *The Spirit of the Laws*, 4.3, 1:32; *Considerations*, 158.
13. *Pensées*, 633, p. 947.
14. *The Spirit of the Laws*, 2.5, 1:18; *Persian Letters*, 114, 22.
15. *The Spirit of the Laws*, 4.3, 1:32; *Persian Letters*, 155.

to those of the seraglio." Still, the will of the despot must prevail. Nevertheless, although the will of the ruler must dominate any despotism, despots do not rule personally, because, while busying themselves with the pleasures of the court, they allow their intermediaries to rule for them. "Here the immense power of the prince devolves entirely upon those whom he is pleased to intrust with the administration." These administrators, or emissaries, of the despot's power must carry that power down to the most local levels, so that the despot, after a fashion, controls all. "Were the governor of a town independent of the pasha, expedients would be daily necessary to make them agree; which is highly absurd in a despotic state."[16]

Sometimes Montesquieu depicted such representatives of the despot's will as administrative functionaries, clerks "whose minds have shrunken into detail"; at other times he pictured such representatives as willful individuals who might well threaten the absolute power of the despot.[17] In either case, if the despotism functions properly, such emissaries exist only to serve the despot. In *The Persian Letters* a prince put this best in addressing the eunuchs who had command over his seraglio: "For what are all of you if not base tools that I can break at my fancy—you, who exist only for so long as you know how to obey; you, who exist in this world only to live under my laws or to die so soon as I shall order." For those living at the bottom of the despotism, it matters little who is the despot, since the power of the despotism strikes them with the same oppressive force. "The invisible ruling power is always the same for the people. Although ten [Asian princes] whose names they do not know may have cut each other's throats one after the other, the people feel no change."[18]

Montesquieu's description of how a despotism is administered shows that his analysis of despotism is at least partly an attack on the monarchies of Louis XIV and Louis XV. Although apparently Montesquieu had evidence suggesting that in some Asiatic despotisms eunuchs did in fact administer government offices, the eunuch also served as a splendid metaphor for the Intendants who extended the power of the French monarchy throughout the country. For Montesquieu, eunuchs were literally sterile,

16. *The Spirit of the Laws*, 11.6, 1:152; 5.14, 1:58; *The Spirit of the Laws*, 3.9, 1:26; 5.16, 1:64; 2.5, 1:18; *Considerations*, 125. The checks and balances that Montesquieu championed so famously were more complicated than simple institutional checks and balances because he included allocating power among the various classes. See André Vachet, "Division de pouvoir et intégration social: De Montesquieu à la crise actuel du parlementarisme," *Canadian Journal of Political Science* 1, no. 3 (1968): 261–69.

17. *Persian Letters*, 48, 127.

18. *Persian Letters*, 21, 2, 103.

figuratively unable to create, and metaphorically lacking in all passion and energy,[19] and yet they were also harsh taskmasters of those they controlled—all qualities he attributed to the Intendants of the king. In his *Pensées* it is apparent that Montesquieu saw himself as living in an age when monarchy was collapsing into despotism; he clearly saw the Intendants as instruments of servitude; and in a letter he referred to a key minister under the Regency (1715–23) of Louis XV as *le grand vizir.*[20] Similarly, in a bold and satirical passage in *The Persian Letters,* he likened the French king to a Turkish despot. "The King of France is old. . . . He governs with equal talent his family, his court, and his state. People have often heard him say that, of all the governments in the world, that of the Turks, or that of our august sultan would please him best—so much significance does he attach to Oriental politics."[21]

Montesquieu blamed Louis XI (1423–83) for French servitude, much as Tacitus had blamed Tiberius for bringing despotism to Rome. "The death of Charles VII [who preceded Louis XI] was the last day of French liberty. One saw, in an instant, another king, another people, another political system, another sufferance, and the passage from liberty to servitude was so great, so prompt, so rapid; the means, so strange, so odious to a free nation: one could only look upon all of this as if a spirit of dizziness had suddenly fallen on the entire kingdom."[22] In Montesquieu's long list of the crimes of Louis XI, what stands out is Montesquieu's dislike for the king's attack on the power of the nobility and the privileges of local communities.[23] In other words, Louis XI began the attack upon the intermediate bodies through which a genuine monarchy channels its power. The key to a despotism, of course, is the abolition of such intermediate powers so that the despot can rule subjects directly by appointed administrators. "Abolish the privileges of the lords, the clergy and cities in a monarchy, and you will soon have a popular state, or else a despotic government."[24] Once a monarch such as Louis XI has deprived individuals, corporate bodies, and communities of their rights and privileges, despotism will follow.[25] For example, in *The Persian Letters* Montesquieu referred to the

19. *Persian Letters*, 114.

20. *Pensées*, 588, p. 922; 228, p. 877; *Correspondance*, in *Oeuvres* (Nagel), 3:743. On eunuchs as a metaphor for the king's ministers, see Orest Ranum, "Personality and Politics in the *Persian Letters*," *Political Science Quarterly* 84, no. 4 (1969): 606–27, esp. 624–25.

21. *Persian Letters*, 37. On the concept of despotism as an implicit critique of the French Monarchy, see Althusser, *Montesquieu, Rousseau, Marx*, 75–86.

22. *Pensées*, 595, p. 929; also 669, p. 952.

23. *Pensées*, 595, p. 929.

24. *The Spirit of the Laws*, 2.4, 1:16.

25. *The Spirit of the Laws*, 8.6, 1:113. On Montesquieu's attachment to intermediate insti-

parlements as "ruins that are kicked about underfoot"; these great institutions, which no longer represent the nation and now perform only a judicial function, have "bowed before . . . supreme authority, which has swept all before it."[26]

The intermediate body that Montesquieu cherished most was the judiciary, which, if effective, is always the best protection of individual liberty. The hallmark of monarchy, and indeed what saved the French monarchy from being entirely despotic, is a functioning judiciary. "It is not enough to have intermediate powers in a monarchy; there must be also a depositary of the laws. This depositary can only be the judges of the supreme courts of justice."[27] Whereas in the despotism of Turkey the law was only "the prince's will" and all court cases were "speedily decided," under a monarchy "the trouble, expense, delays, and even the very dangers of . . . judiciary proceedings are the price that each subject pays for his liberty." The best judicial system allows appeals and sees advantages in delays, because eventually emotions of the moment will fade and then juries and judges can offer reasoned decisions "coolly."[28] In Montesquieu's mind, the single distinguishing characteristic of despotism, its hallmark if you will, is the control or the elimination of the judiciary as an intermediate institution between the sovereign and the subject, protecting the latter from arbitrary abuses of power. "Sentences passed by the prince would be an inexhaustible source of injustice and abuse."[29] Again and again, Montesquieu cited the analysis of Tacitus, who demonstrated that Tiberius and other emperors sought immediately to control judicial proceedings but kept the appearance of legality so that they could govern despotically, all while "under the color of justice."[30] Montesquieu's argu-

---

tutions, see William Henry George, "Montesquieu and de Tocqueville and Corporate Individualism," *American Political Science Review* 16, no. 1 (1922): 10–21.

26. *Persian Letters*, 92. Montesquieu enthusiastically supported attempts by the regent, the duke of Orléans, to institute a system of aristocratic councils. See Ranum, "Personality and Politics in the *Persian Letters*," esp. 613. After the duke died in 1725, Montesquieu wrote a friend that, "The death of the Duke of Orléans has made me regret a prince for the first time in my life." *Correspondance*, in *Oeuvres* (Nagel), 3:758.

27. *The Spirit of the Laws*, 2.4, 1:17. On Montesquieu's fondness for the judiciary, see Émile Faguet, *La politique comparée de Montesquieu, Rousseau, et Voltaire* (Geneva: Skatline Reprints, 1981 [1902]), 117–23.

28. *The Spirit of the Laws*, 5.16, 1:65, 6.2, 1:74; *Pensées*, 293, p. 884; *The Spirit of the Laws*, 6.5, 1:77.

29. *The Spirit of the Laws*, 6.5, 1:78. Actually, Montesquieu thought that the perfect despotism would have no laws; instead, the will of the despot would rule along with deeply ingrained mores and customs. *The Spirit of the Laws*, 19.12, 1:297.

30. *Considerations*, 129–30; see also unpublished fragments of *The Spirit of the Laws*, from "Histoire du droit," in *Oeuvres* (Seuil), 806.

ment that a fair judiciary is a powerful restraint against arbitrary power is perhaps his most lasting contribution to theories of tyranny.

Montesquieu certainly regarded the governing functions and privileges of the French nobility as another intermediate institution threatened by the encroaching power of the French monarchy. In fact, the eunuch is a metaphor not only for the harsh Intendants, who represent royal power, but also for an emasculated nobility whose independence Louis XIV captured by bringing them to Versailles. In *The Persian Letters* the first eunuch wrote, "When my first master . . . had obliged me by seductions doubled with a thousand threats to separate me forever from myself, I planned, weary of the most laborious tasks, to sacrifice my passions to tranquillity and fortune." Certainly Montesquieu thought that the French nobility had sacrificed the fiery passions of its ancestors in order to gain the tranquillity and security promised by Louis XIV. Having bought themselves a host of "courtiers" (and thus impoverishing the majority of their subjects), French kings had augmented their power to the exact extent that they drew nobles from their lands and attracted them to Versailles. To Montesquieu, this was a shameful development. "I hate Versailles, because everyone there is small." *The Persian Letters* satirize repeatedly what the nobility had become under Louis XIV. Usbek, one of two fictional Persian travelers in *The Persian Letters,* describes his visit to see "a great noble" in one of his letters. "I saw a little man so proud, who took his pinch of snuff with such haughtiness, wiped his nose so ruthlessly, spat with so much phlegm, petted his dogs in a way so insulting to men, that I could not cease admiring him." Montesquieu's contempt for the nobility, once so proudly fierce and now so arrogant in their docility, was matched only by his dislike for the kings who helped to bring about this transformation. French kings, who had financed their wars by selling titles, paid as much attention to their flattering courtiers as to those who protected their kingdom. "Often [the king of France] shows preferment to a man who undresses him or who hands him his napkin when he sits down to table over some other who takes cities for him and wins battles."[31]

If despotism can tolerate no intermediate bodies that limit and channel power, that is, if a despotism seeks to rule all directly through administrative emissaries answerable only to the despot, then a despotism must extend the tentacles of government into every province. Such rule, however, immediately threatens the despot. If the despot's appointees possess limited ability, then the despotism will be ineffective, but if these appointees possess great ability, then they can create their own bases of

---

31. *Persian Letters*, 9; *Pensées*, 33, p. 856; 621, p. 945; *Persian Letters*, 124, 74, 37, 24.

power, thus weakening first the absolutism of the despot and perhaps ultimately the despot himself or herself. Nowhere is this dilemma more apparent than in the ways that despots must use force and violence.

Despotisms of course need fear to govern. The principle or motivating force of every despotism is fear, and despotisms must bring their subjects into submission by governing with violence and vengeance, rendering their subjects timid and docile. "When we want to break a horse, we take care not to let him change his master, his lesson, or his pace." In part, a despot brings order with police forces, and Montesquieu regarded despotisms as infamous for their cruelty and and torture. "The severity of punishment is fitter for despotic government, whose principle is terror." But in part, such fear must come from military forces that, despite being incapable of the internalized discipline needed to win wars, are quite capable of putting down revolts and pillaging their own countries. "The pashas . . . lay waste to [the provinces] as to a conquered land. An insolent military arm is ruled only by its own caprice. The fortresses are dismantled; the cities deserted. The countryside is desolate; cultivation of land and commerce are entirely abandoned."[32]

Precisely to the extent, however, that a despot has talented military leaders capable of quelling revolts, a despot's own rule is severely threatened. Any able general with even moderate popularity among the troops is a threat to a lazy, voluptuous, and useless despot sequestered in a seraglio. A despot, noted Montesquieu, who is "shut up in a seraglio" seldom "wages war in person, and hardly ventures to entrust the command to his generals." Montesquieu, of course, saw the problem immediately. Despotisms need armies to keep order—if they had no troops to "bully the rest of their subjects," their rule would not last a month—but despots do not need rival generals, and thus it is difficult to "reconcile the security of the government to that of the prince's person."[33] One possible solution is to have an elite body of troops personally loyal to the despot and ready to strike any threat at any moment. "There should be always a body of faithful troops near the prince, ready to fall instantly upon any part of the empire that may chance to waver. This military corps ought to awe the rest, and to strike terror into those who through necessity have been intrusted with any authority in the empire." Although in theory this may sound workable, in practice this solution presents the same dangers, because the commander of such an elite body can never be trusted entirely. As Usbek writes of the king of France, "he is just as

32. *The Spirit of the Laws*, 5.14, 1:57; 6.9, 1:81; 6.12, 1:83; 6.13, 1:85; 6.17, 1:91; *Persian Letters*, 19.

33. *The Spirit of the Laws*, 5.14, 1:57; *Persian Letters*, 102; *The Spirit of the Laws*, 5.14, 1:59.

afraid of having a good general at the head of his own troops as he would be to have him at the head of an enemy army." As a consequence, the problem of succession, on which most people focus in regard to a despotism, rarely in fact becomes a problem, because few despots survive for very long. Because of the violence of despotisms and because despots have few means by which to defend themselves, despotisms are constantly subjected to military coups and popular violence, both of which Montesquieu apparently labeled as revolutions. "The histories of despotic governments abound with revolutions without civil wars."[34]

Montesquieu depicted a despot so addicted to pleasures, and thus confined to the seraglio or the court, that such a despot is clearly of no use whatsoever in maintaining the despotism. Able ministers, able provincial governors, and able generals are all a threat to seize the despotism, but mediocre administrators and generals cannot protect it. Montesquieu's model of despotism also strays occasionally from picturing the real world of tyranny, ignoring, for example, the elaborate bureaucracies in the Turkish and Chinese empires. Even if we must await Tocqueville to invent the word *bureaucracy,* we need to ask why Montesquieu did not picture despots as ruling through elaborate administrative hierarchies. The answer must be that bureaucracies place intermediate powers between subject and despot, and such a model would have deprived Montesquieu of a model that so dramatically criticized the Intendants of Louis XV. But we also need to ask why Montesquieu did not picture despots as military leaders, instead of seeing them as pleasure-seeking poltroons seduced by the sensuality of the seraglio. We know, for example, that Montesquieu marveled at the efficiency of the Tatars or Mongols, and he certainly had before him the military tyranny of Julius Caesar or Augustus, but such military dictatorships fall completely out of his classification of governments. Indeed, he called military governments the "corruption" of despotic government.[35] Why would he create a model of despotism that could not account for the most famous despots, who were invariably military leaders? Quite probably the reports he had at hand of Eastern courts and seraglios provided him with an irresistible opportunity to liken the luxury of Louis XIV to the sensuality of a sultan.

All of this tells us that Montesquieu's model of despotism served two

34. *The Spirit of the Laws,* 10.16, 1:147; *Persian Letters,* 37; *The Spirit of Laws,* 5.11, 1:56; see also *Persian Letters,* 80.

35. *Pensées,* 239, p. 878; on Montesquieu's attitude toward the Tatars, see *Persian Letters,* 81. For Montesquieu's selective use of the information he had on Asian despotisms, see David Young, "Montesquieu's View of Despotism and His Use of Travel Literature," *Review of Politics* 40, no. 3 (1978): 392–405. Obviously Montesquieu gave us only an inaccurate caricature of Asian governments.

purposes. While it certainly provided, and continues to provide, a highly useful analysis of despotism, it also served the political and rhetorical purpose of subtly attacking the abuses of the French monarchy.

The Means of Control:
Isolation and Socialization

For Montesquieu, friendship was a political virtue appropriate to republics, whereas despotism offered a world without friendship, as Aristotle had suggested. From top to bottom in a despotism, from the despot himself to the poorest of his subjects, all the natural ties between people have been severed. The despot himself is "concealed in his palace," physically isolated from those he rules and psychologically isolated from those in his court who fear his wrath. "Monarch of the Orient, who wishes to be happy all alone! . . . Unhappy is the one who spends his life by himself, . . . who lives in the silence of all that surrounds him; who commands and cannot talk; who seeks a blind obedience and finds a dreadful solitude." Similarly, in *The Persian Letters* the eunuchs, who experience the despotism of the prince but turn around and tyrannize over the wives in the seraglio, frequently lament that they have never known friendship. Said one eunuch, "I had only myself for an intimate friend," and later, "I have scarcely ever known that tie called friendship, [and] I have consciously been wrapped up entirely in myself." The reason for this is political, because friendship, that old Greek and Roman notion of friends acting in common, is a political threat to any tyrant. Under the tyranny of Tiberius, "friendship was regarded as a danger."[36]

Because those accustomed to associating with one another might begin to organize politically, indeed because those who cannot communicate cannot possibly resist despotism, a successful despot finds ways of keeping people isolated from one another. "In despotic states each house is a separate government," wrote Montesquieu, and there is "less communication between young people, who are confined at home." In *The Persian Letters,* after describing Turkey as a place where no one laughs, Montesquieu explained it this way: "This Asiatic sobriety derives from the dearth of intercourse between people. . . . Friendship . . . is practically unknown here. They withdraw to their houses . . . so that each family lives, so to

---

36. *The Spirit of the Laws,* 5.14, 1:58; *Pensées,* 225, p. 877; *Persian Letters,* 9, 15; *Considerations,* 129.

speak, in isolation."[37] In his description of the Persian seraglio, the women, who of course stand metaphorically for the subjects of any despotism, spend their lives isolated from one another, unable to communicate and consequently unable to make some common effort to oppose their servitude. "He keeps each of us closed up in her apartment, and although we are all alone there, he makes us live under the veil. We are no longer allowed to speak to each other, and it would be a crime for us to write to each other."[38] So important is such enforced isolation that Montesquieu even described princes who allowed their wives to travel outside of the seraglio only if enclosed in individual latticework boxes, quite literally isolated and sealed off from the rest of humanity.[39] In other seraglios with less absolute isolation, the rule of eunuchs could bring about a psychological isolation in which each wife suspects the others and each becomes anxious to please and gain the meager favors available under the despotism. "We note that the more women we have under our eyes, the less trouble they give us. A more stringent need to please, less opportunity to band together, more examples of submissive obedience— all of this forges chains for them. Some are even attentive to the behavior of others; it would seem that they work hand in glove with us to make themselves more dependent."[40] Both physical isolation, which is imposed by force, and psychological isolation, which results from mutual suspicion, form the cornerstones of despotism, because they prevent the communication that is a prerequisite for any organized political opposition.

One indication of this psychological isolation of people from one another is the degree to which a despotism fosters deception and dissimulation, an idea seen in Aristotle, Tacitus, and Machiavelli. Because both despot and subjects need false appearances in order to survive, a despotism is a world distinguished by deception, insincerity, role-playing, and pretense. Montesquieu returned to this again and again. Pisistratus tyrannized over the Athenians with the pretense of benevolence, Tiberius seized absolute power under the appearance of legality, Louis XI sought not to govern but to "deceive" by practicing "the art of dissimulation" and by using "false caresses and small flatteries," and Philip II ruled with "the mask of politics." It is advice well taken by any would-be despot. "Princes who have changed the form of the state, who have rendered themselves

37. *The Spirit of the Laws*, 4.3, 1:32; 5.15, 1:62; *Persian Letters*, 34.
38. *Persian Letters*, 156; also 64 and 141. Montesquieu did not think this was only metaphorical; the confinement of women is a sign of despotism. *The Spirit of the Laws*, 16.9–10, 1:256. See also Mark Hulliung, "Patriarchalism and Its Early Enemies," *Political Theory* 2, no. 4 (1974): 410–19.
39. *Persian Letters*, 3.
40. *Persian Letters*, 96.

masters and who want to prevent the people from feeling this, must keep . . . the appearance of a republican state."[41]

Whereas citizens of a republic speak honestly what they are thinking and do not deceive each other,[42] the subjects of a despotism have no such luxury because, if despots deceive in order to maintain their power, subjects deceive in order to gain favors and to survive. In *The Persian Letters* it is Roxanne—the one wife in the seraglio who most dramatically resists the despotism of the prince and his eunuchs—who does the best job of pretending that she enjoys her servitude.[43] After a while, however, such pretense forced upon people is likely to become second nature, and Montesquieu pointedly argued that a despotism is a world in which subjects and despots become both unnatural and insincere. "With us [the women's] characters are all the same because they are forced into a mold. We don't see people as they really are but as they are forced to be." Usbek laments to a friend, "We almost always experience only false sadness and false joy."[44]

If behavior is role-playing, if actions are insincere, and if feelings are unnatural, then indeed despotism is a world of falsehood and pretense, as Tacitus, one of Montesquieu's mentors, suggested. Distortion of language only exacerbates this tendency, thereby further hindering communication and reinforcing psychological isolation. Montesquieu made careful note of this time-honored tactic of tyranny. Whereas the Romans called "allies" those they held in servitude, Julius Caesar labeled his despotism a "magistracy," thus satisfying most people, who "are hardly moved by anything but names." In *The Persian Letters* Usbek criticizes the ministers, or Intendants, of the French monarchy who "gave to injustice and perfidy the name of *necessity*." In announcing her resolve to commit suicide rather than submit any longer to Usbek's tyranny, Roxanne regrets that she had "dared profane the name of virtue by allowing submission to your fancy to be called by that name."[45]

Montesquieu was at his best, however, in demonstrating that people must learn how to be obedient, how to say the right things, and how to play the proper role. For this, he saw two great agents of training or socialization, that is, two great means of teaching customs, manners, and mores: religion and the family. Montesquieu did suggest that religion can

---

41. "Réflexions sur le caractère de quelques princes," in *Oeuvres* (Seuil), 159–62, esp. 159; *Pensées*, 145, p. 870; 129, p. 866; *Considerations*, 129.
42. *Considerations*, 109.
43. *Persian Letters*, 151, 152.
44. *Persian Letters*, 63, 40.
45. *Considerations*, 69, 108; *Persian Letters*, 146, 161.

enhance virtue and be useful both to monarchies and to republics; for example, Christianity accords well with constitutional monarchies, and the Roman Republic "was a ship held by two anchors, religion and morality."[46] Despite such claims, however, Montesquieu's more common attitude toward religion was pessimistic, because he generally maintained that, at best, religions restrain arbitrary rule slightly, whereas, at worst, they reinforce despotic rule powerfully. Although Montesquieu suggested that religion strengthened despotism, in published writings he still carefully blamed religions other than Christianity. "In [despotic states] religion has more influence than anywhere else; it is fear added to fear. In Mahommedan countries, it is partly from their religion that the people derive the surprising veneration they have for their prince." Among the different so-called oriental despotisms stretching from Turkey to China, multivarious religions supplant the legal code, teach a proper submissive morality, and support despotic rule. "The religious code supplies the civil and fixes the extent of arbitrary sway." In other writings, he is even more critical of the role of religion. "The despotic monarch must be religious," he wrote in his *Pensées,* because, as Machiavelli had suggested, virtually no one has ever established a new rule without "recourse to mystery." Indeed, all religions are useful to despotisms, since all religions "prescribe obedience and preach submission"; Catholicism is especially good, for example, at rendering people submissive and ignorant.[47]

Although other writers had demonstrated that religion is useful to despotism, no one before Montesquieu had shown the degree to which the relationships within a family both reflect and reinforce despotic rule. This is another of his most important contributions to theories of tyranny. Montesquieu began his argument about the family where so many other authors had begun, that is, with the Roman family, and he argued that the discipline taught in the patriarchal Roman family was an excellent means for instilling virtue in future citizens. "Paternal authority is likewise of great use toward the preservation of morals."[48] Although patriarchal rule is "natural" for children, however, and perhaps even for the infancy of a society, it must eventually be replaced by love of one's country and respect for its laws. None of this is terribly new, but Montesquieu went on

---

46. *The Spirit of the Laws,* 24.3, 2:29–30; 8.13, 1:119. See also *Persian Letters,* unpublished letter, appendix, 289. For Montesquieu's attitude toward religion, see Robert Shackleton, *Montesquieu: A Critical Biography* (Oxford: Oxford University Press, 1961), 337–55; Andrew J. Lynch, "Montesquieu and the Ecclesiastical Critics of *L'ésprit des lois,*" *Journal of the History of Ideas* 38, no. 3 (1977): 487–500.

47. *The Spirit of the Laws,* 5.14, 1:59; 12.29, 1:205; *Pensées,* 1834, p. 1037; 443, p. 901; *Persian Letters,* 85; "Essay on Causes," in *Oeuvres* (Seuil), 445.

48. *The Spirit of the Laws,* 5.7, 1:48–49; also 4.5, 1:34.

to argue, using the comparative studies that he had available, that different kinds of government require different kinds of authority within the family. For example, in republics, which must teach their citizens self-sacrifice and virtue, Montesquieu found that the members of their families "love each other more," whereas in a monarchy, which seeks to build on the ambitions and glory seeking of its subjects, he found family members less united and more self-seeking. Both the habits and the patterns of authority within the family are simultaneously cause and consequence of political power in the larger society. "Those who raise us are," noted Montesquieu, "manufacturers of our ideas. . . . They constantly give us new ways of being and perceiving."[49]

Even though force might well control behavior for a time, it cannot change the way people think, and consequently a despotism that relies solely on violence and fear can never be lasting. Far better, therefore, to teach people the habits of servitude from childhood. In a crucial letter, one of Usbek's wives reports that she is putting her daughter into the seraglio at age seven. "You can't start too early to cut a young person off from the freedom of childhood." She continues by criticizing those mothers who wait until their daughters are about to be married before confining them to a seraglio, because at that age one can only control behavior with violence, whereas, by training daughters to obedience from childhood, they become accustomed to submission. "Are we to expect everything from the strength of reason and nothing whatsoever from the gentle effect of habit? In vain do they talk to us of the subordinate position in which Nature has placed us. It is not enough to make us feel that. We must practice our role of subordinate."[50] Servitude does not come about naturally, nor can it forever be secured by violence; instead, despotism must use such institutions as the family to inculcate the proper habits of obedience. No despot can hope to have willing subjects, in this case wives who love the prince, unless others, such as families and eunuchs, have begun the whole process of training "by subjugating [the subjects'] minds." In the seraglio, which Montesquieu described as "a uniform existence, without excitement," one which "smells of obedience and duty," base and slavish eunuchs, who are themselves subject to tyranny, set about "destroying [natural feelings of virtue] . . . since the very childhood they tyrannize." Even the pleasures and the moments of joy become "manifestations of authority and subservience."[51]

Having recognized that "families are a government unto themselves,"

49. *Pensées*, 1933, p. 1046; 352, p. 892; "Essay on Causes," 436.
50. *Persian Letters*, 62; also 85.
51. *Persian Letters*, 64, 34.

Montesquieu suggested that the patterns of authority in the family both reflect and help to create the patterns of political authority in the larger society. For example, the practice of primogeniture makes families favor the eldest son and, as a consequence, "destroys that equality among citizens." Similarly, Montesquieu was acutely aware of how family relations promote the inequality of women. Rica, the second of Montesquieu's two fictional travelers, writes to Usbek that only since arriving in Paris has he really known women, that is, only in Europe has he discovered what is natural or authentic about women, because in Persia all women are forced into unnatural molds. "We don't see people as they really are but as they are forced to be."[52] Montesquieu well knew that in families and in the relations between the sexes, women were forced into an unnatural position of submission. In Asia, "domestic slavery and despotic government walk hand in hand." And in his *Pensées* there is an extraordinary sentence: "Despotic government constricts the talents of its subjects and its great men, just as the power of men constricts the talents of women." A despotism necessarily entails "an empire over women."[53] In these discussions, Montesquieu made notable contributions to theories of tyranny, because no thinker before Montesquieu, not even Plato, recognized that a despotic family structure and a widespread oppression of women are essential to establishing and reinforcing a general societal tyranny.

The Delights of Servitude: A Contradiction in the First Theory of Despotism

Montesquieu's despot is obsessed with satisfying ever-increasing desires for sexual pleasures and luxury. Driven by "the most brutal passions," a despot surrounds himself with "comforts" and "throws himself into his pleasures." Although in *The Persian Letters* Montesquieu did outline a female fantasy of a seraglio well stocked with men, he generally thought that the servitude or even "the slavery of women" necessarily accompanies despotism, that under despotism women become "[objects] of luxury" or "the living instruments of men's felicity." And if despots violently seize women as objects of pleasure, they also seize, almost uncontrollably, whatever possessions they desire. "When the savages of Louisiana are desirous of fruit, they cut the tree to the root, and gather the fruit. This is an emblem of despotic government." None of this is ultimately

---

52. *Persian Letters*, 86, 119, 63.
53. *The Spirit of the Laws*, 16.9, 1:256; *Pensées*, 1820, p. 1037.

satisfying. Those driven by cycles of desire followed by gratification find themselves constantly anxious and constantly wanting more because desires act like blackmailers who return again and again. "It is with lust as with avarice, whose thirst increases by the acquisition of treasure."[54]

Montesquieu maintained that, on a more modest level, subjects mirror their masters. Thus, like the despot, the people are pushed by desires or "hurried away by their passions." This is possible because the violence of despotic government rarely reaches down to the ordinary citizen, concentrating itself instead on those with enough wealth or power to threaten the regime. "It is necessary that . . . the lives of the lowest subjects should be safe, and the pasha's head ever in danger." That the subjects of despotism relentlessly chase desires is not surprising. Since Montesquieu regarded any society as an interrelated whole, it would indeed shock him, and us, to find voluptuous despots ruling over self-disciplined subjects. And indeed, Montesquieu suggested that the desires for wealth and pleasure are the signs that republics and monarchies are declining into corruption and quite possibly into despotism. "No sooner were the Romans corrupted than their desires became boundless and immense."[55]

What is surprising, given his often unremittingly bleak picture of despotism, is that he occasionally described the delights of such servitude. The seraglio, as described in some passages, turns out not to be a brutal place but instead a place dominated by lazy and voluptuous princes whose very "indolence . . . renders the eastern seraglios so delightful to those very persons whom they were made to confine." Montesquieu's language here is no aberration. After he moved beyond both the reality and the metaphor of the seraglio, he offered a full-blown analysis of a despotism that was effective and lasting precisely to the extent that it was at least somewhat gratifying. For example, the Romans, as Tacitus wrote, conquered an opposing nation "insensibly"—calling it an ally at first, giving it the appearance of autonomy, providing its leadership with the pleasures of leisure, and thereby rendering "it a subject people without anyone being able to say when its subjection began." The Greeks, for example, "abandoned themselves to senseless delight and believed themselves free in reality because the Romans declared them so." Similarly, "Augustus, a scheming tyrant, conducted [the Romans] gently to servitude."[56] And of course the Romans distracted their subjects from their

<hr />

54. *The Spirit of the Laws*, 2.5, 1:18; *Pensées*, 644, p. 948; *The Spirit of the Laws*, 16.9, 1:256; 7.9, 1:102; *Persian Letters*, 62; *The Spirit of the Laws*, 5.13, 1:57; 16.6, 1:254; *Persian Letters*, 141.

55. *The Spirit of the Laws*, 5.11, 1:55; 3.9, 1:27; 7.2, 1:96; 7.7–8, 1:101.

56. *The Spirit of the Laws*, 15.11, 1:242. *Considerations*, 75, 60, 123. Compare to Tacitus:

servitude with bread and circuses, just as Usbek tells a eunuch to "divert [Usbek's wives] with music, dances, delicious drinks," and "innocent pleasures."[57]

Montesquieu's description of despotism as delightful and gentle is difficult to reconcile with his analysis of despotism as a world of violence, fear, and poverty, a brutal world with neither reliable agriculture nor systematic commerce. In part, Montesquieu was trying to account for the phenomenon of corruption, of how nations fall from virtuous republics or honor-bound monarchies into despotism. Convinced that licentiousness and luxury lead nations to corruption and servitude, he logically described despotism as pleasurable. For example, the people of Rome, as both Tacitus and Machiavelli maintained, remained free so long as they remained virtuous, but "when their morals were corrupted, . . . upon becoming their own tyrants and slaves, they lost the strength of liberty to fall into the weakness and impotency of licentiousness." Similarly, whereas large cities are "extremely pernicious" to republics, since "the mores of a republic are always corrupted there," such cities are useful and appropriate to despotisms. French mores had changed principally because the nobility had left the countryside to take up residence in Versailles and Paris. "One abandoned the simple mores of former times for the vanities of the cities; women stopped the knitting of wool and scorned all amusements that were not pleasures."[58]

Montesquieu's attempt to explain moral corruption accounts only partially for this glaring contradiction between a despotism that is a fearful desert and one that is gently licentious, because Montesquieu did not just mention corruption in passing, but instead offered a far-reaching description of a despotism that depends, not on fear, but on pleasure to solidify the servitude of its subjects. In *The Persian Letters* Montesquieu described the seraglio as an "empire of passion"; the chief eunuch says to Usbek, "[Y]ou are more absolute when you caress than when you threaten." When the despotism of the seraglio is successful—and it is not always so, since it is constantly prone to revolts—it is successful not so much because of force but because the despot creates desires in his subjects that only he can satisfy. After Usbek has left Persia, one of his wives

---

"And so the population was gradually led into the demoralizing temptations of arcades, baths, and sumptuous banquets. The unsuspecting Britons spoke of such novelties as 'civilization,' when in fact they were only a feature of their enslavement." *Agricola*, trans. H. Mattingly and S. A. Handford (New York: Penguin, 1970), 21.

57. *Persian Letters*, 2.

58. *Spirit of the Laws*, 8.12, 1:118; *Pensées*, 311, p. 886; 621, p. 945. For Montesquieu's attitude toward Rome, see Roger B. Oake, "Montesquieu's Analysis of Roman History," *Journal of the History of Ideas* 16, no. 1 (1955): 44–59.

writes that her desires for him returned "each day with renewed violence." She willingly chose servitude because of her devotion to him. "I confess to you, Usbek: a passion much more keen than ambition made me want to please you." Similarly, another wife declares that she is a "slave by the violence of her love." Desperately she writes to Usbek that "it is impossible to go on living in this condition. Fire is flowing in my veins. . . . How miserable it is for a woman to have such violent desires when she is deprived of him who alone can satisfy them."[59]

Using a literary metaphor, Montesquieu depicted a despotism in which people became attached to their servitude, not because of a fearful obedience, but rather because of some genuine pleasure offered by the despotism. This contradiction leads to Montesquieu's second theory of despotism.

Montesquieu's Ambivalence Toward Luxury and Commerce: A Second Theory of Despotism Emerges

Although Montesquieu argued that luxury undermined the self-sacrificing virtue of republics, indeed, that luxury is "fatal" to a republic, he was not entirely critical of luxury, because he saw it as indispensable to monarchies and quite appropriate to despotisms. In monarchies, luxuries help establish the order of inequality, provide rewards for those who have achieved honor in the service of the monarch, and provide labor for the poor who provide luxury. "As riches, by the very constitution of monarchies, are unequally divided, there is an absolute necessity for luxury. Were the rich not to be lavish, the poor would starve."[60] Luxury also brings with it leisure, and with leisure, the development of the arts and sciences. "The effect of commerce is riches; the consequence of riches,

---

59. *Persian Letters*, unpublished letter, appendix, 290; and letters 96, 3, and 7. Montesquieu wrote a startling passage showing the possibilities of what some might call a willing devotion to one's servitude, although it differs by its austerity from Montesquieu's notion of a pleasant despotism. "How comes it that monks are so fond of their order? It is owing to the very cause that renders the order insupportable. Their rule debars them from all those things by which the ordinary passions are fed; there remains therefore only this passion for the very rule that torments them. The more austere it is, that is, the more it curbs their inclinations, the more force it gives to the only passion left them." *The Spirit of the Laws*, 5.2, 1:40–41.

60. *The Spirit of the Laws*, 7.4, 1:97; on luxury as destructive of a republic, see 7.2, 1:96; 21.16, 1:361.

luxury; and that of luxury the perfection of the arts." If luxury is essential to monarchies, however, it is also important to despotisms, as a way in which a despot can reward those who maintain his or her rule. While the despot wallows in "corruption, luxury, indolence, and pleasure," the officials of the despotism are "avaricious" and motivated in large part by the pursuit of luxury and sexual pleasure. Luxury is "absolutely necessary" to despotic states, and in one passage Montesquieu just about defines despotism as a combination of "luxury and arbitrary power."[61]

Montesquieu's attitude toward luxury, however, is not as clear as it first appears, because, although he wrote in *The Spirit of the Laws* that luxury supports monarchy, in other places he suggested that luxury undermines monarchy. This should not surprise us, because Montesquieu himself, who was moderately wealthy, sought no great fortune, looked upon the obsession with wealth as a kind of personally imposed tyranny, and once even wrote that riches are an evil for which one should apologize.[62] And although luxury may well employ the poor in a monarchy, it also contributes to their exploitation. "So that one man may live in delight, a hundred others must labor ceaselessly. A woman has taken it into her head that she must appear at a gathering in a certain attire. From that moment on, fifty workers get no more sleep and are without time to drink and eat." Similarly, Montesquieu looked upon the cities of Europe with "disquiet" and "disgust," because these cities "breathe of avarice, ambition, and passions that torment." With such convictions, it is no wonder that Montesquieu looked upon luxury as capable of corrupting monarchy. "Mores are never very pure in monarchies. This nobility, with its luxury . . . is the source of all corruption."[63]

This idea that luxury can corrupt monarchy also appeared in Montesquieu's famous story of the rise and fall of the virtuous Troglodytes. As long as the Troglodytes remained cooperative, self-sacrificing, and poor, they maintained their virtuous republic. The Troglodytes surrendered their republic, however, and sought a monarch to rule them at precisely the moment when they wanted to satisfy their "ambition, acquire riches, and languish in soft luxury." In a sequel to this story, which he never published, Montesquieu described a further transformation of the Troglodytes' political order from monarchy to despotism. In this sequel, the people appealed to their king to establish "commerce and the arts," and they promised to be moderate and live without excess of "avarice."

61. *The Spirit of the Laws*, 21.6, 1:334; 7.7, 1:101; 15.18, 1:249; 7.14, 1:106; 7.4, 1:98; 15.18, 1:249; see also *Considerations*, 62.

62. *Pensées*, 1135, 1127, 1130, p. 992.

63. *Persian Letters*, 106; *Pensées*, 442, p. 901; 220, p. 876.

The king responded that if both king and people remained virtuous, they would have a wonderful life together, but the king warned the people not to lose their virtue in their quest for riches, because then the king himself would toss off his virtue and "you [the people] would have to wear yourselves out to make me rich." Since Montesquieu regarded luxury, riches, and avarice all as destructive of virtue, clearly he was suggesting, despite some wishful thinking that both people and monarch could remain rich and virtuous, that the self-seeking wish for luxury produces a further decline from monarchy into despotism.[64]

Montesquieu had a very similar ambivalent attitude toward commerce. Evidence from his letters indicates that Montesquieu was something of a merchant himself and engaged in a lucrative wine trade between Bordeaux and England,[65] so predictably he had a great many positive things to say about commerce. For example, because of commerce, the citizens of Marseilles were laborious, just, moderate, and frugal. The "spirit of commerce," Montesquieu suggested, makes every person disciplined and thrifty, and "consequently prevents the growth of luxury." Whereas commerce may corrupt the most virtuous of nations, it improves the moral character of the vast majority of nations, and because commerce imposes self-discipline on citizens, it is appropriate for certain kinds of republics. Thus Montesquieu noted that "great enterprises . . . in commerce are . . . for republican governments."[66] In addition, commerce makes nations flourish, increases the population, and brings peace between nations that are trading partners.[67]

England's commerce also drew Montesquieu's praise. Montesquieu did not know how to classify England; in *The Spirit of the Laws* Montesquieu called England a republic "disguised under the form of a monarchy," but he knew England did not have the virtue required of a republic; in his notes he called it a "mixed monarchy," but he knew England had too much popular government and too few intermediate institutions to qualify as a monarchy; as a consequence, one commentator has correctly concluded that, for Montesquieu, England was "midway between *mon-*

---

64. *Persian Letters*, 24; unpublished letter, appendix, pp. 284–85.

65. *Correspondance*, in *Oeuvres* (Nagel), 3:1429, 1439, 1517–18. See also Shackleton, *Montesquieu*, 201.

66. *The Spirit of the Laws*, 20.5, 1:319; 7.2, 1:96; 20.4, 1:318; 20.1–2, 1:316–17.

67. *Persian Letters*, 115; *The Spirit of the Laws*, 20.2, 1:316. For articles emphasizing only Montesquieu's positive claims about commerce, see Stephen J. Rosow, "Commerce, Power, and Justice: Montesquieu on International Politics," *Review of Politics* 46, no. 3 (1984): 346–66; Peter T. Manicas, "Montesquieu and the Eighteenth-Century Vision of the State," *History of Political Thought* 2, no. 2 (1981): 313–47.

archy and *republic.*"[68] However he chose to classify England, Montesquieu praised it for its freedom, not only because the nobility, the judiciary, and the legislatures limited the executive power of the monarch, but also because England's commerce produced a disciplined ethic that, if it was not exactly like virtue, at least replaced it well. England is "the freest country in the world" precisely because the English "know better than any other people upon earth how to value, at the same time, these three great advantages—religion, commerce, and liberty."[69]

And yet, in his private writings, Montesquieu expressed severe misgivings about England. Here Montesquieu wrote that corruption pervaded all ranks of society, that "money is sovereignly esteemed," while honor and virtue are of little value, and that the English had little respect for religion. Worst of all, "the English are no longer proud of their liberty. They sell it to the king; and if the king gave it back, they would sell it to him again."[70] These passages from his "Notes sur l'Angleterre" suggest grave reservations, although we cannot know the extent of his reservations, since Montesquieu's grandson, as a refugee in England during the French Revolution, destroyed most of the notes for fear that they would offend his English hosts.[71] We do, however, have one other insight to his ambivalent feelings about England. In 1749, he responded by letter to Domville, who had asked Montesquieu's opinion about the future of England. Montesquieu answered that "in Europe the last sigh of liberty will be given by an Englishman," and he went on to suggest that "your liberty is linked to your commerce and your commerce is linked in some fashion to your existence." Montesquieu's *Pensées,* however, contain the draft of a letter to the same Domville, trying to answer the same question about

68. *The Spirit of the Laws,* 5.19, 1:68; *Pensées,* 238, p. 878; M. Masterton, "Montesquieu's Grand Design: The Political Sociology of *L'ésprit des lois,*" *British Journal of Political Science* 2, no. 3 (1972): 283–318, esp. 312–13, 316; also Richter, *The Political Theory of Montesquieu,* 76–77.

69. Montesquieu, "Notes sur l'Angleterre," in *Oeuvres* (Seuil), 331–34, esp. 334; *The Spirit of the Laws,* 20.7, 1:321. It seems to me that the evidence does not support the claim that Montesquieu was a nearly unwavering defender of England, liberalism, and commerce (see, for an example of this interpretation, Thomas Pangle, *Montesquieu's Philosophy of Liberalism* [Chicago: University of Chicago Press, 1973]). And even though Montesquieu was deeply critical of the status quo, he was not a radical republican in disguise (see, for an example of this claim, Mark Hulliung, *Montesquieu and the Old Regime* [Berkeley and Los Angeles: University of California Press, 1976]). Without question, the best book showing Montesquieu's ambivalent attitudes toward England and toward commerce is Keohane's *Philosophy and the State in France,* chap. 14, 392–419.

70. "Notes sur l'Angleterre," 332–34.

71. Franz Neumann, introduction to *The Spirit of the Laws,* xii.

England's future, but here, though Montesquieu praised England, he also said, "[Y]our riches are causing your corruption."[72] Montesquieu definitely was not as enthusiastic about England in private as he was in his published writings, and he certainly felt ambivalent about the English political system and English commerce.

In fact, despite all of his praise for commerce, Montesquieu remained frequently critical both of commerce and of the commercial classes.[73] In his caustic comments about Dutch "avarice" in his travel notebooks he wrote, "The heart of the inhabitants of countries that live by commerce is entirely corrupted."[74] In writing about countries other than England, Montesquieu assumed that commerce destroys republics. "Having become rich sooner than Rome, Carthage had also become corrupted sooner." And if commerce fostered English liberty, it destroyed the liberty of ancient republics, as Tacitus and Machiavelli argued. "Every kind of low commerce was infamous among the Greeks; . . . [it] clashed with the spirit of Greek liberty."[75] Nor did the ancient Romans have any use for commerce. The Romans' "genius, their glory, their military education, and the very form of their government estranged them from commerce. . . . I am not ignorant that men prepossessed with these two ideas, that commerce is of the greatest service to the state, and that the Romans had the best regulated government in the world, have believed that these people greatly honored and encouraged commerce; but the truth is, they seldom troubled their heads about it."[76]

Montesquieu quite simply regarded commerce as a fairly petty undertaking, not worthy of a great people. For example, he quoted Cicero to the effect that it was not proper that the same nation was master of the world and also the greatest commercial power; this would suppose that the people of such a nation "had their heads constantly filled with grand views, and at the same time with small ones, which is a contradiction." Indeed, Montesquieu's writings betray the contempt of the aristocrat for the merchant. Only after the republic had collapsed, he wrote, did Rome become "full of timid *bourgeois*," and similarly he contrasted ancient with modern Greece. The ancient Greeks, "who lived under a popular government, knew no other support than virtue. The modern inhabitants of that

72. *Correspondance*, in *Oeuvres* (Nagel), 3:1245; *Pensées*, 1883, p. 1041.
73. See Keohane, *Philosophy and the State in France*, 408–19.
74. Montesquieu, "Voyage de Gratz à la Haye: Hollande," in *Oeuvres* (Seuil), 326–31, esp. 327.
75. *Considerations*, 44; *The Spirit of the Laws*, 4.8, 1:38; also 4.6, 1:36.
76. *The Spirit of the Laws*, 21.14, 1:358; also *Considerations*, 98–99.

country are entirely taken up with manufacture, commerce, finances, opulence, and luxury."[77]

In one crucial passage, Montesquieu summed up his view. Commerce can coexist for a long time with democracy, he suggested, because commerce promotes good characteristics such as frugality and moderation, but over time commerce will bring luxury, which will destroy all reason for frugality and moderation. "True is it that when a democracy is founded on commerce, private people may acquire vast riches without a corruption of morals. This is because the spirit of commerce is naturally attended with that of frugality, economy, moderation, labor, prudence, tranquillity, order, and rule. So long as this spirit subsists, the riches it produces have no bad effect. The mischief is, when excessive wealth destroys the spirit of commerce, then it is that the inconveniences of inequality begin to be felt."[78] Despite recognizing all the moral, economic, and political benefits of commerce, Montesquieu was suggesting that, over time, commerce creates luxury and together they can corrupt both republics and monarchies, transforming both into a despotism very different from the harsh Asiatic despotism that he more systematically analyzed. In his misgivings about commerce, Montesquieu outlined a second theory of despotism strikingly at odds with the brutal, fearful, and poverty-ridden despotism modeled after a European caricature of Turkey, Persia, and China.

What exactly did he fear commerce might do? First, commerce at best produces a mediocre nation. "Commercial powers can continue in a state of mediocrity a long time, but their greatness is of short duration." Second, commerce renders the citizens or subjects of a nation frivolous because "it is the nature of commerce to render the superfluous useful." In commercial societies people busy themselves with chasing yet more wealth, even though "riches do not bring comforts, but more needs." For Montesquieu this becomes a contemptibly frivolous world in which people are "actuated by an ambition of distinguishing themselves by trifles."[79] Third, commerce brings luxury, a claim that of course sits uneasily beside Montesquieu's claim that commerce prevents luxury. In one passage, Montesquieu said it bluntly: "The effect of commerce is riches; the consequences of riches, luxury." Fourth, Montesquieu suggested that commerce

---

77. *The Spirit of the Laws*, 20.4, 1:318; *Considerations*, 139; *The Spirit of the Laws*, 3.3, 1:21.

78. *The Spirit of the Laws*, 5.6, 1:46.

79. *Considerations*, 47; *The Spirit of the Laws*, 20.23, 1:330; *Correspondance*, in *Oeuvres* (Nagel), 3:794; *The Spirit of the Laws*, 7.1, 1:95.

might well unleash a world based solely on self-interest. In his story of the Troglodytes, Montesquieu had suggested that a society based entirely on self-interest, that is, a society with no internalized sense of morality, would collapse into anarchistic self-seeking. And commerce might introduce a self-interest that undermines morality. "We see that in countries where the people move only by the spirit of commerce, they make a traffic of all the humane, all the moral virtues; the most trifling things, those which humanity would demand, are there done, or given, only for money."[80]

Montesquieu also feared the political consequences of commerce, and as a fifth objection, he worried about the urbanization that invariably accompanies commerce. The Romans had been "corrupted by the luxury of the cities," and Montesquieu complained about cities in which people are "strangers to one another" and in which people forgo sincerity in trying to appear what they are not.[81] Sixth, commerce isolates people because people concerned with their private affairs have little time to devote to public affairs. Montesquieu quoted Xenophon to the effect that people engaged in commerce have no time for their friends or for their communities, and he also noted that "in proportion as luxury gains ground in a republic, the minds of the people are turned toward their particular interests." Seventh, Montesquieu thought commerce to be hostile to citizenship, and he observed that people "grow indifferent to public affairs [when] avarice becomes their predominant passion." Indeed, "with possessions beyond the needs of private life, it was difficult to be a good citizen." Finally, Montesquieu feared that, with commerce, a new class would come to dominate politics. The economic power of the commercial classes unavoidably transforms itself into political power because companies of merchants necessarily "give to the wealth of private persons the weight of public riches." Montesquieu admired Florence because in Florence the nobility still controlled the bourgeoisie, instead of vice versa. For example, whereas "other nations have made their interests of commerce yield to those of politics, the English, on the contrary, have ever made their political interests give way to those of commerce."[82]

<hr>

80. *The Spirit of the Laws*, 20.4, 1:318; 21.16, 1:361; 21.6, 1:334; 20.2, 1:317. For Montesquieu, no society, not even one with the best imaginable laws, can survive without morality. In *The Persian Letters*, 146, he satirized a man who called in a debt and ruined a family, causing the parents to die of grief and rendering the children destitute, but said, "Still I did no more than is permitted under the law."

81. *Considerations*, 40; *The Spirit of the Laws*, 7.1, 1:95. Montesquieu foreshadowed Rousseau's claim that we tyrannize ourselves with our own insincerity. "Éloge de la sincérité," in *Oeuvres* (Seuil), 43–45.

82. *The Spirit of the Laws*, 4.8, 1:38; 7.2, 1:96; 2.2, 1:13; *Considerations*, 98; *The Spirit of the Laws*, 20.10, 1:322; *Pensées*, 52, p. 857; *The Spirit of the Laws*, 20.7, 1:321.

A Second Theory of Despotism

Like ancient writers, but unlike some of his fellow philosophes who believed in a theory of progress, Montesquieu analyzed history in terms of cycles of decline. Most often he saw republics becoming monarchies and then collapsing into despotisms, but he did see the possibility of a monarchy becoming a republic.[83] Not surprisingly, Montesquieu saw himself as living in such an age of decline; born too late both for the virtue of ancient republics and for the honorable and limited monarchy of the French past, he felt confined to *ces temps de barbarie*.[84] "It is the love of country that gave to the histories of Greece and Rome this nobility that our history does not have. . . . When one thinks of the pettiness of our motives, of the baseness of our ways, of the avarice with which we seek vile rewards, of this ambition that is so different from love of glory, one is astonished at the different sights, and it seems that, ever since these two great peoples ceased to exist, men have been cut down a notch."[85] Like Tacitus, to whom he returned again and again, Montesquieu longed for the greatness of the past—and even painted the Roman Republic in such strong and pleasing colors that his picture inspired many of his fellow philosophes—but did not think the reemergence of Cato's republic or Louis IX's monarchy was possible. Instead, he had to analyze and warn against the dangers of the present. In his *Pensées* he copied a line from Tacitus's *Agricola* that described his own situation: "Rome of old explored the utmost limits of freedom; we have plumbed the depths of slavery."[86] Far from thinking that a virtuous republic could be reborn under the ever-enlarging absolutism of Louis XV, Montesquieu resigned himself to holding back the surge of despotism. In a long letter written in 1753, he desperately berated a friend who was afraid to assert forcefully the rights of the Paris Parlement against the crown, and declared to his friend that without these traditional bodies France would experience "the loss of our Constitution."[87]

It would be a mistake, however, to think that Montesquieu feared only the power of the monarchy. Montesquieu assumed that one analyzed politics in class terms, described the dominant classes as "*nobles, bourgeois,*

---

83. See the story of the Troglodytes, *Persian Letters*, 11–14, and unpublished letter, appendix, pp. 284–85; see also letters 102, 131, 136, and *The Spirit of the Laws*, 8.17, 1:121. Melvin Richter correctly noted that "Montesquieu believed that not progress but corruption was the law of history." *The Political Theory of Montesquieu*, 63.

84. *Correspondance*, in *Oeuvres* (Nagel), 3:934.

85. *Pensées*, 598, p. 938.

86. *Pensées*, 1580, p. 1020; Tacitus, *Agricola*, 2.

87. *Correspondance*, in *Oeuvres* (Nagel), 3:1465–69.

laboureurs," and recognized that a new class was becoming increasingly important. The spirit of glory is gone, noted Montesquieu, and "it is the spirit of commerce that dominates today." Indeed, "the passion for growing rich passes along from social class to social class." And Montesquieu did not like it very much. In *The Persian Letters* he noted that neither birth nor reputation counted for much, but instead "the first man of Paris" was the one who could buy the best horses for a carriage. "But when one closely examines the sort of people who have [the most wealth], by dint of despising the wealthy, one comes to have a scorn for wealth."[88] In so many ways Montesquieu is reminiscent of the aristocrat who fears the powerful king and resents the upstart bourgeoisie, who dislikes both monarchs and merchants.

Montesquieu thus saw France as threatened by two forces, a powerful monarchy and an ever-enlarging commercial class, and two different kinds of servitude. On the one hand, by using his model of Asiatic despotism, a harsh despotism founded on a fearful violence that eliminates all intermediate institutions, Montesquieu could warn against the encroachments of the French monarchy. Probably he was not really thinking that France would become like Turkey, but that it might become like Spain.[89] On the other hand, Montesquieu's writings betray another anxiety, an anxiety that a powerful monarch might rule hand in hand, not with the nobility, but with the new middle classes, and that such a despotism would not be a brutal Asiatic oppression but rather a somewhat pleasant European corruption. Just perhaps it would be more absolute to the extent that it seduced rather than forced, to the extent that it pleased rather than brutalized. In an unpublished note, Montesquieu suggested that a despotism would be more effective if it found a basis for its rule other than cruelty, and in his own "general maxims" about politics, he wrote that "fear is a motive that must be used sparingly; it is never necessary to make a severe law when a milder one will suffice."[90] If an absolute power can control its people by some means more lasting than fear, then it might be an even more frightening form of despotism.

Montesquieu was pointing toward a new despotism with the following characteristics. First, it would be controlled by a monarch who ruled hand in hand with the new middle classes. Second, its principle would

88. *Pensées*, 1481, p. 1012; also, 263, p. 880; 1228, p. 997; *Persian Letters*, 106, 88, 98.

89. Hulliung is right in using Spain as a model for what Montesquieu feared France might become. See *Montesquieu and the Old Regime*, 6, 48–53.

90. Montesquieu, "Législation," unpublished fragment from *The Spirit of the Laws*, in *Oeuvres* (Seuil), 799; *Pensées*, 630, p. 946.

not be fear but avarice. Twice in *The Spirit of the Laws,* not more than a few pages after he wrote that fear was the principle of despotism, Montesquieu wrote that "the principal motive of action [in despotic government] is the hope of the conveniences of life."[91] Third, this government would delight in its citizens' pursuing wealth and commerce, because with such private pursuits they would not bother themselves with public affairs. Fourth, people would be isolated from one another, not because of fear and violence, but because the pursuit of wealth and luxury makes people lead private lives. In his notes, Montesquieu complained that all ties between citizens had been severed, that all interests have been "particularized," and that "each man is isolated."[92] Fifth, such a government would eliminate all intermediate institutions and replace them with officials appointed by the central power. Finally, such a despotic government might well endeavor to satisfy its subjects' desires for goods and pleasures; indeed, Montesquieu was beginning to depict a world in which subjects are tied to their servitude, not because of violence, but because such servitude is pleasing. One part of Montesquieu's legacy to Tocqueville and to our century was this notion of a despotism founded not on fear but on gratification, a despotism with a panoply of pleasures much like the seraglio in which the master is more absolute when he caresses than when he threatens.

Conclusion

Numerous similarities of course appear between Montesquieu's discussion of despotism and previous analyses of tyranny. For example, the use of fear and force, the need for military and paramilitary forces, the need to isolate and depoliticize the population, and so forth. But Montesquieu's discussion makes new and distinctive contributions to European theories of tyranny as well. First, Montesquieu changed the vocabulary of tyranny by avoiding the word *tyranny* and purposely using the new word *despotism.* He and other philosophes did so strategically, because they wanted to argue that Louis XIV and Louis XV were more than mere tyrants who used power arbitrarily in their own interests. Instead, they wanted to argue—not terribly convincingly to modern eyes—that French kings were transforming both the French court and French society so profoundly that

91. *The Spirit of the Laws,* 5.17–18, 1:65–66.
92. *Pensées,* 604, p. 939.

France was beginning to resemble some imagined caricature of Turkey, Persia, or China, complete with lavish and degraded courtiers, a thoroughly dependent aristocracy, the absence of all regulated law, a pervasive fear throughout, and a society from top to bottom in which individuals consecrate themselves to the search for sensual pleasure and material comfort. Whereas Montesquieu used the word *despotism* this specifically, by the late eighteenth century Jefferson and others saw no notable distinction between the two words *tyranny* and *despotism* and thus used them interchangeably. While attempting to make the vocabulary of tyranny more precise, Montesquieu contributed to a confusion that emerged with the proliferation of words—soon to include *absolutism, dictator,* and *emperor*—all of which loosely and imprecisely condemned arbitrary power.

Second, after observing Roman and British institutions, Montesquieu gave a resounding critique of the inevitably tyrannical centralization of government power. A monarch's power ought to be checked by a legislative body, common law, positive law, a judiciary, the privileges of an aristocracy, and rights granted to cities, families, and individuals. This is a more extensive and thoroughgoing pattern of checks and balances than Madison knew. Third, and really part of his checks and balances, Montesquieu maintained that the judiciary and the legal system offer the best check to arbitrary power and the best protection for the individual. To the frustration of some who wanted swift and efficient judicial decisions, Montesquieu defended delays and appeals, arguing that these ensured a fair hearing for the individual and a cooly objective evaluation of a case. He recognized, as did Tacitus, that any tyrant or despot must undermine the independence of the judiciary and the legal system. Fourth, Montesquieu feared that the tentacles of centralized power, symbolized in his time by the king's Intendants, would reach down to the local level. How could a society avoid absolute rule of the central government over the individual? His answer was that any constitutional government—a monarchy or a republic—must have legally recognized buffers between the individual and the state, intermediate associations to which the individual can appeal for help. In Montesquieu's time these included classes, guilds, workers' organizations called corporations, groups of all kind, extended families, independent municipalities, and the courts of the judicial system. Despotic government endeavors to eliminate all such buffers between the powerful government and the powerless individual.

Other contributions Montesquieu made toward theories of tyranny point more toward modern developments in the next century. For example, as a fifth contribution, Montesquieu recognized, as did the ancient Romans, that the family was a crucial socializing agent and that any enduring republic must have firm family rules. However, whereas the Romans argued for an extremely patriarchal family, Montesquieu asked whether a republic espousing some degree of equality could thrive if the families themselves were hierarchical and despotic. In particular, he wondered if one could claim to have freedom, in either a monarchy or a republic, if women were oppressed within the family and the society at large. Although Montesquieu hardly gave us an argument for an egalitarian family or for a far-reaching equality of women, his critique did raise questions that led in that direction. And his recognition that a thoroughgoing despotism must teach habits at the family level—"domestic slavery and despotic government walk hand in hand"—was a major contribution to theories of despotism and one not lost on later thinkers.

Sixth, Montesquieu suggested that despotism may find fertile ground in the future because gigantic cities, of which Montesquieu had but a glimpse, seem to lend themselves naturally to rule by despots. Those who live in cities, he suggested, are caught up in commerce and trade, and thus in the private pursuit of wealth. As a result, individuals almost automatically gravitate toward their private homes, leaving the government in charge of public space. Powerless, isolated, and "strangers to one another," cities seem to set forth quite naturally key prerequisites for despotism. Perhaps cities, Montesquieu wondered, create lonely individuals ripe to be controlled by powerful despotic forces, an argument Arendt elaborated in our century. Seventh, Montesquieu asked how a modern republic could function in a commercial world if there was a built-in tension between the private self-seeking of the commercial world and the public duties of the citizen. How could a republic reconcile the fact that there was a conflict between commerce and citizenship, between self-seeking bourgeois and selfless citizen? Both Madison and Tocqueville tried to give answers to this question. Eighth, with his second theory of despotism, Montesquieu raised a question that bothered other thinkers such as Tocqueville and Weber. Can an affluent society that widely distributes wealth and pleasure be despotic by denying freedom and by teaching its subjects what to think and feel? Indeed, can a modern tyranny, one based on providing the population with goods and services, take freedom and dignity from its subjects by caressing instead of threatening? Can there be a tyranny welcomed by its subjects, one rooted in pleasure and avarice, not fear?

And finally, Montesquieu's probing questions—perhaps a realism, perhaps a pessimism—took him outside the Enlightenment faith in progress. It was not at all clear to him the future would be better and more free than the past, that despotism—or other forms of tyranny—might not become the rule in the future and all constitutional government the exception.

6

TOCQUEVILLE
The Pleasures of Servitude

When Tocqueville traveled to North America in 1831 with his best friend, Beaumont, he carried with him not only an undeniable excitement about seeing this boisterous new experiment in democracy, but also a certain aristocratic cockiness that seemed intent on finding flaws in rustic American democracy. Could poorly educated farmers from a fledgling nation sustain a democratic freedom that the great French nation, despite its revolution and despite being the intellectual center of the world, had failed to establish? Although Tocqueville certainly found flaws in this new government—flaws that he elaborated in some detail when he published the two parts of *Democracy in America* in 1835 and 1840—he also found himself irresistibly attracted to this new democracy. Not quite two months after he arrived, Tocqueville wrote to Kergorlay (his oldest friend and an ardent, lifelong Legitimist who always resented the demise of the Bourbons) that his impressions were "more favorable to America than they were during the first days after my arrival. . . . The principles of government are so simple, the consequences are deduced from them with so perfect a regularity, that the mind is subjugated and carried away if it does not take care."[1] Democracy had seduced the aristocrat, although the aristocrat never did yield himself entirely.

Tocqueville most admired the fact that Americans democratically mastered their own political fate. Far from being docile in the face of a monarchy and its bureaucratic representatives (and Tocqueville had read Montesquieu's critiques of Louis XIV's Intendants well), Americans confidently and consciously shaped a political world to fit their needs. "There is not a country in the world where man more confidently takes charge of the future, or where he feels with more pride that he can fashion the universe to please himself."[2] Americans had an admirable internalized discipline that led them to obey the law, but this was a simple matter because they both made the laws and could remake them if it seemed reasonable to do so. "Under their hand, political principles, laws, and human institutions seem malleable, capable of being shaped and combined at will."[3]

Such democratic freedom and citizen control of laws and institutions could only result from widespread political participation. Whereas the citizens of other nations were content with the security to pursue private goods and pleasures, Americans eagerly entered the public world of assemblies and deliberations. "If an American were condemned to confine his activity to his own affairs, he would be robbed of one half of his existence; he would feel an immense void in the life which he is accustomed to lead, and his wretchedness would be unbearable."[4] As a result,

---

1. Alexis de Tocqueville, *Selected Letters on Politics and Society*, ed. Roger Boesche, trans. James Toupin and Roger Boesche (Berkeley and Los Angeles: University of California Press, 1985), 57–58. There are two editions of Tocqueville's "complete" works, neither of which is complete. The first was published by Madame de Tocqueville and edited by Gustave de Beaumont (*Oeuvres complètes d'Alexis de Tocqueville* [Paris: Michel Lévy Frères, 1860–66]). I refer to this edition as *Oeuvres* (B). The second is in the process of publication; it was originally under the direction of J. P. Mayer (*Oeuvres complètes* [Paris: Gallimard, 1951–]). I refer to this edition as *Oeuvres* (M). Wherever possible I have used available English translations.

It should be noted that one can find the ideas for this chapter's discussion of Tocqueville's theory of despotism, although organized in entirely different ways, in my previous works "The Prison: Tocqueville's Model for Despotism," *Western Political Quarterly* 33, no. 4 (1980): 550–63; "Why Could Tocqueville Predict So Well?" *Political Theory* 11, no. 1 (1983): 79–104; and *The Strange Liberalism of Alexis de Tocqueville* (Ithaca: Cornell University Press, 1987). Some passages in this chapter have been taken from these works.

2. Tocqueville, *Journey to America*, ed. J. P. Mayer and A. Kerr, trans. George Lawrence (Garden City, N.Y.: Doubleday, 1971), 186.

3. Tocqueville, *Democracy in America*, ed. Phillips Bradley, trans. Henry Reeve, Francis Bowen, and Phillips Bradley, 2 vols. (New York: Vintage Books, 1945), 1:45; also, *Selected Letters*, 57.

4. *Democracy*, 1:260.

American citizens were politically wiser than any other people because they daily received a practical political education. Just as one learns a language by speaking it, so one learns the habits of democratic participation only by participating. The jury, for example, "is a school where the people come to learn their rights," and municipal institutions enabled Americans "to know the laws by participating in the act of legislation." Similarly, "town meetings are to liberty what primary schools are to science; they bring it within the people's reach."[5] A people long denied any part in municipal government—a description Tocqueville readily applied to the French people of the nineteenth century—will know very little about the practical matters of governing. Thus, in regard to the 1848 Constituent Assembly, composed of many of the most intelligent men of France, Tocqueville half-jokingly remarked that nine hundred "American peasants chosen at random" would know more about practical political matters.[6] Like Aristotle and Machiavelli, Tocqueville thought that political participation was essential to freedom and to the healthy development of all the intellectual and moral potentials of the citizen.

The intelligent participation of American citizens created an enormous popular energy that Tocqueville also admired. "No sooner do you set foot upon American ground than you are stunned by a kind of tumult. . . . Everything is in motion around you; here the people of one quarter of a town are met to decide upon the building of a church; there the election of a representative is going on; a little farther, the delegates of a district are hastening to the town in order to consult upon some local improvements; in another place, the laborers of a village quit their plows to deliberate upon the project of a road or a public school."[7] In contrast to citizens living under the authority of a national and centralized administration, who must apply to the national government to build a road or repair a church,[8] Americans gather immediately to address such concerns themselves. "The republic is everywhere, in the streets as much as in Congress. If there is something blocking the public way, the neighbors on the spot form a body to discuss it; they appoint a commission and put the trouble to rights by the collective effort sensibly directed."[9] While Tocqueville admitted that a centralized administration can offer a nation a certain efficiency in the routine affairs of government, consistency in

5. *Journey to America*, 246, 304; *Democracy*, 1:330, 63.
6. Tocqueville, *Recollections*, ed. J. P. Mayer and A. Kerr, trans. George Lawrence (Garden City, N.Y.: Doubleday, 1971), 127.
7. *Democracy*, 1:259.
8. Tocqueville, *The Old Regime and the French Revolution*, trans. Stuart Gilbert (Garden City, N.Y.: Doubleday, 1955), 62.
9. *Journey to America*, 43. Here Tocqueville was quoting his friend Francis Lieber.

policy, a plodding perseverance in completing tasks, and a skill at securing order and stability, nevertheless it can never accomplish what energetic democratic participation can accomplish. By decentralizing government and encouraging participation, one makes sure that thousands of citizens—not just dozens of functionaries—become actively involved in the political world. Decentralized participation may do "fewer things well, but it does a greater number of things. . . . Democracy does not give the people the most skillful government, but it produces what the ablest governments are frequently unable to create: namely, an all-pervading and restless activity, a superabundant force, and an energy which is inseparable from it and which may . . . produce wonders."[10] Whereas Machiavelli argued a people's army was invincible, Tocqueville suggested that a people's government was relentlessly energetic.

Democratic participation also helps to bring about intelligent and self-reliant citizens. If citizens refuse to rely on a distant and centralized government but instead assume the responsibility for democratically solving public problems, then they develop self-confidence, the ability to cooperate with their fellow citizens, a practical understanding about the political world, and the knowledge necessary for deliberating in assemblies. "One of the happiest consequences of the absence of government . . . is the ripening of individual strength which never fails to follow from it. Each man learns to think and act for himself without counting on the support of any outside power."[11] This self-confidence carries over into the private world, where individuals are quite willing to change occupations, learn new skills, and pride themselves on the fact that they can do many different things. If the big manufacturing cities of Europe were producing men and women stunted by a stifling division of labor, rural America was producing jacks-of-all-trades. Individual Americans often built their own homes, plowed their own fields, made their own clothes and tools, and even engaged in a variety of occupations ranging from farmer to merchant to lawyer to physician. "This is prejudicial to the excellence of the work," concluded Tocqueville, "but it powerfully contributes to awaken the intelligence of the workman."[12]

In addition to praising all the benefits of participatory government at the local level, Tocqueville praised the Americans' ability to gather into voluntary associations. "Wherever at the head of some new undertaking you see the government in France, or a man of rank in England, in the

10. *Democracy*, 1:261–62.
11. *Journey to America*, 38–39.
12. *Democracy*, 1:442–43.

United States you will be sure to find an association." Since Tocqueville regarded these associations as a buffer between the comparatively powerless individual and a potentially coercive state, he saw associations, in effect, as a modern replacement for Montesquieu's more traditional intermediate powers between monarch and subject. "An association for political, commercial, or manufacturing purposes, or even for those of science and literature . . . by defending its own rights against the encroachments of the government, saves the common liberties of the country."[13]

Tocqueville carefully avoided, however, adopting the modern pluralist notion that associations—by lobbying, compromising, and influencing the electoral process—actively represent the interests of passive citizens in governmental decision making. Tocqueville most admired associations because they serve as an additional arena in which citizens are active; indeed, he called the "art of association" the "mother of action."[14] In an imaginary political landscape dominated by Tocquevillian associations, people are not passive, while associations supposedly represent their interests, but instead citizens actively and energetically use the powers of associations to carry out their intentions. "The power of the association has reached its highest degree in America. . . . It is never by recourse to a higher authority that one seeks success, but by an appeal to individual powers working in concert."[15] Indeed, Tocqueville despised those associations in Europe that were rigidly hierarchical, while he admired those in the United States that have "established a government." "The members of [European] associations respond to a watchword, like soldiers on duty; they profess the doctrine of passive obedience; say, rather, that in uniting together they at once abjure the exercise of their own judgment and free will. . . . He who in given cases consents to obey his fellows with servility and who submits his will and even his thoughts to their control, how can he pretend that he wishes to be free?"[16] If members of associations cannot meet directly, they may have to govern themselves through representatives, uniting in "electoral bodies" and selecting "delegates to represent them in a central assembly."[17] No real Tocquevillian association, however, will consist of passive members who have paid their dues for the privilege of sitting back as spectators, while the elite leadership of the association actively enters into the political process.

13. *Democracy*, 2:114, 2:342.
14. *Democracy*, 2:125.
15. *Journey to America*, 219.
16. *Democracy*, 1:205.
17. *Democracy*, 1:199.

Nor did Tocqueville see associations as primarily pursuing the material self-interests of their membership, but instead, associations pursue mainly, although not exclusively, public ends. When he discussed associations, Tocqueville emphasized not those that lobbied for some narrow self-interest but those that cooperatively acted for their vision of the common good, which explains why he regarded townships, cities, and counties as premier, even prototypical, associations. The following passage highlights the predominantly public nature of the associations Tocqueville had in mind: "Americans of all ages, all conditions, and all dispositions constantly form associations. They have not only commercial and manufacturing companies, in which all take part, but associations of a thousand other kinds, religious, moral, serious, futile, general or restricted, enormous or diminutive. The Americans make associations to give entertainments, to found seminaries, to build inns, to construct churches, to diffuse books, to send missionaries to the antipodes; in this manner they found hospitals, prisons, and schools."[18] In sum, Tocqueville admired associations for the very reason he admired democratic participation in local government: associations constituted another outlet for the enormous and constructive popular energy he found in America and another way in which Americans could collectively control their own political universe. In effect, two of the pillars that upheld democratic freedom in America were municipal government and associations.

A third pillar had to do with the character of the people, what motivated the American people, something that appears most clearly in what the French call *les moeurs,* an elusive word that is only inadequately translated by our word *mores.* Not only does this word indicate customs, habits, and manners, but also the character or spirit of a people.

> I have previously remarked that the manners of the people may be considered as one of the great general causes to which the maintenance of a democratic republic is attributable. I here use the word *customs* with the meaning which the ancients attached to the word *mores,* for I apply it not only to manners properly so-called—that is, to what might be termed *the habits of the heart*—but to the various notions and opinions current among men and to the mass of those ideas which constitute their character of mind. I comprise under this term, therefore, the whole moral and intellectual condition of a people.[19]

18. *Democracy,* 2:114, 1:198.
19. *Democracy,* 1:310.

Neither institutions nor laws are sufficient for establishing and maintaining a democracy, but instead one needs the habits of freedom found only in the mores. "I am quite convinced that political societies are not what their laws make them, but what sentiments, beliefs, ideas, habits of the heart, and the spirit of men who form them, prepare them in advance to be." To try to establish freedom without the habits of freedom is exasperating and perhaps futile. "But how difficult it is to establish liberty solidly among peoples who have lost the practice and even the correct notion of it! What greater impotence than that of institutions, when ideas and mores do not nourish them."[20] Perhaps more than any other French thinker, Tocqueville believed that mores are of greater importance than laws in maintaining a society and that to alter society significantly, one needs to transform the mores dramatically, a difficult task indeed. Because one cannot transform habits and mores rapidly, significant change comes only incrementally and in a period of time spanning many generations. As he said of the United States, "it is evident that nothing but a long series of events, all having the same tendency, could substitute for this combination of laws, opinions, and manners a mass of opposite opinions, manners, and laws."[21]

And yet, despite all of his praise for this new democracy, despite his nearly boundless admiration for the popular participation fundamental to American democracy, he feared that in the long run democracy might well bring about a despotism of a new kind. Toward the end of the second part of *Democracy in America,* after hundreds of pages of analysis, Tocqueville introduced his gravest misgiving. "I think, then, that the species of oppression by which democratic nations are menaced is unlike anything that ever before existed in the world; our contemporaries will find no prototype of it in their memories. I seek in vain for an expression that will accurately convey the whole of the idea I have formed of it; the old words *despotism* and *tyranny* are inappropriate: the thing itself is new, and since I cannot name it, I must attempt to define it."[22] While Tocqueville admired American democracy, he feared certain tendencies that he regarded as inseparable companions of this democracy. This Dr. Jekyll could indeed become Mr. Hyde. But what exactly were his fears? How did these fears coexist with his undeniable admiration for American society? And what kind of analysis led him to think that democratic freedom might slowly evolve into an unprecedented democratic despotism?

20. *Selected Letters,* 294; *Oeuvres* (M), vol. 8, pt. 3, *Correspondance d'Alexis de Tocqueville et de Gustave de Beaumont* (1967), 543.

21. *Democracy,* 1:436.

22. *Democracy,* 2:336.

Democracy as Government by the Middle Classes

It is well known that Tocqueville used the word *democracy* in a variety of ways, not all of them consistent. He used it to mean majority rule, equality of political power, the absence of fixed classes, and an irresistible tendency toward equality. Tocqueville's use of the word *democracy,* however, always bore the unmistakable imprint of Guizot, a great French historian (and later a conservative French statesman) whose lectures on European history and the philosophy of history Tocqueville attended from 1828 to 1830. Guizot had suggested that the history of Europe during the previous centuries had been marked by the decline of the landed aristocracy, the movement toward greater equality, and the rise to prominence of the Third Estate, which included, of course, the bourgeoisie. Thus, the key to French history was class conflict between aristocrat and bourgeois, a lesson not lost on Marx, who openly acknowledged a debt to Guizot.[23] All of this culminated, for Guizot, first in the French Revolution and later in the rise to power of the bourgeoisie during the July Monarchy of Louis Philippe (1830–48). Throughout Tocqueville's writings one can see these same themes, although Tocqueville did disagree with this analysis when he contended that this class struggle and this march toward equality would not end with the middle classes comfortably in power. In fact, Tocqueville suggested well before Marx that demands for equality, especially from the working classes, would characterize European politics for the foreseeable future. "There are men who see in the Revolution of 1789 an accident and who, like the travellers in the fable, sit down to wait until the river has passed. What an empty illusion! Our fathers did not see the birth of this Revolution and we will not see it end. It will roll along for more generations still with its unsettling floods. It has been more than six hundred years since it was given its first impulse."[24]

Whether Tocqueville used the word *democracy* to describe increased economic equality or equality of political power or the absence of fixed classes, the shadow of Guizot always remained. The word *democracy* meant many things for Tocqueville, but among these things, it certainly meant the rise of the middle class to political and economic power. "Seen as a whole from a distance, our history from 1789 to 1830 appears to be forty-one years of deadly struggle between the ancien régime with its

23. Marx, in a letter to Joseph Weydemeyer, March 5, 1852.
24. Tocqueville Manuscripts Collection, Beinecke Rare Book and Manuscript Library, Yale University, C.V.H., Paquet no. 3, Cahier no. 3, p. 23.

traditions, memories, hopes and men (i.e., the aristocrats), and the new France led by the middle class."[25] As late as 1853 Tocqueville wrote to Beaumont of the continuing French Revolution, which he characterized as the ever-increasing dominance of "the bourgeois classes and the industrial element over the aristocratic classes and landed property."[26] In the United States, said Tocqueville, "the whole of society seems to have turned into one middle class," and "what never occurred elsewhere, the whole community is simultaneously engaged in productive industry and commerce."[27] Indeed, he referred to the American republics as "companies of merchants formed to make a prosperous business."[28] American democracy, he suggested, demonstrated once and for all that "the middle classes can govern a state" with "practical intelligence," but this is "*in spite of their petty passions, their incomplete education and their vulgar manners,*"[29] a passage clearly revealing Tocqueville's aristocratic contempt for the commercial classes.

Nor was Tocqueville's analysis confined to one side of the Atlantic. In fact, Tocqueville pointedly suggested that the ruling middle classes of the United States and France were remarkably similar.[30] The French government of his time, something he once called the "bourgeois state," exhibited the "narrow atmosphere of a bourgeois and shopkeeper's aristocracy whose egoism and corruption equalled the lack of enlightenment."[31] In a letter written in 1847, Tocqueville said of France that the middle class "is

25. *Recollections*, 5. For a good discussion of the varied meanings Tocqueville gave to the word *democracy*, see James T. Schleifer, *The Making of Tocqueville's "Democracy in America"* (Chapel Hill: University of North Carolina Press, 1980), chap. 19. For discussions on Tocqueville's debt to Guizot, see André Jardin, *Alexis de Tocqueville, 1805–1859* (Paris: Hachette, 1984), esp. 81, and Edward T. Gargan, *De Tocqueville* (New York: Hillary House, 1965), 26–34. For a comparison between Tocqueville's historical method and that of Guizot, see François Furet, *Interpreting the French Revolution*, trans. Elborg Forster (London: Cambridge University Press, 1981), 135–39.

26. *Selected Letters*, 287.

27. *Journey to America*, 290; *Democracy*, 2:37. As Raymond Aron points out, Tocqueville was astonished to find a society in which everyone worked for a living. Aron, *Montesquieu, Comte, Marx, Tocqueville*, vol. 1 of *Main Currents of Sociological Thought*, trans. Richard Howard and Helen Weaver (Garden City, N.Y.: Doubleday, 1968), 286–87.

28. Yale Tocqueville Collection, C.V.H., Paquet no. 3, Cahier no. 4, p. 23.

29. *Journey to America*, 271 (emphasis added).

30. *Oeuvres* (M), vol. 6, pt. 1, *Correspondance anglaise*, 320–21; see Cushing Strout, "Tocqueville's Duality: Describing America and Thinking of Europe," *American Quarterly* 21, no. 2 (1969): 87–99.

31. Tocqueville, *The European Revolution and Correspondence with Gobineau*, ed. and trans. John Lukacs (Gloucester, Mass.: Peter Smith, 1968), 152; R. Pierre-Marcel, *Essai politique sur Alexis de Tocqueville* (Paris: Librairie Félix Alcan, 1910), 369 (from an unpublished fragment).

becoming little by little, for the rest of the nation, a little corrupt and vulgar aristocracy, by which it seems shameful to let oneself be led."[32] And in another letter and in his *Recollections,* which he did not intend for publication, Tocqueville declared that the bourgeoisie of the July Monarchy was "the most selfish and grasping of plutocracies" and "treated government like a private business."[33]

Tocqueville, who was an aristocrat by birth and whose lineage could be traced at least to the fifteenth century, found himself greatly disenchanted to be living among all these merchants and manufacturers. Tocqueville ridiculed *ce pay de boeufs et de vendeurs de boeufs,*[34] and he felt like a stranger in his own country.

> Have you not noticed while travelling, Madame, the impression that one receives upon arriving in the morning in a strange town where everything is new and unknown to you—the men, the language, the mores; you are in the midst of a crowd, and nevertheless, you are more overwhelmed by the feeling of solitude than if you were in the heart of a forest. This is precisely what often happens to me in the midst of my compatriots and my contem-

---

32. *Selected Letters,* 188. Given such statements, it is astonishing to see someone claim Tocqueville as a defender of the bourgeoisie. For example, Maxime Leroy, *Histoire des idées sociales en France,* vol. 2, *De Babeuf à Tocqueville* (Paris: Gallimard, 1950).

33. *Correspondence and Conversations of Alexis de Tocqueville with Nassau William Senior, from 1834 to 1859,* ed. M.C.M. Simpson, 2 vols. in 1, 2d ed. (New York: Augustus M. Kelley, 1968 [1872]) 1:134; *Recollections,* 6. In one passage Tocqueville praised the political effects of commerce. "But I can find no example of a manufacturing and, above all, a trading people who have not been free. . . . So there must be a hidden relationship between those two words: *liberty* and *trade." Journeys to England and Ireland,* ed. J. P. Mayer, trans. George Lawrence and K. Mayer (Garden City, N.Y.: Doubleday, 1968), 105. Tocqueville wrote this just after he had visited England, but back on French soil and nestled in his library of French and ancient authors, Tocqueville wrote scarcely another word that would support this view. Nevertheless, critics still overstate Tocqueville's praise for commerce. See, for example, Melvin Richter, "The Uses of Theory: Tocqueville's Adaptation of Montesquieu," in *Essays in Theory and History: An Approach to the Social Sciences,* ed. Richter (Cambridge, Mass.: Harvard University Press, 1970), 93–102; also Marvin Zetterbaum, *Tocqueville and the Problem of Democracy* (Stanford: Stanford University Press, 1967), 130–37. Jean-Claude Lamberti correctly notes that Tocqueville's fears for the future of democracy relate to his dislike for the bourgeoisie. See Lamberti, *Tocqueville et les deux démocraties* (Paris: Presses Universitaires de France, 1983), 47–54, 189–98, 288–89. See also Georges Lefebvre, "A propos de Tocqueville," *Annales historiques de la révolution française* 27, no. 4 (1955): 313–23; Albert Salomon, "Tocqueville's Philosophy of Freedom," *Review of Politics* 1, no. 4 (1939): 400–431; idem, "Tocqueville, 1959," *Social Research* 26, no. 4 (1959): 449–70.

34. *Oeuvres* (M), vol. 15, pt. 2, *Correspondance d'Alexis de Tocqueville et de Francisque de Corcelle et correspondance d'Alexis de Tocqueville et de Madame de Swetchine* (1983), 138.

poraries. I sense that there is hardly any point of contact between their manner of feeling and thinking and mine. I have kept lively tastes that they no longer have; I still love passionately what they have ceased to love; I have a more and more invincible repugnance for what suits them more and more. It is not only the times that have changed; it is the entire race that seems to have been transformed.[35]

To Tocqueville, France had traded aspirations to intellectual and political greatness for the comforts created by commerce. Whereas the French of the eighteenth century concerned themselves not with commerce and industry but with ideas and hopes for greatness, in his own time his contemporaries busied themselves with the petty private pleasures of the moment. "What strikes me most about our days is not that people do such small things, it is that they do not better conceive the *theory* of grand things."[36] All the immense achievements in industry and science notwithstanding, Tocqueville could see no progress in his century. "If the brilliant talkers and writers of [the seventeenth century] were to return to life, I do not believe that gas, or steam, or chloroform, or electric telegraph, would so much astonish them as the dullness of modern society."[37]

Although Tocqueville's distaste for this new world of the bourgeoisie is easily documented, his own personal distaste is less important than his analysis suggesting that the new world of the middle classes brought key characteristics that, over time, would transform democracy into despotism. Tocqueville was suggesting, in effect, that the commercial ethic was incompatible with participatory democracy, that in the long run democracies might well exchange freedom for a comfortable security in an egalitarian despotism.

Privatization and the Eclipse of Public Life

In the middle of his *Old Regime* Tocqueville outlined clearly the difference between his century and the previous one. "Eighteenth-century man had little of that craving for material well-being which leads the way to

35. *Oeuvres* (M), vol. 18, *Correspondance d'Alexis de Tocqueville avec Adolphe de Circourt et avec Madame de Circourt* (1983), 103.

36. *Oeuvres* (M), vol. 11, *Correspondance d'Alexis de Tocqueville et de Pierre-Paul Royer-Collard: Correspondance d'Alexis de Tocqueville et de Jean-Jacques Ampère* (1970), 60–61; *The European Revolution and Correspondence with Gobineau*, 109.

37. *Correspondence . . . Senior*, 2:85.

servitude." Whereas the landed aristocracy had dominated eighteenth-century France, the bourgeoisie rose to power during the nineteenth century, and with it rose an acquisitive ethic—a "craving for material well-being"—that pervaded all classes of society. "The passion for physical comforts is essentially a passion of the middle classes; with those classes it grows and spreads, with them it is preponderant. *From them it mounts into the higher orders of society and descends into the mass of the people.*"[38] But why did Tocqueville think that such an obsession with accumulating goods and pleasures might well "lead the way to servitude"?

To begin with, this acquisitive ethic fastens people to their private affairs and leaves them with little interest, or time, for public participation. "What strikes me most," Tocqueville wrote to a friend, "is a nearly complete suspension of the collective and national life. Each is retired and as if buried in his private affairs." Thus, the immediate result of this obsession with accumulating physical comforts is a privatization of life that leads rapidly to an indifference or apathy toward public affairs and the decision making of public bodies. No one dreams of greatness, of great literary or political accomplishments, but instead, "the great majority of men of my own age merely want to get on with their small affairs." With each concerned only for his or her private affairs, egoism becomes the predominant motive in society. Tocqueville called egoism "a sweet, peaceful, and tenacious love of one's private interests," and although egoism was compatible with many private virtues, in general it led to "honest men and poor citizens."[39]

In short, Tocqueville thought one could not be both self-seeking bourgeois and selfless citizen, that the acquisitive ethic of bourgeois society would destroy citizenship. "A man absorbed by the cares of making money has always been a timid or indifferent citizen."[40] Since society subtly defines the good life as one rich in private excitements and private successes, people have no time or inclination or energy to extract themselves from their private concerns in order to participate in government.

There is, indeed, a most dangerous passage in the history of a democratic people. . . . The time will come when men are carried away and lose all self-restraint at the sight of the new possessions they are about to obtain. . . . It is not necessary to do

---

38. *The Old Regime*, 118; *Democracy*, 2:137 (emphasis added).

39. *Oeuvres* (B), vol. 7, *Nouvelle correspondance*, 288; *The European Revolution and Correspondence with Gobineau*, 189; *Oeuvres* (M) 11:64.

40. Seymour Drescher, ed. and trans., *Tocqueville and Beaumont on Social Reform* (New York: Harper & Row, 1968), 195.

violence to such a people in order to strip them of the rights they enjoy; they themselves willingly loosen their hold. The discharge of political duties appears to them to be a troublesome impediment which diverts them from their occupations and business. If they are required to elect representatives, to support the government by personal service, to meet on public business, they think they have no time, they cannot waste their precious hours in useless engagements; such idle amusements are unsuited to serious men who are engaged with the more important interests of life. These people think they are following the principle of self-interest, but the idea they entertain of that principle is a very crude one; and the better to look after what they call their own business, they neglect their chief business, which is to remain their own masters.[41]

Tocqueville was suggesting that democracy has two key characteristics in tension with each other: citizenship and commerce. Over time, there is a tendency for the demands and pleasures of the commercial ethic to undermine the ethic of citizenship, that is, for private interests to bring an eclipse of public life. Like Aristotle, whose categories he seems to have borrowed, Tocqueville claimed that in a free and democratic country citizens participate in the public space of the polis, whereas tyrants endeavor to transform citizens into subjects by sequestering them in the private household. Like Machiavelli, he feared that citizens would abandon public space, although not because of violence and fear.

Consider Tocqueville's disenchantment with French parliamentary life. Despite wishing fervently for a politics grounded in debates between principled statesmen and grand political parties that had different visions of the common good, Tocqueville found around him only politicians busying themselves with the pursuit of petty and narrow self-interest. To Tocqueville, a politics based solely on miserable day-to-day interests was unequivocally repugnant. "I cannot tell you, my dear friend, the disgust I feel in watching the public men of our day traffic, according to the smallest interests of the moment, in things as serious and sacred to my eyes as principles. . . . They frighten me sometimes and make me ask myself whether there are only interests in this world, and whether what one takes for sentiments and ideas are not in fact interests that are acting and

---

41. *Democracy*, 2:149. Such a passage should make it clear that Tocqueville did not find Bonapartism the chief threat to freedom, as some argue. See, for example, Melvin Richter, "Toward a Concept of Political Illegitimacy: Bonapartist Dictatorship and Democratic Legitimacy," *Political Theory* 10, no. 2 (1982): 185–214.

speaking."[42] In his famous speech of January 1848, the speech in which he predicted the forthcoming revolution, Tocqueville argued that "public mores are changing," because "private interests now lurk behind every opinion about the common good." Slowly but surely an ethic had emerged that suggested individuals with political power had every right to use that power for their own private interests. Once individuals perceive politics as an arena in which a plurality of interests compete for the means of satisfaction, public corruption occurs because "interest has replaced disinterested feelings in public life," greed supplants all cooperation for the public good,[43] and citizens mock all legislative decisions, seeing them not as careful and principled choices for the general good but merely as victories of the strongest. The political order will no longer be a commonwealth, but a chase after private wealth. Or, as Tocqueville put it in an earlier speech, "And besides, Gentlemen, are therefore so many words needed to prove that in substituting private interest for the general interest, one depraves society?"[44]

France, Tocqueville suggested, was becoming *une troupe de soliciteurs,* an aggregation of individuals distinguished by no consistent views of the general good and incapable of forming political parties with distinct perspectives. "In substituting, as you are doing, private interest for general interest . . . what is it that you are doing? You are undermining parties. . . . Now, do you think, Gentlemen, that a free society can live without parties?" When the France of the past witnessed parties—and Tocqueville thought of parties as groups with distinct and principled perspectives on political issues, not as organized election machines—politics had a certain grandeur and distinction; Tocqueville, for example, regarded the period from 1789 to 1830 as one long struggle between "the old feudal aristocracy and the middle class." Such a struggle gave birth to what he called "great" parties. "Between these two classes there was a long-stand-

42. *Selected Letters,* 129. Tocqueville did praise enlightened self-interest, but that does not mean he wanted a politics based on self-interest, as some have suggested: for example, Pierre-Marcel, *Essai politique sur Alexis de Tocqueville,* 131; Zetterbaum, *Tocqueville and the Problem of Democracy,* 130–37; J. P. Mayer, *Alexis de Tocqueville: A Biographical Study in Political Science* (Gloucester, Mass.: Peter Smith, 1966 [1939]), 22–24; Max Lerner, "Tocqueville's *Democracy in America*: Politics, Law, and the Elite," *Antioch Review* 25, no. 4 (1965–66): 543–63.

43. Tocqueville, "Speech Pronounced in the Chamber of Deputies on January 27, 1948," appendix 3 of *Democracy in America,* trans. George Lawrence (Garden City, N.Y.: Doubleday, 1969), 750.

44. *Oeuvres* (B), vol. 9, *Études économiques, politiques,* 380–82. Tocqueville certainly thought such moral corruption would be hastened by large industrial cities. See Seymour Drescher, *Tocqueville and England* (Cambridge, Mass.: Harvard University Press, 1964), 47, 66.

ing separation of status, memories, interests, passions, and ideas. There had to be great parties—there were."[45]

Tocqueville made a fundamental distinction between "great parties" and "little parties," similar to Machiavelli's distinction between parties and factions. Great parties, according to Tocqueville, affirm or question the most fundamental political assumptions and values upon which a political culture rests. "What I call great political parties, those concerned with principles and not with their consequences, with general questions and not with particular cases, with ideas and not with men, those parties generally have nobler traits, more generous passions, more real convictions, and a look of more frankness and boldness than the others." Little parties, by contrast, busy themselves with quarreling about day-to-day material interests, and "as they are not sustained or dignified by lofty purposes, they ostensibly display the selfishness of their character in their actions." Although little parties avoid the potentially destructive turmoil of grand parties and thereby produce a "great gain in happiness," Tocqueville doubted they brought about a similar gain in morality. When he was in periods of personal despair about the future, he probably preferred to content himself with the stability offered by little parties. More often, however, he noted the absence of noble purpose in such parties, their characteristic of "dishonourable selfishness," and the fact that they "do not rest upon principles, but upon material interests"; in these moments he embraced great political parties for their "generosity" and their quests for political greatness. Under the July Monarchy he despaired that a "single class" dominated all political decisions, producing a "lull in the political world" by removing all principles from politics and leaving mere interests. "As every matter was settled by members of one class, in accordance with their interests and point of view, no battlefield could be found on which great parties might wage war."[46]

Thus, according to Tocqueville, the acquisitive ethic brought into the world by the commercial classes fastens individuals to their private concerns, undermines citizenship, reduces politics to a quarrel about material self-interest, and produces little political parties with no grand vision about the common good, but instead only strategies for minor legislative advantage. While certainly Tocqueville thought this was a miserable and

45. *Oeuvres* (B), 9:380–82; Drescher, ed., *Tocqueville and Beaumont on Social Reform*, 175.
46. *Journey to America*, 250; *Democracy*, 1:182; *Journey to America*, 251, 164; *Democracy*, 1:184; Drescher, ed., *Tocqueville and Beaumont on Social Reform*, 175–76; *Recollections*, 11–12. For a good discussion of parties, see Jack Lively, *The Social and Political Thought of Alexis de Tocqueville* (Oxford: Clarendon Press, 1962), 134–43.

paltry spectacle, he also thought the overall tendency to be, in the long run, dangerous to freedom.

Isolation and Powerlessness

Although Tocqueville recognized that democracy had broken down the hierarchy of feudal society and, in the process, had introduced a great deal of equality into the social world, at the same time democracy had severed traditional ties between people and rendered each isolated and powerless. He noted, for example, that *individualism* was a modern word reflecting a modern development. "That word *individualism* which we have coined for our requirements, was unknown to our ancestors, for the good reason that in their days every individual necessarily belonged to a group and no one could regard himself as an isolated unit."[47] *Individualism* was a new word appropriate to a new society witnessing centrifugal forces flinging individuals into private worlds and fastening them there. Even though Tocqueville knew that the world could not return to an aristocratic past, even though he preferred ties of equality to ones of hierarchy, he confessed an admiration for the "sweet and paternal relations" of previous centuries. In the old aristocracies, one could not escape a web of ties to others. "Aristocratic institutions, moreover, have the effect of closely binding every man to several of his fellow citizens. . . . Aristocracy had made a chain of all members of the community, from the peasant to the king; democracy breaks that chain and severs every link of it."[48]

While democracy broke down the hierarchical and paternalistic groups and classes that had characterized aristocratic society, in the process it left all individuals equal, isolated, and powerless. In an 1840 letter to Royer-Collard, Tocqueville wrote, "I have never seen a country in which the first manifestation of public life, which is the frequent contact of men among themselves, is less to be found." Elsewhere he says that the private pursuit of wealth ensures that individuals live apart; "more and more each seems to retire into himself and to isolate himself."[49] Because each is

47. *The Old Regime*, 96. On the concept of individualism, see Steven Lukes, *Individualism* (Oxford: Basil Blackwell, 1973); for a superb discussion of the effects of individualism and egoism on democratic citizenship, see Lamberti, *Tocqueville et les deux démocraties*, 192–98, 220–27, 238–43, and idem, *La Notion d'individualisme chez Tocqueville* (Paris: Presses Universitaires de France, 1970); for insight into Tocqueville's struggle with these terms, see Schleifer, *The Making of Tocqueville's "Democracy in America,"* 177, 228–30, 240–43, 250–59.

48. *Oeuvres* (B), 7:436; *Democracy*, 2:105.

49. *Oeuvres* (M), 11:89; *Oeuvres* (B), 9:375–76.

isolated and alone, each is equally powerless. "When the inhabitant of a democratic country compares himself individually with all those about him, he feels pride that he is the equal of any one of them; but when he comes to survey the totality of his fellows and to place himself in contrast to so huge a body, he is instantly overwhelmed by the sense of his own insignificance and weakness. The same equality that renders him independent of each of his fellow citizens, taken severally, exposes him alone and unprotected to the influence of the greater number."[50] Likening the people of his time to "dwarfs" riding on a wave, Tocqueville suggested that virtually no one was powerful enough to influence events. "We live in a time and in a democratic society where individuals, even the greatest, are very little of anything"; it was a century of "grand movements . . . in the middle of which each man feels himself so weak and so small."[51]

The privatization of society and the isolation of individuals in effect left a political vacuum, into which stepped the central government. "It is the government alone that has inherited all the privileges of which families, guilds, and individuals have been deprived." In the ancien régime, the privileges of families, guilds, parishes, workers' corporations, and classes had managed to check the central power. "As long as family feeling was kept alive, the opponent of oppression was never alone; he looked about him and found his clients, his hereditary friends, and his kinsfolk." In fact, even if a former despot such as the so-called absolutist Louis XIV had wanted to control and direct every community and every individual, it would have been impossible because of poor means of communication, an imperfect system of administration, and the recalcitrance of Montesquieu's intermediate bodies that are an inevitable part of aristocratic society. "No sovereign ever lived in former ages so absolute or so powerful as to undertake to administer by his own agency, and without the assistance of intermediate powers, all the parts of a great empire."[52] All of this changes after democratic society dissolves all these traditional intermediate bodies and leaves individuals alone and powerless in the face of a powerful, centralized government. "What strength can even public opinion have retained when no twenty persons are connected by a common tie, when not a man, nor a family, nor chartered corporation, nor class, nor free institution, has the power of representing or exerting that opinion, and when every citizen, being equally weak, equally poor, and equally isolated, has only his personal impotence to oppose to the orga-

50. *Democracy*, 2:11.
51. *Oeuvres* (M), vol. 8, pt. 2, 369; *Oeuvres* (B), 9:115.
52. *Democracy*, 1:11, 340; 2:334.

nizing force of the government?"[53] Since the power of all previous governments was checked by traditional intermediate bodies, only with the advent of democracy does the world have the dreadful possibility of witnessing a truly absolutist government.

If this qualitatively new despotism emerges, it will base itself on the
twin foundations of isolation and powerlessness. Despotism has always
sought to isolate and separate subjects so that they cannot organize an
effective opposition, but whereas Aristotle, Tacitus, and Machiavelli saw
tyrants creating the requisite isolation by force and violence, Tocqueville
declared that such isolation would come all too easily, almost automatically, in the new democratic world. "Equality places men side by side,
unconnected by any common tie; despotism raises barriers to keep them
asunder."[54] Both the collapse of traditional group ties and the private pursuit of wealth, which is the necessary companion of the acquisitive ethic,
make isolation and powerlessness inevitable. The Tocquevillian despotism will need comparatively little force because it can isolate and control subjects comfortably.

> I seek to trace the novel features under which despotism may
> appear in the world. The first thing that strikes the observation is
> an innumerable multitude of men, all equal and alike, incessantly
> endeavoring to procure the petty and paltry pleasures with which
> they glut their lives. Each of them, living apart, is as a stranger to
> the fate of all the rest; his children and his private friends consti-
> tute to him the whole of mankind. As for the rest of his fellow
> citizens, he is close to them, but does not see them; he touches
> them, but he does not feel them; he exists only in himself and for
> himself alone; and if his kindred still remain to him, he may be
> said at any rate to have lost his country.
> Above this race of men stands an immense and tutelary power,
> which takes upon itself alone to secure their gratifications and to
> watch over their fate.[55]

The most fundamental characteristics of the acquisitive ethic—individualism, private pursuit of wealth, self-interest, and isolation—were, to
Tocqueville, the indispensable conditions for the new despotism. In the
introduction to his *Old Regime,* written during Louis Napoleon's very
bourgeois Second Empire, which Tocqueville despised, Tocqueville of-

---

53. *Democracy,* 1:340.
54. *Democracy,* 2:109.
55. *Democracy,* 2:336.

fered his last systematic description of the despotism he feared, and he revealed even to the casual reader his conviction that the isolation of the new despotism had its roots in the soil of bourgeois society.

> For in a community in which the ties of family, of caste, of class, and craft fraternities no longer exist, people are far too much disposed to think exclusively of their own interests, to become self-seekers practicing a narrow individualism and caring nothing for the public good. Far from trying to counteract such tendencies despotism encourages them. . . . It immures them, so to speak, each in his private life and, taking advantage of the tendency they already have to keep apart, it estranges them still more. . . . Love of gain, a fondness for business careers, the desire to get rich at all costs, a craving for material comfort and easy living quickly become the ruling passions under a despotic government. . . . It is in the nature of despotism that it should foster such desires and propagate their havoc.[56]

When Tocqueville linked "interests," "narrow individualism," "private life," "love of gain," and "business careers," he quite clearly was illustrating that the acquisitive ethic of the bourgeoisie was not only incompatible with participatory democracy but also the key factor in the new despotism that he feared.

Only with this in mind can one understand Tocqueville's idea of the tyranny of the majority and his famous statements "[F]reedom of opinion does not exist in America" and "I know of no country in which there is so little independence of mind and real freedom of discussion as in America." Tocqueville contended that aristocratic society was characterized by groups and classes to which each individual belonged, and as a result, aristocratic society necessarily displayed a diversity of opinion. Families, guilds, provinces, classes, and so forth, clung to differing views of the world and usually demanded of their members an adherence to this view. "The Middle Ages were a period when everything was broken up, when each people, each province, each city, and each family tended strongly to maintain its distinct individuality." After these groups and classes dissolved, however, individuals found themselves stripped of the support of traditional groups and alone in the face of a single, dominant public opinion. "The same equality that renders him independent of each of his fellow citizens taken severally exposes him alone and unprotected to the influence of the greater number. . . . A sort of enormous pressure of the

56. *The Old Regime*, xiii.

mind of all upon the individual intelligence."[57] Tocqueville did not think Americans tended toward uniformity of thought because they were naturally more "conformist" than other peoples. Rather, he argued that whereas in previous societies artisans used to conform to the standards of their guild and aristocrats to the manners of their class, in democratic society all conform to a dominant and uniform pattern of ideas and sentiments that embrace the entire society.

> In aristocracies men often have much greatness and strength of their own; when they find themselves at variance with the greater number of their fellow countrymen, they withdraw to their own circle, where they support and console themselves. Such is not the case in a democratic country; there public favor seems as necessary as the air we breathe, and to live at variance with the multitude is, as it were, not to live. The multitude require no laws to coerce those who do not think like themselves: public disapprobation is enough; a sense of their loneliness and impotence overtakes them and drives them to despair.
> . . . The majority do not need to force him; they convince him.[58]

Thus, not only do isolation and powerlessness lead to a despotism that takes away political freedom, but they lead as well to a uniformity of thinking, or a despotism of the mind. Previous tyrants used force and violence to control the behavior of their subjects, even if the thoughts of their subjects remained free. But democracy "has perfected despotism itself, though it seemed to have nothing to learn." Now, in the "tyranny [of] democratic republics . . . the body is left free, and the soul is enslaved."[59]

Living in an age when mass-circulation newspapers were just beginning to flourish, Tocqueville knew the importance of the communications media in establishing a uniformity of opinion. Long before radio and television, it bothered him that a newspaper "can drop the same thought into a thousand minds at once." He warned that if a nation relied on only two or three sources of information or a city had only one major newspaper—which he referred to as the "centralization" of the sources of information—then freedom of opinion would be illusory, because opinions would not be freely chosen by individuals but would instead be "formed" for them by distant powers over which they had no control. If in fact a despo-

57. *Democracy*, 1:275, 273, 451; 2:11. See Morton J. Horwitz, "Tocqueville and the Tyranny of the Majority," *Review of Politics* 28, no. 3 (1966): 293–307.
58. *Democracy*, 2:275–76.
59. *Democracy*, 1:274.

tism can control not only public behavior but private thought, then, un-like all previous despotisms, there will be no escape to a private freedom simply by closing the doors of our private homes. Not only will this des-potism be the "absolute master of public life," but it will also "penetrate from all sides into private life."[60] Not content with destroying all public freedom, the new despotism will subtly control our private opinions, all while giving us the illusion that we have freely chosen these opinions.

Centralization of Government as a Prerequisite for Despotism

Although communities in the United States distributed power with some rough measure of equality and attempted to encourage participation, in France most people (hardly citizens, in Tocqueville's eyes, and more like spectators) gazed upon the public world as if it were an uninteresting stage production in which only a few were graced with the right to act. Europe could boast only of the spectacle of nations composed of "set-tlers, indifferent to the fate" of public affairs, leaving judgments about schools, churches, local finances, community affairs, and certainly na-tional decisions to "a powerful stranger whom [they call] the govern-ment." French government was centralized government that "preponder-ates, acts, regulates, controls, undertakes everything, provides for everything, knows far more about the subject's business than he does himself—is, in short, incessantly active and sterile."[61] In most cases, Tocqueville suggested that France could see her possible future by study-ing the United States, but in this case the reverse is true, because Tocqueville thought that something like French centralization of govern-ment was an almost inevitable characteristic of democracy. "A demo-cratic people tends toward centralization, as it were, by instinct. It arrives at provincial institutions only by reflection." Stripped of the web of ties,

---

60. *Democracy*, 2:119; 1:192–94, 200; Yale Tocqueville Collection, C.V.c., Paquet no. 5, p. 4.
61. *Democracy*, 1:96; *The Old Regime*, 253. Tocqueville distinguished between a central-ized government, which speaks for the nation and deals with general laws and principles, and a centralized administration, which enables the tentacles of the central government to meddle in local affairs; he approved of the former and disapproved of the latter (*Democracy*, 1:89–92). I shall ignore this distinction, however, because (1) after *Democracy in America* he rarely made the same distinction and usually ignored it himself, using merely the word *centralization*, and (2), in practice, as Tocqueville's own analysis indicated, it is hard to see how a centralized government could avoid giving birth to a centralized administration. For a fine discussion of Tocqueville's idea of centralization, see Schleifer, *The Making of Tocque-ville's "Democracy in America,"* chap. 10.

privileges, groups, and intermediate bodies that once protected individuals in aristocratic society, individuals in democracies find no buffer between them and the state. "After the destruction of classes, corporations, and castes, [the state] appeared as the necessary and natural heir to all the secondary powers. . . . The idea of centralization and that of the sovereignty of the people were born on the same day." Indeed, "whenever a nation destroys its aristocracy, it almost automatically tends toward a centralization of power." Although isolation and powerlessness are prerequisites, it is centralized government that finally "fashions despotism and destroys citizenship."[62]

In his analysis, Tocqueville admitted that the United States would arrive at centralization more slowly than other nations. Because the United States had no democratic revolution in which the bourgeoisie used a powerful centralized state to wrench political power from the hands of an aristocracy and, in fact, "had no aristocracy to combat"—in this, it was an exception—the United States temporarily managed to avoid centralization. In other nations the middle classes and the aristocracy fought over state power and sought to harness themselves to this power in order to further their class interests.

> The people endeavor to centralize the public administration in the hands of the government, in order to wrest the management of local affairs from the aristocracy. Towards the close of such a revolution, on the contrary, it is usually the conquered aristocracy that endeavors to make over the management of all affairs to the state, because such an aristocracy dreads the tyranny of a people that has become its equal and not infrequently its master. . . . As long as the democratic revolution lasts, there is always one class in the nation, powerful in numbers or in wealth, which is induced, by peculiar passions or interests, to centralize the public administration.[63]

While this meant, according to Tocqueville, that Europe established centralized government more quickly, it did not mean that the United States would avoid the nearly irresistible tendency toward concentration of political power in the national government.

Tocqueville outlined several broad reasons for this inevitable centralization. All of these show that Tocqueville feared the long-run tendency of

---

62. Tocqueville, *Memoir, Letters, and Remains*, no trans. given, 2 vols. (Boston: Ticknor & Fields, 1862), 1:234 (from his essay "France Before the Revolution"); *Oeuvres* (B), 9:14; *The Old Regime*, 60; Yale Tocqueville Collection, C.V.b., Paquet no. 13, p. 1.

63. *Democracy*, 2:315–16.

the demands of the new industrial world to conflict with the prerequisites of democratic citizenship. First, because the acquisitive ethic has brought about the isolation of individuals and eliminated intermediate bodies, only the government is active. Wrenched from the extended families, guilds, communities, and classes that once supported them, individuals feel alone and powerless, and thus their hopeful gaze falls to the government, no longer to a local group that might offer assistance. "In this predicament he naturally turns his eyes to that imposing power which alone rises above the level of universal depression."[64] Called upon frequently to offer more and more assistance, the government can only get larger. Second, governments centralize because members of the middle class solicit the central government on behalf of their private interests. Notwithstanding the fact that nearly everyone is, in principle, hostile to the centralization of government power, in practice each person or each interest group wishes to make an exception in the particular case in question and thus implores the government to rush any and all assistance, obviously augmenting governmental powers.

> Such persons will admit, as a general principle, that the public authority ought not to interfere in private concerns; but, by an exception to that rule, each of them craves its assistance in the particular concern on which he is engaged and seeks to draw upon the influence of the government for his own benefit, although he would restrict it on all other occasions. If a large number of men applies this particular exception to a great variety of different purposes, the sphere of the central power extends itself imperceptibly in all directions, although everyone wishes it to be circumscribed.
>
> Thus a democratic government increases its power simply by the fact of its permanence. Time is on its side; every incident befriends it; the passions of individuals unconsciously promote it; and it may be asserted that the older a democratic community is, the more centralized will its government become.[65]

This rather clever notion that each person will seek to make an exception to the principle of government noninterference in his or her own particular case relates directly to a third reason for centralization. Once the love of wealth dominated all other passions in this new commercial world, Tocqueville suggested, people would clamor for government to enforce

64. *Democracy*, 2:311.
65. *Democracy*, 2:311–12 n. 1.

the order essential to their accumulation of goods and pleasures. "The increasing love of well-being," Tocqueville argued in *Democracy in America,* caused "democratic nations to dread all violent disturbances." This in turn "disposes the members of the community constantly to give or to surrender additional rights to the central power," which seems to be the only body able to protect their property.[66]

Fourth, Tocqueville maintained that centralization is indigenous to industrial society, or to be more precise, it would be indigenous as generations passed and industrial growth continued. The central government would be summoned both to mediate disputes between owners and workers (although he never claimed government to be a neutral arbiter) and to alleviate the misery arising from the cycles of prosperity and poverty. The "one great cause" of governmental centralization in Europe would arise from industrialization. Industrialization brought with it cycles involving "sudden alterations of plenty and want," and it produced working conditions that frequently tended to "sacrifice the health and even the life" of members of the working class. As a result, Tocqueville suggested that industry would require governmental regulation, although one might wonder why local governments, instead of the national government, could not undertake this regulation. Nevertheless, the regulation of industry would be the greatest single cause of centralization. "Thus, the manufacturing classes require more regulation, superintendence, and restraint than the other classes of society, and it is natural that the powers of government should increase in the same proportion as those classes."[67]

Tocqueville most feared a state cursed with the twin terrors of large aggregations of industrial power and a highly centralized government, two centralized powers that might alternate in teaching docility. "Manufactures govern us, [centralized governments] govern manufactures." Indeed, "equality increasingly extends its dominion everywhere—except in industry, which is moving in a more aristocratic direction every day," and capital slowly becomes "concentrated in a few hands." Because such concentrations of economic and political power are essential to despotism, Tocqueville could say that "it would seem as if despotism lurked within [the manufacturing classes] and naturally grew with their growth."[68]

Finally, not only will governments centralize for reasons unique to the new commercial society, they will also centralize for age-old reasons. For example, wars and crises always centralize. War necessarily concentrates

66. *Democracy,* 2:310–12.
67. *Democracy,* 2:327.
68. *Democracy,* 2:331; Drescher, ed., *Tocqueville and Beaumont on Social Reform,* 200; *Democracy,* 2:328–29.

power in the hands of a bureaucratic and technological elite, and it subverts the habits of participatory democracy. "War does not always give over democratic communities to military government, but it must invariably and immeasurably increase the powers of civil government; it must almost compulsorily concentrate the direction of all men and the management of all things in the hands of the administration. If it does not lead to despotism by sudden violence, it prepares men for it more gently by their habits. All those who seek to destroy the liberties of a democratic nation ought to know that war is the surest and shortest means to accomplish it. This is the first axiom of the science."[69] Other sorts of crises tend to centralize, especially the crisis that is the lifelong companion to an obsession for wealth: the perpetual fear of a drop in the standard of living. Eventually, argued Tocqueville, all democratic participation will be put aside, and government will become the guardian of the economy, the nation a machine for producing wealth. At every turn, however, Tocqueville regarded the long-run tendencies of commerce and industry as the ones most likely to transform democracy into despotism.

Tocqueville of course feared the potential, arising from centralization, for plain old-fashioned tyranny. But Tocqueville despised any centralization, even if benevolent *and* popularly elected; "to create a representation of the people in every centralized country is, therefore, to diminish the evil that extreme centralization may produce, but not to get rid of it." Tocqueville feared oppression, but he feared a societal sedation even more. He always considered Russia the most formidable enemy of liberty because its centralization both oppressed and anesthetized men and women. "Uniformity in liberty has always seemed boring to me, but what can be said of complete uniformity in servitude, of these [Russian] villages that are so perfectly alike, populated by people who are so perfectly similar, doing the same things, in the midst of the deepest slumber of intelligence? I confess to you in a whisper that I would prefer disordered barbarism."[70] Mill praised Tocqueville for persuasively demonstrating that democracy's vigilance should be focused not on "anarchy or love of change, but Chinese stagnation [and] immobility." Thus, China and India, the former distinguished by "immobility" and the latter "petrified," also emerged as Tocqueville's preliminary models for the dangers of stagnation in modern democracies.[71] In suggesting that the new commercial

69. *Democracy*, 2:284.
70. *Democracy*, 2:338; *Selected Letters*, 302.
71. *Oeuvres* (M), vol. 6, pt. 1; *Democracy*, 1:94, 2:48–49; *Oeuvres* (M), vol. 3, *Écrits et discours politiques*, 509 (from *L'Inde*). See also Drescher, ed., *Tocqueville and Beaumont on Social Reform*, 183.

world of Europe was in danger of collapsing into a suffocating and motionless Asiatic despotism, Tocqueville was obviously following his mentor, Montesquieu, who had used a similar analysis, and caricature, of the dangers of Asiatic stagnation in order to criticize the abuses of the French monarchy.

Tocqueville, however, did not really worry about an ancient form of Asiatic despotism, but instead about a modern administrative despotism that would be only a distantly related descendant. He feared a political world in which powerful industry and powerful government jointly dominated powerless individuals. Worst of all, of course, would be the nationalization of industry and some form of state socialism in which the state directed all industry and all employment. As the writer who quite probably invented the word *bureaucracy,* Tocqueville worried that centralization would continue "till the very men who from time to time upset a throne and trample on a race of kings bend more and more obsequiously to the slightest dictate of a clerk."[72] This last passage, one of the most forceful in Tocqueville's writings, discloses his fear. By sapping popular energy and inculcating docility, centralized administration invariably extinguishes all capacity for popular democratic participation.

The Delights of Servitude

The image of Tocqueville as a bookish man, floundering in the political world while content only in some study stuffed with ancient authors, omits the fact that, in his friend Royer-Collard's words, "literary glory" could never satisfy Tocqueville's hunger for "political glory." Tocqueville, in fact, exhibited an urge for excitement, passions, and powerful emotions: "When I return to regular habits, the monotony is fatal to me; I am possessed by an internal restlessness. I must have bodily or mental excitement, even at the risk of my life. The desire for strong emotions becomes irresistible."[73] Tocqueville was, of course, active in the political world; he served in the Chamber of Deputies for nine years, and he edited the newspaper *Le Commerce* with an avowed purpose of restoring grandeur to France; yearning for grand political events, he helped direct the fighting in the streets in 1848 (after which his father said, "Alexis does not

72. Tocqueville, *Democracy,* 2:332; see also Drescher, ed., *Tocqueville and Beaumont on Social Reform,* 183. On Tocqueville's possible invention of the word *bureaucracy,* see George Wilson Pierson, *Tocqueville and Beaumont in America* (New York: Oxford University Press, 1938), 713.

73. *Oeuvres* (M), 11:110; *Memoir, Letters,* 1:373.

know what fear is"), and as foreign minister, he despaired that France enjoyed the memory of greatness without recognizing its limited power to reattain it.[74] To Beaumont he confided, "You know what a taste I have for great events and how tired I am of our little democratic and bourgeois pot of soup." In the midst of the 1848 Revolution, he said, "Perhaps a moment will come in which the action we will undertake can be glorious." To Kergorlay he confessed a wish for noble action. "Oh! How I wish that Providence would present me with an opportunity to use, in order to accomplish good and grand things, whatever dangers Providence might attach to them, this internal flame I feel within me that does not know where to find what feeds it."[75] In short, Tocqueville longed for personal greatness, he certainly wished France to undertake grand intellectual and political endeavors, and he despaired that he saw only a sleepy stagnation emerging around him.

Tocqueville was suggesting that comfortable tranquillity might well be the gravest danger to political freedom. For example, as calamitous as he believed war to be, he thought that from war could spring noble actions and sacrifices that show a wondrous side to the human character. To a friend, Tocqueville wrote of the Crimean War, "What gigantic efforts! What energy, what manly and heroic virtues come spontaneous from the breast of these societies that seemed to sleep in material well-being."[76] And in *Democracy in America,* he paused to make the astonishing claim, "I do not wish to speak ill of war: war almost always enlarges the mind of a people and raises their character. In somes cases . . . it must be considered as a necessary corrective to certain inveterate diseases to which democratic communities are liable." Similarly, Tocqueville praised domestic turmoil as being useful to freedom. Although people who busy themselves with accumulating wealth think that "the turmoil of freedom" threatens them, in fact it is a sign of a healthy political order. Freedom, Tocqueville argued, "is generally established with difficulty in the midst of storms; it is perfected by civil discord." By contrast, tranquillity is often a sign of despotic government. "I readily admit that public tranquillity is a great good, but at the same time I cannot forget that all nations have been enslaved by being kept in good order." In a startling passage, Tocqueville suggested that leaders actually expose their nations to mo-

74. *Oeuvres*, (M), vol. 8, pt. 1, 538; ibid., pt. 2, 13; *Recollections*, 169–206, passim; *Correspondence . . . Senior* 1, 63; *Oeuvres* (M), vol. 8, pt. 2, 201.

75. *Selected Letters*, 143, 210, 105. See also Harold Laski, "Alexis de Tocqueville and Democracy," in *The Social and Political Ideas of Some Representative Thinkers of the Victorian Age*, ed. F.J.C. Hearnshaw (London: George Harrap, 1933), 100–115.

76. *Oeuvres* (M), vol. 6, pt. 1, 148.

ments of danger in order to inject energy into the body politic. "I think, then, that the leaders of modern society would be wrong to seek to lull the community by a state of too uniform and too peaceful happiness, and that it is well to expose it from time to time to matters of difficulty and danger in order to raise ambition and give it a field of action."[77]

War, turmoil, "matters of difficulty and danger"—one begins to recognize that Tocqueville welcomed almost anything that would counteract the European and democratic tendency toward stagnation, the tendency, in Baudelaire's words, to fall asleep on a heap of riches. Tocqueville's much-feared stagnation has its roots in the hungering for security and private possessive pleasures that accompanies bourgeois society. While some, said Tocqueville, fear that modern societies will be chaotic and forever changing, he worried that "mankind will be stopped and circumscribed; that the mind will swing backwards and forwards forever without begetting fresh ideas; that man will waste his strength in bootless and solitary trifling, and, though in continual motion, that humanity will cease to advance." His fear, in other words, was that people will "give way to a cowardly love of present enjoyment," becoming both unwilling and unable to attempt anything bold or great or remarkable.[78] Whereas the American of 1831 "confidently [took] charge of the future" and "[fashioned] the universe to please himself,"[79] over time democratic men and women would have neither sense of the past nor vision of the future, but instead would be fastened to the present enjoyment of goods and pleasures. And the cause of this? Certainly Tocqueville blamed the acquisitive ethic of the middle classes. "Eighteenth-century man," as I noted earlier, "had little of that craving for material well-being which leads the way to servitude."[80]

The long-run tendency that Tocqueville thought might undermine democratic government was the commercial tendency. Tocqueville traced all the key points of the new despotism—(1) isolation, (2) powerlessness, (3) centralized government, (4) a willingness to submit to any government that will secure one's property, and (5) the obsession with wealth and pleasure—to the acquisitive ethic of the bourgeoisie. "Thus men are following two separate roads to servitude; the taste for their own well-being withholds them from taking a part in the government, and their love of that well-being forces them to closer and closer dependence upon those who govern." Although the passion for wealth was an inveterate

77. *Democracy*, 2:283; 1:256; 2:149–50, 261.
78. *Democracy*, 2:277–78.
79. *Journey to America*, 186.
80. *The Old Regime*, 118.

trait of the bourgeoisie, it spread from the bourgeoisie to all classes in society. The word *passion* is important here, because Tocqueville thought that wearisome bourgeois society had eliminated all possible human passions with the exception of the single passion for accumulating wealth. About eight months before his death, Tocqueville wrote, "It requires strong hatreds, ardent loves, great hopes, and powerful convictions to set human intelligence in motion, and, for the moment, people believe strongly in nothing, they love nothing, they hate nothing, and they hope for nothing except to profit at the stock exchange."[81]

Tocqueville was describing a new despotism in which people were tied to their servitude by their very satisfactions, indeed a despotism that was built and buttressed by the fact that it could provide gratifications to a pacified people. Although in one passage Tocqueville feared "a yoke heavier than any that has galled mankind since the fall of the Roman Empire," he generally argued that the new despotism would be distinguished by its "sweetness." Although this despotism would use violence occasionally, its strength would derive not from force but from material enjoyments it could provide; not from fear, but bribery. "Civilization, instead of preparing men to live without any master except themselves, seems to have been useful only for sugarcoating and legitimizing their servitude."[82] In discussing the notion of a delightful servitude, certainly Tocqueville was influenced by Montesquieu. In the seraglio of Montesquieu's *Persian Letters* each woman eagerly busies herself with prolonging and perfecting her submission, simply because she feels a "dreadful need" for the satisfactions bestowed for good behavior. As a eunuch writes to his master, "you are more absolute when you caress than when you threaten."[83] But Tocqueville, who regarded Tacitus as a model historian, might well have borrowed from Tacitus the notion of a tyranny that simultaneously pleases and degrades. Tacitus wrote that Rome conquered the Britons through temptations such as baths and banquets, things the Britons thought of as civilization even though they were in reality the instruments of their servitude.[84]

And yet Tocqueville knew he was living neither under Tiberius nor even Louis XV, and the industrial revolution of his own century was

81. *Democracy*, 2:325; *Selected Letters*, 376.

82. *Memoir, Letters*, 1:377; *Oeuvres* (M), vol. 8, pt. 3, 228; Tocqueville letter in Richard Laurin Hawkins, ed., *Newly Discovered French Letters of the Seventeenth, Eighteenth, and Nineteenth Centuries* (Cambridge, Mass.: Harvard University Press, 1933), 199.

83. Montesquieu, *The Persian Letters*, ed. and trans. J. Robert Loy (Cleveland: World Publishing Co., 1961), letter 96.

84. Tacitus, *Agricola*, trans. H. Mattingly and S. A. Handford (New York: Penguin, 1970), 21. Tocqueville regarded Tacitus as a model historian. See *Oeuvres* (M), 18:288.

bringing with it an exponentially greater potential to deliver satisfaction to a docile and degraded population. If Montesquieu feared an Asiatic stagnation, Tocqueville feared an historically new and very European stagnation, based on a centralized government able to dominate people by gratifying them.

> Above this race of men stands an immense and tutelary power, which takes upon itself alone to secure their gratifications and to watch over their fate. That power is absolute, minute, regular, provident, and mild. It would be like the authority of a parent if, like that authority, its object was to prepare men for manhood, but it seeks, on the contrary, to keep them in perpetual child-hood: it is well content that the people should enjoy themselves, provided they think of nothing but enjoyment. For their happi-ness such a government willingly labors, but it chooses to be the sole arbiter of that happiness; it provides for their security, fore-sees and supplies their necessities, facilitates their pleasures, manages their principal concerns, directs their industry, regu-lates the descent of property, and subdivides their inheritances: what remains, but to spare them all the care of thinking and all the trouble of living?[85]

This condition "degrades men without tormenting them," for it transforms human beings who might be active makers of history into satisfied beasts. "The will of man is not shattered, but softened, bent, and guided; men are seldom forced by it to act, but they are constantly restrained from acting. Such a power does not destroy, but it prevents existence; it does not tyrannize, but it compresses, enervates, extinguishes, and stupefies a people, till each nation is reduced to nothing better than a flock of timid and industrious animals, of which the government is the shepherd."[86] In the end people with nearly limitless potential to control their lives and achieve both intellectual and political greatness merely busy themselves with the petty gratifications of private life.

---

85. *Democracy*, 2:336 (I have altered this translation slightly). Tocqueville's conclusion is remarkably similar to that of Herbert Marcuse, who wrote: "If the individuals are satisfied to the point of happiness with the goods and services handed down to them by the administra-tion, why should they insist on different institutions[?] . . . And if the individuals are pre-conditioned so that the satisfying goods also include thoughts, feelings, and aspirations, why should they wish to think, feel, and imagine for themselves?" Marcuse, *One Dimen-sional Man* (Boston: Beacon Press, 1964), 50.

86. *Democracy*, 2:337.

A Despotism Without an Identifiable Despot

Is there a despot for Tocqueville's despotism? Tacitus criticized Roman emperors, Machiavelli wrote against Italian princes, and Montesquieu feared French monarchs; did Tocqueville also write to warn against the threat of some identifiable person or class? One might make a case that Tocqueville feared a despotism by the bourgeoisie. When Tocqueville visited factories in Manchester, he noted many of the miseries that Engels observed later—the hovels, the damp cellars serving as homes for as many as fifteen people apiece, the streams filthy with factory waste—all of which horrified Tocqueville. "Here is the slave, there is the master: there the wealth of some, here the poverty of most. . . . From this filthy sewer pure gold flows. Here humanity attains its most complete development and its most brutish; here civilization works its miracles, and civilized man is turned back almost into a savage."[87] In *Democracy in America* he argued that if a new aristocracy were to arise, it would be an aristocracy of manufacturers, one of the "harshest that ever existed in the world," a vulgar and corrupt aristocracy completely lacking in all high feelings. However much the poverty of the working classes in Manchester startled Tocqueville, he was shocked more by the degradation of both classes of men, that is, some men happy to live in splendor by reducing others to a brutish state of filth and starvation. When he declared that the new aristocracy of manufacturers "impoverishes and debases" the worker, he feared the debasement every bit as much as the impoverishment, because the new bourgeois order tended to smother the wonderful human potentials for courage, intelligence, and creativity.[88]

> When a workman is unceasingly and exclusively engaged in the fabrication of one thing, he ultimately does his work with singular dexterity; but at the same time he loses the general faculty of applying his mind to the direction of the work. He every day becomes more adroit and less industrious; so that it may be said of him that in proportion as the workman improves, the man is degraded. What can be expected of a man who has spent twenty years of his life making heads for pins? And to what can that mighty human intelligence which has so often stirred the world be applied in him except it be to investigate the best method of

87. *Journeys to England and Ireland*, 92–96.
88. *Democracy*, 2:171.

making pins' heads? . . . in a word, he no longer belongs to himself but to the calling that he has chosen.[89]

Marx also criticized the division of labor and blamed capitalism for producing things at the cost of so much human potential. Tocqueville had many of the same misgivings. "It would seem as if the rulers of our time sought only to use men in order to make things great; I wish that they would try a little more to make great men; that they would set less value on the work and more upon the workman."[90] And yet Tocqueville, who was indeed critical of the bourgeoisie, tended in this case to blame not capitalism per se but the demands of the industrial process itself.

This is characteristic of Tocqueville. Although he might have offered a class analysis and openly blamed the bourgeoisie, because it was the class that had clearly risen to political power, Tocqueville instead focused on a process that was developing beyond anyone's control. In general, he depicted this new despotism as faceless and without identifiable despots, like Kafka's world or Foucault's vision of a servitude in which everyone is entangled but no one does the tangling. Tocqueville saw no one, not even the most fortunate member of the privileged classes, as standing apart from the web of servitude that included isolation, powerlessness, the chase after wealth, and the dictates of a centralized and bureaucratic administration. Even though the key developments that accompanied the rise of the bourgeoisie may have been responsible for the demise of democracy, that did not mean that the bourgeoisie could escape this all-encompassing despotism.

In fact, perhaps the most pernicious and most deceptive characteristic of this despotism would be its eagerness to announce itself in the name of freedom. The very ideology designed to buttress this despotism would ostensibly embrace freedom as its most basic conviction, until those in servitude believed themselves to be free. Of course, as Aristotle, Tacitus, and Machiavelli had noted earlier, retaining the forms of freedom has always helped to conceal the fact that the substance has been drained. "Every student of history knows that this phenomenon is a common one; rulers who destroy men's freedom commonly begin by trying to retain its forms—and so it has been from the reign of Augustus to the present day."[91] Tocqueville even argued that the new despotism might well be an elected one and that however preferable that might be to a nonelective

89. *Democracy*, 2:168–69.
90. *Democracy*, 2:347.
91. *The Old Regime*, 45.

despotism, this would not change the despotic character of society. In the absence of municipal freedom, the debates of national legislatures offer only the appearance of freedom, as the senate did under the Roman Empire. The new despotism, even if benevolent and elected, would slowly but relentlessly corrupt people until they could neither act nor think for themselves.

> Our contemporaries are constantly excited by two conflicting passions: they want to be led, and they wish to remain free. As they cannot destroy either the one or the other of these contrary propensities, they strive to satisfy them both at once. They devise a sole, tutelary, and all-powerful form of government, but elected by the people. . . . they console themselves for being in tutelage by the reflection that they have chosen their own guardians. . . .
>
> By this system the people shake off their state of dependence just long enough to select their master and then relapse into it again. . . .
>
> . . . It is in vain to summon a people who have been rendered so dependent on the central power to choose from time to time the representatives of that power; this rare and brief exercise of their free choice, however important it may be, will not prevent them from gradually losing the faculties of thinking, feeling, and acting for themselves, and thus gradually falling below the level of humanity.[92]

Tocqueville labeled this "theatrical representation,"[93] a wonderful phrase suggesting that the new despotism creates servitude with the illusion of freedom. Elections only help to foster this illusion that individuals have control over their lives, allowing them to hasten back to their private worlds, to fill their lives with goods and pleasures, and to pretend to themselves that they are free. Although Tocqueville argued that the bourgeoisie brought with it an acquisitive ethic, isolation, powerlessness, and the centralization of government, he thought that the new despotism would oppress even, perhaps especially, these commercial classes. What will make this despotism suffocating, insidious, and lasting is the fact that its subjects will not recognize their subjection but instead will live comfortably with the illusion of freedom and busy themselves with the private pleasures of accumulating wealth.

92. *Democracy*, 2:337, 339.
93. Yale Tocqueville Collection, C.V.c., Paquet no. 5, p. 50.

Conclusion

In many ways Tocqueville offered the most original discussion of tyranny since Aristotle. First, like Aristotle and Machiavelli, Tocqueville observed that tyrannies must isolate subjects in their private spheres, thereby rendering them powerless to communicate and to organize opposition. But in contrast to classical thinkers, he did not think the modern urban and industrial world would need to do this with violence and threats of violence. Tocqueville argued, in effect, that the commercial world of the bourgeoisie automatically, at least as time passes, leads to the eclipse of public life, the loss of public space, and the sequestration of individuals in their private homes, busying themselves with their private affairs. Although building on the suggestion by Montesquieu that those concerned with making money are poor citizens, Tocqueville could observe this new urban, industrial, and commercial world and note that the acquisitive ethic is, all by itself, a tremendous centrifugal force flinging people out of the public space into their private homes. In brief, without violence and without planning, bourgeois society automatically establishes the two most basic prerequisites for despotism—isolation and powerlessness. It was Tocqueville's fear that the commercial societies of Europe and the United States would invariably become ripe for tyranny without any tyrant doing the ripening.

Second, theorists of tyranny from Plato to Montesquieu focused on the ways that tyrants control the behavior of their subjects—using spies and police, making use of religion, undermining the judicial system, and so on. Whereas previous writers thought tyrants could control the behavior of their subjects, and perhaps some of their thoughts, no thinker before Tocqueville—with the possible exception of Rousseau—warned that a qualitatively new despotism could control the thoughts, and sometimes the feelings, of its subjects. With the tyranny of the majority, said Tocqueville, "the body is left free, and the soul is enslaved." And with Tocqueville's recognition that the centralization of the media (and he was writing in a time when the circulation of newspapers was soaring) could "drop the same thought into a thousand minds at once," he at least had a glimpse of how future tyrants might use the propaganda features of modern mass media.

Third, as one of the first theorists of tyranny writing after the industrial revolution, Tocqueville could see new seeds of tyranny in industrial economies. In part, like Montesquieu or Rousseau, he could not imagine free government or democracy working in large and impersonal cities. Cities of strangers who work in horrid manufacturing jobs and die early—this was no avenue to freedom. Beyond this, he recognized that individuals were certainly threatened by abuses of governmental power, as every theorist of tyranny knew, but surely individuals were also threatened by the new concentrations of private economic power—either as powerful entities in themselves or as corporations with enormous leverage over the central government. As Tocqueville put it, "manufactures govern us."

Fourth, while Tocqueville did fear private economic power, he most feared the much more powerful concentrations of political and administrative power in the central government. As noted above, Tocqueville gave a number of reasons why he thought democratic government over time must centralize. Like Montesquieu, he hoped for intermediate bodies or associations as a buffer between the individual and the state, but his own analysis led to the conclusion that these bodies would weaken and disappear, leaving each of us alone in the face of concentrated governmental power.

Fifth, the tyranny Tocqueville feared was not a brutalizing and terrorizing tyranny familiar in history, but rather a pleasant and gratifying stagnation in which humanity is immobilized, "petrified," and capable of nothing great, neither good nor evil. Like Montesquieu and like Tocqueville's cousin Chateaubriand, he used a caricature of China to suggest his fears of a despotism that changes little in several centuries, where the human intellect thinks nothing new, and where men and women dare nothing adventurous. Tranquillity without greatness, present gratification with no vision of the future. Tocqueville did not fear the tyranny of a Bonaparte, but instead the tyranny of the clerk or bureaucratic functionary. And he did not think this new tyranny would rule by fear, as Montesquieu suggested, but instead the new tyranny would tie us to our servitude by the very gratifications it provided. It would be more insidious and degrading to the extent that it caressed rather than threatened.

Sixth, Tocqueville was mindful of advice given by Aristotle, Tacitus, and Machiavelli to the effect that all tyrannies attempt to give the appearance of normality, indeed the appearance of freedom and constitutionality. In fact, Tocqueville thought elections, which were good, would hardly threaten this tyranny, but instead only give the illusion of freedom, something he called "theatrical representation," or the pretense of free choice. Similarly, individuals would pursue their private interests, make decisions as consumers and investors and entrepreneurs, and thus have nearly complete freedom of choice in private matters; free to mind our own business, but not free to tend to our "chief business which is to remain [our] own masters." Never has a servitude rallied its subjects under such a bold banner of freedom.

Finally, Tocqueville was perhaps the first to recognize that the world might see tyrannies without an identifiable tyrant, an insight amplified later by Weber and Foucault. After reading Tocqueville's writings on a new despotism, one puts down the book and tries to imagine the structure of such a despotism. Is there a despot? Does he or she have advisers? Does he or she need spies and paramilitary forces? And so on. None of this seems necessary. It is a despotism without an identifiable despot, a web in which each individual is caught without anyone precisely doing the catching. In it we find only a centralized administration, a bureaucratic structure, that thinks it is providing for the common good, and decent people who do not recognize that they are both experiencing and extending tyranny as they work day by day.

7

MARX

Despotism of Class
and Workplace

Like Tocqueville, who described a faceless and bureaucratic despotism with no identifiable despot, Marx also broke with classical thinkers who spoke of a single tyrant and with Montesquieu, who discussed the nature of the single despot. Instead, Marx set out to analyze "the despotism of capital,"[1] by which he meant mainly a despotism of the capitalist class over all others, but also the impersonal structure of despotism imposing itself on the individual in factories, by public and private bureaucracies, and by the demands of new machines and technology. Marx used a class analysis of both history and politics, but as should be amply clear by now, Marx was by no means the first to use a class analysis. Plato and Aristotle had maintained that a city must harmonize and balance class interests, and Montesquieu and Tocqueville, at least to some extent, had reacted as aristocrats who perceived political and economic threats from the new commercial classes. Even though thoroughly familiar with Aristo-

---

1. Karl Marx, *Capital: A Critique of Political Economy*, vol. 1, trans. Samuel Moore and Edward Aveling (New York: Modern Library, 1906), 440. Although Marx's *Capital* has three volumes, references in this chapter are to volume 1 unless otherwise indicated.

tle's class analysis, and even though deeply indebted to Montesquieu's approach to understanding societies, Marx's analysis bears more resemblance to Machiavelli's discussions of class conflict; he labeled Machiavelli's *History of Florence,* for example, a masterpiece.[2] In place of Hegel's notion that contradiction and conflict between ideas propel history, Marx quite easily substituted the notion that class conflict moves history forward, and in his own time he relentlessly criticized what he regarded as a despotism of the capitalist class over working men and women. All previous history, to be sure, had been characterized by class despotism, but in the past such despotism had disguised itself with pious religious pronouncements and political convictions about the inevitability of hierarchy. In the nineteenth century, the bourgeoisie had established a class despotism with few disguises. "The bourgeoisie, wherever it has got the upper hand, has put an end to all feudal, patriarchal, idyllic relations. . . . In one word, for exploitation, veiled by religious and political illusions, it has substituted naked, shameless, direct, brutal exploitation."[3]

Marx's central criticism of capitalism was neither that it robbed working people nor that it denied them elementary personal freedoms. Certainly he thought capitalism did both, but more important, Marx condemned capitalism because it murdered what is most beautiful in human beings, the potential for creativity and intelligence. The fulcrum by which he judged capitalism he borrowed from Aristotle. Not only did Marx embark on two lengthy studies of Hegel, whose most fundamental philosophical assumptions were those of Aristotle, but he also did his doctoral dissertation on post-Aristotelian philosophy. Thus, as a young man struggling to free himself from Hegel's influence, Marx declared that "modern philosophy has only continued work that Heraclitus and Aristotle had already begun," and as a mature thinker in *Capital,* Marx still could call Aristotle a "great thinker" and "the greatest thinker of antiquity."[4] Like Aristotle, Marx looked for the proper political and economic soil out of which human potential for greatness could flower mightily, but unlike the more cautious and conservative Aristotle, Marx was angry at opportunities lost, that the potential for a qualitatively new freedom was being squandered and transformed into a miserable new form of servitude.

In our days everything seems pregnant with its contrary. Machinery, gifted with the wonderful power of shortening and fructifying

2. Karl Marx and Frederick Engels, *Selected Correspondence,* 3d rev. ed., ed. S. W. Ryazanskaya, trans. I. Lasker (Moscow: Progress Publishers, 1975), 91.

3. Karl Marx, *Selected Writings,* ed. David McLellan (Oxford: Oxford University Press, 1977), 223 (from Marx and Engels, *The Communist Manifesto*).

4. *Selected Writings,* 19; *Capital,* 68, 446.

human labor, we behold starving and overworking it. The new-
fangled sources of wealth, by some strange weird spell, are
turned into sources of want. The victories of art seem bought by
the loss of character. At the same pace that mankind masters
nature, man seems to become enslaved to other men or to his
own infamy. Even the pure light of science seems unable to shine
but on the dark background of ignorance. All our invention and
progress seem to result in endowing material forces with intellectual life, and in stultifying human life into a material force.[5]

Whereas Aristotle had seen the Greek polis as the proper political setting
in which those fortunate enough to be citizens could be free, Marx
thought that the development of science and the labors of history had
brought humankind to the brink of socialism and thus to a qualitatively
new freedom founded on a social and political order in which none would
have to be slaves and all could be free. One of Marx's lifelong heroes was
Prometheus, and in a sense Marx posed as a modern-day Prometheus
seeking a mythological rematch with the gods, once again stealing the fire
that would liberate humanity. Only this time he would expose the gods as
merely the illusory creations of men and women themselves, and he
would show that, not fictitious gods, but classes and the economic relations among classes stood in the way of human freedom. When circumstances were right, men and women would use the insight Marx provided
to emancipate themselves. Using Kantian language, he spoke of "the categorical imperative to overthrow all circumstances in which man is humili-
ated, enslaved, abandoned, and despised."[6]

Alienation and Marx's View of Human Nature

In a footnote approximately three fourths of the way through *Capital,*
Marx paused to ridicule Bentham's view of human nature. "Bentham
makes short work of it," Marx scoffed. "With the dryest naïveté he takes
the modern shopkeeper, especially the English shopkeeper, as the normal

5. *Selected Writings*, 338; also *Capital*, 445, 482; *The Economic and Philosophic Manuscripts of 1844*, ed. Dirk J. Struik, trans. Martin Milligan (New York: International Publishers,
1964), 110 (henceforth cited as *1844 Manuscripts*).
6. *Selected Writings*, 69 (from "Toward a Critique of Hegel's *Philosophy of Right*"). Marx
and Engels chose the word *communism* because in the 1840s the word *socialism* indicated
something like a middle-class reform movement. With subsequent changes in the connotations of both words, it is quite proper to speak of Marx as a philosopher of socialism. See
George Lichtheim, *Marxism: An Historical and Critical Study*, 2d rev. ed. (New York: Praeger,
1965), 60, 99.

man."[7] Behind this sarcasm lies Marx's deep disagreement with Bentham's conception of human nature, and indeed, although Bentham's simple-minded crassness can hardly be called typical, Marx was quarreling with the most basic assumptions of English liberalism from Hobbes and Locke into the nineteenth century. Whereas English liberals from Locke to Bentham thought of human nature as fixed and static, as selfish and moderately aggressive, Marx borrowed from the views of Aristotle and Hegel and looked upon human nature as capable of change and development. If Locke saw human beings as basically the same in all times and places, Marx took an open-ended view and suggested that, in the proper setting, all human beings could become—and indeed, in a sense, have a need to become—intelligent, creative, and cooperative.

Marx assumed that men and women are first and foremost producers, not in the narrow sense of producing goods and services, but in the broader sense of producing, laboring upon, and creating the world—economic, political, religious—that surrounds them. "Men can be distinguished from animals by consciousness, by religion or anything else you like. They themselves begin to distinguish themselves from animals as soon as they begin to *produce* their means of subsistence. . . . As individuals express their life, so they are. What they are, therefore, coincides with their production, both *what* they produce and *how* they produce."[8] By itself this notion offered neither a dynamic nor an open-ended view of human nature, but Marx suggested that something happens to men and women in this process of laboring to construct their world. To begin with, it is not labor per se that distinguishes human beings, but instead intelligent labor. Spiders and bees construct and produce, "but what distinguishes the worst architect from the best of bees is this, that the architect raises his structure in imagination before he erects it in reality." Even more important, unlike bees, human beings develop and augment their powers in interaction with the world. As we actively work to transform the world, we simultaneously transform ourselves and develop our intellectual capacities. "By thus acting on the external world and changing it, he at the same time changes his own nature. He develops his slumbering powers and compels them to act in obedience to his sway."[9]

Two assumptions behind Marx's argument stand out. First, although Marx's argument is not identical with that of Aristotle, it is similar. Like

7. *Capital*, 668.
8. Marx and Engels, *The German Ideology*, ed. C. J. Arthur, no trans. given (New York: International Publishers, 1970), 42.
9. *Capital*, 198. See G.W.F. Hegel, *The Phenomenology of Mind*, trans. J. B. Baillie (New York: Harper & Row, 1967), "On Lordship and Bondage," 228–40.

Aristotle, Marx assumed that humans are rational beings who develop this rationality by acting in the world, but unlike Aristotle, Marx focused neither on political activity nor on theoretical wisdom. Instead, Marx saw men and women as producers, although to be sure Marx saw such production as best accomplished in a community of equals. Second, Marx's view that human nature can develop over time is far more open-ended and far less defined than Aristotle's view. Aristotle was certain that he knew what a completed human being was, and he felt confident that the finest Greek polis was the natural setting that could best develop such individuals; but Marx, here borrowing what he called the "rational kernel" of Hegel's theory of history, could not begin to define limits to human perfectibility. In a sense, Hegel and then Marx had set Aristotle's dynamic view of human nature into historical motion. Though Aristotle could describe a fully developed human being, Marx could not, simply because history itself is open-ended and therefore the seemingly limitless possibilities of human development stretch well beyond the imagination of any single thinker in any single historical era. How then to formulate this view of human nature? Marx apparently made two different philosophical efforts, the first of which, found not exclusively but most frequently in his early writings, was his concept of alienation, a concept that traveled into Marx's vocabulary by way of Aristotle, Rousseau, Hegel, and Feuerbach.

In criticizing Hegel, Feuerbach had suggested that the secret of religion resided in the wishes of human beings; for example, because human beings were powerless, their wishes created an all-powerful god, and because human beings felt alone in a hostile world, they created a loving god. Religion, Feuerbach thought, was simply the manifold manifestation of human wishes and hopes, and what human beings lacked and wished for—to be omnipotent, omniscient, loving, and so forth—they projected onto a supreme being of some other world. "Religion is the solemn unveiling of man's hidden treasures," wrote Feuerbach, "the revelation of his most intimate thoughts, the open confession of what he secretly loves."[10] In a different political and economic world we would not need to project these wishes onto God, because we ourselves could be powerful, wise, and loving. In sum, religion reveals what human beings essentially are, and are capable of becoming; religion reveals the human essence. When Marx initially broke from Hegel, he used a Feuerbachian analysis.

---

10. Ludwig Feuerbach, *The Essence of Christianity*, ed. E. Graham Waring and F. W. Strothmann, trans. Marian Evans [George Eliot, pseud.] (New York: Frederick Ungar, 1957), chap. 2, 11.

> The foundation of irreligious criticism is this: man makes religion, religion does not make man. . . . [Religion] is the imaginary realization of the human essence. . . .
>
> Religion is the sigh of the oppressed creature, the feeling of a heartless world, and the soul of soulless circumstances. It is the opium of the people.
>
> The abolition of religion as the illusory happiness of the people is the demand for their real happiness. The demand to give up the illusions about their condition is a demand to give up a condition that requires illusion . . .
>
> The criticism of religion disillusions man so that he may think, act, and fashion his own reality as a disillusioned man come to his senses; so that he may revolve around himself as his real sun.[11]

For both Feuerbach and Marx, religion was a form of alienation. Although we are the creators of religion and the authors of this religious world, we cannot recognize ourselves in our creation, and thus the world towers over us as an alien, reifed, and tyrannical force. Similarly, we remain alienated from, or strangers to, what we potentially and essentially are—powerful, intelligent, and loving people. In other words, we are alienated from what it is to be human, or the human essence.

This is, of course, Aristotelian language. Aristotle thought that a life according to reason as a citizen in a Greek polis was the defining or essential characteristic of what it is to be human; to live such a life is to live as one ought, to achieve the proper end of life, to attain or actualize the human essence. Similarly, Marx wrote that individuals are alienated from their "species life," that is, from the characteristics most essential to the human species. "Productive life" or "free, conscious activity is man's species character. Life itself appears only as a *means* to life." Therefore, individuals forced into stifling labor under capitalism remain alienated from "the human essence," from the ways in which men and women ought to live and work, and Communism is therefore "the real *appropriation of the human essence* by and for man." Once again, Marx is complaining not so much that capitalism robs from working men and women but that capitalism destroys the creative potential that defines the very essence of what it is to be human. "*An enforced increase of wages* . . . would therefore be nothing but *better payment for the slave,* and would not win either for the worker or for labor their human status and dignity."[12] By

---

11. *Selected Writings*, 63–64 (from "Towards a Critique of Hegel's *Philosophy of Right*").
12. *1844 Manuscripts*, 113–14, 134–35, 117–18.

contrast, in a better world, free and unalienated labor is an end in itself and deeply satisfying. "Supposing that we had produced in a human manner; each of us would in his production have doubly affirmed himself and his fellow men. I would have: (1) objectified in my production my individuality. . . . (2) In your enjoyment or use of my product I would have had the direct enjoyment of realizing that I had both satisfied a human need by my work and also objectified the human essence and therefore fashioned for another human being the object that met his need. . . . and thus in my own activity [I would] have realized my own essence, my human, my communal essence."[13]

Marx saw individuals as alienated in three broad ways. First, men and women are alienated from the defining characteristic of human beings, that is, the act of producing. For Marx, an individual's labor should be a creative expression of himself or herself, an affirmation of who that individual is; labor should not simply be the means to some subsequent gratification but rather should itself be a source of satisfaction. Instead, capitalist production reverses all of this, and labor becomes coerced drudgery.

> Labor is *external* to the worker, i.e., it does not belong to his essential being; . . . in his work, therefore, he does not affirm himself but denies himself, does not feel content but unhappy, does not develop freely his physical and mental energy but mortifies his body and ruins his mind. The worker therefore only feels himself outside his work, and in his work feels outside himself. . . . His labor is therefore not voluntary, but coerced; it is *forced labor*. It is therefore not the satisfaction of a need; it is merely a *means* to satisfy needs external to it. . . . the worker's activity [is] not his spontaneous activity. It belongs to another; it is the loss of his self.[14]

Although some writers have suggested that there is a decisive break between the young Marx and the old Marx—a young Marx who was wielding the humanistic categories of Hegel and Feuerbach, categories found for example in the discussions of alienation, and an old and mature Marx

---

13. *Selected Writings*, 121–22 (from "On James Mill").
14. *1844 Manuscripts*, 110–11. Marx actually spoke of four forms of alienation: (1) alienation from the act of laboring, (2) alienation from other human beings, (3) alienation from the products of our labor, and (4) alienation from our species being, or the essential characteristic of our species (i.e., labor). I have simply merged numbers 1 and 4. For a good contemporary argument about the labor of workers being under the control of external forces, see G. A. Cohen, "The Structure of Proletarian Unfreedom," *Philosophy and Public Affairs* 12, no. 1 (1983): 3–33.

who had discarded such categories in favor of a new scientific analysis of history[15]—in fact this same concept of alienation surfaces in every period of his life. In *The German Ideology* (1845–46) Marx spoke of the need for an economy grounded in the "all-round development of individuals"; in the *Grundrisse* (principally 1857–58) he bemoaned the fact that "the creative power" of the individual worker confronted him or her as "an alien force"; in the first volume of *Capital* (1867) he criticized the capitalist economy for perpetuating forms of labor that abolished the free play of the intellect; and in his "Critique of the Gotha Programme"(1875) he quite possibly lifted a phrase right out of his early notebooks when he suggested that under socialism "labour [will] become not only a means of life but life's prime want."[16]

In every period of his life, Marx's chief concern was liberating the creative potential smothered inside each individual.[17] Although Aristotle spoke of the life of reason for those few lucky enough to be citizens, whereas Marx endeavored to release the creative potential in each of us, their arguments remain similar. Each thought that some large quantity of human potential for greatness, great achievements in philosophy and politics and art and literature, had been needlessly stifled by political and economic conditions that tyrannized over humanity. In Marx's case—and this is certainly the most inspiring part of his philosophy—he refused to relinquish an abiding belief that in the body of ancient slaves or medieval serfs or nineteenth-century textile workers or women denied freedom in virtually every century, there lived, sadly oppressed and undiscovered, thousands of Shakespeares and Newtons. With the proper political and economic order, all might be artistic, and those with genius would emerge in much greater numbers. Marx did not think that "each should do the work of Raphael, but that anyone in whom there is a potential Raphael should be able to develop without hindrance."[18]

The second kind of alienation that Marx outlined was the alienation of human beings from one another. "An immediate consequence of the fact

15. This argument about a radical split between the young Marx and the old Marx has been made most famously in Louis Althusser, *For Marx*, trans. Ben Brewster (New York: Pantheon, 1969).

16. *German Ideology*, 117; Marx, *The Grundrisse*, ed. and trans. David McLellan (New York: Harper & Row, 1972), 81; *Capital*, 462; *Selected Writings*, 569 (from "Critique of the Gotha Programme").

17. Jon Elster suggests quite rightly that Marx's model for the new Communist individual was someone like Leonardo da Vinci, and he also notes, "Self-realization through creative work is the essence of Marx's communism." See Elster, *Making Sense of Marx* (Cambridge: Cambridge University Press, 1985), 89, 521, 267.

18. *German Ideology*, 108–9.

that man is estranged from the product of his labor, from his life activity, from his species being is the *estrangement of man* from *man*." This notion of alienation was in part a protest, indeed almost a moralistic protest, against a new industrial and urban world in which individuals seemed pitted one against the other. "Competition," wrote Marx, "separates individuals from one another," and "the only force that brings [people] together and puts them in relation to each other, is the selfishness, the gain and the private interests of each."[19] When Marx and Engels wrote in *The Communist Manifesto* that capitalism "has left remaining no other nexus between man and man than naked self-interest, than callous 'cash payment,'" they were referring to famous lines from Thomas Carlyle, a conservative and disenchanted Romantic thinker who was horrified at the loss of traditional, although certainly paternalistic, ties between people.[20]

As always, however, Marx offered much more than a moralistic argument. Again, like Aristotle, Marx maintained that individuals develop their own potentials for intelligence, creativity, and cooperation in a community of equals. Rather than see others as obstacles to our own freedom and to our own satisfaction, Marx suggested that in a free community we would learn from others and look upon others as resources helpful to our own development. "Only in community [with others has each] individual the means of cultivating his gifts in all directions. . . . In a real community the individuals obtain their freedom in and through their association."[21] If the proper, human setting for the development of individual intelligence and creativity is a community of equals, this setting has not been possible in the past both because of the necessity of class relations and because of economic scarcity. Past history has witnessed not only class conflict but also human conflict against nature, and both classes and scarcity necessarily perpetuated antagonistic relations between people. With socialism, however, which brings an end to classes and makes possible some sort of comparative economic abundance (about which, more later), history will experience "the *genuine* resolution of the conflict between man and nature and between man and man."[22] By perpetuating class conflict and cre-

19. *1844 Manuscripts*, 114; *German Ideology*, 79; *Capital*, 195.

20. *Selected Writings*, 223 (from *The Communist Manifesto*); Thomas Carlyle, *Selected Writings*, ed. Alan Shelston (New York: Penguin, 1971), 193 (from "Chartism," published in 1839).

21. *German Ideology*, 83; see Nancy Schwartz, "Distinction Between Public and Private Life: Marx on the *zoon politikon*," *Political Theory* 7, no. 2 (1979): 245–66.

22. *1844 Manuscripts*, 135. Communism should also end the exploitation of women, and in fact "the relation of man to woman is *the most natural* relation of human being to human being. It therefore reveals the extent to which man's *natural* behavior has become *human*, or the extent to which the *human* essence in him has become a *natural* essence." *1844 Manuscripts*, 134.

ating artificial scarcity, capitalism forces people into antagonistic relations in which each person seeks to become an alien power controlling his or her fellows. "Every person speculates on creating a *new* need in another, so as to drive him to a fresh sacrifice, to place him in a new dependence. . . . Each tries to establish over the other an *alien power,* so as thereby to find satisfaction of his own selfish need."[23] Rather than treat others as ends in themselves, in quite literally a Kantian sense, we look upon others as means to our private gratification; and rather than recognize that another's independence can only help us develop our own intelligence and creativity, we regard others as barriers we must destroy or hurdle. In these ways, we remain alienated from our fellows. And yet Marx saw in the workers' movements within capitalist society the germ of a new and cooperative social order that would eliminate this form of alienation.

> When communist *artisans* associate with one another, theory, propaganda, etc., is their first end. But at the same time, as a result of this association, they acquire a new need—the need for society—and what appears as a means becomes an end. In this practical process the most splendid results are to be observed whenever French socialist workers are seen together. Such things as smoking, drinking, eating, etc., are no longer means of contact or means that bring together. Company, association, and conversation, which again has society as its end, are enough for them; the brotherhood of man is no mere phrase with them, but a fact of life, and the nobility of man shines upon us from their work-hardened bodies.[24]

The third form of alienation that Marx identified was alienation from the products of our labor. After pouring ourselves into the objects we produce, these objects return to confront us as "*something alien,* as a *power independent* of the producer." First, this means that the products of a worker's labor come back to control the worker, that the worker's own labor "exists *outside him,* independently, as something alien to him, and that it becomes a power on its own confronting him." But second, this means that we become powerless. Despite creating these objects, we become controlled and tyrannized by them. "It is clear that the more the worker spends himself, the more powerful becomes the alien world of objects which he creates over and against himself. . . . It is the same in religion. The more man puts into God, the less he retains in himself. The

23. *1844 Manuscripts,* 147.
24. *1844 Manuscripts,* 154–55.

worker puts his life into the object; but now his life no longer belongs to him but to the object."[25]

What can we make of this complicated and at times opaque language? In what sense do the products of our labor—food and clothes and machines and houses—tyrannize over us? On the one hand, there is in Marx's argument a bit of nostalgia, quite widespread in this Romantic period of the nineteenth century, for the medieval artisan who inserted his or her personality into both beginning and completing the object, a piece of furniture, for example, that he or she then sold to an identifiable customer. While William Morris romanticized such labor and placed this creative process at the center of his socialism, Marx could neither go that far nor entirely escape such idealized nostalgia. "Owing to the extensive use of machinery and to division of labor," reads the *Manifesto*, "the work of the proletarians has lost all individual character, and, consequently, all charm for the workman."[26]

On the other hand, Marx was making a more complicated argument, derived from Hegel, about the ways in which men and women ought to control their world. To understand this notion of being alienated from the products of our labor, we must recognize that our labor produces not just commodities but also customs, political constitutions, economic systems, and even religions. Marx put this well in his critique of the political radical and sometimes anarchist Pierre Joseph Proudhon. "M. Proudhon has very well grasped the fact that men produce cloth, linen, silks. . . . But he has not grasped that, in accordance with their productive forces, these men also produce the *social relations* amid which they manufacture cloth and linen." Or, in a passage quoted earlier, Marx noted that "man makes religion, religion does not make man." Like Hegel, Marx was suggesting that human beings (subjects) have always been the authors of the political, economic, ideological, and religious worlds (the objective world), but human beings have never recognized the objective world as their creation. To put a simple idea into complicated Hegelian language, the subjects of history remain strangers in an alien objective world that they themselves have created. To be alienated from the products of our labor is to be tyrannized by our own creations. "Man's own deed becomes an alien power opposed to him, which enslaves him instead of being controlled by him." Or as Frankenstein's monster said, "You are my creator but I am your master; obey!"[27]

25. *1844 Manuscripts*, 108.

26. *Selected Writings*, 227 (from *The Communist Manifesto*).

27. *Selected Correspondence*, 36; *German Ideology*, 53; Mary Shelley, *Frankenstein* (New York: Signet, 1983 [1816]), 160.

To take a simple example, it should be clear that the Constitution of the United States is a document, not handed down from God nor demanded by nature, but instead written by some very brilliant men at a particular moment in time. This document could be altered drastically if the men and women of another time so wished, or it could be discarded altogether. What was equally clear to Marx, and perhaps less so to us, was that social customs, economic systems, philosophical theories, and religions are also the creations of men and women, and they too should be altered or discarded if they fail to meet the needs of the people of any given epoch. For Marx, both Christianity and capitalism only tyrannized over human beings, and although each was historically useful, both should be discarded at some future time. Instead, these products of our labor often appear to us as heaven-sent, or self-evident, or necessary, or in absolute accord with the demands of nature. In a sense, the products of our labor stand out as things that control us, instead of vice versa, a process that Marx called "reification." Although we should be "masters" of our creations, we submit as "slaves."[28] A time will come, however, when we will recognize that we, as subjects, can create the objective world willfully and consciously, and at that moment human beings will construct the future democratically and artistically, an idea that meshes nicely with Marx's notions that we should live in a community of equals and that our labor should be an artistic expression of ourselves. Such a time will signal the end of class history and the beginning of human history. It will depend, however, not only on the proper economic conditions but also on a vast alteration in consciousness, a new moment in Hegel's march of Reason. "When the worker recognises the products as being his own . . . it will be an enormous progress in consciousness, . . . in the same way that . . . slaves became aware that they were persons."[29] It will be the end of alienation because neither our own labor nor the products of that labor, nor our fellow citizens, will confront us as alien and hostile forces.

Marx's Idea of Freedom

The notion of labor as a meaningful and satisfying expression of oneself rather than as boring drudgery is obviously attractive, but is it practical? Is drudgery not an inevitable part of the human condition? Will people, or

28. *Selected Writings*, 115 (from "On James Mill").
29. *Grundrisse*, 110. The best discussion of the concept of alienation is in Bertell Ollman's *Alienation*, 2d ed. (Cambridge: Cambridge University Press, 1976).

at least some people, not always have to labor from dawn to dusk to extract a living from nature? And if this is true, then is not Marx's yearning for a world of unalienated labor only the dreamy hopefulness of a Romantic?

In fact, as a contemporary said, "Marx had nothing of the dreamer about him,"[30] and Marx well knew that socialism would be impossible and alienation would be inevitable as long as men and women were forced to labor long hours in order to conquer scarcity. In all previous historical epochs, the best cultures could only free a few from the labor process and then only at the price of condemning the vast majority to lives of endless and thoroughly alienating labor. As Aristotle suggested, male citizens could be free only on the condition that slaves, servants, artisans, and women were not. Capitalism infuriated Marx because, after dramatically increasing productivity so that, for the first time in history, large numbers might be freed from the labor process entirely or at the very least experience a great reduction in time devoted to labor, capitalism found ways to increase and intensify demands on working men and women.

> "If," dreamed Aristotle, the greatest thinker of antiquity, "if every tool, when summoned, or even of its own accord, could do the work that befits it, just as the creations of Daedalus moved of themselves, or the tripods of Hephaestos went of their own accord to their sacred work, if the weavers' shuttles were to weave of themselves, then there would be no need either of apprentices for the master workers, or of slaves for the lords." . . . Oh! those heathens! They understood . . . nothing of political economy and Christianity. They did not, for example, comprehend that machinery is the surest means of lengthening the working day. They perhaps excused the slavery of one on the ground that it was a means to the full development of another. But to preach slavery of the masses, in order that a few crude and half-educated parvenus, might become "eminent spinners," "extensive sausage-makers," and "influential shoe-black dealers," to do this, they lacked the bump of Christianity.[31]

Capitalism played an indispensable historical role by developing science and technology to the point at which human beings could finally win, with comparative ease, its millenia old struggle with nature. Hence Marx

---

30. Cited in David McLellan, *Karl Marx: His Life and Thought* (New York: Harper & Row, 1973), 177.
31. *Capital*, 445–46.

labeled capitalism a "great civilising influence," insofar as it developed economic productivity to the point where human societies could "subdue [nature] to human requirements."[32]

If ever someone shared the Baconian and Enlightenment optimism that progress in science and technology would bring moral and intellectual progress, it was Marx. Indeed, he wanted as much automation as was possible. "The historical vocation of capital"—or, to use Hegelian language, capitalism's role in its world-historical moment—will be fulfilled when economic productivity permits "shorter working hours for the whole of society . . . so that the sort of labour in which the activities of men can be replaced by those of machines will have ceased."[33] Of course, Marx saw capitalism as only assembling these productive forces, whereas he believed that socialism could develop these productive forces more efficiently both because cooperative enterprises are more efficient than authoritarian factories and because a "fully developed individual" can bring a breadth of intelligence and creativity to the work process that capitalism—relying on workers rendered unimaginative and ignorant by the division of labor—cannot. At issue, however, was the use of technology to eliminate unnecessary labor time. It was a question "of reducing the necessary labour of society to a minimum. The counterpart of this reduction is that all members of society can develop their education in the arts, sciences, etc., thanks to the free time and means available to all." The phrase "free time" with Marx is pregnant with new significance because it is literally time freed from the labor process and time in which to be free: "free time, i.e. time for the complete development of the individual."[34]

> In fact, the realm of freedom actually begins only where labour which is determined by necessity and mundane considerations ceases. . . . Freedom in this field can only consist in socialised man, the associated producers, rationally regulating their interchange with Nature, bringing it under their common control, instead of being ruled by it as by the blind forces of Nature. . . . But it nonetheless still remains a realm of necessity. Beyond it begins that development of human energy which is an end in itself, the true realm of freedom. . . . The shortening of the working-day is its basic prerequisite.[35]

32. *Grundrisse*, 94.
33. *Grundrisse*, 85.
34. *Capital*, 534; *Grundrisse*, 142, 148.
35. Marx, *Capital: A Critique of Political Economy*, vol. 3, ed. Frederick Engels, no trans. given (New York: International Publishers, 1967), 820.

Although there is no such thing as absolute abundance (can everyone have a house with a view of the Golden Gate Bridge?), certainly Marx thought that human freedom could only exist where there was comparative abundance and after society had reduced the average work week from perhaps sixty to forty to ten hours.

In this, there was an excitement in Marx that has inspired his followers ever since. In all previous history, most men and women had had to labor from dawn to dusk in order to survive. Only with the productivity that came from science, technology, and the organization of labor could humankind liberate itself from one of the world's most ancient tyrannies, the tyranny of forced labor, a curse described over and over again in literature, perhaps most famously in Genesis of the Hebrew Bible. No century before the nineteenth, thought Marx, could have possibly emancipated men and women, because no other century could solve this intractable problem of necessary, life-consuming labor. But with the nineteenth century, humanity had an unprecedented opportunity for a qualitatively new human freedom, if only a rational socialist society could use science and technology for the general interest instead of leaving capitalism to perpetuate a narrow class interest. For Marx, just as humanity was completing its long historical journey, just as humanity was arriving at the brink of a new human freedom, capitalism had stubbornly summoned all kinds of clever resistances to perpetuate its despotism over other classes. Marx wrote with the anger and passion of a man who could get a glimpse of the new world, but always and only through the confining bars of the old.

But what precisely did Marx mean by this word *freedom*? To Marx, *freedom* had always been a word saturated with ideological overtones and useful to the dominant class in any society. To Roman patricians the word *freedom* meant the right to be citizens protected by Roman law, the right for men of property to deliberate in the senate, and the right to conquer the Mediterranean world; to feudal lords the word *freedom* helped to secure local privileges vis-à-vis the monarchy, and it helped to enforce the duties of laboring serfs; and to the bourgeoisie the word *freedom* signified the right to private property and perhaps the right to elect members of the bourgeoisie itself to "represent" the nation. "By freedom is meant, under the present bourgeois conditions of production, free trade, free selling and buying. . . . This talk about free selling and buying, and all the other 'brave words' of our bourgeoisie about freedom in general, have a meaning, if any, only in contrast with restricted selling and buying, with the fettered traders of the Middle Ages."[36] In other words, in

---

36. *Selected Writings*, 233 (from *The Communist Manifesto*).

all past societies and all past philosophies the concept of freedom has had only limited significance as an ideological defense of the dominant class.

This does not mean that Marx dismissed bourgeois theories of freedom entirely, because, as a good Hegelian, Marx saw the human world winding its way step by painful step toward liberation, and thus John Locke was a limited but progressive step forward from Jean Bodin. Although a bourgeois republic is an instrument for a despotism of the bourgeoisie, it is still an improvement over the more hierarchical and more despotic feudal monarchies. Marx even urged workers "calmly and resolutely [to] improve the opportunities of republican liberty." In speaking of political democracy, especially of democracy in North America, in a passage soon after he referred to Tocqueville, Marx suggested: "Political emancipation is of course a great progress. Although it is not the final form of human emancipation in general, it is nevertheless the final form of human emancipation inside the present world order."[37]

Could Marx himself sketch a theory of human freedom that is not bound to the interests of one class or to the demands of one period in history? Not entirely. Having claimed only to foresee the end to class history and the beginning of human history, having suggested that both history and human emancipation are and always will be dynamic and ever changing, Marx did not pretend to know how qualitatively different human beings in future centuries might redefine the idea of freedom. With his notion of alienation, however, he thought he could transcend class-based theories of freedom and talk about the initial stages of human emancipation.

These initial stages of human liberation would have three broad characteristics addressing the three different forms of alienation that Marx outlined. First, human freedom requires labor to be a spontaneous expression of oneself. Clearly this means an end, or at least a drastic reduction, of forced labor, but it does not mean that free individuals will spend their time passively entertained. To illustrate, Marx always used an example from the arts. "Really free labour, the composing of music for example, is at the same time damned serious and demands the greatest effort." Whether one uses one's free time—again, time in which to be free—to

37. Marx, *Civil War in France: The Paris Commune* (New York: International Publishers, 1968), 34; *Selected Writings*, 47 (from "On the Jewish Question"). Steven Lukes argues brilliantly that Marx condemned all morality of *Recht* (law or right) as just an ideological prop to the rule by the dominant class, but that Marx in fact argued for a morality based on his notion of human emancipation. Lukes is quite persuasive in arguing that a key weakness in Marx's argument is his dismissal of any theory of rights. See Lukes, *Marxism and Morality* (Oxford: Clarendon Press, 1985), chaps. 4 and 5, pp. 48–99, also p. 29.

paint or to study physics or to learn to play shortstop (or quite probably all three), one will pour one's personality into such chosen pursuits. Only spontaneous activity that occurs beyond the demands of necessity can really be called free, human labor; "man produces even when he is free from physical need and only truly produces in freedom therefrom." Although socialism is routinely condemned for stifling all individuality, Marx certainly *thought* that socialism would bring about "rich individuality . . . whose labour thus itself appears not to be labour any more but a full development of activity." Although Fourier was wrong to maintain that work can become play, he was wise enough to recognize that "free time—which includes leisure time as well as time for higher activities—naturally transforms anyone who enjoys it into a different person."[38]

Second, one attains such human emancipation only in a community of equals. "Man is in the most literal sense of the word a *zōon politikon,* not only a social animal, but an animal which can develop into an individual only in society."[39] While such a community of equals certainly allows people to cooperate to attain goals that are of a general importance and that cannot be undertaken alone, the diversity within this community is also an invaluable resource from which we learn our own unique potentials and interests. Thoreau in the woods knows only his own thoughts, but the socialist individual learns from people with a multitude of different talents. In a passage to which I referred earlier, Marx said that "[o]nly in community [with others has each] individual the means of cultivating his gifts in all directions; only in the community, therefore, is personal freedom possible."

Finally, freedom necessitates that people control the products of their labor, that is, consciously construct the political and economic world that best meets their needs. Under capitalism, of course, "the process of production has the mastery over man, instead of being controlled by him." To overcome this problem, Marx wanted people to plan production, to decide quite consciously what production best meets the needs of the citizenry. "The life-process of society, which is based on the process of material production, does not strip off its mystical veil until it is treated as production by freely associated men, and is consciously regulated by them in accordance with a settled plan."[40] If right now we experience a world as reified—as a thing that controls us—then we must cooper-

38. *Grundrisse,* 124; *1844 Manuscripts,* 113; *Grundrisse,* 86, 148.

39. *Grundrisse,* 17; see also *Selected Writings,* 53 (from "On the Jewish Question"), where Marx said that bourgeois society "leads man to see in other men not the realization but the limitation of his own freedom."

40. *Capital,* 92–93.

atively de-reify the world, or regain control over it. Engels, who was often quite good at summarizing Marx's thinking, put it quite well:

> With the seizing of the means of production by society, produc- tion of commodities is done away with, and, simultaneously, the master of the product over the producer. . . . The whole sphere of the conditions of life which environ man, and which have hith- erto ruled man, now comes under the dominion and control of man, who for the first time becomes the real, conscious lord of Nature, because he has now become master of his own social organisation. . . . Man's own social organisation, hitherto con- fronting him as a necessity imposed by Nature and history, now becomes the result of his own free action. . . . Only from that time will man himself, more and more consciously, make his own history. . . . It is the ascent of man from the kingdom of necessity to the kingdom of freedom.[41]

Genuine freedom lies first in recognizing that we are the authors of the social and political world and second in consciously and cooperatively shaping that world to meet human, and not class, needs. To use Marxian language, freedom requires the de-reification of the world.

Toward a Theory of Human Needs

No matter what any individual reader may think of Marx's theory of alien- ation and his concept of freedom, a suspicion may lurk that Marx has offered just one more theory of human nature, an attractive one perhaps, but still merely another theory to take its place on the shelf of the history of ideas. Did Marx offer any evidence to support his theory? Does all this talk about being alienated from the human essence not rest upon Aris- totle's teleological notion that God and nature have outlined a purpose

---

41. Robert C. Tucker, ed., *The Marx-Engels Reader*, 2d ed. (New York: W. W. Norton, 1978), 715–16 (from Engels, *Socialism: Utopian and Scientific*). Marx had always asserted, against Hegel, that ideas do not determine the way we live, but instead that the way we live (including the economic and class basis of society) determines what we think; but in this last moment of class history and the beginning of human history, ideas do in fact shape circumstances. This is a dramatic break with Marx's claims that "[i]t is not the conscious- ness of men that determines their being, but, on the contrary, their social being that deter- mines consciousness," and that "[l]ife is not determined by consciousness, but conscious- ness by life." *Selecting Writings*, 389 (from "Preface to *A Critique of Political Economy*"); *German Ideology*, 47.

for human beings to attain? Has not Marx let his hopes sketch a pleasing picture of human nature?

Marx worried about these very questions. In his writings of 1843–45 Marx had justified his theory of human nature by talking about the "human essence" and humankind's "species-being," but by 1846, when he and Engels wrote *The German Ideology,* he had discarded such philosophical language. Somewhat startlingly he criticized himself in the opening lines of the preface: "Hitherto men have constantly made up for themselves false conceptions about themselves, about what they are and what they ought to be. They have arranged their relationships according to their ideas of God, of normal man, etc. The phantoms of their brains have got out of their hands."[42] In *The German Ideology* Marx jettisoned much of his philosophical speculations in favor of examining human beings empirically, historically, and dialectically, that is, in favor of examining human beings as they have labored and produced. "As individuals express their life, so they are. What they are, therefore, coincides with their production, both with *what* they produce and with *how* they produce." For Marx, only by investigating human beings historically and empirically can we understand what human beings have been and might be, and anyone who discards this approach in favor of philosophical speculation about "Man" has merely "abandoned the realm of real history and returned to the realm of ideology." Years later both he and Engels would liken this approach to that of Darwin, whose scientific studies, said Marx, dealt a "death-blow" to all teleological speculation.[43]

This does not mean that Marx abandoned his early conception of human nature, but rather he now set about to justify it without using the language of Aristotle, Hegel, and Feuerbach. In what is widely referred to as Marx's theory of "historical materialism," Marx now began to examine in exactly what ways human beings interact with the material and economic world. The materialist assumption that men and women are the products of circumstances, that we are creatures of our environment, is half-right; in addition, we are the creators of our circumstances. "Circumstances make men just as much as men make circumstances."[44] Throughout history, the relation between human beings and their material circumstances has been dialectical, meaning that although men and women are shaped by the world, they also labor to transform the world, and in the process they also transform themselves. In this process of laboring upon the world, men and women satisfy their needs and also begin to

---

42. *German Ideology,* 37.
43. *German Ideology,* 42, 119; *Selected Correspondence,* 115.
44. *German Ideology,* 59.

recognize new needs. "The satisfaction of the first need . . . leads to new needs; and this production of new needs is the first historical act."[45]

This word *need* now became pivotal in Marx's attempts to justify his theory of human nature, because he now argued that men and women seek expressive labor, a community of equals, and control over their own creations, not because these achievements allow us to fulfill some alleged "human essence," but because we *need* these things. In this, Marx distinguished between natural needs and needs that emerged historically; in his own century, "the place of natural needs has been taken by needs that are historically produced."[46] Marx was suggesting that after the labor of centuries, men and women had finally developed means of production advanced enough to meet our most basic and natural needs with comparative ease. Having satisfied these elementary needs, however, human beings discover that they have higher needs, such as a need for creativity, community, or democratic control over their lives. Engels, for example, talked of "needs not yet understood by [the proletariat], but only vaguely felt."[47] In short, humankind will discover an irresistible need for a world without alienation.

In a sense the world has always been propelled by needs, although in the past such needs have been class needs. The bourgeoisie, for example, felt a driving economic and political necessity to end feudal relations of production and the absolute monarchies that defended the feudal classes. Similarly, needs will push the proletariat toward revolution. "A radical revolution can only be a revolution of radical needs." For human emancipation, however, narrow class needs will not suffice, because a proletarian revolution that simply establishes another class despotism is hardly the path to freedom. "So where is the real possibility of German emancipation? We answer: in the formation of a class with radical chains, . . . [a class] that has a universal character because of its universal sufferings and lays claim to no particular right, because it is the object of no particular injustice but of injustice in general." Because it is the heir of all previous laboring classes, because it is the class designated by history to bring an end to class history, the needs of the proletariat are not class needs but the needs of all humanity. The proletariat will be driven by an "urgent, no longer disguisable, absolutely imperative need" to build a new

45. *German Ideology*, 49. Marx retained this notion of historically developing needs throughout his life; see his 1880 "Comments on Adolph Wagner," in *Selected Writings*, 581.
46. *Grundrisse*, 86.
47. Engels, introduction to Marx, *Class Struggles in France, 1848–1850*, no trans. given (New York: International Publishers, 1964), 15.

political and economic world that will establish the conditions for human emancipation. As a result, "the question is not what this or that proletarian, or even the whole of the proletariat at the moment considers as its aim. The question is what the proletariat . . . will be compelled to do."[48]

This last point is very important. Marx did not think of himself as a utopian dreaming up blueprints for better worlds. One cannot successfully reestablish Spartan austerity in the lap of European luxury, as Rousseau had noted, and one cannot persuade self-seeking bourgeois to live in selfless cooperatives, as Fourier and Owen had supposed. A philosophy is viable only if it is in accord with the circumstances of a given historical moment, that is, only if it expresses the needs of an age. "A theory will only be realized in a people in so far as it is the realization of what it needs. . . . It is not enough that thought should tend toward reality, reality must tend toward thought."[49] As a consequence, Marx thought of his philosophy as grounded in an understanding of history, scientifically accurate, and thoroughly expressive of what the proletariat—and ultimately humankind as a whole—would feel a need to undertake. Far from being a dreamy utopia, his philosophy was the only one, he thought, that was realistically attuned to the demands of history.

How does one come to understand the scope of human needs? Like a good Hegelian and Feuerbachian, Marx thought that he received a glimpse of these needs by means of religion, art, and of course philosophy. Like Feuerbach, Marx concluded that religion has secretly expressed human wishes and human needs, while we have consistently projected our own potentials onto some illusory deity. "Man has found in the imaginary reality of heaven where he looked for a superman only the reflection of his own self." Similarly, in noting that great art does not merely reflect class interests, he suggested that such art gives us glimpses into timeless concerns and needs of the human race. Finally, Marx repeatedly said such things as "the realization of philosophy coincides with its disappearance" and "you cannot transcend philosophy without realizing it."[50] Because philosophy is a critical tool, because philosophy exposes the explosive possibilities of a given epoch, because philosophy delineates the needs and wants of any era, and because philosophy ultimately depicts the full panorama of human needs, when these human needs are realized philos-

---

48. *Selected Writings*, 70, 72, 135 (from "Towards a Critique of Hegel's *Philosophy of Right*" and Marx and Engels, *The Holy Family*).

49. *Selected Writings*, 70 (from "Towards a Critique of Hegel's *Philosophy of Right*").

50. *Selected Writings*, 63, 68, 14 (from "Towards a Critique of Hegel's *Philosophy of Right*" and notes for his doctoral dissertation). For Marx on art, see *Grundrisse*, 44–46.

ophy as we know it will lose its historical function. "As philosophy finds in the proletariat its material weapons, so the proletariat finds in philosophy its intellectual weapons, . . . the proletariat cannot transcend itself without realizing philosophy." Religion, art, and philosophy all give us glimpses into enduring human needs that become more and more clear with each stage of history. "The world has long possessed the dream" of what it needs, and "humanity is not beginning a new work, but consciously bringing its old work to completion."[51] How much he remained a Hegelian!

We finally must ask what Marx meant by the word *need*? How does a need differ from a desire? Do we not have needs *for* something, and if I need food for survival, then for what do I need expressive labor? Marx provides no clear answer to these questions, but what answer he gave is probably closer than he ever imagined to Plato's notion that a fully developed human being is one who has attained some sort of completeness or health. For example, in his brilliant essay "On the Jewish Question," Marx argued that political emancipation in a capitalist economy was not human emancipation, largely because such a world was still demanding of us the impossible, that is, that we simultaneously be both selfless citizen and self-seeking bourgeois: "He has a life in the political community, where he is valued as a communal being, and in civil society, where he is active as a private individual, treats other men as means, degrades himself to a means, and becomes the plaything of alien powers."[52] While certainly Marx was arguing the impossibility of a genuine community of equals in a society dominated by one class—and especially a class that necessarily promoted an acquisitive and self-seeking ethic—he was also suggesting that these twin demands of being a selfless citizen and a self-seeking bourgeois were in some sense unhealthy. As Rousseau had said, "let us reflect what must be the state of things, when men are forced to caress and destroy one another at the same time."[53] Marx's discussion of human needs must ultimately rest on some understanding, grounded in his investigations of how human beings change during history, of what it means for a human being to be completely fulfilled or healthy. "It will be seen how in place of the *wealth* and *poverty* of political economy comes the *rich human being* and the rich *human* need. The *rich* human being is

51. *Selected Writings*, 73 (from "Towards a Critique of Hegel's *Philosophy of Right*"); *Selected Writings*, 38.

52. *Selected Writings*, 46 (from "On the Jewish Question"). See Karl Löwith, *Max Weber and Karl Marx*, trans. Hans Fantel (London: George Allen & Unwin, 1982 [1932]), 83–90.

53. Jean-Jacques Rousseau, *The Social Contract* and *Discourses*, trans. G.D.H. Cole (New York: Dutton, 1950), 275 (from *A Discourse on the Origin of Inequality*).

simultaneously the human being *in need of* a totality of human manifestations of life—the man in whom his own realization exists as an inner necessity, as *need.*"[54]

Despotism of the Workplace

Marx suggested that the "traditional" mode of making things, found in Europe in the Middle Ages, was one in which the individual artisan worked "independently, and without recognizing any authority over him." However suffocating and class-ridden such traditional villages were, however paternalistic the guildmaster might have been, the individual artisan had a modest independence. By contrast, the modern worker under industrial capitalism was subjected to the "despotism" of the "bourgeois class," the "bourgeois State," the individual "bourgeois manufacturer," the supervisor on the shop floor, and the machine itself.[55] By using the word *despotism* in this way, Marx refused to confine the concept of despotism to the political world and quite logically extended it to the world of production. Having confined their citizens to oppressive and authoritarian economic organizations for most hours of most days, capitalist societies could not reasonably call themselves democratic and their citizens free. For Marx, factory labor was a new form of tyranny that hid behind the notion that workers freely and voluntarily made a contract for a fair wage.

> The slavery in which the bourgeoisie has bound the proletariat, comes nowhere more plainly into daylight than in the factory system. In it all freedom comes to an end both at law and in fact. The workman must be in the factory at half past five. If he comes a few minutes late, he is punished. . . . The despotic bell calls him from his bed, calls him from breakfast and dinner. And how does he fare in the mill? There the master is the absolute lawgiver. . . . the courts say to the workman: Since you have entered into this contract voluntarily, you must now carry it out. . . . These work-

54. *1844 Manuscripts*, 143–44. For a good discussion of Marx's theory of human needs, see Elster, *Making Sense of Marx*, 68–92; also Agnes Heller, *The Theory of Need in Marx* (New York: St. Martin's, 1976); Vernon Venable, *Human Nature: The Marxian View* (New York, 1945); Joseph J. O'Malley, "History and Man's 'Nature' in Marx," in *Marx's Socialism*, ed. Shlomo Avineri (New York: Lieber Atherton, 1973), 80–100.

55. *Capital*, 393; *Selected Writings*, 227 (from *The Communist Manifesto*).

men are condemned to live, from their ninth year till their death, under this mental and bodily torture.[56]

"The previously independent" worker is now subjected to "the discipline and command of capital," which is nothing less than a "despotism" of "the workshop."[57]

As one who grew up in Germany hating Prussian authoritarianism, Marx could think of no way to condemn this factory despotism more than to say that it recreates the "barrack discipline"—think of his phrase "despotic bell"—of the presumably Prussian army. "An industrial army of workmen, under the command of a capitalist, requires, like a real army, officers (managers), and sergeants (foremen, overlookers), who, while the work is being done, command in the name of the capitalist."[58] Like an army, factory discipline uses a hierarchical system of authority to control the time and motion of the workers, eliminating all independence and creativity. The worker becomes a piece of the machinery, or, in an Aristotelian sense, the human being takes on the characteristics and functions of a tool.

What should merely be means by which to improve human life— science, technology, machinery, the techniques of organizing people— instead serve only narrow class interests. Not only does capitalist production deny to workers any time and all conditions for intellectual and physical development, but it even brings about early exhaustion and premature death, lengthening working time only to produce a shortening of life time. Marx put this well in one of his more passionate passages. "They mutilate the labourer into a fragment of a man, degrade him to the level of an appendage of a machine, destroy every remnant of charm in his work and turn it into hated toil; they estrange from him the intellectual potentialities of the labour-process in the same proportion as science is incorporated in it as an independent power; they distort the conditions under which he works, subject him during the labour-process to a despotism the more hateful for its meanness; they transform his life-time into working-time, and drag his wife and child beneath the wheels of the Juggernaut of capital."[59] Marx was passionately angry that human beings, with such potential to be creative and intelligent actors in the world, had become tools used by the capitalist class, even tools serving other tools.

56. *Capital,* 464 (from a passage in which he was quoting Engels). For an excellent historical study of the working class becoming accustomed to the dictates of time, see E. P. Thompson, *The Making of the English Working Class* (New York: Vintage, 1966).
57. *Capital,* 396, 391; also 364.
58. *Capital,* 463, 364.
59. *Capital,* 708.

"In handicrafts and manufacture, the workman makes use of a tool, in the factory, the machine makes use of him."[60] Nowhere is this diminution of men and women and this smothering of human potential more apparent than in the detailed division of labor required by factory production. Some form of the division of labor has always been present. Only the modern factory system, however, perfected the division of labor, forcing men and women with marvelous and wide-ranging potentials for intelligence and creativity into the specialized work necessary for efficient production. The modern factory "converts the labourer into a crippled monstrosity, by forcing his detail dexterity at the expense of a world of productive capabilities." Or, in a passage Marx borrowed from a contemporary, "the subdivision of labor is the assassination of a people."[61]

Again, although Marx complained that capitalism was robbing working men and women, he expressed even greater outrage that capitalist production was forever stifling unexplored worlds of human potential. Capitalism was fast rendering "generations of human beings stunted, short-lived, swiftly replacing each other, plucked, so to say, before maturity"; it was teaching girls and boys from childhood to adapt their "movements to the uniform and unceasing motion of an automaton"; or, as one of Adam Smith's mentors put it, "we make a nation of Helots, and have no free citizens."[62] All of this echoes his early writings in which he complained that the "production of too many useful things produces too large a *useless* population." Most dramatically perhaps, Marx quite respectfully quoted Adam Smith himself, who had first outlined the advantages of the division of labor in the opening chapters of *The Wealth of Nations* but had, much later in that volume, honestly acknowledged the human costs of this production technique. "The man whose whole life is spent in performing a few simple operations," wrote Smith, "has no occasion to exert his understanding. . . . He generally becomes as stupid and ignorant as it is possible for a human creature to become."[63]

Reminding us of Aristotle, Marx called the factory a despotism because it was a hierarchical and authoritarian organization—like Aristotle's household, serving the interests of one person or at least one class—that

60. *Capital*, 461; see also Gerald A. Cohen, "Bourgeois and Proletarians," *Journal of the History of Ideas* 19, no. 2 (1968): 211–30.
61. *Capital*, 396, 399.
62. *Capital*, 295, 460, 389.
63. *1844 Manuscripts*, 151; *Capital*, 397–98. An acquaintance told a story in which Marx watched a man perform a detailed task at a machine, asked the man if he ever did any other job, and was told that he did not. "His power of thinking," Marx said, "is changed into muscular memory." See McLellan, *Karl Marx: His Life and Thought*, 427.

stifled the unfolding of human potential. Marx's theory of human nature and human needs clearly lies behind this critique of factory despotism. Although the division of labor forces men and women into highly specialized activity, in fact each person, according to Marx, has a wide variety of talents and interests that will remain slumbering and undeveloped under capitalism. Against Plato, Marx suggested that the division of labor "develops a one-sided specialty into a perfection, at the expense of the whole of a man's working capacity."[64] After a socialist society has brought about some sort of comparative abundance, that is, after technology and science have completed the conquest of nature and freed us from a lifetime devoted to the division of labor, we can develop all sides of our multivarious personalities. Only then will we know what humankind is capable of creating and what any single individual is capable of becoming, as Marx put it so well in a famous, Romantic passage.

> For as soon as the distribution of labour comes into being, each man has a particular, exclusive sphere of activity, which is forced upon him and from which he cannot escape. He is a hunter, a fisherman, a shepherd, or a critical critic, and must remain so if he does not want to lose his means of livelihood; while in communist society, where nobody has one exclusive sphere of activity but each can become accomplished in any branch he wishes, society regulates the general production and thus makes it possible for me to do one thing today and another tomorrow, to hunt in the morning, fish in the afternoon, rear cattle in the evening, criticise after dinner, just as I have a mind, without ever becoming hunter, fisherman, shepherd or critic.[65]

In a sense, the division of labor is like a symptom of an illness because, in confining us artificially to one specialized function, it renders us less than human or less than completely healthy.

Class Despotism

Nothing seems quite so familiar in Marx as the claim that the "history of all hitherto existing society is the history of class struggles." At any one time, one class more or less securely dominates all others. In the nine-

---

64. *Capital*, 384.
65. *German Ideology*, 53.

teenth century, with the success of the 1830 Revolution in France, "the bourgeoisie had conquered political power" in both France and England; the French monarchy under Louis Philippe, for example, was nothing more than a "bourgeois monarchy."[66] Nor did it make much difference whether the visible form of government was a monarchy or a republic, and after France triumphantly established the Second Republic in 1848, it soon "revealed that here *bourgeois republic* signifies the unlimited despotism of one class over other classes."[67] Such a class analysis is a dramatic break with those attempts, especially by Aristotle and Montesquieu, to classify governments according to whether the one, the few, or the many ruled. According to Marx, all of these governments—monarchies, aristocracies, democracies—were only different formal manifestations of class tyranny. Using this class analysis, Marx claimed that the nineteenth century had simplified the class struggle. If in previous societies several classes all made demands at once—as, for instance, in Rome, where patricians, knights, plebeians, and slaves all came into conflict—bourgeois society had simplified the class struggle all while intensifying it. "Society as a whole is more and more splitting up into two great hostile camps, into two great classes directly facing each other: Bourgeoisie and Proletariat."[68]

All of this sounds wonderfully simple, and in fact it is too simple. To begin with, in Marx's own historical and political analyses he did not talk of "two great classes," but instead analyzed the roles played by anywhere from a half-dozen to a dozen classes. Consider just one passage taken from his famous study of the political struggles in France leading up to Louis Napoleon's coup in 1851. "The bourgeois republic triumphed [after June 1848]. On its side stood the aristocracy of finance, the industrial bourgeoisie, the middle class, the petty bourgeoisie, the army, the *lumpen proletariat* organized as the Mobile Guard, the intellectual lights, the clergy and the rural population. On the side of the Paris proletariat stood none but itself."[69] What are we to make of such a passage? If we count every group that Marx mentions as a class, we find him mentioning ten classes in two sentences. If they are not classes, then are they groups

66. *Selected Writings*, 222 (from *The Communist Manifesto*); *Capital*, 19; *The Eighteenth Brumaire of Louis Bonaparte*, no trans. given (New York: International Publishers, 1963), 23.
67. *Eighteenth Brumaire*, 24; also 48.
68. *Selected Writings*, 222 (from *The Communist Manifesto*).
69. *Eighteenth Brumaire*, 23. The best analysis of the various classes on which Marx focuses his attention is Hal Draper's *Karl Marx's Theory of Revolution*, vol. 2, *The Politics of Social Classes* (New York: Monthly Review Press, 1978). Even Draper does not discuss the full range of classes that Marx mentioned, and Draper gives us no way to distinguish between classes and factions of classes.

that can *sometimes* act independently of their class origins? If they are not groups, are they no more than factions of major classes? If they are factions of some major class, and if they can have interests of their own, then why can we not call them classes?

Although Marx remains silent on these questions, we can safely draw two conclusions. First, in analyzing the roles of many classes, factions of classes, and groups, Marx himself wielded a very sophisticated and complicated class analysis, hardly confining himself to his famous polemical claim that bourgeois society witnessed "two great classes" confronting each other. Second, Marx never gave a clear definition of class. Three paragraphs from the end of volume 3 of *Capital* Marx asked, "What constitutes a class?" After suggesting that a class might be defined by its source of revenue—that, for example, wages distinguish the working class, profit from capital the capitalist class, and rent from land the landlord class—he abandoned the idea; otherwise he would have had to consider physicians and government officials, who also have distinct sources of revenue, as separate classes. At that point, on page 886 of the third volume, the manuscript breaks off inconclusively.[70] Marx had previously attempted to define class by source of income, and he even spoke in *Capital* of "ideological" classes "such as government officials, priests, lawyers, soldiers, etc."[71] All of these attempts ended unsatisfactorily, however, not only because including in the working class those who earn wages would be to define wage-earning industrial managers as members of the proletariat, but also because defining class by source of income creates an endless and ultimately useless multiplication of so-called classes. Did Marx really want to think of lawyers as a class separate from the bourgeoisie whom they generally served? Even if Marx did not give us a perfectly clear definition of class, however, that hardly means his analyses of nineteenth-century political economy are fatally flawed.

By the time of *The German Ideology,* Marx had concluded that political struggles are merely the reflection of larger class struggles. "It follows from this that all struggles within the State, the struggle between democracy, aristocracy, and monarchy, the struggle for the franchise, etc. etc. are merely the illusory forms in which the real struggles of the different

70. *Capital*, 3:886.
71. *Capital*, 487; *Grundrisse*, 34. Even the best modern defenses of Marx offer little clarification. See, for example, Ollman, *Alienation*, 120–27; G. A. Cohen, *Karl Marx's Theory of History: A Defence* (Princeton: Princeton University Press, 1978), 73–77. Cohen's claim—"A person's class is established by nothing but his objective place in the network of ownership relations, however difficult it may be to identify such places neatly"—is typical, and not very helpful.

classes are fought out among one another."[72] Although we are accustomed to having modern-day Marxists criticize elections as only fictitious conflict, as only the opportunity—in Marx's own words—to select "once in three or six years which member of the ruling class was to misrepresent the people in Parliament," in fact Marx thought that sometimes elections succeeded in "unchaining the class struggle." Still, despite bold words about democracy and freedom, underneath the nineteenth century's "mock democratism" one still found the "real despotism" of one class over all others.[73] Marx sarcastically criticized what he called *parliamentary cretinism,* the tendency to think that majority votes in parliament are all-important in determining the course of history, when in fact economic development, advances in technology, wars, revolutions, and of course class struggle are far more important determinants of history.[74]

While it might appear that the central political issues are monarchy versus republic or "the eternal rights of man" versus the necessity of order, such debates offer only a "superficial appearance which veils the class struggle."[75] The appearance of freedom was, for Marx, a crucial ideological tool by which classes dominated. Classes create ideologies, or systems of ideas, that justify their claims and privileges, and individuals generally adopt the system of ideas appropriate to their position in the class structure.

> Upon the different forms of property, upon the social conditions of existence, rises an entire [ideological] superstructure of distinct and peculiarly formed sentiments, illusions, modes of thought and views of life. The entire class creates and forms them out of its material foundations and out of the corresponding social relations. The single individual, who derives them through tradition and upbringing, may imagine that they form the real motives and the starting point of his activity. . . . And as in private life one differentiates between what a man thinks and says of himself and what he really is and does, so in historical struggles one must distinguish still more the phrases and fancies of parties

72. *German Ideology,* 54; see also Engels, introduction to *Eighteenth Brumaire,* 14 [written 1885].

73. *Civil War in France,* 59; *Class Struggles in France,* 54; *Civil War in France,* 25.

74. Engels and Marx, *Germany: Revolution and Counter-Revolution,* ed. Eleanor Marx, no trans. given (New York: International Publishers, 1969), 92–93; Marx, *Eighteenth Brumaire,* 91. Marx, of course, was making an excellent point; have any parliamentary decisions in the last four decades been as important as the invention of television or the microchip?

75. *Eighteenth Brumaire,* 46.

from their real organism and their real interests, their conception
of themselves, from their reality.[76]

In any given moment in history, the dominant ideas reflect the interests
of the dominant class. "The ideas of the ruling class are in every epoch
the ruling ideas [but not the *only* ideas], i.e. the class which is the ruling
material force of society, is at the same time its ruling *intellectual* force."
Those who control the "material production" of any society also control
the "mental production" and use these ideas to dominate other classes.
One can see this, for example, in law, which is supposed to embody timeless standards of justice, but in fact merely expresses the ideas and needs
of the dominant class. "Your jurisprudence is but the will of your class
made into a law for all." In part, "ideological representatives" of the ruling
class, such as educators, intellectuals, journalists, and lawyers, actively
defend and justify such class rule.[77] More important, time and tradition
simply make such class rule seem inevitable, as if it were some unalter-
able law of nature, like gravity. "The advance of capitalist production
develops a working-class, which by education, tradition, habit, looks
upon the conditions of that mode of production as self-evident laws of
nature." While certainly Marx knew that a class ruled with force, this form
of ideological or "intellectual bondage" was probably a more effective and
durable buttress to class tyranny.[78]

The previous discussion makes it sound as if Marx thought that there
was one unified class that ruled, but in fact Marx was adept at showing
the ways in which privileged classes vied for political power, the ruling
class split into factions, and various classes formed alliances. When the
Legitimists, or Bourbons, ruled France before 1830, for example, they represented "big landed property," but when the house of Orléans came to
power with the 1830 Revolution and the July Monarchy, "high finance,
large-scale industry, large-scale trade, that is, *capital* [governed] with its
retinue of lawyers, professors and smooth-tongued orators."[79] Although
these two factions of the ruling class talked about principles of monarchy
and which family had the strongest claim to rule, in fact these ideas only
obscured the fact that the battle was between two different factions of the

76. *Eighteenth Brumaire*, 47.
77. *German Ideology*, 64; *Selected Writings*, 234 (from *The Communist Manifesto*); *Class
Struggles in France*, 34; *Eighteenth Brumaire*, 64.
78. *Capital*, 809; *Germany: Revolution and Counter-Revolution*, 70. On the meaning of
ideology, see Louis Dupre, *Marx's Social Critique of Culture* (New Haven: Yale University
Press, 1983), 216–28; George Lichtheim, "The Concept of Ideology," in *The Concept of Ideology and Other Essays* (New York: Random House, 1967).
79. *Eighteenth Brumaire*, 46–47.

bourgeoisie. "If each side wished to effect the *restoration* of its *own* royal house against the other, that merely signified that each of the *two great interests* into which the *bourgeoisie* is split—landed property and capital—sought to restore its own supremacy and the subordination of the other. We speak of two interests of the bourgeoisie, for large landed property, despite its feudal coquetry and pride of race, has been rendered thoroughly bourgeois by the development of modern society."[80] Although certainly Marx contended that the July Monarchy had excluded landed property from political power, he also maintained that the interests of capital itself had split, with the financial aristocracy, or the bankers, controlling the government and the industrial bourgeoisie in opposition. If banking interests greatly enjoyed government indebtedness and high interests rates, industrial concerns did not.[81]

Although Marx analyzed splits within the ruling class, it was still a ruling class that dominated all others despotically. And if many thought that a republic would cure all the ills engendered by monarchy, Marx declared that, to the contrary, the Second Republic was the political form at last discovered in which these two antagonists—Legitimists and Orleanists, landed property and industry—could dominate other classes more efficiently and to their mutual benefit. Parliament, wrote Marx, was more than neutral ground on which these two antagonists could meet; it was "the unavoidable condition of their *common* rule" over other classes. "Here, in the bourgeois republic, which bore neither the name *Bourbon* nor the name *Orleans,* but the name *Capital,* they had found the form of state in which they could rule *conjointly.*"[82]

A key phrase here is "the form of state," because we finally need to ask how exactly Marx thought the ruling class related to the state. Here we enter the murky area of Marx's theory of the state.

The State as an Instrument That Facilitates Class Despotism

In *The Communist Manifesto,* Marx and Engels wrote that "the executive of the modern State is but a committee for managing the common affairs of the whole bourgeoisie."[83] Although this was a simplistic analysis of the

---

80. *Eighteenth Brumaire*, 48.
81. *Class Struggles in France*, 33–36.
82. *Eighteenth Brumaire*, 96, 36.
83. *Selected Writings*, 223 (from *The Communist Manifesto*). For modern debates between

role of the state, appropriate to a polemical pamphlet, this remark and others similar to it have sparked a blaze of debate about exactly how Marx analyzed the bourgeois state. Consequently, one key dilemma for all scholars studying Marx centers around how literally one is to take such a sentence; is the state a strictly subordinate instrument for class domination, or does the state sometimes pursue a course independent of the interests of the dominant class?

Quite probably because of his early and confrontational encounters with the bureaucratic and police representatives of German states, Marx always detested the all-powerful and centralized modern state. In his early works criticizing Hegel, Marx said that bureaucrats are the "Jesuits" of the state (which, in his mind, was the strongest possible condemnation), and he argued that despite Hegel's claim that the state and its officials would represent the general or "universal" interest of a nation, in fact bureaucratic representatives of the state merely chase after their own private aims. Far from gazing up at "Reason," bureaucrats swim about immersed in "careerism."[84] Although centralized government originated in the days of feudalism, "the military-bureaucratic government machinery [was] forged in opposition to feudalism." Not only did Marx detest the repressive functions of this state, he also resented that "this appalling parasitic body" directed all common activities—the building of bridges, the construction of schools, the management of local concerns—that would better be left to citizens themselves.[85] All previous revolutions, because they were bourgeois revolutions in which the bourgeoisie used state power to destroy feudal privilege, only enlarged this state power. The socialist revolution, wrote Marx, "will no longer attempt to transfer the bureaucratic-military apparatus from one hand to another, but *to smash* it, and this is the precondition for every real people's revolution on the Continent."[86]

Marxists about theories of the state, see Ralph Miliband, *Marxism and Politics* (Oxford: Oxford University Press, 1977), esp. chap. 4, 66–117; Nicos Poulantzas, *State, Power, Socialism* (London: Verso, 1980 [1978]), esp. pt. 2, 123–60; Isaac Balbus, *Marxism and Domination: A Neo-Hegelian, Feminist, Psychoanalytic Theory of Sexual, Political, and Technological Liberation* (Princeton: Princeton University Press, 1982), esp. chap. 3, 84–125; Martin Carnoy, *The State and Political Theory* (Princeton: Princeton University Press, 1984), esp. chaps. 4–5, pp. 89–152.

84. *Selected Writings*, 31 (from "Critique of Hegel's *Philosophy of Right*").

85. *Eighteenth Brumaire*, 121, 131, 122. See Perry Anderson, *Lineages of the Absolutist State* (London: New Left Books, 1975).

86. *Selected Correspondence*, 247; see also *Eighteenth Brumaire* 122; *Selected Writings*, 552 (from the notes for *Civil War in France*). When we see how much Marx detested tyrannical, centralized states, it is cruelly ironic that twentieth-century revolutions in his name have created just such states.

It was generally, although certainly not always, Engels who made the most straightforward claims that the state was invariably the instrument used for one class to dominate others. "In reality, however, the state is nothing but a machine for the oppression of one class by another, and indeed in the democratic republic no less than in the monarchy." Or, as Engels put it in a letter, the bourgeoisie keeps the proletariat in "servitude" not only by economic exploitation but also by "the power of the state—the army, the bureaucracy, the courts."[87] When Marx made this claim, he was generally more circumspect. In his writings on the Second Empire and the Paris Commune, for example, he noted that state power had previously been checked by feudal privileges and before 1830 by divisions within the ruling class. Only after 1830 did "state power [assume] more and more the character of the national power of capital over labour, of a public force organised for social enslavement, of an engine of class despotism." Under the Second Republic the state furthered "class terrorism," and by the time of the Second Empire the state become the "organized force of the slavery of labour" and the "horrid machinery of class domination."[88] For Marx, it was too simple to say that the state was *always* just an instrument of class domination.

While Marx certainly agreed with Engels that functionaries of the state were generally agents of class despotism, he was more willingly to see the state itself as checked by class disputes, and he recognized that the state nearly always pursued, and sometimes even succeeded in obtaining, interests independent from those of the dominant class. Consider just one passage in which Marx analyzes the state in three different ways. "But under the absolute monarchy, during the first Revolution, under Napoleon, bureaucracy was only the means of preparing the class rule of the bourgeoisie. Under the Restoration, under Louis Philippe, under the parliamentary republic, it was the instrument of the ruling class, however much it strove for power of its own. Only under the second Bonaparte does the state seem to have made itself completely independent."[89] From

---

87. Engels, introduction to *Civil War in France*, 22; *Selected Correspondence*, 244. On the fact that Engels's view of the state differed from Marx's view, see Michael Levin, "Marx and Engels on the Generalised Class State," *History of Political Thought* 6, no. 3 (1985): 433–53; also Richard N. Hunt, who talks about Engels's notion of a "class state" versus Marx's notion of a "parasite state." *The Political Ideas of Marx and Engels*, (Pittsburgh: University of Pittsburgh Press, 1974), 125–31.

88. *Civil War in France*, 54–55; *Selected Writings*, 553 (from the notes for *Civil War in France*).

89. *Eighteenth Brumaire*, 122. This claim that Louis Napoleon's state had independence from the bourgeoisie does contradict Marx's description of the Second Empire in his *Civil War in France*.

Louis XIV to Napoleon, the state bureaucracy actually subverted the landed aristocracy and feudalism itself; from the Restoration to the Second Republic, the state bureaucracy was an instrument of class rule, even though it actively sought its own interests; under Louis Bonaparte, the state assumed an independent role, although Marx later added that the state under the Second Empire assisted the peasantry and the middle classes, all while it facilitated capital development by the bourgeoisie.[90] Obviously, Marx did not think a simple formula explained all historical circumstances.

Marx had always believed that the state could act somewhat independently of the dominant class. In the *Grundrisse* he remarked that the American state "was from the start subordinated to bourgeois society and to bourgeois production, and could never pretend to a purpose of its own." From the context it is clear that he thought that this strict subordination of the American state set it apart from European states. In France, from the Restoration to the Second Empire, the state had in fact been the instrument of class domination; but with volatile splits within the ruling class, the bourgeoisie actually wished for the imposition of order so as to pursue its private affairs. They did indeed get the order, but also a new form of despotism. "France, therefore, seems to have escaped the despotism of a class only to fall back beneath the despotism of an individual." Under Louis Bonaparte, "the executive authority . . . made itself an independent power," and the state established itself as a power "separate from and independent of society."[91] The state under the Second Empire became a parasitic body that hardly took orders from the bourgeoisie. "But the state parasite received only its last development during the Second Empire. The government power with its standing-army, its all-directing bureaucracy, its stultifying clergy, and its servile tribunal hierarchy had grown so independent of society itself. . . . It appeared no longer as a means of class domination, subordinate to its parliamentary ministry or legislature. Humbling under its sway even the interests of the ruling class, . . . the state power had received its last and supreme expression in the Second Empire."[92] For the bourgeoisie, the state was "humiliating." Having destroyed the workers' press, the bourgeoisie now lost its own press; having used police repression to control popular discontent, it now felt the effects of police arrests; having forbidden the freedom

90. *Eighteenth Brumaire*, 122–23, 131–32.

91. *Grundrisse*, 48; *Eighteenth Brumaire*, 121, 106, 131; *Selected Writings*, 554 (from the notes for *Civil War in France*). See Hal Draper, *Karl Marx's Theory of Revolution*, vol. 1, *State and Bureaucracy*, chaps. 15–18, 339–464; also Martin E. Spencer, "Marx on the State: The Events in France Between 1848–1850," *Theory and Society* 7, nos. 1 and 2 (1979): 167–98.

92. *Selected Writings*, 552–53 (from the notes for *Civil War in France*).

of assembly, it now complained when its own meetings were dispersed; having subverted the jury system, it now found no independent courts to which it might appeal.[93] Marx did not carry this notion of independence too far; Louis Bonaparte's state neither replaced the dominant class nor greatly damaged its material interests. Just as under the Second Republic, when "the *material interests* of the French bourgeoisie [were] interwoven in the closest fashion" with the "parasitic" state that "enmeshes, controls, regulates, superintends and tutors civil society," so the state under Louis Bonaparte *facilitated* the interests of the bourgeoisie. "Industry and trade, and hence the business affairs of the middle class, are to prosper hothouse fashion under the strong government." Just as parliamentary government under the Second Republic allowed the two factions of the ruling class to unite and dominate together, and just as rule by the aristocratic classes in England furthered the material interests of the industrial bourgeoisie,[94] so Louis Bonaparte's state may have attained a certain independence, but it still necessarily facilitated the interests of the ruling class. "In reality, [the Second Empire] was the only form of government possible at a time when the bourgeoisie had already lost, and the working class had not yet acquired, the faculty of ruling the nation. . . . Under its sway, bourgeois society, freed from political cares, attained a development unexpected even by itself. Its industry and commerce expanded to colossal dimensions."[95] Despite the fact that the Second Empire frequently pursued economic and political interests independent of the wishes of the bourgeoisie, in no sense could this state have survived, according to Marx, had it not simultaneously furthered the interests of the dominant class. Its independence, in other words, was limited.

Thus, for Marx, the state was usually just an engine for class despotism, but sometimes the state was an arena for refereeing disputes between factions of the ruling class, sometimes it pushed the interests of the dominant class but was constricted by political demands of other classes, sometimes it was an active force for organizing the interests of the dominant class, and sometimes it succeeded in attaining a significant independence from the dominant class. For survival, however, the state always needed to be at least an instrument for facilitating the material interests and economic despotism of the ruling class. This did not mean, however, that Marx thought of the working class as merely passive in its servitude.

93. *Eighteenth Brumaire*, 118–19; *Selected Writings*, 551–57 (from the notes for *Civil War in France*).
94. *Eighteenth Brumaire*, 62, 132, 48; *Selected Writings*, 328.
95. *Civil War in France*, 56; *Selected Writings*, 553 (from the notes for *Civil War in France*).

The Role of the Working Class

If all political struggles are only the manifestation of larger class struggles, then certainly the working class needs to be factored into this political equation, because Marx obviously did not think that the working class
remained docile and servile when confronted by the despotism of capital.
For example, Marx took much of parliamentary legislation seriously, and
while he generally regarded such decrees as legislation on behalf of the
dominant class, he saw the working class itself as sometimes compelling
legislative victories. "After a thirty years' struggle, fought with most admirable perseverance, the English working classes, improving a momentary
split between the landlords and money-lords, succeeded in carrying the
Ten Hours' Bill." Even if this was conservative reform, that is, reform
designed to forestall more radical demands, it was genuine reform with
genuine benefits. "The immense physical, moral, and intellectual benefits
hence accruing to the factory operatives, half-yearly chronicled in all the reports of the inspectors of factories, are now acknowledged on all sides."[96]
That Marx took seriously this power of the working classes to compel legislation is seen in his much too optimistic statement that "universal suffrage is
the equivalent for political power for the working class in England" and that
universal suffrage would thus be a "socialistic measure." Because Marx took
legislation seriously, he could say in an 1872 speech that some countries
such as the United States and England might well attain socialism through
peaceful legislative procedures,[97] although such a pronouncement was an
aberration. He almost always asserted that, just as in previous bourgeois
revolutions, working class revolutions would need to use force.

How did Marx envision the working class bringing about such a revolution and with it their own emancipation? Marx's entire theory of revolution resists summary within so narrow a compass as this chapter; nevertheless, for present purspose it is sufficient to note the following. Marx
sought to form workers' organizations and workers' parties, all of which
were to be run by the workers themselves. Although Lenin later talked of
the necessity of an elitist party leading the workers, Marx generally had
no use for such elitism. "The emancipation of the working classes must
be achieved by the working classes themselves. We cannot therefore cooperate with people who openly state that the workers are too unedu-
cated to emancipate themselves and must be freed from above."[98] Both

---

96. *Selected Writings*, 535 (from the "Inaugural Address to the First International").
97. *Selected Writings*, 332, 594.
98. *Selected Correspondence*, 307; see Hunt, *The Political Ideas of Marx and Engels*, chap.
8, 259–83; contrast with the authoritarian party structure Lenin advocated in *What Is to
Be Done?* [1902].

organizing for the revolution and the revolution itself are important because by these processes workers transform themselves, casting off old ideas and assumptions and discovering their driving *need* for a socialist society. "The alteration of men on a mass scale is necessary, an alteration which can only take place in a practical movement, a *revolution*; this revolution is necessary, therefore, not only because the *ruling* class cannot be overthrown in any other way, but also because the class *overthrowing* it can only in a revolution succeed in ridding itself of all the muck of ages and become fitted to found society anew."[99] In a another passage, Marx likened the workers of the nineteenth century to the Jews whom Moses led through the wilderness. The working class of his generation, said Marx, "has not only a new world to conquer, it must go under, in order to make room for the men who are fit for a new world."[100] Again and again Marx emphasized that successful revolutions are not the result merely of willful activity, that we cannot make up dreams about what we would like the future to be and then simply shape that future by force of will. Robespierre and the other French revolutionaries were doomed to fail, largely because they thought that sheer moral will could construct society according to some ideal blueprint, and thus ever-augmenting economic development and the interests of a new industrial class easily crushed their ideal of recreating an austere and virtuous Roman Republic.[101] Marx inherited this conviction from Hegel, who had offered a similar critique of Rousseau and who also stressed that great historical changes, or revolutions, come about successfully only if they meet the historical demands or needs of a given epoch. As Marx wrote in his youthful writings: "We do not then set ourselves opposite the world with a doctrinaire principle, saying: 'Here is the truth, kneel down here!' It is out of the world's own principles that we develop for it new principles. . . . We merely show it what it is actually fighting about."[102] Or, as I noted earlier in this chapter, Marx did not think it mattered what the working class thought it was going to create; what was important was what it would feel compelled to create as it began to feel an undeniable need to make a new society that would emancipate human potential. Despite aching to create a stage for virtuous Romans, French revolutionaries pulled back the curtain to see self-seeking bourgeois. As a consequence, Marx's

---

99. *German Ideology*, 94–95.

100. *Class Struggles in France*, 114. For a more complete discussion of Marx's theory of revolution, see Hunt, *The Political Ideas of Marx and Engels,* and Draper, *Karl Marx's Theory of Revolution,* 2 vols.

101. *Selected Writings,* 125; *German Ideology,* 62; Marx, *The Poverty of Philosophy,* no trans. given (New York: International Publishers, 1963), 125; *Selected Correspondence,* 318.

102. *Selected Writings,* 37.

proletarian revolution was, at least in his mind, thoroughly realistic and completely in harmony with historical demands and necessities, because it sought to do no more than give birth to a new society already gestating in the womb of the old. The working class has "no ideal to realise, but to set free the elements of the new society with which old collapsing bourgeois society itself is pregnant." Or, as Marx put it sarcastically in his preface to *Capital*—sneering at those utopian socialists such as Cabet and Fourier who planned ideal societies down to details such as where to put the toilets—he had no intention of "writing recipes . . . for the cookshops of the future."[103]

While Marx thought that socialism was certainly in tune with the demands and needs of his own historical moment, that did not mean that socialism was inevitably around the corner. He recognized that capitalism could stave off worker unrest by conservative reform—a Ten Hours' Bill, universal suffrage, a progressive income tax, and the encouragement of reformist and co-opted trade unions. Capitalism was also adept at dividing the working class, either by paying one portion more and thus forming a conservative "worker aristocracy" or by playing on ethnic hostility such as the hostility of English workers toward Irish workers or of white American workers toward blacks. Finally, workers themselves were frequently the victims of "corruption" or of a "bourgeois infection" in which they became, not revolutionary, but only interested in privately adapting to and profiting from the status quo.[104] Socialism would emerge only after "15, 20, 50 years of civil war," a long process in which workers transformed both themselves and society. Workers "know that in order to work out their own emancipation, and along with it that higher form to which present society is irresistibly tending by its own economical agencies, they will have to pass through long struggles, through a series of historic processes, transforming circumstances and men."[105]

What can we say about the new socialist society? In a sense, we can say comparatively little about a higher form of socialism because such a society will be the creation—almost literally an artistic creation—of working men and women who will resemble us only about as much as

103. *Capital*, 21; *Civil War in France*, 62; also *Selected Writings*, 135, 140–41 (from Marx and Engels, *The Holy Family*). On Marx's radical vision, but his refusal to depict the future, see Lukes, *Marxism and Morality*, 36–47.

104. *Class Struggles in France*, 68; Draper, *Karl Marx's Theory of Revolution* 2:60–65, 105–110; *Selected Correspondence*, 220–24, 295; *Selected Writings*, 585. Lenin argued that capitalism had bought off the revolutionary tendencies of the working class by paying one sector—a worker aristocracy—very high wages from profits made in imperial adventures abroad. Lenin, *Imperialism: The Highest Stage of Capitalism* [1917].

105. *Selected Writings*, 298; *Civil War in France*, 61–62.

nineteenth-century businessmen resembled the feudal lords of the Middle Ages. To ask to know exactly what socialist society will be like is similar to asking Picasso, when he was alive, what he would be painting twenty years in the future. We can know, however, characteristics of socialism just as it emerges from capitalism, because it will have birthmarks resulting from its long period of gestation. "What we have to deal with here is a communist society, not as it has developed on its own foundations, but, on the contrary, just as it emerges from capitalist society; which is thus in every respect, economically, morally, and intellectually, still stamped with the birth marks of the old society from whose womb it emerges." Still, it is worth remembering that Marx saw these early stages as merely the end to class history, or "prehistory,"[106] and the beginning of human history, where human beings will continue to change and to develop in ways we cannot predict.

Marx noted three general characteristics of this early socialism. First, all people will be paid according to the amount of labor contributed.[107] Second, socialism will accelerate the development of science and technology in order to reduce the amount of necessary labor and to diminish the demand for a division of labor, smoothing the way for a time when society can end alienation. Third, workers will control the factories, something we might well call socialist democracy or economic democracy. Here Marx saw the seeds for a community of equals, and he praised the cooperative movement for showing, within the womb of the old society, a glimpse of the new. "The co-operative factories of the labourers themselves represent within the old form the first sprouts of the new." Indeed, cooperatives have shown the world that "production on a large scale, and in accord with the behests of modern science, may be carried on without the existence of a class of masters."[108]

Marx's conception of the government or political system or organizational form that will be present in socialist society, however, remains ambiguous and has been the subject of much controversy. To begin with, because Marx regarded politics as the reflection of the class struggle, he concluded—at least in some passages—that with the classless world of socialism there could be no politics. "The working class . . . will substitute for the old civil society an association which will exclude classes and

106. *Selected Writings*, 568, 390 (from "Critique of the Gotha Programme" and "Preface to *A Critique of Political Economy*").
107. *Selected Writings*, 568 (from "Critique of the Gotha Programme").
108. *Capital* 3:440; *Selected Writings*, 536 (from "Inaugural Address to the First International"); see Shlomo Avineri, *The Social and Political Thought of Karl Marx* (Cambridge: Cambridge University Press, 1968), 174–84. Marx similarly said that unions, by teaching cooperation, could be "schools for socialism." *Selected Writings*, 538.

their antagonism, and there will be no more political power properly so-called, since political power is precisely the official expression of antagonism in civil society." Later in his life, while he quarreled with the anarchist Bakunin, who said that the chief enemy of human freedom was the inevitably oppressive, centralized modern state and who accused Marx of unwittingly establishing a new tyranny under the guise of a workers' state, Marx answered that there will be no government and no state under socialism. Instead, "the distribution of general functions [will] become a business matter which does not afford any room for domination."[109] While Marx's words remind us of Engels's claim that the state will "wither away" and Lenin's suggestion that the state will be replaced by the "administration of things," in fact Marx's claim was neither. When Marx wrote that the state will "dissolve," the word he used was the Hegelian word *aufheben*, by which he meant that the state will be transcended and preserved in some qualitatively different form.[110] Fuzzy as this sounds, certainly he had in mind the end to the class struggles that characterize what we know as politics, workers controlling factories, citizens controlling communities, and *someone administering the economy* in order to ensure efficient production. The key question here is whether Marx envisioned centralized control over the economy and hence some planning elite that might constitute a new and dominant class.

There is a side to Marx that envisioned some sort of centralized administration or some sort of central control, something we can see in three different ways. First, it seems logical to assume that when Marx talked about a planned economy, he talked about an economy that needs planners.[111] Second, Marx sometimes spoke of nationalization of industry and property, which again will require centralized administration. The proletariat will "centralize all instruments of production in the hands of the State, i.e., of the proletariat organized as the ruling class. . . . Of course, in the beginning this cannot be effected except by means of despotic inroads on the rights of property." Finally, Marx and Engels used the infamous and unfortunate phrase of "dictatorship of the proletariat." Perhaps the most famous use of this phrase is in Marx's "Critique of the Gotha Programme." "Between capitalist and communist society lies the period of the revolutionary transformation of the one into the other. Correspond-

109. *The Poverty of Philosophy*, 174; *Selected Writings*, 563. In his *State and Revolution* (1917), Lenin remarked that administering the state could be an easy matter, shared on a rotating basis among all citizens.

110. Hunt, *The Political Ideas of Marx and Engels*, 79–84; Avineri, *The Social and Political Thought of Karl Marx*, 202–20.

111. For example, *Capital*, 92.

ing to this is also a political transition in which the state can be nothing but the revolutionary dictatorship of the proletariat."[112] Although scholars have laboriously demonstrated that neither Marx nor Engels envisioned such a dictatorship's entailing either widespread use of violence or denial of civil liberties, this phrase has remained troublesome well into the twentieth century. In particular, because Lenin made belief in the dictatorship of the proletariat a sort of political litmus test for whether one was a Marxist, the phrase is linked directly to Bolshevism and Communist tyranny in the Soviet Union.

In all of the writings of Marx and Engels, this phrase appears only sixteen times, and two respected scholars have examined all of these passages in great detail.[113] A summary of this scholarship includes the following characteristics of the dictatorship of the proletariat: it would entail majority rule, not rule by some elite; it would be characterized by the kind of extralegality that is necessary in dismantling any government and setting up a new one; although such a dictatorship would employ force, it would not employ large-scale violence, much less terror; it would not suspend civil liberties, such as freedom of the press; and it would be temporary—in fact, Marx and Engels probably used the very word *dictatorship,* with its original Roman connotation of rule limited by time, as we would use the phrase *provisional government.* Only one passage in Marx's writings—a passage in which he speaks of violence and of "[crushing] the resistance of the bourgeoisie"—seems to disturb these conclusions.[114] This passage serves to remind us that Marx was a revolutionary who did envision and sanction the use of violence for the purpose of overthrowing class despotism. If he expected to use force to counter the resistance of the bourgeoisie, then we may justifiably wonder how he would plan and organize this use of force and whether this would lead to new forms of centralized and perhaps despotic authority.

If Marx in some passages spoke of centralized administration, the predominant thrust of Marx's writings leads to the rejection of centralized states, large bureaucracies, and rule by elites. Behind every part of his writings, from his theory of alienation to the notion that workers must

112. *Selected Writings,* 237, 565 (from *The Communist Manifesto* and "Critique of the Gotha Programme"); also *Selected Correspondence,* 63–64 (from a letter to Joseph Weydemeyer).

113. Hal Draper, "Marx and the Dictatorship of the Proletariat," *New Politics* 1, no. 4 (1962): 91–104; Hunt, *The Political Ideas of Marx and Engels,* chap. 9, 284–336.

114. Quoted in Elster, *Making Sense of Marx,* 448. This sort of comment certainly bolstered Lenin's position; by contrast, Rosa Luxemburg drew more upon Marx's notion that the working class must emancipate itself. See Luxemburg, *The Russian Revolution, and Leninism or Marxism?* (Ann Arbor: University of Michigan Press, 1961).

emancipate themselves, is the conviction that men and women must be in control of their own destinies. So there is a second side to Marx, a far more prevalent side, that suggests people can control their lives democratically in smaller, decentralized socialist communities. For example, as I have already shown, Marx wanted a workers' revolution not simply to take over the state but to "smash it," and he wanted to eliminate the "parasitic state" with its "trained caste" of bureaucratic officials.[115] Most important, in his elegy for the defeated Paris Commune of 1870–71, Marx praised handsomely what can only be called socialist democracy. He fully approved of universal suffrage, the emphasis on democratic participation in municipal and local governments of all kinds throughout France, the election of a working-class government with working-class representatives, the ability to recall representatives at any moment, and the abolition of a standing army in favor of a people's militia.[116] "All France would have been organized into self-working and self-governing communes, the standing army replaced by the popular militias, the army of state parasites removed, the clerical hierarchies displaced by the schoolmasters, the state judge transformed into Communal organs, the suffrage for national representation not a matter of sleight of hand for an all-powerful government, but the deliberate expression of the organized communes, the state functions reduced to a few functions for the general national purposes."[117] Marx thought that this very democratic government would seek to establish socialism and put down any resistance; indeed, it was "the political form at last discovered under which to work out the economical emancipation of labor" and "the rational medium in which that class struggle can run through its different phases in the most rational and humane way." As Engels put it in 1891, if one wants to know what Marx meant by the phrase "dictatorship of the proletariat," then "[l]ook at the Paris Commune. That was the Dictatorship of the Proletariat."[118]

Both of these sides of Marx—the first that tends toward centralization and the second that advocates democratic decentralization—sit in uneasy tension in his writings. If one needs to organize violence to overthrow despotism, does one end up with a society based on organized violence? If society has centralized planning, does this necessarily lead to

115. *Selected Correspondence*, 247; *Civil War in France*, 54; *Selected Writings*, 554–55 (from the notes for *Civil War in France*).

116. *Civil War in France*, 54–69.

117. *Selected Writings*, 556 (from the notes for *Civil War in France*).

118. *Civil War in France*, 60; *Selected Writings*, 557 (from the notes for *Civil War in France*); Engels, introduction to *Civil War in France*, 22. There is indeed much evidence for Hunt's claim that Marx's "ideal polity" was "a radical democracy without professionals." *The Political Ideas of Marx and Engels*, 82.

a new tyranny of bureaucrats and planners? It is important to remember that, for Marx, no political and economic system was an end in itself, and even socialism was desirable only as a means to the full development of human potential,[119] whereas capitalism was a form of despotism precisely because it inhibited such development. Late in his life he offered one passage that can serve as a summary of his beliefs. "In a higher phase of communist society, after the enslaving subordination of the individual to the division of labour, and therewith also the antithesis between mental and physical labor, has vanished; after labour has become not only a means of life but life's prime want; after the productive forces have also increased with the all-round development of the individual, and all the springs of co-operative wealth flow more abundantly—only then can . . . society inscribe on its banners: from each according to his ability, to each according to his needs!"[120] It is cruelly ironic that such a fierce proponent of human emancipation and such a ferocious opponent of despotism would have so many erecting modern forms of despotism in his name.

Conclusion

Although Marx borrowed much from Aristotle, Machiavelli, and Montesquieu, he refined and added to these ideas so compellingly and with such a dramatically fresh perspective that the orginality in his theory of tyranny is striking and powerful. First, Marx was one of the first theorists since Aristotle to offer a well-structured philosophical foundation for his analysis of tyranny, an analysis that ultimately shared more with Plato and Aristotle than he might have acknowledged. Like these two great Greek thinkers, Marx—steeped in Greek philosophy himself—argued that tyranny is the political and economic order that least meets the needs of its population. While Marx disagreed substantially with Plato and Aristotle as to what human needs are, the structure of his argument is remarkably similar; in the proper political and economic order, men and women will become fully human, will become completed, will become healthy in both a physical and psychical sense. Relying on Aristotelian and Hegelian premises, Marx at first thought he could discover philosophically some timeless and enduring human essence from which we are alienated, but by the time he and Engels wrote *The German Ideology*,

---

119. *1844 Manuscripts*, 146.
120. *Selected Writings*, 569 (from "Critique of the Gotha Programme").

Marx had jettisoned his earlier metaphysical claims. Instead, Marx thought he could objectively, even scientifically, discover human needs in history, some of which are constant and some of which emerge as humankind advances. Such an approach led Marx to differentiate between what we might call elemental and more advanced human needs, for example, a need for food and shelter versus a need for a community of equals and for unalienated labor.

Despite difficulties in deciding what a human need is—for example, how does it differ from a desire?—Marx's approach, rooted in Greek philosophical assumptions, opens the discussion of tyranny in broadly new directions. It is now possible to classify tyrannies, indeed grope for a hierarchical ranking of tyrannies, according to which human needs they deny. For example, surely it makes sense to say that a tyrant who condemns his or her subjects to starvation, poverty, violence, and cruel death is somehow *more tyrannical* than a capitalist community that secures basic needs for most of its citizens but blocks the way to the development of higher needs such as needs for unalienated labor, for creativity, for a community of equals, and for democratic control over one's world. Marx made such distinctions implicitly. Notwithstanding his anger at capitalism, he certainly thought the Asiatic despotisms of India's caste system and China's class system were, in some basic sense, more tyrannical.

Why would Marx, with his intellectual roots deep in Greek soil, spin off into such new directions? In part, the answer lies in the influence of Hegel, who convinced Marx that qualitatively new needs emerged in history, which the Greek cyclical view of history could not account for. More important, Marx was battling an enemy to which the Greeks had understandably surrendered, namely, the tyranny of nature, and this battle also pushed him in different directions. Like a new Hebrew prophet, he allied himself with the wisdom of science and thundered against the oldest tyranny over humankind, the tyranny articulated in Genesis, nature's tyranny, which compels most of us to labor from dawn to dusk and to die an early death. For Aristotle only a few could be free, because the many must labor to conquer nature. But with all the confidence of Bacon, Condorcet, and the Enlightenment, Marx thought that surely science and technology could liberate all of us from most of nature's necessities, transporting us to a new world with a qualitatively new freedom, a world in which all men and women can become fulfilled, unalienated, healthy. Free time—time freed from labor out of necessity, and thus time in which to be free—would not be confined to male property owners. For Marx every other vision of liberating humanity from tyranny—Aristotle's polis, Tacitus's rule of law, Machiavelli's republic, Tocqueville's democracy—

liberated us only partially, because each of these visions assumed a continuation of scarcity and thus a division between the few with leisure and the many with drudgery. Only narrow class interests, only a misuse of science and technology by the capitalist classes, stood in the way, Marx thought, of the liberation of humanity.

Marx's second great contribution to theories of tyranny lies in updating and refining the class analyses of Aristotle and Machiavelli. Ambiguous as his discussion of classes was, Marx changed forever the vocabulary with which we discuss tyranny. Who after Marx could seriously argue that a tyrant ruled alone, without allying himself or herself with key classes, or factions of classes, or groups, like the military, that may resemble privileged classes? How could one discuss tyranny after Marx without asking about the economic interests of those with influence and those who are nominally the political leaders? How could one speak of political parties and interest groups without investigating their relations to classes or divisions within classes? As Chapter 10 shows, none of the early analyses of Nazi Germany claimed that Hitler held total power himself, and indeed, because of Marx, thinkers like Neumann and Arendt spoke of the bargaining, balancing, and betraying that Hitler had to do with classes, factions, and so on.

Third, Marx asked new questions about the role of the state. Is any state totally controlled by a single tyrant? He hardly thought so. Can a state be a neutral umpire bringing objective reason to bear on administrative duties? Certainly not. In fact, Marx maintained that one will find complicated interactions between the state and the changing configurations of classes and factions within the political economy at large. Whereas most often the state directly serves class interests with decrees and force, sometimes the state defends a parcel of interests that remain independent of the interests of the dominant class. And Marx even warned, like Weber later, that the modern state—"this appalling parasitic body"—can choke all efforts toward decentralized citizen participation with its bureaucratic tentacles. Certainly he may have smoothed the way for such a strangling state with his talk of a planned economy, and certainly his discussions of what a socialist state will look like are frighteningly unsatisfying, but after Marx, no one could seriously talk about tyranny without seeing the interaction among classes, factions, interest groups, and the state bureaucracy itself.

Fourth, thinkers such as Machiavelli and Montesquieu had noted how useful, in many cases, religion was to tyrants, by teaching subjects to obey and sometimes what to think. No one before Marx, however, had offered such a sophisticated genealogy of ideas. In claiming that ideas reflect class interests, that every class puts forth an ideology to justify its interests or its rule or both, Marx sullied the purity of ideas. Ideas just might be smartly dressed soldiers for deeper economic interests, and class tyrannies may rule effectively because they teach us how and what to think. No longer could one pretend that ideas reflected only an objective reasoning process—though Marx did not entirely deny that this could occur—but rather theorists of tyranny had to grapple with how and to what extent systems of ideas related to the interests of classes and factions. Even thinkers who disagreed with his analysis had to grapple with his arguments before they could proceed, and as a result, once more, the entire discourse used to analyze tyranny had changed.

Fifth, Marx implicitly undermined the neutrality of language. Whereas Tacitus had brilliantly noted that tyrants distort language, Marx added that all language is suspect, that neutral discourse is impossible, because key words—such as *freedom, equality, rights*—are heavily laden with meanings derived from the ideology supporting the dominant class. Until we understand the class interests behind public discourse, we will remain in "intellectual bondage." For example, Marx certainly thought it was fine for Tacitus and Montesquieu to defend an independent judiciary and an objective legal code, but in Marx's opinion Tacitus and Montesquieu could only lead us to partial emancipation—emancipation from an outright brutal tyranny—leaving us in the hands of a legal system far from neutral and objective that daily defended the interests of powerful classes. "Your jurisprudence is but the will of your class made into a law for all."

Sixth, by focusing on the "despotism" and "discipline" of the workshop, Marx made it almost impossible for thinkers to talk as if tyranny were merely or mainly a political phenomenon. Not only does tyranny tell us what to think, it controls our very movements by disciplining workers to the bell on the clock, to the commands of industrial sergeants, to the rhythms of machines, and to the motions one needs for one's function in the division of labor. Even though not all previous theorists had ignored such aspects of tyranny, Marx's emphasis was something new. Building on Montesquieu, who had talked of the role of family and the status of women, it was as if Marx hastened to link what we might call the macropolitics of tyranny to the micropolitics of tyranny. By emphasizing workshop discipline, the subordinate position of women in the family, and the ways in which ethnic tension (between, say, British and Irish workers) benefit dominant classes, Marx made certain that no serious thinker after him could simply gaze high upon the summit of the political and military power of the single tyrant. One has to train one's theoretical microscope on the daily commands of tyranny, the ways it insinuates itself into our most private moments.

Finally, taken altogether, these contributions show that Marx really insisted on not only a political sociology of tyranny but also the examination of the structure of tyranny, because the "despotism of capital" that he deplored was a unified and interrelated whole. Like Montesquieu and Hegel, Marx saw all the key elements of a society—politics, economics, technology, religion, family, habits, literature, art, and so on—as dynamically interrelated. One would hardly find egalitarian families in a tyranny, and hierarchical economic relations mirror tyrannical political rule. It is as if society can be conceived of as a vast and complicated cultural mobile in which each element influences and is influenced by every other.[121] Changing one piece of a mobile changes the balance of all others. Similarly, to change one aspect of a tyranny thoroughly—for example, the discipline of the workshop or the subordinate status of women—one needs to make certain that changes ripple throughout the entire structure of tyranny, including politics and economics, law and religion, and so forth. To change a single aspect of tyranny, one has to change the whole. This insight that tyranny is a structural whole was not entirely new— Plato certainly saw it—but Marx, by exploring it so thoroughly, again altered significantly the ways in which subsequent thinkers would speak of tyranny.

121. I have borrowed the idea of a cultural mobile from the late Yosal Rogat.

8

FREUD
The Reproduction of Tyranny

Even a casual reading of Freud's letters confirms that Freud was habitually indifferent to what we ordinarily think of as political matters. Political parties, elections, legislative decisions, and international relations seldom drew a comment from Freud. In this, as in so many other ways, he reminds one of Plato. Both Plato and Freud regarded the world of politics as a sordid world in which people chased apparent but invariably disappointing and illusory satisfactions; both suggested that despite highminded debates and the earnest profession of solemn principles, political actors are ultimately driven by crass passion and base instinct; both consequently concluded that the political world, subordinate as it is to the psychic world, is of mere secondary importance; and finally, since both saw the political world as offering only frustration and danger, both recommended that individuals seek a psychic peace and harmony—at least as much as one might attain—apart from the bustle of politics. Just as the followers of Socrates or Plato scorned the world of politics in order to know themselves, so the followers of Freud seek a self-interested psychological health that stands utterly outside the political life so warmly praised by Aristotle, Machiavelli, and Tocqueville. Freud preached, as one of his finest critics suggested, an apolitical "medical egoism."[1] Although Freud seemed indifferent to ordinary political concerns, he brashly contended that his science of psychoanalysis had unearthed the secrets of both human history and politics. Freud suggested that human history offered the spectacle of the same drama endlessly repeated, that is, the presence of erotic and aggressive instinctual demands and the inevitable repression of these demands imposed upon individuals by every culture. Political clashes were only a small part of this larger historical conflict, only one scene in this ancient drama continually replayed. Freud regarded political quarrels as mere reflections of tensions between father and son or, as he rather dubiously extended this formula, between leader and mob. Freud's political world was just the household writ large, complete with paternal domination and with children both resenting and yearning for this apparently omnipotent paternal authority.

Despite appearing indifferent to politics, Freud offered conclusions about human psychology that have profound political implications. If Freud is right, then we will always witness in the political realm only the patterns of authority we see in the traditional household, namely, fathers dominating wives and children. And in the larger society infantile masses

1. Philip Rieff, *Freud: The Mind of the Moralist* (New York: Viking, 1959), 255. Two scholars, Carl Schorske and William McGrath, argue convincingly that Freud, who was a very political person as a young man, turned away from political aspirations that were hopeless, because he was both liberal and Jewish. Science and psychoanalysis became the vehicles for a threefold personal triumph over his father, snobbish European aristocracies, and anti-Semitic elites who had denied his political ambition. See Carl E. Schorske, "Politics and Patricide in Freud's *Interpretation of Dreams*," *American Historical Review* 78, no. 2 (1973): 328–47. Schorske used this article as a chapter in a book that illuminates beautifully the time in which Freud was writing; see Schorske, *Fin-de-Siècle Vienna: Politics and Culture* (New York: Knopf, 1980). Also William J. McGrath, "Freud as Hannibal: The Politics of the Brother Band," *Central European History* 7, no. 1 (1974): 31–57, and idem, *Freud's Discovery of Psychoanalysis: The Politics of Hysteria* (Ithaca: Cornell University Press, 1986), esp. chaps. 2 and 5. For a challenge to this view, see Stanley Rothman and Phillip Isenberg, "Sigmund Freud and the Politics of Marginality," *Central European History* 7, no. 1 (1974): 58–78. For a good summary, in addition to Schorske's book, of the cultural background to Freud's work, see Harry Trosman, "Freud's Cultural Background," in *Freud: The Fusion of Science and Humanism*, ed. John E. Gedo and George H. Pollock (New York: International Universities Press, 1976), 46–70. Certainly Freud saw himself as an explorer and an adventurer, and it does make sense, therefore, to say that he channeled a youthful political radicalism into a defiant intellectual radicalism. "I am not really a man of science," Freud wrote, "not an observer, not an experimenter, and not a thinker. I am nothing but by temperament a *conquistador*—an adventurer, if you want to translate the word—with the curiosity, the boldness and the tenacity that belong to that type of being." Quoted in the introduction, by Lionel Trilling, to Ernest Jones, *The Life and Work of Sigmund Freud*, ed. Lionel Trilling and Steven Marcus (New York: Basic Books, 1961), xi.

will seek to obey, and occasionally rebel against, leaders who take on idealized dimensions of the lost father. Sons may rebel against their fathers, and daughters may swear to themselves that they will never submit passively as did their mothers, and yet despite little sound and only smoldering fury, sons come to dominate as did their fathers, while daughters yield as did their mothers. In this way the authoritarian nature of the family—grounded, thought Freud, in human nature—repeats itself generation after generation and reproduces itself in the larger political world. Thus we can know, said Freud, that past forms of domination will also prevail over the future. If Freud is right, then we are faced with the inevitability of inequality and, as a consequence, the impossibility of what Tocqueville thought of as democratic freedom and what Marx regarded as socialist freedom. Most important for our purposes, Freud presented a pessimistic analysis that suggested the inevitability of tyranny, because every culture necessarily offers us a picture of the great many dominated by a very few. Worse still, because civilization demands from each of us the renunciation of the great majority of our erotic and aggressive instincts, in effect each of us internalizes the authority of our fathers—using the agency of the mind that Freud called the superego—until each one of us becomes both ruler and subject, all while civilization teaches us to tyrannize over ourselves.

A "Scientific" Portrait of Human Nature

Freud, of course, offered psychoanalysis to the world as a science, claiming that the insights of psychoanalysis both explained and were derived from his clinical experience, his historical readings, his excursions into the findings of anthropology, and his studies of mythology and literature. Psychoanalysis scientifically decoded the heretofore jumbled mysteries of human nature. Despite invoking the authority of science in making his pronouncements about human nature, Freud offered nothing especially original in his view of human nature, and indeed, despite a new "scientific" vocabulary, his conclusions remind us of Hobbes or Bentham.

Human beings, suggested Freud, live almost always according to the "pleasure principle," that is, they seek pleasure and avoid pain. Like a good utilitarian, Freud maintained that people invariably seek happiness and that they define happiness as "an absence of pain and unpleasure" coupled with "the experiencing of strong feelings of pleasure." While Freud was notorious in his use of imprecise language—for example, in the ways in which he frequently used the words *happiness, pleasure, sat-*

isfaction, and *need* as if they were interchangeable—his conclusion was quite clear. "As we see, what decides the purpose of life is simply the programme of the pleasure principle."[2] Freud most readily set himself apart from thinkers such as Hobbes and Bentham by assuming, first, that what we seek to satisfy are not merely "desires" but "instincts" (another notoriously imprecise word) and, second, that sexual pleasure "has thus furnished us with a pattern for our search for happiness."[3] Nevertheless, Freud has presented us with the not so hidden ethical assumptions of the English utilitarians, because by and large, said Freud, individuals judge an action to be good if it increases pleasure and decreases pain. Although he was pessimistic about how much pleasure or happiness individuals might ever obtain, he could at least praise, as a goal for modern civilization, "the decrease of suffering."[4]

2. Sigmund Freud, *Civilization and Its Discontents*, trans. James Strachey (New York: W. W. Norton, 1962), 23; also idem, *Beyond the Pleasure Principle*, trans. James Strachey (New York: Bantam Books, 1959), 21, and idem, *An Outline of Psychoanalysis*, trans. James Strachey (New York: W. W. Norton, 1949), 19.

3. *Civilization and Its Discontents*, 29; *An Outline of Psychoanalysis*, 19–24. For good discussions of Freud's theory of instincts, see Paul Ricoeur, *Freud and Philosophy: An Essay on Interpretation*, trans. Denis Savage (New Haven: Yale University Press, 1970), 115–57, and Ronald de Sousa, "Norms and the Normal," in *Freud: A Collection of Critical Essays*, ed. Richard Wollheim (Garden City, N.Y.: Doubleday, 1974), 196–221.

4. Sigmund Freud, *The Future of an Illusion*, ed. James Strachey, trans. W. D. Robson-Scott (Garden City, N.Y.: Doubleday, 1964), 88. Did Freud offer a moral system? There seem to be four possibilities. First, implicit in the notion of the pleasure principle is a utilitarianism similar to that of English utilitarians from Hobbes to Mill. Second, Freud spoke of "categorical imperatives," by which he meant, not Kant's moral principles discovered by a priori reasoning, but almost universally accepted taboos, dating to primitive times, against such acts as murder and incest (see Freud, *Totem and Taboo*, trans. A. A. Brill [New York: Vintage, 1946]), 32, and idem, "The Ego and the Id," trans. Joan Riviere, in *A General Selection from the Works of Sigmund Freud*, ed. John Rickman [Garden City, N.Y.: Doubleday, 1957], 210–35, esp. 228; also Jerome Neu, "Genetic Explanation in *Totem and Taboo*," in *Freud: A Collection of Critical Essays*, ed. Wollheim, 366–91). Third, Freud spoke of moral rules—again these ancient taboos—originating in a "kind of agreement" or social contract in which, among primitive tribes, each individual agreed to renounce certain dangerous instinctual gratifications if every other individual would do likewise (see *Totem and Taboo*, 186–87). Finally, Freud sometimes suggested that all moral systems, like religions, were illusions and that the strongest individuals were those capable of recognizing the underlying nihilism of the world (see Rieff, *Freud: The Mind of the Moralist*, 320–24, and Tracy Strong, "Psychoanalysis as a Vocation: Freud, Politics, and the Heroic," *Political Theory* 12, no. 1 (1984): 51–79). My own view is that Freud's reasoning process led him to adopt some sort of nihilism, a view that all moral systems are illusions. His debts to Nietzsche, it seems, called for this much. Nevertheless, throughout his work there are moral and political assumptions—about human nature, about the goal of life being the utilitarian goal of maximizing pleasure and minimizing pain, about a tacit social contract being the base of society, and so forth—that constitute a strong defense of utilitarianism and liberalism. Disenchanted with

In later years Freud divided the human mind into "agencies," or "mental provinces," and he called the agency that most represented the pleasure principle the id, a word that he traced back to Nietzsche. Because he acknowledged that the id is not some identifiable part of the brain, he found himself describing this agency of the human personality by means of analogies. The id "is the dark, inaccessible part of our personality. . . . We approach the id with analogies: we call it a chaos, a cauldron full of seething excitations . . . it has no organization, produces no collective will, but only a striving to bring about the satisfaction of the instinctual needs subject to the observance of the pleasure principle."[5] In the id we find only instincts seeking satisfaction, no sense of good or evil (much like Hobbes's state of nature), no notion of time (a not so subtle challenge to Kant), and certainly no instinct for self-preservation. Left uncontrolled, the id would blindly pursue even pleasures leading to self-destruction.[6]

If the unhindered pursuit of the pleasure principle can lead to self-destruction, then there must be some agency that takes into account the demands of the external world, an agency of the mind that demands prudence in the pursuit of one's desires. Freud called this agency the ego, the organizing entity of the human personality. While the ego certainly welcomes pleasure and the avoidance of pain, it demands that the id take into account the realities of the external world, and thus Freud suggested that the ego acts upon the reality principle. "Under the influence of the ego's instincts of self-preservation, the pleasure principle is replaced by the *reality principle.*"[7] The ego acts to ensure the preservation of the organism by sounding the alarm of anxiety, sometimes demanding flight from danger and sometimes demanding the postponement of satisfaction until a more appropriate time. "To adopt a popular mode of speaking, we might say that the ego stands for reason and good sense while the id stands for the untamed passions."[8]

---

both capitalism and Bolshevik experiments, Freud noted in a 1930 letter, "I remain an old-style liberal" (quoted in Walter Kaufmann, *Discovering the Mind*, vol. 3, *Freud Versus Adler and Jung* [New York: McGraw-Hill, 1980], 67; see also Rieff, *Freud: The Mind of the Moralist*, 247–50; Joel Schwartz, "Freud and Freedom of Speech," *American Political Science Review* 80, no. 4 [1986]: 1227–48).

5. Sigmund Freud, *New Introductory Lectures on Psychoanalysis*, trans. James Strachey (New York: W. W. Norton, 1965), 65 (lecture 31); *An Outline of Psychoanalysis*, 14.

6. *New Introductory Lectures*, 66–67 (lecture 31).

7. *Beyond the Pleasure Principle*, 26. Here is a rare instance in which Freud spoke of an "instinct" for self-preservation, which simply illustrates how ambiguous Freud's terminology frequently was.

8. *New Introductory Lectures*, 68 (lecture 31); *An Outline of Psychoanalysis*, 14–16.

While the human organism needs the energy derived from the desires of the id, it needs to control this energy so as to avoid self-destruction. To illustrate this proper (although frequently unattainable) relation between the id and the ego, Freud borrowed a metaphor from Plato. "The ego's relation to the id might be compared with that of a rider to his horse. The horse supplies the locomotive energy, while the rider has the privilege of deciding on the goal and of guiding the powerful animal's movement."[9] Freud used an additional analogy for this conflict between ego and id, an analogy that more clearly illustrates his own political elitism. "Our mind . . . is no peacefully self-contained unity. It is rather to be compared to a modern State in which a mob, eager for enjoyment and destruction, has to be held down forcibly by a prudent superior class."[10] Behind these analogies are classical and conservative assumptions that lawless passions must be controlled by superior reason in order for human beings and human societies to be free.

The ego, however, must struggle not only against the imperatives of reality and the wishes of the id, but also against the demands of a severe conscience, or superego, the third agency of the mind described by Freud. Like Plato, who sought psychic health by harmonizing reason, spirit, and desire, Freud suggested that in those few individuals who attain mental health we find the ego maintaining an uneasy harmony amid the demands of reality, the id, and the superego. "We are warned by a proverb against serving two masters at the same time. The poor ego has things even worse: it serves three severe masters and does what it can to bring their claims and demands into harmony with one another. These claims are always divergent and often seem incompatible. No wonder that the ego so often fails in its task. Its three tyrannical masters are the external world, the superego and the id."[11] Very few individuals, according to Freud, can attain the balance or internal harmony that he called health.

While we commonly equate the words *conscience* and *superego,* they are not exactly synonymous, because Freud assigned a broad cultural

---

9. *New Introductory Lectures,* 68–69; also "The Ego and the Id," 215. For a good discussion of the similarities between Plato's discussion of the soul and Freud's agencies of the mind, see Philip Rieff, "Freudian Ethics and the Idea of Reason," *Ethics* 67, no. 3, pt. 1 (1957): 169–83. Rieff correctly notes that Freud's ego does not embody Plato's speculative reason, but instead mere bourgeois prudence.

10. Quoted in Rieff, *Freud: The Mind of the Moralist,* 59; also Freud, *The Problem of Anxiety,* trans. Henry Alden Bunker (New York: W. W. Norton, 1963), 19.

11. *New Introductory Lectures,* 69 (lecture 31); also "The Ego and the Id," 232; *An Outline of Psychoanalysis,* 16–17. For an excellent discussion of Freud's "agencies" of the mind, see Irving Thalberg, "Freud's Anatomies of the Self," in *Freud: A Collection of Critical Essays,* ed. Wollheim, 147–71.

role to the superego. Freud suggested that originally all children submit to the authority of parents, especially to an "all-powerful father who wields the power of punishment," an authority that demands of us the renunciation of most of our erotic and aggressive instincts. Later such renunciation becomes internalized, and the superego becomes "the authority which replace[s] and continue[s] that of the father." As a consequence, the superego recaptures what parental authority regarded as right and wrong, and when it demands that we adhere to these standards, it certainly resembles what we think of as one's conscience. And yet the superego is much more, because it ensures that the individual becomes the bearer of the standards, not just of the parents, but of the culture at large. "The parents' influence naturally includes not merely the personalities of the parents themselves but also the racial, national, and family traditions handed on through them as well as the demands of the immediate social *milieu* which they represent." A statement such as this makes it absurd to claim, as some critics have, that Freudian theory cannot account for historical change or cultural differences. Freud later noted that the superego also represents "the tastes and standards of the social class" to which the parents belonged, and he also added that certain parental substitutes, such as teachers and people from public life, also contribute to the normative standards upheld by the superego.[12] Freud remained ambivalent in his judgment of the superego. On the one hand, he applauded the superego because it offers what he called an "ego ideal" and demands achievement of each of us, indeed, because it pushes us toward both a moral life and intellectual accomplishment. "The superego is the representative for us of every moral restriction, the advocate of a striving towards perfection—it is, in short, as much as we have been able to grasp psychologically of what is described as the higher side of human life." In this sense, the superego seems to be an agency of the mind that contributes to moral and intellectual success. On the other hand, Freud condemned the superego as a reactionary force that conserves the past, demanding that we conform to past values and reconcile ourselves to the world of our fathers. The superego makes certain that each of us, as we journey into the future, carries the baggage of the past. Those with a strong superego "are turned from being opponents of civilization into being its vehicles."[13] In other words, the superego ensures that the future always resembles the past, that the tyranny of the father is carried forward with each new generation.

---

12. Sigmund Freud, *Moses and Monotheism*, trans. Katherine Jones (New York: Vintage, 1967), 153; *An Outline of Psychoanalysis*, 17, 123.
13. *New Introductory Lectures*, 59 (lecture 31); *The Future of an Illusion*, 13.

Such tyranny manifests itself most of all in the phenomenon of guilt. "The tension between the harsh superego and the ego that is subjected to it, is called by us the sense of guilt; it expresses itself as a need for punishment." While the superego certainly punishes people with guilt for any deeds they might have done, the vast majority of individuals, according to Freud, torment themselves with guilt simply because of wishes or intentions. "Even when a person has not actually *done* the bad thing but has only recognized in himself an *intention* to do it, he may regard himself as guilty."[14] So much is the superego intent on punishing individuals for erotic and aggressive desires, so much does the superego demand that we live up to the impossible and idealized standards of the ego ideal, that we punish ourselves with guilt just because we judge our wishes to be wicked. Indeed, those who lead the most meticulously moral lives are frequently those who most damningly condemn themselves. "Ultimately it is precisely those people who have carried saintliness furthest who reproach themselves with the worst sinfulness." Ironically the internalized guilt instilled by the superego is all out of proportion to any real punishment that our parents would have imposed. "It is a remarkable thing that the superego often develops a severity for which no example has been provided by the real parents, and further that it calls the ego to task not only on account of its deeds but just as much on account of its thoughts."[15]

Although most of us do not torment ourselves as much as does the extreme neurotic, none of us, according to Freud, can escape the internalized torment of conscience that originates in the superego. No civilization could survive if individuals wantonly sought to satisfy their sexual and hostile desires, and thus civilization uses the superego as an agency within us to preserve itself, despite significant cost in terms of our happiness. While the superego therefore preserves civilization by checking our most dangerous unconscious impulses, in the process it tyrannizes over us. "Civilization, therefore, obtains mastery over the individual's desire for aggression by weakening and disarming it and by setting up an agency within him to watch over it, like a garrison in a conquered city." The tyranny that Freud lamented was an internalized tyranny, a tyranny that we are forced to impose on ourselves, because we can only learn to check our erotic and aggressive impulses by becoming fiercely "tyrannical" toward ourselves.[16]

14. *Civilization and Its Discontents*, 70–71, 75.
15. *Civilization and Its Discontents*, 73; *An Outline of Psychoanalysis*, 121.
16. *Civilization and Its Discontents*, 71; also *New Introductory Lectures*, 98 (lecture 32); "The Ego and the Id," 231.

Civilization Threatened by Human Instincts

Freud's understanding of human nature led him to reverse the long held assumption that consciousness is the dominant factor in determining human behavior. Indeed, the unconscious—complete with aspirations and desires, hatreds and loves, that date in part to infancy—is far more central. And in the unconscious we find a timelessness, because the loves and angers of childhood sit in at least equal prominence with similar emotions from adulthood, much as if Rome, the Eternal City, witnessed the buildings from the Republic, the Renaissance, and the twentieth century coexisting right now side by side, new and glistening.[17] Often unbeknown to us, past unconscious wishes frequently determine present behavior. "Thus a man who has spent his childhood in an excessive and since forgotten 'mother-fixation' may all his life seek for a woman on whom he can be dependent, who will feed and keep him."[18]

While we may certainly repress these unconscious desires, sublimate them, or act upon them in other oblique ways, these desires from the unconscious ultimately determine who we are and how we act, and thus to know human beings we must explore "the much trampled soil from which our virtues proudly spring." This, however, is not a pretty sight. Although we disguise the reality of human motivation under pious pronouncements and moral tales told by schoolteachers and nursemaids, in fact "experience teaches us that the world is no nursery" and that indeed an insightful understanding of the human unconscious is almost too horrifying to announce openly, because, Freud concluded, each one of us harbors both incestuous and homicidal wishes. One of Freud's favorite lines was from Goethe's *Faust:* "After all, the best of what you know may not be told to boys."[19]

The incestuous and homicidal wishes more or less hidden in each of us are, of course, what Freud called Oedipal wishes, and these remain remarkably similar across time whether we look at so-called primitive tribes or supposedly modern civilized nations. "Being in love with one parent and hating the other" remains the inevitable lot of every human

17. Rieff, *Freud: The Mind of the Moralist,* 7–8, 38; *Civilization and Its Discontents,* 17.

18. *Moses and Monotheism,* 95. For good discussions and critiques of Freud's concept of the unconscious, see A. Shalom, "Culture and Psychoanalysis," *Review of Metaphysics* 39, no. 4 (1986): 715–28; also Thomas Nagel, "Freud's Anthropomorphism," and Jean-Paul Sartre, "*Mauvaise Foi* and the Unconscious," in *Freud: A Collection of Critical Essays,* ed. Wollheim, 11–24 and 70–79.

19. Freud, *Interpretation of Dreams,* ed. and trans. James Strachey (New York: Avon Books, 1965), 659; *New Introductory Lectures,* 148 (lecture 35); *Interpretation of Dreams,* 175.

being.[20] Unlike so many of his critics, Freud was well aware that the complexity of family relations promoted loves and hatreds that went beyond the strict Oedipal formula of loving one's mother and hating one's father. When other children appear, the Oedipus complex expands and becomes a family complex. "A boy may take his sister as love-object in place of his faithless mother. . . . A little girl takes an older brother as a substitute for the father who no longer treats her with the same tenderness as in her earliest years; or she takes a little sister as a substitute for the child that she vainly wished for from her father."[21] In making any claim at all about an Oedipus complex, Freud had to put forth the shocking suggestion that infants feel sexual drives and wishes. And Freud meant to shock. After acknowledging that he could have saved himself much bother by using the more acceptable word *erotic,* he said "I did not want to, for I like to avoid concessions to faintheartedness."[22]

Freud suggested that by nursing and caressing the male child, the mother invariably but unintentionally seduces the child, arouses sexual desire in the child, and becomes his first lover. "By her care of the child's body she becomes his first seducer. In these two relations lies the root of a mother's importance, unique, without parallel, laid down unalterably for a lifetime, as the first and strongest love-object and as the prototype of all later love relations—for both sexes."[23] In his quest to love his mother the male child discovers his father as a rival, feels a desperate anger toward his father, and wishes that he were gone. This wish for the absence of the father is the initial wish for the death of the father, because the child, not understanding the concept of death, knows merely that dead people are

20. *Interpretation of Dreams*, 294; *Totem and Taboo*, 171. Freud did talk of an "Electra complex" (*An Outline of Psychoanalysis*, 99) for women, that is, a woman loving her father and hating her mother. Freud, however, almost always used the phrase "Oedipus complex" to describe the phenomenon of loving one parent and hating the other. Nevertheless, his claim of an exact symmetry between the way boys and girls are raised is thoroughly unsatisfying. In my opinion, the three best books criticizing Freud's analysis of women are Simone de Beauvoir, *The Second Sex* (New York: Knopf, 1953), Juliet Mitchell *Psychoanalysis and Feminism* (New York: Pantheon Books, 1974), and Nancy Chodorow, *The Reproduction of Mothering: Psychoanalysis and the Sociology of Gender* (Berkeley and Los Angeles: University of California Press, 1978).

21. Sigmund Freud, *A General Introduction to Psychoanalysis*, rev. ed., trans. Joan Riviere (New York: Washington Square Press, 1952), 343 (lecture 21).

22. Sigmund Freud, *Group Psychology and the Analysis of the Ego*, trans. James Strachey (New York: Bantam Books, 1960), 30. For a good discussion of Freud's theory of infantile sexuality, see Raymond E. Fancher, *Psychoanalytic Psychology: The Development of Freud's Thought* (New York: W. W. Norton, 1973), chap. 5, 134–64.

23. *An Outline of Psychoanalysis*, 90. The female child's experience is obviously not the same, because fathers do not nurse daughters.

"gone" and do not return.[24] As the male child grows older, the moral code of a now-developed superego makes him react with horror at the incompletely suppressed realization that from infancy he has had and continues to have incestuous and homicidal wishes toward those who have been closest to him.

Obviously the satisfaction of human instincts poses a threat to civilization. Civilization cannot survive a sexual free-for-all. "Society can conceive of no more powerful menace to its culture than would arise from the liberation of the sexual impulses and a return of them to their original goal." And the building of civilization requires hard work, which can only be imposed upon people if we divert, harness, and channel their sexual energy.

> We believe that civilization has been built up, under the pressure of the struggle for existence, by sacrifices in gratification of the primitive impulses, and that it is to a great extent forever being re-created, as each individual, successively joining the community, repeats the sacrifice of his instinctive pleasures for the common good. The sexual are amongst the most important of the instinctive forces thus utilized: they are in this way sublimated, that is to say, their energy is turned aside from its sexual goal and diverted towards other ends, no longer sexual and socially more valuable. But the structure thus built up is insecure, for the sexual impulses are with difficulty controlled; in each individual who takes up his part in the work of civilization there is a danger that a rebellion of the sexual impulses may occur, against this diversion of their energy.[25]

Not only is society threatened by an ever-present and incipient sexual chaos, but each of us is a potential rebel who, by seeking private sexual fulfillments, threatens to undermine the habits of disciplined work, which must be imposed if civilization is to flourish.

Although Freud did worry occasionally about how a "rebellion of the sexual impulses" might threaten civilization, he focused most often on the dangers presented by our aggressive instincts. After analyzing dreams, Freud came to the conclusion that among "normal individuals" the "temp-

---

24. *An Outline of Psychoanalysis*, 91; *Interpretation of Dreams*, 288–92. Freud was happy to discover a passage from Diderot: "If the little savage were left to himself, keeping all his foolishness and adding to the small sense of a babe in the cradle the violent passions of a man of thirty, he would strangle his father and lie with his mother" (quoted by Freud in *An Outline of Psychoanalysis*, 97).

25. *General Introduction*, 27 (lecture 1); also *Civilization and Its Discontents*, 50–51.

tation to kill others is stronger and more frequent than we had suspected." Indeed, Freud maintained that we have an inherent instinct to aggression, that "man's natural aggressive instinct, the hostility of each against all and of all against each," threatens to undermine the orderly workings of civilization. Even though Christianity admonishes us to love our neighbors as we love ourselves, it is an unreasonable demand because it is impossible to fulfill, and in regard to the commandment that we love our enemies, Freud was delighted to quote Heine: "One must, it is true, forgive one's enemies—but not before they have been hanged." Freud saw himself as providing scientific evidence supporting the notion that people are naturally aggressive and self-seeking, and he relentlessly drew the obvious conclusion: "In consequence of this primary mutual hostility of human beings, civilized society is perpetually threatened with disintegration."[26]

Freud spent a lifetime being hostile to Christianity in general and Catholicism in particular, but ironically, not since Christian theologians such as Augustine and Calvin argued for a rigid doctrine of original sin had any great thinker presented such a bleak picture of human nature. Even Hobbes, who certainly depicted men and women as intensely self-interested, thought that most individuals were fairly peace-loving and were forced to violence only by a lawless few. Freud refused to offer such a minor consolation.

> Men are not gentle creatures who want to be loved, and who at the most can defend themselves if they are attacked; they are, on the contrary, creatures among whose instinctual endowments is to be reckoned a powerful share of aggressiveness. As a result, their neighbor is for them not only a potential helper or sexual object, but also someone who tempts them to satisfy their aggressiveness on him, to exploit his capacity for work without compensation, to use him sexually without his consent, to seize his possessions, to humiliate him, to cause him pain, to torture and to kill him. *Homo homini lupus.* ["Man is a wolf to man."] Who, in the face of all his experience of life and of history will have the courage to dispute this assertion?[27]

The answer, of course, is that many, even many who regarded themselves as pessimists about the human condition, have had the courage to dispute such an extreme claim.

---

26. *Totem and Taboo*, 92; *Civilization and Its Discontents*, 69, 90, 56–57, 59; Paul Roazen, *Freud: Political and Social Thought* (New York: Vintage, 1968), 268–73.

27. *Civilization and Its Discontents*, 58.

Nevertheless, Freud concluded that one price of civilization is the repression of most of this aggressiveness, a repression that necessitates the development of a harsh superego, which "turns the aggressiveness inwards" and torments us due to "the fatal inevitability of the sense of guilt." If Freud is right, then either we can unleash our aggression outward toward others, or we can succeed in checking our outward aggression only by turning the punishing conscience inward. "It really seems as though it is necessary for us to destroy some other thing or person in order not to destroy ourselves, in order to guard against the impulsion to self-destruction. A sad disclosure indeed for the moralist!" Freud's conclusions led him to a radical pessimism. "Belief in the 'goodness' of human nature," suggested Freud, "is one of those evil illusions" that contradicts historical evidence and personal experience and thus does more harm than good, even though it may temporarily sooth our doubts and quiet our fears.[28] Freud maintained repeatedly that a large part of what constitutes a human being can only be called evil. To those who disagree he sarcastically noted, "For 'little children do not like it' when there is talk of the inborn human inclination to 'badness,' to aggressiveness and destructiveness, and so to cruelty as well. . . . Nobody wants to be reminded how hard it is to reconcile the undeniable existence of evil . . . with His all-powerfulness or His all-goodness." Because this last sentence seems aimed at Christian thinkers who wrestled with the problem of theodicy, or how an omnipotent and benevolent god can allow evil to exist, it is again ironic that Freud also arrived at a conclusion very close to the Christian notion of original sin. Freud did acknowledge not only the evil impulses in human beings but also the checks on those impulses, and he added, moreover, that we "dwell upon the evil in human beings with greater emphasis only because others deny it."[29]

What kind of evidence did Freud offer for this pessimism? First, his interpretation of dreams. As is well known, Freud defended the ancient assumption that dreams have a meaning we can fathom and rejected the conventional "scientific" wisdom of his own time that suggested otherwise. After arguing that dreams have a meaning that, with considerable skill and effort, we can interpret correctly, he concluded that dreams are the "royal road" to understanding the desires of the unconscious and that "a dream is a (disguised) fulfillment of a (suppressed or repressed) wish."[30]

---

28. *Civilization and Its Discontents*, 77, 79; *New Introductory Lectures*, 94, 92 (lecture 32).

29. *Civilization and Its Discontents*, 67; *General Introduction*, 153–54 (lecture 9).

30. *Interpretation of Dreams*, 132, 647, 194. For the best discussion of Freud's notion of interpreting dreams, see Ricoeur, *Freud and Philosophy*, 3–36, 87–114, 159–77; also Frederic Weiss, "Meaning and Dream Interpretation," in *Freud: A Collection of Critical Essays*, ed. Wollheim, 53–69.

But when he interpreted dreams in his clinical practice, Freud found frightening wishes in the human unconscious: raging hatred, wishes for revenge, death wishes against those dearest to the patient, and so forth. "These censored wishes," concluded Freud, "seem to rise from a veritable hell." While all of us have these criminal wishes as we sleep, only the wicked few act upon these wishes during the day, something that confirms "Plato's dictum that the virtuous man is content to *dream* what a wicked man really *does.*"[31] These wishes by and large remain unknown to us as adults because, whereas incestuous and homicidal desires had dominated our waking thoughts as infants, they were later forced into the unconscious and "banished into the night." As he put it in a letter, when he was preparing to write *The Interpretation of Dreams,* he explored the "depths of human instinct," an experience that was "sobering, at first even frightening."[32]

Second, Freud used evidence from historical experience, especially the experience of war, to support his pessimistic conclusions about human nature. In his 1915 essay "Thoughts for the Times on War and Death," Freud suggested that war quickens the heart, makes life seem more valuable as we confront death in an immediate sense, and hence relieves the boredom of modern routine. "Life has, indeed, become interesting again; it has recovered its full content." In addition to this, however, war releases our suppressed and primitive passions, because it "lays bare the primal man in each of us." Since the community no longer objects to cruelty and slaughter, our savage impulses sally forth to commit barbarities that otherwise would be literally unthinkable. But because these passions are always latent, poised at the ready whenever society relaxes the bonds of the superego, humankind will never eliminate war. For example, despite Enlightenment optimism that the interests of a mutually beneficial commerce would put an end to war, "it would seem that nations still obey their passions far more readily than their interests."[33] Certainly the senseless brutality of World War I reinforced his pessimistic conclusion that human nature is a key reason for the perpetuation of warfare. "And now look away from individuals to the great war still devastating Europe: think of the colossal brutality, cruelty and mendacity which is now allowed to spread itself over the civilized world. Do you really believe that a handful

31. *General Introduction,* 150 (lecture 9); *Interpretation of Dreams,* 658; also *General Introduction,* 153 (lecture 9).

32. *Interpretation of Dreams,* 606; Freud, *Letters of Sigmund Freud,* ed. Ernst L. Freud, trans. Tania and James Stern (New York: Basic Books, 1960), 366.

33. Sigmund Freud, "Thoughts for the Times on War and Death," in *The Standard Edition of the Complete Psychological Works of Sigmund Freud,* trans. James Strachey (London: Hogarth Press, 1957), 14:273–302; see 14:290–91, 299, 280–81, 288.

of unprincipled place-hunters and corrupters of men would have succeeded in letting loose all this latent evil, if the millions of their followers were not also guilty?"[34] Years later, on the last page of *Civilization and Its Discontents,* he wondered whether the viciousness of human nature coupled with the immense technological developments of warfare might not culminate in people actually "exterminating one another to the last man."[35]

Third, after reflecting on clinical evidence, Freud came to the rather bold conclusion that human beings have a death instinct that manifests itself ultimately either as violence toward ourselves or toward others. Before about 1920 Freud saw no reason to believe either in an instinct for self-preservation or in an instinct for death; the pleasure principle assures that the human organism stays alive long enough to attain pleasure, and death will come soon enough. Although he continued to deny an instinct for self-preservation, in his startling 1920 book, *Beyond the Pleasure Principle,* he first came to argue that there is an independent instinct that seeks either our own death or aggression toward others. The first and primary instinct, Freud suggested, might well be a wish to return to some initial state, to return to a state of quiescence (what Freud called the "Nirvana principle"), which turns out to be a state of inanimate matter. The first instinct is "the instinct to return to the inanimate state." Of course, this is an instinct for death, and "we are left with the fact that the organism wishes to die only in its own fashion" (a claim almost certainly borrowed from Nietzsche's admonition to die at the right time). By positing a recurring opposition between life instincts (i.e., sexual instincts) and ego instincts (i.e., death instincts), Freud concluded with another dualistic theory of human personality. With tenuous evidence at best, Freud continued by arguing that the death instinct is not just an instinct to kill oneself but also an instinct of full-blown aggression toward others. Freud regarded sadism, for example, as a phenomenon of the death instinct aggressively serving sexual ends.[36] Life, history, and the human condition are primarily the results of this interplay between love instincts and death instincts, Eros and Thanatos.

> This aggressive instinct is the derivative and the main representative of the death instinct which we have found alongside of Eros and which shares world-dominion with it. And now, I think, the

34. *General Introduction,* 153 (lecture 9). Ironically, the pacifist Freud initially greeted World War I with enthusiasm. See Jones, *The Life and Work of Sigmund Freud,* 336.

35. *Civilization and Its Discontents,* 92; see also a letter to Romain Rolland, *Letters,* 341–42.

36. *Beyond the Pleasure Principle,* 65–72, 98, 108, 95; also the introduction by James Strachey to *Civilization and Its Discontents,* 7–9.

meaning of the evolution of civilization is no longer obscure to us. It must present the struggle between Eros and Death, between the instincts of life and the instinct of destruction, as it works itself out in the human species. This struggle is what all life essentially consists of, and the evolution of civilization may therefore be simply described as the struggle for life of the human species. And it is this battle of the giants that our nurse-maids try to appease with their lullaby about Heaven.[37]

Incest, cannibalism, and homicide must be psychologically inhibited precisely because the desire to commit these acts is so powerful; they must be made unthinkable to our conscious minds precisely because they are so delightful to our unconscious. Neurotics, in glimpsing these wishes within themselves, feel only "horror" at the thought that they direct these wishes toward those held most dear, and yet such wishes are the common stock of all humankind.[38]

Because Freud argued that aggression was part of human nature, he criticized sharply the claims by Marxists and other socialists that the equalization of property and the supposed abolition of classes would eliminate human aggression. "Aggressiveness was not created by property." While he thought some reduction in the inequality of wealth might help ameliorate human aggression, he maintained it was a foolish illusion to think that this would transform what he regarded as unchanging human nature. Quite prophetically he observed in 1930 that "one only wonders, with concern, what the Soviets will do after they have wiped out their bourgeois."[39]

What saves us, then, from destroying ourselves and living in a world of orgiastic sexuality? First, repression, but here humankind pays a high cost in terms of guilt and unhappiness. A second and far more constructive way to check these potentially harmful instincts is through sublimation. Freud's theory of sublimation rests on the premise that human be-

37. *Civilization and Its Discontents*, 69; also *Beyond the Pleasure Principle*, 78, 93. For an excellent discussion of Freud's hypothesis of a "death instinct," see Ricoeur, *Freud and Philosophy*, 281–338.

38. *General Introduction*, 353 (lecture 22); *Totem and Taboo*, 43, 48; *Future of an Illusion*, 12–15.

39. *Civilization and Its Discontents*, 60–62, 90; also "Why War?" in *Standard Edition*, 22:203–15, esp. 22:211. It is worth noting that Freud also detested the previous czarist dictatorship. See Ronald W. Clark, *Freud: The Man and the Cause* (New York: Random House, 1980), 33. Freud's childhood heroes were historical or literary figures who often opposed tyranny—"the Carthaginian general, Hannibal; Marcus Brutus, the defender of the Roman Republic; and Karl Moor, the protagonist of Schiller's *The Robbers*." McGrath, *Freud's Discovery of Psychoanalysis*, 59.

ings do not have some instinct for progress. "There is unquestionably no universal instinct towards higher development observable in the animal or plant world." Rather, human society has "advanced" or "progressed" (words that must be put in quotation marks because Freud sometimes doubted whether modern life is qualitatively different from so-called primitive life) only because (1) human beings have been pushed by the reality principle (Ananke, or necessity) and (2) we have been driven by the frustration of our instincts to seek satisfaction in roundabout ways. Although we seek the gratification of primary desires, perhaps killing our fathers and sleeping with our mothers, these satisfactions remain unavailable to us. Instead we propel ourselves forward, settling occasionally for substitute satisfactions, but perpetually remaining restless and unsatisfied since no copy ever meets the standards of the original.

> What appears in a minority of human individuals as an untiring impulsion towards further perfection can easily be understood as a result of the instinctual repression upon which is based all that is most precious in human civilization. The repressed instinct never ceases to strive for complete satisfaction, which would consist in the repetition of a primary experience of satisfaction. No substitutive or reactive formations and no sublimations will suffice to remove the repressed instinct's persisting tension; it is the difference in amount between the pleasure of satisfaction which is *demanded* and that which is actually *achieved* that provides the driving factor which will permit of no halting at any position attained, but, in the poet's words, "Presses ever forward unsubdued."[40]

In a challenge to the Enlightenment vision of progress, Freud seems almost delighted to suggest that human societies advance only because of the frustration of some thoroughly unsavory instincts.

By using the word *sublimation* to describe this roundabout and substitute satisfaction of instincts, Freud placed himself squarely in the German tradition, in this case following Nietzsche, who, in choosing the word *aufheben* to talk about the sublimation of one's will to power, had borrowed in turn from Hegel. To sublimate (*aufheben*) a desire is to preserve that desire and yet channel it into an acceptable form. The sexual instincts, for example, "are in this way sublimated, that is to say, their energy is turned aside from its sexual goal and diverted towards other ends, no longer sexual and socially more valuable." Freud frequently maintained

---

40. *Beyond the Pleasure Principle*, 74–77. The quotation is from Goethe's *Faust*.

that intellectual and professional achievement occurred because of the continued frustration and consequent sublimation of instinctual desires. "Sublimation of instinct is an especially conspicuous feature of cultural development; it is what makes it possible for higher psychical activities, scientific, artistic or ideological, to play such an important part in civilized life."[41]

Sublimation is, of course, especially important in regard to the aggressive instincts, and once again Freud apparently borrowed from Nietzsche. While criticizing Christianity and modern European civilization for smothering what is bold, ambitious, and passionate in human beings, Nietzsche noted that only those capable of what is ordinarily called evil will accomplish anything noble and grand. Similarly Freud noted that "the pre-existence of strong 'bad' impulses in infancy is often the actual condition for an unmistakable inclination towards 'good' in the adult." Children who are often the "most pronounced egoists" ultimately become community leaders, precisely because society succeeded in inducing them to sublimate their especially powerful aggressive impulses in acceptable ways. In a disturbing passage, Freud wryly noted that "most of our sentimentalists, friends of humanity and protectors of animals have been evolved from little sadists and animal-tormentors."[42]

Freud maintained that human societies have checked harmful instincts in a third way, by opposing the aggressive instincts with the erotic instincts. As I have shown, Freud saw two kinds of instincts—the aggressive or death instincts and the erotic or life instincts. Whereas Freud certainly included sexual instincts among these erotic instincts, he widened this category of erotic instincts to go well beyond what is narrowly sexual. Both *libido* (the Latin word for "lust" or "love") and *eros* (one Greek word for "love") indicated for Freud sexual love, self-love, friendship, love for family, love for country, and even love for some abstract notion of humankind. Eros is a unifying force combining "single human individuals, and after that families, then races, peoples and nations, into one great unity, the unity of mankind."[43] Freud readily acknowledged his debt to Plato, who expressed a similar view of Eros in his *Symposium,* although Freud ventured well beyond Plato in suggesting that these life instincts, or Eros, can check the death instincts, or Thanatos. The aggressive instincts "make human communal life difficult and threaten its sur-

---

41. *General Introduction,* 27 (lecture 1); *Civilization and Its Discontents,* 44, 26–27; see also *An Outline of Psychoanalysis,* 114.

42. "Thoughts for the Times on War and Death," 282.

43. *Civilization and Its Discontents,* 69; see also *Group Psychology and the Analysis of the Ego,* 29, and *Beyond the Pleasure Principle,* 78.

vival. . . . Luckily the aggressive instincts are never alone but always alloyed with the erotic ones."[44] Freud was far from suggesting that people become altruistic—or even loving toward family, friends, and community—when their erotic instincts control their aggressive instincts. Rather, he argued that we can learn that checking our aggression and gaining the love of others is in our self-interest. "By the admixture of *erotic* components the egoistic instincts are transformed into *social* ones. We learn to value being loved as an advantage."[45]

Elitism

Does anyone, in some meaningful sense, become completely healthy? Even if individuals manage to control their instinctual drives by means of repression or sublimation, do they survive this process unscarred? Only rarely. All of us live with some degree of unhappiness and some degree of resentment toward a civilization that has bullied us into curbing our desires, and all of us live with a residue of guilt, the legacy of the superego. The beleaguered ego, we recall, must serve three tyrannical masters. "Thus, an action by the ego is as it should be if it satisfies simultaneously the demands of the id, of the superego and of reality, that is to say if it is able to reconcile their demands with one another."[46] Rarely, according to Freud, does this occur satisfactorily. If anything, the controls of civilization ordinarily succeed all too well, and we live a more or less neurotic existence, tied to Oedipal wishes of a long past childhood and dominated, even tormented, by the parental commands embodied in the superego. A healthy person, therefore, is one who has controlled the desires, the passions, of the id and has escaped from blind submission to the superego, that is, one who has escaped the tyranny of our fathers. Whereas most adults free themselves to some extent, few do so entirely.

> From the time of puberty onward the human individual must devote himself to the great task of *freeing himself from the parents*; and only after this detachment is accomplished can he cease to be a child and so become a member of the social community. . . . These tasks are laid down for every man; it is noteworthy how seldom they are carried through ideally, that is, how seldom they

44. *New Introductory Lectures,* 98 (lecture 32); *Beyond the Pleasure Principle,* 100–101; "Why War?" 209.
45. "Thoughts for the Times on War and Death," 282.
46. *An Outline of Psychoanalysis,* 16–17.

are solved in a manner psychologically as well as socially satisfactory. In neurotics, however, this detachment from the parents is not accomplished at all; the son remains all his life in subjection to his father, and incapable of transferring his libido [from his mother] to a new social object. In the reversed relationship the daughter's fate may be the same. In this sense the Oedipus complex is justifiably regarded as the kernel of the neuroses.[47]

Freud regarded completely healthy individuals as something like heroes, individuals strong enough to cast off the commands of the superego and establish a new system of values for themselves and often for others. Indeed, the first act of individuality and the first act leading to moral autonomy is the rebellion of the son against the father,[48] and thus the healthiest individual is that rare person who has overcome the authority of the father. While the masses seek a father figure to obey, "a hero is a man who stands up manfully against his father and in the end victoriously overcomes him." Freud's model here was Moses. Moses overcame the authority of his father, "conceived the plan of founding a new empire," "gave commands and forced his religion on the people," and ultimately "[stamped his] people with its definite character and determine[d] its fate for millenia to come." Just as Nietzsche's Overman rejects the standards of good and evil forced upon him by a slavish majority and then creates new values, so Freud's hero casts off the authority of the past in order to outline a new future. Although certainly historical development (however much of this Freud thought was possible) has many causes—including modifications of climate, demographic change, and economic development—"how impossible it is to deny the personal influence of individual great men on the history of the world."[49]

One should not overlook how much Freud wished to see himself as a hero, perhaps as a Moses who this time brought a new science, and not a religion, to the ignorant and the hopeful. In an 1884 letter to his future wife, Martha Bernays, Freud wrote, "But I know what's driving me; the heart is well again, the giant strong again, gigantically strong. Are you laughing at me for calling myself a giant?" Two years later he proudly wrote Bernays that his friend and first mentor, Josef Breuer, had discovered in Freud "an extremely daring and fearless human being. I had al-

---

47. *General Introduction*, 345–46 (lecture 22); see also Sigmund Freud, *The Sexual Enlightenment of Children*, trans. E.B.M. Herford et al. (New York: Collier Books, 1963), 41 (from an essay called "Family Romances").

48. Rieff, *Freud: The Mind of the Moralist*, 194, 260. Freud named his own son after the revolutionary Oliver Cromwell.

49. Freud, *Moses and Monotheism*, 9, 140, 32, 57, 136, 65, 137–38.

ways thought so, but never dared tell anyone. I have often felt as though I had inherited all the defiance and all the passions with which our ancestors defended their Temple and could gladly sacrifice my life for one great moment in history." If we analyze Freud with his own psychoanalytic tools, it is easy to conclude that he had something of a Moses complex. When Freud expressed his wish to have a "marble tablet" placed on the house in which he discovered how to interpret dreams,[50] is it not likely that he wished his marble tablet announcing the science of psychoanalysis at least to rival, and possibly to supplant, the stone tablets with which Moses announced the Hebrew commandments?

Both Freud's arguments and his personality lead irresistibly to a powerful elitism. If one equates a healthy ego with a life of reason, then—again, like Plato—only a few are capable of reason, and most are driven by desire; if few are capable of establishing their own moral precepts by which to live, then most will curb these desires by submitting to the tyranny of the superego. Indeed, Freud's snobbery is inescapable. As a young man he wrote that "it is neither pleasant nor edifying to watch the masses amusing themselves; we at least don't have much taste for it any more." In a work written late in his life, he expressed the same sentiments: "For masses are lazy and unintelligent; they have no love for instinctual renunciation and they are not to be convinced by argument of its inevitability."[51]

Freud's misogyny and his disdain for the intellectual and professional capabilities of women only reinforce this conclusion. In an early letter to Bernays he took John Stuart Mill to task for likening the oppression of women to the oppression of African Americans. "Any girl," wrote Freud in rather syrupy language, "even without a vote and legal rights, whose hand is kissed by a man willing to risk his all for her love, could have put him right on this. It seems a completely unrealistic notion to send women into the struggle for existence in the same way as men. Am I to think of my delicate, sweet girl as a competitor?" "Nature," he suggested, has "appointed woman by her beauty, charm, and goodness" to the roles of wife, mother, and homemaker. Years later he tried to bolster his conclusions, or biases, with the authority of psychoanalysis, but his argument remained essentially the same, namely, that women are "biologically des-

50. *Letters*, 120, 202; *Interpretation of Dreams*, 154.

51. *Letters*, 50; *The Future of an Illusion*, 6. For an excellent discussion of Freud's elitism and the intellectual climate that fostered that elitism, see Philip Rieff, "The Origins of Freud's Political Psychology," *Journal of the History of Ideas* 17, no. 2 (1956): 235–49. While it is true that Freud was an elitist, he was an elitist who also despised traditional European elites and aristocracies. See Schorske, "Politics and Patricide in Freud's *Interpretation of Dreams*," and McGrath, "Freud as Hannibal."

tined" to a homemaking role and generally incapable of a life according to reason.[52]

Throughout his life Freud remained convinced of an "innate and ineradicable inequality of men" that produces a powerful "tendency to fall into the two classes of leaders and followers," the latter of which will always be the "great majority."[53] Leaders, he declared, must set an example of self-renunciation for the masses, so the latter can be persuaded, and coerced, into doing the necessary labor to build civilization. "It is just as impossible to do without control of the mass by a minority as it is to dispense with coercion in the work of civilization." When leaders have "superior insight into the necessities of life" and have mastered their own instinctual wishes, then all goes well, but civilizations fall apart if leaders merely copy the lazy indulgence of the masses.[54] The vast majority stands "in need of an authority which will make decisions for them and to which they for the most part offer an unqualified submission. This suggests that more care should be taken than hitherto to educate an upper stratum of men with independent minds, not open to intimidation and eager in the pursuit of truth, whose business it would be to give direction to the dependent masses. . . . The ideal condition of things would of course be a community of men who had subordinated their instinctual life to the dictatorship of reason."[55] While Freud was far from advocating a harsh rule over the majority, he was defending something like the inevitability of a benevolent authoritarianism; leaders should become members "of the human community" and use "technique guided by science" to promote "the good of all."[56] It is a paternalism in its most literal sense.

If the vast majority is incapable of reason and hence unable to be persuaded of the reasonableness of these leaders, what makes this majority so willing to submit? To begin with, human beings frequently have a strong fear of being alone, a fear probably dating to "the lengthy duration in man of the helplessness and dependence belonging to childhood." Anxiety largely originates in separation from the mother, from that which was secure, and indeed "birth is the source and prototype of the anxiety affect." Even in adult life the individual in danger recalls "the first great anxiety-state of birth and the infantile anxiety of longing for an absent person—the anxiety of separation from the protecting mother." Many

52. *Letters*, 75–76; *New Introductory Lectures*, 99–119 (lecture 33), esp. 105.
53. "Why War?" 212; also *Civilization and Its Discontents*, 60.
54. *The Future of an Illusion*, 5–6. The German word *Masse* has no exact English equivalent, and it is sometimes translated as "mass" and sometimes as "group," as in *Group Psychology and the Analysis of the Ego*.
55. "Why War?" 212–13.
56. *Civilization and Its Discontents*, 24–25.

adult neuroses, especially agoraphobia, are grounded in this anxiety about being both alone and separated from a protective parent, although it should be noted that anxiety about loneliness is a human feeling at least occasionally common to most everyone, even Freud.[57]

Human beings, in other words, are perpetually looking for some unity or community with their fellows because "the individual feels incomplete if he is alone," and yet this unity remains frustratingly elusive. Freud apparently enjoyed repeating Schopenhauer's story about freezing porcupines—unable to get close enough to satisfy their common needs—as an illustration of the human condition. Having come into the world thoroughly narcissistic, our original narcissism never entirely disappears, and we remain at bottom egoistic (every dream, for example, is "completely egoistic") and incapable of entirely joining ourselves with others. And yet despite all of this self-centered aversion toward others, we need to join with our fellows, both because we cannot bear loneliness and because we must free ourselves from a fixation upon past love objects and "begin to love in order not to fall ill."[58] As a result, the individual seeks to become part of a group.

Father and Mob: Political Domination and Authoritarian Family Structures

If, Freud maintained, even adults are driven by unconscious desires and the prevalence of childhood wishes, if most of us can never escape the fears and passions of infancy, then he could make nearly revolutionary observations about phenomena hitherto only incompletely understood, namely, politics and religion. Freud concluded that the political world will always be hierarchical and authoritarian because most people wish to submit to a benevolent authority that will protect them. "We know that the great majority of people have a strong need for authority which they

---

57. "The Ego and the Id," 221; *General Introduction*, 404 (lecture 25); "The Ego and the Id," 234; *New Introductory Lectures*, 73–75 (lecture 32); *Letters*, 310. On the trauma of birth, see *Interpretation of Dreams*, 436, and *The Problem of Anxiety*, 20, 67. After Otto Rank's 1923 book *The Trauma of Birth* gave primacy, even over the Oedipus complex, to the separation anxiety that occurred with birth, he and Freud parted ways. See Clark, *Freud: The Man and the Cause*, 446–60.

58. *Group Psychology and the Analysis of the Ego*, 64; *Interpretation of Dreams*, 301; "On Narcissism: An Introduction," in *Standard Edition*, 14:67–102, esp. 14:85; *Group Psychology and the Analysis of the Ego*, 41–42; *General Introduction*, 423 (lecture 26); on the fear of loneliness and the difficulties in joining with others, see Rieff, *Freud: The Mind of the Moralist*, 57.

can admire, to which they can submit, and which dominates and sometimes even ill-treats them. . . . It is the longing for the father that lives in
each of us from his childhood days." Even a more or less normal adult in
many respects "remains infantile and needs protection" and as a consequence seeks a replacement for that "gigantic" figure who throughout
childhood both preserved and threatened. Just as a child is afraid of being abandoned by the protecting and yet dominating parent, so most
adults have an unconscious wish "to be ruled by one person."[59]

In this respect "primitive" societies differ only marginally from "civilized" societies, a lesson not lost on the structuralist Claude Levi-Strauss,
who shared, and developed, Freud's occasional skepticism about how
much progress the human race had actually attained. Freud disputed anthropological studies that suggested early human societies were herd societies, because in a herd, Freud noted, all are equal and there is no
leader. A human being is thus not a herd animal but "rather a horde
animal, an individual creature in a horde led by a chief." Freud's model
was of course some variant of a patriarchal family, a model suggesting
that human societies always resemble a group (*Masse*) of inferiors "ruled
over despotically" by a powerful and superior father figure. The future
Overmen who tugged at Nietzsche's imagination existed in fact in these
past tyrannical father figures, the despotic leaders of primitive hordes,
who were "of a masterful nature, absolutely narcissistic, self-confident
and independent." Having argued that the wishes and instincts of modern
men and women are, at bottom, no different from those of so-called primitive men and women, Freud concluded readily—perhaps too readily—
that this model of political societies remains largely applicable to political systems of the twentieth century. No great change is possible in
the political world, simply because politics is always the interplay of a
leader and many followers, an authoritarian father figure willing to rule
and a childlike mob willing to obey. "The leader of the group is still the
dreaded primal father; the group still wishes to be governed by unrestricted force."[60]

Freud outlined numerous characteristics of these groups. First, the
members of groups exhibit an alarming submissiveness toward the
leader. In displaying a "passive-masochistic attitude" toward figures of
authority and in attaching themselves emotionally to "their masters,"

59. *Moses and Monotheism*, 139–40, 165–66; *Group Psychology and the Analysis of the Ego*, 65–68. For a good summary of Freud's reasoning here, see Thomas Johnston, *Freud and Political Thought* (New York: Citadel Press, 1965), 40–51.

60. *Group Psychology and the Analysis of the Ego*, 68–69, 71, 76. See Claude Levi-Strauss, *The Savage Mind* (Chicago: University of Chicago Press, 1966).

members of groups wish to surrender their wills, and they have "an extreme passion for authority."[61] Second, in the group one finds infantile regression and hence a re-creation at an adult age of feelings of helplessness—and the corresponding wishes to be cared for—that distinguish childhood. "Infantile feelings," wrote Freud, "are far more intense and inexhaustibly deep than are those of adults." By bringing such infantile longings to the fore, groups present "an unmistakable picture of a regression of mental activity to an earlier stage such as we are not surprised to find among savages or children."[62] Third, just like children confronted by paternal authority, members of groups offer ambivalent attitudes of passive love and sadistic hate toward the leader. Freud best described this attitude in a letter about Dostoevsky, who, Freud thought, demonstrated in his brilliant writings the ambivalence toward authority that characterizes primitive peoples, children, and members of groups. Dostoevsky's "whole life is dominated by his twofold attitude to the father-czar-authority, by voluptuous masochistic submission on the one hand, and by outraged rebellion against it on the other."[63]

Fourth, although individuals become members of a group out of self-interest or narcissism, it is Eros or some form of love that ties a group together. "A group is clearly held together by a power of some kind: and to what power could this feat be better ascribed than to Eros, which holds together everything in the world?" Members of a group even manage to live under the illusion that love binds the entire society and that each is loved equally by the leader. Panic is a phenomenon that severs these "mutual ties" and sets free "a gigantic and senseless fear." Fifth, groups are intolerant toward those who do not belong. While Eros may well bind groups together, the group tightens its bonds by displaying an astonishing hatred toward the outside world. Freud concentrated on the example of religion. "Therefore a religion, even it it calls itself the religion of love, must be hard and unloving to those who do not belong to it . . . cruelty and intolerance toward those who do not belong to it are natural to every religion." Freud made it clear, however, that all groups—even a group such as a scientific society, which is presumably governed by reason—share some of this characteristic intolerance toward outsiders.[64]

In Freud's sometimes simplistic political analysis a group has only a

61. *Group Psychology and the Analysis of the Ego*, 76; *The Future of an Illusion*, 17.

62. *Moses and Monotheism*, 172; *Group Psychology and the Analysis of the Ego*, 62, 70; *The Problem of Anxiety*, 63–77.

63. *Letters*, 333; see also *The Problem of Anxiety*, 30, 36; Rieff, *Freud: The Mind of the Moralist*, 226.

64. *Group Psychology and the Analysis of the Ego*, 31, 36, 39; also 42–43, 71.

leader who dominates a mob—a scheme that hardly leaves room for the intermediate associations of Montesquieu and Tocqueville—and thus a pervasive equality among all these passive subjects constitutes a sixth characteristic of groups; all Catholics imagine themselves to be equal in Christ's eyes, and all soldiers imagine themselves to be equally loved by the commander. "Group spirit," suggested Freud, insists that "no one must want to put himself forward, every one must be the same and have the same."[65] Seventh, one finds a pressure for conformity. Freud always thought that only individuals strong enough to be alone, especially alone both intellectually and morally, could be free, whereas all those dependent on others would remain subservient. "Isolated, he may be a cultivated individual; in a crowd, he is a barbarian." Groups are always distinguished by "the individual's lack of freedom." We see in groups, said Freud, little individuality, little courage, little originality, and much pressure from every individual on every other to bring about conformity, all of which leads to mediocrity and to a "contagion" of irrationality. "How much every individual is ruled by those attitudes of the group mind which exhibit themselves in such forms as racial characteristics, class prejudices, public opinion, etc."[66] An absence of reason becomes the eighth characteristic of groups, which show us "the weakness of intellectual ability, the lack of emotional restraint, [and] the incapacity for moderation and delay." Only solitary individuals make great discoveries, because "groups have never thirsted after truth. They demand illusions, and cannot do without them." The illusion that Freud had in mind most often was religion, but he acknowledged that political ideologies—he mentioned socialism and Marxism in this regard—also often serve as illusions that satisfy our unfulfilled fantasies and wishes.[67]

Finally, groups have the capacity to unleash aggressive passions, as if every group were a potential lynch mob and as if groups could toss society, almost overnight, into a Hobbesian state of nature. In a group that has become agitated, the individual is encouraged "to throw off the repressions of his unconscious instinctual impulses . . . in which all that is evil in the human mind is contained as a predisposition." In part, Freud is merely expressing his approval of an educated elite and his disapproval of the undisciplined mob. "The mob gives vent to its appetites," Freud wrote, "and we deprive ourselves." In a complete reversal of Aristotle and Machiavelli, Freud almost always depicted the isolated individual as disciplined and rational, while he looked upon groups as potential vehicles for

65. *Group Psychology and the Analysis of the Ego*, 67, 33–34.
66. *Group Psychology and the Analysis of the Ego*, 12, 35, 27, 63.
67. *Group Psychology and the Analysis of the Ego*, 62, 16, 39.

releasing upon society all that is violent and irrational. "A group is impulsive, changeable and irritable. It is led almost exclusively by the unconscious."[68]

How realistic is Freud's argument? His own examples, the Catholic Church and the Prussian army, reveal the weaknesses in his argument. In being so insistent on the model of one father figure and many children, did he overestimate dramatically the equality, even the illusory equality, in these two groups? Using this model, can Freud really account for the phenomenon of modern bureaucracy with all its gradations of authority? And although he acknowledged that a given society will have many groups to which the individual owes allegiance, can his model really explain such a complicated system? Moreover, whereas the Catholic Church and the Prussian army appear to follow the model of leader and led, in what sense are these typical groups? Are all groups so hierarchical? What would happen to his argument, for instance, if he had chosen the American Congregational Church and Cromwell's more egalitarian New Model Army? Finally, while Freud had a lifelong belief in the fundamental irrationality of the Catholic Church, did he really address himself to serious Catholicism, for example, the Catholicism of Saint Thomas Aquinas, or did he always do battle with some popular caricature of the Catholic Church, a caricature in fact that bordered on prejudice?

Freud's model of politics is certainly simplistic, but as a staunch defender of the individual against what he saw as the encroaching irrationality of the political and social world, he ultimately had no use for politics. Ever the follower of Plato, who also sought the psychic health of the individual, Freud was as far as one could get from the arguments of Aristotle, Machiavelli, and Tocqueville that democratic citizenship is a necessary step in developing the intellectual and moral potentials of the individual. Freud had no use for this argument, and it is hard to find a word about citizenship in his writings. His battle was an inner one, a battle designed to encourage self-contemplative individuals to defend a reasonable ego against the wild desires of the id and the irrational prejudice of the superego. As Philip Rieff has pointed out, Freud presented us a model of private man (and I use the masculine on purpose) with no use for the public life of the citizen, a private man who commits "medical egoism" in his quest for psychological health. The Greeks gave to Europe the model of political man, the great Christian thinkers bestowed the model of religious man, English liberals described for us economic man, and Freud gave to the twentieth century the portrait of psychological

---

68. *Group Psychology and the Analysis of the Ego*, 13, 20; *Letters*, 50; *The Future of an Illusion*, 19–20.

man—"anti-heroic, shrewd, carefully counting his satisfactions and dissatisfactions, studying unprofitable commitments as the sins most to be avoided." Whereas Nietzsche gave us a portrait of the Last Man yawning, bored, and content with little pleasures, Freud depicted a Last Man anxious and guilty, constantly checking the egoistic indices on his psychic thermometer.[69]

While Freud's political analysis is not entirely convincing, it is certainly compelling and even chilling in key ways. First, political authority does in some undeniable ways resemble parental authority; we learn sadly from experience that citizens all too easily become subjects willing to submit to dominating leaders. If Freud is even remotely right in his claim that ordinary adults wish to yield to a father figure, then clearly Tocqueville's democracy and Marx's democratic socialism are illusory, and all societies will inevitably be both hierarchical and tyrannical. "If society is held together by its irrational regard for and dependence upon a leader, then society, so far as it is stable, is always, in the broad sense, authoritarian."[70] Second, Freud certainly seems right to focus our attention on the family as a model for political authority and as an indispensable ingredient for the perpetuation of tyranny. Political tyranny may well reproduce itself through the tyranny of a patriarchal family. Children who grow up in hierarchical family structures, for example, apparently do learn to expect and submit to authoritarian political structures.[71] Of course, Freud thought that the patriarchal family was both natural and inevitable, but many feminists and political progressives, while arguing that a more egalitarian family structure might lead to a more egalitarian society, give Freud credit for his insights into the close relation between family structures and political structures. Finally, Freud's parallels between "primitive" social structures and "civilized" social structures, stretched though they may be at times, cannot be dismissed entirely. If democracy and equality are two of our goals, how much indeed have we progressed? And how much will the future resemble a tyrannical past? "For Marx, the past is pregnant with the future, with the proletariat as the midwife of history. For Freud, the future is pregnant with the past, a burden of which only the physician, and luck, can deliver us."[72]

69. Rieff, *Freud: The Mind of the Moralist*, 356–57, 255; Roazen, *Freud: Political and Social Thought*, 231. See also Philip Rieff, *The Triumph of the Therapeutic* (Harmondsworth, Middlesex: Penguin, 1966). For another comparison of the "Last Men" of Nietzsche and Freud, see Rieff, *Freud: The Mind of the Moralist*, 184, 310.

70. Rieff, *Freud: The Mind of the Moralist*, 247.

71. Roazen, *Freud: Political and Social Thought*, 149–57; see also T. W. Adorno, *The Authoritarian Personality* (New York: Harper, 1950).

72. Rieff, *Freud: The Mind of the Moralist*, 215.

Freud's Critique of Religion

When Freud discussed religion, he offered a similar and familiar analysis. Religion originated, Freud suggested, in "the feeling of infantile helplessness" and a longing for some parental protector. "The derivation of religious needs from the infant's helplessness and the longing for the father aroused by it seems to me incontrovertible."[73] Because helplessness continues as children become adults, especially as we face genuine dangers from nature, such as disease and death, adults find themselves recalling a time when they felt helpless and a person who seemed powerful enough to allay their fears. "But man's helplessness remains and along with it his longing for his father, and the gods." If human beings created a religion modeled after the structure of the family, then, just like children, individuals would seek to be special in the eyes of the father figure or god who rules over them. "Now that God was a single person, man's relations to him could recover the intimacy and intensity of the child's relation to his father . . . one wanted to have a reward, or at least to be his only beloved child, his Chosen People. Very much later, pious America laid claim to being 'God's own Country.'"[74]

Moreover, the same ambivalence that one finds in the attitude of the child toward the parent, especially the son toward the father, surfaces in religion. While the son, for example, certainly loves and respects the father, he also hates and fears him because of competition for the love of the mother. Freud regarded it as neither accidental nor coincidental that Christianity claimed the "Son of God" had been sacrificed, since the son is always the most guilty, both because he wishes for the father's death and because in primitive times the sons banded together to commit patricide, the memory of which Freud thought was passed on genetically to subsequent generations. Much later this guilt was expressed by the nebulous phrase "original sin."[75] Religion not only originates in these childhood longings, but it perpetuates a certain infantilism of the human race. "When the growing individual finds that he is destined to remain a child for ever, that he can never do without protection against strange superior powers, he lends those powers the features belonging to the figure of the father; he creates for himself the gods whom he dreads, whom he seeks to propitiate, and whom he nevertheless entrusts with his own protection.

---

73. *Civilization and Its Discontents*, 19; *The Future of an Illusion*, 23; *New Introductory Lectures*, 143–44 (lecture 35).
74. *The Future of an Illusion*, 24, 27.
75. *Moses and Monotheism*, 110, 175.

Thus his longing for a father is a motive identical with his need for protection against the consequences of human weakness."[76]

Freud's discussion of religion betrays his lifelong distaste for Catholicism, and in some ways he posed as an intellectualized and modern-day Hannibal, one of his heroes, who this time would wield the sword of psychoanalysis and actually conquer Rome. Once again some of Freud's insights are remarkable, but the whole analysis hardly bears up under scrutiny. How well does his analysis of God as father figure fit other religions, even major religions such as Hinduism and Buddhism? Does religion always promote childlike behavior, or what Freud called "unconditional submission"? Surely Freud is right in many instances, but the prophets of the Old Testament who courageously resisted injustice are just as much a part of the Judeo-Christian tradition as is childlike passivity. In reality Freud attacked a morally and intellectually simplistic picture of religion and not the religion of Jeremiah and Martin Luther King, of Saint Thomas Aquinas and Pascal.[77]

Freud made more sense when he quit forcing religion into the model of the patriarchal family. Religion originated, he maintained, in the human need to find meaning in life and to offer some explanation of those forces in the universe that frighten us. "One can hardly be wrong in concluding that the idea of life having a purpose stands and falls with the religious system," and Freud had obviously concluded that no such purpose existed. "The moment a man questions the meaning and value of life, he is sick, since objectively neither has any existence."[78] In giving a meaning to life and explaining the universe, however, religion undertakes five different tasks. First, religion satisfies our curiosity and explains to us the origin and nature of the universe. Second, religion convinces us that we are not helpless when confronted by a hostile universe, that we are not

76. *The Future of an Illusion*, 35.

77. *Civilization and Its Discontents*, 32; Rieff, *Freud: The Mind of the Moralist*, 259–63, 282. For example, Freud criticized Tertullian, who claimed, "I believe because it is absurd" (*The Future of an Illusion*, 43), but Freud did not mention that Saint Thomas Aquinas attacked this same unreasoned dogma and was willing to submit his faith to the scrutiny of reason. Much of Freud's argument reflects an intellectual and political climate that was anticlerical, an environment in which science was the weapon for the supposed defeat of religion. See Jan Goldstein, "The Hysteria Diagnosis and the Politics of Anticlericalism in Late Nineteenth-Century France," *Journal of Modern History* 54, no. 2 (1982): 209–39. On Freud's ambivalence toward both Judaism and his own Jewishness, see Sigmund Diamond, "Sigmund Freud, His Jewishness, and Scientific Method: The Seen and the Unseen as Evidence," *Journal of the History of Ideas* 43, no. 4 (1982): 613–34.

78. *Civilization and Its Discontents*, 23; *Letters*, 436. Freud regarded it as "heroic" for an individual, armed by and with psychoanalysis, to live without religion, hence without illusion. See Strong, "Psychoanalysis as a Vocation."

merely playthings "of the over-mighty and pitiless forces of nature." By offering us rituals with which we might appease the gods—prayers, atonements, sacrifices, bribes—religion persuades us that we can in fact have some control over these forces that threaten us. Religious ritual allows us to deny our powerlessness; "life and the universe must be robbed of their terrors." Third, religion comforts us by explaining to us the nature of death and the reasons for the apparently cruel manifestations of fate. Fourth, religion compensates us for the sufferings, and especially the instinctual frustration, necessarily part of life in any society. Finally, religion convinces us that there is, ultimately, a standard of justice operating in the universe. "In the end all good is rewarded and all evil punished, if not actually in this form of life then in the later existences that begin after death. In this way all the terrors, the sufferings and the hardships of life are destined to be obliterated."[79]

Why, Freud asked, are religious beliefs so tenacious? Or, to put it a bit more starkly, why do people of the twentieth century persist in believing that "our wretched, ignorant and downtrodden ancestors had succeeded in solving all these difficult riddles of the universe" that we cannot begin to solve? Freud concluded, as had Feuerbach and Nietzsche before him, that religion thrives precisely because it is grounded in the most fundamental wishes of humankind—the wish to be powerful and not powerless, the wish for justice, the wish for immortality, and so on. Religions "are illusions, fulfillments of the oldest, strongest and most urgent wishes of mankind. The secret of their strength lies in the strength of those wishes." Freud consequently described religions as "illusions," not, he said, because he necessarily thought religions were always false, but because he defined an illusion as a belief "derived from human wishes."[80]

Like an Enlightenment thinker attacking the outlandish tales of priests, Freud in reality regarded religions as no more than mere superstitions that hindered the development of human reason. Religions, he argued, are "mass delusions," "fairy tales," and failed attempts of wishful thinking to master a reality that will bend only to empirical reasoning.[81] Like Marx and Nietzsche, Freud concluded that human beings have created gods and not vice versa and that if the wishes of human beings have been powerful enough to create elaborate religious and moral systems, then just perhaps human reason can create new moral principles—this time unsupported by fairy tales about the gods—by which human societies

79. *The Future of an Illusion*, 22–27, 48.
80. *The Future of an Illusion*, 53, 47–48.
81. *Civilization and Its Discontents*, 28; *The Future of an Illusion*, 45; *New Introductory Lectures*, 148 (lecture 35).

can live. "It would be an undoubted advantage if we were to leave God out altogether and honestly admit the purely human origin of all the regulations and precepts of civilization."[82]

Freud was angry at religion, however, not merely because he thought it was in error, intellectually embarrassing, or even childish, but because it was harmful to human happiness. He thought this was true for a number of reasons. First, after reviewing literally millenia of religious experience, Freud concluded confidently that human beings are less happy and more tormented by guilt because of religion. Religion "has ruled human society for many thousands of years and has had time to show what it can achieve. If it had succeeded in making the majority of mankind happy, in comforting them, in reconciling them to life and in making them into vehicles of civilization, no one would dream of attempting to alter the existing conditions. But what do we see instead? We see an appallingly large number of people are dissatisfied with civilization and unhappy in it, and feel it as a yoke which must be shaken off."[83] Second, religion has made people less tolerant of others and has indeed frequently unleashed aggressive instincts on outsiders—in religious wars, crusades, persecution of heretics, and inquisitions. "It is doubtful whether men were in general happier at a time when religious doctrine held unrestricted sway; more moral they certainly were not."[84] Third, religion stunts the intellectual development of children, which leads, of course, to feebleminded adults. In response to the statement that men and women are irrational and immune to reasonable arguments, Freud answered with a powerful anger: "It is true that men are like this; but have you asked yourself whether they *must* be like this, whether their innermost nature necessitates it? Can an anthropologist give the cranial index of a people whose custom it is to deform their children's heads by bandaging them round from their earliest years? . . . Can we be quite certain that it is not precisely religious education which bears a large share of the blame for this relative atrophy?"[85]

Finally, religion convinces men and women that they are powerless when confronted by the forces of the universe, when in fact they are not. Borrowing from Feuerbach, Freud suggested that humankind has projected everything it wishes to be—omnipotent, omniscient, loving, and so forth—onto some entity called "God" and has then passively accepted the notion that men and women are powerless, ignorant, and sinful. "God

82. *The Future of an Illusion*, 67.
83. *The Future of an Illusion*, 60–61.
84. *The Future of an Illusion*, 61.
85. *The Future of an Illusion*, 77–78.

alone is strong and good, man is weak and sinful."[86] Perhaps in the infancy of the human race the exaltation of God and the denigration of humankind made sense, but no longer, because, with the developments of science and technology, human beings are no longer weak and ignorant. "Today [man] has come very close to the attainment of this ideal, he has almost become a god himself." As a consequence, religion, which encourages "unconditional submission" to superstitious dogma, only binds humankind in an ignorant passivity that is no longer necessary. With the right kind of education, which for Freud especially included science, human beings might become powerful enough to gain some mastery over themselves and their universe.[87]

Freud concluded his dicussion of religion optimistically, because he put what faith he had in science and almost certainly saw himself in the tradition of Copernicus, Newton, and Darwin, all of whose scientific discoveries had brought religious dogma into question. Although science cannot end all problems, it is our best hope. "No, our science is no illusion. But an illusion it would be to suppose that what science cannot give we can get elsewhere."[88] Just as psychoanalysis can treat the individual neurotic by bringing into prominence the ego, or reasonable part of the mind, so perhaps on a broader cultural level society can use reason to overcome the neurosis of religion. "Those historical residues have helped us to view religious teachings, as it were, as neurotic relics, and we may now argue that the time has probably come, as it does in an analytic treatment, for replacing the effects of repression by the results of the rational operation of the intellect."[89] Perhaps with better education even in childhood, if children are brought up "sensibly," people can eventually dispense with harmful illusions and live according to reason. Religion is a legacy of the "childhood of humanity," but nature tells us that children grow into adults. Such new people "will be in the same position as a child who has left the parental house where he was so warm and comfortable. But surely infantilism is destined to be surmounted. Men cannot remain children forever."[90]

86. *The Future of an Illusion*, 62.
87. *Civilization and Its Discontents*, 38, 32. Because Freud gave "scientific" proof of our evil nature, he could hardly argue that we could overcome our sinfulness.
88. *The Future of an Illusion*, 92, 63; *Totem and Taboo*, 115.
89. *The Future of an Illusion*, 72. Freud had an abiding faith in the cultured classes and their superiority to the ignorant masses, but since his death in 1939 "the classes have shown a capacity for fresh barbarisms, and the masses have proved no less docile in their unbelief than they ever were in their belief." Rieff, *Freud: The Mind of the Moralist*, 297. For a superb discussion of Freud's view of religion, see Ricoeur, *Freud and Philosophy*, 230–60.
90. *The Future of an Illusion*, 81; *New Introductory Lectures*, 148 (lecture 35).

The Inevitability of Misery and Tyranny

Despite the uncharacteristic optimism in *The Future of an Illusion,* Freud was most often deeply pessimistic. At the end of *Civilization and Its Discontents* Freud refused to offer his contemporaries consolation—and "at bottom that is what they are all demanding"—because he saw no escape from his pessimistic conclusion that human unhappiness and oppression were inevitable. Although science to a great extent had fulfilled the Enlightenment dream of conquering nature by attacking disease, lowering infant mortality, and increasing life expectancy, this had brought no great increase in human happiness. "What good to us is a long life if it is difficult and barren of joys, and if it is so full of misery that we can only welcome death as a deliverer?"[91] Freud found both insight and amusement in an American advertisement that asked, "Why live, if you can be buried for ten dollars?" Individuals, who invariably seek happiness by acting on the pleasure principle and by seeking instinctual satisfaction, inevitably become miserable. "Life, as we find it, is too hard for us; it brings us too many pains, disappointments and impossible tasks. . . . The programme of becoming happy, which the pleasure principle imposes on us, cannot be fulfilled."[92]

Freud offered barely a shred of hope that political reform, much less political revolution, could alleviate miseries that are rooted in human nature. His own time only reinforced his gloomy convictions. In his later writings he noted that Fascist Italy was witnessing only a new form of brutality, Germany was proving "that retrogression into all but prehistoric barbarism can come to pass independently of any progressive idea," and the Soviet Union had eliminated czarist oppression, abolished religion, and attempted to establish a Communism that would alleviate the misery of the many, but in the process had "subjected [its people] to the most cruel coercion and robbed them of every possibility of freedom of thought." While Freud thought that we might learn from the Bolshevik experiment—quite possibly "that a sweeping alteration of the social order has little prospect of success until new discoveries have increased our control over the forces of Nature and made easier the satisfaction of our needs"—in general he maintained that the "untameable character of human nature" would ensure the failure of all grand political reform.[93]

The source of this inevitable misery lies in the conflict between the

---

91. *Civilization and Its Discontents,* 92, 35.

92. *Letters,* 436; *Civilization and Its Discontents,* 22, 30; see also *The Future of an Illusion,* 21.

93. *Moses and Monotheism,* 67; *New Introductory Lectures,* 159–60 (lecture 35).

demands of any civilization and the individual's recalcitrant instinctual desires, discussed earlier in this chapter. In seeking to protect itself from destruction and in endeavoring to find people to do the work necessary to any society, civilization must demand that individuals renounce most of their instinctual claims. "It is impossible to overlook the extent to which civilization is built upon the renunciation of instinct, how much it presupposes precisely the non-satisfaction (by suppression, repression or some other means?) of powerful instincts."[94] Without such coercion the majority of human beings would refuse to perform the necessary work of society and would cast society back into a destructive war of all against all. "Every individual is virtually an enemy of civilization." The main task of civilization, said Freud, is "to defend us against nature."[95]

Freud posed here as both conservative defender and radical critic of civilization. On the one hand, he defended civilization because he thought that the renunciation of instinct, and the frustration and unhappiness that resulted from this, was inevitable if one hoped for cultural accomplishment—a growth in the standard of living, scientific advancement, a system of justice, the creation of art and literature, and so on. On the other hand, he criticized civilization for excessive demands upon people—to love one's enemy, to abstain from sexuality entirely, and so forth—that lead to excessive misery. After acknowledging that some alleviation of misery is possible, Freud clearly criticized European civilization for demanding that certain groups and classes make entirely unreasonable sacrifices. "It goes without saying that a civilization which leaves so large a number of its participants unsatisfied and drives them into revolt neither has nor deserves the prospect of a lasting existence."[96] In other words, Freud took seriously the thought that civilization may not be worth the trouble, that "what we call our civilization is largely responsible for our misery."[97] Freud ultimately argued that misery and tyranny were the inevitable companions of any civilization. "If civilization imposes such great sacrifices not only on man's sexuality but on his aggressivity, we can understand better why it is hard for him to be happy in the civilization. In fact, primitive man was better off in knowing no restrictions of instinct."[98]

Freud's belief in the inevitability of human misery seems clear enough, but what is the relation between this misery and tyranny? An internalized

94. *Civilization and Its Discontents*, 44; see also "'Civilized' Sexual Morality and Modern Nervous Illness," in *Standard Edition*, 9:181–204, esp. 9:186.

95. *The Future of an Illusion*, 3, 20; also 5, 19.

96. *The Future of an Illusion*, 15–16, 8, 12; Roazen, *Freud: Political and Social Thought*, 209.

97. *Civilization and Its Discontents*, 33, 92.

98. *Civilization and Its Discontents*, 62; also *New Introductory Lectures*, 98 (lecture 32).

tyranny imposed on each of us by a harsh superego is the primary means by which civilization manages to check both our sexual and our aggressive instincts. The tyrannical superego—civilization's agency within us that watches over us "like a garrison in a conquered city"—makes us afraid of strong passions, punishes us for being ambitious or aggressive, denies us sexual pleasure, torments us with guilt for merely wishing to do evil, makes us use up our lives in tiresome toil, forces upon us unthinkingly the past prejudices of our parents, and by eliminating both curiosity and spontaneity renders us insipid conformists, parrots who have learned the lines of history's tiresome drama. Freud's tyranny is thus more terrible than any we have encountered. While we can at least imagine slaying Roman emperors or toppling French monarchs, what do we do when we have been taught to tyrannize over ourselves?

Let us look at the tyrannical consequences in more detail. First, the repression of our instinctual drives. Freud thought the commandment to love our neighbors as ourselves was "impossible to fulfill," and yet the renunciation demanded by the commandment led either to guilt or to a destructive neurosis. "Any restriction of this aggressiveness directed outwards would be bound to increase the self-destruction." What about inhibiting the sexual instincts? In one letter Freud wrote, "I stand for an infinitely freer life, although I myself have made very little use of such freedom."[99] European civilization at present created "anaesthetic men" and "frigid women," people busy both denying and fearing their own sexuality.[100] Despite the extravagance of this passage, Freud generally did not advocate anything approaching a sexual revolution, although he did want an easing of restrictions on sexuality. "The claims of our civilization," Freud said at one point, "make life too hard for the greater part of humanity" because we do not allow for the "animal part of our nature." He continued this passage by relating the story of a small town that owned a marvelous workhorse, with the single bad habit that it ate too many oats. The townspeople decided to break the horse of this bothersome habit by feeding it less each day until one glorious day the horse worked without any food at all. The next day, of course, the horse died. Said Freud, "without a certain ration of oats no work could be expected from an animal."[101] More than a loss of pleasure, of course, Freud was concerned that people

---

99. *Civilization and Its Discontents*, 90, 66; *Letters*, 308.

100. Quoted in Reiff, *Freud: The Mind of the Moralist*, 162; also "'Civilized' Sexual Morality and Modern Nervous Illness," 198.

101. Freud, *The Origin and Development of Psychoanalysis*, in *A General Selection from the Works of Sigmund Freud*, ed. Rickman, 3–36, esp. 35–36.

suffer severe "neurotic illness," precisely because of an excessive "suppression of instincts."[102]

Second, the tyranny of the superego brings with it a bountiful harvest of guilt. "The price we pay for our advance in civilization is a loss of happiness through the heightening of the sense of guilt." In order to control our instincts, the superego punishes us with anxiety and guilt simply when our wishes involve sexuality or aggression that is forbidden, that is, whenever even our hidden thoughts fail to live up to the ego ideal. "Whether one has killed one's father or has abstained from doing so is not really the decisive thing. One is bound to feel guilty in either case, for the sense of guilt is an expression of the conflict due to ambivalence." Such a "fatal inevitability of the sense of guilt" leads to "a permanent internal unhappiness."[103]

Third, civilization must tyrannize over us in order to make us do the work necessary to perpetuate civilization. "The great majority of people only work under the stress of necessity, and this natural human aversion to work raises most difficult social problems." Freud's assumption that work will always be drudgery is obviously far from Marx's assumption that human beings will eagerly free themselves from forced labor, thus ultimately finding labor to be a satisfying end in itself. Freud regarded Marx's view as hopelessly utopian. "For masses are lazy and unintelligent," and only with intelligent leadership can they "be induced to perform the work and undergo the renunciations on which the existence of civilization depends."[104] In disciplining people so that they will work long hours more or less willingly, civilization must train people, Freud thought, to renounce all sorts of gratifications that they would naturally prefer. In some sense disciplined labor makes people unnatural.

Finally, the tyranny of civilization renders adults intellectually deficient. After crushing the sexual curiosity of children and thereby beginning the process of crushing intellectual curiosity,[105] after training people to believe in the fairy tales of religion, after forcing people to accept uncritically the moral dogmas of our parents, it would be foolish to expect curious and creative adults. Indeed, Freud regarded most adults as unthinking robots, feeling anxious about their petty concerns and guilty for their petty passions. "Think of the depressing contrast between the radiant intelligence of a healthy child and the feeble intellectual powers

102. *New Introductory Lectures*, 132 (lecture 34).
103. *Civilization and Its Discontents*, 81, 79, 75; "The Ego and the Id," 229–31.
104. *Civilization and Its Discontents*, 27; *The Future of an Illusion*, 6.
105. *The Sexual Enlightenment of Children*, 17–21.

of the average adult."[106] Such a constriction of the adult mind is all the more sad because Freud presented convincing evidence that everyone had the capacity for great genius and creativity. In his theory of dreams he had "democratized genius," hypothesizing in effect that we all produce a wonderfully original fable every night in our dreams,[107] only to wake up to a life of narrow prejudice. Like Marx, Freud pointed to untapped potentials for creativity, although Freud concluded sadly that the survival of civilization will always demand a tyranny that smothers the creativity in most individuals, necessarily leaving it buried forever.

The Reproduction of Tyranny

Civilization's need for controlling our sexual and destructive instincts, from the extraordinarily conservative Freudian point of view, creates the tyrannical superego. As a first consequence, the past will always prefigure the future. The superego, of course, represents the "cultural past," which means that "during the whole of a man's later life [the superego] represents the influence of his childhood, of the care and education given to him by his parents, of his dependence on them." No matter how much a new generation sets out to rebel, to remake the world in a new image, the dominance of the superego makes certain that the traditions of the past are carried forward. The superego "becomes the vehicle of tradition and of all the time-resisting judgments of value which have propagated themselves in this manner from generation to generation. . . . Mankind never lives entirely in the present. The past, the traditions of the race and of the people, lives on in the ideologies of the superego."[108] While Freud certainly admitted that gradual change was possible, and even talked occasionally about human "cultural evolution," such change was always minimal and peripheral, and thus Freud posed as both daring prophet hoping to free us from the past and as pessimistic Stoic recognizing that this adventure was fated to fail.[109] For example, dreams tells us about the past because they generally originate in the earliest wishes of the the individual. "Nevertheless the ancient belief that dreams foretell the future is not wholly devoid of truth. By picturing our wishes as fulfilled, dreams are after all leading us into the future. But this future . . . has been moulded

---

106. *The Future of an Illusion*, 77–78.

107. Rieff, *Freud: The Mind of the Moralist*, 35.

108. *An Outline of Psychoanalysis*, 122–23; *New Introductory Lectures*, 60 (lecture 31).

109. *New Introductory Lectures*, 130 (lecture 34); Philip Rieff, "The Authority of the Past: Sickness and Society in Freud's Thought," *Social Research* 51, no. 1 (1984): 527–50.

by his indestructible wish into a perfect likeness of the past."[110] The primal wishes of human beings and the domination of the superego are always the central features in the human drama.

Very little new happens under Freud's sun. The attempt to re-create the world and dramatically reduce human suffering is only a "delusion" that invariably founders on the demands of reality;[111] the attempt to break from the past and freely shape one's future ignores the fact that there is always tyranny, that "there are only alternative submissions";[112] and the ideas advocating equality and democracy are, at bottom, only useful weapons in the rebellion of sons against fathers, rebellions that never change the hierarchical patterns of authority. "The conservative implications of Freudian psychology are clear: nothing qualitatively different happens in history. With the leader forced to play father-imago because his followers are children, politics becomes an unchanging strife between the generations."[113] This last sentence indicates the obvious, namely, that the political drama is merely the family drama writ large, that the family is ultimately the agency that perpetuates the tyranny of the superego, dominating father figures, and submissive subjects.

This focus on the family is Freud's greatest contribution to the theory of tyranny, because it is in the family that the oppressive cycle is continued and the patterns of tyranny are reproduced. The key to this lies in the ambivalence of the child toward the parent. Not only does the son resent the father, he also idealizes him and identifies with him. "A little boy will exhibit a special interest in his father; he would like to grow like him and be like him, and take his place everywhere. We may say simply that he takes his father as his ideal."[114] This means, of course, that no matter how much the boy hates his father, no matter how much he rebels against his father, ultimately he comes to resemble him and the cycle continues. Freud recounted a case in which a young man's fear and hatred for his father led him to rebellion, even self-destructive rebellion, until after his father's death. Soon thereafter "he developed an absolutely egotistical, despotic, and brutal personality; . . . He was the exact copy of his father."[115] Similarly, a young woman resented the way she had been raised by her mother, was critical of what her mother had become, and sought to define herself in opposition to her mother. "When this girl married, how-

110. *Interpretation of Dreams*, 660.
111. *Civilization and Its Discontents*, 28.
112. Rieff, *Freud: The Mind of the Moralist*, 274.
113. Rieff, *Freud: The Mind of the Moralist*, 238–39.
114. *Group Psychology and the Analysis of the Ego*, 46.
115. *Moses and Monotheism*, 100; see Roazen, *Freud: Political and Social Thought*, 274.

ever, and became a wife and mother in her turn, we are surprised to find that she became more and more like the mother towards whom she felt so inimical."[116] And thus the family reproduces a future that will always resemble the tyrannical and patriarchal past.

Conclusion

Freud's first and most important contribution to theories of tyranny lies in his discussion of the family. Although Plato and Montesquieu had discussed the importance of the family, no one until Freud made it so central to European discussions about tyranny. It is within the family that the cruel and stifling superego develops; it is within the family that one finds the origin of tyrannical systems of authority; and it is within the family—not the political system and not the class structure—that one finds the roots of the ever-regenerating cycle of tyranny, a tyranny reproduced in each new generation by the family. Freud assumed that tyranny was unavoidable, because he assumed that the patriarchal family was both natural and inevitable. Later thinkers, after discarding Freud's assumption that the patriarchal family is inevitable, still took seriously Freud's notion that family structures invariably resemble political structures, even as these thinkers wished for a more democratic family and society.

Second, whereas other thinkers such as Plato, Tocqueville, and Marx had talked about how we are trained or socialized to accept tyranny, Freud was the first to show the extent to which we emotionally internalize a need for tyranny. Both the family and the society at large make certain that we tyrannize ourselves, that the tyrannical superego oppresses and controls us "like a garrison in a conquered city." While it is important to see us as victims of society, as conquered, as men and women whose very feelings are largely controlled by the internalized tyranny imposed upon us, Freud also wanted us to see ourselves as participants and proponents of tyranny. As Foucault said later, we both experience tyranny and perpetuate it. As victims we carry around an internalized tyranny; as proponents we pass it on and propagate it in others—sons and daughters, sisters and brothers, friends and neighbors, and so on.

Third, after examining religions, political orders, and groups, Freud concluded that we yearn for a father figure to care for us and to protect us. Only a few, Freud maintained, are strong enough and healthy enough to escape the need for rule by a father or father substitute. Although

116. *Moses and Monotheism*, 160–61.

Freud's evidence for this claim is not entirely convincing, it is clear that even if he is partly right, we will always have a world of a few leaders and many led, a hierarchical world in which meaningful equality and democracy are impossible. When the turmoil of revolution abates, suggested Freud, and when the excitement and dust of political reform have settled, the world will still witness strong leaders and the many seeking an "unqualified submission." And thus our choice is not between democracy and tyranny, or between the freedom of liberalism or socialism and tyranny, but rather our future will offer only a choice, as Rieff says, between "alternative submissions."

Fourth, if we have a longing for the father, we also have a longing for the affectionate support—always idealized—of the family. And yet because we must leave the family and separate from it, we suffer, even as adults, from loneliness and separation anxiety. This means that we seek to be part of a supportive group with which we identify, some variation of a primitive horde led by a father figure. "The individual," said Freud, "feels incomplete if he is alone." It is bad enough that such groups breed submissiveness, a regressive and infantile wish for dependence, and a mindless obedience, but even worse, such groups promote their own identity and internally binding affection by defining themselves against outsiders. This leads to tremendous intolerance, Freud noted, of those who are different because of race, ethnicity, religious beliefs, and so forth. In the face of far-flung ethnic, racial, and religious hostility and violence all over the world in the late twentieth century, it is hard to dismiss entirely Freud's claim that all groups are fundamentally hostile, intolerant, and tyrannical toward outsiders. The earliest Greek tyrannies solidified their power by playing off ethnic groups against one another, and Freud specifically offers an explanation for why this racist tactic works so well.

Fifth, whereas most modern scholars would agree that Freud's explanation for the roles and status of women is thoroughly flawed, Freud focused on the family and in many ways accurately described the status of women. I certainly disagree that biology has destined women to the role Freud described, but in noting that women within patriarchal families frequently became submissive, childlike, dependent, intellectually stunted, and afraid of their passions, Freud raised the question—for others to answer—like no thinker since Montesquieu, about what happens to women in the family structure. If his answer is wrong, he at least deserves some credit for alerting others to key questions about women and tyranny.

Finally, Freud noted that for almost all of us—women as well as men—our internalized tyranny does not simply make us submissive and dependent, but also makes us feebleminded and dull. Freud suggested that each one of us at birth had tremendous potential for intelligence and creativity; he could see this potential in children who seemed wonderfully creative and intelligent, and in adult dreams that are elaborate creative productions every night. And yet he regarded most adults around him as intellectually stunted, lacking in all curiosity, childlike, eagerly superstitious, afraid of their passions, and tormented by guilt. It is a sad and sorry picture of what an internalized tyranny does to us.

9

WEBER

The Inevitability of Bureaucratic Domination

It is common to describe Max Weber as the father of modern social science, but this label, accurate as far as it goes, is woefully narrow. It omits Weber as the practitioner of this social science, applying it to virtually every topic from stock market behavior to the sociology of religion; it fails to comprehend Weber's encyclopedic knowledge of cultures ancient and modern, East and West; it misses Weber's lifelong attempt to explain why systematic science and capitalism developed not in the ancient European world or in Asia but in early modern Europe and North America; it overlooks Weber's writing like a prophet from the Hebrew Bible, decrying modern developments but able to offer little hope or consolation; and it omits Weber as a passionate political actor and advocate, a bold defender of Germany's late efforts for empire. Behind his comparatively calm sociological analyses, of which there are certainly thousands of pages, we find the heir to Machiavelli, a thinker who regards politics as the struggle for power between nations, classes, parties, groups, and elites.

Weber's intellectual roots extended deep into the German philosophical tradition, more, perhaps, than he even knew. For example, despite admiring key aspects of a British parliamentary system still manipulated by a farsighted aristocracy, Weber apparently had no inclination to quote the thinkers behind this parliamentary tradition, such as Locke, Burke, or Mill, and Weber similarly paid scant attention to the French tradition from Montesquieu to Durkheim. Two giants of the German philosophical tradition, however, do lurk in the background of Weber's analyses—Marx and Nietzsche. "The honesty of a scholar of our day, and even more of a philosopher of our day can be judged on the grounds of how he defines his relationship to Nietzsche and Marx. He who [states] that he would have been [able] to achieve the most important parts of his own work without the work of both of them, belies himself just as much as the others. The world in which we live as intellectual beings, bears largely the imprint of Nietzsche and Marx."[1] From Nietzsche (whom he curiously mentioned first), Weber took a deep suspicion of the claims of philosophical reasoning, an ultimately nihilistic worldview, a wish to delve beneath the manifest pronouncements in order to examine the latent motives of religious and political leaders, and a more reasonable remnant of Nietzsche's elitist belief in the creative potential of great men. From Marx, Weber borrowed a sophisticated class analysis, much of his critique of capitalism (and, ironically, a way to express his disillusion with socialism), and the belief that economic interests and material forces are of primary importance—but hardly sufficient by themselves—in the developments of history. This notion of historical development is very important. Weber never entirely escaped the Hegelian and Marxian assumption that history "develops" or "advances." Like some sort of strangely pessimistic Hegelian, Weber suggested that history has witnessed the ever-increasing application of instrumental, or technical, reason to more and more areas of human life. Weber hardly meant by this that history embodied Reason in some Hegelian sense, that human life necessarily will become better, more just, and more moral. To say that human soci-

1. Cited in Wolfgang J. Mommsen, The Age of Bureaucracy: Perspectives on the Political Sociology of Max Weber (New York: Harper & Row, 1977), 104 (Weber was reported to have made this statement to a student). On Nietzsche's influence on Weber, see Robert Eden, Political Leadership and Nihilism: A Study of Weber and Nietzsche (Tampa: University of South Florida Press, 1983), esp. chaps. 4–5, pp. 98–173, and Wilhelm Hennis, Max Weber: Essays in Reconstruction, trans. Keith Tribe (London: Allen & Unwin, 1988). For the classic comparison of Marx and Weber, see Karl Löwith, Max Weber and Karl Marx (London: Allen & Unwin, 1982). For Marxist views that Weber was offering an ideological defense of capitalism, see David Beetham, Max Weber and the Theory of Modern Politics (London: Allen & Unwin, 1974), and Herbert Marcuse, "Industrialization and Capitalism," in Max Weber and Sociology Today, ed. Otto Stammer, trans. Kathleen Morris (New York: Harper & Row, 1971), 133–51. For a summary of critiques of Weber from both Left and Right, see Reinhard Bendix and Guenther Roth, eds., Scholarship and Partisanship: Essays on Max Weber (Berkeley and Los Angeles: University of California Press, 1971), 55–69 (an essay by Roth).

eties have become more instrumentally rational (more efficient at attaining given ends) is not at all to claim that societies have become more substantively rational (are the ends chosen "good" ones? a question that will be answered in very different ways). Indeed, the proliferation of instrumental, or technical, reason, in Weber's view, has mainly brought new ways of controlling individuals, especially with the development of systematic bureaucratic domination, and has thus increased the inevitability of more effective tyranny, or domination. "Such concepts of 'will of the people,' genuine will of the people, have long since ceased to exist for me; they are fictitious. All ideas aiming at abolishing the dominance of men over men are 'utopian.'"[2] While Weber's jeremiads warn prophetically against the individual's being swallowed by a bureaucratic structure of domination, they offer little hope of a future promised land.

The State and Politics

One might define the state in many ways. Plato and Aristotle looked upon the polis, or city-state, as designed to cultivate human potential for justice, morality, and greatness; Saint Thomas Aquinas wished the state to provide order, social justice, and an environment in which citizens could live a Christian life; Locke sought a state that would defend individual rights of person and property; Hegel thought the state should embody Reason; and Marx saw the state as an instrument of class tyranny. Defining the state by the purposes one wished it would serve, according to Weber, was both arbitrary and irrelevant. A state is simply the organization that monopolizes the legitimate sources of violence within a given territory. "A compulsory political organization with continuous operations will be called a 'state' insofar as its administrative staff successfully upholds the claim to the *monopoly* of the *legitimate* use of physical force in the enforcement of its order."[3] After arguing that every state possesses various "value systems ordering matters other than the directly economic disposition of goods and services," Weber maintained that the specific

2. Cited in Mommsen, *Age of Bureaucracy*, 87. Carl Mayer makes a persuasive case that Weber was a Kantian in regard to his methodology in the social sciences, but Mayer skims too quickly over the Hegelian themes in Weber's theory of history. See Mayer, "Max Weber's Interpretation of Karl Marx," *Social Research* 42, no. 4 (1975): 701–19.

3. Max Weber, *Economy and Society*, 2 vols., with pages numbered consecutively, ed. Guenther Roth and Claus Wittich, trans. Ephraim Fischoff et al. (Berkeley and Los Angeles: University of California Press, 1978), 54, and idem, "Politics as a Vocation," in *From Max Weber: Essays in Sociology*, ed. and trans. H. H. Gerth and C. Wright Mills (New York: Oxford University Press, 1946), 78.

content of these value systems—from a Platonic notion of justice to a Lockean defense of property rights—is "conceptually irrelevant."[4] Whether conceptually precise or ruthlessly realistic, Weber's definition of a state is certainly somber, and it leads readily to his pessimistic conclusion that in all cases "the state is a relation of men dominating men."[5]

Such a brutally bare-bones definition of a state enabled Weber to avoid setting up supposedly objective standards by which to judge whether a state is good or just or even legitimate. His concept of legitimacy has proved particularly bothersome to his critics because Weber suggested that a state is legitimate and its use of force is legitimate if the subjects *believe* the state and its actions to be legitimate. A state, declared Weber, monopolizes the "means of legitimate (i.e. considered to be legitimate) means of violence." Nor does Weber care if such a belief in the legitimacy of a state is voluntary or manipulated, a distinction probably impossible to make, because every state "attempts to establish and to cultivate the belief in its legitimacy." Weber's claim that a state is legitimate if it is believed to be legitimate allowed him to suggest that Greek tyrants were illegitimate rulers because they were widely perceived to be so, and that Roman tribunes were illegitimate authorities because they challenged a state widely believed to be legitimate. Consistent as Weber's concept of legitimacy may be, it seems to his critics entirely too simple-minded, impossible to verify (does it necessitate a successful rebellion to indicate that subjects no longer believe in the legitimacy of the government?), and entirely too relativistic.[6]

The form of government within a given state was, for Weber, largely a technical question, dependent upon the ends selected by the leaders of a given state. If a nation in the twentieth century sought international expansion as some ultimate goal, Weber once said—in the spirit of Machiavelli—then it might consider either an "absolutist" or a "radical democratic" government as the appropriate means to this chosen end.[7] Just as there are "techniques" of administration and of prayer and of playing mu-

---

4. *Economy and Society*, 902.

5. "Politics as a Vocation," 78; see also Julien Freund, *The Sociology of Max Weber*, trans. Mary Ilford (New York: Vintage, 1969), 218–23.

6. "Politics as a Vocation," 78; *Economy and Society*, 213, 1357; Weber, *General Economic History*, trans. Frank H. Knight (New Brunswick, N.J.: Transaction Books, 1981), 325. For good discussions of Weber's concept of legitimacy, see Susan J. Hekman, *Weber, the Ideal Type, and Contemporary Social Theory* (Notre Dame, Ind.: University of Notre Dame Press, 1983), 51–52, 136–41; and Robert Grafstein, "The Failure of Weber's Concept of Legitimacy: Its Causes and Implications," *Journal of Politics* 43, no. 2 (1981): 456–72.

7. Wolfgang J. Mommsen, *Max Weber and German Politics, 1890–1920*, trans. Michael S. Steinberg (Chicago: University of Chicago Press, 1984), 396.

sic, so there are techniques of governing a state if the goals and values of the state are clearly delineated. For Weber, it simply did not matter very much. "For a rational politician the form of government appropriate at any given time is a technical question which depends upon the political tasks of the nation." Because both the modern state and the modern factory seek to organize the labor of men and women efficiently, it is not surprising that they resemble each other while using the technique of bureaucratic domination. "Sociologically speaking, the modern state is an 'enterprise' just like a factory."[8]

Within the state, individuals engage in politics, which Weber defined as "striving to share power or striving to influence the distribution of power, either among states or among groups within a state." In other words, politics is a battle—"the essence of politics . . . is *struggle*"—for the distribution of power among nations, classes, political parties, and individuals.[9] While Weber certainly acknowledged that economic activity can be exploitative and coercive, in general he sought to maintain the distinction between usually peaceful economic exchange and invariably coercive political action.[10] Although one may discover struggles for power within families or factories or classes, such struggles are not properly political ones, because political struggles ultimately determine who controls—or at least can influence—the use of the legitimate means of violence within a state. "Politics operates with very special means, namely, power backed up by *violence*."[11] Violence, of course, is hardly the only or even the most common means used by those who wield political power, but the threat of force is ever present, and such a threat makes political power unique.

What did Weber mean by the word *power?* "In general, we understand by 'power' the chance of a man or a number of men to realize their own will in a social action even against the resistance of others who are participating in the action."[12] Like Machiavelli and Hobbes, Weber regarded

8. *Economy and Society*, 1383–84, 1394, 65–66.

9. "Politics as a Vocation," 78; *Economy and Society*, 1414, 54–55, 926–39. Weber's definitions of a state and of a "political community" are virtually identical (*Economy and Society*, 54, 901).

10. *Economy and Society*, 64–65, 640, 731.

11. "Politics as a Vocation," 119; also *Economy and Society*, 55; Weber, *The Sociology of Religion*, trans. Ephraim Fischoff (Boston: Beacon Press, 1963), 235; *From Max Weber*, ed. and trans. Gerth and Mills, 334. At fourteen, Weber regarded Cicero's Catilinarian oration as "just one long whimper and lamentation." He found Cicero "without appropriate resolve and energy, without skill, and without the ability to wait for the right moment. For if he had arrested and strangled Catiline at the proper time . . . , the Roman state would have been spared." See Marianne Weber, *Max Weber: A Biography*, trans. Harry Zohn (New York: Wiley & Sons, 1975), 52–53.

12. *Economy and Society*, 926.

the forms of power as nearly limitless. For example, the economic might of a powerful class, a monopoly in a given market, an acknowledged legal "right" that protects one's interests, the monopoly of secret or highly specialized information by a bureaucratic official, the accepted belief that only Brahmin priests can pray effectively, persuasive words used as "weapons" against one's enemies, and of course violence—all of these are forms of power.[13]

Why do individuals seek power? First of all and most commonly, because they want to improve their material interests. In Weber's political world, classes, parties, status groups, and individuals all strive predominantly for material interests, and hence "every policy that ever banked on political gratitude has failed." Second, sometimes individuals or groups seek power in order to bring about what Weber calls "ideal interests," values or ideals vitally important to these political actors. And finally, some relish the "feeling of power," that is, "the knowledge of influencing men, of participating in power over them, and above all, the feeling of holding in one's hands a nerve fiber of historically important events." Weber saw nothing wrong with the love of power, as long as one can bring to this use of power "passion, a feeling of responsibility, and a sense of proportion."[14]

Whereas virtually any competent bureaucratic official can make administrative decisions, Weber thought only a very few—and here we find some remnant of Nietzsche's elitism—are capable of making the most important political decisions. "Politics is always made by a small number of persons. . . . Since the great political decisions, even and especially in a democracy, are unavoidably made by few men, mass democracy has bought its successes since Pericles' times with major concessions to the caesarist principle of selecting leaders."[15] Although Weber acknowledged that the lobbying and electoral activity of political parties or status groups is "political" activity or at least "politically oriented" activity, when he spoke of "politics" he referred to the activities of a political leadership or elite directly trying to use, or perhaps redistribute, the powers of the state. Politics is something only leaders do. This means, of course, that the great mass of people in a modern state are passive, nominally sovereign just like shareholders in a private economic enterprise, but in fact led, manipulated, and dominated. "For it is not the politically

13. *Economy and Society*, 315, 667; *Sociology of Religion*, 14; "Science as a Vocation," in *From Max Weber*, ed. and trans. Gerth and Mills, 145.

14. *Economy and Society*, 1391, 1457, 203; "Politics as a Vocation," 115.

15. *Economy and Society*, 1421, 1452, 1414. For Weber's debt to and differences with Nietzsche's elitism, see Mommsen, "Max Weber's Political Sociology and His Philosophy of World History," in *Max Weber*, ed. Dennis Wrong (Englewood Cliffs, N.J.: Prentice-Hall, 1970), 183–94.

passive 'mass' that produces the leader from its midst, but the political leader recruits his following and wins the mass through 'demagogy.' This is true even under the most democratic form of state." To those critical of bestowing such power on one person or such a small elite, Weber responded that these critics merely harbored a "very petty-bourgeois hostility" to leaders.[16]

Weber was in fact afraid to entrust political decision making to anyone but a charismatic leader. The unorganized mass, or what he called "the democracy of the streets," is simply irrational; even the people in a democracy who are organized into groups and led by party officials are too "emotional" and shortsighted; certainly the German working class and probably all European working classes lack political "maturity"; the bourgeoisie is a "philistine" class that too often exhibits "emotional and senseless cowardice" (Weber cryptically remarked that he did not "deny my pride in [my own] bourgeois descent"); and in contrast to the brilliant British political aristocracy, the German Junker landed class has no aptitude for political leadership.[17] Quite simply Weber could not escape the spell of Bismarck, that "Caesar-like figure" and "political genius" that a nation could reasonably expect to discover only once in a century. He spoke of "the curse of being born *after* a period of political greatness" and of his wish for "*grand* passions" in political matters.[18] While Weber did not expect another Bismarck, he did wish to emulate the British parliamentary system that consistently produced a leadership capable of extending a world empire. Indeed, he almost lovingly described this British leadership. "The ruling party required an ever-ready organization composed *only* of its actually leading men, who would confidentially discuss matters in order to maintain power within and be capable of engaging in grand politics outside."[19]

Weber's focus on an elite political leadership devalued, or turned upside down, his own political sociology, because this focus concludes that only elite leaders engage in politics properly so called, whereas in fact that was not Weber's usual analysis. In other words, Weber's political sociology is extremely detailed and complex, while his occasional equation suggesting that politics is leadership with its hands on the means of

16. *Economy and Society*, 54–55, 1457; "Politics as a Vocation," 114, 77, 91, 99.

17. *Economy and Society*, 1459–61; W. G. Runciman, ed., *Weber: Selections in Translation*, trans. Eric Matthews (Cambridge: Cambridge University Press, 1978), 263–68; *From Max Weber*, ed. and trans. Gerth and Mills, 386–95. For Weber's analysis of classes in Germany, see Karl Jaspers, *On Max Weber*, ed. John Dreijmanis, trans. Robert J. Whelan (New York: Paragon House, 1989), 40–48.

18. *Selections in Translation*, ed. Runciman, 264, 268; cited in Mommsen, *Max Weber and German Politics*, 165.

19. "Politics as a Vocation," 90.

violence is simplistic. To take several examples, Weber analyzed the role of voluntary associations and religious sects in American politics; he noted that the political power of an established church will vary depending "of course upon the power constellation of the status groups concerned"; and he observed that modern bureaucratic officials were beginning to form a separate status group, even a separate caste.[20] In addition, Weber offered a detailed class analysis. For example, when talking of class struggles, Weber distinguished between debtor/creditor struggles more common to the ancient world, commodity/price struggles of the Middle Ages, and wage struggles of more recent centuries.[21] Moreover, his focus on leaders leaves in the shadows his careful analyses of political parties. If status groups reside in the "social order" and classes in the "economic order," then political parties occupy the "sphere of power." The goal of all political parties is to "secure power" so as to attain the interests of its members, contributors, and constituents. "The management of politics through parties simply means management through interest groups."[22]

All of Weber's talk of Caesar-like leaders, elites, and grand politics only indicates how much he personally valued power politics more than democratic constitutions. Politics for Weber is, in the end, not lobbying for votes and legislation, but the struggle for power between the leaders of parties and groups, or classes and nations—and the occasional use of violence. "The state's absolute end is to safeguard (or to change) the external and internal distribution of power. . . . It is absolutely essential for every political association to appeal to the naked violence of coercive means in the face of outsiders as well as in the face of internal enemies. It is only this very appeal to violence that constitutes a political association in our terminology."[23]

Weber longed for grand politics and had no wish to live in a small, unimportant state, no matter how well-governed. He feared after World War I, a war he initially called "*great and wonderful,*" that Germany would be "condemned to remain a small and conservative country, perhaps with a fairly good public administration in purely technical respects, but at any rate a provincial people without the opportunity of counting in the arena of world politics—and also without any *moral* right to do so."[24]

20. *Economy and Society*, 1174–75, 1206–7; *Selections in Translation*, ed. Runciman, 261, 281; *Economy and Society*, 936–38.

21. *From Max Weber*, ed. and trans. Gerth and Mills, 301; Weber, *Economy and Society*, 928–31.

22. *Economy and Society*, 938, 284; "Politics as a Vocation," 94.

23. *From Max Weber*, ed. and trans. Gerth and Mills, 334; see Mommsen, *Max Weber and German Politics*, 396.

24. *Economy and Society*, 1462; cited in Mommsen, *Max Weber and German Politics*, 9–

Weber's discussions of the state, the nature of politics, and the necessity of leadership reflect the political developments of his time, especially recent national unification in German and Italy as well as European imperial expansion. While Weber noted that national security interests and emotional desires for prestige and glory helped foster nationalism and national expansion, he consistently acknowledged that what he called "imperialist expansion" was fueled predominantly by economic interests, by the "profit opportunities" of many groups and classes ranging from banks to overseas traders to munitions industries to key sectors of organized labor. "The universal revival of 'imperialist' capitalism, which has always been the normal form in which capitalist interests have influenced politics, and the revival of political drives for expansion are thus not accidental. For the predictable future, the prognosis will have to be made in its favor."[25] Weber eagerly embraced Germany's efforts to join this European imperial expansion. Great nations, said Weber, must always seek "power above all," and indeed "the preservation of national culture is linked necessarily to power politics," and thus he supported policies leading to "national greatness," lest Germany become a petty state like Switzerland. Even at the risk of war, Germany had a responsibility to see that "English monotony" and "Russian bureaucracy" did not divide the world.[26] Had Weber been content to live in a Switzerland, he might well have defined the state and politics differently, and he might not have focused his gaze so frequently on the fact that political leaders must occasionally use, or threaten to use, the means of violence.

Values and Politics

As indicated earlier, Weber distinguished between "formal," or "instrumental," rationality on the one hand, and "substantive" rationality on the other. An action is instrumentally rational to the extent that it applies

---

10, 191. For Weber's political activities during and after World War I, see Edward B. Portis, *Max Weber and Political Commitment* (Philadelphia: Temple University Press, 1986), chap. 7, 145–70.

25. *Economy and Society*, 919, 910–26.

26. Cited in Mommsen, *Max Weber and German Politics*, 65–77, 191–95, 208. Weber also spoke of the "population problem" leading to a "fierce struggle of man against man" for "the necessary elbow room," and he worried about the "eternal struggle for the survival and the higher breeding of our national species." Cited in Mommsen, *Age of Bureaucracy*, 30. See also Raymond Aron, "Max Weber and Power-Politics," in *Max Weber and Sociology Today*, ed. Stammer, 83–100. For a more generous interpretation of Weber as a defender of liberal democracy, see J. P. Mayer, *Max Weber and German Politics: A Study in Political Sociology* (London: Faber & Faber, 1944), 72–83.

effective means to attain some chosen end; an action is substantively rational to the extent that the observer who judges the action agrees with what Weber called the "criteria of ultimate ends, whether they be ethical, political, utilitarian, hedonistic, feudal, egalitarian, or whatever."[27] An action can be both instrumentally and substantively rational at once—for example, the efficient construction of a bridge that a given observer deems to be a worthwhile endeavor. But an action can also be instrumentally rational but substantively irrational, because an observer may judge that the ends chosen are morally wrong—for example, a well-planned and well-executed invasion of a peaceful country, such as Hitler's invasion of Poland.

Science, social science, and common sense can tell us if an action is instrumentally rational, but—and here is his clearest legacy from Nietzsche—Weber did not think that, in the final analysis, either science or philosophy could tell us which values to embrace, and hence which values we might use to judge if some action is substantively rational. In some final analysis, Weber leaned upon Nietzsche's relativism. "Ultimate *Weltanschauungen* clash, world views among which in the end one has to make a choice. . . . Or speaking directly, the ultimately possible attitudes toward life are irreconcilable, and hence their struggle can never be brought to a final conclusion. Thus it is necessary to make a decisive choice."[28] Shall I find meaning in Christianity or atheism? Shall I embrace Kant's categorical imperatives or Mill's utilitarianism? Shall I defend Bolshevism or pacifism? Weber referred to these values, and of course many more, as "warring gods" from which we must choose. In reality, we look for a prophet or a savior to give the answer, but sadly, "the prophet for whom so many of our younger generation yearn simply does not exist." Like Nietzsche, Weber believed that science and philosophy had succeeded in showing only that reason cannot discover absolute truths and that gods do not exist who can reveal such truths. "Precisely the ultimate and most sublime values have retreated from public life. . . . To the person who cannot bear the fate of the times like a man, one must say: may he rather return silently. . . . The arms of the old churches are opened widely and compassionately for him."[29]

Science and social science are of some help in making such decisions. First, science can often offer empirical evidence to discredit some so-

---

27. *Economy and Society*, 85–86, 24, 30. For a good discussion of instrumental reason versus substantive reason, see Rogers Brubaker, *The Limits of Rationality: An Essay on the Social and Moral Thought of Max Weber* (London: Allen & Unwin, 1984), chap. 2, 49–60.
28. "Politics as a Vocation," 117; "Science as a Vocation," 152.
29. "Science as a Vocation," 153–55.

called value positions. If an individual claims "race x is inferior," science has enough empirical evidence, without some ultimate value choice, to debunk this claim as factually inaccurate. Second, science can show us inconvenient repercussions that necessarily accompany chosen values— for example, an increase in the deaths of young women if abortion is made illegal or the pain caused to fetuses if abortion remains legal. "The primary task of a useful teacher is to teach his students to recognize 'inconvenient' facts—I mean facts that are inconvenient for their party opinions. And for every party opinion there are facts that are extremely inconvenient." Third, science can examine our chosen ends and tell us what means will be necessary to achieve these ends. "Does the end 'justify' the means? Or does it not? [The social scientist] can confront you with the necessity of this choice. He cannot do more." Finally, science can help evaluate the consistency of chosen values. For example, if a man opposes all experiments on animals and also believes in the alleviation of human suffering, science may be able to show that these positions are inconsistent, forcing this man to reevaluate his values. In all these ways, social science is of some use in deciding upon our values, and certainly Weber did not want anyone to choose values lightly, without the kind of uncomfortable wisdom that science can bring to bear on these choices. Teachers of social science "can force the individual, or at least we can help him, to give himself an *account of the ultimate meaning of his own conduct.* This appears to me as not so trifling a thing to do, even for one's own personal life."[30]

Ultimately the individual must choose for himself or herself. Weber quoted Tolstoi: "Science is meaningless because it gives no answer to our question, the only question important for us: 'What shall we do and how shall we live?'" Science and social science can lead us to the intersection of many roads, but we must choose a direction for ourselves. Increasing empirical knowledge, Weber declared, can never answer the most important questions in life, and "the highest ideals, which move us most forcefully, are always formed only in the struggle with other ideals which are just as sacred to others as ours are to us."[31]

Weber argued that reasonable individuals generally adopt one of two broad approaches to choosing values—either an ethic of ultimate ends or an ethic of responsibility. Under what he called an ethic of ultimate ends,

30. "Science as a Vocation," 147, 151–52; Weber, *The Methodology of the Social Sciences,* ed. and trans. Edward A. Shils and Henry A. Finch (New York: Free Press, 1949), 18.

31. "Science as a Vocation," 143; *Methodology,* 57. On Weber's notion of choosing meanings, see Reinhard Bendix, *Force, Fate, and Freedom: On Historical Sociology* (Berkeley and Los Angeles: University of California Press, 1984), chap. 2, 27–45.

Weber lumped together the Christianity of the New Testament, pacifism, Kantianism, and Bolshevism. All of these ethics, according to Weber, regard designated moral actions as intrinsically valuable, as ends in themselves, and none of these ethics examines probable consequences. For example, the pacifist uses only nonviolent means because he or she is convinced this is the only way ultimately of bringing about a world without violence, whereas the Bolshevik may act violently to keep the revolutionary movement alive, trusting that immediate suffering is necessary to bring about a better world without class domination. Weber responded to this ethic of ultimate ends in a number of ways. First, he admitted that there *can be* something incomparably noble about action based on this ethic—the Christian who does love his or her enemies, the Kantian who refuses to lie, and so on. Second, he acknowledged that one cannot prove this ethic to be wrong. But finally, he did not prefer the ethic of ultimate ends, because he thought this approach almost always provided a simplistic answer in an endlessly complex world. Nine out of ten times, Weber found political actors who followed an ethic of ultimate ends to be "windbags . . . who intoxicate themselves with romantic sensations."[32]

Weber much preferred an ethic of responsibility. Here the individual acts upon certain ideals or values, but "one has to give an account of the foreseeable results of one's actions." Because no clear-cut and neverchanging moral rules are available to the moral actor, the ethic of responsibility involves agonizing choice. How one brings values to the personal or political world will change depending upon the means necessary to a chosen end and upon the probable consequences of any action. Such an ethic also involves the recognition that no compromise ethic—some safe middle position—is likely to be one whit more correct than some radical or extreme step. In other words, on some rare occasions, extreme violence may be the correct action. Weber found it "immensely moving" when a political actor weighed all the probable consequences of an action and felt genuine "responsibility with heart and soul" and then announced in Luther's words, "Here I stand; I can do no other."[33]

Weber claimed there was a certain grandeur—as well as frequent tragedy—when political leaders sought to use the ethic of responsibility to bring values and ideals into the realm of politics. Every great political leader must serve some "cause," but to bring this cause to a life of politics is to contract with "diabolic forces," principally because one must use morally dubious means to accomplish anything great. "He who seeks the salvation of the soul, his own and of others, should not seek it along the avenue of politics, for the quite different tasks of politics can only be

---

32. "Politics as a Vocation," 127, 120, 119–25; *Methodology,* 16.
33. "Politics as a Vocation," 120, 127.

solved by violence." Nevertheless, he thought grand politics to be a noble pursuit, and he praised the "beautiful passage" in which Machiavelli eulogized "those citizens who deemed the greatness of their native city higher than the salvation of their souls." A great political leader recognizes that we cannot discover values, and thus sets out, somewhat like Nietzsche's overman, to create new values for a culture—not entirely new, to be sure, but new in some significant way. "The fate of an epoch which has eaten of the tree of knowledge is that it must know that we cannot learn the *meaning* of the world from the results of its analysis, be it ever so perfect; it must rather be in a position to create this meaning itself."[34]

Several problems exist for a political leader trying to bring values to bear on political action. First, frustration. "Politics," said Weber, "is a strong and slow boring of hard boards," and thus it is likely that little one hopes for will come about. Still, despite frustration, "man would not have attained the possible unless time and again he had reached out for the impossible." Second, political leaders come to realize that the good things of this world can never all be attained. The Platonic vision that truth, justice, beauty, virtue, courage, wisdom, and freedom are all in harmony simply does not hold for the human world. If one wants socialist equality, one may have to accept a suffocating centralized bureaucracy; if one seeks capitalist productivity, one may get the exploitation of labor; if one encourages individualism, one may simultaneously produce loneliness and the loss of community; and so on. "It is commonplace to observe," noted Weber, "that something may be true although it is not beautiful and not holy and not good."[35] Third, political action is invariably "interwoven" with "tragedy" because the results of one's actions frequently go completely against one's intentions. "The final result of political action often, no, even regularly, stands in completely inadequate and often even paradoxical relation to its original meaning." Weber was fond of noting that political action is not like a cab that one can stop at will, for once in motion political decisions often gain a momentum one cannot control.[36]

Finally, the human world is tragically irrational. Political decisions would be quite simple if one could apply the principles of private morality to public and political actions, if what we generally call "good" actions always produced good results and if what we generally call "evil" always produced evil results. Weber, like Machiavelli, knew that this was not the case. Religious, philosophical, and literary traditions remind us that "the

---

34. "Politics as a Vocation," 117, 125–26; *Methodology*, 57. Weber reportedly read Machiavelli at age twelve. See Marianne Weber, *Max Weber: A Biography*, 45.
35. "Politics as a Vocation," 128; "Science as a Vocation," 148.
36. "Politics as a Vocation," 117–19.

world is governed by demons and that he who lets himself in for politics, that is, for power and force as means, contracts with diabolical powers and for his action it is *not* true that good can follow only from good, and evil from evil, but that often the opposite is true. Anyone who fails to see this is, indeed, a political infant."[37] Sometimes, certainly not always, a great political accomplishment requires what we generally call "evil" means, but no ethic in the world can accurately tell us when the end justifies such means and when it does not. "No ethics in the world can dodge the fact that in numerous instances the attainment of 'good' ends is bound to the fact that one must be willing to pay the price of using morally dubious means or at least dangerous ones—and facing the possibility or even the probability of evil ramifications. From no ethics in the world can it be concluded when and to what extent the ethically 'good' purpose 'justifies' the ethically dangerous means and ramifications."[38] Weber despaired of those who unthinkingly mouthed the maxim that the end never justifies the means; that is, he despaired of that "soft-headed" and "unutterably philistine" belief that great political leaders can simply apply everyday private morality to decisions of state.[39] Great political leaders are those who can bring ideals and values to politics, but they know that occasionally one must use the violent means of politics, the latent physical force that defines a state, to accomplish anything great.

Weber, of course, brought his own values to his political analyses. In particular, Weber wanted to preserve individual rights and individuality, both of which were threatened by an ever-increasing bureaucratic domination. But what is the nature of this bureaucratic domination? And what is its origin? To answer these questions we must look at Weber's analysis of the rise of capitalism and the development of what he called rationalization.

The Rise of Capitalism

The single intellectual problem to which Weber returned again and again remains like a leitmotif throughout his writings: why did capitalism *and*

---

37. "Politics as a Vocation," 122–23.
38. "Politics as a Vocation," 121.
39. *Selections in Translation*, ed. Runciman, 267. On Weber's view that the political world is irrational, see Freund, *The Sociology of Max Weber*, 25–32. In a letter to Hannah Arendt, Jaspers wrote that Weber "acquired this usually suppressed meaning from the Old Testament: that God was not only experienced in the covenant as law-giving and merciful, but evil like a devil." See *On Max Weber*, 185.

certain techniques that accompanied capitalism develop only in the West in the seventeenth century and not in China, India, the ancient European world, and so on? While Weber acknowledged that some elements of capitalism and capitalistic undertakings have always existed in the world, from Egypt to Babylon and from India to China, "the Occident has developed capitalism both to a quantitative extent, and . . . in types, forms, and directions that never existed elsewhere." Of course, the reader wonders immediately how Weber has defined capitalism. Is it, for example, the impulse to earn maximum profit? No, that impulse "has existed among waiters, physicians, coachmen, artists, prostitutes, dishonest officials, soldiers, nobles, crusaders, gamblers, and beggars." Instead, Weber defined capitalism as the rational pursuit of profit almost as an end in itself. "Capitalism is identical with the pursuit of profit, and forever *renewed* profit, by means of continuous, rational, capitalistic enterprise."[40] Weber saw himself as modifying Marx. Whereas Marx had suggested that feudalism naturally and inevitably gave birth to capitalism, Weber, with far more detailed and sophisticated historical sources available to him, had examined what I shall loosely call feudalism in China, India, and the ancient world and sought to explain why these other forms of feudalism had not naturally and inevitably given birth to capitalism. Weber's simplified answer is well known. The feudal economies of Asia and the ancient world were hindered by "spiritual obstacles" from developing full-fledged capitalism. To take only one of Weber's examples, the Hindu caste system undermined "the possibility of systematically organizing a commercial enterprise along the lines of a rational business economy," whereas "ascetic Protestantism" gave "ethical sanction for economic rationalism and for the entrepreneur."[41]

One key element—certainly not the only one—that encouraged the demise of European feudalism and the rise of capitalism was a Protestant ethic that reinforced material conditions already present in European economies. Weber was very careful about the limits of his argument. Although he agreed with Marx that class struggles, economic interests, and technological advancements were the most decisive factors in historical development, he argued against what he called a "naïve historical materialism" that claimed these were the only factors of importance. Economic forces alone cannot explain historical change, because one must take into account "political, religious, climatic and countless other non-

---

40. Weber, *The Protestant Ethic and the Spirit of Capitalism*, trans. Talcott Parsons (New York: Scribner's, 1958), 17–21. On Weber's claims about the uniqueness of Europe, see Freund, *The Sociology of Max Weber*, 140–49.

41. *Protestant Ethic*, 26–27; *Sociology of Religion*, 42.

economic determinants."[42] In looking at the role of the Protestant ethic in developing capitalism, Weber pointedly said that he was examining only "one side of the causal chain," that he was accentuating only one of a "combination of circumstances," and that it was not his "aim to substitute for a one-sided materialistic an equally one-sided spiritualistic causal interpretation of culture and history."[43] Weber emphasized, in fact, the "limits to the power of religion" in bringing historical change. Religion can only assist in bringing about an economic transformation if there are already "present in the existing relationships and constellations of interests certain possibilities of, or even powerful drives toward, such an economic transformation."[44] Weber's careful qualifications to his analysis have not stopped his critics from charging that he regarded Protestantism as by itself sufficient in causing capitalism. Fernand Braudel, for example, has written, "For Max Weber, capitalism in the modern sense of the word was no more and no less than a creation of Protestantism or, to be even more accurate, of Puritanism. All historians [sic] have opposed this tenuous theory, although they have not managed to be rid of it once and for all. Yet it is clearly false."[45] This description of Weber's work is simplistic nonsense.

Weber noted at least fourteen prerequisites or codeterminants that existed in Europe before Protestantism assisted in the birth of capitalism. First, a system of private property—"land, apparatus, machinery, tools, etc. as disposable property of autonomous private industrial enterprises."[46] Second, cities or the "city-commune," which, "in the full meaning of the word" appeared only in the Occident. Weber put special emphasis on the medieval city that developed markets, autonomous law, and "a distinct 'bourgeois' estate."[47] Third, the development of an urban economy—as opposed both to a household economy and to a national economy—that includes markets, trade fairs, and, most basically, trade that is "very an-

42. Protestant Ethic, 55; Methodology, 70–71.

43. Protestant Ethic, 27, 13, 183.

44. Sociology of Religion, 208.

45. Fernand Braudel, Afterthoughts on Material Civilization, trans. Patricia Ranum (Baltimore: Johns Hopkins University Press, 1977), 65–66. For a comparison of Weber and Braudel, see an essay by Roth in Guenther Roth and Wolfgang Schluchter, Max Weber's Vision of History: Ethics and Methods (Berkeley and Los Angeles: University of California Press, 1979), 166–94. Weber's complex analysis renders a single case study problematic, for example, Rex A. Lucas, "A Specification of the Weber Thesis: Plymouth Colony," History and Theory 10, no. 3 (1971): 318–46. A more convincing attempt to critique Weber is Richard Ashcraft, "Marx and Weber on Liberalism as Bourgeois Ideology," Comparative Studies in Society and History 14, no. 2 (1972): 130–68.

46. General Economic History, 276.

47. Economy and Society, 1226, 1322–23.

tagonistic" to the "tightly-knit structure of the feudal hierarchy."[48] Fourth, a mobile labor force. Capitalism needed a "free labor market," which was necessarily in opposition to a manorial system that restricted the mobility of peasant labor. In England, this problem was solved with enclosure laws, the creation of surplus labor for the cities, and a system of "compulsory labor" that taught individuals the "discipline" of factory work.[49] Fifth, rapid population growth that in Europe, unlike in China, came at just the right moment, creating a needed labor force and not an excessive number of unwanted consumers. Sixth, "mass market demand," helped in European history by the price revolution of the sixteenth and seventeenth centuries, which gave agricultural producers more money for their crops, while it kept the prices of finished products more or less stable.[50]

Seventh, a system of "calculable law," so that a merchant might "depend upon calculable adjudication and administration." In this instance, the highly developed legal system under feudalism helped the development of capitalism, although Weber gave great credit to Protestant sects for defending the rights of the individual against the state, for helping to create "formal legal equality," and for a defense of property rights, all of which eventually undermined feudal law and encouraged a legal system more conducive to later capitalism.[51] Eighth, "the separation of business from the household," a development that fostered more efficient use of the labor force.[52] Ninth, the "art" of accounting, or double-entry bookkeeping, which Weber stressed repeatedly. Weber argued that this crucial development in the history of capitalism arose first in medieval Italy and could not be found in Babylonia, India, or China, because in Asia "the trading association remained a closed family affair and accountability was therefore unnecessary."[53] Tenth, the emergence of banking as not just a safe depository of funds or a way to transfer funds but as a way of financing money-making enterprises, a development that arose in medieval Genoa and Renaissance Florence.[54]

Eleventh, the development of science and technology. On the one hand,

---

48. *Economy and Society*, 1093, 1214–18; *General Economic History*, 220.

49. *General Economic History*, 94, 306–7.

50. *General Economic History*, 310–11, 352.

51. *General Economic History*, 277; *Economy and Society*, 1101, 1208–10. See Sally Ewing, "Formal Justice and the Spirit of Capitalism: Max Weber's Sociology of Law," *Law and Society Review* 21, no. 3 (1987): 487–512.

52. *Protestant Ethic*, 21–22.

53. *General Economic History*, 224–25; *Economy and Society*, 1322; *Protestant Ethic*, 21–22.

54. *General Economic History*, 254–66.

Weber pointedly rejected an argument of technological determinism by dismissing the crude Marxist claim that "the hand-mill requires feudalism just as the steam-mill necessitates capitalism." Steam mills, noted Weber, can well exist under state socialist economies, and hand-mills existed under every type of prefeudal economy. On the other hand, Weber recognized that capitalism was "strongly influenced by the development of technical possibilities, . . . [and was] dependent on the peculiarities of modern science." While he knew, of course, that key scientific discoveries were not unique to Europe, the practical and productive use of these discoveries was welcomed by nascent "capitalistic interests." Science and technology, for Weber, were necessary but hardly sufficient prerequisites for the development of capitalism.[55] Twelfth, the availability of key natural resources. Had Europe not discovered coal and iron at key moments, then modern capitalism might never had appeared, and "thus iron became *the most important factor* in the development of capitalism."[56]

Thirteenth, a special class—the burghers of the middle ages—that had an interest in rational economic production. Weber steadfastly maintained that "the concept of citizen has not existed outside the Occident, and that of the bourgeoisie outside the modern Occident." Within Western medieval cities, the burghers were the "carriers" of modern democracy, just as wealthier peasants had been the key force for democracy in antiquity. Weber defined these burghers as "all those who shared the 'bourgeois' burdens owing to the king (guard and military duties, court service, tax payments) with the other townsmen." This class of burghers became the source of military power independent of king and lord, of demands for political rights and representation, and, above all, of the demand for economic independence. Among other roles, the burgher became the modern *homo economicus,* and Weber even remarked that the Reformation was "codetermined" by the economic interests of this class. Capitalism developed first in England, where this class was comparatively little encumbered by the monarchs and their officials, and took longer to emerge in countries such as France, where a bureaucratic state could hinder this class more effectively.[57]

Finally, Weber insisted that the state must play a key role in allowing capitalism to develop, that the state must overcome those classes opposed to capitalist production. Weber distinguished between patrimonial-

55. *Economy and Society,* 1091; *Protestant Ethic,* 24–25.
56. *General Economic History,* 304–5 (emphasis added).
57. *Protestant Ethic,* 23; *Economy and Society,* 1347, 1278, 1261–67, 1354, 1196, 1097–110. Weber also noted that the proletariat, as a class, first developed in the Occident. See *Protestant Ethic,* 23.

ism and feudalism, although he acknowledged that feudalism was a variant of patrimonialism. Patrimonialism was a state in which authority was immediately dependent on an identifiable ruler, whereas feudalism was a state that gave great autonomy to a system of decentralized authority. In Europe, at least up to the French Revolution, and in a country such as China, Weber saw what he called a patrimonial bureaucratic state. Both patrimonialism and feudalism were hostile to capitalist production, but over time the patrimonial state came to be dominated by a centralized bureaucracy of trained officials that was not threatened by capitalist classes. Thus, capitalism developed either as in England, where plutocratic notables gained political power, or more slowly but just as surely in countries such as France, where professional bureaucracies of the patrimonial state finally defeated the privileged classes of feudalism. In each case the role of the state was crucial, and in the end the bureaucratic state lived harmoniously with capitalism as both dominated Europe. "But no country and no age has ever experienced, in the same sense as the modern Occident, the absolute and complete dependence of its whole existence, of the political, technical, and economic conditions of its life, on a specially trained *organization* of officials."[58] Capitalism and bureaucracy were victorious together. In his own time, the bureaucratic nation states of Europe were quite eager to pursue the capitalist interests of empire.[59]

All of these fourteen prerequisites or codeterminants—only some of which Weber saw developing first in Europe—constituted the fertile soil from which capitalism grew in Europe. Weber still doubted that by themselves these important codeterminants would have engendered capitalism, had it not been for one last factor unique to Europe—a religious ethic that reinforced the tendency to develop capitalism. Only in Protestant Europe and North America did Weber see religion unintentionally promoting, not hindering, the emergence of capitalism.

After decades of exhaustive studies of the world's religions, Weber concluded that there were "only two consistent avenues for escaping the tension between religion and the economic world in a principled and *inward* manner." First, a contemplative mysticism in which one attempts to be a vessel of God in order to possess what is holy. The mystic characteristically withdrew from a corrupt world into a passive asceticism where labor was generally viewed as a distraction from the contemplation needed for salvation. Although Weber acknowledged that such mysticism

58. *Protestant Ethic*, 16; *Economy and Society*, 1010–109, esp. 1085–92; *From Max Weber*, ed. and trans. Gerth and Mills, 298; *Protestant Ethic*, 72; *General Economic History*, 347–49.
59. *Economy and Society*, 346.

could be found in Europe, he saw it as characteristic of almost all Asian religions and their sects. Second, one could attempt to resolve the tension between religion and the economic world by active asceticism. Here one attempted to do God's bidding in the world, to undertake a vocation outlined by God, and one became not a passive vessel of the holy but an active tool of the divine. Weber illustrated the difference between contemplative mysticism and active asceticism by contrasting Dante with Milton. Whereas the poet in the *Divine Comedy* arrives in paradise and "stands speechless in his passive contemplation of the secrets of God," the characters in *Paradise Lost,* after being expelled from paradise, announce that they have work to do and a world to make.[60]

Protestantism, as an example of active asceticism, offered a "moral justification of worldly activity," particularly through Luther's concept of the calling *(Beruf)*. An individual with a calling regarded work in this world not as something to be shunned but indeed as a divine command.[61] While labor in one's calling certainly enhanced capitalist productivity, it did more than that, according to Weber, to encourage the development of capitalism, because over time the habits engendered by laboring in one's calling produced men and women for whom labor became an end in itself. In brief, Protestantism altered human nature. "Labour must, on the contrary, be performed as if it were an absolute end in itself, a calling. But such an attitude is by no means a product of nature. It cannot be evoked by low wages or high ones alone, but can only be the product of a long and arduous process of education. Today, capitalism, once in the saddle, can recruit its laboring force in all industrial countries with comparative ease. In the past this was in every case an extremely difficult problem."[62] In traditional societies men and women labored until they met their needs and then quit working, but Protestantism taught men and women to discipline themselves and to regard labor as an end in itself and, as a secondary consequence, "to earn more and more money" without regard to need. It is, of course, but a short step to Weber's notion that a capitalist is one who looks upon earning money and making profit as if they were ends in themselves. The capitalist "gets nothing out of his wealth for himself, except the irrational sense of having done his job well. But it is just that which seems to the pre-capitalistic man so incomprehensible and mysterious, so unworthy and contemptible."[63] Not the

60. *Protestant Ethic*, 87–88; *From Max Weber,* ed. and trans. Gerth and Mills, 332, 333, 323–25, 285.
61. *Protestant Ethic*, 81, 84–85.
62. *Protestant Ethic*, 62.
63. *Protestant Ethic*, 60, 70–71.

Renaissance but instead the Reformation managed to "transform the soul of man," and Protestantism became "a powerful, unconsciously refined organization for the production of capitalistic individuals."[64]

The early Protestant was enjoined to labor in this world and certainly to profit from such labor, but to shun all enjoyment of the wealth that ensued. Individuals must be in the world but not of it, to labor in their worldly callings but to keep their eyes on the importance of the next world. "Wealth is thus bad ethically only in so far as it is a temptation to idleness and sinful enjoyment of life, and its acquisition is bad only when it is with the purpose of later living merrily and without care. But as a performance of duty in a calling it is not only morally permissible, but actually enjoined."[65] Protestantism demanded of its believers, not the celibacy of the medieval monk, but certainly marriage, mainly for the sake of procreation, and certainly the avoidance of sexual pleasure; not poverty, but certainly the elimination of idleness, luxury, and even the enjoyment of one's wealth; not the subdued life of the cloister, but certainly the curbing of spontaneity, art, and emotion. "The clear and uniform goal of this asceticism was the disciplining and methodical organization of the whole pattern of life." Weber quoted one observer who sought to sum up the Reformation. "You think you have escaped from the monastery, but everyone must now be a monk throughout his life."[66]

No ethic could more readily bring about the labor discipline needed for capitalism and, as individuals made money they could not enjoy, the savings necessary for capital investment. "When the limitation of consumption is combined with the release of acquisitive activity, the inevitable practical result is obvious: accumulation of capital through ascetic compulsion to save."[67] Weber acknowledged that by the eighteenth and nineteenth centuries the proliferation of wealth under capitalism had reinforced a secularism that destroyed the religious roots of the capitalist ethic, and he saw at work only the practical religiosity of a Franklin when, for example, Americans regarded it as good for business and for the obtaining of credit to attend church and to be honest, punctual, and frugal. "The religious root of modern economic humanity [was] dead; today the concept of the calling is a *caput mortuum* in the world." The promise of the eighteenth and nineteenth centuries was the Enlightenment promise of material progress for all who were hardworking, a false promise to the middle and working classes of eternal happiness in material abundance.

---

64. *General Economic History*, 368.
65. *Protestant Ethic*, 163; also 53.
66. *Sociology of Religion*, 183; *General Economic History*, 366.
67. *Protestant Ethic*, 172.

The "boiling heat" of modern capitalism was linked, not to religion, but to the "heedless consumption of natural resources," but still, even though the original religious stimulation to capitalism had faded, it remained a historically important element in capitalism's development.[68]

But why had the motivation for adopting this ethic of worldly asceticism been so strong? Weber found the answer to this question in the effects of Calvin's original doctrine of predestination. Calvin's doctrine stated that not a drop of rain fell without the express consent of God, that each was predestined either for eternal damnation or to be among the elect in Heaven, that no individual could earn salvation either by good works or by faith, and that salvation was always unearned, freely bestowed by a merciful God. Each of us deserves damnation, and each of us can do nothing to help attain salvation; we cannot even turn toward God and have faith without God's grace, which is never deserved. That means, of course, each of us is utterly alone, without reassurance from church, priests, or sacraments. "In its extreme inhumanity this doctrine must have had one consequence for the life of a generation which surrendered to its magnificent consistency. That was a feeling of unprecedented inner loneliness of the single individual . . . he was forced to follow his path alone to meet a destiny which had been decreed from him for eternity."[69]

In the generations after Calvin, this doctrine became unbearable, and while ministers continued to put forth the doctrine of predestination, they also suggested that one could find reassuring signs that one was among the chosen. If one continued to resist temptation and continued to battle sin, it was a sign that one might be among the elect. If one did good works for the community, these could not earn the grace of God or salvation, but they were signs that one had God's favor. Good works were "the technical means, not of purchasing salvation, but of getting rid of the fear of damnation." Ironically, a doctrine of predestination that might lead to a passive fatalism, spurred enormous activity in the world as each individual sought to obtain reassurance on the single most important question in one's life. "Waste of time is thus the first and in principle the deadliest of sins. The span of human life is infinitely short and precious to make sure of one's own election. Loss of time through sociability, idle talk,

---

68. *General Economic History*, 368–69; *Protestant Ethic*, 52, 175; *From Max Weber*, ed. and trans. Gerth and Mills, 304–7, 366. In a 1904 letter from Oklahoma, Weber wrote, "With almost lightning speed everything that stands in the way of capitalist culture is being crushed." Cited by Marianne Weber, *Max Weber: A Biography*, 293.

69. *Protestant Ethic*, 104.

luxury, even more sleep than is necessary . . . is worthy of absolute moral condemnation."[70]

What single activity became the most important in this effort for reassurance? Labor in one's calling. Protestant ministers after Calvin suggested that success in one's calling—an enterprise, after all, in which one did God's bidding—was a sign that one was among the elect. From here it was but a short step to the claim that profitability in one's business indicated that one had God's blessing, and if God showed one of His elect a way to make a higher profit, then one must obey God with all available energy. In this key way the Protestant ethic inadvertently provided enormous energy and intelligence to the developing capitalism. "The religious valuation of restless, continuous, systematic work in a worldly calling, as the highest means to asceticism, and at the same time the surest and most evident proof of rebirth and genuine faith, must have been the most powerful conceivable lever for the expansion of that attitude toward life which we have here called the spirit of capitalism."[71]

If Protestantism supplied a motivating energy for profitable labor in one's calling, it also provided a moral justification of the capitalist economic system. By urging each to work in his or her calling, Protestantism reinforced the growing specialized division of labor; by praising those who undertook profitable enterprises, it belittled aristocrats and gave providential sanction to the self-made businessperson; by claiming that God favored those who prospered, it broke the traditional ethic that sneered at the habits of acquisition; and by supporting the new economic order, it gave the capitalist "comforting assurance that the unequal distribution of goods of this world was a special dispensation of Divine Providence."[72] To workers diligently laboring in their individual callings and suffering from "ruthless exploitation," Calvinism and capitalism offered "the prospect of eternal salvation."[73]

By drawing a contrast between Eastern religions and Protestantism, Weber also was attempting to show how ideas, at key junctures, can become a powerful force in history. Weber claimed that Asian religions looked upon the world as something always present and eminently unchangeable, a "great enchanted garden" that one was to adapt to, unite with, or revere. By contrast, the early Protestant thought the world was something originally created and still changeable, and indeed, the Puritans thought God had commanded them to change the world and bring it

---

70. *Protestant Ethic*, 115, 157–58; also *Sociology of Religion*, 203.
71. *Protestant Ethic*, 172, 162; *Economy and Society*, 1198–200.
72. *Protestant Ethic*, 177, 163, 171.
73. *General Economic History*, 367.

into accord with His laws.[74] Ordinarily ideas have little effect on historical change, even ideas as dramatically different as these. Weber agreed with Marx that the economic interests of classes and status groups, the struggles of parties and elites, technological change, patterns of trade, demographic changes, and so forth, are generally the determining factors in history. But at key moments in history, when the balance of all these material forces is precarious, ideas—or what Weber called ideal interests, that is, the interests that classes, groups, and individuals have in attaining certain goals and ideas—can matter. Material interests remain the locomotive force in history, but at these key moments ideas can push history in a slightly different direction, a difference that can become highly significant, just as a slight nudge to an arrow at its initial launching can change its ultimate destination dramatically. "Not ideas, but material and ideal interests, directly govern men's conduct. Yet very frequently the 'world images' that have been created by 'ideas' have, like switchmen, determined the tracks along which action has been pushed by the dynamic of interests." In the seventeenth century, the ideas of one city— Calvin's Geneva—originated independently of any class interests or any Marxist economic substructure and became an "effective force" in history and "influenced the development of material culture" in Europe overwhelmingly.[75] This was encouraging to Weber because it meant the future was open-ended, at least to some small degree, and perhaps one nation or one political party or one charismatic leader, at some crucial moment, could temporarily forestall Weber's fear of bureaucratic domination.

The Rationalization of the World

Although Weber was certainly interested in the origins of modern capitalism, he was at least as interested in key developments that accompanied capitalism into the world, developments he loosely labeled the rationalization of the world. What did Weber mean by this word *rationalization*? He did not mean that human beings had become more moral or more rational in some philosophic sense, and he certainly did not mean Europe

---

74. *Sociology of Religion*, 178–79, 270; *From Max Weber*, ed. and trans. Gerth and Mills, 336–40.

75. *From Max Weber*, ed. and trans. Gerth and Mills, 280; Weber, *Protestant Ethic*, 90–92; *Economy and Society*, 285. For a good critical commentary on Weber's thesis in his *Protestant Ethic*, see Herbert Luethy, "Once Again: Calvinism and Capitalism," in *Max Weber*, ed. Wrong, 123–34; also Reinhard Bendix, "Japan and the Protestant Ethic," in *Scholarship and Partisanship*, ed. Bendix and Roth, 188–206.

had become better in some absolute sense. Rationalization is the process of developing efficient techniques and of applying instrumental reason to every aspect of the social, economic, and even natural world—from law to art, from bookkeeping to banking, from organizing the finances of political parties to organizing men and women by means of bureaucracies— in the interest of the efficient attainment of given ends. Weber illustrated it this way. Rationalization does not mean we know more about the conditions under which we live than, say, did an early American tribe. "The savage," in fact, "knows incomparably more about his tools." But rationalization of the world means that if we do not know how a radio or a refrigerator works, we *could* know, because we are certain that scientific and instrumental reason has constructed the world around us. "Hence, [rationalization] means that principally there are no mysterious incalculable forces that come into play, but rather that one can, in principle master all things by calculation. This means the world is disenchanted. One need no longer have recourse to magical means in order to master or implore the spirits, as did the savage, for whom such mysterious powers existed. Technical means and calculations perform the service."[76]

Whereas rationalization and the use of instrumental reason certainly existed before capitalism, in what Weber called traditional societies, the application of instrumental reason in virtually every sphere of life in the interests of efficiency, and especially economic efficiency, came into the world with capitalism. Rationalization thus became a "revolutionary force," overturning superstitions, religions, and traditions and no longer allowing "the unthinking acquiescence in customary ways."[77] Weber's studies convinced him that whereas non-Western cultures exhibited "philosophical and theological wisdom of the most profound sort" as well as creative discoveries in science and the arts, only in the West did this sweeping rationalization occur. Only in the West or at least first in the West, according to Weber, science developed fully; mathematical principles were applied to astronomy; the concept of "rational proof" was applied to geometry; the concept of experiment was used in the natural sciences; the practice of medicine rested on biological and biochemical discoveries; Thucydides and others developed a rational historiography; Aristotle and others outlined systematic political classifications; Roman law began a system of rational jurisprudence; the rationalization of music, including the "formation of the tone material on the basis of three triads with the harmonic third," occurred; "the rational use of the Gothic vault as a

76. "Science as a Vocation," 139. On the concept of rationalization, see Freund, *The Sociology of Max Weber*, 17–24, 278–83; and Löwith, *Max Weber and Karl Marx*, 40–60.
77. *Economy and Society*, 1116, 30, 71.

means of distributing pressure" in architecture was developed; painters developed "the rational utilization of lines and spatial perspective"; the use of the printing press for newspapers became widespread; entrepreneurs developed capital accounting and bookkeeping; "the rational capitalistic organization of (formally) free labour" emerged; and finally, "rational structures of law and of administration" were first developed. Weber suggested that all of these developments either accompanied capitalism into the world or were used, promoted, reinforced, or further developed by capitalism.[78]

Weber said repeatedly that the rationalization that took place in Europe did not make Europe or European culture one whit superior to other cultures. Technical progress might well mean moral or aesthetic regress; because a development is instrumentally more rational, it is not necessarily substantively more rational. "It is not true," for example, "that the work of art of a period that has worked out new technical means, or, for instance, the laws of perspective, stands therefore artistically higher."[79] Similarly, Weber did not claim that Western law or administration or political economy was better because more instrumentally rational. Nevertheless, if the rationalization of the world does not make life better, it is a crucially important development in history, a "development having *universal* significance and value."[80] Again the pessimistic Hegelian theme is visible in Weber's work. After reading Weber's *General Economic History,* for example, one puts down the work and forgets the voluminous detail, only then to see the recurring themes or arguments—that the economic, industrial, and administrative worlds are all becoming more instrumentally rational, and thus that reason of a sort is systematically and irreversibly developing throughout history, but that the world is not becoming better or more substantively rational. In fact, rationalization brings with it new and more disturbing forms of domination, or tyranny.

In his famous lecture "Science as a Vocation," Weber offered an abbre-

---

78. *Protestant Ethic,* 13–31. For a good discussion of Weber's key question—why did capitalism and rationalization arise in Europe?—see Wolfgang Schluchter, *The Rise of Western Rationalism: Max Weber's Developmental History,* trans. Guenther Roth (Berkeley and Los Angeles: University of California Press, 1981), esp. 1–12. Karl Loewenstein relates an illustrative anecdote about meeting Weber: "During our chat he must have noticed that I was interested in music . . . he began to block out a sociology of music for my benefit . . . I had thought that music flows from emotional and aesthetic sources; and I now drank in his words as he explained that music, too, has rational and sociological foundations." Related in Loewenstein, *Max Weber's Political Ideas in the Perspective of Our Time,* trans. Richard Winston and Clara Winston (Amherst: University of Massachusetts Press, 1966), 93.

79. *From Max Weber,* ed. and trans. Gerth and Mills, 137; *Methodology,* 35–38.

80. *Protestant Ethic,* 13.

viated history of reason in the West. For Socrates and Plato, reason, or science, was to be the tool for discovering beauty, truth, happiness, and justice. During the Renaissance, reason was a way both to true art and to a meaningful relation with nature. At about the same time, reason and science endeavored to discover the meanings God had put into nature, and hence reason was a way to God. And in the Enlightenment, reason and science promised to bring a world of plenty and thus engineer human happiness. For Weber, all the grandiose dreams and promises of reason had collapsed. Only a "few big children in university chairs" thought that reason could discover beauty and justice, or bring a meaningful relation to nature, or find the intentions of God; and "after Nietzsche's devastating criticism of those 'last men' who 'invented happiness,' I may leave aside altogether the naïve optimism in which science . . . has been celebrated as the way to happiness." Reason succeeded only in disenchanting the world, in uprooting mysteries, superstitions, and religion, but reason proved itself quite incapable of giving meaning to life. Tolstoi, according to Weber, saw this most clearly in his broodings about whether death had meaning for modern men and women. In traditional societies, where all important questions had an answer, one could die meaningfully—fulfilled and "satiated with life"—after living through clearly defined cycles of life, whereas in modern societies, with endless technical change euphemistically called progress, death has no meaning and one is never "fulfilled," but at most "tired of life."[81] Once again Weber is the disciple of Nietzsche. All the bold claims of European philosophers, that they could use reason to discover substantive truths, proved false, and the world has been left with only instrumental reason and science—precisely that which is meaningless.

And yet this uncontrolled development of instrumental reason, this rationalization of the world, is frighteningly important because it defines our world. Nowhere is this more clear than in the way the West manages to organize individuals efficiently—with bureaucracy. Certainly other societies experienced bureaucracies—Egyptian officials who surveyed the Nile, Chinese officials who regulated rivers and canals, officials under the

<hr />

81. "Science as a Vocation," 139–43. On the concept of disenchantment, see Sheldon Wolin, "Postmodern Politics and the Absence of Myth," *Social Research* 52, no. 2 (1985): 217–39. Wolin elsewhere argues that disenchantment leads readily to a politics based mainly on power ("Max Weber: Legitimation, Method, and the Politics of Theory," *Political Theory* 9, no. 3 [1981]: 401–24). Mark Warren, also discussing the concept of disenchantment, suggests that it may lead to what he calls "bureaucratic nihilism" ("Max Weber's Liberalism for a Nietzschean World," *American Political Science Review* 82, no. 1 [1988]: 31–50). See also Arthur Mitzman, *The Iron Cage: An Historical Interpretation of Max Weber* (New York: Knopf, 1970), 219–52.

Roman Empire—but not to the extent of the modern world after capitalism. The key development in the rationalization of the world, and the
development that most distressed Weber, was the rise to preeminence of
bureaucratic organizations in the state, in political parties, in corporations, and in factories, and although such pervasive bureaucracies accompanied capitalism into the world, they were destined to outlast that
economic system.[82] It is this aspect of rationalization that most frightened
Weber, and the theme of the individual threatened with oppression and
stultification by a new form of bureaucratic domination threads its way
through all of his writings. Bureaucracy has become the only conceivable
way to organize men and women in the modern world. "Since bureaucracy has a 'rational' character, with rules, means-ends calculus, and
matter-of-factness predominating, its rise and expansion has everywhere
had 'revolutionary' results. . . . The march of bureaucracy accordingly
destroyed structures of domination that were not rational," that is, not
instrumentally rational.[83]

Domination

In attempting to translate Weber's use of the word *Herrschaft* into English,
his translators have tried "legitimacy," "domination," "imperative control," and "leadership," but they have agreed only that there is no exact
equivalent in English. I translate *Herrschaft* as "domination" because it
conveys his pessimistic view that in every social order individuals are
greatly controlled and have, at best, a limited freedom. Weber defined
domination as "the probability that certain specific commands (or all
commands) will be obeyed by a given group of persons." Behind such a
definition stands Weber's assumption that in every society there are a few
who issue commands and a great many who obey, and thus Weber was
willing to suggest that domination is "a special case of power" and to
equate domination with "*authoritarian power of command.*" Weber willingly acknowledged that every form of successful domination rests on a
foundation of some "minimum of voluntary compliance," including the
formally free contracts or agreements of employers and workers, lords
and vassals, and so forth.[84] Despite the formally free character of such

---

82. *Protestant Ethic*, 16.
83. *Economy and Society*, 1002–3; see Mommsen, *Max Weber and German Politics*, 61. For
a good discussion of the development of capitalism and rationalization, see Reinhard
Bendix, *Max Weber: An Intellectual Portrait* (Garden City, N.Y.: Doubleday, 1960), 71–99.
84. *Economy and Society*, 212, 941, 946, 212, 61–62, 53–54.

contracts, Weber used the term domination to suggest that there is always control, subordination, and oppression in every society, although certainly the harshness of the subjection is not always the same.

Every successful form of domination must inculcate what Weber called discipline, defined as "the probability that by virtue of habituation a command will receive prompt and automatic obedience in stereotyped forms, on the part of a given group of persons." Once again Weber's assumption is that the majority is generally unthinking, that discipline necessarily entails "uncritical and unresisting mass obedience" in which "all personal criticism is unconditionally suspended." Men and women are "trained" for "submission" or "habituated" to "blind obedience," and their actions under a system of discipline become predictably "uniform." Although Weber did not paint a complimentary picture of what happens to men and women after they are trained for discipline, he consistently maintained that discipline is a part of every viable social order. "Discipline in general . . . is impersonal. Unfailingly neutral, it places itself at the disposal of every power that claims its service." As with domination, however, the extent of discipline varies. Weber claimed, for example, that the discipline of the feudal lord over the vassal was "limited."[85]

Weber noted many historical precedents of modern discipline. Church rulers, whenever in power, sought to "domesticate" their subjects (especially women in convents) in all matters "great and little"; medieval monasteries served the purpose of "disciplining [the monk] in the service of his otherworldly master" (and to the profit of his master in this world); and successful military leaders from the Spartans to the Bolsheviks sought an all-encompassing military discipline.[86] Military training, which Weber had abhorred in his youth, is the model for all discipline. "Military discipline gives birth to all discipline. The *large-scale economic organization* is the second great agency which trains men for discipline. No direct historical transitions link the Pharaonic workshops and construction projects . . . with the Carthaginian-Roman plantation, the mines of the late Middle-Ages, the slave plantation of colonial economies, and finally the modern factory. However, all of these have in common the one element of *discipline.*"[87]

Again Weber's pessimism stands out; to link the modern factory with the Pharaohs' building projects and medieval mines is implicitly to criticize the Enlightenment view of progress. Indeed, with modern rationalization the discipline of the modern factory can be even more extensive.

85. *Economy and Society*, 53, 1148–49, 1079.
86. *Economy and Society*, 1176, 1152–53.
87. *Economy and Society*, 1155.

American "scientific management," for example, calculated how to extract maximum profitability from the motions of an individual worker. "The psycho-physical apparatus of man is completely adjusted to the demands of the outer world, the tools, the machines—in short, it is functionalized, and the individual is shorn of his natural rhythm." In brief, compared to the discipline of the feudal manor, that of the modern factory is worse. "Thus, discipline inexorably takes over ever larger areas as the satisfaction of political and economic needs is increasingly rationalized." Again a familiar theme: as domination and discipline become more complete, they "eradicate" individuality.[88]

Weber frequently used the phrase "structure of domination," indicating, like Montesquieu or Marx, that a social order of domination is an intricate whole in which the constellation of classes and interest groups is directly related to and reinforced by the law, religions, beliefs, habits, and so forth. Although Weber admitted that one might find what one loosely calls domination in lecture halls and drawing rooms and erotic relationships, he did not want to broaden the definition of domination that much. Like Marx, Weber saw economic and class interests as the ordinary basis of domination. "Not every position of economic power, however, represents domination in our sense of the word. Nor does domination utilize in every case economic power for its foundation and maintenance. But in the vast majority of cases, and indeed in the most important ones, this is just what happens." On such an economic foundation rests a ruling minority, an administrative staff ("every domination both expresses itself and functions through administration"), and a state ("the modern state is a compulsory association which organizes domination").[89]

Although Weber did refer to "Sultanist despotism" and did write about tyrants, it is precisely because he was well aware that the words *despot* and *tyrant* had specific origins and meanings in the classical world that he tended to avoid applying them, because of what he considered their limited accuracy, to the modern world. Occasionally he used the words *tyranny* and *domination* interchangeably, but most often he used the words *tyrant* and *tyranny* in their specific Greek meanings. A tyrant was someone widely perceived to be ruling illegitimately, someone who ruled by making allies with some classes against others. Typically, the Greek tyrant joined the middle classes and debtor classes against the nobility, whereas in Italian city-states, the only other case in which he used the

---

88. *Economy and Society*, 1156, 1149.
89. *Economy and Society*, 941–54, 942, 948; "Politics as a Vocation," 82.

word *tyrant,* the tyrant, or prince, pitted the nobility and the masses against the new burgher class.[90]

When Weber used the word *tyranny,* he could point to a specific and identifiable tyrant. But he used the concept of a structure of domination, at least in part, to escape the old notion that a tyranny always needs an identifiable tyrant. For example, under what he called "the domination of capital" and in general under modern forms of bureaucratic domination, men and women are dominated and disciplined not so much by an individual or even a class as by impersonal and intangible forces such as markets, institutions, technical requirements such as specialization, and an internalized ethic. Thus, at least in the modern world, Weber—like Tocqueville and Marx earlier, and like Foucault later—sought to describe a new form of tyranny without an identifiable tyrant. "Most of the time this [domination of capital] appears in such an indirect form that one cannot identify any concrete master." Weber was quite fond of Wagner's phrase "masterless slavery" as a description of the domination of capital.[91]

Every structure of domination has at its foundation not only economic interests but also a widely accepted system of beliefs that legitimizes the pattern of domination. "In general, it should be kept clearly in mind that the basis of every [domination], and correspondingly every willingness to obey, is a *belief*" that lends legitimation and prestige to the given structure of domination. Every group or class that benefits from power or domination has a need to justify itself, to convince itself and those subject to this power that any inequalities or advantages or apparent injustices are deserved, legitimate, or at least inevitable. If those who rule are successful, the dominated will believe the structure of domination to be legitimate and will take the beliefs of their rulers as maxims of their own conduct. Sometimes religion can accomplish this. "What the privileged classes require of religion, if anything at all, is this psychological assurance of legitimacy," or "in short, religion provides the theodicy of good fortune for those who are fortunate."[92] Nevertheless, whether Weber focused on religion or a secular ethic, he wanted to stress beliefs, ideas, habits, and ideologies—an "ethos"—almost as much as economic interests, although he generally admitted that such an "ethos" grew out of and reinforced the economic and political interests of the dominant groups and classes. Again, Weber had little confidence in the "masses," whose

90. "Politics as a Vocation," 82; *Economy and Society,* 1316–17, 1267–71, 1305–9.

91. *Economy and Society,* 1186–88; *Sociology of Religion,* 234–35.

92. *Economy and Society,* 263; *Sociology of Religion,* 107; *From Max Weber,* ed. and trans. Gerth and Mills, 271; *Economy and Society,* 953–54, 946.

"natural state" is to think critically about the structure of domination only in times of crisis and acute struggle of classes and groups. Although Weber admitted that there will always be social conflict and conflict between ideas and that hence no structure of domination can attain its desired uniformity of opinion, still he maintained that the great majority of individuals are "conditioned to obedience."[93] To take one example: like Tocqueville, Weber admired American voluntary associations that prevented society from becoming "a formless sand heap of individuals" and kept alive a diversity of opinion, but such a pattern of associations was destined to be a nostalgic exception under modern structures of domination. Instead, isolated individuals trained and disciplined by the structure of domination would be forced, quite literally on pain of "extinction," to work in a specialized role of the division of labor, to accept the belief that a growing standard of living was central to the good life, and to follow an ethic of self-interest, because any oppositional ethic of genuine spiritual asceticism or brotherliness or cooperation was becoming both impossible and unimaginably utopian.[94]

Although Weber insisted that there has always been domination, he feared that "in the womb of the future" the potential of a qualitatively new and quantitatively more extensive type of domination will be ripening. Although such a domination accompanied capitalism and rationalization into the world, it seems certain to outlast the former while it builds upon the latter. The world, said Weber, "is busy fabricating the shell of bondage which men will perhaps be forced to inhabit some day, as powerless as the fellahs of ancient Egypt." On the one hand, he was referring to a rationalized bureaucratic administration that might take over both the state and all economic enterprises, "fettering" each individual to his or her job, class, and occupation.[95] On the other hand, Weber emphasized that such a tyranny would not be simply forced upon us from without, but its legitimacy would be accepted because of a system of beliefs that accompanied capitalism into the world. "Man is dominated by the making of money, by acquisition as the ultimate purpose in life," that is, by an ethos of capitalism that insists upon individuals' postponing gratification in order to make money. The new domination that he feared originated, in part, in an "unexampled tyranny of Puritanism" that brought forth an "unbearable" control of the individual. The frequent claim that the Reformation undermined the control of the Catholic Church over everyday life

93. *Economy and Society*, 1104, 953–54; *Methodology*, 26; "Politics as a Vocation," 80.

94. *From Max Weber*, ed. and trans. Gerth and Mills, 310, 331; *Economy and Society*, 1186–88.

95. *Economy and Society*, 1402.

overlooks the fact that the Reformation brought new forms of control, "a regulation of the whole of conduct which, penetrating to all departments of private and public life, was infinitely burdensome and earnestly enforced."[96]

In seeking to destroy the spontaneous enjoyment of life, Calvinism became a religion of introspective watchfulness, a religion that insisted individuals attain "methodical control" over their impulses, indeed a religion of moral bookkeeping in which individuals both literally and figuratively noted down temptations, sins, and good works, trying to balance saintly books. This "rational planning of the whole of one's life" originated in religious commands, but became an internalized ethic for a new economic world. "The Puritan wanted to work in a calling; we are forced to do so. For when asceticism was carried out of monastic cells into everyday life, and began to dominate worldly morality, it did its part in building the tremendous cosmos of the modern economic order."[97] Having thrown off its religious trappings, this new economic order has retained the internalized discipline and the assumption, crucial in Weber's mind to both capitalism and socialism, that the pursuit of wealth is paramount to the good life. All of this has become an "iron cage," a new sort of bondage or tyranny. But men and women of the modern world, arrogant in their technical mastery of the world, do not realize the human cost of these accomplishments. Weber, however, was appalled at the probable destiny of the world, a "mechanized petrification, embellished with a sort of convulsive self-importance."[98]

Three Types of Legitimate Domination

Weber sorted out different types of legitimate domination by "the kind of claim to legitimacy typically made by each," and he found three "pure types" of legitimate domination, which he called traditional, charismatic, and legal-rational-bureaucratic. One will almost always find a mixture of these types—a traditional village usually relies on a charismatic leader, a charismatic leader like Napoleon might rule along with a strict legal and bureaucratic apparatus, and so forth. Nor did Weber seek to place these three types in some evolutionary order. In Lenin's Soviet Union, for example, one found powerful elements of traditional rule, charisma, and bureaucratic domination all mixed together. Weber, instead, was offering

---

96. *Protestant Ethic*, 53, 36–37.
97. *Protestant Ethic*, 117–19, 153–54, 181, 124, 166.
98. *Protestant Ethic*, 181–82, 29.

"ideal types" that deliberately accentuated, and even exaggerated, the distinctive characteristics of each kind of legitimate domination.[99]

Traditional domination rests on "the authority of the 'eternal yesterday,' i.e. of the mores sanctified through unimaginably ancient recognition and habitual orientation to conform." Key characteristics in this type are (1) the reliance on age-old rules simply because of an unquestioned belief in their sanctity, (2) customary law in which one sets out to discover previous rules and precedents, and (3) rule by one—here we find pure patriarchalism and patrimonialism—with a staff personally loyal to the leader, who embodies tradition.[100]

Charismatic domination is rule by one individual who is regarded by his or her followers as at least exceptional and perhaps divinely inspired. "The term 'charisma' will be applied to a certain quality of an individual personality by virtue of which he is considered extraordinary and treated as endowed with supernatural, superhuman, or at least specifically exceptional powers or qualities." Charismatic leaders must prove themselves repeatedly to their followers or disciples by political victory, military success, evidence of spiritual powers, and so forth. If success or proof is elusive—for example, failure in battle, or a sequence of floods or droughts that signifies a lack of favor from the gods—charisma will vanish. Although followers or disciples of a charismatic leader have an emotional tie to that leader, such emotional attachment cannot outlast repeated failure and must be reinforced by successes or benefits.[101]

Every charismatic leader is a prophet who opens up new worlds, attempts to take his or her followers beyond the everyday economic routine, indeed embarks on some sort of adventure. Because the charismatic leader and his or her followers see themselves as on a mission over and against the routines and rules of the past, "charismatic authority repudiates the past, and is in this sense a specifically revolutionary force." Charisma changes beliefs and thus "revolutionizes men 'from within' and shapes material and social conditions according to its revolutionary will." In the emotional adventure of charisma, both leader and followers shun the routine world of rational economic acquisition (although frequently there is booty to be divided) and establish no career patterns and no permanent institutions. That is not to say that charismatic leaders are not themselves sometimes greedy or do not have self-seeking staff members

99. *Economy and Society*, 213–15, 263, 1113; *Methodology*, 44–45.

100. "Politics as a Vocation," 78–79; *From Max Weber*, ed. and trans. Gerth and Mills, 226–38. For an excellent discussion of traditional domination, see Bendix, *Max Weber: An Intellectual Portrait*, 330–81.

101. *Economy and Society*, 241–43.

around them, and, as Weber noted, at least since the time of Crassus calculating financiers have sponsored charismatic leaders. But whether the charismatic leader is Saint Francis or Cromwell, Napoleon or a pirate, charismatic leadership works against rationalized economic production.[102]

All of this makes charismatic domination unstable. Can the charismatic leader continue to prove himself or herself? Can he or she satisfy both the ideal and the material interests of both staff and followers in the long run? How does the charismatic leader solve the problem of succession? Weber suggests that charismatic domination begins to wane from the moment of its inception, and eventually charisma is routinized, which means that it is transformed either into traditional domination or into legal-rational-bureaucratic domination. In other words, the adventure must end in a new routine of institutions. As charisma recedes, a new domination "congeals into a permanent structure." While the most important individuals and classes that supported the charismatic leader will consolidate their gains politically and economically, the majority of followers—as in the cases of Spartans, Jesuits, Cromwell, or Napoleon—will simply face a new form of discipline. "The charismatically dominated masses, in turn, become tax-paying subjects, dues-paying members of a church, sect, party or club, soldiers who are systematically impressed, drilled and disciplined, or law-abiding 'citizens.'" Because of its inherent instability, and because it cannot satisfy the long-term economic interests of its followers, charismatic domination inevitably perishes. "Every charisma is on the road from a turbulently emotional life that knows no economic rationality to a slow death by suffocation under the weight of material interests: every hour of its existence brings it nearer to this end."[103] Still, for Weber, the charismatic leader, however dangerous such leadership is upon occasion, was a source of hope, simply because such a leader can wrench people from routine and point out a possible new mission.

Weber labeled the third type of legitimate domination legal-rational-bureaucratic, although he frequently referred to it as simply bureaucratic domination. Of course there are significant differences between various kinds of bureaucracy—civilian and military, state and political party, church and factory, and so forth. But Weber sought to describe and analyze not the average bureaucracy—and consequently not all bureau-

102. *Economy and Society*, 243–45, 1111–16, 1132.

103. *Economy and Society*, 1146, 1122, 1120, 246–52, 1120–22, 1146–50. For excellent discussions of charismatic domination, see Edward Shils, "Charisma, Order, and Status," *American Sociological Review* 30, no. 2 (1965): 199–213, and Joseph Bensman and Michael Givant, "Charisma and Modernity: The Use and Abuse of a Concept," *Social Research* 42, no. 4 (1975): 570–614.

cracies will resemble his description—but instead an ideal type of bureaucracy that deliberately accentuates the distinctive characteristics of bureaucratic domination. While Weber acknowledged that constructing ideal types involves some conscious subjective choices about what is important and distinctive, he nonetheless regarded ideal types—of feudalism, capitalism, Calvinism, or individualism and so on—as inescapable methodological tools in sociological or historical analysis. The ideal type "serves as a harbor until one has learned to navigate safely in the vast sea of empirical facts."[104]

Weber's ideal type of bureaucracy has at least ten different characteristics. First, bureaucracy exhibits a clearly defined and developed hierarchy. "The principles of *office hierarchy* and of channels of appeal stipulate a clearly established system of super- and subordination in which there is a supervision of the lower offices by the higher ones."[105] Second, within the hierarchy one finds a vast specialization of function in which each individual has a prescribed and specialized task. Although Weber repeatedly said that he liked bureaucratic officials and civil servants, he did not present a flattering picture of them or of this bureaucratic world peopled by "scribes of all sorts." "The individual bureaucrat cannot squirm out of the apparatus into which he has been harnessed . . . the professional bureaucrat is chained to his activity in his entire economic and ideological existence. In the great majority of cases he is only a small cog in a ceaselessly moving mechanism which prescribes to him an essentially fixed route of march."[106] Third, the official within the bureaucracy normally looks upon his or her job as a "career"—complete with a fixed salary, a defined pension, and security—and looks forward to moving from "lower, less important and less well paid, to higher positions."[107] Fourth, bureaucratic domination signifies the final differentiation of the place of work from the household, of official duties as a public "vocation" separate from private life—all of which Weber (in contrast to Aristotle and Machiavelli, who would see virtually no "public" sphere in Weber's world) calls the separation of the public and private spheres.[108]

Fifth, the entire structure of bureaucratic domination requires a

104. *Methodology*, 104; *Economy and Society*, 1399, 4–15; *Methodology*, 72, 81, 92, 101–7. On Weber's methodology and the use of ideal types, see Hekman, *Weber, the Ideal Type, and Contemporary Social Theory*, 18–60, and Talcott Parsons, "Value-Freedom and Objectivity," in *Max Weber and Sociology Today*, ed. Stammer, 27–50.

105. *Economy and Society*, 957, 220.

106. *Economy and Society*, 957, 987–88, 119, 136, 1413–17.

107. *Economy and Society*, 963.

108. *Economy and Society*, 375–79, 998.

smoothly functioning system of laws, which arose in the West, at least in its modern form, when "bourgeois interests" demanded "an unambiguous and clear legal system" in the battle against the nobility. Bureaucracy develops only along with a predictable legal system, trained legal specialists, and a professional class of lawyers, who—except in extraordinary times such as the French Revolution—defend "the side of 'order,' which in practice means they will take the side of the 'legitimate' authoritarian political power that happens to predominate at the given moment." Sixth, the broader legal system is mirrored within the bureaucracy by an "impersonal order" of rules and regulations applied, at least in theory, equally to all and without the favoritism of patrimonial administration. Seventh, the rules and regulations generally detail the credentials necessary for an official's career. Schools and universities may appear independent, but they become training grounds, dutifully offering the appropriate degrees and specialized fields of study, thus serving both government and industrial bureaucracies.[109]

Eighth, the rules also spell out the available means of compulsion, and thus ensure "strict and systematic discipline and control" of each official.[110] Ninth, disciplined by training and rules, the official in the ideal type of bureaucracy performs his or her function impersonally, with neither hatred nor passion, neither affection nor enthusiasm. "When fully developed, bureaucracy also stands . . . under the principle of *sine ira et studio.* Bureaucracy develops more perfectly, the more it is 'dehumanized,' the more completely it succeeds in eliminating from official business love, hatred, and all purely personal, irrational, and emotional elements which escape calculation. This is appraised as its special virtue by capitalism."[111]

Tenth, bureaucratic officials have no power by virtue of ownership of the means of administration, although some high-ranking officials do have power as a result of their knowledge. Bureaucracies are of course awash in written documents ("the files"), and bureaucrats maintain power from two different kinds of knowledge in these files. Specialized and technical knowledge, for example, gives the bureaucrat the authority of a specialist confronting amateurs—for example, citizens or elected officials. Beyond that, official secrets give bureaucratic officials power. "The concept of the 'office secret' is the specific invention of bureaucracy. . . .

---

109. *Economy and Society*, 847, 876, 217–18, 775; "Politics as a Vocation," 94; *Economy and Society*, 217–18, 956–58, 988, 999–1000, 220.
110. *Economy and Society*, 221, 968.
111. *Economy and Society*, 975, 225.

Bureaucracy naturally prefers a poorly informed and hence powerless parliament."[112] For these reasons, Weber could conclude, "[i]n the modern state the actual ruler is necessarily and unavoidably the bureaucracy."[113]

A Future of Bureaucratic Domination

Weber acknowledged that bureaucratic domination, in some form or other, has an ancient history, and he specifically mentioned ancient China, ancient Egypt, the Roman Empire, and the Roman Catholic Church. The earliest bureaucracies in Mesopotamia, Egypt, and China—"hydraulic bureaucracies"—arose to meet the needs of regulating irrigation from rivers essential to the economy. But these were patrimonial bureaucracies and thus were "imperfect," not fully rational in a technical sense—for example, officials had no special training and were generally loyal favorites of the rulers. The technically rational "bureaucratic structure is everywhere a late product of historical development."[114] Rationalized bureaucratic domination, with most or all of the ten characteristics noted above, came into the world only with capitalism, and indeed, capitalist classes both relied upon bureaucratic organization within the factory and also used the state bureaucracy of absolute monarchs to wrest power from feudal classes. "Though by no means alone, the capitalistic system has undeniably played a major role in the development of bureaucracy. Indeed, without it capitalistic production could not continue. . . . Its development, largely under capitalist auspices, has created an urgent need for stable, strict, intensive, and calculable administration." In fact, Weber said unequivocally that "progress toward capitalism" is the criterion for economic modernization, while "progress toward bureaucratic officialdom" is the yardstick for measuring modernization of the state.[115]

Like a prophet from the Hebrew Bible, Weber described and warned against the "continual spread" of bureaucratic domination into all spheres of life—the state and political parties, armies and corporations, churches

112. *Economy and Society*, 992–93, 224–25, 956, 988–89, 220; "Politics as a Vocation," 82.

113. *Economy and Society*, 1393. For a critique of Weber's concept of bureaucracy, see Lloyd I. Rudolph and Susanne Hoeber Rudolph, "Authority and Power in Bureaucratic and Patrimonial Administration: A Revisionist Interpretation of Weber on Bureaucracy," *World Politics* 31, no. 2 (1979): 192–227.

114. *Economy and Society*, 1002, 971–72, 964, 990, 1401; *Sociology of Religion*, 57; *General Economic History*, 57.

115. *Economy and Society*, 224, 1393, 956; "Politics as a Vocation," 84–89.

and hospitals, universities and labor unions. But why does bureaucratic domination continue to spread? Precisely because it is the most technically rational way of organizing men and women, and thus the spread of bureaucracy is just one important part of the rationalization of the world. "The decisive reason for the advance of bureaucratic organization has always been its purely *technical* superiority over any other form of organization. The fully developed bureaucratic apparatus compares with other organizations exactly as does the machine with the non-mechanical modes of production. Precision, speed, unambiguity, knowledge of the files, continuity, discretion, unity, strict subordination, reduction of friction and of material and personal costs—these are raised to the optimum point in the strictly bureaucratic administration."[116] Weber well knew that bureaucracy could seem maddeningly inefficient, so he argued not that bureaucracy was perfect but only that it was the most efficient means possible of organizing men and women. Bureaucracy is "formally the most rational known means of exercising authority over human beings," because it can attain "the highest degree of efficiency" and because it is superior "in precision, in stability, and in the stringency of its discipline."[117]

But technical rationality refers only to the means chosen to bring about given ends. What ends does bureaucracy further? Or what do men and women in modern societies use bureaucracy to accomplish? Once again, his analysis resembles that of Tocqueville. We use bureaucracy to help establish social order. "The increasing demand of a society accustomed to absolute pacification for order and protection ('police') in all fields exerts an especially persevering influence in the direction of bureaucratization." We also ask the state to intervene in the economy—to administer roads and railroads, to oversee modern means of communication, to provide minimal levels of social welfare—and this invariably increases the scope of bureaucracy. And we want an increase in the standard of living, and hence we must have bureaucratic organization in the economy in order to deliver the goods. "To this extent increasing bureaucratization is a function of the increasing possession of consumption goods."[118]

However much people may complain about bureaucratic bungling and red tape, it is, according to Weber, "sheer illusion" to think we can achieve the goals of modern society without bureaucracy. Indeed, bureaucracy has become "completely indispensable." More and more, "the material fate of the masses depends upon the continuous and correct

116. *Economy and Society*, 973, 221–23.
117. *Economy and Society*, 223.
118. *Economy and Society*, 972–73.

functioning of the ever more bureaucratic organizations of private capitalism, and the idea of eliminating them becomes more and more utopian." Bakunin thought naïvely that if we destroyed the files, we could overcome this bureaucratic tyranny; but the need for order, the wish for prosperity, and the training and discipline in both officials and subjects make the continued spread of bureaucracy inevitable. "The choice is only that between bureaucracy and dilettantism."[119]

In fact, Weber literally could not imagine the disappearance of bureaucratic domination. History demonstrates, he claims, that once bureaucracy was firmly established in China, Egypt, or the Roman Empire, it disappeared only with "the total collapse of the supporting culture." And yet all these bureaucracies were comparatively "irrational," so modern bureaucracy, complete with specialized knowledge and detailed training, should be all the more enduring. "Where administration has been completely bureaucratized, the resulting system of domination is practically indestructible."[120] Suppose we vote out one government and vote in another? Bureaucratic domination in the economy remains the same, and, in the state, the old officials will continue to function much as before. Suppose we organize a political party in order to oppose bureaucratic domination? In order to be effective, our political party will necessarily become bureaucratized. "When those subject to bureaucratic control seek to escape the influence of the existing bureaucratic apparatus, this is normally possible only by creating an organization of their own which is equally subject to bureaucratization." Suppose we organize a revolution? Again, Weber claims not much will change. "Even in the case of revolution by force . . . the bureaucratic machinery will normally continue to function just as it has for the previous legal government." Revolution becomes more and more impossible; at most one can have a coup d'état to replace those at the top.[121]

Weber, who had some sympathy for working-class struggles, thought that socialism would only make bureaucratic domination more thoroughgoing. While willing to admit that the capitalist factory was tyrannical and exploitative, Weber thought that a socialist economy would only heighten the level of domination. Would socialism eliminate the "iron cage" in which we labor? "No! The abolition of private capitalism would simply

119. *Economy and Society*, 223, 988.
120. *Economy and Society*, 987, 1401.
121. *Economy and Society*, 224, 264–66, 988–93. One of Weber's students followed up on this insight with the famous thesis of the "iron law of oligarchy," that all organizations over time tend to become authoritarian and oligarchic. See Robert Michels, *Political Parties: A Sociological Study of the Oligarchical Tendencies of Modern Democracy*, trans. Eden Paul and Cedar Paul (New York: Dover, 1959 [1915]).

mean that also the *top management* of the nationalized or socialized enterprises would become bureaucratic . . . there is even less freedom,
since every power struggle with a state bureaucracy is hopeless. . . . The
private and public bureaucracies, which now work next to, and potentially against, each other and hence check one another to a degree, would
be merged into a single hierarchy. This would be similar to the situation
in ancient Egypt, but it would occur in a much more rational—and hence
unbreakable—form."[122] Whether capitalist or socialist, the name one attached to a modern economy—in every case designed to provide order,
build an infrastructure, and distribute consumer goods—would make little difference, because the future offered only the domination of individuals through factories and bureaucracies. For example, despite intentions
to the contrary, the Soviet Union was forced to reintroduce factory discipline and bureaucratic domination—both of which they had denounced
as bourgeois class institutions—just "to keep the state and the economy
going."[123]

Bureaucratic Domination as a
New Form of Tyranny

Weber offered three conflicting views regarding the location of power in
the modern structure of bureaucratic domination. First, Weber pictured
bureaucracy as a machine or a technique that can be used by a single
individual, an economic class, or even a foreign power. Bureaucracy is a
"precision instrument which can put itself at the disposal of quite varied
interests." For example, Bismarck fashioned a bureaucratic machine that
no longer needed him and continued to function smoothly—much to his
dismay—even when he was gone. As simply a technique, bureaucratic
domination is compatible with an old-fashioned dictatorship, class rule,
parliamentary government, factory or office discipline, and even an occu-
pying army. Bureaucracy is "easily made to work for anybody who knows
how to gain control over it. A rationally ordered officialdom continues to
function smoothly even after the enemy has occupied the territory; he
merely needs to change the top officials."[124] Thus, in this first instance,
Weber depicted bureaucracy as a neutral technique at the service of
those who wield economic and political power.

122. *Economy and Society*, 1401–2, 224–25.
123. "Politics as a Vocation," 100; *Economy and Society*, 1400–1402.
124. *Economy and Society*, 988–90, 980–87.

Second, Weber described bureaucracy as difficult to control, as inherently powerful, or at least as a potential source of power for those officials in the higher strata of the bureaucracy. In this instance, it is hardly a passive instrument to be used at will by those with power. "The power position of a fully developed bureaucracy is always great, under normal conditions overtowering. The political 'master' always finds himself, vis-à-vis the trained official, in the position of the dilettante facing the expert." Bureaucratic officials have tremendous power precisely because they possess specialized knowledge, official secrets, and the organizational power of the bureaucracy itself. "In a modern state the actual ruler is necessarily and unavoidably the bureaucracy, since power is exercised neither through parliamentary speeches nor monarchical enunciations but through the routines of administration."[125] Although in this instance Weber ascribed great power to bureaucracy, he still thought that, with difficulty, it could be controlled by forceful effort of political leaders, parliaments, those who head private corporations, and so on.

Finally, Weber depicted bureaucratic domination as a structure of domination over which no one has control, a tyranny without identifiable tyrants. As he said of the "domination of capital," it appears in such an indirect and impersonal way that "one cannot identify any concrete master." Under this structure of domination all are powerless because each one of us is trained and disciplined to perform one function in the overall structure. State bureaucracies, political parties, interest groups, corporate offices, factories, unions, hospitals, universities, churches, and clubs—all exhibit and reinforce the discipline of bureaucratic domination, and each is a part of the total structure. Under such a structure of domination, one cannot locate a clear source of power, even though all seem to experience the effects of tyrannical power. It is the "pacifism of social impotence under the tutelage of the only really inescapable power: the bureaucracy in state and economy."[126]

Ultimately Weber's analysis of bureaucratic domination and discipline leads to the last of these three models, although, when he spoke of plebiscitary democracy and the role of the charismatic leader, he certainly hoped for a strong individual who could resist the suffocation of bureaucratic domination. At any rate, the tyranny of the future, according to Weber, will be nearly unbreakable precisely because of the formal and

125. *Economy and Society*, 991, 1393.
126. *Economy and Society*, 1186, 1403; Edward Shils, ed. and trans., *Max Weber on Universities* (Chicago: University of Chicago Press, 1976), 18–20. See also the excellent article by Peter Breiner, "Democratic Autonomy, Political Ethics, and Moral Luck," *Political Theory* 17, no. 4 (1989): 550–74, esp. 554–55.

technical rationality of bureaucracy. Bureaucracy "is busy fabricating the shell of bondage which men will perhaps be forced to inhabit some day, as powerless as the fellahs of ancient Egypt. This might happen *if* a technically superior administration *were to be the ultimate and sole value* in the order of their affairs." Some, said Weber, fear that the world will witness too much individualism and too much democracy, but "we 'individualists' and supporters of 'democratic' institutions" know that historical and economic forces have made sure that "the trees of democratic individualism do not grow to the skies." In a conflict between individuality and bureaucratic domination, the latter seems to have won. "In American 'benevolent feudalism,' in the German so-called 'welfare institutions,' in the Russian 'factory system,' everywhere the House of Serfdom is at hand."[127] The discipline and training of individuals is so great that, all around him, Weber saw only men and women clamoring for the security and modest prosperity that bureaucratic domination will bring.

> It is still more horrible to think that the world could one day be filled with nothing but those little cogs, little men clinging to little jobs and striving towards bigger ones—a state of affairs which is to be seen once more, as in the Egyptian records, playing an ever-increasing part in the spirit of our present administrative system, and especially of its offspring, the students. This passion for bureaucracy . . . is enough to drive one to despair. . . . It is . . . as if we were deliberately to become men who need 'order' and nothing but order. . . . That the world should know no men but these.[128]

Weber ultimately judged bureaucracy based on what it does to men and women. He suggested that there has always been a tension between the specialist and what he called the "cultivated man," or between the specialized expert and the charismatic individual who has heroic or magical qualities that are not considered "useful" by the specialist. Weber declared, at first, that he was only offering an objective analysis. "The term 'cultivated man' is used here in a completely value-neutral sense; it is understood to mean solely that a quality of life conduct which *was held to be* 'cultivated' was the goal of education, rather than a specialized training in some expertise. Such education may have aimed at a knightly or at an ascetic type, at a literary type (as in China) or at a gymnastic-

127. *Economy and Society*, 1402; *Selections in Translation*, ed. Runciman, 281–83; cited in Mommsen, *The Age of Bureaucracy*, 100.
128. From a speech translated and published in Mayer, *Max Weber and German Politics*, 95–99.

humanist type (as in Hellas), or at a conventional 'gentleman' type of the Anglo-Saxon variety. A personality 'cultivated' in this sense formed the educational ideal stamped by the structure of domination."[129] Weber examined many kinds of "cultivated men." For example, the Chinese sought to cultivate the ideal literary gentleman, "the man who had attained all-around self-perfection, who had become a 'work of art' in the sense of a classical, eternally valid, canon of psychical beauty." The ancient Greeks used the *agōn*, or contest, in athletic competition, in the visual arts, in poetry, in playwriting, and even in conversations that led easily to Socratic and Platonic dialogues. And feudal knights not only received military training but also were expected to offer a significant accomplishment in art and literature, an education that was "the polar opposite of specialized education in a bureaucratic regime."[130]

After outlining the tension between specialists and cultivated individuals, Weber made it amply clear how sad he was that modern rationalization and bureaucratic domination perhaps signal the final triumph of the specialist. In the modern world, for example, Weber clearly mourned the ascension of the dutiful bureaucrat and the decline of the principled and passionate political leader. Weber paraphrased Goethe's view that the victory of the specialist is really an absence of life and "a departure from an age of full and beautiful humanity." All grand ideals have disappeared, and men and women can live only "in *pianissimo*," can only find meaning in the small affairs of family and friends. Weber merely exhibited disgust for this victory of the specialist. "Specialists without spirit, sensualists without heart; this nullity imagines that it has attained a level of civilization never before achieved." We face, he said, a "polar night of icy darkness."[131]

Alternatives?

Weber regarded Marx as one of his mentors, and indeed the influence of Marx is present at every turn. Weber argued that in every social order there is always a dominant class, that the behavior of interest groups is almost always "economically determined," that "the ends of religious . . .

129. *Economy and Society*, 1000–1001; also *From Max Weber*, ed. and trans. Gerth and Mills, 426.

130. *From Max Weber*, ed. and trans. Gerth and Mills, 436; *Economy and Society*, 1368, 1090.

131. *Protestant Ethic*, 181; "Science as a Vocation," 155; *Protestant Ethic*, 182; "Politics as a Vocation," 128.

actions are predominately economic," and that the influence of the material interests of classes "extends (often unconsciously) into all spheres of
culture without exception, even into the finest nuances of aesthetic and
religious feeling." While Marx made errors in his analyses and in his pre-
dictions, these were "errors of genius."[132] It is also apparent that Weber
had no great love for capitalism. Under capitalism the working class is
subjected to a rigorous shop discipline, confined to one specialized function in a stultifying division of labor, dominated by the "authoritarian
coercion" of a centralized management, exploited economically, pacified
politically insofar as its members are trained to pay too much attention to
consumer goods, and, at least in the United States, ruled by a "raw plu-
tocracy." However valuable, the "Rights of Man" so trumpeted by the Enlightenment "made it possible for the capitalist to use men and things
freely." Capitalism, claimed Weber, may be technically rational, but because it requires the exploitation and domination of the worker, it is
substantively irrational. And because capitalism brought bureaucratic
domination into the world, it is no friend to freedom, and he urged working-class organizations to resist domination by a "capital hegemony" in
which the state, the bureaucracies, and the owning classes jointly dominated the majority. Finally, he despised the bourgeoisie as a class lacking
all ideals and incapable of heroism.[133]

Does this mean Weber supported socialist struggles? Hardly. He accepted Nietzsche's notion that class struggles are at least partly born of
resentment, he regarded the shadowboxing of the Social Democrats as
merely providing "a kind of vaccination for the vested interests of the
existing order," and he declared that Rosa Luxemburg belonged in a zoo.
On the one hand, Weber maintained that socialism would not be that
much different from capitalism. Under socialism interest groups would
still clash over questions involving economic self-interest (questions such
as wages, working conditions, and investment decisions), individuals
would still be "administered dictatorially," workers would still experience
"bondage to the machine and a common work discipline," and industrial
enterprises would still exploit those who work. "The lot of the mine
worker is not the slightest bit different whether that mine is privately or
publicly owned."[134] On the other hand, Weber suggested that socialism

132. "Politics as a Vocation," 86; *Economy and Society*, 341; *Sociology of Religion*, 1; *Methodology*, 65; *Selections in Translation*, ed. Runciman, 256.

133. *Economy and Society*, 108–19, 137, 156, 731, 1209, 1320; Mommsen, *The Age of Bureaucracy*, 68; *From Max Weber*, ed. and trans. Gerth and Mills, 372, 392; Mommsen, *Max
Weber and German Politics*, 83, 120; *Protestant Ethic*, 37.

134. *Selections in Translation*, ed. Runciman, 283; *Economy and Society*, 202–3; *Selections*

would most likely be worse. For example, strikes against the state would be impossible, so the dependence of the worker—indeed all citizens—on the state, in this case the bureaucracy of the planned economy, would only increase. In fact, a socialist economy "would retain the expropriation of all workers and merely bring it to completion by the expropriation of the private owners." And, by eliminating private bureaucracies, which offered some check on public bureaucracies, socialism would only consolidate bureaucratic domination. "It is the dictatorship of the official, not that of the worker, which, at present anyway, is on the advance."[135]

Is there any hope? Weber noted several ways one might resist the power of bureaucratic domination. First, like Tacitus, Montesquieu, and Tocqueville, Weber championed a clearly defined legal system protecting specified rights of the individual. "Formal justice is thus repugnant to all authoritarian powers."[136] Second, again like Tocqueville, Weber wanted to use democratic electoral procedures to upset routine bureaucratic appointment. Here Weber mentioned short terms of office, bureaucratic officials subject to recall, rotation of officials, and frequent accountability to elected representatives. As he put it succinctly, "An official elected by the governed is no longer a purely bureaucratic official." Anxious to please an electorate, such officials will not forever subject themselves to the discipline of the bureaucratic hierarchy. Weber sympathetically recounted the wisdom of American workers who preferred corrupt city officials, at least accountable to party bosses, to bureaucratic experts who would "lord it over" them. In other words, they saw advantages in politicizing administrative appointments. "Those American workers who were against 'Civil Service Reform' knew what they were doing; they preferred to be governed by parvenus of doubtful morality rather than by a formally qualified mandarinate."[137] Third, citizen committees, or what Weber called collegial bodies—something like Montesquieu's and Tocqueville's intermediate associations shielding the individual from the state—can serve as watchdogs that limit the autonomy of bureaucracy. A collegial body "unavoidably obstructs the promptness of decision, the consistency of policy, . . . and . . . the maintenance of discipline within the group." Fourth, in extreme cases, perhaps even revolutionary cases, a popular and parallel organization might develop alongside the legitimate state administration,

---

in Translation, ed. Runciman, 252–55; "Science as a Vocation," 124–25; Mommsen, *Max Weber and German Politics*, 305.

135. *Economy and Society*, 139; *Selections in Translation*, ed. Runciman, 260, 255–59.

136. *Economy and Society*, 812, 1208–10. See Ewing, "Formal Justice and the Spirit of Capitalism: Max Weber's Sociology of Law."

137. *Economy and Society*, 960–61, 271; *Selections in Translation*, ed. Runciman, 281–82; *Economy and Society*, 289, 221, 267–70.

thereby checking bureaucratic domination. One might include here Cromwell's New Model Army, the Jacobin Club, the Farmers Alliance, India's Congress Party, and Solidarity in Poland. Weber analyzed the Italian *popolo,* "a state within the state," and the "first *deliberately nonlegitimate and revolutionary* political association." Because such parallel organizations need their own administration, however, they eventually further the process of bureaucratic domination.[138]

Weber did acknowledge theoretical alternatives to bureaucratic domination, although he concluded that these are unrealistic possibilities in the modern industrial world. When one reads Weber closely, it becomes clear that he regarded direct democracy as a form of government comparatively free of domination, in some ways the opposite of domination. "Immediate democracy," at least in its "genuine" form, is "free from domination [*Herrschaft*]." Or elsewhere, he maintained that "direct democratic administration" is an "undeveloped state of domination." In talking about democracy, Weber distinguished between "active" and "passive" democracy, the former characterized by direct rule by citizens and the latter involving elections but leaving real power to political leaders, elites, and party bosses. It is active democracy that opposes bureaucratic domination. "Political democracy strives to shorten the term of office through election and recall, and to be relieved from a limitation to candidates with special expert qualifications. Thereby democracy inevitably comes into conflict with the bureaucratic tendencies."[139] Direct democracy could only be feasible if applied on a small scale. "Only by reversion in every field—political, religious, economic, etc.—to small-scale organization would it be possible to any considerable extent to escape [bureaucracy's] influence." Weber mentioned North American townships, Swiss cantons, a few of the very first soviets, voluntary associations, and universities (!) as just about the only organizations capable of government by direct democracy. All of these examples, he quickly added, are atypical and "marginal."[140]

Weber's usual model for socialism is a highly centralized one, with a planned economy and a centralized bureaucracy. In some passages, however, he acknowledged the theoretical possibility of a democratic socialism of producer cooperatives, which apparently would entail worker-owned and -controlled factories within what is now commonly referred to as market socialism. This too would be a government and an economy

138. *Economy and Society*, 279–80, 1302, 995, 974.

139. *Economy and Society*, 292, 951, 985–86; *From Max Weber*, ed. and trans. Gerth and Mills, 300.

140. *Economy and Society*, 224, 290–93, 948–49.

that would resist bureaucratic domination. While Weber saw the theoretical possibility of a democratic socialism, he saw no realistic way to establish such a form of government. In speaking of consumer cooperatives in Belgium, he admitted that a "consumer socialism" in which consumers ran factories would be a "fundamentally different species" of government, but added, "[I]t remains a mystery where the interest groups are to be found which might one day give it life."[141]

This, ultimately, is Weber's pessimistic conclusion. While he saw theoretical alternatives to bureaucratic domination, and while he admitted that in theory one might create direct democracy or a democratic socialism of workers' cooperatives, he saw no realistic ways such forms of government could exist in the modern world. First, economic inequalities will quickly appear, and then administration and rule will fall into the hands of the wealthy. Second, genuinely democratic forms of government are economically irrational, and with modern demands for an increased standard of living, the population will want the comparative efficiency of bureaucratic administration. Third, a modern economy needs specialists, but with specialists comes bureaucracy. And finally, when one organizes a movement or a political party, even one specifically designed to bring about a world without bureaucratic domination, one can be successful only if the political party is rigorously organized and thus bureaucratic. As a result, the movement or party itself will inevitably plant the seeds of a new bureaucratic domination. One cannot journey in a bureaucratic carriage to a new land without bureaucracy. Weber leaves us alone and facing his "polar night of icy darkness," that is, the inevitability of a new bureaucratic tyranny.

Weber tried to offer one hopeful alternative. How can we preserve some remnant of freedom and individualism in the face of overpowering bureaucracies? Can any power check the influence of bureaucracies? "How will democracy even in this limited sense be *at all possible?*" Weber pinned his hopes on the charismatic leader powerful enough to oppose bureaucratic domination. "What was lacking was the *direction* of the state by a *politician*—not by a political genius, to be expected only once every few centuries, not even by a great political talent, but simply by a politician."[142] Here finally is the hope Weber gave us—the statesman versus the bureaucrat, the hope that a statesman with a vision can gather the sup-

---

141. *Selections in Translation*, ed. Runciman, 255; Weber, *Economy and Society*, 137, 731. For a very different but excellent study of Weber and possible alternatives, see Lawrence A. Scaf, "Fleeing the Iron Cage: Politics and Culture in the Thought of Max Weber," *American Political Science Review* 81, no. 3 (1987): 737–55.

142. *Economy and Society*, 1403–5. See Löwith, *Max Weber and Karl Marx*, 52–60.

port of the masses to overcome a new bureaucratic tyranny. In short, only charismatic domination is a realistic alternative to bureaucratic domination.

Weber thus advocated plebiscitary democracy, or a democracy led by a charismatic leader whose vision is affirmed by the masses by means of a plebiscite. "Plebiscitary democracy—the most important type of *Führer-Demokratie*—is a variant of charismatic authority, which hides behind a legitimacy that is *formally* derived from the will of the people. The leader (demagogue) rules by virtue of the devotion and trust which his political followers have in him personally." The plebiscite itself does not select a leader, but simply affirms the leader and his or her vision, thereby conferring legitimacy. Weber defended both elitism and Caesarism and openly admitted that such a leader is not the servant of the citizenry but its master. The plebiscite "is not an ordinary vote or election, but a profession of faith in the calling of him who demands these acclamations." All modern democracies, he claimed, tend toward Caesarism, and he cited Cromwell, Napoleon, American presidents from Jackson to Teddy Roosevelt, Gladstone, and Bismarck as examples. Finally, plebiscitary democracy eliminates neither class rule nor parliament, although parliaments should have the subordinate roles of preparing budgets, cross-examining bureaucratic officials (and thus attempting to undermine their monopoly of expert knowledge), providing a training ground for future leaders, and defending civil rights.[143]

What are the advantages of plebiscitary democracy? First, it is practical. In modern industrial states, direct democracy is impossible. "The *dēmos* itself, in the sense of a shapeless mass, never 'governs' larger associations, but rather is governed." A plebiscite confirming the legitimacy of a charismatic leader, however, provides a feasible alternative combining charismatic rule with popular accountability. Second, it is efficient, especially in matters of great power politics in foreign affairs. Weber remarked ironically that the much-maligned "night-watchman's state" of England, was able to bring forth powerful charismatic leaders from parliament, and managed to conquer "the best parts of all continents." The charismatic leader is indispensable for great nations. "Large-scale tasks which require quick and consistent solutions tend in general, for good technical reasons, to fall into the hands of monocratic 'dictators.' . . . It is impossible for either the internal or the foreign policy of great states to be strongly and consistently carried out on a collegial basis." Third, a plebiscitarian democracy will draw its finest and most ambitious talents

143. *Economy and Society*, 267–68, 1451–55, 1126–28, 1414–18; "Politics as a Vocation," 107–8.

into politics. In Weber's time, at least in Germany, the most ambitious individuals had no desire to join a powerless parliament or a ministry dominated by bureaucracy, but instead they sought the power located in "giant industrial enterprises, cartels, [and] banks." As Weber said, "why in the world should men with leadership qualities be attracted by a party which at best can change a few budget items . . . ?"[144]

Fourth, a plebiscitary democracy gives a charismatic leader the chance to challenge the march of rationalization and bureaucratic domination. Weber regarded the plebiscitary leader as akin to a prophet, warning against the present and bestowing "coherent meaning" on some vision of the future. In a "godless and prophetless time," this would be no small achievement. The plebiscitary leader Weber hoped for must accomplish a number of goals. He or she must be a statesman who takes power from bureaucracy. "Politicians must be the countervailing force against bureaucratic domination." Moreover, this charismatic leader must focus our gaze on what is *political,* wrenching us from bureaucratic routine and merely *technical* questions. "Bureaucracy failed *completely* whenever it was expected to deal with *political* problems." This means the statesman must formulate a new standard of substantive rationality that will entail a new vision of what is just and and a new vision of what a society wishes to attain, even and especially a vision beyond mere formal economic rationality. And finally, such a leader will inevitably make an attempt to alter the course of history, ever so slightly, like one of those "switchmen" who change the direction of a locomotive. Just as Calvin's Geneva changed history dramatically, so perhaps can a modern charismatic leader. This, ultimately, was Weber's hope for the future—a leader who could impose some vision on history to save us from the twin tyrannies of capitalist bureaucratic domination and, even worse, a Leninist or centralized statism.[145]

Weber gravitated toward his support for plebiscitary democracy, because he feared the new bureaucratic tyranny and because he thought a nation governed by bureaucrats could achieve no national, international, or historical greatness. And he argued that we have only two alternatives in the modern world—a leaderless democracy suffocating under medi-

144. *Economy and Society*, 985, 1407, 278, 1413–14, 961.

145. *Sociology of Religion*, 59; "Science as a Vocation," 153; *Economy and Society*, 1417, 269; *Selections in Translation*, ed. Runciman, 281–82. Weber noted that the statesman "is constantly in danger of becoming an actor . . . and of being concerned merely with the 'impression' he makes." "Politics as a Vocation," 116. For a good discussion of the weaknesses of Weber's theory of democracy, see Jeffrey Prager, "Moral Integration and Political Inclusion: A Comparison of Durkheim's and Weber's Theories of Democracy," *Social Forces* 59, no. 4 (1981): 919–50.

ocrity and bureaucracy, or a leadership democracy capable of greatness. His preference for the latter and his disdain for the former reflect his lifelong admiration for Bismarck, a love for power politics, the spell of Nietzsche's overman, and an inherent elitism. His relentless analysis of why bureaucratic tyranny is inevitable, however, hardly makes his late-twentieth-century readers—who of course have hindsight on the century—eager to embrace the proposition that to save freedom we must harness our hopes to a Caesarist demagogue. And yet his question of how we save individual and democratic freedom in the face of ever-growing bureaucracy remains hauntingly unanswered.

Conclusion

Weber has offered European theories of tyranny several original contributions and some important refinements of previous ideas. First, his key word *Herrschaft,* or domination, suggests that there always has been and always will be domination of the many by the few. While he agreed that theoretically a decentralized democratic socialism with worker-owned cooperatives offers a world without domination, he thought it was impossible to create such a world. "All ideas aimed at abolishing the dominance of men over men," he said, "are 'utopian.'" Although there has always been domination, however, it is not true that all dominations have been equally harsh. Feudal domination, for example, was limited. Weber, like Foucault after him, presented us with the ironical conclusion that despite brave talk in the past two centuries about progress, the domination facing modern men and women is as harsh and debilitating, in a less overtly cruel way, as the Pharaohs' building projects and medieval mines. Second, it follows that Weber is the first thinker I have discussed whose arguments explicitly break from the Enlightenment promise of progress. Despite pessimism in Montesquieu, Tocqueville, Marx, and Freud, all owed major debts to the Enlightenment. But looking much more closely at the detailed changes brought by the individualism of the Reformation and the Rights of Man hailed by the Enlightenment, Weber argued that the first gave to us an "unbearable" and despotic self-vigilance over our inner lives in this "unexampled tyranny of Puritanism," and the latter brought capitalism and with it the discipline of the factory and the domination of administrative bureaucracies.

Third, Weber pointed to the application of science to virtually every area of life—a development he called the rationalization of the world—as the change in history that made this qualitatively new domination possible. Although Weber was in awe at what science could achieve, he had neither a Baconian optimism that saw science as the key to progress nor Marx's view that science was a neutral force that could be used for good and bad. For Weber, if science was hastening to every corner of the human world, it would certainly be used to organize and discipline men and women in new forms of bureaucratic domination. Fourth, his analysis of bureaucratic domination in effect answers Tocqueville's question about who will rule this new and faceless tyranny. It is likely that Tocqueville, who may have invented the word *bureaucracy,* would have marveled at Weber's analysis. The world can witness a tyranny without a tyrant, or a "masterless slavery," said Weber, because we are all subject daily to multiple administrations that impose upon us bureaucratic domination. This ensures that the modern world will be hierarchical, authoritarian, and undemocratic.

Fifth, Weber wanted us to see that this new tyranny is not imposed on unwilling subjects. As long as men and women put so much value on increasing the availability of goods and services, a conviction Weber called an "iron cage," then they will clamor for bureaucratic domination to ensure an efficient delivery of the goods. In very different ways from Freud, Weber—again, like Foucault—also argued that each one of us participates in this domination. Because each of us plays a part in the structure of domination, because each is in some sense a willing "cog," then it is accurate to say that we are all victims of this new tyranny and that we all inflict this tyranny on others. Sixth, Weber argued that there is a structure to this domination, that each component of society reinforces every other, because all are subject both to rationalization and to discipline. Not just state bureaucracies but corporations and labor unions, hospitals and colleges, and so on, are all organized rigorously and bureaucratically, and we will find discipline not just in factories but in offices, schools, universities, and hospitals. Like Foucault later, he explored the micropolitics and the micropractices of tyranny.

Seventh, under this new bureaucratic tyranny each of us from childhood is disciplined so that our bodily motions, our habits, and our thoughts move according to prearranged rules that are strikingly "uniform." We are "trained" for "submission" and unthinking obedience. Society works efficiently because each of us becomes a specialist trained to do one task in an extremely elaborate division of labor. Like Tocqueville and Marx, Weber was horrified at what this does to men and women, at how the world stagnates and becomes petrified, at how it makes each of us a "little cog, little men clinging to little jobs." Every thinker we have examined would agree with Weber, who despaired "that the world should know no men but these." With the victory of the specialist over the "cultivated" person, Weber saw the disappearance of individuals capable of grand thoughts and grand accomplishments in many fields. Life, he said, can now be lived only "in *pianissimo.*"

Eighth, with the rationalization of the world, all previous customs, assumptions, and values have been rigorously analyzed by reason. As a result, the world has become what Weber called disenchanted; that is, all mysteries and superstitions and values have been unmasked, since reason is capable of undermining past assumptions but incapable of establishing absolute values in their place. This leads to a new cynicism in which individuals and nations embrace values only so long as they are useful. As a result, in a disenchanted world, politics—both internally and externally—is only a cynical battle for power and empire. Instead of a clash of principles, politics presents only a battle among self-interested nations, classes, groups, and individuals—all of whom may hide behind the flag of high-sounding values they no longer believe in. Finally, Weber genuinely thought that this new bureaucratic tyranny was unbreakable, that is, that it could not be defeated. While he hoped that a charismatic leader might upset the routine, he gave us no hope that in the long run even such a leader could abolish this new tyranny. Even to attack this tyranny one must establish a political movement organized on rational bureaucratic principles. "Everywhere," said Weber, "the House of Serfdom is at hand."

10

FROMM, NEUMANN, AND ARENDT

Three Early Interpretations of Nazi Germany

"Not a single prophet, during more than a century of prophecies," wrote the Italian critic Giuseppe Borgese, "ever imagined anything like fascism. There was, in the lap of the future, communism and syndicalism and what not; there was anarchism, . . . war, peace, deluge, pan-Germanism, pan-Slavism . . . ; there was no fascism. It came as a surprise to all."[1] As Fromm put it, when Fascism came to power, the world was not only unprepared politically and militarily to oppose it, but also unprepared to understand and explain it "theoretically."[2] And yet, as I have shown throughout this book, there was a many-centuries-old intellectual tradition that sought to analyze the phenomenon of tyranny, and thus, when three of the best early critics of Fascism and Nazi Germany tried to explain these phenomena, they leaned upon the past. I know of no example that could better demonstrate and support the thesis of this book, that is, that there is a little noticed tradition in the history of European political

---

1. Quoted in H. Stuart Hughes, *The Sea Change: The Migration of Social Thought, 1930–65* (New York: Harper & Row, 1975), 70; see also 80–81.
2. Erich Fromm, *Escape from Freedom* (New York: Avon, 1969 [1941]), 23.

thought that focuses on the perennial problem of tyranny. And when three of the most influential early interpreters tried to make sense out of Nazi Germany—Fromm writing as the European war started, Neumann as the world was engulfed in war and death camps became known, and Arendt just after the war was over—all three borrowed ideas from this long-standing discourse on tyranny, all three returned to discussions in this little-known tradition of political theory in order to try and explain Nazi totalitarianism, which seemed like a new species of tyranny coming alive for the first time in history. Fromm borrowed mostly from Freud, Marx, and Weber, although Aristotle's ideas are implicit in his arguments; Neumann turned to Machiavelli, Montesquieu, Marx, and Weber; and Arendt relied upon Plato, Aristotle, Tacitus, Machiavelli, Montesquieu, Tocqueville, and Weber.

None of these three interpretations has survived intact. Fromm's analysis now looks intriguing but too neat and too simplistic; Neumann's interpretation has been the most influential on later historians, but is flawed in important details and too strong in its claims about the role of business in Nazi Germany; Arendt's remains the most ambitious, but the most controversial in that her claims seem overblown, and her political theory mixes poorly with her history. All three interpretations remain influential, however, and all three passed on to contemporary scholars— often unnoticed—the history of theories of tyranny dating to Plato.

Erich Fromm on the Wish to Escape from Freedom

As his first book written in English, *Escape from Freedom* (1941) launched a literary career in which Fromm became immensely popular in the United States as a social critic using the ideas, often disguised, of a so-called humanistic Marx and an obviously revised Freud to comment delicately on contemporary problems. Fromm twice was a member of the now famous Frankfurt Institute for Social Research, once in 1930, when the Institute was still in Frankfurt, and later in the 1930s, after both he and the Institute had emigrated to the United States and Columbia University. Like other members of the Frankfurt School, Fromm sought to understand Fascism in Germany, to explain why millions of Germans "were as eager to surrender their freedom as their fathers were to fight for it." In trying to explain Fascism in Germany and Italy, he concluded that all modern industrial and democratic states were likewise "fertile soil for the rise of Fascism," and thus *Escape from Freedom* is simultaneously an analysis of Nazi Germany and a critique of Western democracies.[3] To put forth this analysis and critique, Fromm, again like some members of the Frankfurt School, sought to develop a "synthesis"—or, as some would put it, an unholy marriage—of the ideas of Marx and Freud in order to explain Nazi Germany. "Together with Einstein," wrote Fromm, "Marx and Freud were the architects of the modern age." Of Marx and Freud, the former "had greater depth and scope."[4] Although Fromm was a very German thinker who overtly relied almost entirely on Marx, Freud, Weber, and a number of other German theorists, his analyses of Nazi Germany also reveal key parallels with the ideas of Aristotle, Tacitus, and Tocqueville.

According to Fromm, Marxists have frequently overemphasized the importance of economic factors, Freud reduced historical and political developments to psychological factors, and Weber put slightly too much emphasis on the role of ideas, especially religious ideas, in historical and economic change (a grossly inaccurate interpretation of Weber). Fromm sought to show just how economic forces, psychological needs, and ideas are interdependent. "Economic forces are effective, but they must be understood not as psychological motivations but as objective conditions: psychological forces are effective, but must be understood as historically conditioned themselves; ideas are effective, but they must be understood as being rooted in the whole of the character structure of members of a social group."[5] The key to Fromm's method was his concept of "social character," which, in an abysmal 1940s automobile metaphor, he called "the transmission belt between the economic structure of society and the prevailing ideas." The "social character" is something like a Weberian ideal type; it is "the nucleus of the character structure which is shared by most members of the same culture" or class.[6] In other words, it tells us the essential psychological type or the key psychological needs of a given culture, class, or status group, and thus Fromm referred to the "character

---

3. *Escape*, 19, 265. One should note, as evidence of the book's popularity, Ashley Montagu's claim, in a 1942 review, that "I regard Erich Fromm's *Escape From Freedom* as one of the most important books published in our time." "*Escape from Freedom*—A Synoptic Series of Reviews," *Psychiatry* 5 (1942): 109–34; see 122.

4. Fromm, *Beyond the Chains of Illusion: My Encounter with Marx and Freud* (New York: Simon & Schuster, 1962), 9–12. For Fromm's relations with others in the Frankfurt School, see Martin Jay, *The Dialectical Imagination: A History of the Frankfurt School and the Institute for Social Research, 1923–1950* (Boston: Little, Brown, 1973), 88–106, and David Held, *Introduction to Critical Theory: Horkheimer to Habermas* (Berkeley and Los Angeles: University of California Press, 1980), 112–15.

5. *Escape*, 325–26.

6. *Beyond the Chains*, 78.

structure" or "social character" (phrases he often used interchangeably) of, say, the German working class. And what inculcates the broader social character into the individual? Like Freud, Fromm gave this role to the family. The family "molds" the individual personality and "represents all the features that are typical of a particular society or class." The parents, by representing the "social character of their society or class," pass to the child the distinguishing traits of that social character.[7]

Fromm regarded Marx's economic and class analysis as primary, although it is as if Fromm took this Marxist analysis for granted, and thus an economic and class analysis only quietly occupies the background of *Escape from Freedom.* In a later autobiographical work Fromm listed matter-of-factly, as causes of German Fascism, Germany's late national unification, the need for raw materials and colonies, the subsequent comparatively late quest for empire, the unity of German industrialists and militarists in these ventures, and how after the economic crises of inflation and unemployment of the 1920s, Hitler united with German industrialists, the landed Junker classes, and the military for another attempt at imperial expansion.[8] In one place or another, Fromm mentioned most of these economic and political causes of Fascism in *Escape from Freedom,* but one has to look with some care because he focused on the psychological roots of Nazism. Still, he declared emphatically, "Nazism is a psychological problem, but psychological factors themselves have to be understood as being molded by socio-economic factors."[9]

Fromm tried to find a middle ground in psychology between behaviorism and Freudianism. Against behaviorism he claimed that human nature was not "infinitely malleable," because human beings have passions or instincts that ensure that human nature has a "psychological dynamism of its own." Against Freud he claimed that what is most important in human beings is not the biological drives or instincts, but the ways in which they are socially modified and channeled. Although human beings have certain biological drives, such as hunger or sex, the passions that make individuals different—the ability to love or the inclination to hate, a yearning for submission or a wish to relate to others as equals—all result from different socializing processes and the different ways in which we relate to others. Thus, there is no "fixed and biologically given human nature," but rather, "man's nature, his passions, and anxieties are a cultural product."[10] Whereas Freud regarded human nature as biologically

7. *Escape*, 308, 33, 314–15.
8. *Beyond the Chains*, 21–23.
9. *Escape*, 232.
10. *Escape*, 27–29; also, 317–19.

and instinctually determined, Fromm saw human nature as historically and culturally determined. As one of his best critics put it, Fromm's psychology was always social psychology, indeed, a Marxian social psychology.[11]

It is now possible to see how economic, psychological, and ideological factors are interdependent. For Fromm, the economic structure and class relations create "social character," or perhaps even different "social characters" for different classes and status groups. Ideas result from social character, but they also react back upon both social character and the economic structure of society. "It is not only the 'economic basis' which creates a certain social character which, in turn, creates certain ideas. The ideas, once created, also influence social character and, indirectly, the social economic structure." Once again, social character is the "intermediary" or the "transmission belt" between the socioeconomic structure and the ideas of a society, class, or status group.[12]

Fromm's argument in *Escape From Freedom* is initially appealing because it is so tidy and clever. Roaming a span of five centuries, from the fifteenth to the twentieth, Fromm sought to show a parallel between economic developments and psychological reactions in both the Reformation and Nazi Germany. Fromm's analysis began with a wildly inaccurate caricature of the Middle Ages—derived from Burckhardt—as the childhood of European history. Just as the child has a "primary tie" to his or her mother, the man of the Middle Ages was tied to "the Church and his social caste," and even though these ties restricted individual freedom, they gave to individuals "security and a feeling of belonging." Fromm depicted the Middle Ages as lacking "individual freedom," because each individual was "chained"—in security and in some contentment—"to his role in the social order." The Renaissance broke these secure ties, and brought about both the freedom and the "individuation" of the individual. "The Italian of the Renaissance became, in Burckhardt's words, 'the first-born among the sons of Modern Europe,' the first individual."[13]

---

11. John H. Schaar, *Escape from Authority: The Perspectives of Erich Fromm* (New York: Basic Books, 1961), 89. For key discussions of Fromm's revision of Freud, see Fromm, *The Crisis of Psychoanalysis* (New York: Holt, Rinehart & Winston, 1970), 30–45; Rainer Funk, *Erich Fromm: The Courage to Be Human* (New York: Continuum, 1982), 13–31; Douglas Kellner, *Critical Theory, Marxism, and Modernity* (Baltimore: Johns Hopkins University Press, 1989), 36–43.

12. *Beyond the Chains*, 86–87; *Escape*, 322–27.

13. *Escape*, 40, 57, 61. Ruth Benedict, in her 1942 review of *Escape from Freedom*, resented this likening of medieval and primitive societies to the infancy of the human race. "I am thoroughly skeptical about the author's thesis that preliterate man was dominated by 'primal ties' which have only recently been outgrown." *Psychiatry* 5 (1942): 112.

Freed from past restrictions, Renaissance individuals had also lost a previous security, or "the sweet bondage of paradise," and they gained an overwhelming sense of aloneness, powerlessness, and doubt. "This growing individuation means growing isolation, insecurity, and thereby growing doubt concerning one's own role in the universe, the meaning of one's life, and with all that a growing feeling of one's own powerlessness and insignificance as an individual."[14] However attractive, such freedom is a burden, and individuals will seek, as Freud suggested, ways to escape from freedom and submit to some new authority. The anxieties of newly won freedom make the individual "ready for submission to new kinds of bondage,"[15] and like Tocqueville's new despotism, Fromm's new tyranny is founded on the twin pillars of isolation and powerlessness.

What brought about the breakdown of the medieval world, along with an onrush of newly won freedom and all of its accompanying anxieties? The development of capitalism. "The Renaissance period," Fromm maintained, "represented a comparatively high development of commercial and industrial capitalism." With this capitalism came new powerful and impersonal forces of monopolies, capital, and the competition of the marketplace. Faced with these new forces, the urban middle classes in particular felt threatened, alone, powerless, and anxious. Fromm declared confidently that the "fear and rage" that the middle classes of the sixteenth century felt against the new developments of capitalism was "in many ways similar" to what the middle classes of the twentieth century felt toward the powers of capital. The middle class, said Fromm, "fighting against the authority of the Church and resenting the new moneyed class, felt threatened by rising capitalism and overcome by a feeling of powerlessness and individual insignificance." Protestantism and Calvinism harnessed these new anxieties by offering a way to escape from the burdens of this freedom.[16]

Fromm's interpretation here is too neat, but extremely clever. The Reformation was a period of crisis and even revolution precisely because social character could not change as rapidly as the economic structure and class relations. The social character of the medieval world—paternalistic and exploitative, but reassuring and secure—no longer fit the new capitalism of the Renaissance and the Reformation. Individuals unready for the ruthless freedom of the marketplace were released there nevertheless, just as young children might be abandoned on dangerous streets. Thus, economic change produced an overwhelming and dislocating anx-

14. *Escape*, 50–51.
15. *Escape*, 296–97.
16. *Escape*, 67–68, 75, 92, 80–81.

iety precisely because the social character born in the Middle Ages lagged behind the new capitalist world, and as a result powerful new "psychological needs" arose—in this case a need, as seen in Freud, to submit to a new authority, a need rapidly answered by the ideas and the institutions of Protestantism.[17] Again, we see the interplay of economic forces, social character, and ideas.

Luther and Calvin—and ultimately Protestantism and Calvinism—represented the newly threatened middle classes and expressed their wish to escape from the burdens of freedom. Like the middle classes he represented, Luther had an "authoritarian character." As Freud suggested, such an authoritarian character, or personality, is characterized by an ambivalence toward authority, namely, both an inclination to rebel against it and a yearning to submit to it (a masochistic component), and by a general love of what is powerful, as well as a wish to dominate anyone who is powerless (a sadistic component). Luther, claimed Fromm, was a "typical representative" of the authoritarian character of the middle classes. "His personality was torn by a constant ambivalence toward authority; he hated it and rebelled against it, while at the same time he admired it and tended to submit to it. . . . He was filled with an extreme feeling of aloneness, powerlessness, wickedness, but at the same time with a passion to dominate."[18]

The authoritarian character of Luther, Calvin, and the middle classes they represented exhibited certain psychological needs that the ideas of Luther and Calvin addressed. Luther declared that human beings are innately evil, lacking in free will, and thus utterly powerless and alone before an all powerful God, and necessarily surrounded by doubt. Our only hope is to try to have faith and then humble ourselves before God and surrender to His power. Luther wanted "to find certainty by elimination of the isolated self, by becoming an instrument in the hands of an overwhelmingly strong power outside of the individual. For Luther this power was God and in unqualified submission he sought certainty." And why were these ideas appealing to, and accepted by, the middle classes? Because a member of the middle class "was as helpless in the face of the new economic forces as Luther described man to be in his relationship to God."[19]

In writing about Calvin, Fromm followed Weber by focusing on the centrality of the doctrine of predestination. Calvin's uncompromising position on predestination both expressed and enhanced the feelings of pow-

17. *Escape*, 83; Schaar, *Escape from Authority*, 92–98.
18. *Escape*, 84; also 102, 190–91, 96, 186.
19. *Escape*, 93–100, esp. 97, 100.

erlessness, aloneness, and insignificance of the middle classes. With no power whatsoever to alter one's fate, one literally is a "powerless tool in God's hands." Fromm repeated Weber's argument that one could find some psychological reassurance, perhaps some sign that one was among the elect, by success in worldly economic activity, and thus a compulsion to work, which Fromm likened to a neurotic ritual, spurred capitalist development even further. Going beyond Weber, Fromm suggested that individuals forced to submit to such a demanding and "despotic" God necessarily develop hostility and resentment directed toward the upper classes, the Catholic Church, and all unbelievers. (By claiming that Luther and Calvin fueled resentment and were among the "greatest haters" in history, Fromm quietly borrowed from Nietzsche.)[20] Protestantism, Fromm concluded, both reflected and reinforced a new social character, or character structure—an authoritarian character that felt isolated and powerless, hostile and resentful, loving all power and wishing to submit to power. "Protestantism was the answer to the human needs of the frightened, uprooted, and isolated individual who had to orient and to relate himself to a new world."[21] In sum, the Reformation signaled a destructive escape from freedom.

Although Nazism was an extreme case of the modern wish to escape from freedom, it grew out of the same "fertile soil for the rise of Fascism" present, according to Fromm, in all modern industrial democracies. In discussing the tyrannical propensities of modern industrial democracies, Fromm detailed many characteristics of capitalism and democracy that remind us of Tocqueville. First, while capitalism was a step toward freedom, it also "made the individual more alone and isolated and imbued him with a feeling of insignificance and powerlessness."[22] Second, in language reminiscent of Weber, Fromm claimed that each individual has become "a cog in the vast economic machine, . . . always a cog to serve a purpose outside of himself." While the white-collar worker has become an "utterly insignificant" cog in a bureaucratic hierarchy, the industrial worker has been "employed" as a tool in an impersonal enterprise.[23] Third, in impersonal corporations, in the anonymity of modern bureaucracies, and as a stranger in vast cities, the individual feels like a "small particle" buffeted by unseen winds.[24] Fourth, invoking Kafka and remind-

20. *Escape*, 108, 115–16.
21. *Escape*, 121; also 106–22. Did this most unflattering depiction of Luther and Calvin originate in part from Fromm's experience of anti-Semitism? See *Beyond the Chains*, 5.
22. *Escape*, 128.
23. *Escape*, 130–31, 146–47, 139.
24. *Escape*, 153.

ing us of Tocqueville and Weber, Fromm asserted that authority has become invisible and that no one seems to have power, and thus "there is nobody and nothing to fight back against."[25] Finally, like Marx, Fromm suggested that we have lost control over the world we have created, that the world has become reified and thus our own creation, like Frankenstein's monster, has come to dominate us. The individual "is not really the master any more of the world he has built; on the contrary, this manmade world has become his master, before whom he bows down."[26]

Alone, isolated, powerless, and pestered by doubt, the individual in modern industrial democracies "feels threatened by gigantic forces and the situation resembles in many ways that of the fifteenth and sixteenth centuries."[27] Individuals have two ready avenues to escape from their anxious freedom—submit to a leader, as in Germany and Italy, or undertake a compulsive conformity, as in the other industrialized democracies. In either case, although one loses individuality and freedom, one gains security, pride in belonging to some larger entity, a feeling of power instead of powerlessness, certainty where there was previously doubt, meaning instead of meaninglessness, and the ability to avoid responsibility for one's decisions. Protestantism, according to Fromm, smoothed the escape. "Once man was ready to become nothing but the means for the glory of a God . . . , he was sufficiently prepared to accept the role of a servant to the economic machine—and eventually a 'Führer.'"[28]

Both before and after Fascism in Germany and Italy, individuals in modern democracies tended toward unthinking conformity. In the majority of cases, Fromm claimed, the individual "gives up his individual self and becomes an automaton." The individual is neither spontaneous nor authentic, but—in a claim reminiscent of Plato—"he is only playing a role that has been handed over to him."[29] Moreover Fromm maintained there was little freedom of thought in modern democracies, and he frankly acknowledged that Marx and Freud taught him the concept of "false consciousness," that is, the ability to believe our manipulated thoughts and feelings are freely and authentically our own. As individuals we do not have original thoughts of our own, our thoughts and feelings "have been put into us from the outside," we learn to want what we are "*supposed* to want," and thus, whereas the individual is convinced that he is free and spontaneous, he is really no more than a puppet who "thinks,

25. *Escape*, 190, 154.
26. *Escape*, 138.
27. *Escape*, 144.
28. *Escape*, 131.
29. *Escape*, 208–9, 279.

feels, and wills what he believes he is supposed to think, feel, and will."[30] Like Tacitus, Fromm thought that the distortion of language reflected this one-dimensional thinking. Betrayal of allies is called "appeasement," military aggression is labeled "defense," and tyrannical governments that ally themselves with us are pronounced "free." "Never have words been more misused in order to conceal the truth than today." Aside from the manipulation of language, what induces us to play roles and repeat indoctrinated phrases rather than to think critically? Like Tocqueville, Fromm answered that it is the fear of public opinion and the fear of being isolated and ostracized. "There is almost nothing a man will not believe—or repress—when he is threatened with the explicit or implicit threat of ostracism."[31] Isolated, powerless, and overpowered with doubt, the individual of modern industrial democracies tends to escape from freedom by submitting to a tyranny of unthinking conformity. Nazi Germany was thus only an extreme—and extremely destructive—case of this pervasive modern wish to escape from freedom by submitting to external authority, the modern wish for a "totalitarian flight from freedom."[32]

In analyzing the causes of Nazi Germany, Fromm focused on economic, psychological, and ideological factors primarily, but his language also suggests, in perhaps another debt to Weber, that the state bureaucracy played an independent role. Fromm frequently used such phrases as rule by "Hitler and his bureaucracy" or simply rule by a somewhat independent "Nazi bureaucracy," and he made it clear in his example of the Soviet Union that a key component of tyranny can be "a powerful bureaucracy" that controls the populace. In a later work, he declared "the alternative is not between 'capitalism' and 'communism' but between bureaucratism and humanism."[33]

Nevertheless, economic and psychological factors were primary, and no explanation of Nazism that ignores either of these two would be adequate. "Nazism is a psychological problem, but the psychological factors themselves have to be understood as being molded by socio-economic factors. Nazism is an economic and political problem, but the hold it has over a whole people has to be understood on psychological grounds." Although he claimed economic factors were primary, he emphasized the "psychology of Nazism." He did mention, however, "the expansive tenden-

---

30. *Beyond the Chains*, 106; *Escape*, 212, 278–79.
31. *Escape*, 266, 300–301; *Beyond the Chains*, 124–27.
32. *Escape*, viii.
33. *Escape*, 242–45, 300–302; *Beyond the Chains*, 181. Fromm continued in this latter work by advocating a "democratic, decentralizing socialism" as the best political and economic system to develop freedom.

cies of German imperialism," the capture of the state by "one political party backed by industrialists and Junkers," key financial support given to Hitler by industrialists who profited from National Socialism, and of course the inflation of 1923 and the depression of 1929.[34]

While Nazism met the economic needs of the capitalist classes, it met the psychological needs of the middle classes. The working class, Fromm maintained, bowed to Nazism grudgingly, neither capable of the strong resistance one might have expected from their numbers nor able to admire strongly the ideology and the deeds of the Nazis. To Fromm, this was no post facto generalization. In 1929, while at the Frankfurt Institute for Social Research, he planned and oversaw a very sophisticated survey of German workers and some members of the lower middle class, and thus he predicted in 1929 "a frightening lack of will to resist among the German workers' parties," because he found too many workers with an authoritarian character.[35] In contrast to the working class, the lower middle classes were "deeply attracted to the new ideology" and "fanatically" drawn to Nazi leaders. For evidence, he drew on his own 1929 survey, which showed white-collar workers the most highly authoritarian in their attitudes toward political leadership and toward those they regarded as weak, such as women, and he also borrowed from a 1933 study by Harold Lasswell. Among "small shopkeepers, artisans, and white-collar workers," Fromm predominantly found an authoritarian social character with "its craving for submission and its lust for power."[36] Although Nazism did not create this authoritarian social character, it did intensify it and capitalize on it.

Before 1918, according to Fromm, members of the lower middle classes found security in identifying with the monarchy, had a clear meaning in their lives through "the authority of religion and traditional morality," and found strength in an "unshaken" family situation. "The individual felt that he belonged to a stable social and cultural system in which he had his definite place." In addition, the economic position of the lower middle classes was perhaps declining, but still "solid enough." While the lower middle classes exhibited an authoritarian social character in submitting to the authority of monarch, religion, and family, it was neither extreme nor terribly destructive. After the defeat in World War I, however, all this

34. *Escape*, 232, 231, 242–43, 238.

35. *Escape*, 233; Fromm, *The Working Class in Weimar Germany: A Psychological and Sociological Study*, ed. Wolfgang Bonss, trans. Barbara Weinberger (Cambridge, Mass.: Harvard University Press, 1984), 43, 226–28.

36. *Escape*, 233–37. See *The Working Class in Weimar Germany*, 118–26, 162–70, 215, 231. For more on Fromm's sources for *Escape from Freedom*, see Don Hausdorff, *Erich Fromm* (New York: Twayne Publishers, 1972), 38–46.

changed rapidly. With the downfall of the monarchy and with challenges to religion and family, the authority on which the lower middle classes leaned collapsed. With the inflation of 1923 and the depression of 1929, all the old values of thrift and hard work no longer seemed to have a place. And with its economic position eroded, the lower middle classes no longer could feel superior to the working classes. The Treaty of Versailles became a symbol for the frustrations and anxieties rooted in these rapid changes in the socioeconomic structure.[37]

"Psychic change is slower than economic change," wrote Fromm, so that rapid socioeconomic changes produced new and pressing psychological needs, especially a need for a new authority—as Freud had suggested—to which the lower middle classes might submit. Fromm's parallel with the Reformation is obvious. Just as the collapse of the Middle Ages brought insecurity and anxiety for which Protestantism was a solution, so the collapse of the social and economic position of the lower middle classes in the 1920s created psychological needs for which Nazism proved to be an extremely destructive answer.[38] True, the vast majority of the entire German population was "seized with the feeling of individual insignificance and powerlessness," and thus Nazism appealed to some members of all classes, but the middle classes were the most intensely devastated, and Nazism based itself most successfully on their needs. Fromm again noted that psychological factors were not the chief cause of Nazism, but rather Nazism was successful precisely because it furthered the economic interests of the industrialists, while it met the psychological needs of other strata of the population, especially the lower middle classes. Nazism "mobilized [the lower middle class's] emotional energies . . . in the struggle for the economic and political aims of German imperialism."[39]

The ideas of Hitler and National Socialism consciously appealed to the psychological needs of the lower middle classes and their authoritarian social character. Hitler intuitively addressed himself to individuals feeling alone, powerless, and insignificant. In the mass meeting, said Hitler, the new adherent "feels lonely and is easily seized with the fear of being alone, [and] receives for the first time the picture of a greater community" to which he or she might belong.[40] In addition, National Socialism built upon that side of an authoritarian personality that has a "sadistic craving for power" and wishes to dominate and rule others. The racist

37. *Escape*, 237–41.
38. *The Working Class in Weimar Germany*, 209.
39. *Escape*, 241–45.
40. *Escape*, 246–58, esp. 248.

doctrines constantly suggesting that Germans ought to dominate or destroy so-called inferior peoples such as Jews and Slavs, and that Germans deserved *Lebensraum,* or living space, to the East, where they might properly rule over such allegedly inferior peoples, easily appealed to this wish to dominate the weak. "What [the masses] want," declared Hitler, "is the victory of the stronger and the annihilation or the unconditional surrender of the weaker." And finally, Hitler and National Socialism consciously appealed to the masochistic side of the authoritarian personality, the wish to escape from freedom, to submit to power, and to surrender one's individuality by submerging oneself in some larger entity. Hitler claimed, for example, that the masses want to "submit to the strong man" and even become a "dust particle" in the service of some superior "force and strength."[41]

In Fromm's analysis of Nazism, once again economic changes produced new psychological needs from which new ideas drew support, although Fromm made it clear that not just Nazi ideology but also Nazi political and military practice appealed to the middle class. Nazism was a destructive tragedy, however, in part because it was a false solution and did not meet the authentic need of German citizens to move beyond negative freedom to positive freedom. Instead, it merely preyed upon apparent or false needs. Isolation, powerlessness, meaninglessness, and frustration persisted because our real needs for developing human potentials for intelligence and creativity, love and friendship, and a community of equals remained unaddressed.[42]

Conclusion

Fromm offered a creative synthesis of Marx and Freud in his analysis, although he also borrowed from Weber and was astute enough to make observations similar to those of thinkers such as Tacitus and Tocqueville. First, his class analysis originated with Marx, but when he focused on middle-class status anxiety, he was leaning on Freud as well. Second, using Freud's writings, Fromm made a convincing argument that anxiety, especially group anxiety, plays a part in politics. When the lower middle classes lost virtually everything they took for granted in the 1920s, their anxiety led them to search for a new identity and new beliefs. Third, Fromm's use of the concept social character—a creative blend of Freud and Marx, along with a poor interpretation of Weber—does indeed offer

41. *Escape,* 246–47, 257–58.
42. *Escape,* 262–63, 207. For good discussions of Fromm's notion of human needs, see Schaar, *Escape from Authority,* 45–52, and Henry S. Kariel, "The Normative Pattern of Erich Fromm's *Escape from Freedom,*" *Journal of Politics* 19, no. 4 (1957): 640–54.

an explanation why social and economic changes can move more rapidly than changes in personal habits and beliefs. Fourth, Fromm certainly made a key point when he said that the Nazis consciously played upon the psychological needs of individuals who were anxious, lonely, powerless, and isolated. Again, he extended Freud's arguments about the needs that groups led by a father figure satisfy in individuals. Fifth, his studies on the authoritarian personality, on how individuals have a need for submission and a wish for power, both a masochistic and a sadistic streak, was another highly innovative application of Freud. And finally, the notion that we must play roles in a tyranny to survive, and the notion that tyrannies distort language—these are insightful observations that Tacitus made of the Roman Empire.

Franz Neumann's Theory of Modern Tyranny

Franz Neumann is perhaps the most overlooked member of the Frankfurt School. One searches almost in vain for scholarly articles on Neumann's thought, and books on the Frankfurt School pay his analyses comparatively scant attention.[43] Such neglect has stemmed in part from the relatively small quantity of Neumann's scholarly publications and in part from the fact he influenced subsequent scholars by being a dynamic teacher of brilliant students (e.g., Peter Gay, Fritz Stern, and many others). In addition, many subsequent scholars apparently embraced the facile assumption that *Behemoth,* a 1942 analysis of Nazi Germany, must have been superseded by works with later dates of publications; too many scholars gave too much weight to the factual inaccuracies of *Behemoth* and thereby failed to appreciate the superbly intricate theoretical analysis; and finally, Neumann became a victim of Cold War scholarship that assumed his "Marxist" analysis of Nazi Germany must be dogmatic propaganda.[44] Certainly some historians of modern Europe have recognized Neumann's importance. H. Stuart Hughes claimed *Behemoth* was "the classic examination of [German] fascism in power," and the French

43. See Keith Tribe, "Introduction to Neumann: Law and Socialist Political Theory," *Economy and Society* 10, no. 3 (1981): 329–47; Ralph Miliband, "Freedom and Coercion," *British Journal of Sociology,* March 1958, 66–72; Jay, *The Dialectical Imagination*; Held, *Introduction to Critical Theory*; and Kellner, *Critical Theory, Marxism, and Modernity.*

Most of this part of the chapter has previously been published as "Franz Neumann's Theory of Modern Dictatorship," *Nature, Society, and Thought* 6, no. 2 (1993): 133–58.

44. Hughes, *The Sea Change,* 100–119; Arthur W. MacMahon, "In Memoriam," *American Political Science Review* 48, no. 4 (1954): 1239–40.

historian Pierre Aycoberry described Neumann's great work as "the first of the classics" and suggested that "in nearly every one of its chapters [one discovers] the seeds of the investigations of later historians."[45]

But while Neumann's *Behemoth* is certainly a seminal analysis of Nazi Germany, it is also, woven amidst his empirical investigation, a great work of political theory, perhaps the best theoretical analysis of tyranny in this century, an analysis obviously leaning upon the previous theoretical work of Aristotle, Machiavelli, Montesquieu, Marx, and Weber. Like others in the Frankfurt School, Neumann sought to use a modified Marxist analysis to understand the origins and functioning of Nazi tyranny, and especially why "the underprivileged masses" came to support Nazism.[46] In a later essay entitled "Notes on the Theory of Dictatorship," Neumann groped toward a more comprehensive theory of tyranny, or what he preferred to call "dictatorship." Showing how well he knew both Aristotle and Montesquieu, he rejected both the words *tyranny* and *despotism,* charging that the former word involved a somewhat arbitrary rejection of governments one believes to be unrestrained and unconstitutional, whereas the latter word is emotionally laden with prejudicial rejections of so-called "Oriental" forms of government. "Tyranny and despotism," wrote Neumann, "have no precise meaning." What he wished to undertake, but could not because of an early and accidental death, was a "systematic study of dictatorship," looking at and comparing the functioning of not only twentieth-century dictatorships but also those from the distant past. At most Neumann could begin the process of outlining "the theoretical problems encountered in the analysis of dictatorship."[47]

His definition of dictatorship was straightforward. "By dictatorship we understand the rule of a person or a group of persons who arrogate to themselves and monopolize power in the state, exercising it without restraint." (Ironically, and confusingly, the Roman dictatorship—with authority and power clearly circumscribed—does not fit Neumann's defini-

---

45. Hughes, *The Sea Change,* 82, 100–119; Pierre Aycoberry, *The Nazi Question: An Essay on the Interpretations of National Socialism, 1922–1975,* trans. Robert Hurley (New York: Random House, 1981), 97; Karl Dietrich Bracher calls Neumann's work a "pioneering study" and "the most important attempt at a socio-economic interpretation" of National Socialism, although he disagrees with some of Neumann's key conclusions. See Bracher, *The German Dictatorship: The Origins, Structure, and Effects of National Socialism,* trans. Jean Steinberg (New York: Holt, Rinehart & Winston, 1970), 7.

46. Herbert Marcuse, preface to Franz Neumann, *The Democratic and the Authoritarian State: Essays in Political and Legal Theory,* ed. Marcuse (Glencoe, Ill.: Free Press, 1957), ix.

47. Neumann, "Notes on the Theory of Dictatorship," in *The Democratic and the Authoritarian State,* 233–56; see 233–35. For parallels and contrasts of Neumann's analysis with that of other members of the Frankfurt School, see Jay, *The Dialectical Imagination,* 143–72.

tion.) Neumann outlined three types of dictatorship, the difference between the first two being similar to Machiavelli's distinction between a prince who wishes for a static, stay-at-home tyranny and a prince who seeks to mobilize popular support for conquest and expansion. First, in a *simple dictatorship* the dictator maintains power almost completely through the predictable means of coercion, including army, police, and a dependent judiciary. Second, in a *Caesaristic dictatorship* the dictator builds up "popular support" and "[secures] a mass base" personally loyal to him or her. Third, in a *totalitarian dictatorship* those with power seek "to control education, the means of communication and economic institutions and thus to gear the whole of society and the private life of the citizen to the system of political domination." Such totalitarian dictatorship may or may not be Caesaristic.[48]

Analyzing dictatorships, Neumann suggested, is more difficult than ever before because more than in the time of Augustus and more than in the era of the Medicis even the cruelest dictatorships dominate and tyrannize while proclaiming themselves defenders of freedom and democracy. Neumann quoted Guizot's famous remark that "no government or party . . . believes it can exist without inscribing [the word *democracy*] upon its banner." Even the worst dictators such as Hitler seek, at some level, "to play the democratic game" and "practice the ritual of democracy." Thus, the most effective dictatorships tyrannize their populations while both mobilizing popular support and convincing citizens that their servitude is a higher and nobler form of democratic freedom. Convincing individuals that their perceived freedom is only disguised servitude is, argued Neumann, no easy task. Finally, in arguing that liberal democracy and dictatorship are not polar opposites, Neumann sought to show that modern dictatorships such as those in Italy and Germany often arise from and flourish upon the political and economic preconditions fostered so routinely by liberal democracy.[49]

To analyze dictatorships Neumann drew upon the theories of thinkers such as Aristotle, Montesquieu, and Marx not only because these writers described accurately many of the practical techniques used by tyrannies to thrive but also because they defined tyranny or dictatorship as a political system that thwarted the fulfillment of human needs and blocked the development of human potential. Aristotle and Montesquieu outlined convincingly how men and women become "dehumanized" under tyranny, willing to embrace a social order that meets neither elemental nor more elevated human needs. Rousseau, Schiller, and Marx offered theoretical

48. "Notes on the Theory of Dictatorship," 233–36.
49. "Notes on the Theory of Dictatorship," 236–37, 248–49.

analyses of a "modern society [that] produces a fragmentation . . . of man himself who, as it were, keeps his different faculties in different pigeon-holes—love, labor, leisure, culture—that are somehow held together by an externally operating mechanism that is neither comprehended nor comprehensible." Montesquieu—whom Hughes mysteriously calls an "unlikely" source of inspiration—taught Neumann of the "ambiguous character of progress," the dubious legacy that the Enlightenment bestowed upon the modern world.[50]

Interwoven with Neumann's discussion of the Nazi dictatorship, therefore, one finds not only an analytical framework but also a political philosophy answering questions about human freedom and human needs. Both a legal scholar and a political philosopher, Neumann defined freedom as (1) the absence of restraints, or, to put it another way, the guarantee of civil rights as a protection from both private economic power and public political power, and (2), in an Aristotelian and Marxian sense, with a nod toward Freud late in his life as he reworked the theories of alienation by Hegel and Marx, the development of human potential and the meeting of genuine human needs. "Freedom is more than the defense of rights against power; it involves as well the possibility of developing man's potentialities to the fullest." Every significant scholar, thought Neumann, must bring a philosophy of freedom to bear on his or her work, and every philosophy must be critical, since nowhere have men and women attained human liberation. "Since no political system can realize political freedom fully, political theory must by necessity be critical."[51] Critical thinking reveals how far short of authentic freedom any society has fallen. Neumann himself hoped for a democratic socialism that would meet the "universal interests" (in a Hegelian and Marxian sense) of humanity, that would bring a "humanization of politics" in which "the words of idealism become history."[52]

Neumann was an emigré from Hitler's Germany, and he was pessimistic about the possibility of immediate and dramatic steps toward human liberation. As a consequence, he sought instead to analyze rigorously the oppression of the present. The analytical framework he used to examine Nazi Germany was derived from a conviction found in Hegel, Marx, and most specifically Montesquieu—the conviction that each society is an

50. Neumann, "Montesquieu," in *The Democratic and the Authoritarian State*, 96–148, see 100–103; idem, "Anxiety and Politics," in *The Democratic and the Authoritarian State*, 270–300, esp. 271–73; "Montesquieu," 104; Hughes, *The Sea Change*, 109.

51. Neumann, "The Concept of Political Freedom," in *The Democratic and the Authoritarian State*, 160–200, esp. 173, 162.

52. Neumann, "Approaches to the Study of Political Power," in *The Democratic and the Authoritarian State*, 3–21, esp. 18; "Anxiety and Politics," 294–95.

interrelated whole in which each individual element from classes to political institutions, from economic production to personality structure, from laws to ideas, reinforces every other. "Each society has, according to [Montesquieu], a specific structure and follows its own inner logic. . . . Each nation being thus an essential unit, it is folly to isolate phenomena and to attempt to understand them if they are not seen in their interdependence."[53] To suggest that society is a "structure" or a "unity," argued Neumann, does not lead one to embrace a static or ahistorical analysis, because change generated by one part of the structure—for example, a need developed by the army or the industrial sector—reverberates and alters the entire structure. In fact, and this is Neumann's Marxian conviction, the class structure and the demands of economic development will be the key determining factors—*not* the sole determining factor—in determining the precise outlines of this social structure and how it demands change over time. Finally, enlivening any interrelated social structure is what Montesquieu called the "spirit" of the society, a complex term embracing morals, customs, behavior, motivations, ideas, indeed the very "character" of a society.[54]

Isolation, Loneliness, and Powerlessness

Neumann found some truth in the retort by Nazi propagandists that liberal democratic societies became no more than "an aggregate of Robinson Crusoes," not pluralistic societies composed of influential groups and associations, but rather atomized scatterings of isolated and powerless individuals. Such atomization formed the foundation, not the cause, of Nazi dictatorship. Just as Montesquieu and Tocqueville had argued that despotism must destroy intermediate institutions between the individual and the state, so Neumann suggested that National Socialism, while carefully defending the class structure of society, consciously sought to atomize individuals "through the destruction of every autonomous group mediating between them and the state." The early-nineteenth-century conservative critics Bonald and de Maistre were right, according to Neumann, in suggesting that liberal democracy and the developing capitalism would create "mass-men," dissociated from one another, unattached and homeless, easily manipulated.[55] While National Socialism could not create this trend toward atomization, it succeeded in accentuating and exploiting it. "Such groups as the family and the church, the solidarity arising

53. "Montesquieu," 119.

54. "Montesquieu," 119–20, 128; "Notes on the Theory of Dictatorship," 250.

55. Neumann, *Behemoth: The Structure and Practice of National Socialism, 1933–1944*, 2d ed. (New York: Oxford University Press, 1944), 42, 366–67.

from common work in plants, shops, and offices are deliberately broken down." How did the Nazis accentuate the modern tendency toward atomization and isolation? First, by simply destroying traditional groups such as political parties, trade unions, and associations of any kind. And second, using fear to create an intense psychological isolation, "making it impossible for anyone to rely on anyone else."[56]

Isolated and lonely, detached from previous ties to families and communities, to groups and associations—the individual still sought to belong to something larger. Indeed, again openly borrowing from Aristotle, Neumann argued that individuals have an objectively identifiable need for meaningful participation in a political community. "Man can realize his political freedom only through his own action, by determining the aim and methods of political power."[57] Denied a genuine political community and thereby an arena for political participation, German subjects under National Socialism embraced the illusory, and ultimately unsatisfying, "people's community," or *Volksgemeinschaft,* allegedly a broader community of the nation transcending class, region, associations, and even families. "The natural structure of society is dissolved and replaced by an abstract 'people's community,' which hides the complete depersonalization of human relations and the isolation of man from man." National Socialism thus actively sought to create a new "type of man determined by his isolation and insignificance, who is driven by this very fact into a collective body where he shares in the power and glory of the medium of which he has become a part."[58]

Of course the "people's community," or *Volksgemeinschaft,* was a propagandistic sham that hardly erased feelings of loneliness. Two companions of such isolation are powerlessness and anxiety. Having experienced defeat in war, devastating inflation and depression, and the disruptions of the Weimar political system, Germans in the early 1930s already experienced "moral, social, and political homelessness." The Nazis quite consciously attempted to accentuate this feeling of homelessness, "to foster helplessness and hopelessness among the people," and thereby to create "an individual who feels himself overwhelmed by his own inefficacy," an individual thus readied to do or believe almost anything. Powerless individuals are easy to control, even more so if they are captivated by anxiety. Here Neumann used Freud to modify Montesquieu. While Montesquieu was correct in noting that all despotisms rely on fear, he might well have added, according to Neumann, that despotism must inculcate and

---

56. *Behemoth,* 400, 524; also "Montesquieu," 106–9.
57. "The Concept of Political Freedom," 186.
58. *Behemoth,* 402.

even institutionalize a "depressive and persecutory anxiety." "The caesaristic movement," wrote Neumann, "is compelled not only to activate
but to institutionalize anxiety."[59]

Such anxiety leads easily to (1) obedience to a leader and (2) a false
sense of unity based on a fomented hatred for a fabricated enemy. Without acknowledging Freud in his earlier work, Neumann maintained that
anxious and powerless individuals look to obey powerful leaders (father
figures?), who will supposedly save them from their helplessness. "It is
not only anxiety that drives men to embrace superstition, but inability to
understand the reasons for their helplessness, misery, and degradation.
. . . Like primitive men, they look for a savior to fend off their misery and
deliver them from destitution." After admittedly borrowing from both
Freud and Fromm in his later work, Neumann suggested that isolated men
and women seek to overcome anxiety through "ego-surrender" to a powerful leader.[60] "But how was the people to be integrated, despite all cleav-
ages of class, party, religion? Only through hatred of an enemy." With the
Bolsheviks too strong and the Catholic Church too entrenched, hatred for
Jews provided essential psychological leverage for uniting anxious individuals. Like Fromm, Neumann focused on status anxiety, the anxiety of
the middle classes—likened to the anxiety in the United States felt by
poor whites in their hostility toward blacks—"doomed" by inflation, depression, and rapid economic and technological change. National Socialism easily channeled this middle-class anxiety into anti-Semitism. "The
Nazi-Fascist movement activated the anxieties of the middle classes and
turned them into channels of destruction which were made legitimate by
means of the masses' identification with a leader, the hero."[61]

In seeking total control over even the individual's private life and
thoughts, totalitarian dictatorship sought to top Pisistratus, who had
boasted that he "told the puppets how to dance." Education became propaganda, while labor became regimentation, as National Socialism sought
total control over the individual "from the earliest childhood to the oldest
man." Neumann most chillingly described this attempt at total control in
the manipulation of leisure, which, far from spontaneous enjoyment, became no more than relaxation so one could collect one's strength for
work.[62] Such control of leisure only symbolized for Neumann the Nazi
attempt to control the most minute details of one's life and thought.
"There must be no social intercourse outside the prescribed totalitarian

59. "Anxiety and Politics," 287; Behemoth, 96; "Anxiety and Politics," 291.
60. Behemoth, 96; "Anxiety and Politics," 288.
61. "Anxiety and Politics," 287, 284–85; "Notes on the Theory of Dictatorship," 251–53.
62. "Notes on the Theory of Dictatorship," 238; Behemoth, 429–30.

organizations. Workers must not talk to each other. They march together under military discipline. Fathers, mothers, and children shall not discuss those things that concern them most, their work. A civil servant must not talk about his job, a worker must not even tell his family what he produces. . . . Even leisure time is completely organized, down to such minute details as the means of transportation provided by the authoritarian Strength through Joy organization."[63]

How could National Socialism hope to bring about such control? Once more isolation, powerlessness, and anxiety were the key factors, because all three made individuals subject to manipulation by mass organization, propaganda, and terror. First, "the atomization and isolation of the individual" rendered the individual lost and lonely in "huge and undifferentiated mass organizations" and therefore "more easily manipulable." Indeed the National Socialist principle of social organization involved driving "workers into huge organizations where they are submerged; they lose their individuality, march, sing, and hike together but never think together."[64] Second, saturated with propaganda, such individuals cannot think critically. "Propaganda creates the conditions of spiritual exhaustion which makes critical thinking impossible, not through its completely insignificant content, but through endless repetition." National Socialism transformed culture and education into propaganda, borrowed from the science of psychology, which had experimented with the "management of men" in order to perfect the manipulation of individuals, and consciously played upon the status anxiety of the middle classes by giving them a theory of Jewish conspiracy and thereby a concrete enemy for their anger.[65] As early as his writing of *Mein Kampf*, Hitler recognized the power of propaganda on isolated individuals. "The mass meeting is necessary if only for the reason that in it the individual . . . feels lonely and is easily seized with the fear of being alone, receives for the first time the picture of a greater community, something that has a strengthening and an encouraging effect on most people. . . . If he steps for the first time out of his small work shop or out of the big enterprise, in which he feels very small, into the mass meeting and is now surrounded by thousands and thousands of people with the same conviction . . . he himself succumbs to the magic influence of what we call mass suggestion."[66]

63. *Behemoth*, 401.
64. "Notes on the Theory of Dictatorship," 245; *Behemoth*, 430.
65. Neumann, "Economics and Politics in the Twentieth Century," in *The Democratic and the Authoritarian State*, 257–69, esp. 267; *Behemoth*, 439; Neumann, "Intellectual and Political Freedom," in *The Democratic and the Authoritarian State*, 201–15, esp. 205; "Notes on the Theory of Dictatorship," 245; "Anxiety and Politics," 287, 293.
66. *Behemoth*, 439.

Finally, individuals who feel alone and powerless, separated from any group that might offer protection, are overwhelmed by the terror used by totalitarian dictatorship, and indeed the Nazis engaged in a process of "isolating the worker and terrorizing him." Terror, or "non-calculable violence," hovering as a "permanent threat" against each individual is essential to such a tyranny.[67] By using terror and genocide mainly but not exclusively against Jews, the Nazis set about "to make the whole people into accomplices"—unsuccessfully, according to Neumann. Anxiety and collective guilt did play an important role, however, because in committing crimes, even those ordered by the authority of the leader and the party, the Nazis transformed the normal anxiety present in any political order into repressed guilt and "a nearly panicky" anxiety that could "be overcome only through unconditional surrender to the leader [which thus compelled] the commission of new crimes."[68]

The Leadership Principle

Despite criticisms of liberal democracy—for its weakness, for its supposed inability to act, for its lack of unity (because liberal democracies are composed of millions of Robinson Crusoes)—Nazi theorists still waved the banner of democracy, proclaiming loudly that National Socialism was a higher form of democracy. Genuine democracy, according to Nazi ideology, embraces equality and "the principle that there is an identity between the rulers and the ruled," and in providing this identity, it creates a unified government, a government that transcends and overcomes the divisions of provinces, classes, parliaments, state institutions, interest groups, and corporations. By this logic only a strong government unified by a leader constitutes genuine democracy. Possessing both legislative and executive powers, the leader could stand "above the petty quarrels of the numerous interests, public agencies, and states." As a principle that allegedly facilitates democracy, leadership was not, according to Nazi theorists, a form of domination, because it unified the nation, brought about the identification of the people with the government, and was based on "voluntary consent." While the people do not authorize the power of the leader, of course, because that would imply the authority to revoke it, they instead merely "recognize" this power. Such unity brought about by surrendering all power to the leader also solved the problems of inaction and political paralysis, leading directly to what Nazi theorist Carl

---

67. *Behemoth*, 424; "Notes on the Theory of Dictatorship," 245.
68. "Anxiety and Politics," 300, 293.

Schmitt called "decisionism," or "action instead of deliberation, . . . decision instead of evaluation."[69]

In Nazi ideology, Hitler as supreme leader "combines the functions of supreme legislator, supreme administrator, and supreme judge; he is the leader of the party, the army, and the people. In his person, the power of the state, the people, and the movement are unified." At first Hitler was merely chancellor, then effectively chancellor and president, then leader for life ("although no one knows whence his constitutional rights are derived"), and finally, "his power is legally and constitutionally unlimited; it is futile to attempt to describe it. A concept that is boundless cannot be rationally defined." Relying on Weber, Neumann noted that Hitler's authority was based on charisma, the belief that "the Leader is endowed with qualities lacking in ordinary mortals. Superhuman qualities emanate from him and pervade the state, party, and people."[70]

In offering a political theory of modern dictatorship, Neumann argued that such powerful, charismatic dictators emerge, not simply because of some innate human urge to accumulate power, but rather when a conjunction of many events creates the preconditions for totalitarian dictatorship. Lord Acton's famous dictum that "absolute power corrupts absolutely" is no more than a "facile half-true generalization." Indeed, the charismatic rule of the totalitarian dictator only "becomes a powerful stimulus once the proper psychological and social conditions are set." By producing atomized societies composed of isolated, powerless, and anxious individuals, liberal democracy and developing capitalism made the modern world ripe for such dictators. Neumann agreed with conservative nineteenth-century thinkers who, appalled at the fragmentation of society, predicted "the most gigantic and the most destructive [despotism] that men have ever seen," and he thought Spengler was right in predicting that Caesarism was a predictable outcome of liberal democracy.[71]

Modern Dictatorship and a Qualitatively New Kind of Terror

Neumann observed several times that Montesquieu was correct in suggesting that fear and violence were the foundations of every despotism. The use of terror, or "noncalculable violence," as a permanent threat

69. *Behemoth*, 42–45, 136, 47–49, 66, 83–84.
70. *Behemoth*, 83–85.
71. "Approaches to the Study of Political Power," 4; *Behemoth*, 85, 195–96.

against each individual creates a climate of fear essential to any dictatorship. Propaganda wears out, said Neumann, and needs to be supplemented by terror. "Violence is not just one unimportant phenomenon in the structure of National Socialist society; it is the very basis on which the society rests. Violence not only terrorizes but attracts." With no organized groups and classes that might conceivably defend themselves, this terror was, of course, highly effective against isolated and powerless individuals. And finally, as I have shown, Neumann drew upon Freud and Fromm to argue that dictatorships seek to exploit the anxieties of isolated individuals and, in effect, to institutionalize both fear and anxiety.[72]

Although violence and fear mark every tyranny, Neumann saw as early as 1941, in writing the first edition of *Behemoth,* that the terror of National Socialism was historically unique. "National Socialism," wrote Neumann, "is the first Anti-Semitic movement to advocate the complete destruction of the Jews."[73] Although Jews were suffering the brunt of the terror, Neumann also noted that Nazi violence, following a racial ideology I have yet to examine, was directed toward Jews first but also toward all allegedly inferior persons, for example, Poles and Slavs, the physically disabled, and the mentally ill. Nazi population policy, for instance, gave two commands—"to the German women, whether married or not, the commandment to produce children; to the S.S., the commandment to kill those who are not fit to live."[74] It is this violence, falling almost exclusively on the innocent and harmless, that set National Socialism apart from previous dictatorships. Neumann made this point by contrasting Nazism to Bolshevism, although we know now he was too generous to the latter. "In this respect, National Socialism and Bolshevism are utterly divergent. Not the persecution of political opponents—which is practiced in both countries—but the extermination of helpless individuals is the prerogative of National Socialism."[75] As he put it in a speech in 1951, we must distinguish between the violence of past tyrannies and that of twentieth-century dictatorships. In the past, violence was a somewhat selective "retributive justice" against identifiable and genuine opponents, whereas in our century it has become "irrational terror" against the innocent. "Between a penal justice, no matter how brutal, and terror there exists not only a quantitative but also a qualitative difference."[76]

---

72. *Behemoth,* 403; "Notes on the Theory of Dictatorship," 245; "The Concept of Political Freedom," 194; "Anxiety and Politics," 291.

73. *Behemoth,* 111.

74. *Behemoth,* 112.

75. *Behemoth,* 112.

76. "Economics and Politics in the Twentieth Century," 266–67.

In the second edition of *Behemoth,* published in 1944, Neumann began to offer some tentative answers to the question why Nazi anti-Semitism was uniquely murderous. First, the Nazis needed an enemy. Not only did they need to direct the hostility of anxious individuals toward an alleged conspiracy, but having supposedly abolished the class struggle, the Nazis needed an enemy against whom the key groups and classes could unite. Such an enemy could be neither too weak nor too strong, and Jews fit this prescription perfectly. Second, Neumann concluded that the Jews were not a scapegoat, because a scapegoat implied some final, expiating sacrifice, whereas terror against Jews only brought more terror against both Jews and many other groups. Instead, concluded Neumann, Nazi anti-Semitism was "the spearhead of terror,"[77] the prototype of terror to be used against other peoples in both imperial expansion and the destruction of free institutions everywhere.

> An understanding of Anti-Semitism is impaired by the widely accepted scapegoat theory, according to which the Jews are used as scapegoats for all evils of society. The slaughter or the expulsion of the scapegoat, however, marks in mythology the end of a process, while the persecution of the Jews, as practiced by National Socialists, is only the prologue of more horrible things to come. The expropriation of the Jews, for instance, is followed by that of the Poles, Czechs, Dutch, French, anti-Nazi Germans, and middle classes. Not only Jews are put in concentration camps, but pacifists, conservatives, socialists, Catholics, Protestants, Free Thinkers, and members of the occupied peoples. Not only Jews fall under the executioner's ax but so do countless others of many races, nationalities, beliefs, and religions. Anti-Semitism is thus the spearhead of terror. The Jews are used as guinea pigs in testing the method of repression. . . . It follows that in this Anti-Semitic ideology and practice the extermination of the Jews is only the means to the attainment of the ultimate objective, namely the destruction of free institutions, beliefs, and groups. This may be called the spearhead theory of Anti-Semitism.[78]

Neumann contended, therefore, that anti-Semitism in Germany was useful to the Nazis and largely contrived, not some indigenous characteristic of the German people. Anti-Semitic legislation proceeded relentlessly but gradually from 1933 on when needed by the Nazis either to

77. *Behemoth,* 551.
78. *Behemoth,* 550–51; also 125–27.

motivate the population or to distract them from larger problems. "Spontaneous, popular Anti-Semitism is still weak in Germany. . . . The writer's personal conviction, paradoxical as it may seem, is that the German people are the least Anti-Semitic of all."[79]

Of Political Parties and Bureaucracies

In totalitarian dictatorship the "monopolistic" political party plays the preeminent role. First, the existence of a party allows the ruling elite to claim to be part of a democratic movement, one that practices the "rituals" of democracy and thus supposedly answers to the people. Second, the party is the weapon of attack against any possible opposition. Because the state bureaucracy, the army, the trade unions, the judiciary, and so forth, are threateningly unreliable, the party can both attack and control these potential sources of opposition. "The monopolistic party is a flexible instrument which provides the force to control the state machine and society and to perform the gigantic task of cementing the authoritarian elements within society together." Before 1934, Neumann claimed, it was not clear whether the party was able to dominate the army, business, the state bureaucracy, and so on, but after the liquidation of the Röhm group in the summer of 1934, it became "abundantly clear that the party had succeeded in monopolizing political power."[80] Writing the second edition of *Behemoth* in 1944, Neumann noted: "The N.S.D.A.P. is today the organization that maintains German society. Without the party, Germany would collapse. Party, State, and Society are, under war conditions, identical. The party provides the ideological leadership; it supplies the huge system of terror; it runs the occupied territories; it provides bread, shelter, clothing, and medical services for air-raid victims; it controls the administration; it administers labor and housing supply; it supervises millions of foreign laborers. In short, it controls all but two fields: the fighting fronts and the economy."[81] Not Machiavelli, Tocqueville, or Weber—all of whom discussed mobilizing political parties—could imagine a political party undertaking so much.

In its third role, the party is the agency that attempts the total control

79. *Behemoth*, 121; see also "Anxiety and Politics," 286.
80. "Notes on the Theory of Dictatorship," 244; "Approaches to the Study of Political Power," 17; *Behemoth*, 80. Neumann clearly changed his views from those he had held when he wrote, in the first edition of *Behemoth*, that the state bureaucracy and the army were the dominant forces (*Behemoth*, 221). Indeed, his claims of an all-powerful party frankly contradict his other analyses in which he located power in the party, the army, the state bureaucracy, and the industrial classes.
81. *Behemoth*, 530.

of society. "The pluralistic principle is replaced by a monistic, total, authoritarian organization." Not only is the party responsible for disseminating propaganda, but it must try to break up traditional organizations, invade the life of the family, and control the most minute aspects of behavior. The best means of achieving this is by replacing genuine organizations that might pose an oppositional threat with spurious organizations, created and controlled by the party, that seek to isolate and control the individual. The Nazis replaced all genuine youth groups with the party-controlled Hitler Youth, independent schools and universities with party-controlled administration and faculty organizations, and similarly created special organizations for lawyers, doctors, small businessmen, and so on. Most telling of all, the Nazis abolished all trade unions, and workers —isolated, unorganized, powerless, and anxious—became meaningless units in the twenty-five-million-member Labor Front. In this the Nazis attempted to "drive the workers into huge organizations where they are submerged." With these artificial organizations, the party sought total control of society, all while doing what Tacitus and Machiavelli suggested —keeping intact the illusory facade of pluralism.[82]

Openly borrowing from Weber, Neumann argued that the National Socialist Party was simultaneously charismatic and bureaucratic: charismatic in providing a leader to mobilize isolated individuals, and bureaucratic in seeking total control over them. Despite noisy ideological denunciations of bureaucracy, National Socialism increased bureaucratization in every sector of society. Just as Weber suggested, the demands of organizing the economy and society increased bureaucratic domination. "We must not be deceived into assuming, however, that centralization of bureaucratic machinery has in any way lessened in Germany, that the party's existence has in any way restricted bureaucratic powers. On the contrary, preparedness and war have noticeably strengthened authoritarian control in the federal, state, and municipal bureaucracies."[83]

Neumann has given us Weber's analysis. Despite repeated attempts by the party either to dispense with or to control state bureaucracy, in the end it could do neither entirely, because such bureaucracy is indispensable to a modern economy. "National Socialism must necessarily carry to an extreme the one process that characterizes the structure of modern

---

82. *Behemoth*, 400, 430; "Notes on the Theory of Dictatorship," 245; *Behemoth*, 398–400, 413–18.

83. *Behemoth*, 80. The Nazis finally did succeed in replacing the traditional Prussian civil servant—"a nihilistic technocrat . . . willing to serve any government"—with officials even more willing to dispense with rules and procedures (ibid., 629–30).

society, bureaucratization."[84] While Neumann took the power that bureaucratic techniques gave to the state and the party to be somewhat obvious, he sought to show what the bureaucratization of life did to ordinary men and women. He took labor as his chief example. By abolishing trade unions that gave individual laborers considerable power, and by enrolling twenty-five million workers in the National Front, National Socialism sought to bring individuals under the control of distant and impersonal bureaucracies. "The Labor Front has driven the process of bureaucratization to its maximum. Not only the relations between the enterprise and the worker but even the relations among the workers themselves are now mediated by an autocratic bureaucracy. . . . The Labor Front has about twenty-five million members. Of what account can the individual be? The bureaucracy is everything."[85] Neumann was exploring, and elaborating upon, the nightmares of Tocqueville and Weber. Modern totalitarian dictatorship has "imprisoned man in a network of semi-authoritarian organizations controlling his life from birth to death," and like Tocqueville, Neumann recognized that modern forms of tyranny would attempt to do this by exacerbating and exploiting the isolation and powerlessness of individuals. "The isolation of the individual characteristic of modern society is intensified to the utmost limit with the help of an immense network of bureaucratic organizations."[86] Neumann's nightmare, however, combined two elements of Weber's analysis of the twentieth century that Weber had not seen as entirely compatible—a charismatic and mobilizing political party coexisting with a society suffocating under bureaucratic domination.

The Less-Than-Totalitarian Society

Although Neumann seemed ambivalent about whether the leader, the party, or the state had the most power, he nevertheless set out to examine the political dynamics behind the "all-embracing totalitarian state," and in the process, he demonstrated that totalitarian dictatorship was neither total nor monolithic. Leader, party, state bureaucracy, army, and police, not to mention key classes with often decisive influence, all shared power. It is one of Neumann's lasting and original contributions to recognize that so-called totalitarian dictatorships offer a precarious politics among key groups and classes. He chose the title *Behemoth*—the land monster of Jewish eschatology and the chaos of civil war as depicted

84. *Behemoth*, 367.
85. *Behemoth*, 418–19, 402.
86. *Behemoth*, 367, 467.

by Hobbes—precisely to show that National Socialism was not the static, monolithic rule of a leviathan, but rather a dynamic system forced constantly into political and economic change, indeed, "a non-state, a chaos, a situation of lawlessness, disorder, and anarchy."[87]

The key to Neumann's analysis is his argument that behind the totalitarian state one finds both a functioning system of monopoly capitalism and thus a definite class structure. In fact, Neumann suggested, European Fascism grew out of both liberalism and capitalism. Much is made, for example, of the negative state, or the night-watchman state, in Locke's political theory, certainly the prevailing theory in British politics until the early twentieth century. But was it really so powerless to act? Indeed, not. This negative state "proved itself capable of preserving the internal security of England, of dealing with the Chartists and the labor movement, and of establishing an immense colonial empire. Surely a strange theory for a so-called negative state which succeeds in maintaining an imperialist policy!"[88] A better interpretation of Locke's theory suggests that the state, which in fact more or less left alone both the economy and the class structure within England, was politically aggressive and even authoritarian in defending the interests of the economy and its ruling classes both at home and abroad. In the late nineteenth and early twentieth centuries, however, the liberal state had to do more. With the advent of a more aggressive imperialism and monopoly capitalism, the state had to use force abroad, leave the economy alone at home, and defend forcefully challenges to the dominant classes from various democratic movements. Out of these actions—that is, out of imperialism, monopoly capitalism, and the liberal state—Fascism arose. "Here are the germs of Fascism. Since the economy needs the state, it wants a state that will not touch economic power relations. Thus one may say that Fascism emerged from the need of the holders of economic power for a strong state which, however, must not be subjected to the control of the people. Fascism did not originate as a reaction to the communist danger, but for the purpose of suppressing the democratic movement which wanted to give rational and democratic shape to the economy."[89] At the time Neumann was writing *Behemoth*, it was fashionable among such writers as Peter Drucker, James Burnham, and Dwight Macdonald to suggest that National Socialism had eliminated capitalism in favor of some sort of state-run economy or a bureaucratic collectivism. Neumann rejected these conclusions. He noted that from the early 1930s Nazi theorists had boasted that National

---

87. *Behemoth*, 221, vii; Aycoberry, *The Nazi Question*, 92–93.
88. "Economics and Politics in the Twentieth Century," 259.
89. "Economics and Politics in the Twentieth Century," 265.

Socialism left the economy alone, and he argued that despite or because of heavy state interference, the basic structure of monopoly capitalism persisted and flourished under Nazi Germany. Fascism in Germany, in short, was used to preserve the class domination of monopoly capitalism. "The German economy of today has two broad and striking characteristics. It is a monopolistic economy—*and* a command economy. It is a private capitalistic economy, regimented by the totalitarian state. We suggest as a name best to describe it, 'Totalitarian Monopoly Capitalism.' "[90]

Borrowing from Marx and Weber, Neumann maintained that behind the Nazi state one found a class structure intact, and thus, the very description "totalitarian" is an ideological veil hiding powerful classes. Far from attempting to create a classless society, National Socialism followed a conscious policy of using elites to control the masses. "National Socialism therefore seeks to carve out from the masses certain elites who receive preferred treatment, greater material benefits, a high social status, and political privileges. In return the elites act as the spearhead of the regime within the amorphous mass."[91] The key elites, of course, lie within the groups that served National Socialism well and profited from it—big industry, the party, the bureaucracy, and the armed forces.

> National Socialism could, of course, have nationalized private industry. That, it did not do and did not want to do. Why should it? With regard to imperialist expansion, National Socialism and big business have identical interests. National Socialism pursues glory and the stabilization of its rule, and industry, the full utilization of its capacity and the conquest of foreign markets. German industry was willing to co-operate to the fullest. It had never liked democracy, civil rights, trade unions, and public discussion. National Socialism utilized the daring, the knowledge, the aggressiveness of the industrial leadership, while the industrial leadership utilized the anti-democracy, anti-liberalism and anti-unionism of the National Socialist party, which had fully developed the techniques by which masses can be controlled and dominated. The bureaucracy marched as always with the victorious forces, and for the first time in the history of Germany the army got everything it wanted. Four distinct groups are thus represented in

90. *Behemoth*, 261, 49, 222.
91. *Behemoth*, 402, 365.

the German ruling class: big industry, the party, the bureaucracy, and the armed forces.[92]

To these four, Neumann cautiously added the landed Junker class, which both helped the National Socialists attain power and profited from the new regime. "The political influence of the Junkers is still strong, though not decisive."[93] By the second edition of *Behemoth* (1944), Neumann still recognized the power of the party, the army, and big business, but thought that the power of the state bureaucracy had "steadily declined." Because Neumann recognized the immense power of what he called "terrorists," he thought that the SS and the Gestapo could not be subsumed under, or declared dependent upon, either the army or the party.[94] In seeking to demonstrate the politics of totalitarian dictatorship, Neumann probably underestimated the power of the leader himself.

Nonetheless, Neumann demonstrated convincingly that behind claims of total control by the leader, uniformity imposed by the party, and the monolithic nature of the state, genuine political conflict existed. While industrialists were happy to eliminate trade unions, they did not like restrictions imposed upon them by the state bureaucracy, and while the army eagerly embraced imperial expansion, it detested meddling by the party. Thus, the ruling class was neither homogenous nor held together by stated ideals or common loyalty, unless it was loyalty to self-interested profit and power.

> Nothing remains but profits, power, prestige, and above all, fear. Devoid of any common loyalty and concerned solely with the preservation of their own interests, the ruling groups will break apart as soon as the miracle-producing Leader meets a worthy opponent. At present, each section needs the others. The army needs the party because the war is totalitarian. The army cannot organize society "totally"; that is left to the party. The party, on the other hand, needs the army to win the war and thus to stabilize and even aggrandize its own power. Both need monopolistic industry to guarantee continuous expansion. And all three need the bureaucracy to achieve the technical rationality [note again

92. *Behemoth*, 361; see also 365–99 for a more detailed discussion of classes in Nazi Germany. Bracher is probably correct in claiming that Neumann's interpretation "runs the risk of misjudging the revolutionary component of National Socialism" by underestimating the transformations in the economy and society that National Socialism brought about. Bracher, *The German Dictatorship*, 7.
93. *Behemoth*, 396.
94. *Behemoth*, 632–34.

the reliance on Weber] without which the system could not operate.[95]

By outlining in some detail these "deep antagonisms within the ruling
classes," Neumann sought to prove the existence of political conflict behind the decisions of the Nazi tyranny. "It is thus impossible to detect in
the framework of the National Socialist political system any one organ
which monopolizes political power."[96] Not only did Neumann seek to
show that the state was less than monolithic, he went on to suggest that
perhaps we could not call the system of National Socialism a state. Perhaps it is only a bargain, a perverse social contract, between these four
ruling groups. Uncomfortable with the political categories of Marx and
Weber as they might apply to National Socialism, Neumann suggested
that perhaps Nazi Germany was becoming merely class rule directly
through the means of the party, the army, and the terror apparatus.

Tyranny and Empire

Neumann argued ultimately that National Socialism had three different economies simultaneously—a competitive economy, a monopolistic economy,
and a command economy. While Neumann called this command economy,
resulting from an "interfering and regimenting state," a "controlled" or
"steered" capitalism, he made it clear that the state controlled and steered
the economy on behalf of industrial interests. If one paid too much attention, Neumann contended, to legal decrees and to pronouncements by government officials, one might erroneously conclude that the state, with nearly
absolute legal authority over business and the economy, actually regulated
the economy in the interests of the broader population. "But law, like language, does not always express reality; it often hides it."[97] Within Nazi Germany, and especially given the complicated relations of state, party, army,
and business, "it is the function of law to veil and hide the antagonisms until
it becomes almost impossible to pierce through the mass of words." Neumann, of course, sought to transport us behind the ideological and propagandistic veil to show "the ever closer connection between private capitalists and the state."[98]

Time and again Neumann showed that business relied upon state interference to consolidate its position: to take the risk out of investment, to
fend of nationalization, to co-opt regulatory agencies, to protect cartels,

95. *Behemoth*, 397–98.
96. *Behemoth*, 469–70.
97. *Behemoth*, 293, 234, 254.
98. *Behemoth*, 254, 298.

to plan, along with the party, against the interests of the working and middle classes, and to make certain that old capitalists such as Krupp and new capitalist enterprises such as the Herman Göring combine flourished. Neumann frequently asserted that private economic power was as dangerous as the power of the state; when a dictatorial state works hand in hand with the interests of the ruling class, the result is a fascist tyranny. "The essence of National Socialist social policy consists in the acceptance and strengthening of the prevailing class character of German society."[99]

If National Socialism promoted the interests of big business, how did labor fare? First, labor by and large refused to support National Socialism, to the "lasting merit of Social Democratic education."[100] Few of the Social Democratic labor leaders went over to National Socialism, and the large majority of trade unionists and supporters of the Social Democrats refused to support Nazi policies. Second, ordinary working men and women did resign themselves to National Socialist polices, largely because the Nazis eliminated unemployment and provided an extensive social security program. "Unemployment assistance, health and accident insurance, invalidity and old-age pensions—that is how National Socialism wins the passive toleration of the masses for the time being. Social security is its one propaganda slogan built on the truth."[101] Third, despite enormous increases in profits for industry, wages were frozen and the standard of living for workers declined. From 1932 to 1938, "productivity . . . more than doubled while income [rose] by merely 66.1 per cent. . . . In sum, the exploitation of the workers . . . measurably intensified." Neumann concluded that National Socialism intended "not only to establish a ceiling on wages but to abolish all social gains made in decades of social struggles."[102] Fourth, as I have shown, the Nazi tyranny destroyed independent trade unions, making all workers powerless members of the gigantic Labor Front. In addition, labor policy glorified a fictional "community" within the individual plant, established puppet "councils of confidence" to increase productivity, and gave authoritarian powers to the "plant leader," generally the employer. "They are devices for the manipulation of the working classes, for the establishment of authoritarian control . . . for the isolation of each individual worker."[103] Finally, labor

99. *Behemoth*, 366–67; "The Concept of Political Freedom," 178. See Held, *An Introduction to Critical Theory*, 53–63; Kellner, *Critical Theory, Marxism, and Modernity*, 69–70.
100. *Behemoth*, 215.
101. *Behemoth*, 432.
102. *Behemoth*, 436, 347.
103. *Behemoth*, 419, 424–25.

laws ensured that the worker had no rights. The worker "cannot choose his place of work or kind of work, he cannot leave at will. . . . Labor has been delivered to authoritarian control, as completely as possible." All of these measures complete what Marx called the despotism of the workplace, and indeed, Neumann argued that Hitler agreed with Spengler's conclusion that the laboring classes were "human vermin" who should work under slavelike conditions twelve hours a day.[104]

What happened to the class struggle? On the one hand, National Socialism sought to buy it off with promises to the masses, but chiefly to the middle classes. The "uprooted middle classes," devastated by inflation and depression, formed the backbone of National Socialist support, and they certainly had the most to gain. "The annihilation of a prosperous middle class [by inflation and depression] turned out to be the most powerful stimulus to aggressive imperialism, for it was the section of the middle class having but little to lose that whole-heartedly supported the drive by heavy industry for rearmament and for imperialism."[105] Nazi propaganda consciously played to these aspirations, by promising, for example, both to the masses at large and to the middle classes more specifically "a share in the coming profits of world conquest." National Socialism also promised the middle classes profits from the "Aryanization," or the seizure, of Jewish property and from the spoilation of Eastern Europe. "Let us exploit, at least, Poles and Russians," thought the middle classes.[106] All promises of prosperity by empire proved to be a sham. While the Nazis awarded the bulk of the spoils from "Aryanization" and conquest in Eastern Europe to the large industrialists, the "middle classes of independent small and middle businessmen (artisans, industrialists, retailers, wholesalers) . . . ceased to exist or [would] cease to exist within a very short period."[107] Members of the middle classes—cruelly corrupt, and always for sale, in Neumann's eyes—fell into the working classes or eagerly joined the SS.

On the other hand, National Socialism sought to disguise class antagonism with an overload of specious—and often racist—ideology. To take but a few examples, the notion of a people's community, or *Volksgemeinschaft,* pretended that the German Reich was attaining a genuine community transcending classes and groups; racial theories attempted to hide class conflict, because inferior races—not classes—became the enemies against whom workers and others allegedly had to struggle; anti-

104. *Behemoth,* 343, 349, 197.
105. *Behemoth,* 217, 201.
106. *Behemoth,* 150, 628.
107. *Behemoth,* 117, 626, 275.

Semitism, more specifically, became a substitute for class struggle, because "by heaping all hatred, all resentment, all misery upon one enemy who can easily be exterminated and who cannot resist, Aryan society can be integrated into a whole"; and finally, the National Socialists put forth the fantastically fictional doctrine of "racial proletarian imperialism," a doctrine depicting "Germany and Italy [as] proletarian races, surrounded by a world of hostile plutocratic-capitalistic-Jewish democracies"—that is, Britain and the United States—against whom the nation as a whole must struggle.[108]

While false promises and spurious ideology were the keys to making imperial expansion acceptable to the German people, Neumann concluded that, opposition or not, a Nazi push for empire was inevitable. Much as the expansive adventures of Machiavelli's princes were the manifestations of the tyrants' efforts to pacify military and financial interests, so "imperialistic war is the outcome of the internal antagonisms of the German economy." Neumann even took a "certain satisfaction" in noting that he predicted this in 1935, when this conclusion was not yet obvious to the rest of the world. Successful imperialist war would bring cheap labor and raw materials for industry, power to the party, grandiosity to the state, and glory to the army—and of course profits for all. The key, of course, was that German industry and the National Socialist Party needed each other.[109] "The imperialistic sections of German society found in the National Socialist party the ally needed to provide the mass basis for imperialism. This does not mean that National Socialism is merely a subservient tool of German industry, but it does mean that with regard to imperialistic expansion, industry and party have identical aims. . . . The National Socialist party is solely concerned with establishing the thousand-year rule, but to achieve this goal, they cannot but protect the monopolistic system, which provides them with the economic basis for political expansion."[110] Just as Germany achieved national unification late in European history, so did Germany come late to its imperialistic ambitions, and thus found the world already divided up among European powers. "When Germany came forward as an active imperialistic force, it found the earth divided among the various military machines. Redistribution . . . required the force of arms and an enormous outlay in blood and money."[111]

It also required ideological justification. Just as the National Socialist

108. *Behemoth*, 125, 186–87, 227, 103, 130.
109. *Behemoth*, 202, 37, 360–61.
110. *Behemoth*, 185, 354.
111. *Behemoth*, 103.

German Workers' Party was neither a workers' party nor socialistic, it was also not nationalistic. "A biological race theory replaced the political theory of nationality." If a racial theory supplants nationalism, then neither national sovereignty nor national boundaries need be accepted. Instead, "the sovereignty of the Germanic race exists wherever there are racial Germans," an idea supposedly justifying "liberating" Germans living in Austria, the Sudetenland, and the Polish corridor. This idea was buttressed by the claim that the German Reich was heir to some idealized past moment of the Holy Roman Empire.[112] In addition, the doctrine of "living space," or *Lebensraum*—roughly the idea that nations ought to share the earth in proportion to their populations and to their greatness and, thus, that a great nation like Germany has a right to colonies in the East—sought to justify expansion into countries of Eastern Europe with little or no German populations.[113] And finally, the claims of racial superiority purportedly gave a right to the so-called Aryan races to dominate and even exterminate Jews, but also Poles, Slavs, and so forth. Under these claims of racial superiority, the Germans had a right, indeed an obligation, to rule over allegedly inferior races. "The theory of German racial superiority and Jewish racial inferiority permits the complete enslavement of the eastern Jews. . . . It actually establishes a hierarchy of races—giving no rights to the Jews, a few to the Poles, a few more to the Ukranians, . . . and full rights to Germans."[114]

Propaganda, Ideology, and the Structure of National Socialism

The subtitle of *Behemoth* refers to "The Structure and Practice of National Socialism," and National Socialist ideology is an important part of this structure. In seeking to control isolated and powerless individuals, the Nazis saw that propagandistic ideology goes hand in hand with terror, indeed is "fused with terror." Propaganda and terror are "two aspects of a single development: the transformation of man into the passive victim of an all-inclusive force which flatters and terrorizes him, which elevates him and sends him into concentration camps." In arguing that propaganda is not really a substitute for terror, but in fact an integral part of it, Neumann called propaganda "violence committed against the soul."[115] By managing to transform genuine ideas and culture into propaganda, by constant repetition of ideological jargon and by substituting "magical celebrations" for independent judgment, the Nazis sought "to prevent the

112. *Behemoth*, 103, 168, 130, 147–50.
113. *Behemoth*, 130, 131–50.
114. *Behemoth*, 126.
115. *Behemoth*, 38, 221, 436.

masses from thinking."[116] Himmler's claim that German subjects should learn no more than to count to twelve and to spell their names—"beyond this, education is dangerous"—illustrates how much the National Socialist Party wanted to think for the entire nation. "In order to manipulate the masses," Neumann concluded, "in order to control, atomize, terrorize them, one must capture them ideologically." This means, of course, that the actions of the German people were not in any sense authentic, because they were manipulated by the leader and the party. "Action without thought is possible only if it is directed and controlled action. . . . Thus controlled it is pseudo-action, for it is not man who acts but a bureaucratic machine."[117]

Nazi ideology was derived from the needs of the ruling classes. First, Nazi arguments that liberal democratic societies are weak (the nightwatchman's state), composed of an aggregate of isolated Robinson Crusoes, divided, and incapable of action—these critiques became only a prelude for surrendering power to a totalitarian state and its leader, supported of course by the party, the army, and big business. Second, the happy picture of a "people's community," or *Volksgemeinschaft,* sought to entice workers by promising them everything socialism did and more—a united community beyond classes, an end to loneliness, a share in the spoils of totalitarian military adventures, and no need for class struggle—without posing any threat to the established structure of power. Third, the doctrine of "racial proletarian imperialism" legitimized a struggle against moneyed power,[118] but sought to transfer it from domestic to international politics as the supposedly proletarian races of Germany and Italy struggled against domination by the plutocratic-capitalistic-Jewish democracies of Britain and the United States. How eager was German business to depict its imperialistic struggles as a mission for the heroic German workers struggling to conquer the traders and financiers of England, German greatness against the petty and sordid virtues of the British bourgeoisie! Fourth, Nazi theorists explicitly contrived the doctrine of *Lebensraum* as an ideological rationalization for imperial expansion. And finally, racial theories not only justified imperial expansion, but by giving superior virtues to the German race, these theories suggested that the Aryan race—not Marx's proletariat, and not democratic men and women—embodied the morality for a new world order.[119]

At every turn, ideas merely served the interests of the ruling classes in

116. *Behemoth,* 467, 402.

117. "Economics and Politics in the Twentieth Century," 267; "Notes on the Theory of Dictatorship," 246; *Behemoth,* 465, 438–39.

118. *Behemoth,* 187.

119. *Behemoth,* 189–93, 187–88, 205, 132.

Germany, and thus were at most a peripheral influence on developments in Nazi Germany. Effective only in manipulating the ruled classes and hiding from them their true interests, these ideological pronouncements of National Socialism were probably not even taken seriously by a large part of the Nazi ruling elite. In the end, no political theory, but only weakly disguised power, justified the rule of National Socialism. "What is left of justification for the Reich? . . . Only the Reich itself remains. It is its own justification. . . . Power is a sufficient theoretical base for more power."[120] I have explored the preconditions and the means necessary for the exercise of this power—isolation, anxiety, bureaucratic domination, terror, and propaganda—but when it came to using this power, the determining forces of Nazi tyranny were ultimately the economic and political interests of big industrialists, the party, the state bureaucracy, and the army.

Conclusion

Neumann's contributions to theories of tyranny are immense, although many of them come from his creative use of the categories set forth by Montesquieu, Marx, Weber, and Freud. First, like Marx, as well as thinkers such as Machiavelli and Tocqueville, Neumann noted that the leaders of Nazi Germany, this most evil of tyrannies, ruled under the proclaimed banner of freedom, the spurious claim accepted by so many that National Socialism was a higher and nobler form of democratic freedom. Second, like Tacitus and Montesquieu, Neumann noted that the tyranny of National Socialism, like all tyrannies, had to subvert the rule of law and the indendence of the judiciary. Third, Neumann was most brilliant in applying the idea he found in both Montesquieu and Marx that a society is a structure with "its own inner logic." Looking behind the ideological veil that claimed National Socialism to be working on behalf of the middle and working classes, Neumann outlined a structure of rule in which the state bureaucracy, the party, big industry, the military, and the Junker landed class all had interests that benefited from the expansionary rule of National Socialism. Fourth, he observed the necessity of a single "monopolistic" party to hold the structure together. Fifth, in an implicit critique of Weber, he noted that National Socialism, in a frightenly clever way, combined an all-encompassing and oppressive bureaucracy with an almost uniquely powerful charisma. Whereas Weber thought these two could coexist, he did not allow for each being so dominant simultaneously. Sixth, borrowing directly from Weber, Neumann noted how skilled National So-

---

120. *Behemoth*, 135, 467; "Approaches to the Study of Political Power," 4–5.

cialism was in applying science, and especially the science of organizing men and women, to their rule. Bureaucracy was everywhere, so that Nazi tyranny "imprisoned man in a network of semi-authoritarian organizations controlling his life from birth to death." Seventh, like Montesquieu and Tocqueville, Neumann saw the tyranny of National Socialism as consciously eliminating intermediate institutions between the individual and the ruling structure. Associations, unions, and clubs were all eliminated by the party, leaving the individual alone, lonely, powerless, and anxious. Eighth, as Freud suggested, individuals who are alone are readily susceptible to the claims of propaganda—that all citizens were part of a greater community (*Volksgemeinschaft*), that Germany found unity in submitting to the leader (as father figure), and so on. Ninth, as Montesquieu had suggested, fear and violence are at the heart of any tyranny, and how much better they work when each individual is required to resist violence alone. What Montesquieu could not predict, however, Neumann observed as early as 1942, that the violence of Nazi Germany—which Neumann called terror—was rare, if not unique, in that it was directed at those who were wholly innocent. Tenth, racial theories defining the German as superior not only to Jews but also to Poles, Slavs, and so forth, by providing isolated individuals with a common enemy, preyed on their need to feel themselves part of a larger whole. Eleventh, racial theories also directly supported the material interests of the ruling classes that sought profit and advantage from empire, and because Germany came late to European imperialism, it had to go to war to redivide the world. Indeed, racial conflict masked class struggle. And twelfth, and most brilliantly, Neumann noticed that no government is entirely totalitarian, that there is a politics—even a chaotic politics—that still remains as the bureaucracy, powerful industrialists, the party, the terror apparatus, and the army quarrel for power and policies with the leader as both player and umpire. Nearly five decades after Neumann had written, political scientists wrote foolishly that totalitarian governments were entirely without politics, without conflict, and without change.

Arendt: Totalitarianism as a New Form of Government

Despite—or perhaps because of—studying philosophy with Heidegger and Jaspers, Arendt became one of this century's most accomplished classical scholars. Like virtually all other great German thinkers, she made an intellectual and philosophical pilgrimage to the ancient Greek world. As a consequence, by bringing classical categories of thinking to her analyses of Nazi Germany, Arendt refreshingly forces us to reexamine the original meanings of words such as *tyranny, despot, dictatorship, authority,* and *freedom.* In her view, "such terms as *tyranny, authority,* and *totalitarianism* [had] simply lost their common meaning," thus allowing political commentators to toss such terms about as they saw fit.[121] Knowing so thoroughly these ancient classifications of government only served to convince her that totalitarianism was an entirely new form of government "different from dictatorships and tyrannies," a new classification—sad as this is for the modern world—unknown to ancient authors. Arendt acknowledged that she resisted such a conclusion as being "extremely unlikely," because "the forms of government under which men live have been very few; they were discovered early, classified by the Greeks and have proved extraordinarily long-lived." Although many who followed Arendt applied the word *totalitarian* to virtually any tyranny, and especially to every Communist country regarded as an enemy in the Cold War, Arendt cautioned that writers should use the word *totalitarian* "sparingly." Indeed, she applied it only to two cases. "Up to now we know only two authentic forms of totalitarian domination: the dictatorship of National Socialism after 1938, and the dictatorship of Bolshevism after 1930 [whose totalitarian features, in her mind, ended with Stalin's death]. These forms of domination differ basically from other kinds of dictatorial, despotic or tyrannical rule."[122]

What makes totalitarianism a new form of government, according to Arendt? The answer involves three features that I explore in more detail later: loneliness, ideology, and terror. First, loneliness. Arendt maintained that if there is indeed a new form of government in the world, it must rest on "an experience which . . . has never before served as the foundation of a body politic." Whereas all tyrannies have used force to isolate subjects in order to control them, totalitarianism came into the world when, with the decline of classes, communities, and families, loneliness had become "an everyday experience of the evergrowing masses of our century." It is this experience of widespread loneliness that is new to the world, and totalitarianism "bases itself on loneliness, on the experience of not belonging to the world at all, which is among the most radical and desper-

121. Hannah Arendt, "What Is Authority?" in *Between Past and Future: Eight Exercises in Political Thought* (New York: Viking, 1961), 91–142, esp. 95–96.

122. Arendt, *The Origins of Totalitarianism,* new ed., with added prefaces (New York: Harcourt Brace Jovanovich, 1973), xxvii–xxviii, 460–61, 419. On Arendt's use of the concept of "totalitarianism," see M. Bittman, "Totalitarianism: The Career of a Concept," in *Hannah Arendt: Thinking, Judging, Freedom,* ed. Gisela T. Kaplan and Clive S. Kessler (Boston: Allen & Unwin, 1989), 56–68.

ate experiences of man." Loneliness, in turn, renders men and women easily susceptible to both ideology and terror.[123]

Ideologies, the second characteristic of this new form of government, "pretend to know the mysteries of the whole historical process—the secrets of the past, the intricacies of the present, the uncertainties of the future—because of the logic inherent in their respective ideas." Whereas tyrannies dominate subjects but leave their private thoughts intact, ideology—aided by loneliness and terror—invades the private lives of men and women, destroys common sense, and with an inflexible consistency manipulates their thinking. "Ideological thinking ruins all relationships with reality. . . . Men lose the capacity of both experience and thought."[124] In addition, ideologies encourage totalitarian movements to discard all the utilitarian and economic motives so central to an ordinary tyranny. Despite ruling brutally, tyrants dominate their subjects according to somewhat predictable selfish interests, whereas the totalitarian dictatorships of both Stalin and Hitler achieved "emancipation from the profit motive" and thus discarded economic and military interests in search of higher ideological goals, for example, racial extermination in the case of Nazi Germany. This fact alone, according to Arendt, makes totalitarianism a new form of government. "No ordinary tyrant was ever mad enough to discard all limited and local interests—economic, national, human, military—in favor of a purely fictitious reality in some indefinite future."[125]

The third characteristic of this new form of government is terror. Whereas tyrannies brutally use violence against real or perceived opponents, totalitarian rule uses terror even, and especially, after "all political opposition [has] been extinguished." Terror and death camps, regarded as useless by the outside world, constitute the key characteristics of totalitarian government, and thus the crimes of totalitarianism differ not just in the "degree of seriousness but in essence." If lawless rule is the essence of tyranny, "then terror is the essence of totalitarian domination," and if tyrannies strive for a severe limitation on human freedom, totalitarian domination, by means of ideology and terror, "aims at abolishing freedom, even at eliminating human spontaneity in general."[126]

Montesquieu, on whom Arendt relied extensively, argued that only tyrannies are destroyed from within, as if devouring themselves, and Arendt

123. *Totalitarianism*, 461, 478, 475; also "Tradition and the Modern Age," in *Between Past and Future*, 17–40, esp. 26.

124. *Totalitarianism*, 469, 474.

125. *Totalitarianism*, 418–19, 411–12; also "What Is Freedom?" 143–72, esp. 163.

126. *Totalitarianism*, 421; Arendt, *Eichmann in Jerusalem: A Report on the Banality of Evil*, rev. and enlarged ed. (New York: Viking, 1965), 267; *Totalitarianism*, 464, 405.

agreed that "totalitarian domination, like tyranny, bears the germs of its own destruction." And yet this new form of government seems destined to persist as a perpetual temptation, "a potentiality and an ever-present danger [that] is only too likely to stay with us from now on," just as monarchies and republics, democracies and tyrannies, have been with us from ancient times.[127]

Imperialism and Racism

The Origins of Totalitarianism, published in 1951, has three distinct parts—"Anti-Semitism," "Imperialism," and "Totalitarianism"—that seem to have very little relation to one another. In letters and lectures, Arendt later explained that anti-Semitism and imperialism, along with racism and the decay of the nation-state, were not in a strict sense *causes* of totalitarianism, but instead "problems" of the modern world for which totalitarian rulers claimed to have found an admittedly terrifying "solution." Thus, anti-Semitism and imperialism form the groundwork for totalitarianism.[128]

Although anti-Semitism was an important part of the groundwork for totalitarianism, imperialism was the most important. Imperialism, and all that went with it, was the key development that led to totalitarianism, that "led to an almost complete break in the continuous flow of Western history as we had known it for more than two thousand years." Imperialism itself, or at least the kind that Arendt dates to the Berlin Conference

---

127. *Totalitarianism,* 478, 467.

128. Elisabeth Young-Bruehl, *Hannah Arendt: For Love of the World* (New Haven: Yale University Press, 1982), 200–204. Arendt wrote *The Origins of Totalitarianism* as a political philosopher trying to explain historical events, and her approach and methodology have severely frustrated many historians. Hughes, for example, complained of her "heavily freighted terminology," insufficient data, factual mistakes, and the fact that the book was "almost entirely innocent of economics" (see *The Sea Change,* 119–25). Aycoberry complained that the book was too descriptive and gave no real account of the causes of totalitarianism, that the very concept was replete with contradictions, and that the book was marred by errors and an "uncertain chronology" (see *The Nazi Question,* 130–33.) George Lichtheim succinctly stated that Arendt was, "to put it mildly, no historian" (cited in Stephen J. Whitfield, *Into the Dark: Hannah Arendt and Totalitarianism* [Philadelphia: Temple University Press, 1980], 53). Readers can find a balanced summary of criticisms directed at Arendt's book in Margaret Canovan, *The Political Thought of Hannah Arendt* (New York: Harcourt Brace Jovanovich, 1974), 38–50. Though the book has factual inaccuracies and other shortcomings, it endures because it offers provocative insight and forces us to ask uncomfortable questions. For what amount to two defenses of Arendt's approach, see David Luban, "Explaining Dark Times: Hannah Arendt's Theory of Theory," *Social Research* 50, no. 1 (1983): 215–48, and Richard H. King, "Endings and Beginnings: Politics in Arendt's Early Thought," *Political Theory* 12, no. 2 (1984): 235–51.

on Africa in 1885, was something new to the world. "Expansion as a permanent and supreme aim of politics is the central political idea of imperialism. Since it implies neither temporary looting nor the more lasting assimilation of conquest, it is an entirely new concept in the history of political thought and action."[129] Arendt observed accurately that this imperialism was not simply the looting of some nations by others (although looting did take place), or conquest in which one assimilates and transforms a conquered nation, or even the old-fashioned empire building of the ancient world. In contrast to those of ancient empires, the institutions of the imperialist home country remained almost entirely separate from the conquered "possessions," but instead served only to exercise loose control over a designated "colonial administration."[130]

While Arendt frequently referred to imperialism as "expansion for expansion's sake," her own analysis defined nineteenth-century imperialism as expansion for profit's sake. "Not ideas," Arendt wrote, "but events change the world."[131] She made it quite clear that no ideal of expansion created imperialism, but instead the economic needs of the bourgeoisie that could not be met within the confines of the nation-state. This is evident even in her brilliant, if at times strained, analysis of Hobbes, as the preeminent theorist of the bourgeoisie, whose claims that the ever-increasing accumulation of property would necessitate an ever-increasing accumulation of power ultimately defended the logic of power politics and imperialism. Imperialism was caused chiefly, according to Arendt, by "the overproduction of capital" and the fact that the bourgeoisie "could no longer find productive investment within the national borders." Thus, Cecil Rhodes's claims that "expansion is everything" and that "I would annex the planets if I could" were grounded not in grand ideals but practical economic interests.[132] "Imperialism was born when the ruling class in capitalist production came up against national limitations to its economic expansion. The bourgeoisie turned to politics out of economic necessity; for if it did not want to give up the capitalist system whose inherent law is constant economic growth, it had to impose this law upon its home governments and proclaim expansion to be an ultimate political goal of foreign policy."[133] Imperialism signaled the triumph of the bourgeoisie. Arendt argued that even after the bourgeoisie had become "the ruling

129. *Totalitarianism*, 123, 125.
130. *Totalitarianism*, 130–32.
131. *Totalitarianism*, xvii; Arendt, *The Human Condition: A Study of the Central Dilemmas Facing Modern Man* (Garden City, N.Y.: Doubleday, 1959), 248.
132. *Totalitarianism*, 135, 124, 139–47.
133. *Totalitarianism*, 126.

class," it declined to exercise its power, preferring instead to pursue its private interests and leave political decisions to state bureaucracies. When the nation-state, however, hindered its economic ambitions and its need for imperialistic expansion, the bourgeoisie sought "to use the state and its instruments of violence for its own economic purposes," and thus with imperialism came "the political emancipation of the bourgeoisie." Unlike Lenin, Arendt saw imperialism as "the first stage in political rule of the bourgeoisie rather than the last stage of capitalism."[134] But why was imperialism so readily accepted by the rest of society? Because imperialism seemed to be "a cure for all evils, an easy panacea for all conflicts," a solution to the problems of outdated political structures, class struggles, and economic crises that were bringing about the disintegration of the body politic. All of these difficulties "made it appear as though imperialism alone were able to settle the grave domestic, social, and economic problems of modern times. . . . The solution of the riddle was imperialism."[135]

Although the needs of the bourgeoisie hastened Europe to expansion, imperialism could not have succeeded without an alliance between what Arendt called the "mob" and capital. "The alliance between capital and mob is to be found at the genesis of every consistently imperialist policy." Arendt used the word *mob* with maddening imprecision, claiming that the mob is distinct from the working classes, the people, and the masses. Instead, the mob is "the refuse of all classes" and "the by-product of bourgeois society, directly produced by it and never quite separable from it." Arendt seemed to use the word *mob* to indicate nihilistic and unprincipled malcontents, easily led by certain intellectuals eager to escape the productive process in quest of a greater cause or a grand adventure, no matter how destructive. "The political principles of the mob, as encountered in imperialist ideologies and totalitarian movements, betray a surprisingly strong affinity with the political attitudes of bourgeois society, if the latter are cleansed of hypocrisy."[136] In other words, the mob is always potentially present in bourgeois society because of the unprincipled egoism underlying bourgeois ideals. Imperialistic adventures united capital and the mob, first and most specifically, in the race for gold in South Africa, which established "the first paradise of parasites." In the British

134. *Totalitarianism*, 123–24, 138.

135. *Totalitarianism*, 147, 157. Throughout her *Origins of Totalitarianism*, the bourgeoisie turns out to be the key villain, not as in the writings of Marx but rather more as in Tocqueville's writings. See George Kateb, *Hannah Arendt: Politics, Conscience, Evil* (Totowa, N.J.: Rowman & Allanheld, 1983), 66–68.

136. *Totalitarianism*, 155–56.

experience, capital dominated the mob, and their rule was generally confined to the overseas empire. By contrast, in the German experience the mob came to dominate capital in a destructive totalitarian rule in the home country. "The German bourgeoisie [threw] off the mask of hypocrisy and openly [confessed] its relationship to the mob, calling on it expressly to champion its property interests."[137]

Imperialism was a disaster. Not only did this move for expansion and power "lay waste the whole globe," but it also helped prepare the way for tyranny or totalitarianism in the home countries. Police forces and armies so useful abroad eventually used violence against citizens at home; secret agents turned from protecting the overseas empire to spying on their fellow citizens. In other words, violence and economic exploitation abroad inevitably degenerated into tyranny at home. And finally, competition in the game of imperial expansion could only bring nations into war with one another. "How a competition between fully armed business concerns—'empires'—could end in anything but victory for one and death for the others is difficult to understand."[138]

To lay the groundwork completely for totalitarianism, and not merely for ordinary tyrannies, Europe needed to add racism to imperialism. Indeed, in the original draft of *The Origins of Totalitarianism,* Arendt described Nazi Germany as an example, not of totalitarianism, but of "race imperialism," a phrase she borrowed from Neumann's *Behemoth.*[139] Imperialism needed racism. Racial doctrines not only inspired the mob, they provided the elite with intellectual justification for the "brutal deeds and active bestiality" of European imperialism. Apologists for imperialism eagerly borrowed from the racist theories offered by thinkers like Gobineau, but, as Arendt acknowledged, "imperialism would have necessitated the invention of racism as the only possible 'explanation' and excuse for its deeds, even if no race-thinking had ever existed in the civilized world."[140] Racism fostered imperialist expansion in two ways. First, by relying on distorted Darwinian theories, racist thinkers defended not only the inevitability of struggle and "survival of the fittest" but also the so-called science of eugenics. Second, racist theories are by nature internationalistic, not nationalistic, because they encourage conflict between races not confined to national borders, for example, white Europeans versus black Africans, or "Aryans" against Jews or Slavs. "From the very beginning, racism deliberately cut across all national boundaries, whether defined by geo-

137. *Totalitarianism,* 151, 156, 225–26, 123–24.
138. *Totalitarianism,* xviii-xx, 125–26, 136–37, 351.
139. Young-Bruehl, *Hannah Arendt,* 203.
140. *Totalitarianism,* 183–84.

graphical, linguistic, traditional, or any other standards, and denied na-
tional-political existence as such."[141]

Arendt argued that racial doctrines had roots extending into the eighteenth century, but that they flourished in all Western nations simultaneously in the nineteenth century. Moreover, "racism has been the
powerful ideology of imperialistic policies since the turn of our century."
An ideology, as Arendt defined it, must offer one single and simple idea
that claims to explain all of history, to solve the riddles of the universe,
and to uncover the hidden workings of either nature or history. Only two
ideologies, in her view, have survived into the twentieth century—one
that claims to explain all of history in terms of class struggle, and one
that explains history as a "natural fight of races." The twentieth century,
indeed, is "witnessing the gigantic competition between race-thinking and
class-thinking for dominion over the minds of modern men." In her opinion, a class-based ideology supported Stalinist totalitarianism, whereas a
race-based ideology supported Nazism.[142]

Some of the most powerful passages in *The Origins of Totalitarianism*
show Arendt's condemnation of racism. While Hitler was certainly ingenious in using "the hierarchical principle of racism," that is, dividing up
the world so that every race except the Jews had some other race to look
down upon, the very thinking itself, not to mention the genocidal deeds
that emerged from it, was detestable. This European attempt "to divide
mankind into master races and slave races, into higher and lower breeds,
into colored peoples and white men," only serves to deny our common
humanity by dividing us up into warring pieces, Germans against English-
men, Slavs against Jews, whites against blacks. "Racism may indeed carry
out the doom of the Western world and, for that matter, of the whole of
human civilization. . . . Race is, politically speaking, not the beginning of
humanity but its end, not the origin of peoples but their decay, not the
natural birth of man but his unnatural death."[143] While imperialism was an
exciting and adventurous game for some (Arendt was fond of quoting
from Kipling's *Mandalay*: "Ship me somewheres east of Suez where the
best is like the worst, / Where there aren't no Ten Commandments, an' a
man can raise a thirst"), it was a murderous game leading eventually not
just to the Holocaust, but more immediately, to take but one example, to
the reduction of the population of the Congo from between twenty and
forty million in 1890 to approximately 8.5 million in 1911.[144]

141. *Totalitarianism*, 156–57, 178, 161.
142. *Totalitarianism*, 158–61.
143. *Totalitarianism*, 241, 152, 157.
144. *Totalitarianism*, 189, 185.

Imperialism eventually came home. Arendt distinguished between two kinds of imperialism, the familiar kind, under which Europe sought to exploit Africa and Asia, and the continental variety, in which racial movements, for example, Pan-Germanism or Pan-Slavism, sought imperial expansion within Europe and across national borders. Arendt saw the Boers of South Africa as the prototype of these movements because they embraced the chief characteristic of these movements—the abandonment of the profit motive in the interest of racial theories. "The Boers remained the undisputed masters of the country: whenever rational labor and production policies came into conflict with race considerations, the latter won. Profit motives were sacrificed time and again to the demands of a race society."[145] Here, Arendt's insight was brilliant, and a fine counter to both Weber and Neumann. This ability to ignore the demands of economic rationalization would be a hallmark of the pan-movements in Europe and especially of the racist policies of the Third Reich. At any rate, Arendt's observation remained: racism and imperialism, a murderous game abroad, formed the groundwork for totalitarianism at home.

> When the European mob discovered what a "lovely virtue" a white skin could be in Africa, when the English conqueror in India became an administrator who no longer believed in the universal validity of law, but was convinced of his own innate capacity to rule and dominate, when the dragonslayers turned into either "white men" of "higher breeds" or into bureaucrats and spies, playing the Great Game . . . the stage seemed to be set for all possible horrors. Lying under anybody's nose were many of the elements which gathered together could create a totalitarian government on the basis of racism. "Administrative massacres" were proposed by Indian bureaucrats while African officials declared that "no ethical considerations such as the rights of man will be allowed to stand in the way" of white rule.[146]

The Key Precondition for Totalitarianism: Loneliness

Anti-Semitism, racism, and imperialism—along with the twin economic disasters of inflation and depression in the Weimar Republic—are all part of the groundwork for totalitarianism, but none of these factors can explain the "mass support for totalitarianism" and the "indisputable popularity" of both Hitler and Stalin.[147] Arendt began her explanation of this by

145. *Totalitarianism*, 204; also 195–97.
146. *Totalitarianism*, 221.
147. *Totalitarianism*, xxiii, 306.

noting, as did Tocqueville, how easily individuals are persuaded and controlled when they are isolated and powerless. "Totalitarian movements are mass organizations of atomized, isolated individuals." Such movements, Arendt maintained, demand an unprecedented and unconditional loyalty, and "such loyalty can be expected only from the completely isolated human being who, without any other social ties to family, friends, comrades, or even mere acquaintances, derives his sense of having a place in the world only from his belonging to a movement."[148]

Although Arendt claimed that Montesquieu made the discovery that tyranny always rests on isolation—"the isolation of the subjects from each other through mutual fear and suspicion"—this argument certainly appeared in the works of Aristotle, Tacitus, and Machiavelli. Nevertheless, the point remains important. Any tyranny requires a "radical isolation" and "the banishment of citizens from the public realm and the insistence that they mind their private business," thus leaving the tyrant alone in charge of public affairs. Such isolation is crucial because it eliminates potential opposition, for "action . . . is never possible in isolation."[149] Just as Tocqueville predicted, the isolation in modern Germany came about quite logically, with the breakdown of traditional communities and the privatization of life that accompanies bourgeois society. Stalin, by contrast, needed to create such "radical isolation" artificially with purges, denunciations of one's former friends and comrades, and thereby mutual suspicion. Stalin's approach, however more murderously extensive, had more in common with traditional tyrannies. Clearly, such physical and psychological isolation is not new to the twentieth century, although it may be in degree, and Arendt made it clear that it extended to the leadership at the top, which was not a tightly knit "gang" but instead a group of isolated individuals fearful of imminent denunciation.[150]

As with Tocqueville, the companion of isolation is always powerlessness. "Isolated men are powerless by definition." Totalitarianism, Arendt claimed, must render each person "powerless . . . degraded into a cog in the power-accumulating machine." Whereas tyrannies and despotisms have always tried to bring equality to their subjects, each equally subjected to the force of the tyrant or the despot, they generally left intact some nonpolitical bonds between subjects, "such as family ties and common cultural interests." Even these ties are unacceptable to totalitarian domination. Unless totalitarianism can control the private lives of its

148. *Totalitarianism*, 323–24.
149. *Human Condition*, 181, 53, 198, 167.
150. *Totalitarianism*, 407, 318, 323, 430–31; Arendt, *On Violence* (New York: Harcourt, Brace & World, 1970), 55.

subjects, its rule will be far from total, and as a consequence, it must eliminate these private ties, regard them as dangerous, indeed stamp out common ties between individuals who love, to take two of Arendt's examples, chess or art. Lovers of chess for the sake of chess are a threat, precisely because they are "not yet absolutely atomized elements in a mass society whose completely heterogeneous uniformity is one of the primary conditions for totalitarianism."[151] Ultimately, terror and ideology complete the process of creating powerlessness by total control over even our private lives and thoughts. "Isolation and impotence, that is the fundamental inability to act at all, have always been characteristic of tyrannies. . . . But not all contacts between men are broken and not all human capacities destroyed. The whole sphere of private life with the capacities for experience, fabrication and thought are left intact. We know that the iron band of total terror leaves no space for such private life and that the self-coercion of totalitarian logic destroys man's capacity for experience and thought just as certainly as his capacity for action."[152]

Totalitarianism can dominate so effectively, according to Arendt, because the men and women of the modern world have a fundamental new experience, new in fact to the history of the world. As I indicated earlier, this new experience is loneliness. "What prepares men for totalitarian domination in the non-totalitarian world is the fact that loneliness, once a borderline experience usually suffered in certain marginal social conditions like old age, has become an everyday experience of the evergrowing masses of our century." Loneliness is neither solitude, which can be a creative dialogue with oneself, nor isolation, which leaves the individual some relation to the world through work or the making of things. The lonely person feels superfluous, has lost any place to call his or her own, and undergoes "the experience of being abandoned by everything and everybody." He or she is left with "only the sheer effort of labor which is the effort to keep alive."[153] Loneliness allows totalitarian rulers to use terror and ideology so successfully. "While isolation concerns only the political realm of life, loneliness concerns human life as a whole. Totalitarian government, like all tyrannies, certainly could not exist without destroying, by isolating men, their political capacities. But totalitarian domination as a form of government is new in that it is not content with this isolation and destroys private life as well. It bases itself on loneliness, on the experience of not belonging to the world at all, which is among the

151. *Totalitarianism*, 474, 146, 322.
152. *Totalitarianism*, 474.
153. *Totalitarianism*, 474–78.

most radical and desperate experiences of man."[154] Arendt made amply clear, by the way, the manner in which she would address the isolation, loneliness, and powerlessness endemic to the modern world. Borrowing from Rosa Luxemburg, Arendt argued that genuine democracy can never come from parliaments and competing parties, but instead must come from those organizations formed spontaneously or defended theoretically by those involved in popular agitation—the revolutionary societies and municipal councils of the French Revolution, Jefferson's wards, the soviets undermined by the Bolsheviks, and the workers' councils of the Hungarian Revolution. All of these "consciously and explicitly desired the direct participation of every citizen in the affairs of the country." Such genuinely democratic bodies secure freedom and undermine the key conditions—loneliness and powerlessness—of tyranny or totalitarianism.[155]

Why did widespread loneliness become a common and unprecedented phenomenon in the twentieth century? Arendt linked this new experience of loneliness to the "transformation of classes into masses and the concomitant elimination of all group solidarity," or, put more simply, the breakdown of classes and groups, all leading to the rise of "mass man" and mass society.[156] Like Tocqueville, Arendt was suggesting that industrialization, urbanization, and capitalism undermined former ties between individuals—classes, communities, groups, and even to some extent families—causing, in short, "communal disintegration." The modern world witnesses the "lonely mass man," or, in a marvelous passage, a "structureless mass of furious individuals who [have] nothing in common." Mass society and loneliness go hand in hand.[157]

Arendt dated this communal disintegration to what she called the "degeneration of the *citoyen* into the *bourgeois*," a complete "victory of bourgeois values over the citizen's sense of responsibility." In the fundamental conflict between freedom and tyranny, this was the central development of the nineteenth and twentieth centuries. After "emancipating [themselves] completely from public concerns," individuals in bourgeois society found themselves confined to private life because of a "withering of

154. *Totalitarianism*, 475.
155. *On Revolution*, 267, 250–54, 260–69, 282–83. For an excellent discussion, sometimes critical, of Arendt's democratic theory, see James Miller, "The Pathos of Novelty: Hannah Arendt's Image of Freedom in the Modern World," in *Hannah Arendt: The Recovery of the Public World*, ed. Melvyn A. Hill (New York: St. Martin's, 1979), 177–208. See also Margaret Canovan, "Arendt, Rousseau, and Human Plurality in Politics," *Journal of Politics* 45, no. 2 (1983): 286–302.
156. *Totalitarianism*, xxxii, 315–16.
157. *Totalitarianism*, 225; *Human Condition*, 233; *Totalitarianism*, 315. For a good discussion of Arendt's use of the term *masses*, see Kateb, *Hannah Arendt*, 70–74.

the public realm." With genuine public space either disappearing or already gone, the *agora,* or meeting place for citizens to discuss public matters, was transformed "into an assemblage of shops like the bazaars of oriental despotism."[158] Individuals consecrating their lives to accumulating wealth cannot engage in public and political action, so the act of consumption, and a consumer society, readily replaced citizenship and political participation. The wish for happiness through accumulation replaced the wish for political freedom, but though "abundance and endless consumption [became] the ideals of the poor; they [were] the mirage in the desert of misery."[159]

Bourgeois society, as Tocqueville had argued, quite naturally brings about two prerequisites for a dictatorship or tyranny—isolation and apathy.

> Indifference to public affairs, neutrality on political issues, are in themselves no sufficient cause for the rise of totalitarian movements. The competitive and acquisitive society of the bourgeoisie had produced apathy and even hostility toward public life. . . . A citizen's duties and responsibilities could only be felt to be a needless drain on his limited time and energy. These bourgeois attitudes are very useful for those forms of dictatorship in which a "strong man" takes upon himself the troublesome responsibility for the conduct of public affairs; they are a positive hindrance to totalitarian movements which can tolerate bourgeois individualism no more than any other kind of individualism.[160]

Bourgeois individualism could hardly, by itself, hold back totalitarian movements, and in fact such individualism was easily eliminated. If bourgeois society, in Arendt's mind, was not sufficient cause for totalitarianism, it certainly helped lay the groundwork by means of isolation, apathy, and indifference to public affairs. The bourgeois wish to be left alone, to use government as a police force to protect one's private space and private interests, easily turns into a wish to abolish the public affairs of the citizen in favor of efficient administration. The polis, the realm of free individuals, disappears; and the household, the realm of necessity and hierarchy, becomes the model for political affairs. The bourgeois wishes simply that "everyday affairs [will] be taken care of by a gigantic, nationwide administration of housekeeping." In this sense, the hope that public

---

158. *Totalitarianism,* 79–80; *Human Condition,* 196, 140.
159. *On Revolution,* 136–37; also *Totalitarianism,* 146, 301.
160. *Totalitarianism,* 313.

institutions will only serve private interests does in fact further total-itarianism, simply by eliminating the distinctions between public and private. "The bourgeoisie's political philosophy was always 'totalitarian'; it always assumed an identity of politics, economics and society, in which political institutions served only as the facade for private interests."[161]

Arendt's point was a simple one. Individuals confined to private life may think that they are free, but isolated and powerless, they are easily manipulated or destroyed. Bourgeois philosophy clings to the idea that at least in one's private enclosure, one is free to think and feel, but in fact, while that may have been true under an ordinary tyranny, it is no longer true in the face of totalitarian ideology and terror. Lonely individuals lose even their capacity for common sense, according to Arendt, when confronted with the straitjacket of ideological thinking. This occurs because individuals need to talk to one another to make sense of the world, and thus human interaction, impossible in a lonely world that has destroyed public space, is essential for independent thinking. Arendt saw only "total conformism" in totalitarian countries, and even went so far as to claim that there was less freedom of thought in totalitarian societies than in the internment camps of democratic countries (Arendt herself was confined in an internment camp in France for about nine months from 1940 to 1941) and even in some concentration camps![162] Certainly a powerful claim, but it illustrates Arendt's contempt for the bourgeois notion that regardless of the collapse of the public realm, one might remain free and independent in a private refuge.

> The philistine's retirement into private life, his single-minded devotion to matters of family and career was the last, and already degenerated, product of the bourgeoisie's belief in the primacy of private interest. The philistine is the bourgeois isolated from his own class, the atomized individual who is produced by the breakdown of the bourgeois class itself. The mass man whom Himmler organized for the greatest mass crimes ever committed in history bore the features of the philistine rather than of the mob man, and was the bourgeois who in the midst of the ruins of his world worried about nothing so much as his private security, was ready to sacrifice everything—belief, honor, dignity—on the slightest provocation. Nothing proved easier to destroy than the privacy and private morality of people who thought of nothing but safe-

161. *Human Condition*, 28; *Totalitarianism*, 336.
162. *Totalitarianism*, 308, 471–77; *Human Condition*, 4, 10; *Totalitarianism*, 296; Young-Bruehl, *Hannah Arendt*, 150–61.

guarding their private lives. After a few years of power and systematic co-ordination, the Nazis could rightly announce: "The only person who is still a private individual in Germany is somebody who is asleep."[163]

A Movement, Not a Political Party

One of Arendt's finest insights into totalitarianism lies in her claim that totalitarianism is a movement, something very different from political parties, which tended to represent the tangible, economic interests of classes and groups. A movement differs from a political party, and even from a nation-state after it has taken over, in that it must, by its own interior logic, change constantly. "It was the nature of the Nazi movement that it kept moving, became more radical with each passing month," so much so that the members of the movement could never keep up and could never predict the next change. Arendt described this as "the perpetual-motion mania of totalitarian movements which can remain in power only so long as they keep moving."[164] Several characteristics flow logically from this principle of constant motion. First, a movement never has a fixed goal or program, but is quite willing, even eager, to "change its policy from day to day." The Nazis scornfully referred to the Weimar Republic as the "time of the System," implying that it was a sterile and static time, followed rightfully by a dynamic moment in history, "the era of the movement." The very "essence of government itself has become motion."[165] Second, even after seizing power, a movement must avoid the ossification that might easily come with the responsibilities of governance. If the movement becomes one more dictatorship, or some variant of absolute government, then change stops and the movement ends. This would not be totalitarianism, that is, total domination of the population, but rather some ordinary tyranny. Thus, the totalitarian ruler must pursue a contradictory task. "He must establish the fictitious world of the movement as a tangible working reality of everyday life, and he must, on the other hand, prevent this new world from developing a new stability."[166] Third, a movement must also avoid bowing to the demands of nationalism, because nationalistic sentiment will transform the movement until the government is similar to that of every other nation-state. Rather, movements stay alive by becoming international and aspiring to global conquest, best expressed, in Arendt's mind, by Trotsky's doctrine of per-

163. *Totalitarianism*, 338–39.
164. *Eichmann*, 63; *Totalitarianism*, 306.
165. *Totalitarianism*, 260, 466.
166. *Totalitarianism*, 391.

manent revolution. If totalitarian regimes "do not pursue global rule as their ultimate goal, they are only too likely to lose whatever power they have already seized."[167] While all three of these characteristics make totalitarianism unstable, they also serve the purpose of total domination.

Even more than parties, movements become "embodiments of ideologies" and "charged with philosophy." Arendt argued that parties embrace more particular class and group interests, thereby focusing more on economics than on ideology, whereas a movement embraces an ideology purporting to explain everything. By depicting itself as above all political parties, a movement claims to represent the general good, as opposed to particular interests, and to have the key to absolute knowledge, as opposed to all partial explanations. "It is this absoluteness of movements which more than anything else separates them from party structures and their partiality. . . . In this stream the difference between ends and means evaporates . . . , and the result is the monstrous immorality of ideological politics." A movement, said Arendt, announces that it stands above the state, political parties, and the people, and is ready to sacrifice all three for the sake of its ideology.[168]

While Arendt saw in totalitarianism an alliance of business and the mob, with the mob having the upper hand, she noted that the elite delighted in watching the mob destroy "respectability." Indeed, the elite— by which Arendt apparently meant something close to *intellectuals*—frequently "let themselves be seduced by totalitarian movements" because of what Arendt called a "justified disgust" with "the ideological outlook and moral standards of the bourgeoisie" and because of a wish to become a part of something heroic and grand, "something historic, grandiose, unique."[169] (Arendt refused to blame the elite for totalitarianism; the ideas of the elite do not cause such historic events, and anyway, the very creativity of the elite made them dangerous to totalitarian movements and hence among the first victims.) Ideological pronouncements that the movement is in accord with law, supposedly either the laws of history or the laws of nature, entice the elite to become part of a grand and world-historical moment. "The law of Nature or the law of History, if properly executed, is expected to produce mankind as its end product. . . . Totalitarian policy claims to transform the human species into an active unfailing carrier of a law to which human beings otherwise would only passively and reluctantly be subjected."[170]

167. *Totalitarianism*, 392.
168. *Totalitarianism*, 249–50, 266.
169. *Totalitarianism*, 333, 339, 328; *Eichmann*, 105.
170. *Totalitarianism*, 462, 399. Despite her wish to clarify political terms, which Arendt did successfully with words like *tyranny*, *authority*, and *freedom*, her use of other words

In the wish to be part of something great and historic, the elite was no different from the rest of society. World War I, followed by disastrous inflation and depression, produced a breakdown of both the class system and the party system. Totalitarian movements moved into this power vacuum, recruited members from those formerly regarded as too indifferent to politics, and actively built on a deep resentment of the status quo. More specifically, totalitarian movements appealed to isolated individuals wishing to be part of something larger, to that "great unorganized, structureless mass of furious individuals" left isolated, powerless, and resentful by bourgeois society. A movement with an ideology is very attractive; "men in the midst of communal disintegration and social atomization wanted to belong at any price." Thus, totalitarian movements are successful, precisely because they organize atomized and isolated individuals and because they can demand unconditional loyalty from such men and women. "Such loyalty can be expected only from the completely isolated human being who, without any other social ties to family, friends, comrades, or even mere acquaintances, derives his sense of having a place in the world only from his belonging to a movement, his membership in the party."[171] Totalitarian movements, in other words, derive strength and support from "mass men," who are frequently "yearning for anonymity, for being just a number and functioning only as a cog." Such individuals long for a "strong man," or a "great leader," and a totalitarian movement readily supplies such a leader, thereby transforming individual men and women into a "horde," a claim that certainly reminds one of Freud.[172]

Arendt located one key precedent for totalitarian movements in the pan-movements, that is, movements attempting to unite some "race" or "people" or "nationality" living throughout Europe, dispersed across established national borders. "Nazism and Bolshevism owe more to Pan-Germanism and Pan-Slavism (respectively) than to any other ideology or political movement." Founded upon a sort of "enlarged tribal consciousness," these pan-movements sought "to unite all people of similar folk origin, independent of history and no matter where they happened to live."[173] Two characteristics of these pan-movements proved to be of great importance to totalitarian movements. First, by seeking to unite a "folk" dispersed across national boundaries, the pan-movements "enthusiastically absorbed the tradition of race-thinking." These pan-movements hailed their people as unique, chosen, and usually surrounded by ene-

---

such as *mob, masses, capital,* and *elite* is notoriously imprecise. See Canovan, *The Political Thought of Hannah Arendt,* 42.

171. *Totalitarianism,* 315, 225, 323–24.

172. *Totalitarianism,* 329, 107, 196, 267, 311–14, 392, 363.

173. *Totalitarianism,* 222–24.

mies, namely, those of different ethnic origins. Like race-thinking, the ideas embraced by the pan-movements denied a common humankind in favor of dividing up humanity into races and peoples supposedly always at war with each other. "Now everybody was against everybody else, and most of all against his closest neighbors—the Slovaks against the Czechs, the Croats against the Serbs, the Ukrainians against the Poles."[174] Second, by seeking territory for their own people, the pan-movements embraced a form of continental imperialism that actually predated the international imperialism of European nation-states. Just as the British and the French had a right to expansion, so did the ethnic nationalities of Central and Eastern Europe. Unable to expand overseas, they claimed a right to expand within Europe itself, an idea clearly leading to Hitler's doctrine of *Lebensraum,* or "living space," the right of the German people to expand to the East.

This continental imperialism, the aspiration of every pan-movement, was irretrievably hostile to existing political bodies, existing borders, and the confining definitions of the nation-state. The Pan-Germans, for example, insisted on the priority of the German people over the German state, insisted that "the only permanent factor in the course of history was the people and not states." Arendt argued that this led ultimately to a major difference between a fascist party dictatorship and a totalitarian movement. While Italian Fascism, to take one example, claimed to be a movement, it was in fact merely a party dictatorship that "seized the state machine without drastically changing the power structure of the country, being content to fill all government positions with party members." Totalitarian movements, by contrast, sought nothing less than the destruction of the state itself, along with the party system supporting the state. To take one key example, Italian Fascists came to rely on the army, the preeminent national institution, while the Nazis succeeded in subordinating the army to paramilitary and police forces, to the agents of terror.[175]

The pan-movements and continental imperialism grew out of a "rootlessness" and "statelessness" that pervaded Central and Eastern Europe. Finding it impossible to draw national borders that would grant each ethnic group its own nation, various treaties lumped many peoples together in one state, for example, Slovaks in Czechoslovakia, or Croats and Slovenes in Yugoslavia. Various ethnic groups, minorities within designated national boundaries, found out quickly that one's rights are protected best if one has a nation-state to call one's own, that abstract human rights hold little sway when confronted by hostile neighbors. Growing out

174. *Totalitarianism,* 224, 257, 268.
175. *Totalitarianism,* 237, 225, 257–63, 412.

of this rootlessness, what Arendt called a tribal consciousness proclaimed that even if a people had no identifiable homeland, it could feel at home wherever members of its tribe happened to live. "The hallmark of the pan-movements was that they never even tried to achieve national emancipation, but at once, in their dreams of expansion, transcended the narrow bounds of a national community and proclaimed a folk community that would remain a political factor even if its members were dispersed all over the earth."[176]

Anti-Semitism came easily to the pan-movements. Their own claims to uniqueness, chosenness, and even holiness came into direct conflict with such claims by Jews, as did their attempts to extend their movements beyond national borders. "The Jews were a perfect model of a nation without a state and without visible institutions. . . . But what drove the Jews into the center of these racial ideologies more than anything else was the even more obvious fact that the pan-movements' claim to chosenness could clash seriously only with the Jewish claim."[177] In the end, however, both the Jews and most of the ethnic groups involved in pan-movements landed in similar situations of persecution, although the Jewish fate was certainly the most horrific. All of these peoples were stateless, easily denationalized, and superfluous in the sense that organized nation-states did not want to accept them. Thus, both Jews and Slavs could be declared enemies to the more elaborate racist thinking of the Nazis, and without a nation to protect them, both groups were ready subjects for terror and murder. "Before [the Nazis] set the gas chambers into motion they had carefully tested the ground and found out to their satisfaction that no country would claim these people. The point is that a condition of complete rightlessness was created before the right to live was challenged." Indeed, Arendt went so far as to claim that totalitarian rule could flourish only where "great masses are superfluous," because after a totalitarian movement becomes totalitarian rule, it needs "enemies" to terrorize and murder.[178]

The Shapelessness of Totalitarianism and the Bureaucracy of Murder

Although the leader is necessary to totalitarian rule, by itself the "leadership principle" is hardly totalitarian, since dictatorships and tyrannies also rely on a strong leader. Still, reliance on the leader is a key organiza-

176. *Totalitarianism*, 232–33, 269–70.
177. *Totalitarianism*, 239–40.
178. *Totalitarianism*, 296–97, 311.

tional principle. "In the center of the movement, as the motor that swings it into motion, sits the Leader. He is separated from the elite formation by an inner circle of the initiated who spread around him an aura of impenetrable mystery." What propels such a leader to power? Neither organizational brilliance nor the ability to command paramilitary forces, both of which are crucial to ordinary tyrants, but rather "an extreme ability to handle inner-party struggles" and to appoint key personnel personally loyal to the leader. Far from relying on the SA for his rise to power, Hitler had to overcome Röhm and other leaders of the SA, just as Stalin had to conquer Trotsky.[179]

Once in power, the leader is indispensable, not so much because of charisma, although that may be crucial, but because the principles of totalitarian organization demand such a position. While those who occupy the highest ranks of a totalitarian hierarchy do not actually believe much of the propaganda, they do believe in organization, and for organizational purposes there must be a leader. The leader "is needed, not as a person, but as a function, and as such he is indispensable to the movement." In contrast to tyrants, who distance themselves from the acts of subordinates, the leader claims personal responsibility for every deed, misdeed, and pronouncement of every official of the movement. "This total responsibility is the most important organizational aspect of the so-called Leader principle, according to which every functionary is not only appointed by the Leader but is his walking embodiment." Of course, if mistakes are made, it is only because of fraud, because some imposter impersonated the leader, and thus, if the leader "wants to blame his mistakes on others, he must kill them."[180] All of this, Arendt recognized, is contradictory, because the leader is simultaneously totally responsible and totally innocent, but nonetheless Arendt argued that such contradictory claims are descriptively accurate. "The real mystery of that totalitarian Leader resides in an organization which makes it possible for him to assume the total responsibility for all crimes committed by the elite formations of the movement *and* to claim at the same time, the honest, innocent respectability of its most naïve fellow-traveler."[181]

This notion that each official in the movement, and eventually each official in the party or the government as well as each key commander in the police and armed forces, is the personal embodiment of the leader's authority necessitates that there be no authoritative bodies between the leader and the masses. The fear, so eloquently expressed by Montesquieu

179. *Totalitarianism*, 364, 373.
180. *Totalitarianism*, 387, 374–75.
181. *Totalitarianism*, 375.

and Tocqueville, that the modern world would witness the disappearance of intermediate institutions between the government and the governed came to full realization in totalitarian rule. "This absence of any authority or hierarchy in the totalitarian system is shown by the fact that between the supreme power (the Fuehrer) and the ruled there are no reliable intervening levels. . . . The will of the Fuehrer can be embodied everywhere and at all times."[182]

What kind of organizational structure could possibly give such total power and responsibility to one person? Arendt distinguished between authoritarian government, tyranny, and totalitarianism in the following manner: an authoritarian government is like a pyramid in which each intervening layer has a certain amount of independent authority; a tyranny resembles a pyramid in which the intervening layers have been eliminated, leaving the tyrant to rule over those equal in their subjection; and finally, totalitarian rule is like an onion-like structure with the leader in the center, surrounded by layers of authority—front organizations, the party bureaucracy, elite formations, and police groups. The "onion-like structure of the movement" ensures that each individual layer of authority is "the front of the next more militant formation."[183]

Actually, although Arendt fell back upon this image of the onion more than once, this image gives the structure of Nazi Germany more coherence than it actually possessed. In other passages, she more successfully borrowed from Neumann in designating "shapelessness" as the key characteristic of Nazi rule. What did she mean by this word *shapelessness?* First, Nazi rule was far from monolithic, but instead had multiple layers of ever-overlapping authority, all held together by the "Führer principle." Certainly, the dual authority of party and state stands out, but beyond that was an apparently designed confusion of authority; the National Socialists created not just a duplication of state and party offices but indeed a "multiplication of offices." As Arendt put it, "The inhabitant of Hitler's Third Reich lived not only under the simultaneous and often conflicting authorities of competing powers, such as the civil services, the party, the SA, and the SS; he could never be sure and was never explicitly told whose authority he was supposed to place above all others."[184] This confusion and multiplication of authority leads to a "shapelessness [that] turns out to be an ideally suited instrument for the realization of the so-called Leader principle." The multiplication of layers of authority only enhances the leader's power because each official and each subject must

182. *Totalitarianism*, 405.
183. *Totalitarianism*, 413; "What Is Authority?" 98–100.
184. *Totalitarianism*, 395–96, xxxii, 398–99.

wait until the leader designates which body has authority at any given moment.[185]

Second, "shapelessness" helps explain that while a building can have a structure, a movement only has motion and direction. That means that the structure of Nazi Germany was constantly changing, or, as Eichmann put it, "everything was always in a state of continuous flux, a steady stream." Arendt called it a "fluctuating hierarchy" in which Nazi leadership continually added new layers of authority and periodically shifted the locus of authority, something seen most clearly in the police organizations, where new controls were "always needed to control the controllers."[186]

> Another advantage of the totalitarian pattern is that it can be repeated indefinitely and keeps the organization in a state of fluidity which permits it constantly to insert new layers and define new degrees of militancy. The whole history of the Nazi party can be told in terms of new formations within the Nazi movement. The SA, the stormtroopers (founded in 1922), were the first Nazi formation which was supposed to be more militant than the party itself; in 1926, the SS was founded as the elite formation of the SA; after three years, the SS was separated from the SA and put under Himmler's command; it took Himmler only a few more years to repeat the same game within the SS.[187]

Such shapelessness is "ingeniously effective." Both the multiplication of authority and the fluctuating hierarchy "make possible the swift and surprising changes in policy for which totalitarianism has become famous. The body politic is shock-proof because of its shapelessness."[188] Although all of this is remarkably inefficient in terms, for example, of rational economic production or Weberian bureaucratic administration, it is astonishingly efficient in securing power for the leader, because the leader can use a variety of institutions at any moment, and the leader alone can determine which bodies have real authority and which only have apparent authority.

Multiple layers of authority, the onionlike structure of authority, also projected the appearance of normality both to the subjects of totalitarianism and to the outside world. Behind every organization for students, teachers, lawyers, physicians, and so forth, stood a party organization

185. *Totalitarianism*, 404.
186. *Eichmann*, 152; *Totalitarianism*, 368–69, 398.
187. *Totalitarianism*, 368.
188. *Totalitarianism*, 408–9.

with the real authority, just as behind the army stood the more authoritative SS. "All of these were primarily duplicates of existing nontotalitarian professional societies, paraprofessional as the stormtroopers were paramilitary."[189] This appearance of normality is little different from that projected by the senate under Tiberius, which retained its pomp but had no real authority. And just as it appears normal from the outside world, so it does from the inside, so that those caught up in the lying and the murdering see no great gap between their beliefs and actions and those of the real world. "The reason why the movements in their prepower, revolutionary stage can attract so many ordinary philistines is that their members live in a fool's paradise of normalcy; the party members are surrounded by the normal world of sympathizers and the elite formation by the normal world of ordinary members."[190]

The mere duplication of authority is a time-honored revolutionary technique. Cromwell's New Model Army, the Jacobin Clubs, Bolshevik-controlled Soviets, Gandhi's Indian National Congress—all formed organizations parallel to established authority, ready to take over in a revolutionary situation. The Nazis were no different.

> The important factor for the movements is that, even before they seize power, they give the impression that all elements of society are embodied in their ranks. . . . The Nazis . . . set up a series of fake departments which were modeled after the regular state administration, such as their own department of foreign affairs, education, culture, sport, etc. . . . together they created a perfect world of appearances in which every reality in the nontotalitarian world was slavishly duplicated in the form of humbug. . . .
>
> . . . The practical value of the fake organizations came to light when the Nazis seized power and were ready at once to destroy the existing teachers' organizations with another teachers' organization, the existing lawyers' clubs with a Nazi-sponsored lawyers' club, etc. They could change overnight the whole structure of German society—and not just political life—precisely because they had prepared its exact counterpart within their own ranks.[191]

The Nazis went beyond mere parallel organizations to multiple layers of authority. Arendt recounted that behind university history departments stood the Munich institute, Rosenberg's institute at Frankfurt, and a spe-

189. *Totalitarianism*, 371.
190. *Totalitarianism*, 368.
191. *Totalitarianism*, 371–72.

cial division of the Gestapo. This instance clearly followed a rule in totalitarian regimes that the more visible the institution, the less authority it
actually has: "The only rule of which everybody in a totalitarian state may
be sure is that the more visible government agencies are, the less power
they carry, and the less is known of the existence of an institution, the
more powerful it will turn out to be."[192]

Once more, while this is inefficient administration, it is extraordinarily
efficient for totalitarian domination, and this distinction is important, because Arendt, who admired Weber enormously and was a close friend of
his wife, Marianne Weber, simultaneously rejected and extended Weber's
conclusions. On the one hand, she implicitly maintained that Weber was
wrong to conclude that charismatic domination becomes routinized as
the demands for rationalizing production become more strident. But on
the other hand, Arendt argued that Weber's model of bureaucratic domination was crucial, first in imperialist expansion and later in the systematic extermination of Jews and others.

The two key elements of imperialism, later combined in totalitarian
rule, were race-thinking and bureaucratic domination. "Two new devices
. . . were discovered during the first decades of imperialism. One was race
as the principle of the body politic, and the other bureaucracy as a principle of foreign domination."[193] Discovered and developed independently,
race-thinking and bureaucracy were essential for imperialism, but no one
until the twentieth century "ever came to realize the full range of potentialities of power accumulation and destruction that this combination
alone provided."[194] Arendt argued that the pan-movements and eventually
totalitarian movements "saw in bureaucratic regimes possible models of
organization." The Pan-Slavs, for example, admired the czarist Russian
bureaucracy as a tremendous machine to be set in motion at any moment
and guided by the hand of one man. With such a power, "whom could we
not force into obedience?"[195] Similarly, Arendt contrasted the old-fashioned bureaucracy of Russia, which "left the whole inner life of the soul
intact," with totalitarian bureaucracy, "which intruded upon the private
individual and his inner life with equal brutality."[196] Despite such claims,
Arendt's own analysis rejected the idea that Nazi Germany was simply
Weberian bureaucratic domination writ large. Multiple layers of authority,
fluctuating hierarchy, and inefficient administration all form a different

192. *Totalitarianism*, 402–3.
193. *Totalitarianism*, 185.
194. *Totalitarianism*, 186.
195. *Totalitarianism*, 247.
196. *Totalitarianism*, 245, 243–44.

genus of tyranny, although the species of bureaucratic domination is still present. Arendt is more convincing in claiming that bureaucratic domination came to be the rule, not in society at large, but in the death camps.

One sentence from *The Origins of Totalitarianism* seemed to provide the basis for her later book, brilliant and controversial, *Eichmann in Jerusalem: A Report on the Banality of Evil.* "For the ruthless machines of domination and extermination," she wrote in *Origins,* "the masses of co-ordinated philistines provided much better material and were capable of even greater crimes than so-called professional criminals, provided only that these crimes were well organized and assumed the appearance of routine jobs."[197] Eichmann, according to Arendt, was a "terrifyingly normal" man, with normal and even "desirable" family relations, far from a pathologically evil person and even far from someone who had some obsessive hatred for Jews. "Except for an extraordinary diligence in looking out for his personal advancement, he had no motives at all." Arendt judged him to have the personality of a "common mailman." He was a career bureaucrat, a jobholder with a family, a man incapable of thinking from another's perspective and thus an average man, not stupid, but nonetheless incapable of thinking beyond a few clichés he had learned by rote. With some luck, his career would have carried him to the administration of a factory or a hospital, and thus he would not have involved himself directly in criminal acts. In fact, Eichmann's career led him "to become one of the greatest criminals of that period," to engage in mass murder, and to become a "cog in the machinery" that produced one of the greatest evils in history—all without being capable of knowing he was committing evil.[198]

Why could this happen? Because Eichmann helped administer "the bureaucracy of murder," that is, because the Nazis actively pursued the "administrative massacres" that the British considered but rejected in India. Arendt argued that every totalitarian government must incorporate bureaucratic domination and thus "make functionaries and mere cogs in the administrative machinery out of men." Like Kafka, she maintained that bureaucratic domination is rule by Nobody, but "rule by Nobody is not no-rule, and where all are equally powerless we have a tyranny without a tyrant." Indeed, rule by Nobody is "clearly the most tyrannical of all"

197. *Totalitarianism,* 337.

198. *Eichmann,* 276, 25–26, 287, 145, 288–89, 48–49, 54, 277–79. On the enormous controversy surrounding Arendt's publication of *Eichmann in Jerusalem,* see Young-Bruehl, *Hannah Arendt,* 339–78; Whitfield, *Into the Dark,* 208–47; Derwent May, *Hannah Arendt* (New York: Penguin, 1986), 101–13. For an excellent discussion of Arendt's book on Eichmann, see Shiraz Dossa, "Hannah Arendt on Eichmann: The Public, the Private, and Evil," *Review of Politics* 46, no. 2 (1984): 163–84.

because no one is responsible, neither the one nor the few in monarchy and oligarchy, neither the best nor the many in aristocracy or democracy. Eichmann was correct in maintaining that in no direct sense did he murder anyone. Rather, from afar, he was responsible for administering a bureaucracy of murder, and in this modern and Kafka-like world, as the court in Jerusalem put it, "the degree of responsibility increases as we draw further away from the man who uses the fatal instrument with his own hands."[199]

The Tyranny of Ideology

The essential content of Nazi ideology, as distinguished from the details that were endlessly complex and frequently changing, is well known. First, Nazi ideology promised to bring a new unity to the nation, one transcending groups and classes, Right and Left. The very name of the party, the National Socialist German Workers' Party, "offered a synthesis supposed to lead to national unity, a semantic solution whose double trademark of 'German' and 'Worker' connected the nationalism of the Right with the internationalism of the Left."[200] Second, the new community promised by Nazi propaganda initially centered on the elusive concept of *Volksgemeinschaft*, a "people's community" in which all racially authentic Germans were equal, that is, a community uniting members of the German race as equals, superior and different to all other peoples. Not only did the *Volksgemeinschaft* prepare the way for an "Aryan" racial society, but it also tried to answer the Marxist call for a classless society, in this case promising the German people that they could unite in equality by subjugating others. "The classless society had the obvious connotation that everybody would be leveled to the status of the factory worker, while the *Volksgemeinschaft*, with its connotation of conspiracy for world conquest, held out a reasonable hope that every German could eventually become a factory owner."[201] Third, the preservation and domination of the German race, and even eventually the "Aryan" race, which was allegedly superior to the German race, was the chief concern of Nazi ideology. Anti-Semitism and opposition to a fictional Jewish world conspiracy became central. Finally, the ideological goal of racial conquest supplanted old-fashioned imperialism, and building on the continental imperialism of the pan-movements, Nazi ideology defended conquest to the East, the right of the German race to *Lebensraum*, or living space, and hence the

199. *Eichmann*, 172, 218, 288–89; *On Violence*, 81, 38; *Eichmann*, 247; *Human Condition*, 37.
200. *Totalitarianism*, 357.
201. *Totalitarianism*, 361.

right of the German race to conquer, and even eliminate, so-called inferior races. The end of bourgeois imperialism coincided with the rise of
ideological and racial imperialism. "The aggressiveness of totalitarianism
springs not from lust for power, and if it feverishly seeks to expand, it
does so neither for expansion's sake nor for profit, but only for ideological reasons."[202]

As hateful as the content of Nazi ideology was, Arendt concerned herself more with the ways in which any ideology tyrannizes over the individual. By Arendt's definition all ideologies claim to have a single principle that explains the uncertainties of the present, solves the riddles of
history, and predicts the future. All ideologies are potentially totalitarian,
and all ideologies remain temptations, because they announce they have
the answer to all problems. (Arendt did come close, in one essay on the
Hungarian uprising, to embracing the Cold War claim that liberalism is
not ideological.)[203] As a result, despite claims about being realistic and
embracing a *Realpolitik,* totalitarian movements rely on ideologies that
have a "contempt for facts and reality." Indeed, totalitarian movements
have no hesitation to change facts at will. Stalin's history of the Russian
Revolution that omitted any mention of Trotsky is perhaps only the most
dramatic example of how factual truth might indeed, with a victory of
totalitarianism, disappear from the world. The world must face, Arendt
suggested, the terrible and demoralizing "possibility that gigantic lies and
monstrous falsehoods can eventually be established as unquestioned
facts, that man may be free to change his own past at will, and that the
difference between truth and falsehood may cease to be objective and
become a mere matter of power." Factuality remains only in the outside
nontotalitarian world because totalitarianism, protected from reality by
its ideology, is "shock-proof" against evidence.[204]

Altering facts to achieve political goals was hardly unique to totalitarianism. Surely every tyrant has done that, although the extent to which it
could be done has certainly been amplified by the technology of propaganda and modern communications. Arendt was suggesting that ideological thinking aided the disappearance of factuality in four ways. First,
lonely individuals severed from common discourse with fellow citizens
lose common sense and latch on to the claims of ideology to the detriment of factuality and evidence. "Ideological thinking ruins all relation-

202. *Totalitarianism,* 458, 354–55.

203. Arendt, "Reflections on the Hungarian Revolution," epilogue to *The Origins of Totalitarianism,* 2d enlarged ed. (New York: World Publishing Co., 1958), 480–510, esp. 482.

204. *Totalitarianism,* xxxii, 333; "What Is Authority?" 100; *Totalitarianism,* 159, 457–59,
469–70, 388, 353; "Truth and Politics," in *Between Past and Future,* 227–64, esp. 231, 252.

ships with reality." Second, ideologies embrace what Arendt called a "tyranny of logicality." If an ideology claims the secret of history to be that of class struggle or a natural struggle of races, then factual claims to the contrary are swept aside. "What convinces masses are not facts, and not even invented facts, but only the consistency of the system of which they are presumably part." As Arendt put it elsewhere, "nothing matters but consistency." Third, ideologies lead to intellectual and political passivity because at bottom they are "desperate efforts to escape responsibility." Claiming to be sanctified by the discovery of "scientific" laws of history or society, ideologies ask us to bow to the inevitable, to become passengers on the train of history and spectators to the battles of nature. These new philosophies of history consist "in describing and understanding the whole realm of human action, not in terms of the actor and the agent, but from the standpoint of the spectator who watches the spectacle." And finally, even more than in an ordinary tyranny, totalitarian regimes can distort language, which, as Tacitus had noted, is a key means of controlling individuals. As Arendt noted, deportation to death camps came to be called "change of residence," "resettlement," and "labor in the East"; mass murder was labeled either "mercy death" or the "final solution."[205]

While the Nazis built upon "the blind conformism of bourgeois society" (what Arendt called the "social slavery" of Americans), they went well beyond such conformism by borrowing from modern advertising techniques and using both propaganda and indoctrination. "The masses have to be won by propaganda," but "wherever totalitarianism possesses absolute control, it replaces propaganda with indoctrination."[206] While ideologies naturally "attract the average," the entire population must learn to repeat in the morning what the leader said the night before, must learn to regard as dangerous thoughts today what was orthodoxy the previous week. Although there may be some cynicism in regard to day-to-day public pronouncements, totalitarian rule is successful only when individuals actually believe general precepts of the ideology, for example, the alleged inferiority of Jews and the worldwide Jewish conspiracy. These ideological lies become "like sacred untouchable truths."[207] In all these ways, ideological thinking assists totalitarianism in doing what no other previous tyranny could do, that is, rule us from within. "Totalitarianism is never content to rule by external means, namely, through the state and a machinery of violence; thanks to its peculiar ideology and the role as-

205. *Totalitarianism*, 468–74, 351, 458, 9; *On Revolution*, 45–46; *Eichmann*, 85, 108; *Totalitarianism*, 345–46, 352, 462–63.
    206. *Totalitarianism*, 141; Young-Bruehl, *Hannah Arendt*, 166; *Totalitarianism*, 341.
    207. *Totalitarianism*, 209, 384.

signed to it in this apparatus of coercion, totalitarianism has discovered a means of dominating and terrorizing human beings from within." Even beyond this, however, totalitarianism would like to transform human nature. For this, concentration camps, whose essence is terror, became "the laboratories where changes in human nature [were] tested."[208]

Terror as the Essence of Totalitarianism

Arendt saw ideological thinking and terror as the key characteristics of totalitarian rule, with the instruments of terror used to carry out, not political or economic goals, but ideological ones. "In order to establish a totalitarian regime, terror must be presented as an instrument for carrying out a specific ideology." Certainly ordinary tyrannies used violence to achieve political order, but Arendt defined terror as the use of violence when it was no longer necessary for establishing political dominance. "Terror is not the same as violence; it is, rather, the form of government that comes into being when violence . . . remains in full control."[209] Arendt learned from Montesquieu that tyranny is the form of government that is the most violent but the least powerful, that is, the least capable of organizing independent men and women for the purpose of conscious political action. Building on Montesquieu, Arendt declared that totalitarianism is that form of government in which manifestations of terror become, not a means to an end, but rather an end in itself. "Propaganda, in other words, is one, and possibly the most important, instrument of totalitarianism for dealing with the nontotalitarian world; terror, on the contrary, is the very essence of its form of government."[210]

Like Montesquieu, Arendt maintained that fear becomes the key motive force in this modern despotism called totalitarianism. "Nobody, not even the executors, can ever be free of fear." Mutual suspicion between friends, eyeing one's neighbors as potential informers, fearing that even a family member is potentially an *agent provocateur* who will entice one to say something dangerous—Arendt's description is powerful. "This atomization . . . is maintained and intensified through the ubiquity of the informer, who can be literally omnipresent because he no longer is merely a professional agent in the pay of the police but potentially every person one comes into contact with." However chilling, her description is not entirely new, but rather reminds us of Tacitus and Montesquieu. It is a

208. *Totalitarianism*, 325, 458.
209. *Totalitarianism*, 6; *On Violence*, 55.
210. *Totalitarianism*, 344; *On Violence*, 41–46; *On Revolution*, 174.

world in which all individuals are automatically suspect, simply because every human being has the capacity to think.[211]

This fear is derived, of course, from the overwhelming power of police forces, which rule the home country as if it were a conquered land. "Above the state and behind the facades of ostensible power, in a maze of multiplied offices, underlying all shifts of authority and in a chaos of inefficiency, lies the power nucleus of the country, the superefficient and supercompetent services of the secret police."[212] But even this is not qualitatively new in the history of the world, because even in authoritarian governments the secret police can become a state within a state. What is new and different is the way in which police power and the use of terror accelerate just when they seem superfluous, that is, when the population has become subdued and obedient. In other words, totalitarian terror is new because the regime uses it not mainly against political opposition but also, when the opposition has disappeared, against those who are wholly innocent. "A fundamental difference between modern dictatorships and all other tyrannies of the past is that terror is no longer used as a means to exterminate and frighten opponents, but as an instrument to rule masses of people who are perfectly obedient . . . its victims are innocent even from the point of view of the prosecutor."[213] Arendt's analysis is a criticism of Weber's view that violent and tyrannical regimes would become more moderate as they faced the day-to-day problems of efficient administration and economic production. By contrast, Arendt argued that the very horror of totalitarian terror lies in the fact that it increases with victory over the opposition, that it "reigns over a completely subdued population."[214]

This happens because totalitarian regimes use terror not merely to achieve political goals, but ideological ones. In contrast to all previous tyrannies, not political and not even military considerations, but ideological ones determine the enemy, and thus even in the face of military setbacks and the destruction of the Germany economy, Hitler could rejoice as the SS established death camps and began to exterminate Jews. "Neither military, nor economic, nor political considerations were allowed to interfere with the costly and troublesome program of mass exterminations and deportations."[215] It is the primacy of racial and ideological extermination over utilitarian ends that sets totalitarianism apart from pre-

211. *Totalitarianism*, 6; *On Violence*, 55; *Totalitarianism*, 430–31.
212. *Totalitarianism*, 420.
213. *Totalitarianism*, 6.
214. *Totalitarianism*, 344.
215. *Totalitarianism*, 411.

vious tyrannies and makes it seem almost unbelievable to the outside world. What previous tyranny, in the midst of war and confronted by crushing economic and military necessities, could divert desperately needed resources to establishing death camps and transporting millions of victims? Such actions had "an air of mad unreality" to the outside world. "The incredibility of the horrors is closely bound up with their economic uselessness. . . . This atmosphere of madness and unreality, created by an apparent lack of purpose, is the real iron curtain which hides all forms of concentration camps from the eyes of the world." In short, the horror of totalitarianism lies in this combination of ideological thinking plus terror. Only such a combination enabled Himmler and his forces to take enormous moral pride in mass murder but regard as immoral the theft of so much as a cigarette.[216]

Unlike the violence of an ordinary tyranny, the ideological terror of totalitarianism has no end, because there must always be new enemies to liquidate for the totalitarian movement to remain a movement. "If it were only a matter of hating Jews or bourgeois, the totalitarian regimes could, after the commission of one gigantic crime, return, as it were, to the rules of normal life and government. As we know, the opposite is the case. . . . The Nazis, foreseeing the completion of Jewish extermination, had already taken the necessary preliminary steps for the liquidation of the Polish people." Arendt noted, for example, that the Nazis had already compelled Poles to wear a badge with a *P*, similar to the Jewish star. Indeed, not only were the Poles and the Slavs deemed unfit to live, but so was much of the German population. The Germans, according to Nazi ideology, were not a master race, but rather they too needed to be ruled by a master race not yet born. "Not the Germans were the dawn of the master race, but the SS. . . . the 'Aryan' world empire, as Hitler would have put it, was in any event still centuries off." In other words, the Nazis scheduled much of the German population itself for terror and liquidation.[217]

Arendt's analysis reflected Plato's fear that if the nihilism implicit in the Sophists' arguments were let loose upon the world, all would be permitted. Going beyond such nihilism, the Nazis set up laboratories of terror to see what human beings might be capable of, to show that all is possible. "What binds [the Nazi elite] together is a firm and sincere belief in human omnipotence. Their moral cynicism, their belief that everything is permitted, rests on the solid conviction that everything is possible."[218] The death

216. *Totalitarianism*, 445, 422–23, 429.
217. *Totalitarianism*, 424, 412, 391; also *Eichmann*, 217–18.
218. *Totalitarianism*, 387.

camps, more specifically, were experiments with what is possible, experiments that the human imagination may have previously conceived but that men and women had heretofore never undertaken on such a scale. Armed with science but guided by the wildest fantasies that Plato said came to us in our nightmares, the Nazis sought "hideous discoveries in the realm of the possible." No single element in the apparatus of terror, except this, was new. Massacres of the population have occurred throughout history; the extermination of native populations was systematic in Africa, the Americas, and Australia; even concentration camps originated with the Boers in South Africa and were used against the African population.[219] "All these elements they utilize, develop and crystallize on the basis of the nihilistic principle 'everything is permitted,' which they inherited and already take for granted. But wherever these new forms of domination assume their authentically totalitarian structure they transcend this principle, which is still tied to the utilitarian motives and self-interest of the rulers, and try their hand in a realm that up to now has been completely unknown to us: the realm where 'everything is possible.'"[220] All of this Arendt calls a "radical evil" virtually impossible for us to understand. As Arendt was fond of quoting from David Rousset, who was a concentration camp survivor, "normal men don't know that everything is possible."[221]

Plato argued that a tyrant does in broad daylight what the rest of us dream at night. That contention, it seems, is the basis of Arendt's analysis. Although all reasonable adults in Nazi Germany knew that the death camps existed, the details remained shrouded in mystery, almost literally beyond belief. The operations of these camps, the experiments in these laboratories of the possible, were held in secrecy. "The only strictly guarded secret in a totalitarian country, the only esoteric knowledge that exists, concerns the operations of the police and the conditions in the concentration camps." How many of the normal individuals around us, asked Arendt, would acquiesce to the existence of such camps if, like Eichmann, they could have career advancement? Is it possible, she wondered, that these factories of death correspond to the "secret desires" of the masses in our century? In other words, do the death camps, which "are the true central institution of totalitarian organizational power," allow the police forces of this new form of tyranny to act the way Plato feared, to do during the day what the rest of us dream at night?[222]

219. *Totalitarianism*, 436, 298, 440–41.
220. *Totalitarianism*, 440.
221. *Totalitarianism*, 443, 459, 436, 303, 440–41.
222. *Totalitarianism*, 435, 437–38.

Suddenly it becomes evident that things which for thousands of years the human imagination had banished to a realm beyond human competence can be manufactured right here on earth, that Hell and Purgatory, and even a shadow of their perpetual duration, can be established by the most modern methods of destruction and therapy. To these people (and they are more numerous in any large city than we like to admit) the totalitarian hell proves only that the power of man is greater than they ever dared to think, and that man can realize hellish fantasies without making the sky fall or the earth open. . . .

Nothing perhaps distinguishes modern masses as radically from those of previous centuries as the loss of faith in a Last Judgment: the worst have lost their fear and the best have lost their hope. Unable as yet to live without fear or hope, these masses are attracted by every effort which seems to promise a man-made fabrication of the Paradise they had longed for and of the Hell they had feared.[223]

While Arendt saw the camps as a hell constructed to inflict "the greatest possible torment," more than that she saw them as experiments with how much one can alter human nature. "The concentration camps are the laboratories where changes in human nature are tested." Although Arendt was certainly horrified by the "blind bestiality" of the early camps run by the SA, whose torture seemed to exhibit hatred or resentment toward those heretofore deemed superior, she thought "the real horror began" when the SS took over and an almost understandable bestiality gave way to "an absolutely cold and systematic destruction" of individual men and women, and even of human dignity.[224] It was, of course, the bureaucracy of death that administered Nazi wishes that their victims leave no trace on earth, that they die anonymously, that the uniqueness of the individual be denied by being prodded into cattle cars and forced to strip naked, and that a martyr's death become virtually impossible. Thus, the camps were designed not just for torment and not just for extermination, but for "the ghastly experiment" of obliterating human spontaneity, that human "power to begin something new out of [one's] own resources," something determined neither by the past nor by the environment. The goal, therefore, was to transform human beings into things. "Nothing then remains but ghastly marionettes with human faces, which all behave like the dog

223. *Totalitarianism*, 446.
224. *Totalitarianism*, 445, 458, 453–54.

in Pavlov's experiment, which all react with perfect reliability even when going to their own death, and which do nothing but react."[225]

The camps, which seem so useless to the outside world, turn out to be central to totalitarianism because only in the camps can totalitarianism manifest total power, total domination over human beings. "The uselessness of the camps, their cynically admitted anti-utility, is only apparent. . . . Total power can be achieved and safeguarded only in a world of conditioned reflexes, of marionettes without the slightest trace of spontaneity." When victims, both Jewish and non-Jewish, go "to their death like sheep," when camp inmates see no possible meaning in either resistance or martyrdom but remain passive and subdued, hundreds of thousands of them, each "in absolute solitude," then the regime demonstrates its ability for total domination. The SS men "know that the system which succeeds in destroying its victim before he mounts the scaffold . . . is incomparably the best for keeping a whole people in slavery. In submission. Nothing is more terrible than these processions of human beings going like dummies to their death. The man who sees this says to himself: 'For them to be thus reduced, what power must be concealed in the hands of the masters,' and he turns away, full of bitterness but defeated."[226]

Arendt was not optimistic. Totalitarianism, she suggested, is a new form of government that will always be with us, as both a threat and a temptation. Yet new human beings will still be born with the capacity for action, which, for Arendt, entailed both the ability to interrupt the causal chain, thus beginning something anew, and the capacity for virtuosity or mastery over events. Even though totalitarianism will remain a potential threat, and even though it might some day reduce all human beings to things, Arendt could be cautiously optimistic just because human beings are born with the capacity to bring about a beginning, something she called "natality." This is the miracle that saves the world from ruin, because with the birth of each new child comes the ability to begin again. Arendt fondly quoted a passage in which Plato said, "the beginning is like a god which as long as it dwells among men saves all things."[227]

---

225. *Totalitarianism*, 438, 455, 433–35, 451; *Eichmann*, 232. Arendt noted with irony and anger that someone, even someone Jewish, who actually committed a crime was better off than a totally innocent person shipped off to the death camps. The criminal had some rights and dignity. Ibid., 214, 227.

226. *Totalitarianism*, 456–57; *Eichmann*, 10–11; *Totalitarianism*, 451, 455. The final quotation of this paragraph Arendt took from David Rousset.

227. *Human Condition*, 222; "Tradition and the Modern Age," 18; "What Is Freedom?" 169, 153–54; *On Violence*, 30–31; *Totalitarianism*, 479; *Human Condition*, 157, 209; *On Revolution*, 213. For a good discussion of Arendt's views on action, freedom, and natality, see Robert Grafstein, "Political Freedom and Political Action," *Western Political Quarterly* 39, no. 3 (1986): 464–79.

Conclusion

Arendt's brilliant analysis of Nazi Germany borrowed from almost every thinker I have explored—Plato, Aristotle, Tacitus, Machiavelli, Montesquieu, Tocqueville, Marx, and Weber. Freud alone she seemed not to use. How did she apply these ideas in such an original fashion? First, her thorough knowledge of Greek civilization allowed her to claim that totalitarianism was an entirely new form of government and that the centuries-old classifications laid out by Plato and Aristotle needed to be revised. Second, she focused on the isolation and powerlessness predicted by Montesquieu and Tocqueville, the notion that individuals will have few, if any, ties to their fellow citizens, but she went beyond this analysis to the fact that so many modern men and women experience extreme loneliness. Third, Arendt argued that lonely individuals are particularly susceptible to ideological thinking. Whereas she would agree with Marx that ideologies might originate as defenses of class interests, she went well beyond that—which is not to say she was right—to say that ideological thinking pretends to explain the mysteries of history with alleged laws of history (class thinking) and nature (race thinking). Lonely individuals too easily grasp on to the supposed laws of ideological thinking, to the simplistic but all-explaining nature of ideologies, and to the distortions of language by all ideologies. In other words, lonely individuals have trouble thinking for themselves, and thus ideological thinking in effect destroys their private lives and thought. Fourth, National Socialism could easily control individuals by violence and terror, as Aristotle, Tacitus, Machiavelli, and Montesquieu had suggested. Arendt distinguished between two types of terror. On the one hand, isolated individuals, alone and powerless, become readily obedient when threatened by violence. But on the other hand, totalitarian governments use terror against wholly innocent people to demonstrate their power. As Plato had suggested, a monstrously tyrannical regime will act out in the daytime what the rest of us occasionally dream at night, and the death camps sought to prove that totalitarian regimes could destroy all humanity, all spontaneity in individuals, and as such, the death campus were centrally important to the regime.

Fifth, Arendt brilliantly described the Nazi state as like an onion—or alternatively a shifting shapelessness—with the outer layers appearing normal, while the real power always resided in deeper layers. Front organizations, thoroughly subverted labor organizations, puppet professional associations—all these did what Aristotle, Tacitus, and Machiavelli suggested; that is, they gave the appearance of normalcy to the outside world while shielding what real changes in power and authority had taken shape. Sixth, her distinction between a state, a party, and a movement was ingenious, perhaps an application of Machiavelli's notion of a mobilizing army and party. Parties and states, she said, behave as Weber suggested; eventually they seek the routine production of goods and stability of power. Movements, by contrast, change constantly because they are propelled not by economic and power considerations but by an ideology that is necessarily expansionistic. The movement must change and expand and conquer anew to stay a movement. Seventh, in another explicit critique of Weber, Arendt suggested that ideological movements do not succumb to the pressures of rationalized production and stable bureaucratic rule, but instead can pursue ideological goals such as the extermination of Jews, even when these goals go against rational economic and military demands. Eighth, she did see the bureaucratic operation of the death camps as closer to Weber's description of bureaucracy rationally pursuing—in this case, horrifying—ends.

Ninth, her discussions of imperialism seem to rely heavily on Marx, Lenin, and Weber, although she analyzed the component of racism better than any of these thinkers. In suggesting that Nazi Germany came late to European imperialism and was pushed to find *Lebensraum* in Europe, she was not far from Neumann's analysis. But finally, her very original and brilliant analysis of what she and Neumann called "race imperialism" led her to ingenious observations about Europe and race-thinking. What she called continental imperialism, as distinct from the international imperialism of European powers in the nineteenth century, grew out of ethnic nationalism and the pan-movements, for example, Pan-Germanism. These became what one could call ethnic internationalism, as each ethnic group sought its own territory for the protection of its citizens. This led to Nazi continental conquest, to make room first for Germans and then so-called Aryans. By implication ethnic nationalism and the hatred of ethnic groups for one another will be with us for a long time, a sobering thought for the late twentieth century, when ethnic conflict has swept the world.

Every great and original thinker makes new analyses but also borrows from the past. Arendt was no different. However brilliant her analyses, she borrowed from this tradition in European political thought that repeatedly analyzed the perennial problem of tyranny.

CONCLUSION

THINKING ABOUT TYRANNY

After examining the analyses of tyranny of a dozen political theorists, the first and most obvious question to ask is, What is a tyranny? This straightforward question is exasperatingly difficult to answer. The definition of tyranny remained remarkably stable until the Enlightenment. Plato, Aristotle, Tacitus, and Machiavelli saw tyranny as rule by one person contrary to the general good. Montesquieu was a pivotal figure who saw despotism in the contemporary rule of French monarchs but also feared the sweet and centralized administrative tyranny that might be produced by a new urban and industrial world. With the nineteenth century, various thinkers used the word *tyranny* to warn against new threats. Marx condemned class rule, Tocqueville worried about a faceless tyranny without an identifiable tyrant, Weber decried the impersonal mechanism of bureaucratic tyranny, and Freud pronounced sadly that we always internalize tyranny and thus tyrannize over ourselves. Nor do these thinkers agree on what tyranny is *not*. Tocqueville defended a certain type of liberal democracy, but Plato saw every democracy as one evil step short of tyranny; Montesquieu defended a constitutional government in which monarch and nobility shared power, but Machiavelli regarded all rule by princes and nobles as tyrannical; and so the contradictions continue. And to compound the confusion further, Aristotle, Tacitus, Machiavelli, and Montesquieu generally perceived tyranny as something externally and often violently imposed upon a resentful population, whereas Plato, Tocqueville, Marx and Freud saw tyranny as internally imposed and sometimes willingly accepted by a population ignorant of its true needs.

What could all these theories of tyranny have in common? Are all these theorists analyzing anything that is remotely similar? Or was Hobbes correct when he observed that "they that are discontented under *Monarchy*, call it *Tyranny*,"[1] a statement suggesting that a person using the word *tyranny* is merely indicating that he or she does not like the government in question.

All manner of tangling confusion follows when we plunge into the jumbled thicket of our modern vocabulary of tyranny. To be fair, such confusion is not entirely new. As noted in the Introduction, by the time of the Declaration of Independence, Jefferson used the words and phrases *tyranny, absolute tyranny, absolute despotism,* and *absolute rule* as if they were synonymous. What is new is the degree to which such confusion has multiplied. Whereas the words *tyrant, tyranny,* and *despot* all originated in ancient Greece, the words or phrases *despotisme, absolutisme, dictatorship, totalitarianism,* and *authoritarian government* were either invented or, in the case of the word *dictator,* given a distinctly new connotation in the last three centuries directly in response to new and threatening political developments. Not surprisingly this has resulted in a political and politicized lexicon of words that, at least for most writers, has lost all precision, so much so that one can find bandied about any number of labels—dictatorship, one-party rule, autocratic rule, praetorian government, rule by a strong man, absolute government, totalitarianism—applied almost indiscriminately to the same political order.

In attempting to make sense of this confusion, I have become convinced that the word *tyranny* is an old and venerable word that should neither be discarded nor looked upon as quaintly anachronistic, as it so often has been recently. Obviously the problem of tyranny is not identical over time; Stalin did not rule like Tiberius. Nevertheless, while our modern vocabulary wants to emphasize discontinuity and novelty, I have argued instead for considerable continuity amidst obvious historical change and variation. Tyrannies have in fact oppressed men and women in strikingly similar ways in any century one chooses to examine. As I suggested in the Introduction, we might liken tyranny to an ever-recurring and very frightful melody, and then conclude that history has only witnessed frequent variations and considerable innovation on a familiar theme. As a result, I regard these modern descriptions of government—*despotism, dictatorship, totalitarianism*—as only varieties of tyrannical government, and I cautiously suggest that we can think about tyranny more clearly if we escape from the hopelessly muddled modern vocabulary of tyranny and return instead to key analyses or theories of tyranny, both ancient and modern.

I suggest this not because I have some dogmatic conviction that earlier thinkers harbored some special truth, but rather because it is one way to

---

1. Thomas Hobbes, *Leviathan*, chap. 19.

wrench ourselves from what one could call the liberal democratic prejudices of the late twentieth century. For example, in response to the question of what is the opposite of tyranny, most modern commentators will
almost unthinkingly answer "freedom" or "democracy" and even use
these two words as if they were interchangeable. Leaving aside how notoriously imprecise these words *freedom* and *democracy* are in contemporary discourse, we at least know that their meanings for us generally have
roots in the liberal tradition. But, to take just two examples, neither Plato
nor Aristotle saw tyranny as the opposite of freedom—at least not freedom in some Lockean sense—but rather regarded tyrannical government
as the opposite of a government that cultivates justice, virtue, excellence,
and human greatness. Similarly, few of the thinkers we have discussed
regarded "democracy" as the opposite of tyranny. Plato detested the mediocrity of democracy, Aristotle depicted the dangers of excessive equality, Tacitus sought a lawful rule by an elite, Montesquieu defended constitutional monarchy, and Marx regarded liberal democracy as merely one
more class tyranny. Reading ancient and early modern writers helps us to
think more clearly about tyranny by rubbing the rust off of long unexamined assumptions.

Returning to ancient authors also helps us find common ground among
what in the final analysis are very different and irreconcilable theories of
tyranny. Initially all similarity looks impossible. What could Plato and
Machiavelli, Tocqueville and Marx, or Freud and Weber have in common?
So clearly do these thinkers walk different paths in developing their theories of tyranny, they might well resent the suggestion that occasionally
their paths run parallel, along common ground. But consider Aristotle's
simple statement that captures the Greek understanding of tyranny. "Tyranny is just that arbitrary power of an individual who is responsible to no
one, and governs . . . with view to its own advantage, not to that of its
subjects, and therefore against their will." Although it is certainly important to note that Aristotle saw a tyrant as ruling over unwilling subjects
and as ruling arbitrarily—that is, unchecked either by law or by constitutional devices—the heart of this definition is the claim that a tyrant is
one who rules in his or her own interest, not in the general interest. In
addition, Aristotle regarded tyranny as the perverse counterpart of monarchy, and therefore, in his scheme of classifications of government, tyranny was the "worst" form of government known to humankind.[2]

If tyranny is the worst form of government, the one that least governs
in the general interest, then we might reframe this definition and still be
true to the thinking of Plato and Aristotle by saying, "Tyranny is that form

2. Aristotle, *Politics*, 1295a19–23; 1289b2.

of government that most thwarts, or least furthers, the development of justice as well as human virtue, excellence, and greatness." Having made our escape from the tangling assumptions of the liberal tradition, that is, having for the moment avoided thinking of individual rights and elections and representative government as the opposites of tyranny, we have perhaps found some common ground. Each thinker we have examined objected to tyranny precisely because it is the form of government that most impedes the development of justice, excellence, and greatness. Obviously we have found only a small patch of common ground, because what these writers regarded as just, excellent, and great certainly differs dramatically, as do their arguments about what political, economic, and social preconditions must exist in order to achieve these human goals. Small patch of ground though it is, this strikes me as a more fruitful way of thinking about tyranny than the usual opposition of tyranny to liberal democracy, because this formulation reminds us that tyranny is evil not just because it kills or brutalizes individuals, and not just because it denies human rights that most of us support, but also because it takes us as far away as possible from some higher goals of humanity.

An opportunity presents itself. If we could stretch the Greek formulation of tyranny just a little farther—and probably this does not stretch it past the breaking point—to say that "tyranny is the form of government that least meets human needs," we would have the possibility of more rigorously defining tyranny and even of having classifications of tyranny. Montesquieu, Tocqueville, Marx, Fromm, Neumann, and Arendt would all agree with Plato and Aristotle that tyranny is the form of government that least fulfills human needs. Each one of these thinkers, while certainly condemning tyrannies that use fear and violence to sustain their rule, also describe as tyrannical a political order that meets basic physical needs but fails, for whatever reason, to fulfill what we might call higher human needs.

Although this line of inquiry is perilous, it is also suggestive and fruitful. If, for example, someone such as Abraham Maslow were correct and we could empirically discover lower and higher needs, ranging from physical needs for food and shelter to more lofty needs for "self-actualization," then we might indeed construct a hierarchical classification for tyrannies. In trying to think clearly about tyranny, there would be considerable advantage in categorizing tyrannies according to the kinds of human needs they deny. At the lowest level we could classify tyrannies that kill and brutalize not just potential political opposition but even the innocent; at a second level we might find tyrannies that are less violent but that systematically impoverish large portions of the population while denying subjects rudimentary protections of the law; at a third level we might find tyrannies that more or less leave individuals alone but fail to provide health care, education, and basic social services; and finally, we might have a last classification of tyranny in which a government has the capacity to fulfill human needs but neglects, for whatever political and economic reasons, to do so. In some ways, such a project is really in the spirit of the early Greek analyses of tyranny. Both Plato and Aristotle argued that one could not attain excellence in a polis that itself did not approach excellence—that one would rarely, if ever, find a great citizen in an unhealthy political order—and both thought that the subjects of a tyrannical government were the most in need, the least developed, the least natural, and in some broad sense the least healthy. As Plato put it, tyranny embodies the "extreme illness of a city," and the subjects share the illness with the tyrant. Similarly, Maslow concluded that "a man who is thwarted in any of his basic needs may fairly be envisioned as simply sick."[3]

While I believe that this notion of tyranny as a political order that most denies human needs is a very helpful way to think more clearly about tyranny, I cannot convince myself that it can ever be precise—and empirically verifiable—so that we could produce a theory of tyranny offering a hierarchy of classifications according to the needs that various tyrannies denied to their populations. That would be a scholarly tour de force simplifying the world of tyranny for even the most skeptical reader! But I decline to do this for two reasons. First, theories of higher and lower human needs, in my view, ultimately rest on unproven and unprovable metaphysical postulates about human nature and the goals men and women "ought" to attain. This holds true, I think, both for Aristotelian teleologies as well as for the more fully "human needs" that Marx claimed would emerge as history develops. And second, classifying tyrannies according to the needs they deny ultimately stretches the word *tyranny* until it is unrecognizable. After all, for Aristotle and the Greeks, "tyranny is a kind of monarchy which has in view the interest of the monarch only," and Greek thinkers certainly acknowledged a variety of classifications of government that did not best meet human needs—for example, aristocracies and oligarchies—but which were emphatically not tyrannical in their eyes.[4]

As I showed in the Introduction, a typical tyranny according to Greek

---

3. Plato, *Republic*, 544c; Abraham Maslow is cited in Patricia Springborg, *The Problem of Human Needs and the Critique of Civilisation* (London: Allen & Unwin, 1981); see 184–97, esp. 190.

4. Aristotle, *Politics*, 1279b6–7; see Springborg, *The Problem of Human Needs and the Critique of Civilisation*, 1–18, 94–117, 245–51.

thinking in the fourth century B.C.E. had a number of characteristics: rule by one person, rule over an unwilling population, arbitrary rule unrestrained by constitutional bodies, arbitrary rule unrestrained by an independent judiciary or a well-defined legal code, and rule in the interest of the tyrant and not for the general good.[5] The first and second characteristics of this definition of tyranny have not weathered the centuries unchallenged. By the early twentieth century Tocqueville, Marx, and Weber had no longer focused on a one-person tyranny, but rather a class tyranny or an amorphous and impersonal tyranny, a tyranny in which all are dominated but no one person does the dominating. And Montesquieu, Tocqueville, Marx, and Freud—in fact, even Plato—argued that subjects sometimes welcome their servitude and thus believe their tyranny to be their liberation. If we take into account the qualifications subsequent thinkers have made to this Greek description of tyranny, however, this description stands as perhaps the best we can do—as long as we are willing to broaden, and leave open, the concept of the general good. More detail is probably not possible. Nor should we expect agreement regarding what constitutes the general good, because different writers will bring different philosophical assumptions and arguments to their studies of tyranny. As I said above, almost all thinkers agree that tyranny is the form of government that most hinders the development of justice and human virtue, excellence and greatness, although they hardly agree on how to define these terms.

There is, in fact, far more agreement on what constitutes a tyranny than on what is the *opposite* of tyranny. To borrow a famous remark about pornography: we may not be able rigorously to define tyranny, but almost all of us know it when we see it. For this reason, Hobbes's claim that in effect all definitions are arbitrary, that one person's tyranny is another's legitimate government, is historically inaccurate. One can find in fact broad, although not unanimous, agreement among thinkers who have identified and analyzed tyrannies. If we may leave aside the fawning apologists who cling to any regime, few observers disagree about classifying a government as tyrannical when they see it.

In the final analysis a definition of tyranny is less important than a clear and careful analysis of how a given tyranny works and what it does to the people subjected to it. In this conclusion it seems worthwhile to go back over the kinds of questions our various thinkers asked about tyranny, as well as the suggestions they made about resisting and defeating tyranny.

Who rules a given tyranny? Broadly speaking, the theorists reviewed here have given three different answers to this question—a single tyrant, a class, or an impersonal structure that dominates society and is uncon-

5. See A. Andrewes, *The Greek Tyrants* (London: Hutchinson & Co., 1956).

trolled by any single person or class. The theorists I have examined all knew that each of these answers is too simplistic. Borrowing from Montesquieu and Marx, Neumann suggested that every tyranny—even one nominally ruled by a single person—has a structure of power with an inner logic of its own. Probably the first question our theorists asked of a given tyranny, therefore, was, what is the structure of power, what constellation of classes, groups, political parties, and so forth, come together to make up this structure? How do individuals and classes in such a structure hold it together and perpetuate it?

Consider rule by a single tyrant. Strictly speaking, not even Greek theorists thought a single tyrant ruled alone. No tyrant can dominate successfully without paramilitary forces, an army controlled either by personal loyalty or direct self-interest, some kind of political party to mobilize one's supporters, alliances with certain classes or groups, a state administrative structure, and so on. Machiavelli was right in suggesting that such a tyrant does not engage in activity properly called "political," but rather he or she is adept at the "art of the state," that is, using the state apparatus to manipulate and coordinate this structure of power without being swallowed by the inevitable conflicts. In her analysis of Nazi Germany, Arendt was persuasive in suggesting that a tyrant can enhance his or her rule by a structure that is shapeless and constantly fluctuating, so that no one but the leader knows which layer of an onionlike structure—state, party, or secret police—has authority at any given moment.

A class tyranny also has a structure. The key question here is, how do the nominal political figures, political parties, state administration, and so forth, reinforce rule by a dominant class? How does opposition from other classes manifest itself? And by what means does a class perpetuate its rule—by force, by ideological indoctrination, and so on? Finally, consider the worry best expressed by Tocqueville and Weber that the world will see a tyranny without an identifiable tyrant, oppression without an oppressor. Why is it that individuals and classes have little or no influence over a world in which all are caught in hierarchical and bureaucratic structures? What historical conditions produced such a tyranny? Is opposition impossible, and if so, why are these administrative structures so tenacious?

Are there customs and habits that support a tyranny? Both Plato and Aristotle thought that individuals would reflect their civic cultures, that they would resemble their governors, and hence, it was virtually impossible for a virtuous and excellent individual to emerge from a violent and licentious tyranny. Both Tacitus and Machiavelli spoke of the "character" of the ancient Roman Republic, a character of discipline, austerity, and concern for the common good taught first by the patriarchal Roman family and reinforced by religion, political institutions, and the military. Both thought that one could not have freedom without an internalized discipline; license led to servitude.

Montesquieu and Tocqueville, by focusing on the customs, habits, and *moeurs* of a nation, argued most forcefully that it is the character of the people—and not their laws and institutions—that will determine if a people is fiercely free or if it suffers a submissive servitude. In the smallest examples—such as the custom of children electing leaders in games, or the need of French villagers of the ancien régime to petition Paris for permission to fix a church—one can discern the habits of freedom or the practices of despotism. Beautifully written constitutions will not help freedom one whit if not supported by an ethos of freedom; elaborate laws cannot fill the void left by the absence of *les moeurs* that support freedom.

Each thinker examined agreed that—however it is conveyed, and whatever the content—there is indeed an ethos of tyranny that teaches us fear, resignation, and the supposed inevitability of submitting to tyrannical rule. And most would agree with Montesquieu that changing these *moeurs,* changing this ethos of tyranny, even if possible, will always take a frustratingly long time, perhaps entire generations. "Politics is a smooth file," wrote Montesquieu, "which cuts gradually."[6]

How does a tyranny depoliticize its subjects? Aristotle, Tacitus, Machiavelli, and Tocqueville all suggested that tyrannies can function successfully only if subjects are isolated from one another, powerless because they cannot organize potential opposition. For Aristotle, this meant that tyrants must find a way to keep subjects out of the public realm (the polis) and confine them to their private spheres (the household). Tyrants must transform a political order in which citizens meet in the polis as equals into household rule that is by nature hierarchical and despotic. As Tacitus put it, over the course of several centuries Rome changed from a republic (*res publica*) to an empire in which the emperor ruled Rome as if it were a private household (*res privata*). Or, as Machiavelli suggested, tyrannies must find ways to eliminate citizen access to public space—city halls, public auditoriums, parks, streets, and so forth.

What are the various ways in which tyrannies bring about depoliticization, isolation, and powerlessness? First, as Tacitus and Machiavelli suggested, tyrants can use force, and prohibit public meetings, abolish asso-

6. See Roger Boesche, "Why Did Tocqueville Think a Successful Revolution Was Impossible?" in *Liberty, Equality, Democracy,* ed. Eduardo Nolla (New York: New York University Press, 1992), 165–86, esp. 182.

ciations and clubs, and thus use fear and violence to confine individuals to the private sphere. Second, Tacitus and Arendt observed the "psychological isolation" that resulted when one feared the violence and terror of the secret police. If even our friends and families are potential informers, each of us is irredeemably alone and hence incapable of honest conversation. Third, Plato and Aristotle pointed out that an imposed economic scarcity forces subjects to work from dawn to dusk, effectively eliminating time for public and political activity. Fourth, Tacitus and Montesquieu suggested that large cities by their very nature become impersonal gatherings of strangers, so that urbanization by itself breaks down traditional ties between individuals, thus effectively isolating them. Fifth, Montesquieu and Tocqueville feared a powerful centralized administration that would abolish or break up intermediate associations, that is, those groups that serve as a buffer between the individual and the state. This would leave atomized and powerless individuals directly confronting the administrative power of the state. Borrowing from Montesquieu, Neumann noted that the Nazi state abolished intermediate associations that were participatory and confined each individual, from birth to death, in hierarchical, authoritarian, and bureaucratic organizations. Sixth, Tocqueville argued that the acquisitive ethic acts as a centrifugal force flinging men and women into their private spheres and fastening them there. The very acquisitive ethic that produced prosperity in the new commercial and industrial world is by itself a private pursuit that undermines citizenship. Too busy with their private affairs, the middle classes abandon the public sphere willingly in order to gain private comforts and security. Thus, urban and industrial nations automatically produce isolated and powerless individuals, readied for subjection to tyranny. Seventh, Arendt, extending Tocqueville's argument, suggested not only that urban and industrialized societies naturally created literally tens of thousands of lonely people whose lives had little meaning, but that such individuals were eager to find meaning and a sense of belonging in a political movement offering simplistic ideological answers to complicated problems. And finally, both Freud and Fromm argued that by nature we fear separation and are thus alone and anxious and that therefore we have a pathological need to join with any group that will relieve us of choice and responsibility, even groups that further solidify the tyranny around us.

How much and what kinds of violence does a tyranny use? Aristotle, Tacitus, and Machiavelli regarded violence as essential to every tyranny, and they noted that tyrants almost always surround themselves with a bodyguard, paramilitary forces, a secret police, spies, informers, and the regular military. So much had he learned from ancient tyrannies, Montesquieu called fear the chief motivating principle in a despotism. And yet violence is of course not the same in every tyranny. Some questions that one who is analyzing tyranny must ask include the following: Does a tyranny employ professional spies and informers, or is the atmosphere of the tyranny so frightful that virtually every person is afraid and consequently willing to inform on neighbors and friends? In the latter case, of course, mutual suspicion leads to extreme psychological isolation. Is the violence selective and occasional, or is it daily and widespread? Machiavelli suggested that one might even measure the effectiveness of a tyranny by how little violence the tyrant needs to use to instill fear in his or her subjects. If a tyranny needs only occasional violence against potential opposition, it will be more successful, meaning more stable and long-lasting, than a tyranny in which violence is never ending and all-encompassing. Does the tyrant understand what Machiavelli might have called the economy of violence? That is, does the tyrant know when it is imperative "not to be good," in which case he or she must use violent means to uphold the state, and, by contrast, when one has the luxury of being "good" as defined by traditional criteria? For example, Machiavelli thought it took little violence for a tyrant to take over a people accustomed to servitude, whereas by contrast anyone who wants to establish a tyranny in a formerly free country must be willing to devastate the population with violence. Does a given tyranny engage in a day-to-day violence that is not apparent? Marx and Weber, for example, certainly noted the overt violence in class rule, but they focused on the despotism and discipline of the workplace as a systematic source of violence, against both the body and the mind, masking itself as a voluntary contract. Thinkers such as Tacitus, Montesquieu, and Tocqueville took for granted that all tyrannies would undermine an independent judiciary as well as all legal protections of individual rights.

To what extent does a tyrant rely on a professional military and police force instead of a popular army and militia? Relying on professionals may be more efficient, but every tyrant must worry that the head of the secret police or the general in charge of the army will seek to supplant the tyrant. As Machiavelli noted, tyrants must rely on good generals, but successful generals create danger both for the tyrant and for themselves. Relying on a popular army and militia, as Plato, Freud, and Fromm pointed out, makes the entire society complicit in the crimes committed and binds the group more tightly together by guilt. However, any tyrant must fear an armed populace, which has obvious opportunities to organize and oppose the tyranny. Finally, how can we explain what Neumann and Arendt regarded as a new phenomenon in history, namely, the systematic and scientific slaughter of those who are wholly innocent, indeed a slaughter undertaken *after* the population has been pacified? Both Neumann and Arendt blamed racist beliefs, and Arendt focused on an ideology of racism in which history and nature allegedly commanded an Aryan race to exterminate or dominate Jews, Poles, Slavs, and so forth. Arendt also saw the death camps, which seem so irrational to outsiders, as an essential component of totalitarianism demonstrating its absolute power.

Several thinkers I have examined thought that tyrannies would be long-lasting only if violence was at a minimum and the chase for pleasures and comforts depoliticized the population. Plato argued that tyranny was like cookery; while we may need a physician undertaking harsh treatments to bring health, we instead seek cooks who promise us pleasures and pander to our desires. Tacitus saw Rome conquer the Britons with baths and banquets, corrupting them in order quietly to bring them to servitude, and he thought bread, circuses, and the chase for physical pleasures made the tyranny of the empire palatable, if not welcomed, by the Roman populace. Both Montesquieu and Tocqueville feared a tyranny that was sweet and not violent, that caressed more than it threatened, but that left the population childlike, satisfied, though petrified, incapable of anything great. To paraphrase Baudelaire, Europe might well gratefully fall asleep on a heap of riches.

How do tyrannies use deception, discourse, and language? One task of any tyrant is to create a world of reassuring appearances. How do tyrannies do this? Both Aristotle and Machiavelli gave to a tyrant the well-known advice that it is not important to *be* religious, law abiding, merciful, and frugal, but it is important to *appear* to be so. Both Tacitus and Tocqueville noted that every tyrant who converted a republic to a tyranny—for example, Augustus—tried to keep the appearance of little change by having the legislative representatives debate and courts deliberate, even though both institutions had lost all power and independence. Tocqueville once suggested that a tyranny could continue functioning even if elections took place as usual, because the elected officials would be as powerless as the rest of us, a condition of governance he called "theatrical representation." In other words, elections can sometimes be the fluff of freedom and not its substance. And Arendt noted the importance of front organizations in convincing the subjects of Nazi Germany that not much had changed, that their political world was still functioning in a normal fashion.

Tyrannies also attempt to hide the reality of servitude by distorting language and limiting discourse. Tacitus most effectively described the ways in which the language of politics become blurred and distorted under tyranny. In a famous sentence condemning Rome, he called attention to the corruption of language: "To robbery, butchery, and rapine they give the lying name of 'government'; they create a desolation and call it peace."[7] Tacitus also maintained that under a tyranny one cannot find orators, but instead mere rhetoricians, because true orators must be able to ask substantial and important questions and go beyond mere flattery. Similarly, by suggesting that tyrannies eliminate leisure time, or the time needed for deliberation, Aristotle argued that tyrannies eliminate certain kinds of questions, especially practical questions that concern themselves with what is the good life and how citizens of a polis might bring it about. Instead, subjects in a tyranny can only ask technical questions about perpetuating the present regime.

If tyrannies distort language and limit discourse, then we can hardly expect subjects to develop carefully crafted critiques of their situation. Although he worried about a tyranny of a majority, Tocqueville worried more about what he thought of as centralization of sources of information. The more newspapers and magazines a nation had—and we could add here radio and television stations—the more free it was likely to be, according to Tocqueville, and he feared the day when the news was monopolized by a handful of sources. By arguing that all political discourse serves economic or class needs, Marx scoffed at the supposed neutrality of language. What the ruling class calls equality is in fact an extensive class despotism, and what the factory owner calls a fair wage is in reality only well-disguised exploitation. For different reasons, Tocqueville, Marx, and Neumann all noted that modern tyrannies ruled effectively while proclaiming themselves to be higher and more genuine forms of freedom. Arendt saw a danger in what she called ideological thinking. In criticizing ideological thinking, Arendt was really focusing on the "science" of Marxism-Leninism, in which we must submit to the "laws of history," or the racist thinking of National Socialism, under which we must submit to pseudo-Darwinian "laws of nature." Ideological thinking makes critical thinking and even common sense impossible. Facts that confound the tenets of an ideology must be stretched or broken to fit the logical straitjacket of ideology. Once more, the distorted discourse of tyranny deceives us and hides the reality of the world from us.

What role does the family play in a tyranny? Plato was the first European thinker to have the insight that family structure reinforces the broader political structure, that is, that the private household has profound public and political repercussions. For example, he saw a more egalitarian family as leading to democracy (which of course he detested), whereas a more aristocratic family might lead literally to rule by the best. For Greek thinkers in general, despotism was proper rule for the family

7. Tacitus, *Agricola*, trans. H. Mattingly and S. A. Handford (New York: Penguin, 1970), 30.

because the father as despot was perfectly appropriate as a benevolent ruler over slaves, servants, women, and children. Montesquieu borrowed this insight but criticized it. He was among the first modern thinkers to argue that the family is a school for creating and perpetuating despotism, which is appropriate rule neither for the family nor for society at large. Scattered among his writings, and especially in his *Persian Letters,* Montesquieu's ideas for the family were daring for the eighteenth century. The family, he suggested, teaches the habits of obedience necessary for despotism, it sanctions the practice of boys dominating girls and of men ruling women, and it reinforces the notion that hierarchy and despotic rule are natural and unavoidable. All of these notions Montesquieu called into question, without, of course, advocating anything like a democratic or egalitarian family.

No one raised these questions in such a profound way as did Freud. For Freud the political structure quite logically mirrored the family structure, and he regarded the patriarchal family as both natural and inevitable. By maintaining that in some sense most of us remain childlike, yearning for a father figure to rebel against but ultimately someone to whom we may submit, Freud argued that the family structure emotionally internalized a need for hierarchy, a strong leader, and tyranny. In effect, tyranny is reproduced from generation to generation by the patriarchal family. Implicitly Freud asked what happens to girls and women in the family structure, although he thought a submissive role was natural, and hence appropriate, for both. Subsequent thinkers built on Freud's insight that the family reproduces the inequality of women, and they argued that a more democratic and egalitarian family would give to women a more equal role in society at large. Fromm extended Freud's ideas more directly to historical and political developments by arguing that a people can have a social character that, in times of crisis, makes them look to an authoritarian leader from whom they may find security through submission.

Why are some tyrannies static and content with stability at home, whereas others are expansionistic and imperialistic? Machiavelli was perhaps the first to make a distinction between static and mobilizing tyrannies, between, for example, the stay-at-home Sparta and the expansionistic Roman Empire or, in our own century, between Franco's Spain and Nazi Germany. Whereas static tyrannies seek to depoliticize the population, mobilizing tyrannies must rely on the energy and participation of the population, although this must be done in a controlled fashion. Whereas static tyrannies rely on a professional army loyal to the tyrant, mobilizing tyrannies must use a popular army—which poses risks for the tyrant— but again strictly guided by the tyrant's military objectives.

How have theorists explained mobilizing tyrannies? First, Machiavelli explained expansionistic tyrannies by a wish for greatness, glory, and grandeur. Although he did not ignore economic factors entirely, he clearly saw them as secondary. Second, Tocqueville made a distinction between great parties, which are motivated by grand ideals, and little parties, which are motivated by petty economic and class interests. Great parties, in Tocqueville's mind, can do great good or great evil, but they certainly are more likely to be expansionsitic. Third, Weber saw political and economic interests leading—quite appropriately, in his mind—to imperialist expansion. Fourth, Neumann explained Nazi Germany's aggressive militarism by the needs of the dominant classes in Germany, as well as Germany's political and economic needs for empire, because a united Germany came so late to Europe's imperial race for territory.

And finally, Arendt offered perhaps the best explanation for a nation's mobilizing for empire. While Arendt did not ignore a nation's urge for greatness and glory, and while she did not overlook economic interests, she focused mostly on what she called ideological factors, in this case an ideology based primarily on racist assumptions. What justified Europe's imperial exploitation of countries in Africa, Asia, and Latin America was some combination of religious ideals that stressed the importance of conversion to Christianity, cultural ideals about the superiority of the West, and racist notions about inferior peoples' need to be ruled by superior whites. Arendt explicitly criticized Weber. Weber thought that all nations would eventually succumb to the pressures of a rationalized production of goods and services, but Arendt showed that racist ideals, including conquest and extermination, can take precedence over rational economic and political concerns. Sadly, racial and ethnic hostility has been a part of tyranny since Greek tyrannies saw Dorian portions of the population suppress non-Dorians. Neumann regarded racism as something usually reinforcing economic and class interests, especially by hiding the problems of class behind destructive racial and ethnic clashes. Freud saw ethnic hostility as a more primal emotion. Groups establish their identities, Freud thought, by their hostility toward the Other, by hostility toward perceived enemies. In the late twentieth century, when ethnic hostilities seem to be sweeping the entire world, this is a saddening thought.

What happens to men and women oppressed by tyranny? While it is true that many feel the violence of police and prisons under tyranny, what else happens to ordinary men and women? First, Tacitus suggested that under some tyrannies all moral character disappears, and subjects indulge in lusts of all kinds out of a sense of hopelessness about the future. Plato spoke of tyrants pacifying the population by cookery, that is, by flattering desires; Aristotle and Tacitus said that one could pacify a population by diversions and amusements; and Montesquieu and Tocqueville suggested that despots encourage avarice and private greed so that subjects will not oppose absolute rule. Second, Plato, Tacitus, and Neumann suggested that in order to survive, subjects engage in role-playing, and that they become actors acting out the parts they think the tyrant wants to see, so they do not arouse suspicion. Third, almost every theorist focused on the ways in which it is hard to be an independent thinker in the face of propaganda, a controlled media, and a pervasive ideology. While it might seem like a variant of Tocqueville's tyranny of the majority, in fact it is tyranny by a minority that is seeking to tell the majority how to think.

Fourth, Marx, Weber, and Neumann turn our attention to what Foucault called the micropolitics of tyranny, that is, what happens to workers in the workplace, to ethnic minorities, and to women. For example, Weber saw the discipline of modern factories as every bit as exploitative and oppressive as work in the mines of ancient Rome or the labor of serfs in the Middle Ages. And Weber saw discipline as everywhere—in factories and farms, in schools and offices. Both Marx and Weber saw men and women in factories become tools of their tools. In this micropolitics of tyranny, theorists focus not on what a tyrannical government does to us, but on what private power does to men and women in factories, to women in families, and to ethnic minorities in cities. Fifth, Weber and Freud anticipated an argument later made more explicit by Foucault. Tyranny is something we all experience, but it is also something we daily inflict on others in our families, our factories, and our offices. It is not something simply descending from above. And finally, as Freud suggested, men and women subjected to tyranny become dull and mediocre, or, as Weber suggested, incapable of greatness. This takes us back to the very definition of tyranny offered by Plato and Aristotle, that is, tyranny is the form of government that least satisfies human needs, that least develops the human capacity for justice, excellence, and greatness.

Having talked so much about how tyrannies work, we risk overlooking a rather obvious historical fact. Tyrants and tyrannies do not last forever, and they are hardly changeless, as some who talked of the "unchangeability" of Communist totalitarianism have found to their intellectual chagrin. In fact, the job of a tyrant is perilously difficult. The tyrant indeed engages in what Machiavelli called the art of the state, but it is an art in which solving one problem almost always provokes another, as a child who squeezes a balloon in one spot only makes it bulge out on the other side. This becomes obvious to the students in my seminar on theories of tyranny when my students try playing the role of successful tyrant to exasperating results. How does the tyrant rely on leaders in the secret police and the military without being supplanted by one or the other? How can the tyrant create fear and terror without provoking desperate revolt? If the tyrant uses assassination and extermination, how can he or she avoid getting caught in this atmosphere of fear? How can tyrants ally themselves with one class without offending others? Can the tyrant use religion and an established church without yielding significant power to religious authorities? If tyrants are intent upon gaining enormous wealth for themselves and their allies, will they not create poverty for the middle and lower classes and risk provoking a revolt? How can a tyrant foster ethnic and class conflict without dissolving the country he or she seeks to rule? While a tyrant may seek to control workers in state-controlled unions, how will the tyrant prevent these unions from gaining real and significant power? Tyrants certainly need to rely on efficient state administrations, but how can they do this without yielding power to state bureaucracies? How can tyrants create the appearance of independent courts without giving them genuine independence? Or again, can tyrants create apparently independent media without creating opportunities for real independence? If tyrants choose to maintain the traditional family, do they not risk resistance from women, and if they do not maintain traditional families, do they not risk resistance from church authorities and others? How can a tyrant use an effective political party without fearing its power? How can a tyrant rely on the power of a political party that organizes the people without bringing the people together, thus giving them an opportunity to organize themselves? While the tyrant needs factories and cities, will this not invariably bring subjects together, outside of the private household, so they can organize? How can tyrants harness the energies of a population without the people becoming an organized, and perhaps armed, threat to the tyrants themselves? Can a tyrant really appear religious, law abiding, and frugal without being so? Does a tyrant not risk being lulled into complacency when his or her subjects learn to play roles in order to survive, when they appear energetically committed to the regime, though in fact they are only sullenly obedient? Most important of all, how can the tyrant depoliticize his or her subjects? What if the tyrant wants to mobilize for conquest?

As noted, tyrants do not last forever, and the job of a tyrant is risky and difficult. Tyrants are like jugglers: they try to keep many balls in the air, but of course, eventually one or more is bound to fall.

Every problem for a tyrant is an opportunity for those who oppose tyranny. Although tyrants certainly have attempted to depoliticize the population, they must bring subjects together in factories, churches, and neighborhoods, thus providing opportunities for creating the intermediate bodies and associations that Montesquieu and Tocqueville so admired. Here is a possibility for creating public space. If tyrants seek to mobilize the energies of the people, then the people have opportunities to organize themselves independently. If a tyrant allies himself or herself with the upper classes, then one can organize more easily among the middle and lower classes. Whenever a tyrant must rely on religious authorities, this provides an opportunity to use religion and the church to organize opposition. If a tyrant tries to establish tame unions, organizers can try to give these unions significant power. When a state administrative body has some independent authority, one can use its rules and practices to protect individuals and groups. If tyrants want the appearance of an independent judiciary, then organizers have an opportunity either to expose the dependence of the judiciary or to make it genuinely independent. To the extent that the official media seems controlled and untrustworthy, alternative forms of media will be more easily trusted and relied upon. When tyrants rely on the traditional family, this provides opportunities in the late twentieth century for women to organize themselves. If the tyrant tries to separate subjects by ethnic hostility, this also provides opportunities to organize ethnic groups in opposition to the regime. Because we know that every tyranny, even so-called totalitarianism, always has a politics among the elite, organizers can hope for, and capitalize on, conflicts between the tyrant, the army, the secret police, business, the state, and so forth. Admittedly, none of this resistance and opposition is easy, but neither is managing a long-lasting tyranny.

It seems to me that this long discussion of tyranny calls the Enlightenment view of progress into question. If tyranny is always with us like some macabre companion or, to choose another metaphor, like an ever-recurring outbreak of disease, then in what sense can we look forward to the day when tyranny is defeated finally and unequivocally? Weber and Freud suggest that there will always be forms of tyranny or domination, and if we have moments of freedom, in general we simply lunge from one species of domination to the next. Even worse, it seems that in the twentieth century tyranny has tended too often toward genocide, so it is possible that new tyrannies will be worse, that in this case the disease fends off all attempts at treatment and merely is more virulent with each return. Aristotle saw this possibility centuries ago. An evil tyrant might be safer and wiser, suggested Aristotle, if he or she committed "crimes so great and terrible that no man living could be suspected of them: here too no precautions are taken. For all men guard against ordinary offences, just as they guard against ordinary diseases; but no one takes precautions against an offence that nobody has ever yet committed."[8] I have likened

8. Aristotle, *Rhetoric*, 1372a25–29.

tyranny to some frightful and recurring melody that always seems to accompany humankind, and this seems like an appropriate metaphor. But just as there is tyranny, so is there opposition to tyranny, so if there is indeed a frightful melody, there is also the powerful and hopeful song of human freedom and excellence.

AFTERWORD

Since I began writing this book in 1986, the following major events have occurred. Ferdinand Marcos was ousted in 1986 by so-called People Power in the Philippines, and Corazon Aquino won the free elections that followed; in 1989 General Augusto Pinochet in Chile lost an election that put an end to sixteen years of rule by a military junta; also in 1989 General Alfredo Stroessner fell from power in Paraguay after thirty-five years of rule; in 1989 the Berlin Wall came down and Germany united; between 1989 and 1991 Communist regimes in Czechoslovakia, Poland, Hungary, Romania, Bulgaria, and Albania all crumbled; quite dramatically, the tyrant of Romania, Nicolae Ceausescu, was arrested, tried, and executed in December of 1989 (and the transcript of these events clearly indicates he was so blind to his tyranny that he actually believed he was beloved and good for his country!); just as gratifying and almost as surprising, Václav Havel was elected president of Czechoslovakia in 1989, and Lech Walesa president of Poland in 1990; most dramatic of all, the Soviet Union had its first elections in 1989, and after an attempted coup in August of 1991, the Communist Party collapsed, the Soviet Empire completed its process of splintering, and Boris Yeltsin was chosen president of Russia; the United States armed forces ended Manuel Noriega's rule in Panama in 1990; Nicaragua had free elections in 1990, and Violeta Barrios de Chamorro defeated the Sandinista leader Daniel Ortega; the century's longest-lasting tyrant was Emperor Haile Selassie, who ruled Ethiopia for more than fifty-seven years, from 1917 until his overthrow in 1974 (he was regent for his female cousin for the first fourteen years, until he was named emperor); in 1991 the Leninist thugs led by General Mengistu, who replaced Haile Selassie, were removed by a popular revolt, and Ethiopia's first free elections followed in 1994; similarly, under United Nations' supervision Cambodia had free elections in 1993, although the genocidal Khmer Rouge still threaten civil war; and finally, happily, and perhaps least predictably, Nelson Mandela was elected president of South Africa in 1994.

Despite these historically important gales of freedom, all is hardly perfect with the world, and tyranny has not disappeared. Jean Claude "Baby Doc" Duvalier was chased out of Haiti in 1986, but a promising democracy could not last and was replaced by a military tyranny (as I write these words, United States' troops have just landed in Haiti to restore elected president Jean-Bertrand Aristide); in May and June of 1989, students and workers all over China demonstrated and agitated for democracy, but their efforts were crushed brutally in Beijing's Tiananmen Square and elsewhere by a Communist Party that does not want political reform; Iraq's tyrant, Saddam Hussein, invaded Kuwait in 1990, was defeated militarily in 1991, but still remains firmly in power in 1994; the twenty-one-year tyranny of General Muhammad Siyad Barrah in Somalia ended in 1991, only to be followed by a chaos that was nearly a Hobbesian war of all against all, although United States troops did restore some order after 1992; what was once Yugoslavia broke into warring and tyrannical ethnic factions in 1991–92.

In 1994, we have seen the following: In Rwanda, the majority Hutu government and military engaged in ethnic, and near genocidal, murder by killing hundreds of thousands of Tutsis and moderate Hutus; despite an organized general strike in Nigeria, a military junta will not let the elected president take power; after almost a half century in power, North Korea's Kim Il-Sung died, but so far the Communist tyranny has remained intact; in Burma, the military continues to rule (General Ne Win was in power from 1962 to 1988), ignoring the elections in 1990, in which the opposition, led by Nobel Peace Prize winner Aung San Suu Kyi, won decisively; in Cuba, Fidel Castro remains in power; in Iran, an oppressive theocracy still reigns; in Libya, Colonel Muammar Gadafy still rules; a military tyranny in the Sudan continues to impose unfathomable misery of starvation and civil war on the South of the country; in Syria, Hafez al-Assad is as strong as ever; in Vietnam, one sees economic reform but no signs of political reform; and in Zaire, President Mobutu Sese Seko is a brutal tyrant whose country has fallen apart into feuding pieces. And despite the fall of Communism, in 1994 an uneasy mood has descended on many former Communist countries, a mood that suggests people might willingly embrace some form of authoritarian rule—similar to rule by Communist parties, but without Communist ideology—in exchange for peace and economic security. Former Communists made election gains in Poland, Hungary, and what was once East Germany; in Uzbekistan, in Kazakhstan, and to a lesser extent in the Ukraine, former Communist Party officials still rule, although they are wearing new hats.

Several observations come to mind. First, the political theorists in this book can help us to understand all of these events; nothing is so totally new in history as to be a shock. Although many—indeed, almost all—of those in the academic and journalistic worlds from the 1940s to the 1980s told us that so-called totalitarian countries were immune to change, Neumann and Arendt, as I have shown, saw political clashes and even constant movement in what they regarded as these less-than-totalitarian countries. Whereas the collapse of Communism in the period 1989 to 1991 surprised nearly everyone, it would have surprised Neumann and Arendt much less. Second, the events of the last eight years indicate that the galaxy of tyrannies is ever changing; that is, a given constellation of tyrants cannot remain intact forever. As this book indicates, it is difficult and unusual to establish a long-lasting tyranny—Haile Selassie, Kim Il-Sung, Spain's Francisco Franco, and Stroessner notwithstanding—because every decision a tyrant makes strengthens one aspect of his or her tyranny but weakens another. Once more, it is like trying to juggle balls forever, when of course one or more of the balls is bound to fall.

Third, it is comparatively easy to kill or overthrow a tyrant, but extremely difficult to establish a free or just political order, a society that genuinely addresses human needs. The people of Haiti drove out "Baby Doc" Duvalier in 1986, but eight years later the United States' armed forces are taking it upon themselves to "restore" a democracy that has never existed in Haiti. Similarly, it was comparatively easy—and wise—for Romanians to execute Ceausescu in 1989, but Romania now appears directionless, a country that does not know what to do next. None of this would surprise our political theorists; almost all agonized over the nearly impossible task of political regeneration, that is, taking a corrupt political order and making it virtuous, just, or free. As Machiavelli said, "nothing is more difficult than to initiate a new order of things." Even if one succeeds in removing a tyrant, nevertheless one must still overcome what Montesquieu, Marx, Weber, and Neumann called the structure of tyranny, and one must alter what Tacitus, Montesquieu, and Tocqueville labeled the character, the habits, the customs, and the mores of tyranny.

Fourth, after observing tyrannies over the last decades, one must conclude sadly that many are founded upon racial or ethnic hatred for the Other. Germans against Jews, white South Africans against black South Africans, the Khmer (Cambodian) people against the Vietnamese, Serbians against both Croats and Bosnians, Armenians against Ajerbaijanis, Slovaks versus Hungarians, Turks against both Kurds and Armenians, and Hutus against Tutsis. Is Freud right when he says that we unite affectionately with one group only by exhibiting intolerance and hatred for others?

And finally, the events of the last eight years show just how right Aristotle, Machiavelli, Tocqueville, and Arendt were in claiming that a free people must literally occupy public space—streets, parks, meeting halls, city council meetings, and so forth. The Filipino people finally overthrew Marcos when they took to the streets, persuaded the military to support them, and captured a key television station. Similarly, black South Africans won the vote only after years of public demonstrations and running street battles with the police and the army. And in the failed coup in Russia in 1991, Boris Yeltsin dramatically and heroically stood on a tank in front of a huge crowd in Moscow and persuaded the military to yield public space to the people. By contrast, Chinese students and workers could not transform their victories in public squares into an alliance with either the Communist Party or the military, and they were finally driven by violence out of Tiananmen Square. As I watch the streets of Haiti on television, I can literally see a battle for public space between the Haitian police and the civilian population. As the police sweep on to the next block, people emerge from their private homes to seize back the street— public space—the police just left. Of course, as Aristotle, Machiavelli, Tocqueville, and Arendt said, one must have institutions that permanently allow citizens to control public space, public debate, and public decisions, and one must teach citizens the habits of participation in public life. That is more difficult.

September 23, 1994
Los Angeles

INDEX